LY SKETCH.

LONDON, WEDNESDAY, MAY 6, 1914.   [Registered as a Newspaper.]   ONE HALFPENNY.

AND NOW: THE LOVE-STORY THAT CHANGED IRISH HISTORY AND DELAYED HOME RULE.

CHARLES STEWART PARNELL, WRITTEN BY OW, KATHARINE PARNELL (MRS. O'SHEA).

Copyright in Great Britain and the U

Katharine O'Shea.

BRIEF BIOGRAPHIES OF THE PRINCIPAL PEOPLE.

rcc
his c
enew
nes ch
curred
e charge

eabha

ll, the Irish leader, a
in County Wicklow. A
me family as the English
name and the two Parnells,
enry, who fought with
the Union. Elected for
leader of the party in

fterwards Mrs. Parnell),
H. O'Shea. Daughter of
ood and sister of Field-
Wood. In 1880 was living
at Eltham in a house
rovided by her Aunt Ben.

a Catholic Whig. Elected
1880. A noted rider to
Sold out of the Army
od managed a bank and
where a branch of his
In 1880 was living prin-

Aunt Ben, widow of Mr. Benjamin Wood and patron of George Meredith. A stately lady of the old times, living the life of a literary recluse at Eltham.

The O'Gorman Mahon, one of the most remarkable figures in the Parliament of 1880-1885. After having been in the House with O'Connell fifty years before had led a wild and adventurous life all over the world. Was reputed to have once been Lord High Admiral and Generalissimo of a South American Republic.

William Ewart Gladstone. At the time the story opens the great Liberal leader was seventy years of age. Recently in opposition to the Disraeli Government, he was just about to form a Cabinet.

MY FIRST MEETIN WITH PARN

pirit the taint of excuse
rather the victim than
O'Brien

selves in her service to earn for her a name that should no longer be a byword and
the nations.

In these columns I am giving to th
my lover and myself tha   Mr.

In
ive
With Parnell as her chief the Ireland ne roused might indeed be a scourge of whips to British Government, but without him this Irel was undoubtedly a scourge of scorpions.

THE ELTHAM TREATY.

l came out of Kilmainham on ged at Eltham, and, as Willie wa er of the olive-branch to the Gov

tters From The "Uncrowned King."

ell came to stay with
Dublin as occasion
him to come, and I
palms to make my

strong then, a few
roat, and looked,
indoor garden,
ery day. It then
sing this of giving
with it. He evi
mitted that he

Captain O'Shea is in Paris, and, if so, when do you expect his return?.. I have had no shooting, weather too wet, but shall try to-morrow, when you may expect some heather. .... Somehow or other something from you seems a necessary part of my daily existence, and if I have to go a day or two without even a telegram it seems dreadful.
I want to know how you intend to excuse yourself for telling me not to come on pose if I must return. (To Ireland going on purpo unhappil

April 28th

Our Queen
Sister came yesterd
who
count
d him

he was going to
in days or a fortnigh
after my return – I send y
this news as I know it
comfort my own littl

CHARACTERS IN THE STORY.

Charles Stewart Parnell, the Irish leader. Protestant landlord in County Wicklow. member of the same name and the two Parn poet of the same name and Henry, who fought Sir John and Henry, who fought Grattan against the Union. Electe Meath 1875. Became leader of the party 1880.

Mrs. Katharine O'Shea (afterwards Mrs. Parnell), wife of Captain W. H. O'Shea. Daughter of the Rev. Sir John Wood and sister of Field-Marshal Sir Evelyn Wood. In 1880 was living with her children at Eltham in a house (Womersh odge) provided by her Aunt Ben.

Captain W. H. O'Shea, a Catholic Whig. Elected for West Clare in 1880. A noted rider to in races Sold out of the Army

HOUSE.
of the Phœnix Park

cir
rrow
rrow
tch
ow
o
n

Ireland's Misfortune

Ireland's Misfortune

THE TURBULENT LIFE
OF KITTY O'SHEA

Elisabeth Kehoe

ATLANTIC BOOKS

LONDON

For CFK

First published in Great Britain in hardback and trade paperback in 2008 by Atlantic Books, an imprint of Grove Atlantic Ltd.

Copyright © Elisabeth Kehoe 2008

1 3 5 7 9 8 6 4 2

A CIP catalogue record for this book is available from the British Library.

Hardback ISBN: 978 1 84354 486 9
Export and Airside ISBN: 978 1 84354 561 3

Family Tree by Mark Rolfe © Mark Rolfe Technical Art.

Designed by Nicky Barneby @ Barneby Ltd
Set in 12/15pt Monotype Bell
Printed and bound in Great Britain by MPG Books Ltd, Bodmin, Cornwall

Atlantic Books
An imprint of Grove Atlantic Ltd.
Ormond House
26–27 Boswell Street
London WC1N 3JZ

www.groveatlantic.co.uk

Contents

CONTENTS

List of Illustrations

1. Sketch of Katie. Author's own.
2. Rivenhall. Author's own.
3. Avondale. Hulton Archive / Getty Images.
4. Mrs Anna Maria Wood. Author's own.
5. Lady Wood. Author's own.
6. Captain William Henry O'Shea. Author's own.
7. Charles Stewart Parnell. Author's own.
8. Members of the Irish Home Rule Party. Mary Evans Picture Library.
9. Kilmainham Gaol. Topham Picturepoint / TopFoto.
10. William Ewart Gladstone. Mary Evans Picture Library.
11. Joseph Chamberlain. Mary Evans Picture Library.
12. Political cartoons. Punch Limited / TopFoto.
13. Katherine Parnell. Courtesy of the National Library of Ireland.
14. Marriage certificate. General Register Office © Crown copyright material is reproduced with the permission of the Controller of HMSO and Queen's Printer for Scotland.
15. Parnell's funeral. Mary Evans Picture Library.
16. Clare O'Shea. Kilmainham Gaol Museum.
17. Assheton Maunsell. Kilmainham Gaol Museum
18. Katie O'Shea. Author's own.
19. Katie on the south coast. Author's own.

Acknowledgements

The Institute for Historical Research at the School of Advanced Study at the University of London is a tremendous resource for many historians and I am grateful to be a Visiting Fellow there. The Centre for Contemporary British History within the IHR has been a wonderfully stimulating environment in which to teach and to conduct research and I should like to thank my colleagues for their help and support, in particular Dr Michael Kandiah, Virginia Preston, Dr Tanya Evans, Dr Kate Bradley and Dr Andrew Smith. Also at the IHR I would like to thank Liza Filby for her valuable assistance with my research, as well as the librarians for helping me to track down so many books and other materials. Most of all I wish to express my huge gratitude to Professor David Cannadine whose sound advice and unwavering support have proved once again to be invaluable.

I would like to thank Dr Matthew Kelly and Professor David Cannadine for kindly reading the manuscript and making very valuable suggestions and corrections. Of course, the remaining errors are mine.

Ciara Kerrigan, Elizabeth Kirwan, and all of the archivists at the National Manuscripts Library in Dublin were extremely helpful. I am grateful to the past curator of the Kilmainham Gaol Museum, Pat Cooke, and to archivist Niamh O'Sullivan and supervisor Niall Bergin, for so generously sharing the Parnell collection held there. Librarians and archivists at the British Library, the London Library, the University of Birmingham Library, the University of London Library, and the National Library of Ireland also richly deserve and have my heartfelt appreciation. I would particularly like to thank Honora Faul in the Prints and Drawings Department in the National Library of Ireland for her help. Thank you also to the archivists at the Essex Record Office. Manuscript quotations on pages 287, 341, 352, 353, 355 and 357 are reproduced with the Permission of The Board of The National Library of Ireland. I also gratefully acknowledge permission to quote from the following: the Joseph Chamberlain Manuscript Collection at the University of Birmingham; the Parnell Collection at Kilmainham Gaol Museum, Dublin; and the Gladstone and Grosvenor Papers at the British Library, London.

I am grateful to Professor David French at University College London for sharing his expertise on the British military generally and the 18th hussars specifically. Professor Patrick O'Shea from St Mary's University in Winona, Minnesota, kindly helped me with O'Shea geneaology and history. I would also like to thank Donald Cameron for lending me very interesting Parnell material from the Cameron family archive in Ireland.

I am indebted to the large number of scholars who have published work on Irish history. This ever-growing body of work has proved immensely useful and inspiring. Although there are many historians whose research and analysis have been of great import to me, I should particularly like to thank those whose works were essential for this book. They are – among many others – Paul Bew, D. George Boyce, Frank Callanan, S. J. Connelly, Jane McL. Coté, Roy Foster, Alvin Jackson, Theodore Hoppen, Robert Kee, Matthew Kelly, Carla King, Donal McCartney, Seán McConville,

Margaret O'Callaghan, Alan O'Day, Pauric Travers, and Sally Warwick-Haller. See the Bibliography for the many other historians and authors whose works were consulted for this biography.

Toby Mundy at Atlantic Books was as ever a terrific publisher. Louisa Joyner was an editor extraordinaire. Also at Atlantic Books I would like to warmly thank Emma Grove and especially Sarah Norman. Thanks are also due to Chris Shamwana at Ghost for designing the beautiful cover, Helen Gray for copyediting, Celia Levett for proofreading, Mary Hamilton for typesetting, Meg Davies for the index and Mark Rolfe for the family tree. My agent, Tif Loehnis at Janklow & Nesbit, provided me with every encouragement and much enthusiasm for this project, for which I am deeply appreciative.

This book is dedicated to CFK, who deserves it and much, much more. May the long time sun shine upon you.

WHEN YOU ARE OLD

When you are old and grey and full of sleep,
And nodding by the fire, take down this book,
And slowly read, and dream of the soft look
Your eyes had once, and of their shadows deep;

How many loved your moments of glad grace,
And loved your beauty with love false or true,
But one man loved the pilgrim soul in you,
And loved the sorrows of your changing face;

And bending down beside the glowing bars,
Murmur, a little sadly, how Love fled
And paced upon the mountains overhead
And hid his face amid a crowd of stars.

William Butler Yeats

A Note on Nomenclature

Katharine Wood, later O'Shea, and then Parnell, was never called 'Kitty'. Referring to her as 'Katharine' and 'Katie' follows the course adopted by her own book. Her family and friends called her Katie, and it is by this name that she will be referred to primarily, throughout the book. In public, of course, she was known formally as Miss Wood, Mrs O'Shea and finally, Mrs Parnell.

There is an inherent difficulty in applying Katie's usage of 'Willie' and 'Parnell' in her memoir. The former is essentially private, and the latter public or formal. Charles Stewart Parnell's siblings referred to him as 'Charles' or even 'Charley' in their works, but elsewhere he was always known as Parnell. William O'Shea, on the other hand, was presented in Katharine's book in a personal light. She constantly referred to him in print as 'Willie'. She did not, however, apply the same practice when referring to her lover. This has resulted in a real imbalance of perception. Parnell retained a dignity in her account that was very much lacking for her first husband.

This work has attempted to redress this balance, referring to O'Shea by his formal name when discussing his public life. In the complete absence of any references to Parnell in print by anything other than his last name by Katharine and his colleagues, I have chosen to refer to him by his surname as well – with the understanding that this is not an ideal representation.

Mistress of the Irish Party

$\mathcal{B}$ Y 1889, IRELAND WAS FINALLY — after years of heartache and bloodshed — teetering on the brink of independence. For decades, this island and the 'Irish Question' had preoccupied nationalists and dominated British politics, causing enormous social and political controversy on both sides of the Irish Sea. Opinion over independence was divided — often bitterly so — in both England and Ireland. The nationalist struggle was carried across the Atlantic too, and in America countless Irish emigrants took up the fight. Thousands of dollars were sent across the ocean to finance the battle for independence, along with soldiers and revolutionaries prepared to fight for their motherland's freedom. A resolution to Ireland's struggle for independence was proving frustratingly elusive.

Now, after years of bloody conflict, insurrections and assassinations, the Irish nationalists were at long last tantalizingly close to achieving the independence they had sought. They had been led in their quest by the charismatic Irishman, Charles Stewart Parnell. This Protestant landowner had, against all the odds, succeeded where for centuries so many others had failed. Parnell was an aloof and taciturn man who, through sheer force of will and personality, had brought together his often unruly and divided followers. They were at last on the verge of hard-won success.

The auspices of the brilliant Irishman had put pressure on the Liberal leader Gladstone to grant Home Rule – a form of limited independence. He was confident that he would shortly be elected to his third term in power, and he hoped that his administration's proposed Irish legislation would bring decades of Irish nationalist disappointments to an end. For Parnell, it seemed only a matter of time before the Irish nationalists triumphed, and he would become the 'Uncrowned King' of a new nation.

But there was a private side to the Irish leader that the public knew nothing about. For ten years, he had been conducting a clandestine affair with the English woman Katharine O'Shea, wife of one of his parliamentary colleagues. And now, just as Parnell was on the verge of political success, Captain Willie O'Shea decided to take vindictive action. At the end of 1889, with Irish independence within reach, O'Shea sued his wife for divorce and named Parnell as co-respondent. A massive scandal followed. Exaggerated salacious details of the affair were avidly reported by the press and eagerly seized upon by the opponents of Home Rule. The debacle reverberated through the two lands and across the sea to America, where Irish-American nationalists watched in growing dismay as their leader was publicly scorned and humiliated.

As hopes for an independent Ireland dimmed, retaliatory anger grew. In Ireland the initial disbelief was swiftly followed by a sense of despair. Katharine was blamed by the English and Irish alike for her part in the disaster. She became a figure of loathing, derisively referred to as 'Kitty' by her many enemies, to suggest childishness or licentiousness. The revered leader was thought to be a victim of 'the wiles of a loose woman'. Parnell's detractors – Irish, English and American – claimed that, for Katie's sake, the hopes and dreams of a nation had been squandered, perhaps lost for ever. One of Parnell's previously loyal lieutenants claimed in disgust that Katharine had become the mistress of the Irish Party. She became the scapegoat, blamed for a selfish and ill-considered determination to place her love affair above society's conventions and, worse still, above the cause of Irish nationalism.

Thus, Katharine O'Shea made her mark in history: the ignominious woman who brought down one of Ireland's greatest bids for independence. There were many reasons for the failure to achieve some form of Home Rule at this time, but the scandalous affair and Parnell's subsequent humiliating downfall played into the hands of his enemies. Indeed, many Irish nationalists were tempted then – and later – to look outside Irish politics to explain their failure. They claimed that it was because of Katie's infidelity that Ireland was 'lost' for another thirty years. During that time, countless lives were sacrificed and the nation, when eventually granted independence, became not one country but two, controversially divided between North and South. Katharine's affair with Parnell changed the course of history. But it also gained renown as one of the world's great romances. In 1925, *The People* newspaper published a series of great love stories, 'The World Well Lost for Love'. The very first of the series began with the 'wonderful love story of Charles Parnell – the uncrowned king of Ireland – and Kitty O'Shea'. The headline read: 'A Beautiful Woman's Smile That Altered Ireland's History'.[1]

Her scandalous love story, with its shattering repercussions, lends further drama to an already extraordinary life. Many believed that it was Katharine O'Shea's wanton disregard for convention that betrayed the hopes of a nascent nation. It is this defiance of society and its dictates that make Katharine such a dramatic and compelling figure. Indeed, she later commented: 'For the Irish Party I have never felt anything but pity – pity that they were not worthy of the man and the opportunity, and, seeing the punishment that the years have brought upon Ireland, that their craven hearts could not be loyal to her greatest son.'[2]

In the context of the Victorian era, with all of its societal constraints and reverence for the institution of matrimony, what gave this remarkable woman her sublime confidence and self-belief? Katharine O'Shea chose to ignore convention, and to live a complicated, secret double life as the mistress of a very famous man for years. Yet, far from seeking to hide and excuse her scandalous lifestyle, she expected instead to take her place at Parnell's side as the Uncrowned Queen of Ireland.

Ireland has known at any rate one English she-wolf… who has brought more misfortune on our country than all the coercion of Mr. Balfour.

T. M. Healy, *Irish News*, 30 September 1891

He did not make any 'dying speech', or refer in any way at the last to his 'Colleagues and the Irish people', as was erroneously reported. I was too broken then and too indifferent to what any sensation-lovers put about to contradict this story, but, as I am now giving the world the absolutely true account of the Parnell whom I knew and loved, I am able to state that he was incapable of such an affectation so complete. The last words Parnell spoke were given to the wife who had never failed him, to the love that was stronger than death.

Katharine Parnell, 1914

CHAPTER ONE

A Vicar's Daughter

$\mathcal{K}$atharine, or Katie – as she was known – was born at Glazenwood in Essex, some 45 miles from London, on 30 January 1845. She was a product of the mid-Victorian age, and her early influences were those of her immediate family. The Wood family were members of the privileged upper-middle-class world of the landed gentry, although they were not themselves landowners. Around them, nineteenth-century England was in flux, driven by industrialization that was accompanied by urbanization and other significant changes to people's lifestyles. Katie's parents inhabited the more traditional life of the countryside elite. Her father, Sir John Page Wood, had inherited the baronetcy some two years before Katie's birth. He was an Anglican vicar, and in 1832 had been appointed to the vicarage of Cressing in Essex. Soon after their youngest daughter was born, he and his wife, Emma, née Michell, moved with their family to Rivenhall, close to Witham, also in Essex.

It was a large family. Katie was the last of thirteen children. Like many of their contemporaries, the Woods had a good number of children, but many of them did not live long. Emma Wood had given birth to six children in rapid succession, of whom only two survived. She then had another six; so eight siblings altogether were alive at the time of Katie's birth. Two years later, however, Emma lost two further offspring: her seventeen-year-old daughter Clarissa, and eldest surviving son, Frederick. Katie thus grew up with six surviving siblings: Maria (always called Polly), Francis (known as Frank), Charles, Evelyn, Emma and Anna. Katie was the baby of a family where the loss of children had caused great grief. Of thirteen live births, only seven children survived to adulthood.

Emma Wood was by all accounts a devoted mother. With Queen Victoria, herself the mother of nine children, at the helm, Victorian society placed great importance on the virtues of motherhood.[1] Emma was especially fond of the youngest of her boys, Evelyn, Katie's senior by seven years and Katie knew that her brother was her mother's favourite.[2] She was very much her father's pet, and later wrote: 'As a matter of fact, my mother was so entirely wrapped up in Evelyn that I think I was jealous, even though I had my father so much to myself.' Katie described her childhood as idyllic. The home where she grew up was spacious and beautifully situated. She was raised in a domestic environment where the values of the hearth and home were encouraged.[3] Although her mother, Emma, had considerable artistic and literary talent, she exercised these activities from within the home.

Money, however, was a constant preoccupation for John Wood's household. This was because there was never enough. The Wood family were middle class, in that they did not perform manual labour, nor rely solely upon income generated by land ownership. In fact, John Wood owned no land at all, and the family lived either in accommodation provided by the Church or, later, in a house that was rented. John Wood had little family money and needed to live on his earnings. The life of a clergyman in 1840s England was one of comfort but not luxury. However, John Wood's salary at the time of his youngest daughter's birth was about £700, which was the revenue from his position at St Peter's, Cornhill, London, and did not include his salary from the Cressing parish. That income put him in the top 1.2 per cent of the population. Just less than 1 per cent of income recipients of England and Wales earned between £300 and £1,000 in 1867. Indeed, even by 1911–12, merely 2 per cent of all employees and professional persons in Britain earned as much as £200 per annum.[4] And yet the Wood family found it difficult to maintain a rather grand lifestyle, in a large country house.

Katie's grandfather was Sir Matthew, Baron Hatherley of Hatherley House, Gloucestershire. He had three sons, of whom John was the eldest. A self-made wealthy man, Sir Matthew Wood had helped John by providing him with an entrée to royal circles. Alderman Wood, as he was then known, had become a firm supporter of the unfortunate Caroline, the rejected spouse of the Prince Regent, later King George IV.[5] George and Caroline had separated in 1795, within a year of their marriage. Bitter years followed, during which her husband sought to be rid of her. Many Radicals espoused her cause.

Matthew Wood was a strong Radical who nevertheless maintained his allegiance to the Whig Party. He was very successful in both his business and his political life, and was twice elected Lord Mayor of London. Wood was an ambitious man – of a 'vehement and somewhat pushing disposition' – and became a prominent figure on the social and political landscape, largely through his base as a member of the Fishmongers (the traditional Whig company).[6] He publicly and forcefully championed Caroline's cause, and was largely responsible for encouraging her to return to England from the continent in 1820 to fight for her title and position, even offering her refuge in his own home in South Audley Street in London. This act of public support was commemorated with china plates, which were circulated throughout the nation. They bore his portrait and were inscribed: 'M. Wood, Esq., Twice Lord Mayor of London, who patriotically gave up his house to her Majesty, Queen Caroline, upon her arrival in London on the 6th of June, 1820.'[7]

His son John had taken holy orders after coming down from Cambridge, and Matthew arranged for him to take the position of Caroline's private chaplain. After the trauma of George IV's coronation – from which she was successfully excluded – Caroline became increasingly weak and ill. She sacked some of her loyal attendants and, most unusually, made John Wood Chamberlain and his wife, Emma, Mistress of the Robes in July 1821. One of her supporters believed that this nomination was due to her passion for their child.[8] This is indeed possible: family history records that Caroline 'used to take pleasure in making little garments for young Mrs. Wood's baby'.[9] For the rest of her life, the Queen remained 'on terms of the closest intimacy with the Wood family', and it was noticed that her 'genuine, if somewhat capricious, kindness was freely extended to the children and grandchildren of the man she regarded as her benefactor'.[10] When Caroline died later that year, in August 1821, both father and son attended her remains all the way from England to Brunswick, where she was laid to rest.[11]

John Wood was proud of the family's connection to royalty. There were a number of mementoes of the late Queen in Rivenhall. Her 'unfinished knitting' was carefully 'preserved for many years in its little work-basket as a token of her womanly kindness in her last unhappy days',[12] and John Wood had removed a red carnation from the table of one of Queen Caroline's dinner parties, which he carefully kept in a vase under a glass shade. With the flower were two Doulton figures. Both represented the Queen, standing and crowned, with a roll in her hand. On the one was written 'My hope is in the People'. The other was engraved: 'My hope is in my People'.[13]

The family preserved the heirlooms, and Katie related in her memoir how she had kept the knitting box until it was stolen from her possession.[14] Other treasured pieces carefully preserved included a picture of Caroline's funeral cortège passing through London. There was also a jewelled snuffbox and a ring. These had been gifts from Caroline to Sir Matthew Wood, and he in turn left the ring to his son John. It was inherited on Sir John's death by his own son Charles, whose daughter recounted that her father 'constantly wore this ring on his tie when it came into his possession, and we were never tired of asking him to open its little crown and show us the tiny piece of Queen Caroline's hair'.[15]

John Wood was appointed Rector of St Peter's, Cornhill, in 1824. It is likely that once again his father helped him, as the appointment was made by the Common Council of the City of London. The Episcopal Church of England and the Presbyterian Church of Scotland were fighting hard to maintain their established status. Although a large number of distinct Christian denominations existed, the predominant four groups were Anglicans, old Dissenters (dating back to the sixteenth and seventeenth centuries – including Baptists, Congregationalists, Quakers and others), new Dissenters (mainly Methodist) and Roman Catholics. Anglicans by and large constituted the establishment, and religious persuasions tended to align politically. Broadly speaking, Dissenters tended to be more individualist, and to favour lower taxation and laissez-faire economic policies. As the Dissent movement grew in size, its aspiration expanded from being the religion of barns to being 'infected with the ambition of becoming the religion of cathedrals'.[16] The growing respectability of many of these sects did little to commend them to the Church of England. The Anglican cleric and novelist Charles Kingsley spoke dismissively of Baptist pastors as 'muck enthroned on their respective dung hills'.[17] At the same time, the nineteenth century saw a significant growth in the Catholic population – greatly influenced by the large numbers of Irish immigrants. In 1850, Pope Pius IX appointed a full hierarchy of Catholic bishops.[18] Catholic communities showed the highest rate of church attendance, and under the new organizational structure formed large communities linked in faith as well as by cultural values.

Thus, during the time that Katie's father ran his parish, the Church of England was experiencing the changes brought about by the growing confidence of non-Anglican Protestants and the increasing population of Catholics.[19] Common to all these Christian denominations was a characteristically Victorian preoccupation with class. Anglicanism was perceived by many to be the religion of the ruling elite. Anglican bishops were appointed after discussion between the Prime Minister and Queen Victoria, who held strong views. In many churches, pew renting was common, and the best seats were reserved for those prepared to pay. The Anglican clergy were slow to grasp that much of the disenfranchisement felt by the working class and labouring poor was due to the gulf between them and Church leaders.

Victorian men were attracted to the clerical life, as evidenced in the rise of the number of clergymen from 14,613 in 1841 to 24,232 fifty years later.[20] A large proportion of these clerics were graduates of the Universities of Oxford and Cambridge; during the 1840s nearly three-quarters of the Oxbridge graduates chose the priesthood and, in 1841, 86 per cent of ordinands came from these two universities.[21] Compensation had risen throughout the eighteenth century and by the 1830s the median income of English incumbents was £275.[22] When John Wood was appointed Rector of St Peter's, the *Essex Chronicle* reported on 12 November 1824 that the living was worth from £700 to £800 a year.[23] This was a very good living, and the young couple settled in London.

As an Anglican cleric, John Wood was typical of his time and generation. He espoused a middle-class lifestyle that was costly, enjoying hunting, for example, an expensive sport. Wood was conservative in his politics and his views. With two short exceptions, he supported the government when the Liberal Party was in power, from 1846 to 1866, and took pride in his standing in the community and served as a magistrate. His granddaughter would later write: 'Sir John was a most popular man, and beloved by all who knew him; the old villagers still declare that he always had a cheery word for them when they used to "make him their obedience".'[24]

In 1833, Reverend John Wood obtained the living in Cressing, in Essex, while continuing to retain that of St Peter's, where he left a curate in charge when the family left London and moved to Cressing. This additional revenue would have helped the family's coffers, and the motivation to take on the Essex position was probably financial. Certainly, Emma's sister Maria did not believe that her sister had been altogether pleased by the move. Maria visited the Wood family in August 1833 and wrote to her friend Mrs Pascoe that although the vicarage was 'pretty and convenient', with 'orchard trees gleaming with fruit', the landscape viewed from the windows would, she felt, 'be dismal in the winter when they have nothing to see but the naked shoots barren as lances'. Maria did not think that her sister was happy, concluding:

I must console myself by reflecting that if John had not had the living he could not have gone there. As the 'uses of adversity' may be sweet, I trust they may prove so to her, for she seems to me to be buried with all her faculties in full life; but she has had the good sense and good taste not to make a single complaint either in her letters or in conversation.[25]

The household was rather isolated, and Emma was unable to leave the children for long. Journeys were tiring. Maria wrote of how her sister had travelled to see her in February 1835. The trip had involved a 52-mile drive in a pony chaise, driven by her servant. Emma had brought two children and a nursemaid, leaving the other three youngsters at home with their father. 'She and John never leave home at the same time,' Maria explained, 'as five children are too many to carry on a visit.' Travel of this kind was never easy – Maria was worried about the journey home, 'as the weather is very tempestuous'.[26]

The vicarage in Cressing proved to be too small for the growing family, and so the Woods moved to a house called Glazenwood, where Katie was born, later described as a 'charming house with the most beautiful gardens I have ever seen in a place of moderate size'.[27] Wherever she lived, Emma was industrious and indefatigable in her efforts to educate her children. Maria wrote admiringly of an occasion when her niece Clarissa, aged seven, had played piano with her mother, including 'five or six variations' of 'Away with Melancholy', the March in 'Puritani' and a number of pieces on her own, without a music sheet. Another of Emma's daughters, Maria, had construed fourteen verses of the Latin testament – correctly. The children's aunt was impressed, writing: 'When I tell you that these various branches of instruction are given by Emma, you will agree with me that there are few like her.'[28] Evenings at home in the Wood household were spent by the fireside, as described by Emma to her sister: 'John with Clarissa on one knee and Emma on the other; Freddie netting large nets to preserve the cherries, Maria leaning over my chair asking me to play at verses, and Frank sitting on my lap with my paint-box open before him'.[29]

Soon after Katie was born, the family moved from Glazenwood to Rivenhall Place, also in Essex. Family lore has it that the move took place after Sir John had sent out his son Charles on a pony to look for a bigger house. Apparently the boy returned, saying that he had found the perfect place, which his mother would love, 'because it has a waterfall down the front stairs'.[30] It was the property of a family friend, Lord Western, and had so long been unoccupied that it was practically a ruin. The Wood family took the house on an extended tenancy after agreeing to make the necessary repairs. The house was enormous, containing forty rooms and halls.

In this pleasant place, the Wood family enjoyed country pursuits together. They were keen hunters. Katie wrote of how she befriended the hares, but never 'confessed my unsporting behaviour to any of the household, as my brothers always hunted when at home, and my sister also'.[31] Katie was provided with a pony of her own, and she rode daily on her mount, Eugenie.

Both the surrounding countryside and the landscape and horticulture of Rivenhall were a delight. There were beautiful gardens, as well as a lake and a park of 100 acres. In front of the library window was a large 'peony tree' whose pink blossoms were the size of 'dinner plates'.[32] Other peonies mingled with a 'dark crimson bush' to make a 'fine show'.[33] The many colourful plants included white oriental poppies as well as yellow and wine-coloured dahlias. A fine feature within the grounds was a sun-dial which had been purchased by Sir John, made from one of the old piers of London Bridge.

The large lake provided constant entertainment for the children and many visitors, and fishing was especially enjoyed. Katie's niece recollected how their coachman used a hook tied to the end of his whip to catch fish on visits to Rivenhall.[34] In the winter the lake froze and the children looked forward to skating. The sport was very popular with the family and Katie's brother-in-law, Sir Thomas Barrett Lennard, had a rink laid down at his own property at Belhus Park, near Rainham in Essex.

The Wood residence was not only beautiful, but also warm and welcoming. Years later Katie described it: 'In the large hall of Rivenhall logs burnt in the great open fireplaces. Out of this hall opened a smaller one from which the broad shallow oak stairs led to the upper rooms… The drawing room was hung with my mother's paintings'.[35] The long dining room was home to pictures by the French military artist Edouard Detaille, including paintings that depressed the younger children, such as *Après le Combat* and the *Salut aux Blessés*. The walls of the hall and many of the other rooms also displayed Emma Wood's paintings – according to her granddaughter the rooms were 'literally papered with them'.[36] Her pictures could be melancholy too: the drawing room featured a huge canvas, covering an entire side of one wall, entitled *The Ordeal by Touch*. Its subject was a man, 'very blue and dead, with blood flowing from his side at the murderers' touch',[37] and the people around were depicted with horror in their faces.

Emma was industrious and talented. In addition to her painting, she was a novelist whose works were later published, and a 'fine musician'.[38] When the Woods were living at Peckham, Emma's sister Maria wrote: 'My chief and favourite companion is Emma, than whom it would be difficult to find a person more gifted both in intellect and accomplishments.'[39] In addition to the oils, Emma painted watercolours, featuring subjects that were mainly classical, including *Actaeon surprising Diana and her Nymphs*. These watercolours were carefully hung, with little velvet curtains on tiny brass rods in front of them to prevent fading. Emma's prowess was such that she was invited to be an early exhibitor in the rooms of the New Water Colour Society in 1833, where her pictures were much admired. The brothers Finden engraved a number of her works. Although Emma's husband John apparently complained 'of the misery of having married an artist', her sister Maria believed that he was in fact 'proud as a peacock of her handiworks'.[40]

Katie wrote that her childhood might have been solitary had it not been for her close relationship with her father, for whom she had intense admiration: 'My brothers and sisters were all so much older than myself – most of them married, with children of their own – and my mother was so absorbed in her brilliant boy Evelyn, the affairs of her elder daughters and her own literary work, that had it not been for my father I should have been a very lonely child.'[41] These observations from Katie, written many years later, are quite misleading. In fact, she had two siblings quite close in age to her, her sister Anna and brother Evelyn, and older siblings visited frequently. They played games. She records that 'My brothers loved to tease me', and that 'Evelyn was specially adroit in bewildering me.'[42] Katie's recollections constantly provide glimpses of a childhood that was anything but lonely.

She described her childhood winter nights at Rivenhall: 'My father used to sit by the fire reading his *Times*, with his great white cat on his knee, while I made his tea and hot buttered toast, and my mother and sister Anna read or sketched.' Nor was Katie left out of this cosy domesticity: 'I used to write the plots of tragic little stories which my "Pip" [her father, Sir John] used to read and call "blood-stained bandits," owing to the violent action and the disregard of convention shown by all the characters concerned.'[43] Thus Katie had a flair for the dramatic – and an attraction to the rebel – at a young age, and it is clear that she was encouraged within the security of the family circle.

Katie recounted a tale of a family friend, Sir William Peel, who had inadvertently given offence by remarking on how like a mushroom Katie looked in her large new hat. In order to 'hide her mortification', she recalled, she had brought out her largest cat to show him. '"Oh, what an ugly" – then, seeing my face of reproach, he hastily continued – "but *very* fine cat!"' What is particularly revealing is the following observation: 'To this day when members of the family wish to make excuses for any inexcellence they remark hopefully, "but *very* fine cat!".'[44]

From a careful reading of her story, it would seem that Katie was a well-loved, indulged child. She had thirteen cats in addition to her pony. She took singing lessons, and her mother enjoyed her young daughter singing French operatic music to her. When she was older, Katie read her mother and sister Anna's novels, reporting that they 'used to let me read and criticise, at which I felt greatly honoured'.[45]

Emma Wood, in addition to her own obvious talents, was clearly an enthusiastic supporter of the efforts of her offspring. When Katie set Longfellow's poem 'Weariness' to music, she later wrote that she was 'so encouraged by my mother's praise of the setting that I sent the poet a copy'.[46] Great was the youngster's delight when the famous man wrote to thank her, saying that hers was the best setting of that piece that he had ever heard. Emma Wood wrote to a friend of how much she enjoyed her children's successes: 'One always likes to have one's children praised. It is a kind of extended selfishness. When my children beat me at chess, I say, what wonderful children I have brought into the world!'[47]

Katie's parents took a dynamic approach to her general culture and education. She had informal lessons from her father, who had 'never-ending patience' in answering her questions. 'Looking far back to my childhood', she penned, 'I can now see how he used to direct my reading, without my being in the least aware of it, and how he drew me on to questions of countries, places, and men that led continually to further interest and desire for knowledge which he never failed to supply.'[48] Her 'happiest' days, she claimed, were when she and her father took long walks and hunted for wild flowers.

My father knew a great deal about botany and taught me the names of the flowers I collected, their old English names and the derivations of them. I have still the books he gave me, that I might learn more of the flowers which grow without cultivation, and the power of observation he awoke in me then has been a great solace to me through life.[49]

Sir John was a serious classical scholar, but he was also great fun. His granddaughter recorded how he constantly delighted his children by putting their sayings and doings into doggerel verse, then making little tunes to fit the words.[50] Katie adored her father and recalled that he had been a 'tall, handsome old man with merry blue eyes and a ready smile'.[51] She remembered with pride being taken with him when he addressed political meetings, stating, 'he became a great influence in the county during election times'. Katie loved being in the limelight too. 'I remember', she recorded, 'when he was to speak at a political meeting, how he laughed as he tied me up in enormous orange ribbons and made me drive him there, and how immensely proud of him I was.'[52]

Katie published a memoir in 1914 and provided an interesting perspective on how she saw her life. It was clearly important to her to present herself in a positive light. This of course is a common characteristic of autobiography, but her sense of self-importance is extraordinarily pervasive. In the first place, this work was meant to be a biography of Charles Parnell, yet a large portion was given over to her own story. She constantly casts herself in an admiring light: she brought ears of wheat to 'two old friends who were too feeble to glean it for themselves'. These 'old people' as well as the farmer were, she said, 'great friends' of hers. The Rivenhall curate was also her 'great friend'.[53] Another admirer was Reverend Thomas Gosse, who took her father's place as curate at Cressing, and taught Katie about astronomy. A gentleman friend of her sister's, a Colonel of the Light Dragoons, made Katie a present of her first 'grown-up' book, *Vanity Fair* – 'a first edition, illustrated, which I then prized very greatly, and which I still have'.[54] The Master of Hounds, Mr Honeywood, was another 'great friend', as was the Hon. Grantley-Barkley. This 'dear old man' was, Katie recorded, completely besotted by her, and wrote her long letters. He also wrote to her mother 'inquiring of my welfare and the direction of my education'. Katie kept many of the verses that he composed in her honour.[55]

Katie frequently went to stay with her sister, Emma Barrett Lennard, and her husband, Sir Thomas. Emma was a good ten years older than her younger sister, and had married when Katie was eight. The Barrett Lennards were very wealthy and had two fine homes: a house in Brighton, and their country seat, Belhus. They also owned an estate in Ireland, in Clones, County Monaghan, which had been in the family since the sixteenth century.[56] 'She was always very kind to me', Katie recalled, 'and I used to love going to visit her at her house in Brighton.'[57] Emma had an excellent singing voice, and was a talented composer. She wrote many songs, and set to music various poems, including Tennyson's 'Crossing the Bar'.[58]

The Wood family talents were musical, artistic and literary. It was a logical outreach to extend their abilities to the performance of amateur theatricals. From 1860 to 1869 the family gave theatrical performances for various charities. At that time, such amateur theatricals were a rarity and the 'Belhus Dramatic Corps', as they

styled themselves, caused something of a sensation. The Barrett
Lennards hired professional actors and actresses to coach them.
This extra work was undoubtedly welcome. Then, as now, most
actors found it difficult to get regular work. Although a small
number of thespians became star actors, others were paid very
little. It was a hard existence, and actors sometimes starved.[59] The
comic actor John Clarke was called upon to advise the company, in
1861, on a burlesque of *Romeo and Juliet*. Robert Keeley, another
actor, helped them in the spring of 1862, on a play entitled *Plot and
Passion*. At first, the corps played at Rivenhall and at Belhus. As
their confidence grew, they expanded their repertoire, and
performed near home, at Chelmsford and Colchester, even London.[60]
Katie's niece (the daughter of her brother Charles) lamented that
she had been 'too young' to attend the performances, but could 'well
remember my mother taking us to the woods to pick basketfuls of
primroses and periwinkles which she made into immense lilac and
yellow bouquets to throw on the stage at an evening performance,
the newspapers afterwards stating that the actors were deluged
with floral offerings.'[61]

It was a delightful family venture, and it reinforced the slightly
bohemian and unconventional aspects of Katie's upbringing.
Emma Wood was a keen supporter of these theatrical endeavours
and Katie recounted how her 'devoted mother, who was
wonderfully clever with her brush, left her beloved pictures and
novel-writing, and set to work to paint the scenery for our play'.[62]
Indeed, Lady Wood was, according to her youngest daughter, much
the heart of the enterprise. 'She never grew impatient', recalled
Katie, 'but painted serenely on, coaching us, greeting her guests
gaily from her elevated position, and pairing off men and maidens
with an unerring intuition that stilled the bickerings that naturally
arose in the scramble for the best parts.'[63] Katie admired her
mother, who kept her good looks as she grew older. She was, Katie
later wrote, 'a very attractive woman with large grey eyes and jet-

black hair… a woman scorning throughout her life all the cosmetic adjuncts to feminine beauty, she was rewarded by nature with the preservation of her good looks in old age.'[64]

Katie basked in the self-confidence that a sheltered and supportive environment provided. In describing a dinner with Mr John Morley (later Lord Morley), she explained that her family felt that this 'brilliant' young man's 'tense intellect kept them at too great a strain for pleasurable conversation'. Because she was the youngest and because, according to her sister Anna, 'no one expects you to know anything', she was asked to entertain him. Katie's true feelings shone through in her recounting of the tale: 'So I calmly invited John Morley to walk with me, and, as we paced through the park from one lodge to the other, my companion talked to me so easily and readily that I forgot my role of "fool of the family", and responded most intelligently to a really very interesting conversation.'[65]

In addition to the theatricals, Katie was enjoying many aspects of becoming a young lady. She was given a sitting room of her own, where she could be 'undisturbed' and receive her own friends. She wrote of how their servant, Tim Bobbin, put down a carpet for her, and hung white curtains, 'afterwards filling the window seats with the best flowers he could get'. As ever, family members were kind to Katie. Her sister-in-law, Minna, married to her brother Charlie, lined the new curtains in pink fabric for her. Katie's private room 'glowed with colour'.[66] Katie was not only well loved by her family but popular with others. She craved admiration, and probably revealed more than she meant to when describing how, when younger, she had tried to impress her sister's fiancé by putting a red fez on her 'golden curls' and galloping on her pony past the dining room where he might look out and 'see and admire the intrepid maiden'.[67] She announced in her memoir that she received 'many valentines'. Katie described how one year she received, 'amongst innumberable [sic] other valentines', a 'gorgeous' one from their servant Tim Bobbin. She gave this one, a 'wonderful affair of satin, paper-lace, and orris-root scent, the 'place of honour'.[68]

And then, at the age of fifteen, she met Willie O'Shea.

CHAPTER TWO

The Parnells of Avondale

CROSS THE IRISH SEA, on the wooded estate of Avondale
in County Wicklow, Charles Stewart Parnell was at this
time fourteen years old. The Parnells were true landed gentry, who
had been at Avondale since 1795. The estate of nearly 4,000 acres
was noted for its beauty, and for the spectacular site of the house,
above a deep river gorge. Avondale, built in 1777, was a spacious
home; above the central hall was a gallery in which a band played
at dances, and there was a library, with a billiard-table. Charles
Parnell spent his early life enjoying the typical pleasures of a young
country gentleman, playing cricket, hunting and fishing. There
were eleven children, but the marriage of Charles's parents, John
and Delia Parnell, does not seem to have been a happy one.

John Parnell was a traditional country gentleman, descended
from a long line of Parnells, who had been in Ireland since the
time of the Restoration, around 1660.[1] Such Anglo-Irish families
were mainly Protestant landowners, who had settled in Ireland
and by the eighteenth century had gained considerable political
and economic ascendancy over the Catholic indigenous population.[2]
The second Sir John Parnell (1744–1801), who in 1785 became
Chancellor of the Irish Exchequer, and in 1786 was sworn a

member of the British Privy Council, broke with the government in opposing the Act of Union, and died soon after taking his seat at the new Parliament in Westminster, at the end of 1801.[3]

The Parnell line continued to be distinguished enough, and wealth steadily accrued to the family through enterprise and astute marriages. William Parnell, Charles's paternal grandfather, inherited the estate of Avondale in County Wicklow in 1795. He was a respected liberal landlord, and was MP for Wicklow from 1817 to 1820. Although he died before Charles was born, he left behind a number of pamphlets and a novel, which supported his views on the need both for reform in Irish rural life and for concessions to the Catholics. Charles's father, John Henry Parnell, continued the family tradition of mildly reformist liberal politics and benevolent landlordism. He was Master of Foxhounds and a keen cricket player.

While travelling in America in 1834 with his cousin Lord Powerscourt, the twenty-three-year-old Parnell met Delia Tudor Stewart, the eighteen-year-old daughter of the famous American naval hero, Commodore Charles Stewart, the son of Ulster emigrants who had left Belfast and settled in Philadelphia. The Commodore, who had run away to sea in his youth, had had a successful career, capturing two British warships in 1815, for which he was awarded a Gold Medal from Congress. He was later made an Admiral, and served in the navy until his retirement – although his record was not unblemished and included a court martial in 1826. He married Delia Tudor in 1815, and they had two children, Delia and Charles. The marriage was not a happy one, however, and Delia was brought up by her mother after her parents separated.

The Tudors had settled in Boston in colonial times, and Delia enjoyed the privileged life of the social elite. She and her mother lived in Washington, DC, and although they were not exceptionally well off, they were well connected and sufficiently prosperous to enjoy the social pleasures of the Washington and New York seasons, as well as summers in Boston with relatives and in Maine with Mrs Stewart's sister, Mrs Hallowell Gardiner.[4] The engagement to John Henry Parnell was not, she later claimed, welcomed by her mother, who believed that she could do better, but the Anglo-Irishman was a man of substantial property, of which the estate at Avondale was the core. Her grandmother wrote to another daughter that John Henry Parnell was connected with 'the nobility of Ireland'.[5] The couple were married in the fashionable Grace Church in New York on 31 May 1835.

Thus Charles and his siblings, although not from a particularly wealthy background, nevertheless formed part of an elite class in Ireland. The Anglo-Irish were often educated in England and Charles – the seventh child and third son – was, at the age of seven, sent there to boarding school. His mother, Delia, seemed lacking in maternal instincts, and, when Charles was only seven, she effectively abandoned the family home to install herself in Paris. Then, when Charles was thirteen, his father died unexpectedly. Delia remained in Paris when not travelling to America, and family life must have been rather grim for the Parnell children, who were still based, outside of term time, at Avondale. Charles's brother, John Howard Parnell, wrote how even the routine of meals fell apart while they were still quite young:

We all got into a terribly disorganized habit as to meals during our days together at Avondale, after our father had died and our mother had gone to America. The only meal during the day at which all the family and visitors were certain of meeting was dinner, which we generally had about eight o'clock in the evening.[6]

Thus, the close-knit family cosiness enjoyed by Katie was not something that Charles Parnell experienced. The life of Anglo-Irish families like the Parnells was quite different from anything Katie would have known. By the mid- to late-nineteenth century, the historical dominance of such Anglo-Irish families was on the wane. Their entitlement to privileges as well as the lands they held was increasingly challenged, and the general unease about their position in Ireland had been emphasized by struggles for Catholic emancipation in the early nineteenth century.

The Parnells were at the middling to lower end of the landowning scale, and they did reside in Ireland, whereas many of the wealthy landowning Anglo-Irish families did not. This absentee landlordism caused particular problems, especially during hard times. Ireland was still essentially rural in the mid- to late-nineteenth century and the economy was primarily agricultural, with almost three-quarters of the male population engaged in farming. In England, by comparison, well under a quarter of men were so employed, and only just over half the population of England and Wales lived outside towns of 2,500 or more.[7]

But families like the Parnells had made an effort to integrate into local life, while their position as employers of large numbers of people led to greater proximity and some social integration within the local community. The servants at Avondale, for example, lived with the family. Charles was extremely fond of his nurse, Susan, and believed in her native cures. He 'accepted the peasant lore of Ireland with the simplicity of a child'.[8]

A young woman such as Katie would have lived a country life in Ireland characterized by outdoor pursuits with some home learning, and in that respect her lifestyle would have been much like that of Charles Parnell's sisters. Evening parties and country-house entertainments featured largely, much as they did in England. What would have been quite different, however, was the proximity to real misery that many resident landowning families in Ireland experienced. Although there was poverty in England in the mid-nineteenth century, there was nothing comparable in scale to the mid-century famines in Ireland. Millions died or emigrated after the potato blights of 1846–9 left the people starving. The 'Great Famine' (1845–9), as it became known, was a tragedy that left a powerful legacy of anger and a deep sense of betrayal. Many of those whose families suffered, and those who emigrated, blamed the British establishment for its laissez-faire economic policies and for ostensibly not doing enough to help Ireland.[9] The miseries and perceived injustices of the Great Famine left great bitterness and division through many parts of Ireland.

Some local landowning families did help, however, forgoing rents, and providing soup kitchens, as well as work, for their tenants. In Wicklow, fragmented land ownership and fertile soil meant that the experience of the famine years was more muted than in other parts of Ireland; in 1883, there were twenty landowners of over 3,000 acres who were resident there, and a number of large commercial families, including the Guinesses, Latouches and Jamesons, lived in the county. Wicklow had estates that were larger in median size than those of most other counties, and the number of absentee landowners was lower. In addition, there were a significant number of 'middling gentry' families, many of whom were Protestant. This had important repercussions during the famine years, when Wicklow was relatively speaking better off than most other parts of Ireland, and recovered more quickly.[10] Nevertheless, emigration and premature death from disease and starvation on a massive scale formed, and continued to form, a distinctive and melancholic element of the nineteenth-century Irish experience.[11]

Ireland's main urban development was Dublin, on the Irish Sea. Originally a Viking settlement dating back to the ninth century, Dublin was a fine residential city, which had experienced a second cycle of rapid growth from the 1590s to the 1820s. Dublin's population in the early nineteenth century approached 250,000 (with a further 150,000 in the surrounding county), so it was a very large city – although not quite on the scale of London, whose population was close to 900,000 at this time (representing 10 per cent of the total population).[12] Eighteenth-century Dublin drew benefit, in terms of its growth, from the political aspirations of the ruling Ascendancy. The development of the city continued with the construction of the Parliament House that began in 1729,[13] the Four Courts, the College and Dublin Castle. The central thoroughfares were refashioned into wider streets and two central trunk canal systems were built. Dublin was the leading port and national centre for distribution of goods and printed information. It held a significant role in the provision of financial services during the commercialization of Irish agriculture as well as a monopoly of certain professional services, such as the provision of higher education and the courts of law. The ruling elite wintered in Dublin and their presence underpinned the city's prosperity, while the parties and entertainments they required sustained a large variety of craftsmen and artisans.

But the loss of its own parliament – legislated through the Act of Union in 1801[14] – had by all accounts a negative impact on the city, although other factors also contributed to its relative decline in the nineteenth century as an important political centre for the Protestant Ascendancy. Dublin continued nevertheless to thrive: gas lighting arrived in 1825, and people thronged to private mansions for dinners, concerts and other parties. There were processions, parades and ceremonies. The retail trade was sophisticated and varied: display arcades housed Dublin silversmiths and goldsmiths, and Irish lace, poplins and linens could all be purchased. Fashionable ladies and gentlemen enjoyed walks through the city's beautiful park, St Stephen's Green, in the centre, as well as the magnificent Phoenix Park, where one could hire carriages.

A favourite occupation of the elite, and also for those of the lower echelons, was hunting and attending the races. The Duke of Stacpoole recalled:

The winter of 1881 saw me installed in Dublin at the Shelbourne Hotel for some months, to hunt with the Meath and Ward hounds... The

Kildare Hunt Races, better known as 'Punchestown', are held near Naas in April every year, and are the most sporting of all race meetings in Ireland. The course is laid out over a natural hunting country which comprises fences of all sorts, while the view from the stand is of world-wide fame... Great numbers of English and foreign visitors came to Ireland for Punchestown, as they did for the other big social and sporting event – the Dublin Horse Show.[15]

There was a craze in Dublin in the 1880s for coaching-parties. The pastime took off in 1878 when Captain Seeds set up his four-in-hand. Coaching tours from the posh Shelbourne Hotel – on St Stephen's Green – to Bray, on the Wicklow coast, set forth on fine mornings. In 1886, Squire Thompson, of Clare Hall, Raheny, offered his own coaching tour. Also setting off from the Shelbourne, Thompson – the reputed best coachman living – took his parties to Kilmacanogue, inland in the Wicklow hills. He later diverted his route to the coastal town of Greystones.[16] Evening entertainments were enlivened by Dublin's thriving theatres. The Gaiety, opened in 1871, soon became the most fashionable and popular. Top London companies brought their shows to Dublin. The D'Oyly Carte company brought its Gilbert and Sullivan productions to the Gaiety, to great acclaim. Dublin audiences had a reputation for discernment and wit, and greeted musicals as well as great drama with enthusiasm.[17]

Although no longer in its Ascendancy heyday, mid- to late-nineteenth-century Dublin prospered. The flourishing middle classes – many of them Catholic professionals – continued to spend money and build houses. The landed gentry, although somewhat decreased in numbers and relative importance, continued to dominate the elite social season. Regimental balls and other evening entertainments were patronized, sustaining the market for fashionable finery, while carriage-riding, hunting, watching the races, as well as shopping and the theatre, provided pleasurable activities for the leisured middling gentry in these post-famine years. But this agreeable lifestyle was reaching its end, and it became increasingly difficult for the gilded – predominantly Protestant – elite to ignore the clamour for social and political change.

Much has been written about the influences of his early life on Charles Parnell's political views. It is generally believed that despite Delia Parnell's American outlook and her father's naval success against the British (with whom he was actually very friendly, happily entertaining the captains whose ships he had captured), she was in fact a confirmed Anglophile. Despite her well-known disregard for convention (she seems to have regarded herself as a charming *enfant terrible*, and she was certainly fond of expressing her views on any subject), she made sure that her daughters were presented at Queen Victoria's court. She was an enthusiastic participant in Ireland's elite Anglo-Irish social life, and regularly attended dances, dinners and other receptions at Dublin Castle while she resided in Ireland. As one of Parnell's excellent biographers has concluded – after detailed study – there seems 'little ground' for assuming that Delia Parnell's 'political beliefs were an important factor in the upbringing and conditioning of the Parnell children'.[18] And indeed Charles Parnell himself admitted that even in his early manhood he was 'not very interested in politics'.[19]

CHAPTER THREE

Katie Wood and Willie O'Shea

$\mathcal{K}$ ATIE WOOD WAS AN ATTRACTIVE young woman, although perhaps not beautiful. Her features were slightly on the heavy side, but her assets were her 'thick curling hair' and a 'lovely English-rose complexion'.[1] Her wit and self-confidence, bolstered by her family's indulgence, were much in evidence. She was sociable and outgoing, and enjoyed meeting her family's many friends. Her brother Francis (known as Frank) was in the 17th Foot Regiment and stationed at Aldershot. Katie and her sister Anna went to stay with him, and Katie later wrote of how she had 'greatly enjoyed seeing the cavalry, with all the officers and men in full dress'.[2] This occasion, in 1860, was, according to Katie's memoirs, when she first met Willie O'Shea, a Cornet in the 18th Hussars. She was fifteen, and had accompanied her brother's wife to see a small drama acted by the officers, and there were 'many of the 18th Hussars, who paid us much attention'.[3]

Katie's recollections of her first meeting with Willie were published many years later, though her account was riddled with discrepancies. She claimed that she was not especially taken with her future spouse on their first meeting, finding the 'elderly and hawk-eyed colonel of the regiment far more interesting than the younger men',[4] yet, when recalling a meeting with Willie some time later, she wrote of how she immediately noticed and 'was pleased' with 'his youthful looks and vivacity'. His 'dress' pleased her as well, and was, in her view, 'extremely becoming… a brown velvet coat, cut rather fully, sealskin waistcoat, black-and-white check trousers, and an enormous carbuncle and diamond pin in his curiously folded scarf'.[5] It was clear that Willie O'Shea had made a strong impression on Katie, and certainly watercolours portray him as an extremely handsome and self-confident man, resplendent in tight-fitting uniform.

Katie was attracted, and eager to impress him. She recounted how she had been 'nettled' at his condescension towards her, and had 'promptly plunged into such a discussion of literary complexities, absorbed from my elders and utterly undigested, that he soon subsided into a bewildered and shocked silence'.[6] In the course of the few days of the visit, Katie wrote that they became 'very good friends' and that she had been 'immensely pleased' when, on parting, he had presented her with 'a really charming poem written about my "golden hair and witsome speech"'.[7] Very soon Katie and Willie became a courting couple. After her theatrical performances, Katie recalled how Willie would present her with 'most beautiful bouquets…, and, in the pretty fashion of those days, bees and butterflies were so mounted as to appear hovering over the rare exotics'.[8] The following summer, Katie went to stay with the Barrett Lennards at Belhus, and once again met up with her suitor.

But Willie O'Shea was not considered a suitable match for Katie, and her father's response to seeing the poem Willie composed for his daughter was not encouraging. 'Ah, too young for such nonsense', he reportedly told Katie, adding, 'I want my Pippin for myself for years to come.'[9] Subsequently, Katie could not quite decide how to present the story of the courtship. She declared that she had seemed to slide passively into the relationship. 'Unconsciously we seemed to drift together', she wrote. 'Week after week went by in our trance of contentment', she claimed, adding, 'I did not look forward, but was content to exist in the languorous summer heat.'[10] Indeed, she felt that it was O'Shea who made the running. One day, she wrote, he kissed her 'full on the lips' in front of two other officers. One of them, whom she named only as 'E. S.', was a man to whom she was 'attracted', and who, moreover, had paid her 'considerable attention'.[11] Claiming to have been 'furious', Katie recalled how she had ridden home, vowing never to speak to her beau again. But after hearing his explanation and apologies, she was all too ready to forgive him; this was 'in keeping with the dreamy sense I had of belonging to Willie'.[12]

In their financially straitened circumstances, the Wood family's hope would have been for Katie to marry someone with good prospects, someone from – at the very least – the same social class. Katie was very well connected. Her father's brother, William Page Wood, had been knighted in 1851 (he later became Baron Hatherley of Hatherley, when he was made Lord Chancellor in 1868), and he and his wife were frequent guests of Queen Victoria. Katie's brothers were also distinguished. Evelyn, who had joined the navy at age fourteen, became the most well known and successful of Katie's siblings. A veteran of the Crimean War, the Indian Mutiny (during which he won the Victoria Cross), the Zulu War, and the relief of Khartoum, he became Field Marshal Sir Evelyn Wood in 1903. Another brother, Charlie, was a farmer who later became a successful businessman. Katie's sister Emma was not only an accomplished musician and composer, but had married an extremely wealthy man and raised a large family. Her sister Anna became a novelist of repute and the eldest sister, Maria, married a military man, Colonel Chambers, in 1847 and lived for many years in India.

There may have been additional sensitivity about Katie's choice of suitor because, even though the family were members of the upper-middle-class elite, her origins were unusual compared with those of the more conventional landed gentry. Her mother Emma's family, the Michells, had a slightly rackety background. Emma's father had run away from home as a boy and joined the Navy. In 1783, promoted to Lieutenant, Sampson Michell joined the service of the King of Portugal. He rose quickly, became an Admiral, and eventually Commander-in-Chief of the Portuguese Navy. When on leave he met and married Anne Shears, and the young couple were apparently 'very poor' and settled in Exeter. They had two sons and three daughters and, after a time, the family moved to Lisbon. Thus, both Maria and Emma Wood spent their early years abroad. Emma 'often talked' about the pleasure of those days, her granddaughter recalled, and 'told how she used to eat the golden fruit of the passion-flower. Late in life she had a plant of it in her greenhouse at Rivenhall, and astonished us by picking and eating the golden seed pods, which we had thought were poisonous.'[13]

The family left Portugal when Emma was very young. Sampson settled his wife and children in Truro, Cornwall, then followed the Portuguese King to Brazil. He died there on duty, in January 1809, at the age of fifty-four. His eldest son, Frederick (who became Admiral Sir Frederick Michell), was nineteen, and his youngest child, Emma, was only seven. Sampson's advice to his son, written in his affectionate letters home to his family in 1808, was simple: 'Never get into debt. Do your duty to God and your country.' His descendants apparently treasured this advice from one who 'had little to leave beyond the fine example of a blameless life'.[14] Frederick supported his sisters, and, according to his sister Maria, did so dutifully, in order to strictly fulfil the 'injunctions of my father, who used to say to his sons, "I spend on your education all the money I might have saved for your sisters. It will be your part, therefore, to take care of them".'[15]

Clearly, Katie's family history, despite its conventional appearance, was rather more bohemian than that of most middle-class Englishwomen. And shortage of cash was a chronic and persistent difficulty. Even when Sir Matthew Wood died in 1843, and Reverend

John Wood succeeded to the baronetcy, the family were still in 'financial difficulties'. The governess was sent away, and Evelyn had 'little instruction' until he attended the Marlborough Grammar School.[16] Over time, John and Emma Wood increasingly relied on her sister, Maria, for help with the family finances. Emma's sister had married John's uncle, the wealthy Benjamin Wood. Family lore has it that when John met and fell in love with Emma, his father Matthew sent his brother Benjamin to warn John off the match. Instead, Benjamin fell in love with Emma's elder sister, Maria. Benjamin and Maria were very happy together, but they had no children. They were extremely fond of John and Emma's family. Marie Wood took a keen interest in Emma's children, and was committed to helping her sister.

Benjamin Wood had made a fortune in hops, and became Liberal MP for Southwark. Benjamin took his parliamentary responsibilities very seriously, and was often away working. Maria wrote to a friend: 'I do love him and with an affection which has been won by a mind "pure in its last recesses," by a heart utterly destitute of selfishness'.[17] Her beloved husband's health was poor, however, and Maria worried about him. She wrote to Emma that he looked ill:

for long anxiety and fatigue leave traces on the countenance at fifty-four, which are not soon effaced, particularly when illness is accompanied by the sleeplessness which is always an attendant on his. Last night was the first which was not almost all spent in walking about the room or in reading... After the Parliament has settled what is to be done, I hope he will be able to go from home for a short time, and that change of air and of scene will restore his sleep, and with it strength and health.

Benjamin's health was indeed sufficiently precarious for him to consider his sister-in-law's future. He wished to reassure Emma, Maria continued, telling her that Benjamin 'told me all he wished

I should do, should he die before me. "You will be kind", he said, "to John and Emma, and the children – they will probably want assistance, and as far as you can, I should wish you to give it." The following evening brought the unexpected intelligence which will place you above the want of assistance from any one. I thank God for it, for your sake, and have thought every day since, of the comfort with which you must wake in the morning, and think that your dear children will be provided for.'[18]

Benjamin Wood died in 1845, the year that Katie was born. Thus, all Katie's life, her family knew of, and expected to benefit by, the generosity of Maria, known as 'Aunt Ben'. Aunt Ben lived at Eltham Lodge, which was a beautiful old house at Eltham in Essex. She had the lease for life of this lovely property, which was in fact owned by the Crown. The rent was £630 a year in 1874. With its magnificent carved oak staircase and many oak-panelled rooms, it was a most desirable residence. On more than one occasion, there were efforts made by Crown deputations to dislodge her. These met with no success.[19] Aunt Ben lived for many years in her luxurious dwelling, always happy to receive members of family. Katie and her siblings knew that Aunt Ben was rich, and that she would help them. One of the tangible manifestations of this aid was the promise of £5,000 to each child upon their marriage. This would be Katie's only marriage settlement.

While Katie was possibly considering marriage to Willie O'Shea, there were other obstacles to such a union, apart from her family's probable disapproval. There was the problem of Willie's religion, for example. He was a Roman Catholic and, although not especially devout, he had been brought up in the faith and showed no signs of leaving it. His mother was a fervent believer, and was even made a Countess of Rome, a courtesy temporal title given by the Pope to lay people for services rendered to the Church. For Katie, the daughter of an Anglican vicar, to consider a 'mixed' marriage into a Catholic family would have been an enormous step.

Anti-Catholicism was rife in Britain, and 'mixed' religious marriages were much frowned upon. There was still considerable suspicion about a religion that owed its allegiance to Rome. A great burst of anti-Catholicism had broken out in 1845, the year of Katie's birth, brought about by Sir Robert Peel's proposal to increase state funding for the Catholic seminary at Maynooth, in Ireland, from £9,000 to £26,360 a year, and also to place that funding on a more secure basis than had previously been the case.[20] Public outcry against the proposed reforms was huge, and over 10,000 petitions with 1,284,296 signatures were presented.[21] The restoration of the Catholic hierarchy in 1850 led to further outrage. The Whig Prime Minister, Lord John Russell, did little to calm feelings. Serious anti-Catholic riots broke out in November 1850 and the following month 2,626 English memorials were presented to the Queen protesting against the hierarchy. These memorials collected 887,525 signatures.[22] Feelings ran high, exacerbated by a growing band of anti-Catholic lecturers who toured Britain in the 1850s and 1860s. One of the most famous of these was an Irishman, William Murphy, who arrived in England in 1862. He told his rapt listeners that 'every Popish priest was a murderer, a cannibal, a liar, and a pickpocket'.[23] Although popular protest eventually declined, unenthusiastic attitudes towards Catholics remained.

A further complication of marrying a Catholic concerned the requirement for a conversion or, at the very least, a commitment to raise any children as Catholics. Despite their reservations, however, Katie's parents were not really in a position to criticize the young man. Willie was a great favourite and a frequent guest of the Barrett Lennards. Like him, John and Emma Wood often benefited from the lavish hospitality offered to them at Belhus. Emma and her husband Thomas were generous to her parents, who regularly stayed with them for months at a time.

Sir Thomas Barrett Lennard was a keen connoisseur and breeder of horses. His hobby was to collect hunters from Ireland, break them in, and then sell them at an annual sale at Belhus. 'He obtained some splendid animals', wrote Emma to a friend, 'and many letters afterwards from hunting men, testify to their appreciation of Sir Thomas's fine judgement of horseflesh.'[24] The 'Belhus sale of Hunters' was, according to Emma, always attended by a 'large number of sportsmen and masters of hounds', even if not always a financial success. On these festive and lively occasions, Sir Thomas would give a champagne luncheon in a big tent.[25]

Willie O'Shea was a 'crack' steeplechase rider, and he schooled young horses on the Downs above Brighton, where the 18th Hussars were stationed. His expertise was such that he trained not only his own, but the horses of other men. Katie remembered that 'his "way with a horse" and his good hands were generally appreciated among his brother officers'.[26] Evelyn, also a friend, had apparently introduced Willie to his youngest sister, by saying that he was 'the only man who sat properly "over the brook" at the Aldershot races'.[27] His prowess stood him in good stead in his friendship with Sir Thomas. When Willie was thrown from his steeplechaser and suffered serious injury, it was Sir Thomas and his wife Emma who went to Preston Barracks to nurse him. As soon as he could be moved, Willie was taken to the Barrett Lennards' town residence in Brighton, where he stayed for six weeks. When he was ready, he was brought to Belhus to convalesce.

Katie described how she had heard of Willie's accident, 'and for six unhappy weeks I did little else than watch for news of him'.[28] When she and her sister Anna went to see him as he was accompanied to Belhus, he was, apparently, 'too weak to speak'. He did manage, however, to slip a ring from his finger to hers, 'and pressed my hand under cover of the rugs'. When she went again to visit him for a dinner party at Belhus, she was 'shyly glad to meet him again and at his desire to talk to me only'. After dinner, while the others were 'all occupied singing and talking', Willie slipped a 'gold and turquoise locket on a long gold and blue enamel chain round my neck'. Katie wrote: 'It was a lovely thing, and I was very happy to know how much Willie cared for me.'[29]

At this point, there could be little question that the relationship was serious. Well-bred young women in Victorian Britain did not casually accept personal presents from men. Willie was clearly smitten, and Katie herself, despite her reluctance to show too much enthusiasm in her memoir, was in love. The courtship then took a curious turn, if Katie's memoirs are to be believed. Katie implied that her parents sanctioned the relationship, which is unlikely and also contradicted by other evidence. Another family member recounted that the couple fell 'deeply in love', but that Lady Wood opposed the match.[30] By Katie's account, she and her mother travelled to Brighton where she spent much time riding on the Downs, often in the company of her beau: her mother hired a horse from the livery stable for her, 'so that Willie and I had long rides over the Downs together'.[31] Although she did not go so far as to say that this had been her mother's intention (it almost certainly was not), she did imply as much. What is far more likely is that Emma Wood began to realize how much time her daughter was spending in the company of O'Shea, and decided to remove her from Brighton. John Wood could have had something to do with this decision. Katharine recorded that her father 'soon wrote to say how dull he was without us, and we went home'.[32]

Katie wrote that she did not see Willie for a short time, because of his father's death. When she did come upon him, at a 'small dance', he 'monopolised me the whole evening, and called at the house to see me the next day'. She then went on to say that a 'curious distaste' for the love affair had 'grown up' within her, and that she felt a 'desire to be left free and untrammelled by any serious thoughts of marriage'. She 'wished him away' when he looked fondly at her. When her mother, who 'understood me better than anyone', interviewed Willie that day, Katie said that she felt a 'feeling of relief' as he left, having 'merely said good-bye to me in passing down the stairs'. Her feelings were perhaps more honestly expressed in her conclusion to the episode: 'With all the unreasonableness of girlhood I felt a sudden sense of regretful vanity that Willie's last glimpse of me then was while I was wearing a most unbecoming black silk jacket, much too large for me.'[33] Willie O'Shea went off to Valencia, and sent Katie some 'Farewell' verses, which, interestingly, she kept all those years until publishing them in her memoir of Charles Parnell.

The affair might have ended there, but for John Wood's death in February 1866. His health had been faltering, and later that year he fell very ill. The family had been staying for one of their long visits, this one of many months' duration, at Belhus. John Wood began by travelling to Cressing once a week to fulfil his parochial duties, but was soon obliged to give up the visits. He sank swiftly, according to Katie, and she spent her days by his side. She was distraught when he passed away, and, according to her recollections, had to be carried out of the room by the doctor. She may then have been given a sedative and slept for a long while until, some time later, she opened her eyes 'to see Willie and my sister bending over my bed'.[34]

Willie had brought her a King Charles spaniel, and she 'contented' herself 'with curling round in bed with my new treasure'. Katie wrote that she had later heard that her mother and sister had telegraphed for Willie, 'as they feared that, after my long attendance on my father, I should fall ill when he died'.[35] It is possible that Katie was so ill that her mother did telegraph to summon her disappointed suitor to return from Spain. It is perhaps more likely that, ill and depressed at her beloved father's demise, she had begged her mother to send for Willie. Furthermore, it is distinctly possible that it was John, even more than Emma, who had objected to Willie's courtship (having been unenthusiastic from its inception), and, with his death, an obstacle had been removed.

Katie was badly shaken by her father's death. She wrote:

The loss of my father was my first real sorrow and I wandered miserably round his study, where everything was as he had left it, including the things he had so lately touched – the letter-weight, pressed down on the answered letters and those now never to be answered; his sermon case; his surplice folded on his table ready for the next services at the Church, now for him never to take place.[36]

She and her father had been so close, and it was to her that he made his request that she destroy his papers and sermons. She took the papers down to the lake in the cold winter evening, weighted them with stones, and watched them sink, 'only to come to the surface again in distant and darker shadows'.[37]

John Wood's demise also brought to the fore the vexatious problem of money. Emma was left without income – 'almost penniless',[38] as Katie described. Her mother had spoken sadly of her financial predicament one day as Katie entered her room. '"We must sell the cow, and, of course, the pig", my eldest sister (Emma) replied in her sweet, cheerful voice, which produced a little laugh, though a rather dismal one, and our sorrow was chased away for the moment.'[39] Fortunately, Maria Wood came to the rescue. Aunt Ben, on hearing of their troubles, 'settled a yearly income' on her sister, wrote Katie, 'thus saving her from all future anxiety, most of her children being provided for under our grandfather's – old Sir Matthew Wood's – will'.[40]

Emma Wood, always industrious, now turned her hand to writing novels. In this she was very successful. From the years 1868 to 1879 she produced a large number of books, many in multiple volumes, and, according to her granddaughter, she received an income of £300 a year right up till the last tome.[41] It was a fairly unusual pursuit for an upper-middle-class woman and female authors in Victorian times occupied an ambiguous place in the public sphere. Earning money in the publishing market was considered 'unfeminine'. The respectability of female novelists was thus suspect – as evidenced by the fact that many of them wrote under pseudonyms. And almost all the women who published claimed to do so for a good reason.[42]

With her mother thus occupied writing her novels, and without her father's company, Katie spent a quiet year at Rivenhall after his death in February 1866. At the end of the year, she, her mother and Anna went to stay in Brighton. Anna had married, in 1858, Captain Charles Steel,[43] whom she had left after a matter of weeks, never to return. It was a strange story, and never fully explained. All that is known is that she had returned home after the honeymoon, and 'no persuasion nor threats could ever induce her to return'. Her husband supposedly tried several times to 'claim' her, and family lore has it that one day Evelyn, out with his sister Anna, came upon her husband. When Steel tried to join them, Evelyn apparently knocked him down, and was subsequently fined for assault.[44]

In 1873, when Katie was eighteen, there seems to have been further trouble with Colonel Steel. Katie's eldest sister, Maria, wrote to her mother, Emma, in 1873, that 'What you tell me of poor Anna's affair is very untoward, but I would try not to let it be distressing… With such a person as Colonel Steele [sic] seems to be, a compromise I fear would be no security, as Mr. Teesdale told me apropos of some other case, that the law did not recognise any agreements to separate, and that either of the parties might break it at his or her pleasure… so let us DO what should be done, and then hope for the best.'[45] Marital discord, especially that which resulted in separation, was generally considered scandalous. Extreme marital incompatibilities did, of course, occur, but it was unusual for a young woman to abandon her husband. It was even more unusual to receive the goodwill of her family, and the fact that the Wood family was understanding and supportive of Anna's decision indicates that there was probably ill treatment. Their behaviour also indicates, however, that the environment in which Katie grew up was rather more tolerant of some social deviance than that of her more staid Victorian neighbours.

Anna became a novelist too, publishing several novels and some poetry, to considerable critical acclaim and commercial success. She also wrote for newspapers, and she settled companionably with her mother at Rivenhall to write and to take care of their innumerable pets. Emma and Anna had sixty dogs, kept outside the house 'in numerous little brick houses, each of which had a stove attached, always lit on winter nights, and a long wire netting day-run in front'.[46]

Katie, meanwhile, resumed her romance in earnest. Soon after their arrival in Brighton, Willie had returned from Spain, and called on her 'at once'.[47] 'I now yielded', she wrote, 'to Willie's protest at being kept waiting longer.'[48] Her primary objective in writing this seemed to have been to present Willie as the pursuer, and she the pursued. What this sentence also makes clear, however, is that Willie *had* been kept waiting. This implies that he must have had some encouragement, a sentiment Katie did not dispute. Thus she had her wish, and married William Henry O'Shea on 24 January 1867. It was less than a week before her twenty-second birthday, and just under a year after her father had died. The couple were married in Brighton, at the parish church of St Nicholas, in a Church of England ceremony. This was an extremely important concession for Willie to make. When Katie's brother Evelyn had chosen to marry the Hon. Paulina Southwell, a Roman Catholic, Aunt Ben had refused to give him the £5,000 promised to all the Wood children upon marriage. Such was the dependence of her nephews and nieces on her generosity that Evelyn seems to have been quite financially embarrassed by this refusal. Fortunately for him, his generous brother-in-law, Sir Thomas Barrett Lennard, offered to come to his aid.[49]

A similar predicament was avoided by some finessing on Katie's part. The ceremony was indeed Church of England, but it would seem that she promised to raise any children of the union as Catholics. This would not have pleased her aunt, but seems to have enabled Willie to overcome any scruples. However, neither his mother nor sister attended the wedding: they would not 'lend their countenance to a "mixed" marriage'.[50] There were many wedding gifts, which Katie described in her book. Her 'mother, brothers and sisters' gave her 'beautiful presents'. Her wealthy sister, Emma Barrett Lennard, provided the trousseau, a generous gesture, as her mother was certainly not in a position to spend the large sum required. Willie gave his new wife a 'gold-mounted dressing bag'. Her 'old Aunt H.' (presumably her Uncle Hatherley's wife) sent her a gold and turquoise bracelet, and sister Anna gave Katie a 'carbuncle locket with diamond centre'.[51] Clearly, once the match had been agreed upon, both families made the best of what they felt to be an undesirable union. After the wedding, the couple set off to begin their honeymoon at Holbrook Hall, a residence lent to them by Sir Seymour Fitzgerald.

CHAPTER FOUR

Mrs O'Shea

T HE O'SHEA (PRONOUNCED O'SHEE) family were originally
landowning Irish Catholics, whose rights and position in
society had steadily eroded over the years. Legislation against the
rights of Catholics, known as penal or popery laws, originated in
the late seventeenth century, and were designed to protect
Protestant dominance in Ireland.[1] Catholics were forbidden to hold
weapons,[2] and a second law forbade them from going overseas for
the purposes of education (to prevent continental alliances).
Catholics were also forbidden from teaching or running schools
within Ireland. The Act to Prevent the Further Growth of Popery,
of 1704, was the most severe. It prohibited Catholics from
purchasing land, inheriting land from Protestants or from taking
on leases of more than thirty-one years. The Act was strengthened
by another piece of legislation in 1709 which introduced the
'discoverer'. This was a legal procedure by which a Protestant could
'discover' a disregard of the penal laws by a Catholic and thereby
claim his interest in their land.[3]

The nationalist leader and barrister Daniel O'Connell ('the Great
Liberator') led the campaigns for Catholic emancipation. His

brilliant oratory and organizational skills drove forward a mass movement, which achieved some of its goals in 1829.[4] Yet despite the legislation more favourable to the positions of Catholics, many of the landowning families had already slowly lost revenue and position. The landowning Catholics had been the primary target of the penal laws, and by mid-eighteenth century their number had been decimated.[5] Many converted to Protestantism so that they could own and inherit land. In addition to their particular struggle as Catholic landowners to maintain prestige and high status, the agricultural depression following the end of the French wars of 1793–1815 led to more economic hardship for most landowners. By 1844, there were 1,322 estates – with a rental income of £904,000 (which may have represented 10 per cent of the whole) – that were being managed by the courts, usually in preparation for sales of the land to pay off creditors.[6]

The O'Shea family was one of those who had lost their estates and their income. Henry O'Shea, Willie's father, and his two brothers, John and Thaddeus, were thus members of an impoverished class, and had to make their own ways in the world. Henry, as the eldest, had taken it upon himself to sort out the problems left on his father's death. On 'finding the estates mortgaged up to the utmost limit', he 'bound himself to a solicitor in Dublin, worked hard, and in due course became himself a fully qualified solicitor'. He did 'extremely well', developing a 'perfect genius for pulling together estates that appeared to be hopelessly bankrupt'.[7] Nationalist lawyer and politician Tim Healy (who started out as Parnell's secretary but later became his bitter enemy) was probably being vindictive when he referred to Henry O'Shea as 'a Limerick pawnbroker designated by an unsavoury Gaelic nickname'.[8] It would appear, however, that Henry made his money by profiting from the salvaging of bankrupt estates. In Ireland's post-famine years, this was a legitimate, rather than laudable, way to make one's fortune. In fact, the Catholic mercantile and manufacturing classes were far less affected by the social and legal climate than the Catholic aristocracy. There was a thriving Catholic middle class in Ireland, which by the late nineteenth century had gained considerable prominence and prosperity. Henry O'Shea's move into a profession was therefore a sensible and realistic assessment of his opportunities for advancement and generation of reliable income.

Henry's brother John preferred to take his chances in foreign climes. He immigrated to Spain and settled there, marrying Dona Ysabel Hurtado de Corcuera, and had five children.[9] John was successful; he founded a bank and 'prospered exceedingly'.[10] There was thus a branch of the O'Shea family based in Madrid, as well as an earlier one in France. Willie grew up travelling constantly between these countries and had a number of Spanish-speaking first cousins. There was little contact, however, with the third brother, Thaddeus. He was, according to Katie, the 'black sheep of the family, wasting his substance in gambling and in breeding unlikely horses to win impossible races'.[11]

Henry O'Shea married Catherine Quinlan, originally from Tipperary, and also a Catholic. Catherine Quinlan was an exceedingly devout woman, who adhered to an ultramontane form of Catholicism. This favoured a close association with the Vatican, and an adherence to papal rather than national or diocesan authority. Ultramontanism had come to prominence in Ireland in the mid- to late-eighteenth century, when the popes sought to increase Church centralization.[12] Much of Ireland's rural Catholic population accommodated the demands of the Church by merging the ritual with their existing belief system still in practice throughout Ireland. A parallel world of superstition and ritual had been kept alive through oral tradition for centuries, but this rich culture of kings and heroes and legends of fairies became absorbed or marginalized by a priesthood increasingly focused on a modern, literate approach to worship. Ancient magic was incorporated into religious amulets and Christian symbols. Fairy forts became holy shrines, and traditional festivals were merged into Catholic holy days.

Yet, although the clergy were very successful in dominating their flocks, the old culture remained pervasive, especially in rural areas. The horrific tale of how in 1895 a twenty-six-year-old woman, Bridget Cleary, was tortured and burned by her husband and members of her own family – in a supposed attempt to rescue her from the fairies – provides evidence of strong superstitious practice as late as the turn of the century.[13] Fairy belief was part of a rich oral cultural tradition – they were usually invisible, sometimes just a little smaller than humans, and sometimes tiny, as the Irish scholar Angela Bourke explained:

They had their origin when the rebellious angel Lucifer and his followers were expelled from Heaven… Like figures in a film that is suddenly stopped, the expelled angels falling towards Hell halted where they were: some in mid-air, others in the earth, and some in the ocean and there they remain. They are jealous of Christians, and often do them harm, but are not totally malevolent since they still hope to get back to Heaven one day… Fairies are not human, but they resemble humans and live lives parallel to theirs… they keep cows, and sell them at fairs; they enjoy whiskey and music; they like gold, milk and tobacco, but hate iron, fire, salt and the Christian religion, and any of the combination of these mainstays of Irish rural culture serves to guard against them.[14]

Belief in the fairies – who stole children and young women to leave withered changelings in their place – was a response to life's imponderables, as Bourke points out: 'Fairies belong to the margins, and so can serve as reference points and metaphors for all that is marginal in human life. Their underground existence allows them to stand for the unconscious, for the secret, or the unspeakable, and their constant eavesdropping explains the need sometimes to speak in riddles, or to avoid discussion of certain topics.'[15]

The Catholic clergy were, however, increasingly trained to take a more modern view, and to discourage such ancient superstitious practices. St Patrick's College, the Catholic seminary at Maynooth, trained hundreds of Irish Catholic priests (by 1826 it had over 400 students), many of them recruited from the tenant farmer class. There was also a vigorous church-building programme throughout the nineteenth century. By the latter half of the century, the Catholic Church in Ireland was guiding its parishioners to an increasingly standardized and modern religious devotional practice. Group-centred, semi-pagan devotions, such as patterns (a local festival at a holy well) and wakes, were discouraged. And the highly ritualized Catholic ritual – as encouraged by the papacy and promoted by a trained clergy through Sunday sermons with regularized devotional practice – was welcomed by the Irish Catholic population generally.

Catherine Quinlan was deeply religious, and a rather serious-minded woman. Her daughter-in-law described her as 'a bundle of negations wrapped in a shawl – always a very beautiful shawl'. Although Katie wrote that Willie's father had been 'the very kindest of fathers', clever, just and honourable, she had little to say in her mother-in-law's favour. 'Even when I first knew her', she recalled, 'she and her daughter were evidently convinced that she was very old and feeble, although she could not have been much more than middle-aged, and if there had been no daughter to lean upon I do not think she would have desired to lean.' Even allowing for Katie's evident dislike of the woman, a convincing portrait of a rather sour creature emerges. 'She was destitute of any sense of humour, and highly educated, always, I think, an unhappy combination', Katie continued, 'and her only definite characteristics were her assiduous practise [*sic*] of her religion and her profound sense of my undesirability as a daughter-in-law.'[16]

Henry and Catherine had two children, William Henry, known as Willie, and his younger sister, Mary. Katie had equally choice words to describe her sister-in-law. Mary was 'sadly deficient in humour, and wore herself and her friends out in her endeavours to make bad Catholics out of indifferent Protestants'. Mary had, Katie believed, 'taken conscientious advantage of her meticulously thorough education, was a human library of dry and solid information, and was as ignorant – and as innocent – of the world at twenty-eight as she must have been at eight.' Despite Mary's obvious drawbacks, Katharine claimed that the two 'had a certain liking for one another', and that 'had she not shared her mother's conviction as to my "undesirability", I might have become fond of her'. Still, Katie's trenchant observations of Willie's sister continued:

She was betrothed to an Italian of old family and of the blackest of the black Roman society. I believe she was devoted to him in her quiet, methodical way, but after her third attack of acute rheumatic fever, leaving behind it the legacy of heart disease, shortly before they were to be wedded, she decided that her state of health would render her but a drag upon her prospective husband, and that she would ask him to release her from her promise... She died a few years later in much suffering but perfect happiness.[17]

The upper ranks of Irish society tended to be schooled in England and Willie was duly sent to St Mary's College, Oscott, in Warwickshire. Oscott had as its dual mission the training of the pastoral clergy, and the provision of a thoroughly Catholic education, 'to ensure a lofty tone of morality among the pupils, and next, to furnish a liberal education as distinct from what would be described as commercial or professional'.[18] Katie commented that Henry's 'only fault' might have been in giving his children 'so foreign an education they lost somewhat of the Irish charm which he possessed so strongly himself'. 'He spoke with a brogue that was music in the ear', she continued, in contrast with 'his son's clear, clipped English'.[19] Katie declared that Willie had 'no natural taste for learning', but in fact his surviving school records for the five years that he was at St Mary's show that he was 'well above average in scholastic ability, usually second in the monthly class placings, never less than fifth'.[20] At Oscott, students were taught English language and elocution, as well as foreign languages. Here Willie excelled, helped, no doubt, by his travelling to Spain and France to visit family members. Indeed, his mother had decided to make her home in Paris and lived there with her daughter Mary. Like that of his sister, Willie's command of the French language was of an extremely high standard, and, as Katie reported, his 'cosmopolitan education had given him an ease of manner and self-assurance that made him popular with his contemporaries'.[21]

Willie's social advancement was clearly important to his devoted father. When Willie returned to Dublin, where his father was working, he entered Trinity College, the first Irish university established on a permanent basis, founded in 1592. Although Queen Elizabeth I had expressed the hope that it would provide for the education of all Ireland's youth, regardless of religion, it was modelled on a Cambridge college and its student body was firmly Protestant. Catholics were admitted after 1793, but it was not until 1873 that all religious tests were abolished. At the time of Willie's brief university career, Trinity College was still very much the university of the Protestant Ascendancy.[22]

Although not a Protestant – nor a landowner – Willie had aspirations that characterized members of the social group known as 'Castle Catholics'. The Castle referred to Dublin Castle, where the British Viceroy worked and entertained Ireland's elite. The Castle season, as it was known, ran from January to March and viceregal hospitality was lavish. In addition to dinners and parties, there were stylish regimental balls held at the magnificent building in the centre of Dublin. Those who enjoyed such elegant festivities were predominantly Protestant, hence the exceptions being marked out as 'Castle Catholics'.[23]

In 1858, Willie's father had bought him a commission in the 18th Hussars of the British Army, reportedly paying £5,000 for the commission of Cornet. A Cornet in the cavalry was the equivalent of Ensign, the lowest subaltern rank in the regiment.[24] Officer commissions could be bought in the Guards, and in infantry and cavalry regiments; commissions in the Royal Engineers and the Royal Artillery were awarded only to those who successfully completed a course at the Royal Military Academy at Woolwich. A man bought his commission and then paid for each subsequent increase in rank, the obvious disadvantage being that this allowed for wealth to override competence. Yet the frequent victories of the British Army, operating under the purchase system, led many to believe in its worth. The Duke of Wellington was famously a strong supporter of the scheme.

Since its official creation in 1689, the army had occupied a complex position on the British political and social landscape.[25] After the people of England had been subjected to the military dictatorship of Cromwell's Major Generals, the governing elite was determined that the army should never be in the hands of professional soldiers. To this end, purchase was established so that only men of property, and with a vested interest in perpetuating the stability of the nation with its existing systems, would be allowed to become officers. The practice reached its height in the 1850s. There was some talk of reform after the problems publicized following the Crimean War, where some officers were accused of incompetence that had resulted in needless suffering and deaths. But the government also believed that the system had its advantages. With private means, officers would, it was thought, be less inclined to steal, loot or pillage. In addition, the investment by these officers in purchasing the commission meant that, in order to recoup the initial outlay on leaving the service, they would need to maintain the status quo. Any possibility of the army participating in a revolution or coup would thus be diminished.

In 1858, when Willie O'Shea obtained his commission in the 18th Hussars, the British Army had just emerged from the Crimean

War (1853–6). Until that conflict, Britain had been largely at peace for the four decades after the resounding victories in the French and Napoleonic Wars that ended in 1815. And, unlike the navy, the army was not used as an instrument of foreign policy. Its secondary position thus reinforced public and political indifference to the institution. Parliamentary preoccupations focused on reducing costs, so that reform was inevitably slow. The 18th Hussars were considered a dashing and fashionable regiment. Light dragoons, or hussars as the 18th later became, were always special troops. First raised in the mid-eighteenth century, they were used for reconnaissance and scouting. They soon garnered a reputation for courage in the charge and the light dragoon regiments that were formed fought all over the world. These troops distinguished themselves during the Napoleonic Wars, as well as in the Crimea, and in India. Sportsmen were preferred cavalry officers and the 18th Hussars prized great horsemanship, as one would expect. The officers of the 18th looked quite magnificent in uniform. From 1700 onwards these were inspired by Hungarian fashion: the dress outfits of blues, yellow and gold comprised a jacket with heavy horizontal gold braid on the breast, and gold Austrian knots on the sleeves. There was a matching *pelisse*, which was a short-waisted overcoat (often worn slung over one shoulder). White gloves and a helmet with upstanding plumage completed the uniform, along with a scabbard and sword. The officers were shod with well-polished high riding boots.

While Katie and Willie were courting, he was a dashing officer in a glamorous regiment. According to Katie, Willie's father had counselled his son to 'First become a smart officer; secondly, do what the other men do and send the bill in to me!'[26] Willie was, she wrote, 'keen about his work in the regiment, and took an honest interest in all that pertained to it'.[27] This was probably an accurate assessment of the situation as she understood it; Katie would have had a reasonably good understanding of military life, with two brothers and an uncle, Frederick Michell, on active service. She had experienced at close quarters the risks of a military career: her brother Evelyn had been sent out to the Crimea in HMS *Queen*. Severely wounded in June 1855, he had returned to England and resigned his appointment in the navy. He then joined the army, and was gazetted to the 13th Light Dragoons who were at the time fighting at Scutari. Back again in the Crimea with his new regiment, where he held the rank of Cornet, Evelyn was struck ill with pneumonia and typhoid. Sir John and Emma set out to see him as soon as they heard the news. In addition to the dangers of the journey, there was considerable discomfort. Maria Wood later described her sister's misery:

She suffered so much travelling to Paris, that five hours spent there were passed in retching, from which she had to rise and proceed twenty-two hours and a half without stopping, and at Marseilles, where she stayed the night, the bedroom was so offensive that she could not go to bed. A most stormy voyage of ten days took her to Scutari.[28]

To compound her agony, Emma found that, once arrived in Constantinople, they could not get to see their son at Scutari, due to the foul weather conditions. She wrote to her brother-in-law, Lord Hatherley, from Constantinople, where she and John were staying at the Hotel du Globe: 'I am looking anxiously over the Bosphorus to see if there will be a possibility of crossing to-day... So we sat silently in our room, looking on the large red building that contained our dearest child, but unable to get any very recent intelligence.'[29]

When Emma finally did get to see her son, she was appalled at his condition. He was 'terribly emaciated' with ulcers on his spine and hips. She demanded the right to stay with him and, according to family history, 'crossed swords somewhat sharply' with Florence Nightingale, head of the Nursing Staff in the Crimea. The family believed that Emma's nursing saved her son's life, and she returned with him to England as soon as she could.[30]

When the Indian Mutiny broke out in May 1857, Evelyn was so anxious to go out that he transferred from the 13th Light Dragoons, who were not to go to India, to the 17th Lancers, who were. Maria Wood recorded in October 1857 that 'Poor Emma says that she feels she shall never see him again, which I think most probable, for he is not twenty yet, and has not regained the strength he lost from his wound at the Redan, and from his long fever at Scutari. Yet she says she should despise him were he not anxious to go.'[31]

O'Shea, on the other hand, did not come from a military family, and there must be some question about his motivation for joining the army. In 1858, the 18th Hussars were stationed in England, and Willie spent much of his time riding in the regimental races in which the 18th were 'so successful'. In an attempt to help his son acquire a 'greater sense of responsibility', Henry O'Shea purchased for him the next rank up, that of Captain. Apparently this was unsuccessful in curbing Willie's spending, which soon resulted, according to Katie's recollections, in some £15,000 of debt. Henry had paid the amount, 'without cavilling', but proposed that Willie should 'in future make his ample allowance suffice for his needs, even if it necessitated his leaving the regiment'.[32] Willie agreed, and did in fact leave his regiment, shortly before he and Katie married.

Most army officers possessed a private income. The low rates of pay (junior officers received about £100–200 per annum), the high cost of living and the expensive uniforms meant that officers were dependent on outside sources of revenue. Cavalry officers such as Willie had to pay for a charger – usually two – as well as a personal servant and groom, and for their furniture. Officers were also expected to contribute to the high cost of running the canteen, or mess, clubbing together to buy food, to pay for the chef, and to meet the cost of the mess band.[33]

The mess was an important feature in establishing and perpetuating a regiment's identity. Regiments had reputations that ranked them in the army's social pecking order, according to the lavishness of their fixtures and furnishing and the costliness of their wines and provisions. In 1892, a 'subaltern serving with 1/Somerset Light Infantry at Gibraltar noted that in terms of the hospitality its mess offered "we go in for being rather crack and are on much better terms with the 60th & 42nd than we are with the more 'scug' 82nd".'[34] Social life in the officers' mess was governed by rigid rules. Officers were forbidden to 'talk shop' or discuss 'contentious' subjects such as politics or religion. Guests could be introduced only according to a strict protocol. Entertaining was, however, an important function of the mess. Before 1914 most regiments held a formal dinner five nights a week and a regimental guest night was held once a week.

It was not an option for an officer to neglect his contribution to the gentlemanly social life of the mess or to fail to keep up with other expensive pursuits, such as hunting.[35] When Willie's father was unable to meet the high costs associated with his son's military career, it meant that his son had to face up to the fact that he was not in a position to take his place as a gentleman officer. Although cutting back on personal expenditure must have been an option for Willie, his share of the costs of the officers' mess and other expenses simply had to be honoured. And it is important to take into account the relative expenditure of those with whom Willie shared a lifestyle as well as a career. It is likely that being an 18th Hussar on a shoestring was as unfeasible as it must have seemed unattractive.

Thus Willie's challenges began early in his adult life. It seems clear that his expectations largely exceeded his work ethic, and that to realize his lifestyle ambitions he needed substantial income. And his problems were more than financial: he seemed ill equipped, by nature and by habit, to deal with his ambitions methodically. Henry O'Shea died in 1865 and Willie left the army soon after, receiving £4,000 for selling his commission.[36] When he married Katie, early in 1867, he was without an occupation. The Irish politician Tim Healy wrote later that 'When Sir Evelyn proposed the match to his subaltern, O'Shea at first pleaded that he was too poor to marry, but was assured that Miss Wood possessed £30,000.'[37] This was most unlikely. Willie had never been Evelyn's subaltern and, furthermore, O'Shea, as a close friend of the family, cannot have been unaware of their financial situation, especially after John Wood's death.

The couple took their honeymoon at Holbrook Hall, lent to them by Sir Seymour Fitzgerald. Katie later wrote that this had been 'a kindness that proved unkind, as the pomp and ceremony entailed by a large retinue of servants for our two selves were very wearisome to me'.[38] They had been bored, she recollected, hemmed in by bad weather and not enough to do. This does not mean, however, that the early days of the marriage were unhappy. Katie wrote that Willie had taken one of their wedding gifts, the bracelet from Aunt H. [Hatherley], and said '*this* will do for the dog' and 'snapped it round the neck of my little Prince'. Some time later, she and her new husband had gone to call on her aunt. Katie recalled that her aunt had broken off in mid-sentence, and fixed a 'surprised and indignant eye on my dog'. She had 'forgotten all about Prince's collar being Aunt H.'s bracelet, and only thought she did not like my bringing the dog to call, till I caught Willie's eye'. He had, to her consternation, 'all at once taken in the situation, and became so convulsed with laughter' that she had 'hustled him off'.[39] The recounting of this episode of conspiratorial naughtiness rang true, and demonstrated a clear affection between Katie and her new spouse.

Household advice manuals for the period suggested an expenditure of about £585 to set up a middle-class home.[40] Couples typically waited until they had the means to establish themselves independently before they married. The necessary funds were often provided by sufficiently well-to-do parents, or, with difficulty, through savings. The groom was expected to provide his wife with an establishment of her own. This did not necessarily mean buying a house. In fact only 10 per cent of the population at this time owned their homes. The poorest members of society paid weekly rents, and many of the better off took renewable seven-year leases.[41] In addition to the costs of renting a suitable property were those of equipping it for living. The challenge this presented to most middle-class men was reflected in the fact that at mid-century the average age of a groom was almost thirty.[42] Aunt Ben's generous marriage settlement was thus of critical importance to Katie and Willie's wedding plans.

Instead of setting up a household, Katie and Willie embarked on an entirely different course of action. When the couple married, they had Katie's settlement of £5,000, and an income of £120 a year.[43] The proceeds from the sale of Willie's commission were invested in his Uncle John's bank, in Spain. The timing of this investment is not entirely clear, but in any event the couple decided that they would move to Spain so that Willie could pursue the partnership in O'Shea and Co. There was no suggestion in her memoir that Katie was unhappy at the idea. It was, she wrote, 'too good an offer to be refused', so she had said goodbye and gone with Willie to stay a few days in London before leaving.

While there, Willie's mother and sister called on them. Katie recorded that they had brought her 'beautiful Irish poplins which were made into gowns' as well as a 'magnificent emerald bracelet' and '£200 worth of lovely Irish house-linen'.[44] These were handsome gifts, and Katie conceded that her in-laws were 'most generous'. Nevertheless, she wrote in her usual direct style that she then, 'and always, acknowledged them to be thoroughly good, kind-hearted women, but so hidebound with what was, to me, bigotry, with conventionality and tactlessness, that it was really a pain to me to be near them'.[45] Catherine and Mary O'Shea were, it would seem, rather strait-laced and conservative. One can imagine that the O'Sheas were shocked by the Wood family theatricals, by Anna Steele's abandonment of her marriage, and by Katie's strong independent streak. As Katie herself wrote, 'I admired them for their Parisian finish… and for their undoubted goodness, but, though I was rather fond of Mary, they wearied me to death.' She also observed that Willie's mother and sister 'very plainly disapproved of me'.[46]

The journey to Spain was described as a great adventure. The couple crossed the English Channel to the French port of Boulogne, where they remained for a few days so that Katie could recover from her seasickness – although it is of course possible that she had become pregnant, which would account for her descriptions of illness that plagued her for quite some weeks. If she had indeed become pregnant, she must have subsequently miscarried, as there was no child born to them until some years later. For whatever reason, Katie's first days abroad were spent in a hotel bed. Willie was not an inconsiderate husband. When leaving her to rest in the room while he went to have some lunch, he ordered refreshment to be delivered by a maid, 'as he knew that I, not being used to French customs, would not like a waiter to bring it'. When it turned out to be a manservant – who let himself into the room with a passkey – she was horrified, making 'agitated protests in very home-made French'. The servant was kind, and Katie was made comfortable, such that she was 'able to laugh at Willie's annoyance on his return to find the waiter once more in possession and removing the tray'.[47]

The couple then travelled on to Paris. They spent time visiting Willie's mother and sister, who lived there. The O'Sheas did their best to make Katie welcome, and found her a French maid, Caroline. Katie wrote of how her new maid helped her to dress her long hair most elaborately in 'the latest French fashion'. Willie 'insisted' upon it, Katie wrote, much to her 'annoyance', because she did not consider it 'becoming to me'. The maid 'was also much occupied in making the toilet of my little dog'. This was far more appealing. Katie fawned on her pet, and wrote that Prince, a 'lovely little creature', went everywhere with her. The animal was an annoying lapdog of the first order. Katie wrote that he was 'as good and quiet as possible when with me, but if I ever left him for a moment the shrill little howls would ring out till the nearest person to him would snatch him up, and fly to restore him to his affectionate, though long-suffering, mistress'. The pet was also Katie's fashion accessory. Caroline would tie 'an enormous pale blue bow' on the animal after combing him.[48]

The O'Sheas also welcomed their new in-law by taking her to see the sights of the French capital. Katie's fondness for her dog and her strong-willed insistence on bringing him everywhere with her could, however, be a trial. When her mother-in-law, and sister-in-law took her to visit the Cathedral of Notre Dame, Katie wrote 'as a matter of course Prince was in my arm under my cloak'. She let the dog down to run as they left the church, whereupon her mother-in-law 'nearly fainted'. Catherine O'Shea, whose devotion and dedication to the Church was such that she had been made a Comtesse de Rome, turned to her daughter-in-law, exclaiming, 'You took the dog into the *church*! Oh, Katie, how wrong, how *could* you! Mary! what shall we do?' Katie was unrepentant, declaring that 'you must excuse me if I remind you that God made the dog; and I seem to remember something about a Child that was born in a stable with a lot of nice friendly beasts about, so you need not have gone back to pray for me and Prince, I think!' She had then 'stalked off'. Katie's sense of humour never deserted her entirely, and she admitted in her memoir that the 'dignity' of her departure had been 'rather spoilt by my not having sufficient French to find my own way home, and having to wait at the carriage for them'.[49]

She was perhaps somewhat lacking in thoughtfulness. This is understandable in someone so young and inexperienced, but Katie used her memoir, published over thirty years later, to add interpretative comments to her stories. She rarely expressed anything other than total certitude in the rights of her views and behaviour. It also seemed difficult for her to be anything other than entirely vindicated. In a later note to the anecdote, she said that her sister-in-law had made her a gift of a Parisian bonnet, which Katie described as a 'peace offering'. The present cheered Katie greatly – she was, she wrote, 'happy in the knowledge' of how 'extremely pretty' she looked wearing the hat, made of white lace, trimmed with pink roses and fastened under the chin with pale blue ribbon ('the very latest fashion of the moment').[50]

She and Willie continued their travels and went on to the French seaside resort of Biarritz, on the Atlantic coast. The couple took a suite, and the bedroom and sitting room looked out over the sea, with 'great waves breaking on the rocks' just under the windows. A few days after their arrival, Katie was once again ill, and confined to her bed, this time with whooping cough and pneumonia. Once again, everything was done to make her comfortable during her illness. An English doctor was brought in. A chambermaid of the hotel, a local Basque girl, was made Katie's 'devoted' nurse. Donkeys were driven into the hotel's courtyard every morning from Bayonne, so that fresh asses' milk – 'the only nourishment' Katie could take – was provided for her. Her convalescence was a 'pleasant time', while she particularly enjoyed the 'great red cherries' brought to her by her nurse. Willie occupied himself by taking long walks during her illness and made 'really good' sketches. When Katie was better, he brought her out on long drives through the countryside, through 'winding wooded roads' where she could admire the 'sea showing its boundless grandeur through the tall trees on the broken cliff'.[51]

When she had recovered, the couple continued on to Madrid, and Katie professed to find the scenery greatly interesting. She enjoyed seeing 'lank fir trees with cups tied on them to catch the exudations of resin', as well as the 'vineyards with all their profusion of promise'. It was all 'wonderful' to her 'untravelled mind'.[52] She was very annoyed, however, to arrive in Madrid, 'dusty and untidy', only to be met straight away by Willie's Spanish relatives. To compound their faux pas, the Spaniards even annoyed the dog, which was also 'very tired, and disinclined to respond with any cheerfulness to the Spanish tongue which assailed us on every side'. Katie was exhausted after two days and nights in the train and wished to make a better impression on her new relatives than being found 'in an old lace bonnet with a red rose stuck rakishly on one side'. To make matters worse, Willie's aunt had brought her two daughters, Margharita and Pepita. 'They, of course, were cool and fresh', commented Katie with some feeling, 'and their pretty lace mantillas contrasted well with my dusty train-worn headgear.'[53]

Willie's family had arranged for his wife to be seen by a doctor at her arrival. The consultation was not a success as Katie was 'too cross and tired' to try to remember the Spanish Willie had taught her. Her husband 'came to the rescue' and took the doctor away. When the aunt and cousins came in to see her, Katie felt that this was the 'last straw'. She recalled how she had said to Willie, 'with a polite smile', that if he did not take 'these people away at once I shall howl'. Her alarmed spouse 'frantically told his aunt that he was hungry', and with that they took him away and left her 'in peace'.[54]

Katie rapidly recovered from whatever illness had troubled her, and settled down next morning at the hotel to eat a large breakfast of coffee, poached eggs and French rolls. She set out to explore and visited the Prado art gallery. In the evening Willie's extended family threw a large party in her honour. Katie wore a bright blue poplin gown and a diamond star in her hair. She was 'pleased and excited' at her reception – guests included cousins she had not already met, and many friends of the family. They were all 'most warm' in their greetings, Katie wrote, and she was 'naturally gratified' at their 'very obvious admiration' of her. She found John O'Shea, Willie's uncle, a 'typical Irishman'. Like his brother Thaddeus, he was an 'inveterate gambler' and he played cards for such high stakes that it was a source of 'perpetual distress' for his family.[55] The O'Sheas were lively risk-takers, and Willie was no exception. He brought Katie out to see the sights, despite the political unrest that pervaded the capital. She wrote of how shots might ring out as they were strolling through the Prado, and of how people would then fly in all directions. One evening, a 'volley of bullets' fell among them, and she described how her husband had caught up her dog and, seizing her hand, led her to safety by making her 'run hard up queer little side streets to our hotel'. Willie left her in the room and went out to investigate. Two ministerial buildings had been attacked, but the 'slight outbreak' of the Republicans had been quashed by soldiers. In her memoir, Katie wrote that she had not been alarmed, and that she had been 'sufficiently young' to have found it all 'very picturesque and interesting'.[56]

In this memoir, Katie referred frequently to her youthfulness during those early married years. She was twenty-two during her travels to Spain; not, by the standards of the time, especially young. When Willie admired the children playing in the gardens, wishing 'he might have many', she claimed that she was 'too young to find them interesting'. The real point was that Katie was most interested in herself. She was experiencing all sorts of delightful things, and was undeniably self-absorbed. Even when describing Margharita O'Shea's engagement, she could not help assigning herself an important part. She pointed out that although the young woman had looked 'very lovely', she had been 'pale as usual'. Katie had come to the rescue, by pinning crimson carnations into her hair, thus providing 'the contrast needed to render her strikingly beautiful'.[57]

Katie and Willie seemed to have been happy living in Madrid. They enjoyed spending time with his family, and Katie liked the lifestyle in the Spanish capital. Robert Lytton, the diplomat and great friend of Katie's sister, Anna Steele,[58] visited Madrid that same year, in 1868, and commented very favourably on the city. He liked 'the very little' he had seen of Spain, he wrote to Anna in May 1868, 'and even the very little more I have seen of Madrid, which is a very much handsomer and more animated town than I expected to find'. 'Indeed', he added, 'it is all animation morning and night, and full of display.' The city, he wrote, was 'like a pretty Provincial who has been to Paris, and come back quite *à la mode*, with her head rather turned, and a decided flair for spending more money on herself than the *gros bon homme* who pays the dressmaker can afford; his estate suffers perhaps, but at least his pretty wife seems to enjoy herself.' As had Katie, Robert Lytton visited the Prado, and commented that the gallery was 'even more crowded with carriages, horses and pretty faces every evening than Rotten Row or the *Bois* [no doubt the Bois de Boulogne, in Paris]'.[59] Katie had much admired the attractive Spanish women with their 'grace' and the 'dark, animated beauty of their eyes'.[60] So, too, did Lytton, who wrote of 'pretty faces… as brilliantly decorated as fireflies.'[61]

Spain had a lack of modernity that many visitors found enchanting. The nation's slow development was evidenced by its relatively late industrialization compared to England and continental nations. Images of Spain as a somewhat backward but mysterious and alluring place grew, especially after the Napoleonic Wars (1808–15) when many British and French veterans returned home and published memoirs of their time in the Iberian Peninsula. These stories were often exaggerated accounts of 'danger and exoticism'. Interest in Spanish culture also increased as Spanish artistic treasures began arriving in London and Paris. Some of this was plunder from the wars and some was in the form of gifts, such as those presented to the Duke of Wellington by the Spanish government. Writers such as Victor Hugo romanticized the nation further. Spain became, in the eyes of foreigners, a 'land of gypsies, highwaymen, proud beggars, flamenco dancing, bullfighting, public executions by strangulation, monks acting as Carlist guerrilla fighters, passionate and dangerous women perfectly depicted by Mérimée in his novel *Carmen* which Bizet later converted into an opera'.[62]

Yet this nation was full of contradictions. Profoundly traditional and Catholic, it was also a hotbed of revolutionary activity. The wars against Napoleon had destabilized the nation, and there followed struggles between the absolutist supporters of the monarchy and the Liberals who were determined to implement a new constitutional system. The nation was thrown into internal turmoil. This complex conflict, in which the parties were divided into groups with different interpretations and aims, was not resolved until the first Carlist War (1833–40), which saw a victory for the Moderate division of the Liberal Party. The Moderate victory lasted until 1868, the year that Katie and Willie spent in Madrid. During the rule of this Liberal regime, significant changes were made. There were many shortcomings to the regime, and they resulted in revolution in 1868. But there were also, despite the internal divisions among the Moderates, and disagreements with other political parties and factions, considerable achievements. The Moderates were committed to making significant changes to the infrastructure of Spanish society and implemented important administrative and legal changes to its governance.

The liberalizing of the banking system was one of such changes and it was no doubt the reason why Willie's uncle had invited him to join in his bank's expansion. The banking industry in Spain had developed very rapidly after a revolution in 1854. New banking legislation was enacted in 1856, and two types of banking institutions emerged. The first group of banks was limited to one per city, and these were authorized to issue banknotes following strict rules about gold and silver holdings. These institutions were also allowed to make loans and discount bills. The other banks that emerged after the 1856 legislation were credit societies, modelled on the French Crédit Mobilier. They did not have the right to issue banknotes but were authorized to participate in many other kinds of business activity.

The banking system sustained remarkable growth after the new laws were introduced. From five or six banking societies in 1855, there were some sixty establishments ten years later. This growth was, however, based on an over-reliance on investment in the railroads and national debt. When the economy faltered, towards 1864, there followed a crisis in the banking industry. Many establishments closed their doors, leaving millions in unpaid debts.[63] This contributed to an increasingly unstable economic and political situation. Years of unrest led to the further revolution in 1868.

It was at this time that Willie and Katie left Spain, after living there for nearly a year. The reason for their departure, Katie claimed, was due to 'some dispute about the business arrangements of Willie's partnership in his uncle's bank'. Willie then 'withdrew altogether from the affair' and they decided to return to England.[64] Katie's justification for leaving Spain suggested – perhaps inadvertently – a possibility of incompetence or irresponsibility on Willie's part, especially given his lack of success in later business dealings. Although Willie's banking partnership was not a success, it should be noted that political events might have played a more important role in the couple's decision to return home than Katie allowed by her account.

CHAPTER FIVE

Golden Opportunities

O N THEIR RETURN TO ENGLAND in 1868 the couple took a
house in Clarges Street, just off Piccadilly in central London.
Katie wrote of how this was a temporary measure, while they
looked for a suitable property from which Willie could run a stud
farm. He was 'very fond of horses', she explained, 'and understood
them well'. He was also an entrepreneur who was prepared to start
a business of his own. Katie seemed enthusiastic, writing that she
was 'delighted at the idea of his getting some really good brood
mares and breeding race-horses'.[1] The couple settled on
Bennington Park in Hertfordshire. This, their first real home, was
a very substantial property. It was a pretty place, Katie recorded,
'with two fine avenues of trees in a small park leading up to a
comfortable house'. There was also a 'lovely rose-walk' which 'led
to the glasshouses and kitchen gardens'. In addition to the stables
alongside the house, there were 'after them the long rows of loose
boxes, the groom's and gardener's cottages'. Paddocks 'opened on
and adjoined the park'.[2]

There they purchased thoroughbred mares, hoping to breed a
future champion, presumably using some cash that Willie was able
to withdraw from his uncle's business or perhaps from Katie's

marriage settlement from her Aunt Ben. In 1868, before the Married Women's Property Act of 1882 was made law, married women could not own property independently of their husbands. Whatever source of funds was used to finance their new business, Katie threw herself into the life with gusto. She recorded how when the foals arrived, she would give them bowls of warm milk. She spent 'many happy hours' with the horses, and she and her husband shared 'great hope' of many racing victories that would be theirs.

The lifestyle appealed to Katie. Her own pony was sent to her from Rivenhall, and Katie 'found her very useful trotting through the Hertfordshire lanes to return the calls of the country people'. Willie gave her a mare, called Brunette, for Katie to use with a cart.[3] She took an active part in the business. Willie was frequently away at the races, so she walked round every day in his absence, in order to report on the condition of the mares. One of the stallions was so difficult, apparently, that only she could manage his 'wicked' temper. On occasion the head man would have to ask her 'to come and soothe the beautiful brute, who was as gentle as a lamb with me'.[4]

Horse racing was an important pastime and a growing industry. It became increasingly popular in the second half of the century. The rapid expansion of the railroads had revolutionized racing in England, facilitating the transport of spectators to the courses. From less than a thousand miles of track in operation in 1839, the nation's network grew to 13,500 miles by 1870.[5] Grooms, trainers and jockeys increasingly travelled by train after 1840. Betting on horse racing became less confined to a minority wealthy elite, as larger numbers of spectators travelled to Doncaster, Epsom, Newmarket and other venues. Special trains were laid on to transport thousands of eager enthusiasts on race days – a leading fixture could attract crowds of 80,000 to a Bank Holiday event.[6] As more courses opened the number of fixtures rose (sixty-two new events were added to the turf calendar in the 1850s, another ninety-nine in the 1860s and a further fifty-four in the 1870s).[7] There were no entrance fees paid by spectators to this nationwide circuit of major races. The great attraction for the large numbers of working-class enthusiasts was the betting. Illegal sweepstakes had been replaced in the 1840s by betting shops where odds were displayed, and by the 1850s there were 150 such establishments operating in the capital alone.[8]

Victorian reformers disapproved of gambling, although this commercial and modern development was less objectionable than the disreputable and untrustworthy activities of the past. Now, the electric telegraph (completed in the 1850s) allowed results to be known immediately and a specialized press served the industry. The *Sporting Life* was founded in 1859 and the famous "Pink 'Un" in 1865. The lifestyle values associated with the turf were regarded with particular concern by many of the Victorian middle class.[9] Historian and social scientist Harold Perkin claimed that the drive to 'soften' manners – particularly from the late-eighteenth century to the mid-nineteenth century – was led by a wish to curtail what were seen as hindrances to the social and economic development of the nation. The increasingly dominant middle-class values, as embraced by the bourgeoisie, precluded a society in which 'the aristocracy and working class were united in their drunkenness, profaneness, sexual indulgence, gambling and love of cruel sports'.[10] Betting shops were thus outlawed in England in 1853, although the upper classes – who placed bets privately on the course or through clubs – and the working class, who used street runners acting for illegal bookies, both continued to place their bets. By the 1880s working-class gambling had become very widespread.[11]

Owning horses was, of course, costly. There were the expenses associated with training, stabling, feed and veterinarians' bills, the costs associated with racing, including the cost of entry to races, and jockeys' fees as well as the expense of colours, saddles and other equipment. Also to be taken into account were travelling costs and stabling at the course, together with the initial capital outlay of purchasing a racehorse. Although a higher price usually implied a higher-quality animal, this was not always the case. And the costs of keeping a racehorse were the same, whatever their performance.

Yet the risks were often part of the appeal. Successful owners could anticipate the value of their bloodstock would rise, and this is where O'Shea and other breeders hoped to make their profit. But it was a world filled with uncertainty. Most owners knew it was unlikely that they would cover their costs, but this did not stop them from indulging their passion, and hoping for winning form. The uncertainty of turf performance was increased by the lack of knowledge prior to the late nineteenth century on how breeding worked. Mendel's work on genetics was published in 1865, but not fully understood until many years later. The first major attempt to incorporate genetic knowledge into horse breeding did not occur until Bruce Lowe's 'figure system' of the 1890s.[12]

Breeders such as Willie O'Shea in the late 1860s did not have a scientific or quantitative basis for their business, nor did they fully comprehend that qualities could be passed on through the female line as significantly as through that of the stallion. It was thus an uncertain business, and a difficult environment in which to make money. Most of the very wealthy owners did their own breeding, and it was those who could not afford to do so who turned to the professional breeders. Most sales of racehorses came from farmers for whom breeding from one or two mares brought in some additional income. Other horses came from breeding companies, many of which were established after Mr Blenkiron's famous Middle Park Stud, begun in 1856, had achieved some considerable success. It was the privately bred racehorses, however, that achieved the most convincing results on the racecourse. The breeding companies were not terribly successful at producing outstanding horses – probably because they had neither the time nor the money enjoyed by the wealthy private breeders who could afford to take a long view. A further handicap was their habit – for reasons of cost – of using the same stallion for all their mares, regardless of suitability. The rich private breeder, on the other hand, took care to select stallions they believed to be physically and physiologically suited to their mares.

Those without the capital cushion and regular revenue to sustain them suffered in a competitive environment. Willie's business faltered under the predictable problem of high costs. He employed some twenty stable lads as well as a head groom. In addition to the breeding operation, the O'Sheas kept horses for their friends, which increased the costs of running the business. As Katie pointed out, their 'expenses were so heavy, both in the house and in the stables'. A further difficulty was O'Shea's unwillingness to collect money owed by his friends. 'Willie was never very good at dunning friends for money owed', Katie wrote, 'and as we had many brood mares, not our own, left with us for months at a time, the stable expenses, both for forage and wages, became appallingly large.'[13]

Although Willie found it nearly impossible to call in what he was owed, he could not ignore the expenses due. He was 'perpetually worried', according to his wife, 'by forage contractors, the shoeing smith, and the weekly wage bill, besides the innumerable extra expenses pertaining to a large stable'.[14] There was nothing feckless in Katie's description of a man who was constantly fretting over costs, and who demanded that she report to him on the mares' condition every day. He also used his many contacts in the racing world and brought his sporting friends home to be entertained, an important part of the business.

Katie later wrote of how she had dared to be different, and liked to mix up the guests in unexpected ways at such parties. She took pleasure, she wrote, in sending 'a stiff and extremely conventional "county" madame, blazing with diamonds and uninspiring of conversation, in to dinner with a cheery sporting man of no particular lineage and a fund of racy anecdote'.[15] Entertaining both the county set – who needed horses for hunting – and the more rackety and less reputable racing fraternity was an important element to the O'Sheas' enterprise. Katie seems to have fulfilled her responsibilities with aplomb, if not reverence. Although Willie besought his wife 'to be more careful', she recalled how it used to 'make me happy to give some of the accompanying daughters a good time among the "ineligible" men we had about'. These were men, she acknowledged, who were mostly 'without "two sixpences to rub together"; but nevertheless very gay-hearted and pleasant companions'. Katie had clearly not left her own somewhat bohemian background far behind her on marriage. Her unusual party arrangements, she claimed, made 'a change for the dear prim girls'. In looking back on those days, Katie concluded that she and Willie – 'a good-looking young couple' – were no doubt 'of great interest to all these dull people'.[16]

Despite their best efforts, the farm was running out of money. Willie frequently threatened to sell the mares, much against Katie's urging. 'He used to stare gloomily at me', she wrote, 'and swear gently as he wished there were more profit than peace in their maternity and my sentimentality.'[17] He forgot his worries, however, in the pleasure he took in schooling the yearlings. Both he and Katie 'agreed always to hold on as long as possible to a life we both found so interesting'.[18]

But the business did not improve. According to Katie, her husband began betting heavily in an attempt to raise cash. This was a common tactic used by owners who were losing money. In his well-respected Badminton Library volume on racing,[19] the Earl of Suffolk declared that the 'great majority' of racing owners gambled 'to a greater or lesser degree'.[20] It was not often, however, a particularly successful way to earn money. In addition to his losses thus generated were the heavy expenses of maintaining his stud farm. The overdraft grew larger, until one day, Katie reported, their 'kind-hearted' bank manager, hitherto 'such a good fellow', for whom they had given a breakfast at his hunt, insisted on the clearing of the debt.

In the past Willie had been able to give Mr Cheshire, the bank manager, 'something on account' whenever he had been 'very pressing', but this was no longer possible. Although Willie had maintained friendly relations with his bank manager, who had accepted their hospitality, the more businesslike climate of industrialized Britain meant that cordiality was not enough. After consultation with Cheshire and 'another friend', Willie decided that the mares would all have to be sold. It was, Katie wrote, a 'heavy blow', and as the 'long string of thoroughbred mares' was led away she 'kissed their muzzles for the last time', and 'cried bitterly'. Her 'poor' husband watched them go, she said, 'with a miserable face'.[21] When the horses failed to sell, however, the situation became critical. Bankruptcy loomed.

Katie's mother Emma wrote to her great friend the journalist E. S. Dallas (he often sent her two letters a day, and she owned three thousand of them) that her youngest daughter was 'ruined'.[22] Fortunately, Katie's wealthy and loyal brother-in-law, Sir Thomas Barrett Lennard, came to the rescue. He bought the mares for £500 and they were sent to his estate at Belhus. The business was wound down. The servants were paid off, although Katie was not left entirely bereft. She retained the services of her childhood maid, Lucy, her French maid, Caroline, and their 'faithful' stud-groom Selby, who all travelled with her to Brighton.[23] Other members of Katie's family rallied and Aunt Ben took a house for her at Brighton, close to her sister Emma Barrett Lennard. The family was no doubt particularly sensitive to her predicament because she was expecting her first child. Katie gave birth to a son, Gerard, on 4 April 1870, in the house rented for her by Aunt Ben. She was 'very ill' afterwards and her mother came to stay with her. She made, Katie recollected, a 'lovely water-sketch' for her while she was there.[24] Although Katie wrote that she was consoled in her sorrow over the loss of the Bennington Place enterprise by her 'beautiful babe', she made no mention of Willie's reaction to the birth of his firstborn son.

By now, the winding up of Willie's stud farm was finalized and the business venture was no more. A young solicitor, Charles Lane of the firm Lane and Monroe, had been brought in to manage the process. According to Katie, Charles Lane took it upon himself to call on her uncle William, now Lord Chancellor. Lane apparently asked Lord Hatherley to assist the O'Sheas in their 'financial difficulties'. Although Uncle William was, Katie wrote, 'much astonished' at the request made by the 'obviously nervous' solicitor, the young man went on to suggest that Captain O'Shea might be given a 'lucrative appointment'.[25] Katie later claimed that it had never even occurred to her to turn to her uncle for aid. This may or may not have been the case. What is certain is that her uncle was a powerful man. The post of Lord Chancellor was at that time one of the most important of the land:[26] he was the Keeper of the Great Seal,[27] the chief royal chaplain and advisor to the Crown on spiritual and temporal affairs, Speaker of the House of Lords, and he held responsibilities for the Church of England, including the appointment of clergymen in those ecclesiastical livings under the patronage of the Crown, and of those which were under his own patronage. Lord Hatherley was by all accounts extremely devout (it was noted that he and his wife attended the quarter to eight morning service in Westminster Abbey every single day) and hardworking. He was also known to be rather a dour fellow. One contemporary noted that he was 'a mere bundle of virtues without a redeeming vice'.[28]

When Lane came to the O'Sheas with a 'substantial cheque and a kind message' from Lord Hatherley, Katie wrote that she and her husband 'were as surprised as we were pleased', despite the news that there was no job to be made available for Willie.[29] Her strict and sober uncle did not promote those he believed to be unsound. Emma Wood wrote to her friend Dallas that her brother-in-law had turned down her request for a living for a man whose 'character is stainless' simply because this man did not believe in the eternity of punishment. Her son Evelyn had, however, agreed with his uncle's judgement.[30] It was unlikely that O'Shea, with his gambling debts and failed business record, would have appeared a suitable candidate for any position recommended by the Lord Chancellor.

Willie was thus without employment and they continued to live in Brighton. Katie wrote that she was mindful of cost and moved the family out of the expensive house her aunt was renting for them, to cheaper accommodation on the Marine Parade. She was struck by the large number of refugees from France who had fled to England, many of them living in Brighton. In July 1870 the French Emperor Napoleon III had reluctantly gone to war with Prussia.[31] The conflict was a disaster for the French, and within a few months the capital was threatened. Those who had the means to do so fled the city and crossed the Channel. Many of them landed at Brighton, where they stayed in hotels and boarding houses. Jennie Jerome – who later became the mother of future Prime Minister Winston Churchill – had been living with her mother and sisters in Paris, and recollected in her memoirs how depressing the evacuation had been. 'Our friends scattered, fighting, or killed at the front', Jennie recalled, 'it was indeed a sad time.'[32] France was defeated and Paris surrendered on 28 January 1871. Prussian troops marched down the Champs Elysées to the Place de la Concorde, singing 'Die Wacht am Rhein'. To make a bad situation worse, civil violence broke out shortly after. Many civilians as well as troops were killed, and buildings destroyed, including the Tuileries and Hôtel de Ville.

Katie was attended by her French maid, Caroline, who had remained with her mistress. The servant – whose 'hardest task', Katie wrote, had been to dress her hair and wash the dog – 'now with the utmost cheerfulness took to cooking, scrubbing, cleaning and being literally a maid-of-all-work'. The O'Sheas were also served by their old groom, Selby, who now found that he 'did anything that needed doing, helping in the house, valeting his master'. When Katie's pony was sent to her, it was looked after by Selby, who 'installed himself as stable-boy as a matter of course'. The two servants also made it 'their first duty' to keep little Gerard 'amused'. All in all, Katie acknowledged that despite their fall from affluence, she and her husband were 'very comfortable', thanks to what she called 'these faithful friends'.[33]

Aunt Ben continued to pay the rent, and it was decided to take a small house at Patcham, just out of Brighton, where Katie could keep her pony. She rode in daily to visit her sister Emma, who was also living in Brighton. But she was bored with her life, writing that she also suffered from great loneliness at this time, as Willie was often away – 'on various businesses'.[34] This state of affairs was unsatisfactory to her, and she told her husband that she wished to join him in London. The family moved to Harrow Road, till they had time to find something 'less depressing'.[35] Insufficient funds continued to plague them. After moving to London, Willie fell very ill. During his convalescence, Katie recollected that a moneylender had called to 'have some acceptances of Willie's met'. When she explained that she was unable to do so, Mr Calasher renewed on her signature alone, and later told them that the Captain could pay the monies owed, with an added 6 per cent, when he was 'able'. This kindness, Katie wrote, was much appreciated by the O'Sheas, and she was glad that they had been able to repay the money within a year.

Despite her 'inexperience' at nursing, it was Katie that Willie chose to have beside him, rather than his mother or sister, whose 'presence irritated the patient so intensely'.[36] Willie's health gradually improved and in 1872 the family moved away from Harrow Road – an abode that Katie had disliked, as there were 'constant' processions of hearses on the way to Kensal Green Cemetery. Their finances mysteriously improved as well. The couple moved with their son to a house in Beaufort Gardens in

Knightsbridge, where they redecorated and hired new staff. A butler joined the establishment, and Caroline returned to her 'light duties' and, indeed, 'reigned over a staff of maids'.[37]

Now Katie's complaint was not of loneliness, but of too much social activity. Her husband 'insisted' on making new acquaintances, and the couple soon found themselves 'in a social whirl of visits, visitors and entertainments'.[38] Unlike her experiences in Patcham, where Katie had fretted over the loss of her 'busy life at Bennington' and from 'want of companionship',[39] now the problem was that she had never liked society. She also declared that her husband *did*, and therefore thoroughly revelled in their new life. Meanwhile, the couple's second child and first daughter, Norah, was born on 10 January 1873.

In her memoir, Katie's complaints about Willie's behaviour escalated after their move to Beauchamp Gardens. She referred to his desire for social companionship and stimulation, and claimed that he even brought her home after a dance or reception and left her there, alone, as he went out again. On the one hand, she remarked on how much Willie savoured social occasions, yet she was forced by him to attend functions at her uncle's home by herself. Indeed, Katie, in a remark that contradicted a previous assertion, stated that she and her husband 'were a great deal' at the Lord Chancellor's house, 'both at "functions" and privately'. Given that the Lord Chancellor hosted 'the pick of the intellectual world of the day... with the necessary make-weight of people who follow and pose in the wake of the great', it seems hardly credible that society-loving Willie would systematically forgo these events.[40]

But Katie was clearly enjoying being in London. A second daughter, Carmen, was born on 4 August 1874 and, like her brother and sister, she was baptized in a Catholic ceremony. Katie's sister Emma was living in London, having taken a house in Whitehall Gardens, and their sister Anna came up to town to see them regularly. 'I saw a great deal of them', wrote Katie, 'and was happier and more amused than I had been for some time.'[41]

Unfortunately, the happy interlude was interrupted by illness and more financial worries. Katie fell ill during a cold winter following the birth of her third child, and was advised to move to warmer climes. Aunt Ben once again came to the family's aid, and sent a cheque. Katie and the children, along with nurses, moved to the Isle of Wight for the winter. She wrote that Willie, having installed them all in lodgings at Ventnor, then left for London. She added that her spouse was 'too busy' to come to Ventnor, and that she eventually became depressed: it was decided to move the family closer to 'home'. Accompanied by her nephew, the family travelled to Hastings. When they had been settled at St Leonard's, her relative 'informed his Uncle Willie of the whereabouts of his family'.[42] Aunt Ben, who lived at Eltham, was still paying Katie's expenses, and, as Katie's health improved, she and Willie visited her frequently. According to Katie, one day Aunt Ben proposed to provide her niece with a home near her, so that Katie could be her 'constant companion'.[43] This arrangement must have seemed like an answer to the O'Sheas' prayers.

The agreement was not informal. An arrangement was made after consultation with the County Court Judge and one of Aunt Ben's nephews who was responsible for her business transactions. Aunt Ben bought Katie a house at the other side of her park, and settled a regular income on her. She also agreed to pay for the children's education. In return, 'Swan', as Aunt Ben liked to call Katie, would be her daily companion. It was an offer that suited both parties, especially the O'Sheas, and one would have to question whether hopes of pecuniary advantage had lain behind all those visits made by the pair to the wealthy woman. Certainly the outcome was a positive one for Katie. She now had a home, an income and provision for her children, independent of her husband's fortunes. Katie did not disclose the amount paid over to her by her aunt, but she lived a comfortable life on the income thus afforded. Her situation was an unusual one in some respects but Katie had by this arrangement rather neatly solved her financial crisis. Middle-class women in the Victorian era did not usually work outside the home. Fathers and husbands took the responsibility for providing the family income.

Women, on the other hand, were characterized by their 'feminine' qualities, such as submission and dependence,[44] although many unmarried women and widows had to earn their keep. There were few suitable paid positions, the most common of which was that of governess. This employment was considered respectable, but was poorly remunerated, and there were not enough jobs available. Some women earned their living by running their own business. These tended to cater to an upmarket clientele, and were usually run as female-oriented establishments, such as dressmakers.[45]

An interesting exception to this was the female novelist, and Katie had observed at first-hand the resourcefulness of her mother and sister, while wealthy Aunt Ben provided another example of independence available to some women within the Victorian norm. Katie's experience of income generation was therefore not typical of her class.

In the absence of a reliable income from her spouse, Katie chose an option that satisfied her desire to provide a comfortable life for her family. She described her new routine, stating that she went to her aunt in the morning, returning for a visit to her children at lunchtime. If Willie were in Eltham, she would later join him for dinner. It was a quiet existence, and Aunt Ben's regime rather severe. She was a French and Latin scholar, who also enjoyed translating Greek verse. Katie's life assumed a regular and uneventful rhythm. She was with her aunt, she later wrote, 'nearly the whole of the day – reading to her, writing for her, wheeling her up and down the great tapestry room, or walking quietly in the grounds'.[46]

Aunt Ben was strong-willed. She insisted that her servants attend church, and made them learn verses or collects, which had to be recited every Sunday evening. Katie described how uncomfortable this ritual was: 'The servants hated these excursions into culture, and, from the man-servant, whose "piece" always lacked aspirates, to the kitchenmaid, round, crimson, and uncomfortable, whose "portion" always halted despairingly in the middle, they kept their resentful gaze fixed upon me, who held the book – and the thankless office of prompter.'[47] Indeed, the elderly lady was something of a tyrant. No one was allowed to tread on the polished wood floors of her house, and guests had to skip from carpet to carpet to avoid doing so. This diktat extended to her 'gentleman readers', who called once weekly to read aloud from the classics. The author George Meredith was one such reader, and was paid £300 a year to read to her once a week. Katie described how the distinguished author occasionally rebelled against the order and tiptoed across the hall 'under the scandalised gaze of the footman'.[48] Aunt Ben's demands were considerable, and she had a gate made in the park fence so that her niece could come and go more quickly. When Katie was absent for a long period due to illness, her aunt was 'disconsolate'. The feeling was mutual: Katie professed to be 'very glad' to get back to her aunt once more – 'someone who wanted me always'.[49]

Willie had not, however, given up his entrepreneurial ambitions. He set up a company in Spain in order to develop some mining interests there. There was more than a hint of wariness in Katie's account of the venture: she wrote that her husband 'always drew up a prospectus excellently', and that indeed, 'on reading it one could hardly help believing – as he invariably did – that here at last was the golden opportunity of speculators'.[50] In fact, O'Shea did manage to attract capital to the scheme. Investing in mining and other commercial enterprises was an increasingly popular way for the upper middle classes to generate income. Revenue from landed estates had been falling since the 1870s, as agricultural rents dropped. This was due in large part to increased competition from cheap grain that was carried in from North America at 'unprecedently low freight rates'.[51] The agricultural industry had long been the mainstay upon which the upper classes derived their income, and also their power and status. The decline in agricultural revenues forced many to look elsewhere for income.[52] Unlike many of these patricians, Willie did not seem to have felt distaste at earning his living. In fact, he seems to have embarked on his Spanish mining venture with enthusiasm.

Katie's account of the enterprise was detailed and revealed a focused participation on her behalf. 'Acute' business friends had invested amounts varying from £1,000 to £10,000, she wrote. Their 'old friend', Christopher Weguelin, took a strong interest in the venture.[53] Willie was away in Spain for eighteen months, and during that time, Katie was asked to liaise with the investors in England. She paid 'frequent visits' to London to see Weguelin, and to 'place the constant demands for new machinery in as ingratiating a way as possible before various members of the "board"'.[54]

Katie was sufficiently involved in the business to write later about the specific difficulties faced by her husband. Machinery was sent from England without critical spare parts, meaning that workers sat expensively idle in Spain, with useless machinery. Katie was pressed by her furious spouse to show his reports to the company directors. After Willie had invented a machine to extract sulphur from the ore, Katie drew up a report, and had it verified by the firm's engineers. She also used her more feminine talents to help with the venture. One of the directors – whom Katie named only as 'Mr. C' – suggested that she make one of her 'ripping' meat pies for the fellow directors. Although she did produce the 'gorgeous beefsteak pie', for which she had been 'famous among my friends since childhood', it failed to move the businessmen. Mr C reported: 'the pigs wolfed that scrumptious pie, and then, though I said you'd made it, declared that old Father William was to be ordered home at once, and the mines closed'.[55]

Her husband returned from Spain after another setback. Although they were pleased to see one another, 'the wearing friction caused by our totally dissimilar temperaments began to make us feel that close companionship was impossible'. By 'mutual agreement', Willie took rooms in London, and visited Eltham at the weekends. One of Charles Parnell's colleagues (and subsequent bitter enemy), Tim Healy, later wrote that Katie had embarked on an affair with Christopher Weguelin while Willie was in Spain.[56] Although Healy was completely misinformed about Katie's life, and never even met her, the story gained some circulation at the time of her divorce. It is difficult to ascertain the truth of the assertion. Katie's later behaviour does open up the possibility of a previous extramarital affair, especially if her husband was absent for eighteen months, but there is no available evidence to support the claim of Katie's infidelity.

Meanwhile Katie continued to act as hostess for Willie, and travelled to London to do so. They entertained at Thomas's Hotel, in Berkeley Square. She was well known there, having stayed at the establishment with her parents on trips to the capital. 'I used to help Willie with his parties', she recollected, 'and to suffer the boredom incidental to this form of entertainment.' But she preferred to receive guests at Eltham, 'where one had more time to talk'.[57]

CHAPTER SIX

The Rise of Charles Stewart Parnell

WILLIE O'SHEA WAS AT THIS TIME 'longing for some definite occupation'. He knew a number of 'political people' and on a trip to Ireland early in 1880 he was 'constantly urged by his friends' to try for a seat in Parliament. But it was one thing to have political ambitions, and quite another to pay for them. O'Shea wrote to his wife of his concern that 'the expenses would be almost too heavy for us to manage'. Katie replied, 'strongly encouraging him to stand'; she believed that a political career would give her husband an occupation he would enjoy and was not displeased that it would also keep them apart.[1]

It is most likely that Willie sought his wife's blessing because he needed her financial support. Katie's continuing good relationship with Aunt Ben was undoubtedly an important factor in the decision to run for a parliamentary seat. MPs were unpaid in 1880, and also had to meet the expenses of their campaigns. Indeed, Katie recalled that, after the election, when both Willie and his friend, The O'Gorman Mahon, had won their seats, they asked Katie to find £2,000 to meet their costs. The O'Gorman Mahon told her 'he was almost penniless – this announced by him with the grand air of a conjuror – and that Willie, with more zeal than discretion, had guaranteed the whole of the expenses for both'.[2] Katie promised to do what she could to get her aunt to help.[3]

At this time, the Irish political arena was an exciting one. The Irish Franchise Act of 1850 had increased the Irish electorate from 45,000 to 164,000 and the Reform Act of 1868 further raised the numbers allowed to vote. By 1871, 16 per cent of the adult male population were enfranchised (compared to 34 per cent in England).[4] By the 1870s, Irish political parties were still attempting to harness the impetus for change into their own political agendas. There were a number of interests that would benefit from political representation. From the principle of 'tenant right' to the enunciation of the 3 Fs – fair rent, fixity of tenure, and freedom of sale – the desire to achieve reform to the existing system and structure of land ownership and management was a permanent feature of the Irish political landscape throughout the century.

The clergy – who as sons of tenant farmers were often inclined to support land reform – were not always inclined (or allowed) to support campaigns for political reforms, especially in the latter half of the century. Under Archbishop, and then Cardinal, Paul Cullen, the Church moved away from overt support for political change. Cullen was a committed ultramontanist and he dominated the Irish Catholic Church from the 1850s through to the late 1870s. He believed that Church and State should be kept separate, yet firmly opposed any political movements that did not serve the interests of the Church. This was one of a number of reasons why the Church played an increasingly ambiguous role in the factional struggles for political dominance in Ireland.

Another political arena focused on the numerous campaigns to restore some form of limited legislative independence to Ireland. An example of this was the 'repeal' movement (which specifically campaigned for a repeal of the Act of Union and the restoration of a separate Irish parliament), led by Daniel O'Connell. The movement had fizzled out by the 1850s after a lack of success, but struggle for a form of independence continued in various other ways. 'Young

Ireland' was a romantic nationalist group, active from 1842 to 1848, which focused on the *Nation* newspaper. The 'Young Irelanders', led initially by Thomas Davis, Charles Gavan Duffy and John Blake Dillon, were mainly middle-class graduates and of both Catholic and Protestant origin. They sought to infuse the Irish population with a cultural identity, through a promotion of national literature and by a revival of Gaelic, the Irish language.[5] The 'Young Irelanders' (as opposed the 'Old Irelanders' led by O'Connell) staged a rebellion in 1848 which was swiftly suppressed. The leaders were arrested and transported to Australia.[6] Their movement, although unsuccessful, nevertheless laid the foundation for much of the cultural revival explicitly linked to Irish nationalist aims that was to follow. Also, members of the movement contributed to the foundation of what became the Irish Republican Brotherhood.

Members of this emerging, secret, revolutionary movement, active from the 1850s, were known as Fenians – a reference to the warriors of ancient Ireland. Fenianism originated in the United States, where the difficulties of integration experienced by many of the Irish immigrants had kept their attention centred on 'home' and the political situation there. Men such as John O'Mahoney, Michael Doheny, Joseph Deniffe and James Stephens were the leaders of this movement. Stephens launched a revolutionary society in Dublin on St Patrick's Day, 17 March 1858. Known as 'The Society', 'The Organization' or 'The Brotherhood', it was dedicated to secrecy and the establishment of an independent Irish republic. The title Fenian was used when a parallel branch was set up in New York by John O'Mahoney, but was subsequently used to describe the movement in Ireland as well.

In 1867 a weak attempt at a rising in Ireland – first in February, then on 4–5 March – was a failure. After this setback, internal divisions hindered further activity by the Fenian movement. There was, for example, considerable debate over whether it was most expedient to strike at England in Ireland or Canada, which was resolved only after failed interventions in Canada in 1866, 1867 and 1871. The Fenians attempted to reorganize after 1871 and by 1873 established themselves as the Irish Republican Brotherhood, with a formal Constitution that provided for this secret revolutionary society to be governed on a democratic basis with a partially elected supreme council.[7]

The tradition of revolutionary societies in Ireland was not new. The Society of United Irishmen, made up of Protestants and Catholics, was established in 1791, and led by men such as the legendary patriots Theobald Wolfe Tone and Robert Emmett. It had as its ideology a new radicalism inspired by the French and American Revolutions, and sought parliamentary reform and the removal of English control over Irish affairs. A failed insurrection in 1798 was the culmination of their revolutionary efforts,[8] and following this some 1,500 people were executed, transported or flogged. The rebellion, which is believed to have resulted in 30,000 deaths overall and represented one of the most violent periods in Irish history, became a rallying point for revolutionaries. Other secret societies had been a feature of Irish rural life for over 150 years. Defenders, Whiteboys, and Ribbonmen, for example, were all part of a long – albeit localized and intermittent – tradition of agrarian protest that in the latter half of the nineteenth century found expression through the Fenian movement.[9] The Fenians to a large extent thus encompassed the overlapping concerns of agrarian protest and the drive for some form of legislative independence.

The direction espoused by the Fenians did not, however, always appeal to the majority of the population. The Irish Republican Brotherhood (IRB) was explicit in its rejection of support from the Church, for example, and strongly opposed to 'priests in politics'.[10] And the Church was implacably hostile to revolutionaries, threatening members of such groups with excommunication. From the 1860s Cardinal Cullen sought a papal denunciation of the Fenian movement specifically. He got this in 1870.[11] But the rise of Fenianism continued.

From 1865, the movement was supported (and indeed often led) by Irish Americans, men such as John O'Mahoney and James

Stephens. The poor land management practices that had exacerbated the terrible effects of the earlier famines were explicitly blamed by the many emigrants who had fled starvation. They believed that only independence from England would solve Ireland's problems. Many of the Irish-American émigré community longed for the day they could return to a free Ireland, and to this end they provided a steady stream of financial support for revolutionary activity. Clan na Gael was the most important of such sister groups of the Irish Republican Brotherhood and bankrolled the organization.[12] Arms were smuggled from the United States and, as Fenian membership rose, the revolutionaries committed to a rising in 1865. The government responded by launching a series of successful raids in September 1865. The leaders were ultimately found and arrested, but three days after his arrest, the American ringleader James Stephens was spirited out. He was replaced by his friend and fellow Fenian Thomas J. Kelly (born in Galway, Kelly had emigrated to the USA where he served as a subaltern in the Signal Corps of the Union's Army of the Potomac). Once again consignments of arms and men made their way from America to Ireland.

Plans were almost always betrayed, however, by informers and the authorities were well prepared for a new wave of attacks. The revolutionists issued a proclamation of the Irish Republic in London on 10 February 1867. Risings throughout Ireland, including a general insurrection in Dublin on 5–6 March 1867, were unsuccessful, largely due to lack of organization and good intelligence available to the British. Many arrests were made, but the two leaders, Kelly and another American, Captain Timothy Deasy, were rescued on 18 September by an armed gang. The key-holding officer, Sergeant Charles Brett, was shot and killed during the attempt and intense police activity followed. The men involved were arrested and put on trial, and of those convicted three were publicly executed on Sunday 23 November 1867. William O'Meara Allen, Michael Larkin and Michael O'Brien (tried and convicted as Gould) were put to death in front of a crowd of 8–10,000 people, with 500 constables and 2,000 special constables on duty. There were also 500 soldiers present, including cavalry, infantry and two batteries of artillery. The bravery of the men's deaths, and the belief shared by many in Ireland that the shooting had been accidental, meant that the men became hugely admired. The 'Manchester Martyrs', as they became known, galvanized public sentiment and sparked tremendous nationalist feeling.[13]

This represented a turning point, in that popular opinion stood firmly behind the 'Martyrs' – to the extent that a number of high-profile Masses were said for them by Irish Catholic Bishops.[14] This did not go unnoticed in Westminster, where William Ewart Gladstone, Prime Minister from 1868, had already commented that his mission was to 'pacify Ireland',[15] and subsequent legislation included the disestablishment of the Church of Ireland in 1869, followed by the Irish Land Act of 1870.[16] This legislation to improve the lives of Irish Catholics in Ireland weakened the position of the Fenians, whose commitment was to reject any constructive engagement with the British government and to demand independence.

The Irish Protestant Tory barrister, Isaac Butt, saw an opportunity to build on the mass-movement support that Fenianism claimed. He mistrusted the Fenians, and proposed Home Rule as an alternative to the separatist republicanism they espoused. Butt argued that devolved government within the Union would 'satisfy Irish nationalist dignity while allowing Ireland the benefits of imperial partnership with Britain, the strongest and richest nation in the world'.[17] The Home Rule League was established in 1873 and, at the general election of 1874, fifty-nine MPs were returned on Home Rule 'principles'.[18] At first, the IRB worked with Butt through the amnesty movement, which campaigned for the release of Fenian prisoners, and a number of prominent Fenians who had escaped exile in the 1860s became Home Rulers in the 1870s. Some of the revolutionaries realized during the 1870s that a determined commitment to violence would not yield immediate success, and the Supreme Council of the IRB amended their Constitution in 1873 to allow it to 'support every movement calculated to advance the case of Irish independence consistently with the preservation of its own integrity'.[19]

This paved the way for a series of rather uneasy 'new departures', in which the revolutionary nationalists – still funded by the organization's American wing – worked in tandem with the Home Rulers.[20] This shadowy cooperation was never official, but it laid a template for further developments. Cooperation formally ended in 1876, but many Fenians continued the pattern. They would relax their commitment to violence for a time, and often their support would give a strategic boost to the Home Rule movement, in certain regions of Ireland especially. The Home Rule movement, led by Butt, made little discernible progress, however, from 1874 to 1880. Butt used Parliament to issue polite protests, to little avail.

Other Home Rule MPs grew impatient. They were not all gentlemen landlords any longer. Increasingly, the Irish MPs were journalists, merchants and shopkeepers, who had little truck with gentlemanly parliamentary tactics. Joseph Biggar was one example. A prosperous provision merchant from Ulster and Home Rule MP for Cavan, in 1874 he was allowed to join the IRB and he later took a seat on the Supreme Council. At Westminster, much to Butt's discomfort, Biggar initiated the policy of 'obstruction', whereby he would hold up parliamentary proceedings in protest at the government's refusal to legislate on Home Rule. After the Meath by-election of April 1875 he was joined by a new recruit, the Protestant landowner Charles Stewart Parnell. Parnell had taken a sudden decision in 1874 to enter politics. After meeting with the leaders of the Home Rule movement, he stood first for a seat in Dublin, in 1874. He was defeated, and then won his seat for Meath in 1875. In all of his campaigning, Parnell laid great stress on the Parnell family's patriotic record.

He was not a typical landlord MP. He had been sponsored by Patrick Egan, who had been a Fenian since the 1860s but, like many other Fenians, was willing in the 1870s to give Home Rule a try for a limited time. From the outset, therefore, Parnell was knowingly working with revolutionaries, albeit ones who were at this time ostensibly cooperating with MPs to achieve legislative progress via Home Rule. He made a point of building a rapport with militant nationalists.[21] In 1876, he travelled to America, where his purpose was to convey – on behalf of the 'Irish people' – a congratulatory address to the President on the centenary of the American Declaration of Independence. This was refused, but Parnell gained public attention.[22] In addition to collaborating with the American Fenians, Parnell also worked with the radical Fenian Michael Davitt on land reform.

Davitt was a member of the Supreme Council of the radical Irish Republican Brotherhood, and had served a prison sentence for gathering arms. He was committed to radical land reform. Landlords of 1,000 acres and more still owned 81 per cent of the land in 1870,[23] and the fact that many of these landlords were absentees added to the iniquities of the Irish situation. After poor harvests in 1877 and 1878, the west of Ireland was facing famine conditions – which were not helped by the general and industrial depression in the United Kingdom and elsewhere. Credit was being called in, putting tenants under greater pressure.[24] Rents went unpaid, which resulted in an increased number of evictions. In June 1879, the American Fenian and head of the revolutionary Clan na Gael,[25] John Devoy, reached an agreement with Parnell to produce the 'New Departure'. Devoy was an important ally as he was the publisher of the New York *Gaelic American Newspaper*.

The 'New Departure' was an informal agreement that brought together Devoy, Parnell and Davitt.[26] It endorsed full legislative independence for Ireland, compulsory land purchase to allow tenants who wished to do so to buy the land they farmed, and an independent Home Rule Party at Westminster. It was constructed with the foundation of the Land League, established in October 1879 as a means of promoting and coordinating a country-wide campaign against landlordism. Parnell accepted the Presidency of the League. By so doing, he symbolically widened its scope from the issue of land reform to include broader aims of legislative nationalist objectives. It is not certain how much Parnell wished for comprehensive land reform (he was, after all, a landlord himself), but that he saw advantage in linking the agrarian unrest with his political objectives is clear. He declared as much in a speech at Galway, on 24 October of that year, saying that he 'would not have taken off my coat and gone to work if I had not known that we were laying the foundations by this movement for the recovery of our legislative independence'.[27]

The stated purpose of the Land League was to achieve peasant proprietorship, but many of its members harboured from its inception far more revolutionary plans. In New York City, Patrick Ford, the Irish-born influential and controversial proprietor of the *Irish World*, launched a crusade in support, collecting funds.[28] But his paper also preached against England, and railed against those Fenians who disagreed with the diversion of fighting funds (destined to pay for the armed struggle against England)[29] to support the non-payment of rent by Ireland's tenants. In October – while Parnell was travelling throughout Ireland – the 'Transatlantic' correspondent of the *Irish World* thundered:

Behold now 200 Land League branches established through Ireland with at least 500 members in each, and all in full cry against the land robbers... I pray and urge my friends at home and abroad to drop the controversy [over the use of funds], and to unite against the common enemies of our people, the landlords of Ireland and of England, with their forces of armed men at their backs![30]

In August 1880 the House of Lords rejected any reform on the Irish land question in the form of a very moderate Compensation for Disturbance Bill. This lack of cooperation from the English set the scene for a winter of trouble in Ireland. The 'New Departure', in which Parnell played such a key role, continued as an unprecedented 'alliance of Fenians, parliamentarians, Land-Leaguers, Irish-Americans, priests and peasants'.[31] To keep such disparate elements working harmoniously together was a massive challenge, and one historian has likened Parnell's involvement to 'riding a tiger'.[32]

The Irish National (or Parliamentary) Party was by 1880 arguably making some headway in its goals to achieve independence for Ireland.[33] Not all of its members agreed on the exact nature of the objectives or on the methods to achieve them, however. The 1880 general election had returned seventy-year-old William Ewart Gladstone as Prime Minister, and he faced many challenges in his second tenure as the nation's leader, among them a number of internal and external threats to the nation's stability. At this time, there were problems with South Africa,[34] as well as with Ireland.

Meanwhile, the Irish MPs were determined to keep Irish affairs a priority in Westminster. After a meeting of the Irish members in May 1880, Willie O'Shea telegraphed to his wife that he had voted for a new leader. He and twenty-two others had chosen Charles Stewart Parnell. Willie also confided to her his concern that 'Mr. Parnell might be "too advanced"'.[35] And indeed the new leader was seemingly in favour of limited agitation to achieve the goals of land reform.[36] The campaign of agrarian protest, begun in 1879, went from tenant demands for rent rebates to a campaign against landlordism altogether. Much of the activity centred on evictions for non-paying of rent. The Land League generated mass enthusiasm and explicitly linked the tradition of landlordism in Ireland with a privileged, British, elite.

Parnell's position on land reform was in fact complex. As a landowner, he was not in favour of the more revolutionary ideas of peasant proprietorship as espoused by many members of the Land League. But as an astute and moderate politician, he was quick to see the advantages of harnessing the mass movement to a general, nationalist support for constitutional reform. Not all members shared such goals, or, indeed, agreed on the means to achieve greater independence for Ireland. Many people admired the outgoing chairman, William Shaw, who was seen as 'safe' and 'steady-going'.[37]

Parnell's leadership mandate was not therefore overwhelming. Of the fifty-nine nominal Home Rule MPs, twenty-three had voted for him, and eighteen had supported the more moderate Shaw.[38] But the new leader, now elected as President of the Home Rule Confederation of Great Britain in 1877, had gone from strength to strength. By the time that Willie met him, Parnell was a rapidly rising star. He had returned to America in December 1879, with Davitt, on a fund-raising tour for the Land League. After his return home in April 1880, he had gained his seat as MP for Cork City and his election to the party chair followed in May. He was the first Irish leader to meet British MPs on an equal footing in Westminster, as well as being able to generate the mass adoration of the crowds back home, where he was known simply as 'the Chief'.[39]

After his own election to a seat for County Clare, Willie prevailed upon his wife to host small dinner parties for him. Katie was an accomplished hostess. The MP (and Parnell loyalist) Henry Harrison later described her as a woman 'with the full endowment of physical and moral qualities that might be expected from the family of which she came'. She was, he stated emphatically, 'no mere pretty woman'. She was someone with great personality:

Her allure, with her visible strength of type, suggested the empress rather than the nymph. Her intelligence was lively and audacious; her brain quick and far-ranging, competently stocked with rather more than the full usual complement of general knowledge of affairs social, political, literary and artistic (...) She was generous, irascible and high-tempered, and most indulgently kind to others... Of enterprising spirit and of high courage she had full share.[40]

Katie recounted how she had invited Charles Parnell to several of these social occasions. When guests scoffed at how impossible it was to lure the leader to the table, Katie declared that she would succeed where others had failed. She became determined, she later claimed, 'that I would get Parnell to come, and said, amid laughter and applause "The Uncrowned King of Ireland shall sit in that chair at the next dinner I give!"'[41]

One 'bright sunny day' she had driven, with her sister, to the House of Commons. There she sent in her card, asking Mr Parnell to come out and speak to her in the Palace Yard. According to her memoir, their first encounter was portentous. This 'tall, gaunt figure, thin and deadly pale' looked at her, smiling, and his 'curiously burning eyes looked into mine with a wonderful intentness that threw into my brain the sudden thought: "This man is wonderful – and different"'.[42]

The encounter was dramatic and the impact on Katie obviously very strong. When she leaned forward out of the carriage to say goodbye to Parnell, a rose she was wearing fell on to her skirt. Parnell picked it up, and, she wrote, 'touching it lightly with his lips, placed it in his buttonhole'. Years later, she claimed that she had found the rose 'done up in an envelope' with her name and the date transcribed on it, among Parnell's private papers.[43] Whatever the truth of this account, it did not suit Parnell's supporters. One of Parnell's best biographers, F. S. L. Lyons, declared that the story was 'no doubt romanticised'.[44] Nonetheless it was possible, and of course Katie was the wife of a parliamentary colleague, though Captain O'Shea and Charles Parnell were not friends. For Parnell, the first meeting with Mrs O'Shea was undoubtedly momentous.

He wrote to her on 17 July 1880 that soon after this initial meeting, he had been 'quite unable' to leave the House, where important legislation was taking place, adding that his inability to leave was 'notwithstanding the powerful attractions which have been tending to seduce me from my duty to my country in the direction of Thomas's Hotel'.[45]

Photographs and contemporary accounts all portray Parnell as a very handsome man. His political colleagues and even his enemies referred frequently to his charisma. No great orator, he overcame this liability by cultivating an aura of cool aloofness that mesmerized his opponents and awed his many supporters. In a nation that loved oratory, he managed somehow to make a lasting impression in spite of his pedestrian speech-making. At the time of meeting Katie O'Shea, Parnell was a politician well on his way to dominating his party, and was becoming an increasing threat to any British political complacency on the Irish question. For the first time since O'Connell, the island had a leader whom many believed was capable of delivering some form of constitutional independence to her inhabitants. The Land League was gradually being reshaped into a broader organization, which had constitutional aims. It was to become the National League, and from 1882 the generic term Irish Parliamentary Party (or Irish Party) was used, as agrarian protest became integrated into demand for Home Rule.

Although Katie records that she reiterated the dinner invitation, it was Parnell who made the next move. He wrote to her upon his return from Paris, where he had gone to attend his sister's wedding. The subsequent invitation was for a quiet dinner hosted by the O'Sheas. Katie's sister Anna, their nephew Matthew Wood, and the Irish politician and journalist Justin McCarthy were the guests whose names Katie recalled.[46] McCarthy, also a novelist and historian, was Vice-Chairman of the Irish Parliamentary Party from 1879,[47] and a close colleague of the Irish leader. Katie had taken a box at the Gaiety Theatre, as 'we thought it would be a relief for the "Leader" to get away from politics for once'.[48]

It is true that many of the Irish MPs led a life dominated by politics. Most were living away from home, and had only one another for company. The poorer ones socialized little. The funds available for living expenses were so small that most of them lived in London very frugally indeed. Irish MPs' lifestyles had little in common with those of their English parliamentary colleagues. Despite reforms, the House of Commons still resembled a gentlemen's club. Newly elected members 'often likened their early experiences to memories of their first days at public school'.[49] This was unsurprising, since the membership of the lower House (the upper House was clearly an institutional manifestation of the landed aristocracy) was drawn from a narrow constituency. In 1886, only 2 per cent of MPs were working class, and nearly half were from aristocratic and landed backgrounds. Those men who wished to become MPs could not rely on a salary, as MPs were unpaid until 1912.[50] The Irish Party was the exception: many of its MPs were (skimpily) aided by money collected by fund-raising tours in America. T. P. O'Connor,[51] another Irish Nationalist politician and journalist (and an important fund-raiser for the party), recorded the harsh lives of the Irish MPs:

But as to the rank and file of the Party, they were practically paupers. I look back on several of their figures, and there is an ache in my heart when I think of how pathetic and how essentially noble most of them were... There was no Parliamentary subsidy at that time; £400 a year would have been to them a fortune beyond their dreams of avarice. They had to depend accordingly on subscriptions from the public, and these subscriptions were casual, uncertain, and never erred on the side of generosity... I should say the general average was about £240 a year. A good part of this the members had to send home to those poor wives struggling hard to keep a petty business going; the little they kept for themselves they had to use very sparingly. Their method of living was for two of them to take two small bedrooms and a small sitting-room in the cheap district of Pimlico, which had the additional advantage of being near the House of Commons.[52]

At Westminster, Parnell was more at home than those of his compatriots who had not been educated at public school and Cambridge, and who did not, unlike their leader, enjoy cricket and fox-hunting. He was known to dislike dinner parties, but was perfectly at ease in society. Katie described their first evening: they had a 'pleasant dinner', during which they talked of 'small nothings' and avoided 'the controversial subject of politics'. She had been 'really anxious' that her guest should have 'an agreeable evening', and recorded that she had felt great 'relief' when Parnell agreed to accompany them to the theatre.[53] It was in the 'dark corner of the box' that she and the Irishman began to talk. Katie later wrote that she had a 'feeling of complete sympathy and companionship with him, as though I had always known this strange, unusual man'.[54]

One of Parnell's biographers wrote of how Katie had 'advanced a reiterating sense of disappointment' with her relationship with her husband that 'may retrospectively have been given more emphasis than it had definitely acquired at the time'.[55] This perceptive analysis is borne out by an examination of Katie's ongoing behaviour with Willie O'Shea. Although Katie took drives with her new admirer, they 'chiefly discussed' her husband's chances of being returned to his parliamentary seat in Clare. 'Both Willie and I were very anxious', she recorded, 'to secure Mr. Parnell's promise about this, as The O'Gorman Mahon was old, and we were desirous of making Willie's seat in Parliament secure.'[56] Moreover, the arrangement whereby Katie lived with the three children, while Willie stayed up in town, was not so very uncommon. He worked in town, came down regularly to see his family, and took the children to Mass on Sundays. Katie entertained in London to advance her husband's interests. Aunt Ben was extremely conservative, and she was sufficiently happy with these arrangements to pay Willie's election expenses, as well as the rent on his London flat. That Katie and Willie were still close at this stage there is no doubt. When Katie's old nursemaid, Lucy, died, in September 1880 (just months after Katie had met Parnell), it was Willie O'Shea who brought the body down from Essex so that the faithful servant could be buried near Katie's parents in Cressing. There, by Katie's own account, he attended the funeral.

Katie's memoir has provided her biographers and those of Charles Parnell with the only information available on the details of their courtship.[57] Of great interest were the letters that Katie used to bolster and illustrate her narrative. These letters – from her husband and from Parnell – were not always provided in full. In addition to being fragmented, the correspondence was not consistently dated. The letters do, however, have a ring of authenticity.[58] Some time after their first meeting, there was a lunch hosted by Katie's sister Anna, at which Parnell, Justin McCarthy and Katie were guests. She recalled that Parnell had insisted on seeing her home to Eltham, and drove down in a horse-drawn cab on the sunny afternoon. She had not allowed him to stay, as she was unsure of 'what state of confusion the house might be in' and had to 'hurry over the park' to her aunt. He then 'reluctantly returned to London'.[59] However, the two met a few days later, as Katie arrived by train to Cannon Street station in London. Parnell had invited her to take tea with him at the hotel there before proceeding to Thomas's Hotel to have dinner together. When the couple spotted some Irish MPs taking tea at the hotel, the leader invited his guest to his private sitting room. This was a hugely significant development. From the moment that Katie accepted an invitation to Parnell's private room, she moved the relationship out of the arena of respectable behaviour for married women of her era and class. While they were taking tea in his sitting room, her admirer 'lapsed into one of those long silences of his that I was already beginning to know were dangerous in the complete sympathy they evoked between us',[60] a statement which made quite clear Katie's understanding of the risk she was taking.

But the danger was pursued. She and Parnell dined that evening at Thomas's Hotel, and after the meal she returned to her home in Eltham. Parnell left the following morning for Ireland. He wrote to her from Dublin on 9 September, addressing his letter to 'Mrs. O'Shea'. Although the title of address was formal, what followed was not. 'I may tell you also in confidence', he wrote, 'that I don't feel quite so content at the prospect of ten days' absence from London amongst the hills and valleys of Wicklow as I should have done some three months since.' He took care to make his meaning plain, adding that the 'cause was mysterious, but perhaps you will help me to find it, or her, on my return'.[61]

Until he met Katie, Charles Parnell seems to have had only one love affair of importance. He had met and fallen for an American girl, a Miss Woods, from Newport, Rhode Island, on one of his visits to Paris in the summer of 1870. Although he believed that his strong feelings for her were entirely reciprocated, it would appear that this was not in fact the case. The pair met frequently during the Woodses' stay in France, and during a later trip to Rome, but when the young woman returned to America, she simply sent him a short note. Charles Parnell set out for the United States as soon as he could and in 1871 visited her in Newport. He was informed that she would not marry him, and he telegraphed his brother John, who had some years earlier set himself up as a peach farmer in Alabama, with the disappointing news.

Instead of confirming his engagement to the woman he loved, he spent time with his brother, and travelled around the country looking for possible investment opportunities. The episode marked him deeply. It was one of the first confidences that he shared with Katie. He remembered the affair with great sadness, once commenting to a colleague, 'You know I was jilted.'[62] Some of his colleagues certainly believed that the leader was no monk,[63] and there was talk of a dalliance with a barmaid. Tim Healy, claimed that in 1880 he had opened a letter to the leader from 'Lizzie from Shropshire', a barmaid from Manchester. Healy further stated in his published memoirs that he had learned that Joseph Biggar had sent an emissary to 'Lizzie'. This person had supposedly found a woman with a baby living in a garret, with a newspaper picture of Charles Parnell pinned to the counterpane. Although some of Parnell's colleagues believed Healy's account, others most emphatically did not, and claimed the whole story to be a fabrication.[64]

But the overall impression of the aloof Parnell was that he was not a womanizer, and that he was devoted to politics. His colleagues confirmed that their leader was remote, although courteous in a distanced fashion. Michael Davitt called him a 'cold, reserved man'.[65] The Nationalist MP and journalist William O'Brien,[66] who liked him better, explained that the Chief deliberately cultivated such a mystique. He noticed that while on tour in America, Parnell 'had a way of disappearing at the back of the train, and not discovering himself until the business meeting in the evening'. The leader explained, wrote O'Brien: "'All that half the people in an American town want to see in these shows is the man. If they can see him for nothing, you won't find them turning up for the collection.'" O'Brien was absolutely convinced of his colleague's sincerity, writing that there could be 'no grosser misreading of his character than to attribute such traits to cynicism, or to anything except an honest simplicity and directness of purpose, which was not a selfish purpose'.[67] He believed that his colleague was simply 'not a sociable or marrying man'.[68]

And although Parnell used his cool demeanour to promote the Irish cause, he was not entirely lacking in warmth. Justin McCarthy was extremely fond of him, and claimed that he had a 'singular magnanimity of nature and character... absolutely free from vanity or meanness or jealousy or smallness of any kind'.[69]

The Parnells were not a demonstrative family. Charley, as he was known to his family, had sibling relationships that were cordial, but not especially devoted. Two of his sisters, Fanny and Anna, also became ardent nationalists.[70] Although they shared common cause, Parnell spent little time with either of them. He did tell his colleague Tim Healy, the Irish barrister who was his secretary for a short time in 1880,[71] that Fanny was his favourite sister. She, however, complained to the nationalist politician T. D. Sullivan:[72] 'it is no use writing to my brother, for he never reads the letters of any of the members of his own family'.[73] Fanny died unexpectedly in 1882, while living in America where she was the founder of the New York Ladies' League.[74] Anna came back from America to head a Ladies' Land League (LLL) in Ireland early in 1881. She was a fearless and dedicated leader, travelling throughout the country to address meetings and collect funds.[75] She and her brother fell out over the Ladies' Land League and, although he tried at various times to mend the breach, they never spoke after 1882, when he forced the LLL to shut down.[76] John Parnell had also settled in America, where he was primarily interested in experimental agriculture. He, too, saw little of his brother Charles. He travelled to Wicklow for occasional visits, and tried to stay in touch by letter, but recalled that this was difficult: 'even I, when I wished to arrange to meet him, had to do so by telegram, as, if I sent on a letter in advance, he rarely took much notice of it, and I had to go and rout him out wherever he was stopping'.[77]

According to many contemporary accounts, there was a strain of excitability in the Parnell family, who were known to be eccentric and nervy. Poor health ran in the family, and many of Charles's siblings died quite young or were often unwell. Parnell biographer Roy Foster helpfully divided the offspring into two categories. There was a 'strong-minded, individualist' group in which he included Charles, Emily, Fanny, Anna and Hayes (who died when he was fifteen), and they were the 'politically minded' siblings, all of whom stayed single or married late in life. The other group, who married young and were 'more self-effacing and conventional', included Delia, Sophia, Theodosia, and Henry.[78]

Charles was fond of his sister Delia, who settled in Paris. Her life was touched by tragedy, however, and she died soon after the traumatic death of her son Henry in 1882. Sophia died at the age of thirty-two after nursing her children through scarlatina while she was pregnant. Henry, with whom Charles was not close, led a 'shadowy life style' and suffered from a persecution mania, believing that he was constantly being followed.[79] Emily married an alcoholic and led an unhappy, melancholic life, although she stayed in touch with her brother who was kind to her.[80] Theodosia, known as Dosia, was also fond of her brother although they too saw little of one another after her marriage to naval officer Claude Paget.

Tim Healy was astounded at the family relations, writing to his brother Maurice: 'They are the most extraordinary family I ever came across. The mother, I think, is a little "off her nut" in some ways, and, for that matter, so are all the rest of them!'[81] William O'Brien – who became one of Parnell's chief lieutenants – claimed that the 'shadow of madness… hung heavily over one side of the house, if not over both'.[82]

Whatever the mental state of the various family members, it is clear that, as a whole, the relations between them were not based on solid and dependable mutual support. Even where friendly, contact between Charles and his siblings was sporadic. It is significant that he did not choose to confide in any of them about his relationship with Katie. And it was the same with his colleagues, even those with whom he had warm friendships. It is possible that they ignored the signs, because they wished to believe that their cold and somewhat arrogant leader was wedded to the cause, and not subject to the frailties of human emotions. Certainly Parnell chose to keep his private life just that.

CHAPTER SEVEN

Irish Politics

CHARLES PARNELL CONTINUED to press Katie for more of her time. On 22 September – just a short while after they had met in July– he wrote: 'I cannot keep myself away from you any longer,' and asked her to wire him to let him know 'if I may hope to see you to-morrow'.[1] Owing to her nurse's illness Katie could not leave her servant's side and telegraphed 'Mr Parnell' in London to advise him of this.[2] Unfortunately he did not receive her wire in time, and was 'very much troubled' at not having seen her, especially as he had to return to Ireland, adding accusingly, 'I came on purpose for you, and had no other business.' He signed this letter 'Your very disappointed C.S.P.'[3] Belatedly he may have realized how thoughtless his remarks had been, and wrote her again the following day: 'In my hurried note to you last night I had not time to sympathise with you in this troublesome time you have been going through recently.'[4] Although he may well have reconsidered his words, it is equally likely that he worried at not hearing from her. Parnell was already known by his closest colleagues as a man not predisposed to self-examination. T. P. O'Connor described his colleague as neither 'expansive nor introspective. It is one of the strongest and most curious peculiarities of Mr. Parnell not merely that he rarely, if ever, speaks of himself but that he rarely, if ever, gives any indication of having studied himself'.[5]

Whatever the reason, Parnell was certainly keen on pursuing his new love, writing a few days later to tell Katie that he was planning to visit London and would 'renew my attempt to gain a glimpse of you'. To conclude, he added that he would be 'intensely delighted to have a wire from you'.[6] Katie's response to these ardent and demanding missives was not included in her account. Instead, she followed these excerpts with the comment that, meanwhile, 'Willie was in communication with Mr. Gladstone, Mr. Tintern (one of the Liberal agents) and others, in reference to a meeting held by him.'[7] It seems an odd juxtaposition, to say the least.

Life at Eltham, in the meantime, carried on much the same. While Parnell was travelling back and forth to Ireland, Katie was taking care of her aunt and her children. Occasional forays to the capital were the extent of her travels, as she was firmly committed to her domestic duties. It is likely that she was also quite conscious of where her financial security lay. That Katie was inextricably ensconced at Eltham clearly became obvious to Parnell and, if Katie could not free herself to be with him, he would come to her. She wrote that in the autumn of 1880 'Mr. Parnell' came to stay with 'us', meaning that Willie had invited him to stay with them. It seems hard to imagine that an affair took place in such circumstances, with children and servants about, not to mention Aunt Ben next door. It is possible, however, that during this visit the couple fell deeply in love. And, contrary to assertions by Parnell's colleagues and supporters later on, it would seem that he was the pursuer, and not the pursued.

Soon after the Irish leader arrived at Eltham, he fell ill, complaining of a sore throat and, Katie recorded, gazed 'mournfully' on the collection of flowers and plants she had carefully gathered for his arrival. Still, he was 'childishly touched' when she 'at once' had all the offending plants removed.[8] He also complained about the green carpet – a colour he believed to be unlucky. Parnell was known to harbour many such superstitions, as his brother John confirmed: 'One of his most remarkable superstitions was his aversion to the colour green, although it was the national colour of Ireland … He carried to strange limits this dislike to the colour green in any shape or form.'[9] But there were other phobias, among them the number 13, which 'of course, was always an unlucky one, in his opinion. He steadily refused, even at the risk of annoying or offending his host, to sit down thirteen at table.'[10] He had a fear of death and funerals, which was such that he neglected to attend any: 'Funerals always caused him intense dread, and he never could be persuaded to attend one, even when the deceased happened to be one of his most intimate friends.'[11] These dreads and irrational fears included a horror of seeing three candles burning,[12] and, as his brother John pointed out: 'Charley always had a great dread of the bad results that would follow the falling of an object (such as a picture or ornament) without obvious cause.'[13] Yet another fear was of the month of October: 'With regard to October, he always regarded that as an unlucky month, and began to show signs of uneasiness when it approached, often remarking: "Something is sure to happen in October".'[14]

Katie seemed remarkably calm in the face of such fancies. She simply cut out a bit of the green rug, and sent it to London for analysis. It was found to be perfectly fine, 'quite a harmless carpet'.[15] Katie proved a devoted nurse to their guest: 'I nursed him assiduously, making him take nourishment at regular intervals, seeing that these day-sleeps of his were not disturbed, and forcing him to take fresh air in long drives through the country around us.'[16] Still, the narrative does not make clear who initiated these prolonged attentions. It has been posited that Willie was determined to gain advantage from his relationship with the Irish leader, who could help him in his parliamentary career. It would not be the first time that O'Shea had encouraged his pretty, vivacious wife to cultivate and charm men who could help him. The visit lasted many weeks –

Parnell did not leave until December. While based at Eltham, enjoying Katie's ministrations, he travelled back and forth to London, and to Ireland.

Parnell would perhaps have been easy prey. He was a loner, constantly travelling, unaccustomed to the comforts of warm domesticity. Katie was attractive and there is no doubt but that he was smitten. In fact there is a clear note of infatuation in those early letters. But it is important also to recognize that Charles Parnell was a strong-minded individual who at the age of thirty-five was becoming dominant in his party. He ruled in an authoritarian manner, and his MPs were for the most part intimidated by his hauteur. He was a man accustomed to getting his own way. There is little in his letters to suggest that he was chary of expressing his feelings. The fact that Katie included no letters of her own to Parnell can be explained by his habit of losing correspondence. She also claimed to have held many such private letters back from publication.

A key to Parnell's success was his ability to reconcile his position in Westminster, arguing for constitutional reform that would bring about increased independence for Ireland, while at the same time accommodating the more radical supporters for freedom. Many of the agitators for land reform favoured an aggressive, violent response to the perceived injustices perpetuated – in their view – by the ruling Anglo-Protestant class on the Catholic majority. That Parnell, himself an Anglo-Protestant – and landowner – was able to garner the support of the Fenians was a remarkable feat. It was also an unprecedented and difficult juggling act. It was critically important to keep the more revolutionary elements onside, working with him, rather than in opposition.

The autumn spent between Eltham and Ireland was a period during which Parnell made substantive progress in his political agenda. On 19 September, he outlined at a meeting in Ennis, in County Clare, Ireland, the strategy of 'moral Coventry', or, as it was soon to be known, 'boycotting'.[17] Parnell's main objective was to achieve constitutional reform, but he used the winter of 1880–1 to encourage agitation. He wrote frequently to Katie, who reproduced some fragments of his letters. On his return from the Ennis meeting, he wrote that he had received her letters to him, as well as her wire, and told her that she could write him 'even nicer ones with perfect confidence'. He trusted that he would see her the following week, and then asked: 'Is it true that Captain O'Shea is in Paris, and, if so, when do you expect his return?'[18]

A few days later, on Friday evening, another missive was sent. 'I want to know how you intend to excuse yourself', he wrote, 'for telling me not to come on purpose if I must return.' With the forcefulness for which he was known, Parnell continued, 'Of course, I am going on purpose to see you.'[19] He was determined to see her, writing on the Monday (4 October) that he planned to reach London the next day, and hoped to see her on Wednesday 'when and where you wish'.[20] The weather was poor, and he wrote again on Tuesday evening, saying that his crossing had to be postponed. He ended his short note: 'Can meet you in London at 9 to-morrow evening anywhere you say.'[21]

It is significant that Parnell enquired as to Willie O'Shea's whereabouts, and the question lends credence to his acknowledgement of the clandestine nature of his feelings for his colleague's wife. Katie did not claim that her spouse was cognizant at this early stage of her budding relationship with the Irish leader. Furthermore, her statement that Parnell was based at Eltham during this period seems to be contradicted by Parnell's clear intention to see her in London. In his notes to her he made no mention of travelling to her home. How and where they did meet Katie does not say. The next letter from Parnell in the sequence, however, was addressed to 'My Own Love', and dated 17 October. It is clear from its content that the relationship had moved on to one of intimacy. 'You cannot imagine', he wrote, 'how much you have occupied my thoughts all day and how very greatly the prospect of seeing you again very soon comforts me.'[22]

The context of Parnell's growing obsession with Katie was the continuing development in Ireland of a mass movement which he hoped to harness. The Land League meetings in Ireland attracted huge crowds – there were an estimated twenty thousand people at a meeting he addressed in New Ross on 26 September. The town had been decorated to receive him – one of the banners read: 'Let it ring out over hill and dale, God bless our noble chief Parnell!'[23] As he travelled throughout Ireland to attend the Land League meetings, Parnell was greeted by adoring crowds. His triumphant procession was recorded by an English MP who was visiting Ireland at the time: 'Parnell's journeyings can be compared only to the progress of Caesar. Parnell sits erect in the open carriage, accepting the homage of emotional enthusiasm in the streets with almost an Imperial mien.'[24] He was booked for weekend meetings throughout October, expected in Roscommon on the tenth, Longford on the seventeenth, Galway on the twenty-fourth and in Limerick on the thirty-first. He had also planned to attend a special meeting of the farmers of County Cork on 9 October. But he did not return to Ireland that week. At the Saturday meeting, it was Parnell's colleague, the militant agrarian John Dillon,[25] who addressed the farmers. He told them that the leader had asked him to take his place, 'because he is a man the demand for whose presence just at present in all parts of Ireland is so great that he is unable to keep all his engagements'.[26] At Roscommon, the following day, Parnell's place was taken by the MPs Kelly and Commins.

In fact, he did not appear in Ireland until the following Saturday. He travelled with Justin McCarthy to Longford, to a meeting he was due to address there. When he arrived, his friends were taken aback. He had changed his appearance by shaving off most of his beard, except for a narrow strip down each jaw and under the chin. His colleague T. P. O'Connor had visited him earlier that month at Parnell's home in Avondale. He noticed that the leader was showing signs of baldness – to which he was very sensitive.

According to Parnell's biographer Lyons, O'Connor noticed that Parnell had just shaved his head, apparently to make his hair grow thicker. He believed that this changed his appearance so much that this was why his colleagues failed to recognize him.[27]

Certainly Charles Parnell had changed. But those around him did not know why. A naturally reserved man, he did not share his changed circumstances with his colleagues or friends. In fact, at around this time, a Walsall solicitor, W. H. Duignan, asked Parnell why 'he did not get married, and his reply was, "I am married – to my Country and can best serve as I am."'[28] The fact that Parnell was aware of the need to keep absolutely quiet about his love for Katie would indicate that he understood the delicacy of the situation. She later claimed in her book that he did not feel bound by the conventions, and that she and O'Shea had for some time no longer lived as man and wife. How much of this is true is impossible to ascertain. Certainly, there was no precedent in her husband's behaviour to indicate that he was anything but a very proud man, who would not take well to being made to look a fool.

Katie was aware that the new man in her life was famous. She described taking Parnell for a drive in an open carriage through the hop-growing district of Kent. They drove over Chislehurst Common and came across a crowd of Irish 'hoppers'.[29] The Irish leader was greeted by cheering workers. The Irish were 'so inured to privation in their own country', explained Katie, that 'they were very popular among the Kentish hop-farmers, as they did not grumble so much as did the English pickers at the scandalously inefficient accommodation provided for them.'[30]

Parnell's reputation as the defender of the poor of Ireland thus ensured him a hero's welcome. There was a 'wild surge' towards them, wrote Katie, with cries of 'The Chief! The Chief!' and 'Parnell! Parnell! Parnell!' Such was the crowd's fascination with seeing the man in person that their coachman 'jerked the horses on to their haunches for fear of knocking down the enthusiastic men and women who were crowding up – trying to kiss Parnell's hand, and calling for "a few words"'.[31] Katie recalled that the leader had been too unwell to make a speech, but he told the crowds that he was 'glad to see them'. The couple drove off 'amid fervent "God keep your honours!" and cheers'.[32]

It is perhaps unlikely that the workers would have recognized Parnell at this relatively early stage of his career as the leader, though there is nevertheless a ring of authenticity in the details of the story. It is quite probable that such an incident did take place – but perhaps not in the autumn of 1880. Even if the timing of the tale is inaccurate, the fact remains that Parnell was becoming increasingly well known in public.

In Dublin Castle, close to the realities of the situation and frustrated by the government's lack of response to the crisis, Lord Cowper, the Liberal politician who had been appointed Lord-Lieutenant[33] of Ireland in 1880 – at the height of the land crisis – was in sympathy with the concerns of Ireland's poor. So indeed was William Edward Forster,[34] the Liberal who had also taken his post as Chief Secretary in 1880. But they recognized too the threat posed by Parnell and the Land League to British rule of law in Ireland. Indeed, Parnell was increasingly vocal about his ambitions for Ireland. Speaking at Galway on 24 October, he declared:

I expressed my belief at the beginning of last session that the present Chief Secretary, who was then all smiles and promises, should not have proceeded very far in the duties of his office before he would have found that he had undertaken an impossible task to govern Ireland, and that the only way to govern Ireland is to allow her to govern herself.[35]

Lord Cowper later said: 'we considered Mr. Parnell the centre of the whole movement. We thought him the chief, if not the only danger.'[36]

*

It was a real predicament for Gladstone's government. Cowper and Forster urged the Cabinet to take decisive, coercive action against the agitators. But Parnell was a Member of Parliament, and it was almost impossible to prove that he was encouraging illegal, revolutionary activity. 'We did not think he instigated the outrages', admitted Cowper, but we 'thought he connived at them'.[37] He wrote to the Cabinet in early October of the huge increase in agrarian crime in Ireland. He was concerned at how the movement was gaining force, encouraged by large meetings and rallies. 'I would preserve freedom of speech to the very utmost as long as it is confined to general subjects, such as abuse of England, abuse of the Government, or advocacy of political measures, however impracticable; when it has the immediate effect of endangering the lives or property of individuals, it should be stopped.'[38] This was the problem for the government and Forster moved from advocating reform to pressing hard for coercion.[39] The Prime Minister and other Cabinet members were, however, reluctant. And attention was directed elsewhere.

T. P. O'Connor wrote angrily that:

Mr. Gladstone had not a syllable to say on this great struggle: he was at that time too busy with Dulcigno, the difficulties of the Montenegrins, and the humiliation of the 'unspeakable Turk'[40] to bend his mind to the consideration of an island sixty miles off which contained five millions of British subjects, and was making a movement more perilous to British peace than any since the death of the Great Liberator.[41]

Gladstone was not oblivious to the problems of Ireland, but he was concerned about over-extension of the British Empire, and he had other problems. The Liberal election victory in 1880 was decisive, but Gladstone was not immediately asked to form a government. One obstacle had been Queen Victoria, who had written on 4 April to her Private Secretary Ponsonby that she would 'sooner *abdicate* than send for or have any *communication* with *that half mad firebrand* who wd soon ruin everything & be a *Dictator*.[42]

Gladstone did go on to form a government of his choosing – despite the Queen's many complaints about his suggested Cabinet appointments. But unlike 1868, when Gladstone as Prime Minister had declared his mission was to 'pacify Ireland',[43] this time the island was hardly mentioned in his campaigning, or afterwards. There were problems in South Africa, where an armed Boer rebellion began in December. And in Afghanistan the British and Russian Empires struggled for dominance in the region.[44] The Battle of Maiwand – in which nearly 1,000 British and Indian forces lost their lives and a further 161 were wounded – caused great consternation and received much publicity. The dramatic 314-mile relieving march led by General Frederick Roberts saved the day, and the famous subsequent British victory at the Battle of Kandahar on 1 September restored some pride after the shock of defeat at the hands of the native Afghan tribesmen. Maiwand made a big impact on public consciousness and it was immortalized by Rudyard Kipling in his poem 'That Day', written to commemorate the battle.

There was further trouble in Egypt, where Britain had important financial interests, and repeated warnings that the Dual Control exercised by the French and British was breaking down.[45] Grumblings there would erupt by 1882 into full-scale disaster. Ireland, however, maintained a curious status within Britain's imperial mantle. On the one hand, the island was perceived as an extension of liberal British rule, whereby the inhabitants could share the many commercial benefits of a prosperous empire. And indeed, by the time of the Act of Union, more than 85 per cent of all Irish exports went to Britain – and by 1790, nearly two-thirds of Ireland's national debt was lodged with British creditors. It was not just a financial integration; the Irish also made a massive contribution to Britain's armed forces – both as recruits in the ranks and as senior officers.[46]

Yet the island was not fully integrated. One of the most obvious manifestations of this was the appalling poverty that persisted just a short Channel crossing away. The sufferings endured by the Irish population during the mid-century famines had not resulted in legislative changes to improve living standards for the poorest members of society. This was why land reform continued to feature so prominently on the agenda for improvements in the Irish situation. Attempts to initiate such reform met with great resistance.

Parnell's actions throughout the autumn of 1880 increased the intensity of the struggle, and the British Cabinet took notice. Gladstone disagreed with Forster's view that renewed coercion should be combined with agrarian reform. The Cabinet floundered without a clear policy. But the Prime Minister knew that the Irish question could not be avoided. 'It is with regret, and perhaps with mortification', he wrote to Cowper on 24 November, 'that I see the question of land reform again assuming or having assumed its large proportions.'[47] The Cabinet decided to act, and on 23 October it was announced that prosecutions would be instituted. These were to be against Parnell, the militant agrarian Tipperary MP John Dillon (son of the Young Irelander John Blake Dillon),[48] and Biggar. Loyal Parnell supporter and Land Leaguer MP Thomas Sexton was also targeted,[49] and Patrick Egan, the Treasurer of the Land League, was arrested, as were other League officials.

Forster was worried about the effects the arrests would have, and wrote to Gladstone on 8 October that he feared the results would be to generate great enthusiasm for Parnell, as well as driving the moderates into his camp. He believed that the quarrel between the nationalists (separatists) and Land Leaguers would heal, and that increased funds would flow in from America.[50] He also doubted that a conviction against the men would be secured.[51]

Meanwhile, Parnell continued to combine his escalating political rhetoric with his pursuit of his new love. The letters Katie provided from this episode were a curious mix. Those addressed 'My Dear

Mrs O'Shea' were, presumably, those that could be read by her husband. And, indeed, they were innocuous. Parnell was seemingly in correspondence with Captain O'Shea too. On 6 November – just days after the British government had decided to prosecute him – Parnell wrote: 'You can have very little idea how dreadfully disappointed I felt on arriving here this evening not to find a letter from either you or Captain O'Shea.'[52] This two days after a letter, dated 4 November, stated: 'I do not suppose I shall have an opportunity of being in London again before next Thursday, but trust to be more fortunate in seeing Captain O'Shea then than the last time.'[53] At this point, it seems clear that whatever Katie's feelings for Parnell might have been, her husband was not aware of what was going on.

Katie was still focused on obtaining advancement for Willie. Whatever the motivation, her intentions were plain. And her spouse needed help. He was not much liked by his fellow Irish MPs. When the Captain met his new colleagues at the April meeting to select the Party Chairman, he was unknown to most of them, and he was not particularly admired. 'Slightly overdressed', noted T. P. O'Connor; 'laughing, with the indescribable air of the man whom life had made somewhat cynical, he was in sharp contrast with the rugged, plainly dressed, serious figures around him.'[54] O'Shea had begun his constituency work reasonably well. On 5 September 1880, he had attended a large successful land meeting at Milltown Malbay. In recognition of his efforts in helping to get a bill through Parliament to enable a railway line to be built in County Clare, he was warmly cheered and welcomed. A letter from his parliamentary colleague and supporter, O'Gorman Mahon, was read. 'I desire it to be recognized by all', he had written, 'that to the zeal, energy and perseverance of your young member Captain O'Shea is the county indebted for the advantages that must inevitably accrue – He achieved the affair himself and… to him alone should be accorded the well-earned merit of this favourable issue'.[55]

This initial success was short-lived, however. O'Shea had only a limited attendance at Westminster and, after his victory with the railway, there were no further achievements in Ireland for his constituents. This was a critical error of judgement on his part. By far, localism remained a primary feature in politics. Irishmen and women by and large focused on the 'parish pump', that is, on getting better roads, better sewage systems, jobs for friends and relatives and other political favours.[56] For Willie O'Shea to betray so early his fundamental lack of engagement in the local scene was a grave mistake. On 10 October, while Parnell was with Katie in Eltham, O'Shea was absent from a public meeting in Ennistymon in County Clare. The letters of apology were read out. The one from The O'Gorman Mahon was accepted, but that from the Captain was badly received, and there were cries of 'We don't want him for the County again!' A member of the disapproving crowd called out, 'He doesn't care; he's got what he wanted. Is there anyone now to come up and say a word for him?' There was no one inclined to do so. Indeed, the lone reply was, 'He's not worth it.'[57]

Interspersed with the formal letters addressed to 'Mrs O'Shea' were the intimate notes, which began to arrive from mid-October 1880. Parnell wrote on 11 November:

My dearest Love, It is quite impossible for me to tell you just how very much you have changed my life, what a small interest I take in what is going on about me, and how I detest everything which has happened during the last few days to keep me away from you – I think of you always, and you must never believe there is to be any 'fading'.[58]

That their relationship had moved onto another plane was confirmed by his masterful command that she must 'not send me any more artificial letters'. It was not what he wanted, rather he wished for 'as much of your own self as you can transfer into written words, or else none at all'.[59]

It was difficult for them to communicate openly by post. What is interesting to observe is how guarded much of the correspondence had to be. This mirrored Parnell's professional communications. He and other Irish MPs were continually operating at the fringes of legality. Their association with the Fenians was constantly subject to surveillance. Parnell and his colleagues were watched by the English police, and their post was often intercepted. He was thus accustomed to the need for circumspection, especially on paper. Coded communication was a hallmark of the Irish Nationalist movement during this period.

And, of course, there was O'Shea to consider. Parnell was in correspondence with him as well, and referred on numerous occasions to letters and meetings with Katie's husband. The fact that he was so open about this in the letters reproduced by Katie could indicate that he was oblivious to the impropriety of his behaviour. If, as Katie later declared, her spouse was aware of her intimacy with Parnell, this would explain Parnell's lack of circumspection, but there is nothing in Katie's behaviour to lend credibility to the theory that she was prepared to risk her family's security – provided by the immensely conservative Aunt Ben – for the early stages of a new romance. Second, there are formal letters written by Parnell to her that were designed to allay any suspicion, such as one, probably written in November,[60] which merely stated: 'I enclose keys, which I took away by mistake. Will you kindly hand enclosed letter to the proper person and oblige.' Katie footnoted in her book that the 'proper person' was 'Myself'.[61]

In addition, Parnell was certain that his post was being intercepted. He received hundreds of letters and parcels. Katie recounted that he asked her to take care of these – so that she might 'open them and give him only those it was necessary for him to deal with'.[62] Parnell had no office, and no staff to look after his administrative needs. One of his colleagues, Tim Healy, had of course acted as his secretary for a short time, but this arrangement was on behalf of the Land League primarily, and was also short-lived. Parnell was worried too about security and suspicious of most of the letters and parcels sent to him. He insisted that even gifts of eggs be destroyed: 'They might be eggs, but then again they might not.'[63] He was increasingly seen as an agent of revolutionary activity, and some Cabinet ministers believed that he was very dangerous.[64] Cabinet debate intensified as the Land League's activities gained momentum. Forster pushed for renewed coercion linked to agrarian reform. The Liberal Radical Joseph Chamberlain, who held the Cabinet position of President of the Board of Trade, was adamantly opposed.[65] The aristocratic Secretary of State for India, Lord Hartington, was wary of agrarian reforms.[66] But the case for coercion made headway, especially as Forster changed his mind about the use of force. The 'gossip of the period', recollected T. P. O'Connor, was that the Cabinet was divided, and that Chamberlain, along with fellow Liberal Radicals Charles Dilke and John Bright, 'held out steadily and for a long time' against the demands for coercion made by Forster.[67] The increasing number of tenant evictions (which rose from 463 in 1877 to 2,110 in 1880, and then to 5,201 in 1882),[68] combined with the Lords' rejection of the Compensation for Disturbance Bill,[69] led to more alarm at Cabinet level.

Katie recorded that Parnell was distinctly unworried by the confusion. He told her that his arrest and that of his Land League colleagues were 'such a farce' and that 'he could not take it seriously in any way'. He knew that no jury in Ireland would convict him, and he would attend the trials 'chiefly, he said, for the "look of the thing"'.[70] During this period, throughout the autumn of 1880, Parnell continued to travel back and forth between Eltham and Ireland. The stories of the evictions in Ireland, she claimed, 'brought home to me by Parnell himself made my heart sick'. In his 'low, broken monotone', he told her of the 'terrible cruelty of some of the things done in the name of justice in unhappy Ireland'. He spoke of how old people, sick people, women with newborn babies were 'all thrust out from the little squalid cabins which was all they had for home, thrust out on the roadside to perish, or to live as they could'. When she, in her 'English ignorance', asked why they did not go to neighbours or to the workhouse, Parnell would 'look wonderingly' at her as he explained that such places were 'few and far between' in his country, and that neighbours were themselves in the same predicament. There were cases when a 'wife would beg, *and with none effect*, that the bailiffs and police should wait but the little half-hour that her dying husband drew his last breath; and where a husband carried his wife from her bed to the "shelter" of the rainswept moor that their child might be born out of the sight of the soldiers deputed to guard the officials who had been sent to pull their home about their ears'.[71]

Like many of her contemporaries, Katie knew little about Ireland. Even though her husband was Irish, she herself had never set foot in the country. Her knowledge of Parnell's homeland was therefore meagre. And she was not unusually ignorant. Such lack of understanding of the Irish situation extended to the highest political circles.[72] The subject of Ireland drew the attention of the literate English public primarily in terms of the parliamentary time it occupied, or in the newspaper columns it generated. Regular features in *The Times* referred to the distress in Ireland, and also to the agrarian agitation there. On 5 January 1880, the Dublin correspondent telegraphed that an anti-rent meeting had been held at Claremorris, in County Galway. 'It was attended by about 3,000 people', read the report,

who carried mock pikes, guns, and swords, and banners with such inscriptions as 'God save Ireland', 'Stick to your homesteads', and others which have characterized previous meetings. Before the proceedings commenced those present, including many mounted men, went through some military maneuvers in a large field where the meeting was held. Mr. Davitt was the principal speaker and chief attraction. In a long address he went over the ground he travelled in former speeches, denouncing landlordism and declaring that it must be abolished, for until its last vestige was swept off the face of the country there would be no peace, happiness, or contentment for the Irish people.[73]

Regular articles reported the outrages as well as the misery in Ireland. Reaction in England (and Scotland) was often one of exasperation. Lord Forbes of Aberdeenshire wrote on 5 November 1880 to reply to the question asked in the leading article of *The Times* the previous day: 'What is to be done with Ireland?' He thundered:

What would be done if such agrarian outrages as have disgraced Ireland, or anything like them, were to be perpetuated in any parish or district either in England or Scotland? I ask again, would such outrages be tolerated for a moment either in England or Scotland? And, if not in Great Britain, why should they be tolerated in Ireland?[74]

Irish agrarian violence featured increasingly in the English press and inevitably influenced public opinion. Cartoons in the political magazine *Punch* provided consistent reinforcement of the Irish stereotypes – impoverished starving peasants, or dishonest tenants trying to cheat the landlords, or violent, simian thugs.[75]

There was much that smacked of crisis management in Westminster's dealings with Ireland. Sporadic attempts to deal with the agricultural depression and land issues were made, through special inquiries and commissions, but on the whole there was little understanding of the complexities of the problems presented by Ireland, and a concomitant lack of subtlety in dealing with them. The Liberal ministry of 1880 had in addition the immediate challenge of defining whether the Irish problem at that time was economic or political. Such confusion was shared by the English population, who knew little about Ireland beyond what was reported in the press. There had been a large drop in what had been a thriving tourist trade from England to Ireland after the famines. Instead of pleasure-seeking visitors, the island attracted politically minded individuals, such as the author Thomas Carlyle, and journalist and social campaigner Harriet Martineau. Both wrote, in the years immediately following the Great Famine, of the terrible conditions endured by the Irish people.[76] In 1886, a *Times* special correspondent travelled through Ireland and sent back a series of letters that were published in the paper. The correspondent observed the civil unrest and boycotting with dismay. He described how it had been 'the worst tourist season for many years'. He had expected this to be the case, he wrote, due to the difficulty he had experienced 'in procuring a copy of Murray's Ireland before leaving London, even Mr. Standford being unable to produce one, not because the stock was exhausted, but because there is no demand for Irish guide books'.[77] His letters confirmed a general impression of agitation and civil unrest in Ireland. As for many others in England, Katie's information about the island – before knowing Parnell – would have been limited to an image of poverty and backwardness, along with violence and land agitation.

Parnell's actions in supporting the League agitation made the Liberal dilemma more difficult. Forster's gloomy predictions to the Prime Minister and Cabinet colleagues of the corrosive and negative impact of arresting Parnell and other Land Leaguers were accurate. On 23 January 1881 the government case against the Leaguers collapsed. Simultaneously, a subscription to raise money, the Parnell Defence Fund, was launched, and the remarkable sum of £21,000 was quickly raised. Although much of this came from League funds, around two-thirds came through the efforts of the newspaper, *Freeman's Journal*. This important paper began to give consistent support to both the League and its leader, and among the subscriptions it registered in its columns were those of the Archbishops of Cashel and Tuam, as well as the Bishops of Limerick, Cloyne and Ross, and Clonfert.[78]

While Parnell spearheaded this broad-based coalition, he secretly increased his pursuit of Katie. On 4 December 1880, he wrote to her that he had been 'quite homesick since leaving Eltham', and that news from her seemed 'like news from home'. He continued:

You will also be pleased to hear that the special jury panel, of which we obtained a copy last night, is of such a character as in the opinion of competent judges to give us every chance of a disagreement by the jury in their verdict, but we cannot, of course, form an absolute conclusion until the jury has been sworn, when we shall be able to tell pretty certainly one way or the other.[79]

When he left for a trip to Paris later that winter, Katie accompanied him by train for part of the journey. She was anxious about the cold and snow, and wrapped him in rugs as he attempted to rest. She recalled how she had 'loathed the great white expanse that made him look so ill, and I wished I had him at home again, where I could better fight the great fear that so often beset my heart: that I could not long keep off the death that hovered near him'.[80] For a lonely, aloof man, the solicitude and fuss made by this attractive woman must have been very appealing. The 'home' provided by Katie was warm and welcoming. She had bought flowers and potted palms to make the house look well for Parnell's visit.[81] The house acquired for her by Aunt Ben, Wonersh Lodge, was a solid Victorian redbrick villa located on the edge of a park. Katie's staff included the children's governess, the parlourmaid Mary Francis and the cook Ellen Delany from Tipperary. She also took on a new maid at this time, Jane Lennister.[82] Managing such a household with competence and efficiency would require supervision of the staff, regularly inspecting the cleanliness of the premises and managing household supplies and catering.[83] Even with help, Katie was adding a significant burden to her manifold other duties in looking after Parnell so assiduously.

The village of Eltham was just 8 miles out of London, but at that time was a country town, with just a few small shops in the high street. The house was comfortable, with four reception rooms and a large conservatory downstairs. This conservatory was given to Parnell. The front garden was small, but there was a large back garden with stables at the end. The adjoining park provided additional space and privacy. This quiet retreat was no doubt what the tired and reclusive leader wanted. He was, as we have seen, naturally reserved, with few close companions. Although he remained attached to his childhood home, Avondale, all his life, and poured investment into mines and quarries on the estate, he visited there less and less. A reporter from the *World* in 1880 found Avondale so 'barren and neglected' that 'one could fancy that the coverings had just been drawn off the furniture at the expiration of a Chancery suit'.[84] The neglect was partial, however, as in 1882 a *Nation* reporter wrote that improvements were being made.[85] Over the following decade, though, Parnell indisputably made fewer and fewer visits to the Wicklow countryside he loved. His connection to his family home (and to his family) diminished as he spent more and more time in England, although his feelings for Avondale remained strong all his life.[86]

The romance now developed rapidly, if Katie's account is to be believed. There were still two sorts of correspondence. On 27 December, Parnell wrote to 'My dear Mrs O'Shea', while the following day a note was sent to 'My dearest wife'.[87] Both letters expressed great concern for her health. The leader had been 'exceedingly anxious' on the twenty-seventh at not having heard from her that she had arrived home safely after leaving him.[88] He was therefore 'immensely relieved' the following day after receiving a letter, adding that she 'must take great care' of herself for his sake and 'your and my future'.[89] This could be a general reference to her health, or it could mean something more, such as a pregnancy. On 30 December, a letter from Parnell stated that he had been 'in a continual panic lest some dreadful disaster had happened'. He urged his 'poor love' to take 'great care of herself for the sake of *our* future'.[90] If Katie were indeed pregnant at this time, she must have lost the child, as there is no record of a subsequent birth.

Because there is no corroboration of the letters Katie used for her book, it is not possible to verify the accuracy of the dated correspondence. However, during her stated dates of December 1880 and early January 1881, it is quite clear that the liaison was still to be kept secret from Willie. Parnell wrote that he had wired and written to the Captain in Madrid. On 3 January, he wrote that he would have liked to come to see Katie over the New Year, but feared she 'might not be alone'. He proposed to be 'with my own wifie' the following Wednesday.[91]

In fact, Parnell came down to Eltham in January, during which time he met Katie's aunt for the first time. At this point, the household servants were almost certainly aware of the true nature of their mistress's relations with Parnell. The Irish cook was so excited by his presence that Katie persuaded him to see her so that she could settle down to do her work. Ellen fell to her knees and kissed his hands 'much to his horror', recalled Katie, who recorded that Parnell 'disliked it extremely'. He told her 'with some reproach that he had expected to be quite free from that sort of thing' in her house.[92] He had tipped the servants generously that Christmas, and such was their excitement that the leader had to warn them to be discreet. Mrs O'Shea let him 'come down here for a rest', he explained, and 'if people know I'm here I shall be worried to death with politics and people calling'. Both Ellen and the parlourmaid Mary 'promised faithfully' to observe 'absolute silence'.[93]

There remained the problem of Aunt Ben. She was known for her conservative views, and was a stern believer in matrimony. Only the previous year, she had written to her sister Emma (Katie's mother) that the 'irrevocability of the marriage vow makes it frightful, unless there be every chance of its being always considered a silken cord instead of a rusty chain'.[94] So it was all the more essential that Aunt Ben – the sole source of Katie's income – should be unsuspecting. Parnell was thus presented to her quite openly. He did not disappoint. Katie recalled that the elderly woman had been 'much charmed' with him, and that his 'quiet manners and soft, clear voice' had 'pleased her greatly, as also did his personal appearance'. In addition, he later spoke of his admiration of the old woman's 'pretty round arm'. Katie obligingly reported this to her benefactor, who was 'much gratified'.[95]

Meanwhile, Parnell continued his political campaign. The collapse of the government's case against him and his fellow traversers came as no surprise to the British government. At the Cabinet meetings of 30 and 31 December 1881 it was decided that tough measures were required, and the ministers agreed to the suspension of habeas corpus.[96] This was done with reluctance. English politicians did not wish to rely on ad hoc coercive responses to the escalation of violence in Ireland. The importance of a sound legal framework and due legal process was central to good governance and the Cabinet took very seriously its responsibility in using legal measures to impose order on the unruly island.[97] It was increasingly believed that well-organized land agitation in Ireland posed a very real threat to law and order, and an unequivocal response from government was essential to restore confidence to Irish landlords.

The Land League raised its own funds (with help from Irish Americans) and encouraged Irish men and women to take the law in their own hands. In addition the populist land movement was becoming firmly linked – thanks in large part to Parnell – to nationalist aspirations. Thus the movement's rapid gain in credibility and wider public acceptance meant that its leaders were perceived by the Cabinet to be very dangerous indeed. When these leaders implemented, with great success, the tactics of parliamentary obstruction, it propelled the Irish problem into a crisis.

Gladstone had, with difficulty, softened his opposition to land reform in Ireland. He moved to support a radical Land Bill – but only after he had considered other less attractive options. This bill supported tenant demands for the '3 Fs'. After he had decided, however, he became totally committed. The Cabinet accepted the new bill after seeing the report from an inquiry into the Irish land problem, chaired by Lord Bessborough. The Prime Minister worried, however, that the radical solution would not satisfy. On 3 December he told Forster 'the three Fs' in their popular meaning... will I fear break the cabinet without reconciling the leaguers'.[98]

Meanwhile, Parnell expected that the Cabinet would propose legislation, and the Land League's policy was to 'wait and see'. The executive moved funds to Paris, out of British jurisdiction, in January – which is no doubt the trip that Katie referred to when the leader looked so ill – and Parnell adopted an increasingly secretive lifestyle. He took great care to keep few in his confidence about his whereabouts. The Ladies' Land League (LLL) was set up at the invitation of Davitt, to run the Land War in the event of its leaders being imprisoned.[99]

In a speech to Parliament on 7 January 1881, Parnell claimed that the Land League was a legitimate and legal organization. He also declared that there was a conspiracy in the British press to exaggerate the extent of Irish agrarian crime, and that this was because they supported the long-term interests of the landlords.[100] It was not only the press in Britain that condemned the revolutionary drive of the land agitation. Dublin's *Evening Mail* had carried an editorial on 10 June 1879 that denounced the Land League as radical and dangerous, claiming that it was 'a form of Continental Communism'.[101] And disapproval went beyond the Atlantic. The *New York Herald*, *New York World* and *New York Evening Times* all condemned the movement as 'subversive and communistic'.[102]

The population's fears that Irish land agitation would lead to massive social upheaval are easier to understand in the context of the spread of communist theory that was gaining support at this time. Revolutions in France and Germany in 1848, underpinned by radical economic theory that criticized the capitalist model, had shaken Britain. The British Radical movement, driven by the Chartists in the 1830s and 1840s, had never crystallized into a truly threatening force, but the precedent for activism had been established, through mid-Victorian trade unionism, for example.[103] The radical thinker and revolutionary, Karl Marx, wished to further radicalize British workers. He had moved to England in 1849, and had soon turned his attention to the Irish situation. After studying conditions there, he concluded that English landlordism was vulnerable to attack through Ireland. In January 1870, Marx had pressed that a resolution he had written on the Irish question be passed at a special session of the General Council of the International.[104] The resolution was accepted, and its message goes some way to explaining why the British political establishment became so worried about the wider implications of the Land League movement:

Above all, Ireland is the fortress of English landlordism. If it falls in Ireland then it will inevitably fall in England also. In Ireland this operation is a hundred times easier because the economic struggle is concentrated there exclusively around landed property, this struggle is also a national one and the people of Ireland are more revolutionary and embittered than in England. Landlordism in Ireland is only supported by the English army. The moment an end is put to the compulsory union of these two countries, a social revolution will break out in Ireland, although in old fashioned forms.[105]

Although Marx (and his close collaborator Friedrich Engels) did not garner much support during Marx's lifetime, the ideas he expressed struck at the very core of British life. Attacks on private property, whether in Ireland or at home, were dreaded and condemned. Parnell's fears of becoming an outlaw were, therefore, based on a realistic assessment of his situation. He chose to stay within the boundaries of the law as much as possible. At a meeting in February 1881 in Paris, it was decided not to withdraw the party from Westminster after the passing of another Coercion Bill, which suspended habeas corpus. The latest Coercion Bill was another of the Coercion Acts, which formed part of the historical government response to the Irish problem, since the Insurrection Act of 1796, which had imposed the death penalty (replaced in 1807 by transportation for life) on persons taking illegal oaths, and provided for the imposition of a curfew in 'disturbed' districts. Other special measures were also provided by this Act, which was reintroduced – with modifications – in 1807–10, 1814–18 and 1822–5. In 1833 it was replaced by the Coercion Acts, a series of measures commencing with the Suppression of Disturbances Act of 1833, which gave the Lord-Lieutenant special powers in 'disturbed' districts, including the right to allow for detention without trial for up to three months. The legislation, with modifications, was regularly renewed up to 1875. A new approach was taken in 1871 and in 1881, with legislative measures that targeted individuals, and suspended habeas corpus.

Further Acts, including the Prevention of Crimes Act, were in force from 1882.[106] Despite such legislation, Parnell did not believe that pulling back from Parliament would help the Irish cause. By withdrawing to Ireland, the parliamentary momentum would be lost, and his status – and that of his colleagues – would be reduced to that of rebels or conspirators. The impression given in the London papers was that Ireland was a 'hot-bed of sedition'.[107] Neither Gladstone nor Forster believed, though, that there was a direct link between Land League meetings and the outrages. Their private correspondence at this time reflected a more nuanced understanding of the complexity of the situation.[108] The Chief Secretary held to the view, however, that a coercive approach was required in order to ensure control. The government took the public position that a few individuals could be held responsible (a 'controlled conspiracy') – although in private many believed that there was in fact a widespread sympathy for the tenants who resisted landlordism. Gladstone and Forster hoped that by holding a few troublemakers to account the British government might calm the situation and avert a full-blown crisis.

Forster's Coercion Bill was introduced on 24 January, and the following day Gladstone moved that it should take precedence over any other business. This measure was strongly opposed by Parnell and he adopted the obstruction tactics for which the Irish Party was becoming known. He and his colleagues kept the House sitting continuously from 4 p.m. on Tuesday until 2 p.m. the next day. On Thursday 27 January the debate was resumed and on Monday 31 January the government made clear their determination to close the debate on the first reading that night. Parnell protested and once again the House was kept up all night, sitting continuously from 4 p.m. on Monday until 9 a.m. on Wednesday 2 February 1881. This record sitting of forty-one hours was 'the longest on record in the history of the House of Commons and probably of any other legislative body'.[109]

It had become clear that a group of thirty Irish MPs could bring the business of governance to a halt. The bill could be blocked for the whole session. That morning, therefore, the Speaker declared that in the interest of 'the dignity, the credit, and the authority of the House',[110] the debate would be closed. The first reading was put to the vote, and was carried by a majority of 164 to 19. There was great protest from the Irish members. The following day, the Home Secretary announced the arrest of Michael Davitt. Angry outbreaks ensued. Dillon was suspended for disregarding the authority of the Chair and Parnell interrupted the Prime Minister. Scenes of 'indescribable confusion' then occurred and, following the mayhem, thirty-six Irish members (including Parnell) were suspended and ejected from the House. Gladstone finally moved a resolution that effectively put an end to the use of obstruction by the Irish members. This stipulated that urgent public business could be carried out under certain conditions without fear of delays.[111]

Back in Ireland, many expected the Irish leader and his parliamentary colleagues to withdraw altogether from Westminster. The day following the ejection of the Irish members, a representative from the Irish newspaper *Freeman's Journal* asked Parnell whether his party would return to the House of Commons. His reply was: 'If we consulted our own feelings we should retire, but we must do our duty.'[112] If Parnell had been planning to make a bold statement by withdrawing from representative government this would have been the opportunity to do so. The fact that he chose not to has been interpreted as a realistic reflection of Parnell's lack of revolutionary ardour.

Katie wrote of her pride in the Irish leader, whom she watched from the Ladies' Gallery in the House. She had obtained tickets from her husband, or, possibly, from Parnell. It was but six months since they had met, yet Katie was now fully in the leader's confidence. She wrote of how Parnell 'drove quickly to one of our meeting places' so that he could tell her of his plans before she returned home to Eltham.[113]

The expulsion of the party members lasted for only twenty-four hours. Patrick Egan, in his capacity as Party Treasurer, fled to Paris with the Land League funds. Other prominent party members joined him there. Most of the Land League executive – including Biggar, Dillon, and T. D. Sullivan – went there for an emergency meeting. Parnell's movements throughout this critical week were, however, a mystery: his colleagues had no idea of his whereabouts. Tim Healy later complained that he and the others had waited in vain for Parnell for the better part of a week.[114] He recounted how he had brought unopened letters addressed to Parnell to a meeting. When asked to show one of them, he had insisted upon a resolution of the executive before doing so. He stipulated that the letter, written in a woman's hand, should be seen by only two members, Dillon and Egan. After they had read the missive, it was agreed that Biggar and Healy should set off the following day to seek out the leader at the address provided by the letter. Healy describes how he and Biggar set out just as Parnell arrived in a carriage to the courtyard of the Hôtel Brighton on the Rue de Rivoli. The following day Parnell attended the meeting of the executive, 'without apology or explanation'.[115]

Healy later suspected that Parnell had spent much of the time at Eltham. And certainly Katie, unlike Parnell's colleagues, was aware of Parnell's travel plans. On 23 February 1881, he wrote to Katie from the Grosvenor Hotel in London, informing her of his intention to travel to Paris. This short note was addressed to 'Mrs O'Shea' and in it he requested that she write 'as before, and send some addresses'.[116] Evidence that Parnell had indeed been at Eltham is provided by his second letter to Katie that day, in which he asked her to 'Kindly send on my portmanteau with my letters and other things in my room or in the wardrobe to me at Hotel Brighton, Rue de Rivoli, Paris.'[117] He wrote to 'My dearest Katie' two days later that he had received her three letters. From Paris, he wired that he had not understood the meaning of her previous telegram, and that he had received no letter from her. He also wrote further to her that day from the Hôtel Brighton, telling her that she could 'write freely' to his own name care of Thomas Adams & Co. in Paris, who would then forward the letters safely to him. He had been warned, he continued, of a plot, and he was awaiting further information. He told her that he had received five letters in total from her, and advised that it was better not to post her letters at Eltham.

There was no doubt in his mind of the danger of his position. His departure, he wrote, had been 'influenced by information of reliable kind' that he was to have been arrested, and left in jail until habeas corpus was suspended – when he could 'have been again arrested'. He believed that 'they' had 'abandoned this intention', but would make sure before returning. He reported that this had been his third letter to her since his arrival in Paris.[118] Two days later, on 1 March, he wrote to his 'Dearest Love', stating that he had received her four letters. He kept careful track of their correspondence. Her earliest letter to him had been written on Saturday, he wrote, and assumed that she had not written on the Friday. He ended by saying that he was hoping to return to England in two days' time. If he managed to arrive by Thursday, he wrote, 'my Queen may expect to see me about one o'clock'. Katie was clearly suffering from strain. Parnell commented that her letters made him 'both happy and sad, happy to hear from my own, but sad when I see how troubled you are'.[119]

At the Paris meeting, Dillon told Parnell that the Central Branch of the Land League had little faith in the Westminster Parliament, and suggested that Parnell should travel to America.[120] The suggestion was made because it was known that the leader was a restraining influence, but Parnell refused to abide by the resolution. Instead, he proposed to follow a course 'deepening the lines and widening the area of our agitation', which would result in 'a junction between English democracy and Irish nationalism'.[121]

In spite of the leader's confidence and sureness of touch in promoting his policy, his colleagues had become alarmed at his unexplained absence. Healy resigned as his Secretary over the issue of the opened letter and was replaced by Henry Campbell (who was returned as MP for Fermanagh South in 1885). He proved to be discreet and loyal. T. P. O'Connor commented:

Like the faithful partisan he was, and being of a nature almost as suspicious as Parnell's own, he had a certain tendency to watch with a rather jaundiced eye the doings of Parnell's lieutenants... I have an impression that, quite innocently, Campbell may have helped to widen the gulf between Parnell and the few men in Parnell's party who were personally hostile to him.[122]

While in Paris, Parnell ostentatiously met with some French left-wing republican figures, including the author Victor Hugo. Although his dalliance with the radicals appeased some of the more extreme elements of his party, his actions angered conservative nationalists. One of the foremost propagandists of Irish nationalism, Arthur Martin Sullivan (brother of Timothy Daniel Sullivan and proprietor of the Irish newspaper *Nation*, from 1855 to 1874), responded to a public letter by declaring: 'the deep seated sentiments of the Irish people would be *outraged* by any attempt to ally or associate the Irish cause with French Communism or European Revolution'.[123] The 'castle' Archbishop of Dublin, McCabe, claimed forcefully: 'A calamity more terrible and humiliating than any that has yet befallen Ireland seems to threaten our people to-day. Allies for our country in her struggle for justice are sought from the ranks of impious infidels, who have plunged their own unhappy country into misery and who are sworn to destroy the foundations of all religions'.[124]

Although the threat of revolution on British shores was perceived by most politicians to be remote, there was sufficient propaganda to favour a cautious approach to the problems posed by land agitation. Funding from America continued to stoke the engine of Irish nationalism. Because much of the American press disapproved of anti-landlordism, however, Irish nationalists carefully presented an image of a near-starving tenantry. The propagation of the image of a stereotypical starving peasant became a feature of the battle to win hearts and minds in America. The British Cabinet members were keenly aware of the need to tread judiciously, yet there was a determination to legislate. The final debate on introducing the suspension of habeas corpus under the Protection of Person and Property Act was held on 25 February 1881. Forster returned to Dublin on 28 February and on 2 March the Home Secretary, Lewis Harcourt, pushed the ancillary Arms Bill through the House of Commons.

Then the arrests began. Those detained were prominent local Fenians and 'known activists'. Crimes of which they were suspected included 'intimidation against rent, shooting and wounding, attempted murder, boycotting, firing into a dwelling, arson, malicious wounding, attacking dwellings, sending threatening notices, unlawful assembly, riot, treasonable practices, incitement to murder, murder, preventing the payment of rent, maiming cattle, assaulting and beating'.[125] Some 995 persons were detained under the Act during the eighteen months of its existence and the majority of these were held for 'intimidation against rent'.[126]

On 7 April 1881 the Prime Minister introduced his Land Bill.[127] This was Gladstone's second Land Act, and it granted the '3 Fs' and instituted the Land Commission, which had authority to adjudicate on fair rents and also to make loans of up to 75 per cent of the purchase price to tenants wishing to purchase their holdings. As expected, it divided Irish nationalists. Gladstone had agreed to the suspension of habeas corpus with reluctance and he made it clear that he did not believe that the Land League was a criminal conspiracy. What he really wanted was to enact his legislation, and he was keen to enlist the support of the 'good' Land Leaguers. Forster, back in Dublin, was faced with the day-to-day challenges of maintaining order and implementing the unpopular coercion laws. Meanwhile, the Prime Minister was more preoccupied with achieving a successful result on land reform. He believed that accommodation with the nationalists was possible.

During this political tango, Parnell wrote from Glasgow on 19 April to 'Dearest Katie', sending her 'authority' for letters – meaning that she could collect and open them. He was leaving for Dublin, and he trusted that 'his own wifie' had not 'permitted herself to be too unhappy'. He ended his letter by telling her that he was writing 'with her own beautiful face' before him, which he had just kissed. His signature read: 'Always your husband'.[128]

CHAPTER EIGHT

Parnell's Arrest

THE IRISH LAND BILL basically conceded the demands for fair rent, fixed tenure and a freedom of sale, with very modest provision for land purchase, and was the precursor to further land legislation that followed. Healy and others vociferously attacked the bill at first, criticizing its restrictive scope, but later came to support the legislation. Parnell was originally aloof on the matter. At the Land League convention held after the third reading of the bill, he argued for a middle course that neither supported nor opposed the Act. He suggested that the tenants should hold back until after a series of test cases had been brought under the auspices of the League, and addressed meetings throughout Ireland promoting the policy. At the same time, Healy went through the test cases and advised the local lawyers representing the tenants.

But tenants were not convinced of the strategy. An *Evening Standard* journalist – who had accompanied Healy in Fermoy and Mitchelstown – believed that the movement went too far, writing on 14 October: 'Time after time I have seen a sharp farmer's face cloud over doubtfully when he has been told that he should abstain from going into Court until test cases, not affecting in any way the principle upon which his own must be decided, have been heard.'[1] Many farmers were reformers but did not hold with the socio-economic agenda of the radicals – whether that radicalism was communist (nationalizing land ownership) or seeking to destroy landlordism. They were more interested in obtaining an affordable rent. Anna Parnell was shocked and disappointed to be told by a Land League member, 'there's not a single tenant in Ireland who would not pay the rent if he could'. She asked in disgust, 'Then what was the Land League for? And what were we all supposed to be doing? And how was it that the Land League was still going on?'[2]

Charles Parnell's achievement was that he was able to reconcile the divergent interests of the parliamentary party members, Land Leaguers, and tenants. Radicals cohabited with moderate reformists in an uneasy alliance to achieve legislative progress. One of the features of Parnell's successful leadership was his legendary aloofness. This was a product in part of the fact that he was so rarely in Ireland, especially after 1882. His absences increased as his relationship with Katie intensified. She had decided to spend part of the summer with her children in Brighton, and took a house there. Aunt Ben was settled with a friend while her 'Swan' went to the seaside. By the 1860s the fashion for taking holidays at seaside resorts had become very popular. Brighton's West Pier was erected in 1866 and hotels were built to welcome the tourists, including Brighton's magnificent Grand Hotel.

Until the 1870s visitors were mostly middle class, keen on getting plenty of fresh sea air and taking walks along the promenade or in the gardens. As the market developed and became more oriented to the masses, resorts provided more robust entertainments. Winter palaces, dance halls and fairgrounds appeared, along with Punch-and-Judy shows and donkey rides.[3] Brighton remained a resort that catered to a wide range of visitors, and the number of day trippers increased as the railway connection to London improved. In the 1820s, the journey took six hours from the capital to Brighton. In 1841, the Brighton-to-London line was opened and, on Easter Monday 1862, a total of 132,000 people arrived on that day alone. By now, the travel time from London was only two hours.[4] More sedate visitors such as Katie and her family could keep well away from the working classes and their fun-fairs and noisy amusements.[5]

Katie described how she had gone down to Brighton in advance of the children's arrival in order to organize rooms for them. She was startled by a 'tall man' whom she did not at first recognize. It was Parnell – who had cut off his beard in order to avoid recognition. He had wrapped a scarf round his neck and covered the lower part of his face. He had announced himself as 'Mr Stewart' to the hotel landlady.[6] It is not clear whether the disguise and pseudonym were to avoid detection because of his political status – he certainly expected to be arrested at any time – or to hide his identity from anyone interested in his relationship with the wife of a colleague. No further details of the Brighton interlude are available, except for the fact that Parnell had gone on to Cork soon afterwards. Katie recounted that they had had a 'little quarrel' and 'were very unhappy until we had made it up again'.[7] While in Cork, Parnell had had his photograph taken wearing the ring that she had given him.[8]

Parnell was fascinated by architecture, Katie recalled, and spent many hours examining the rebuilding of Brighton Station. He paced and measured and drew up plans to build a similar structure at Avondale to house his cows. Another hobby that occupied him with intensity was 'assaying' small pieces of crystal from the stream at Wicklow.[9] Katie recorded that she had assisted him 'for hours' at this. 'His endeavour to obtain gold from this quartz was rewarded to a certain extent', she wrote, 'but the working was, of course, far too laborious and expensive to be profitable otherwise than as a hobby.' While working at these things, Katie remembered, he was 'absolutely oblivious to the passing of time, and it was with difficulty that I prevailed upon him to take sufficient exercise, or even to take his meals before they were spoiled by waiting'.[10]

By this time Katie and Parnell were behaving as a couple. When the *Freeman's Journal* printed an account of messages passing between him and an American lady, Katie had been upset. He was pained to know that it had caused her unhappiness, and explained:

An old and ugly woman with whom I was very slightly acquainted, but who wanted to put herself *en evidence*, perched herself just behind me, and got a gentleman sitting next to her to hand me down a slip of paper, on which was written some message of congratulation. I only rewarded her with a stare, did not even bow or smile, and certainly sent no communication of any kind in reply. That was all. I will ask my own dearest to believe in me while I am away, and never again to feel unhappiness from want of confidence.[11]

Meanwhile, though, Katie continued to maintain relations with her husband. Willie O'Shea adopted a moderate position on the proposed Land Bill, and supported Parnell. He had spoken in Parliament on 10 January 1881, asserting that, although he was not himself a Land Leaguer, he believed that it was the League that had brought the land reform question, 'one of the most dangerous to the Empire, nearer settlement'.[12] It is not clear how much O'Shea knew of his wife's relationship. On 17 January 1881, however, he took the trouble to tell the Prime Minister's son, Herbert Gladstone – whom he knew well – that Parnell was 'thoroughly honest and not touching a penny of Land League money'.[13] Willie voted with the Party leader on 20 January for a second proposed Irish amendment to the Land Bill. He continued to work within the Party throughout that spring, and on 30 May he wrote to Gladstone, following a conversation he had had with the Prime Minister that afternoon in the House, proposing a plan whereby the Exchequer would compensate those landlords who would reduce their rents to an average of the Griffith's valuations.[14] He claimed to have shown the proposal to Parnell,

who expressed himself satisfied that it embodies the principles by which he yesterday promised that he would stand. I am therefore in a position to promise that the opposition of Mr Parnell's party in the House of Commons will immediately cease and that he will give the Bill an effectual support in Ireland, such support to be loyally afforded even if outwardly and for the moment prudently veiled.[15]

Later that spring, Parnell advanced his own political interests and platform by acquiring a stable of Irish newspapers from the publisher Richard Pigott,[16] using Land League funds to make the purchase. Parnell urged his loyal friend and supporter William O'Brien to take on the editorship of a new paper, *United Ireland*. The first issue of this organ – entirely loyal to Parnell – appeared on 13 August. This acquisition was designed to counter the nationalist paper, the *Nation*, a publication that did not hesitate to criticize him. Now the leader could benefit from the support of a radical newspaper, whose published views, however, could be denied as his own. And, indeed, he later asserted of the paper: 'paragraphs and articles have often appeared of a stronger character than I could have approved, from time to time, and they appear to this day.'[17]

In 1881, however, his personal situation came under attack. Willie O'Shea came to Eltham unexpectedly in July, having heard some 'flying rumours'. Katie claimed that she and Willie had been 'quarrelling because he, my lawful wedded husband, had come down without the invitation that was now (for some years) understood as due to the courtesy of friends, and because he had become vaguely suspicious'.[18] His account, given years later at the divorce court, was that until that time he had had no idea of the relations between his wife and his leader. Katie claimed that her husband had at first encouraged the intimacy. She had been unwilling to invite Parnell to Eltham in the first instance, worrying that the house was 'too shabby' and that the children 'would worry so nervous a man'.[19] However, she had done so to please and help her husband. 'But Willie', she wrote, 'was blind to the existence of the fierce, bewildering force that was rising within me in answer to the call of those passion-haunted eyes.' Although her spouse had known of other men who had admired – or even loved – her, he now grew possessive. When he arrived that day in July, he searched for Parnell. Not finding him, O'Shea 'went into his room, and finding his portmanteau, sent it to London, and left my house, declaring he would challenge Parnell to fight a duel and would shoot him'.[20]

After the furious row, Willie walked all the way to London in the early hours of the morning. He later testified that he had gone to the residence of his sister-in-law,[21] Mrs Anna Steele, at St James's Street, near Buckingham Palace. He then told her what had taken place, and wrote to Parnell 'challenging him to go abroad and fight a duel'. The letter, sent from the Salisbury Club and dated 13 July 1881, read as follows:

Sir,

Will you be so kind as to be in Lille, or in any other town in the north of France which may suit your convenience, on Saturday next, the 16th inst.? Please to let me know by 1 p.m. to-day where to expect you on that date so that I may be able to inform you of the sign of the inn at which I shall be staying. I await your answer in order to lose no time in arranging with a friend to accompany me.

I am, your obedient servant, W. H. O'Shea.[22]

Anna Steele thus became the mediator between the warring couple, and 'exercised herself to settle the differences that had arisen'. She had an interview with Parnell at the Westminster Palace Hotel, and he apparently 'assured her that there were no grounds for the jealous suspicions which Captain O'Shea had formed. He also promised her that in future he would not see Mrs. O'Shea or give any cause for the suspicions that had been excited.'

Anna Steele then persuaded her brother-in-law to return to Eltham to talk to Katie. There ensued a 'stormy scene, in the course of which Captain O'Shea said he would no longer live with his wife'. Katie 'implored' him, however, 'to dismiss the suspicions, the truth of which she emphatically denied'. Eventually he calmed down and 'agreed that their relations should be resumed as before'. Willie travelled back to London with his sister-in-law. He took with him the portmanteau, which he 'flung out at Charing-cross'.[23]

O'Shea was still unhappy at the state of affairs. He wrote again to the Irish leader: 'Sir – I have called frequently at the Salisbury Club to-day, and I find that you are not going abroad. Your luggage is at Charing-cross Station.'[24] Parnell replied, on 14 July 1881:

Sir – I have your letter of yesterday bearing the postmark of to-day. I replied to your previous letter of yesterday morning, and sent my reply by a careful messenger to the Salisbury Club. I would ask you to inquire there again, as I await your reply, and you will find from the contents of the letter referred to that your surmise that I refuse to go abroad is not a correct one.

Yours truly, Chas. S. Parnell.[23]

Parnell kept Katie fully informed of developments, writing:

I replied to Captain O'Shea's note yesterday, and sent my reply by a careful messenger to the Salisbury Club; and it must be waiting him there. He has just written me a very insulting letter, and I shall be obliged to send a friend to him if I do not have satisfactory reply to a second note I have just sent him.

Katie recorded that her spouse 'then thought he had been too hasty in his action'. Knowing that she had 'become immersed in the Irish cause', he changed his mind about the duel and 'merely made the condition that Mr. Parnell should not stay at Eltham'.[26] Katie wrote that as of this pivotal moment, she and her lover 'were one, without scruple, without fear, and without remorse'.[27] This was certainly an exaggeration, as there was still Aunt Ben to consider, as well as the children and her own reputation. In fact, Parnell wrote her a series of letters directly after the contretemps, formally addressed to 'My dear Mrs. O'Shea'. On 20 July he wrote: 'Just a line to say that I am very well and wondering when I shall see you again.'[28] Two days later, he addressed another short missive to 'my dear Mrs O'Shea', telling her that he had received her two letters 'quite safely' and was 'looking forward to seeing you somewhere or somehow to-morrow'. He added that he was 'troubled at everything you have to undergo and trust that it will not last long'.[29]

In spite of what they had told Anna Steele and Willie O'Shea, it was clear that the intimacy continued. On 25 July, Parnell asked her to send him his travelling cap, as he might have to travel to France. The following day he wrote again, saying that he had decided to postpone his trip. Katie's comment was that the letters were 'cypher' to her, letting her know about the duel. The postponement of the trip was therefore to advise her that the duel was not to take place. Thus it took ten days or so to sort things out. It was not until 25 July that Parnell knew that he would not be going to France. This suggests that Willie was quite determined, and not easily dissuaded from his course of action.

Katie was careful thenceforth. All throughout 1881, she wrote, the leader continued to visit her at Eltham. She recorded:

He came home to me now always between the times of his journeyings up and down the country, and if it was not certain that I should be alone he would write me a formal though friendly note or letter that anyone could have been shown, in which was given some word or sign that let me know a place or time of meeting him, either in London or nearer my home.[30]

It is interesting to observe that Katie, whilst obviously distressed at the disruption and conflict, nevertheless seemed quite excited by events. The situation became outwardly calmer, and O'Shea and Parnell continued to work together. Parnell had apparently told Willie that Katie had become 'a medium of communication between the Government and himself', and that he needed to go on meeting her so that she could continue this important task. This would 'render negotiations possible and safe'.[31] Some sort of an agreement must have been reached, as communications between the pair went on through the summer. On 1 August 1881 he wrote that he thought she might have 'some books of mine at Eltham, which I propose going to look for on Monday, about eleven or twelve, unless I hear from you that you can find them for me'.[32] He requested that she reply to the House of Commons. On 17 August he had been 'rendered very anxious' by not receiving any news from her that day. He trusted that nothing had happened to her and that she was 'not ill'.[33] His anxiety was all the more acute because at this point Katie was expecting a child.

A daughter was born to Katie O'Shea on 16 February 1882. The child was, therefore, conceived sometime around the end of April or beginning of May 1881. This would coincide with the time of the holiday in Brighton, and Parnell could well have been the father. Admitting this to her husband might have sparked off the row that led to his demand for a duel. It is quite plausible that Katie decided to confront her spouse with the truth and to demand an accommodation of her new situation. After all, Parnell was by September writing to 'My Own Wifie'.[34] On the other hand, such a compromise would have been entirely out of keeping with Willie O'Shea's character. Katie herself wrote of his attitude regarding her that he was 'content that what was his, was *his* for good or ill'.[35] Hence his demand for satisfaction. Katie's housemaid, Jane Lennister, recalled that as of May 1881 Parnell was in the habit of coming to Wonersh Lodge. She also claimed that he had slept in the spare room, which was connected by a dressing-room to her mistress's own bedroom. When asked whether Mr Parnell had remained there while Mr O'Shea was away, she replied, 'Yes, very often'.[36] But at this point the evidence was not overwhelming. On only one occasion could the maid recall that Mrs O'Shea and Mr Parnell had been in the drawing room alone with the door locked. Further, there is every indication that Willie believed that the baby was his.

Meanwhile, the political agitation continued. On 22 August the Land Bill received royal assent in Westminster. Before leaving for Ireland, Parnell had made as much trouble for the government in the House as he could. He intervened thirty-three times in the three weeks before the amendments proposed by the House of Lords were considered by the Commons. His parliamentary exchanges with the Prime Minister were mostly unfriendly, and the conflict between Parnell and Gladstone was gaining momentum. Although the Prime Minister believed that the Irish leader was in fact a moderating influence on the more revolutionary agitators in Ireland, he was losing patience with his opposition to the Land Bill. There was little social contact between the two men, whose interaction was thus confined to exchanges in the House of Commons; these, as mentioned, grew increasingly acrimonious.

At the end of August, Parnell travelled to Ireland and was soon busy campaigning for a by-election in Ulster. He supported the Home Rule and Land League candidate for County Tyrone, a Unitarian clergyman named Harold Rylett. This prospective member was opposed by a Conservative *and* a Liberal candidate. Parnell had the delicate task, therefore, of supporting a Land League position above the Liberal one, despite the fact that it was a Liberal government that had just passed the much demanded Land Reform Bill. What Parnell and his chief lieutenants wished to avoid was a situation whereby their followers would accept the terms of the Land Act and thus effectively 'decouple the agrarian engine from the Home Rule train'.[37] But there was a need to tread carefully in the north of Ireland, where agrarian reform was welcome – Home Rule less so. Support for Home Rule, in this more industrialized area of Ireland, was unevenly distributed.

The economic conditions in Ulster were dominated by the great industries of textiles, shipbuilding, engineering and foundrywork. The successful entrepreneurs of the Belfast shipping industry – such as William and John Ritchie, Edward Harland, G. W. Wolff and George Clark – came from Britain, and their businesses were closely linked to imperial markets and to a 'British identity'.[38] What historian Roy Foster has called a 'factory culture' of the mechanized flax-spinning industry of Ulster spread to the shirt-making centre of Derry. But in addition to the particular economic links to Britain – constant exchanges of colliers between Britain and the north-west of Ireland for instance – the development of industry in northern Ireland had led to an 'intensely sectional and disputatious workforce'.[39] There were religious divides and even urban sectarian riots in Belfast from the 1850s. Land issues, however, brought Protestant and Catholic together in agricultural Ulster in the early 1880s. Although in Belfast the Presbyterian voter was turning solidly Tory, by 1880 Ulster Liberalism had become a rural party, and therefore one within which Parnell could hope to gain non-sectarian support, on the basis of promised land reform. Speaking at further meetings in Ulster, at Dromore and Enniskillen, he argued selectively in favour of the land reform cause.

At Enniskillen he played the agrarian card. 'What is the end and object of the Land League', he asked, 'for which we struggle?' He answered:

We aim at abolishing rent and making the people the owners of the land of this country. The Government passed an Act in the session just gone by for the purpose of establishing the courts to fix rents. We do not aim at fixing rent because, as I have said, we aim at abolishing it altogether, and as far as the Land Law may reduce the rents, so far will it go in our direction, and if the result of the Land Act should be to reduce the rents by 30% we can fairly call on you to rally again. And with this proof – that a reduction in your rent is the result of two years' work by the Land

League – we can call on you to rally behind us and press on with this work until we have reduced the rent to nothing at all.[40]

Still in Ulster, at Strabane, Parnell argued that the Land Act had been obtained largely due to the efforts of the Land League. He claimed:

If we can teach the tenant farmers how much of it they can possibly use, and how much they ought to reject, then this Land Act properly used and carefully guarded against – insofar as it is likely to produce demoralization into our ranks – would be of importance in encouraging the people, in putting them in a better position to push forward and gain the full platform.[41]

His strenuous campaigning was noted and admired by his colleagues. Sexton commented at a Land League meeting in Dublin on 31 August (from which Parnell had excused himself as he was too busy) that he observed 'with rejoicing that Mr Parnell is exhibiting in this contest that marvellous energy and that stern and uncompromising Irish spirit which has won for him the leadership of the Irish Party'.[42]

Although there were pockets of angry resistance to Parnell's message, the public mostly received him with rapturous enthusiasm. After his speech at Dungannon, on 1 September 1881, the crowd drew him back to his hotel by wagonette. Parnell was careful as ever, nevertheless, while campaigning in the north of the island, to tone down his nationalist discourse. He emphasized the advantages of land reform and this drew a predictably positive response. And even though the Home Rule candidate Dickson lost the election to his Liberal opponent – much to Gladstone's relief – Parnell viewed the results with optimism. 'Two years ago', he declared, 'it would not have been possible for me to have gone through the country and preach the doctrines we preach there and have escaped with our lives.'[43]

Parnell's separation from Katie was surely painful, but he was exceedingly busy in Ireland. He had been so pressed that he had 'not even had time to sleep'. He added, however, that he had 'never been too busy to think of her'.[44] After the Ulster by-election, he was preparing for the National Convention of the Land League, to be held on 15 September. Although some of the Land Leaguers wished Parnell to denounce the Act entirely, he preferred a more cagey approach. 'The Land Act settles nothing,' he declared. 'It leaves everything in an unsettled condition to be a continual source of contention between the landlords on the one side and the tenants on the other.' But he wanted more radical change. 'The cause of the political and social evils which afflict and impoverish our country, is to be found in the detestable system of alien rule so injurious and oppressive to our people.'[45] This kind of talk was precisely what worried Gladstone and the English political establishment. Parnell's position at the Convention was overtly nationalist.

Resolutions securing Ireland's right to self-government, condemnation of coercion, the reassertion of the need to abolish landlordism – all these were passed unanimously. The editor of *United Ireland*, William O'Brien, called the Convention 'in all but name the Sovereign Parliament of the Irish nation'.[46] Parnell trod carefully at the Convention, trying to reconcile extremists and moderates. The danger was that the radicals might so resent a cautious approach to the Land Act that they might choose to take the law into their own hands and instigate and encourage further violence. The real problem with this would be the tainting of Parnell's parliamentary approach with the violent acts of secret societies who were not even associated with the Land League. Many of these extremist individuals resisted any external control.

As well as attempting to promote a platform sufficiently radical to quell such actions, Parnell had also to ensure that Irish-Americans – who provided most of the funds – were in agreement with the League's strategy. Many of the Americans believed that a more dynamic policy was called for. Patrick Ford, in the columns of the *Irish World*, demanded more action and called for a simple tactic: 'No Rent'.[47] Parnell thus needed to buy time during which tenants could test their rent reduction claims in the land courts. He heightened the tone of his nationalist rhetoric. Immediately after the Convention he made a series of speeches, beginning in Dublin on 25 September. There he was greeted by a torch-lit procession – said to have been the greatest demonstration of this kind since the days of the Great Liberator, Daniel O'Connell.

Parnell was becoming a national hero. While in Dublin, he dramatically stopped the cortège outside the Bank of Ireland – where Grattan's Parliament had sat some hundred years previously[48] – and silently pointed his finger. The crowd roared its approval at the gesture, signifying the demand for a return to Ireland of its own Parliament. There could thus be no mistaking Parnell's intentions. Gladstone was unimpressed. Some two weeks later, in a speech given at Leeds, he compared the current and past Irish national leaders:

O'Connell professed unconditional and unanswering loyalty to the crown of England. Mr Parnell says that if the crown of England is to be the link between the two countries it is to be the only link; but whether it is to be the link at all… is a matter on which he has not, I believe, given any opinion whatsoever.[49]

Although disappointed at the Land League's overall response to his Land Act, Gladstone took heart, nevertheless, as the autumn progressed, at the willingness of tenants to present their cases independently to the Land Commission. But Parnell's speeches continued to be inflammatory and many of his colleagues expected his arrest to be imminent.

Throughout the upheavals and political challenges in Ireland, Parnell retained his commitment to Katie. Because she did not choose to explain the exact nature of the relationship between the three parties at this time, it is difficult to know precisely what was going on. What does seem likely, however, is that the situation lacked clarity for all parties. The letters Parnell wrote to Katie throughout this period contained references to what might have been the continuance of her marital relations with her husband. On 10 September, Parnell wrote that he was pleased to know that her 'trouble had not returned since I left', although this could of course refer to a physical ailment or side effect of the pregnancy. Certainly, Katie and Parnell were determined to allay Willie's concerns. Although Katie and Parnell seemingly had more to lose at this point, there was always the question of finances. Aunt Ben was meeting Willie O'Shea's expenses as well as those of her niece. Her continued goodwill and beneficence had become an integral and essential part of both of the O'Sheas' lifestyles.

It was therefore not in Willie's best interests to make too much of a fuss. He may have been more concerned with appearance than with the actual facts of the situation. His demand that Parnell should not stay at Eltham would support this interpretation of his position. And indeed, Parnell's letters to Katie through September and October, just after the duel crisis, make clear that he stayed away. This may have been from fear of arrest, or from the obvious need to spend time on managing a highly volatile political situation back home. It could have been that the lovers had temporarily to separate. His correspondence was mostly reassuring and solicitous. 'Your King thinks very very often of his dearest Queen and wishes her not to be sad', he wrote on 10 September 1881 from Dublin, 'but to try to be happy for his sake.'[50] On 25 September he wrote, 'I send these few words to assure Wifie that her own husband always thinks of her and hopes she is well and happy.'[51]

On the other hand, his tone could be surprisingly unconcerned. He had been away from her, in Ireland, all through September. Considering that 'My Own Wifie' was at the time five months' pregnant, his letter of 4 October from Wicklow struck a rather self-centred note. He penned:

I have satisfied myself, by two separate tests today, that there is a good deal of silver in the dark stone of which there is so much in the old mine. In fact nearly the whole lode consists of this (the miners are working in it in the North Level). I cannot say how many ounces there will be to the ton until I get it assayed, but if there should be six or eight ounces it ought to pay to work.

There were no endearments to follow, save his signature: 'Your Own King'.[52]

Parnell was not alone in attempting to find precious minerals in Ireland. A talk given by G. P. Bevan to the Society of Arts in London in January 1882 discussed the potential of copper and iron mines in Wicklow. A few years later, a select committee meeting on Irish industries examined pyrites and gold also in the Wicklow area.[53] An article in the *Nation* of 20 November 1880 stated of Charles Parnell: 'for years past he has been making borings for lead and in his latest attempt he has succeeded in striking the lode'.[54] Indeed, he invested large amounts of capital into the search, and continued through his lifetime to believe that his land was rich with minerals. He became obsessive in his quest, as Katie described. When asked by Parnell biographer Barry O'Brien about his shooting trips with Parnell, political colleague John Redmond recollected that his leader 'was always looking for gold in Wicklow'.[55]

A few days later, on 7 October, Parnell wrote to Katie that he had called today to see 'him', meaning Captain O'Shea.[56] He had waited for three hours, then called again at eleven o'clock that night. He was writing to make an appointment for the following morning when O'Shea finally materialized. The fact that Parnell, normally aloof and rather forbidding towards his colleagues, was so keen to see O'Shea indicates one of several possibilities. The least likely is that it involved a political matter. A more likely explanation is that the quarrel about Katie had not been resolved and Parnell was anxious about it.

Another plausible reason was his strong desire to ensure that he could see Katie. 'He *says* that he leaves to-morrow (Friday) evening', wrote Parnell, 'and stops to shoot on Saturday in Wales, and goes on Tuesday to Paris to see the Papal Nuncio, who he says has requested him to come.' This would therefore, he wrote, be the last letter he would send her to Eltham – presumably for fear that O'Shea might change his mind and go there. This was a clear indicator that the relationship between Katie and Parnell was still being kept secret – from Willie as well as everyone else. Parnell continued by saying that he hoped to go over to London to see her, and wondered whether he should 'remain in London or go down to you'. He ended by sending 'numerous kisses to my beautiful Queenie'.[57]

Then, on 7 October, the Prime Minister delivered his most hostile attack on Parnell in a speech given at Leeds. He warned his audience that Parnell 'desires to arrest the operation of the Land Act, to stand as Moses stood between the living and the dead; to stand there, not as Moses stood, to arrest, but to spread the plague'. Gladstone was unequivocal in his denunciation of the Irish leader, continuing:

If it shall appear that there is still to be fought a final conflict in Ireland between law on the one side and sheer lawlessness upon the other, if the law purged from defect and from any taint of injustice is still to be repulsed and refused, and the first conditions of political society to remain unfulfilled, then I say, without hesitation, the resources of civilization against its enemies are not yet exhausted.[58]

Undaunted by this attack on the man she loved, Katie wrote proudly of Parnell's riposte. He had responded with 'passion and scorn' in a speech given at Wexford two days later, and had spoken dismissively of the British premier:

It is a good sign that this masquerading knight-errant, this pretended champion of the liberties of every other nation except those of the Irish nation, should be obliged to throw off the mask to-day and to stand revealed as the man who, by his own utterances, is prepared to carry fire and sword into your homesteads unless you humble and abase yourselves before him and before the landlords of this country.[59]

Despite the virulent tone of these mutual attacks, Parnell was sufficiently confident in his future to reassure Katie on 8 October that things in Dublin had been 'settled up pretty satisfactorily', and he trusted 'only to have to make an occasional appearance in Ireland during the rest of the autumn and winter'. He told his lover that he had 'kept his eyes, thought and love' all for her, and his 'sweetest love may be assured that he always will'.[60] That Parnell was able to play the critical and demanding role required of him in Ireland while at the same time maintaining (albeit at a distance) a clandestine romantic relationship is remarkable. The tone of most of his letters indicated quite clearly that he was a man infatuated.

Katie herself wrote of 'the fierce, bewildering force that was rising within me in answer to the call of those passion-haunted eyes, that waking or sleeping never left me'.[61] She had been 'swept into the avalanche of Parnell's love', and although she had 'fought against our love', Parnell would not. She claimed that she had argued against the liaison, for the sake of her children and his work, but he had replied: 'For good or ill, I am your husband, your lover, your children, your all. And I will give my life to Ireland, but to you I give my love, whether it be your heaven or your hell. It is destiny. When I first looked into your eyes I knew.'[62]

Parnell continued to function on two entirely different planes – political and personal. And perhaps the rapturous and adoring reception he was receiving in many parts of Ireland contributed to his sense of exhilaration. After receiving the freedom of the city of Wexford on 8 October, it was Parnell instead of 'the Queen' whose name was 'coupled with the prosperity of Ireland in a variation of the traditional toast'.[63] The demands for reassurance and his risky behaviour – including plans to travel to see her, despite the problems with Willie – would also fit with the pattern of an infatuated man. He wrote to Katie from Dublin on 11 October, after fretting at not hearing from her. 'Your telegram this morning took a great weight off my mind, as your silence made me almost panic-stricken lest you had been hurt by that – and had not been able to get to town.' He was planning on travelling to Kildare, he continued, and promised to send 'Wifie' a wire that Friday. He then planned to cross over to England. 'If I arrive London Friday night', he wrote, 'shall go to the same hotel and shall wait for my darling.' He was, 'Always Your Own King'.[64]

It is more difficult to gauge how Katie felt. She may not even have been sure herself. Her comment about trying to be reasonable about their love is revealing, if perhaps self-serving. She did not, as we know, publish her own letters to Parnell, and this is perhaps because they did not substantiate her story.[65] It is likely that at the time she was more cautious and pragmatic. There were sound reasons for this. She was, of course, married and she had her three children to consider. The eldest, Gerard, was now aged eleven; Mary (known as Norah) was eight and the youngest, Carmen, was seven. Katie was also, technically, the breadwinner, since it was through her relationship with Aunt Ben that all the household income was derived.

When she became pregnant, Katharine was undoubtedly faced with an unpalatable situation. Parnell was a forceful and demanding lover. She had spent a holiday with him at Brighton, during which the child might have been conceived. To tell an infatuated lover that the baby might not be his would have been very daunting. Equally worrying, no doubt, was the possibility of her husband believing that the child was not *his* own. Katie's preoccupation with secrecy would imply that O'Shea was not, at that moment, to be trifled with. There is every chance that Katie was hedging her bets, and waiting to see how her tricky situation would develop.

Events in Ireland played a significant part in the unfolding drama of Katie's life. On 12 October, she recalled, she had been in London – 'to ascertain the movements of the Government'. Her task, she claimed, was to inform Parnell if she heard news of his imminent arrest, so that 'he might destroy any papers that, found on him, might frustrate his plans and cause unnecessary difficulty to those working with him'.[66] When she learned that a Cabinet meeting had been 'hurriedly summoned' she had wired in code to her lover.[67] Katie recorded that she had been terribly worried at the prospect of his imprisonment. Her health, she tactfully wrote, 'was then delicate'. She felt 'an unreasonable fear and loneliness when he was away' from her. The Irish leader had explained to her, however, why 'the turmoil and rebellion in Ireland he had brought to a head in Ireland must be very carefully handled to be productive of ultimate good'.[68] Even so, she 'could not bear the thought of his arrest' and asked him to travel to Holyhead to meet her, writing that she 'felt almost unable to cope with the situation; I was not strong and I was full of anxiety as to the probable effects upon Parnell's health of life in Kilmainham Gaol'. And of course there was the continuing problem of managing her husband. 'In addition to my anxiety', she recalled, 'the deception I had to practise towards Captain O'Shea, seldom as I saw him, told upon my nerves just now.'[69]

After the Cabinet made its decision, Chief Secretary Forster immediately made his return to Dublin, arriving on the morning of Thursday 13 October. Parnell had travelled up to Dublin from Avondale and was staying at Morrison's Hotel. He planned to address a meeting in Kildare the next day. When the porter came to call him the following morning, he was told there were two men waiting for him. When Parnell learned that the two men were in fact a superintendent of the Dublin police (it was actually the celebrated detective, John Mallon), accompanied by a constable, he sent them word that he would dress and be down to them in half an hour. Although the porter urged Parnell to escape through the back door, he declined, on the basis that every entrance would be guarded. The policemen were brought up to Parnell's room, where, according to the *Freeman's Journal*, 'the documents were presented to him with manly courtesy' by Mallon. According to this warrant, Parnell was

to be reasonably suspected of having, since the 30th day of September 1880 been guilty as principal in a crime punishable by law, that is to say: – inciting other persons wrongfully and without legal authority to intimidate divers persons with a view to compel them to abstain from doing what they had a legal right to do, namely to apply to the land court under the provision of the Land Law (Ireland) Act 1881 [to pay rents lawfully due by them][70] to have a fair rent fixed for their holdings committed in the aforesaid Prescribed District (City of Dublin) and being the inciting to an act of intimidation and tending to interfere with the maintenance of Law and Order.[71]

When the detective expressed his concern at what might happen if a crowd collected, Parnell agreed to a discreet departure by cab, and by 9.30 that morning the leader was behind the prison gates of Kilmainham Gaol. One of his last acts before leaving the hotel was to write to Katie. 'My Own Queenie', he penned, 'I have just been arrested by two fine-looking detectives, and write these words to wifie to tell her that she must be a brave little woman and not fret after her husband.' In this hour of crisis, he remained supernaturally calm and reassuring. 'The only thing that makes me worried and unhappy', he continued, 'is that it may hurt you and our child. You know, darling, that on this account it will be wicked of you to grieve, as I can never have any other wife but you, and if anything happens to you I must die childless. Be good and brave, dear little wifie, then.' Parnell signed 'Your Own Husband'.[72]

Parnell had refused to travel to Holyhead to try to see her before his inevitable imprisonment. He would 'not allow' her to take on the 'fatigue of a journey' and 'nor would he go abroad to avoid arrest'. He was convinced that his incarceration would be of 'short duration', and Katie was left to comfort herself 'as I could with his confident spirit and loving messages'.[73] She recorded how a violent storm had swept throughout the south of England. The force of the gale was such that trees were torn out by their roots. Katie did not exaggerate in this instance. The arrest of Parnell coincided with a ferocious tempest that swept through Europe. It was one of the worst recorded since 1855, and wind speeds of 84 mph were recorded at Kingstown Pier in Ireland.[74]

CHAPTER NINE

Kilmainham: Parnell's Incarceration

*S*ending Parnell to prison was a risk for the British government. The previous week, after a particularly inflammatory speech given at Wexford, one of his colleagues had asked the Irish leader for any instructions should he be arrested. Parnell had apparently 'looked through the glass of champagne he had raised to his lips' and replied: 'Ah, if I am arrested, Captain Moonlight will take my place.'[1] The danger of violent, marauding groups taking the law into their own hands was a genuine threat in Ireland and Parnell knew this very well. One of his most significant bargaining chips with Gladstone was the latter's belief that Parnell represented the forces of moderation and was therefore the acceptable face of Irish nationalist aspirations. In addition, the Liberal government was now engaged on a politically unpalatable and rather dangerous course of action. Arresting and imprisoning elected MPs on flimsy and mostly unproven allegations was antithetical to British justice.

So Parnell was treated with caution and respect. He and the large numbers of Land Leaguers who followed the parliamentarians into prison were held in quite favourable conditions.[2] Kilmainham Gaol was a dark, forbidding building located on the Phoenix Park edge of central Dublin. This County of Dublin Gaol had from 1796 served as an institution to imprison common convicted criminals and public executions had taken place within its grounds. Following the rebellions of 1793, 1803, 1848 and 1867, the jail had also served to incarcerate individuals associated with armed resistance to the British presence in Ireland. This meant that criminals convicted of serious crimes, such as rape or murder, as well as for lesser offences, were housed alongside 'political' protesters. Kilmainham Gaol was enlarged in 1867 with the opening of an east wing, its design modelled on that of Pentonville Prison. The 'panoptic' design was a three-storey, barrel-vaulted space, lined on either side with iron galleries and catwalks. The central vista was wide and bright, but the prisoners were held in dark, cramped cells ranged along the sides of the central vaulted area. The design permitted close and constant supervision of prisoners, who were nevertheless hidden away in tiny cells.

Kilmainham Gaol had also housed the many prisoners of the famine years. At the height of the Great Famine, the prisoner body rose from an average of 700 to over 9,000 in 1850. This was a reflection of the desperation of the starving people, who actively sought imprisonment as a means of avoiding starvation.[3] There was thus a particular poignancy to the imprisonment of Parnell and other Land Leaguers at Kilmainham. It was also an imprisonment fraught with symbolism. The heavy heritage of previous rebel incarcerations, added to the memory of the famine years, were part of the Kilmainham experience. Parnell was by his own account well treated at Kilmainham and received many visitors. He also had books as well as writing materials and was not required to do prison work. He was provided with a sitting room that contained two armchairs and a fire. Although the conditions were certainly not luxurious, Parnell was comfortable and in close contact with his political colleagues, whose company he found reasonably congenial.

It was Katie who suffered intensely. Her lover's incarceration posed huge problems for her. It was critical that Aunt Ben should suspect nothing untoward in her niece's pregnancy. This meant that Willie O'Shea had to be either entirely compliant or completely unaware of the question mark over the unborn child's paternity. 'I lived a curiously subconscious existence', she wrote, 'pursuing the usual routine of my life with my aunt, but feeling that all that was of life in me had gone with my lover to prison.'[4] In an unlikely coincidence, Willie arranged to have dinner with her at Eltham the evening of Parnell's arrest. He rushed from London to give his wife the news. She had gone out, she recalled, to collect the evening papers and had found her husband at home on her return. He was 'extremely pleased to be able to announce to me that Parnell had been arrested that morning'.[5] There is an unmistakable ring of sincerity in her depiction of Willie's reaction to the news. He was 'so fiercely and openly joyful' that her maids – 'ardent Parnellites' – were 'much shocked'. Katie wrote of how, despite being 'terribly overwrought', she had managed to get through dinner 'amicably enough'. Her husband had, however, spent the evening decrying the 'wickedness and folly of Parnell's policy and the way the Irish question should really be settled, and would be if it could be left in his hands and those who thought with him'.

The difficulty with Katie's account of their interaction at this point in time is how poorly it squares with her sporadic insistence (to Parnell's biographer, Henry Harrison, for instance) that Willie not only knew of the affair but also encouraged it in order to gain personal advantage. It could be of course that O'Shea was very unwillingly compliant once he had understood how serious the relationship had become. The forceful character of Parnell, and his notorious *hauteur* in justifying his actions, could have annoyed the Captain considerably. Pacifying her spouse might have been part of the price that Katie had to pay for her security. 'He observed me closely as he criticised Parnell and his policy', she observed, 'and reiterated his pleasure in knowing he was "laid by the heels".'[6]

It could also be that Willie was testing the waters and remained suspicious of his wife. 'I had to be careful now,' she claimed, 'Willie became more solicitous for my health, and wished to come to Eltham more frequently than I would allow.' A further substantiation of the memoir's central tenet – that her husband was unaware of her liaison – was her assertion that he hoped that the baby's birth would 'seal our reconciliation'.[7] This completely contradicts her later assertion to Henry Harrison in 1891:

There was no bargain; there were no discussions; people do not talk of such things. But he knew, and he actually encouraged me in it at times. I remember especially one particular occasion, very early in the affair, when he wanted to get Mr. Parnell's assent to something or other and he was urging me to get this assent, he said, 'Take him back with you to Eltham and make him all happy and comfortable for the night, and just get him to agree'. His air, his manner, made his meaning unmistakable to me. He knew too, of course, that Mr. Parnell was staying with me when he was not. How could he fail to know?[8]

Katie told Harrison that Parnell 'was prepared – for my sake and reluctantly enough – to keep up appearances with the outside world and to avoid scandal... He hated all the concealments and pretence of concealments.' It was to satisfy Willie's honour that 'assurances' were given to him. 'I always realised', explained Katie, 'that it was necessary to do everything possible to preserve appearances and to prevent the truth being publicly forced' on her spouse. And, although he was unhappy about it, her lover 'fell in with every suggestion for avoidance of public scandal'. For, in truth, none of them wanted that. 'With my aunt there, a scandal was not to be thought of – we could not afford to risk the consequences.'[9]

But now Katie was in a dreadful position. Parnell was away for an indefinite period, while she awaited her baby's birth. She was left alone to deal with her family – including Aunt Ben – and with a suspicious husband. But Charles Parnell's arrest had aroused an intense response in Ireland. Soon his lieutenants, the prominent Land Leaguer Thomas Sexton (a brilliant public speaker and Home Rule MP for Sligo),[10] James O'Kelly, William O'Brien and John Dillon, ended up in Kilmainham as well. Unknown to any of them, or indeed to any of his thousands of devoted supporters, Parnell was actually relieved to have been incarcerated at this moment. Despite his anxiety for Katie, he was pleased with this outcome, as he was worried about the escalation of the agrarian attacks. He had insisted on posting his letters before entering the jail, and he wrote to Katherine of his true feelings about the arrest. Even allowing for the possibility that he was merely trying to reassure her, the words ring true: 'Politically it is a fortunate thing for me that I have been arrested, as the movement is breaking fast, and all will be quiet in a few months, when I shall be released.'[11]

It would have caused huge consternation had his thoughts been made public, but he was certainly correct about the problems created by the League. By this time, the rule of law was faltering in parts of Ireland. The Irish correspondent of *The Times* described the League as 'a very distinct and potent government which is rapidly superseding the Imperial government... It rules with an iron hand and with a promptitude which enforces instant obedience.' Even more worrying for Forster – dealing with the problems from Dublin – and his Cabinet colleagues back in Westminster, was their lack of control over the situation. 'There is a Government *de facto*', the article continued, 'and a Government *de jure* – the former wielding a power which is felt and feared, the latter exhibiting the paraphernalia and pomp, but little of the reality of power.'[12]

The blow of the arrests had fallen so quickly in Ireland that the Land League executive was immediately confronted with the problem of how to contain and direct the people's anger and frustration. In addition, there were many problems within the League itself and complaints were arising of mismanagement. How to proceed in response to Gladstone's Land Act continued to be the critical decision. In the end, it was decided to issue a manifesto calling on all tenants to pay 'No Rent' until the government had restored the Irish people constitutional rights. Katie recorded that Parnell was 'really opposed to it', and Dillon 'openly so',[13] but the majority of those incarcerated at Kilmainham did approve of it. There was pressure from Patrick Ford in America and Patrick Egan in Paris who both supported a 'No Rent' campaign.[14] The manifesto was duly signed and published in *United Ireland* on 17 October.

It would almost certainly have been clear to Parnell that such a manifesto would never work. He had always tried to steer a middle course, and at this point his intentions were hard to decipher. But as a result of the manifesto the British government suppressed the Land League. Parnell's prediction that 'Captain Moonlight' would take his place had proved correct, and secret societies increased their activities in rural Ireland. Even before its suppression, the fast-growing League had evolved into a rather shaky structure. Now, with its leadership in jail, local factions and private feuds predominated. The Ladies' Land League tried to step into the breach, as intended, but found that their task mainly consisted of disbursing relief payments and court expenses to tenants fighting eviction notices.[15]

The suppression of the League made the situation worse. Arrests all over Ireland rose dramatically. The jubilation in England that had greeted Gladstone's announcement of Parnell's arrest was replaced by increased concern within Parliament and the Cabinet at the escalation of violence. Despite Forster's insistence on the importance of continued coercion, there were many doubters. The Prime Minister agreed with the coercion measures at first, but with considerable doubts, and it did not take long for him to regret the policy. Gladstone's son Herbert recorded in his diary on 23 March 1882:

talk with father about coercion. He agrees that our party won't stand the renewal of the present act. He told me what I had never heard, that he had all along been opposed to this kind of coercion by suspension of habeas corpus. He thought the action too big, wide and strong for it [coercion] to be successful. It is good versus secret societies but not against an open, organised, almost national conspiracy like the Land League. He would have altered the law in regard to inciting to break contracts and mischievous speeches and made these offences punishable by summary jurisdiction with severe sentences. I am sure he was right, but he declared that he was almost alone in his view in the cabinet.[16]

This sentiment was some way from the premier's original statement upon Parnell's arrest. Gladstone had declared then that he had been informed 'that towards the vindication of the law, of order, of the rights of property, and the freedom of the land, of the first elements of political life and civilisation, the first step has been taken in the arrest of the man who has made himself pre-eminent in the attempt to destroy the authority of the law'.[17] And, indeed, the public face of the League was an ugly one.

There was also a class differential that negatively influenced the governing elite. With the exception of Parnell, most of the League executive was of lower-class origin. Both the Treasurer, Patrick Egan, and Thomas Brennan, the Secretary, had started out as junior commercial clerks in Dublin. Thomas Sexton – one of the League's chief organizers – was the son of a policeman and had a first job as a railway clerk. John Barry, who organized support for the League in Britain, was the son of a Wexford coastguard. In Parliament, two of the League's strongest supporters were Joseph Biggar and John O'Connor-Power. Biggar was a grocer from Belfast and O'Connor-Power was probably the illegitimate son of a Royal Irish Constabulary man and was brought up in

Ballinasloe Workhouse. As noted previously, Davitt had worked in a Lancashire cotton mill as a boy, where he had lost his arm in an accident, while John Devoy, in America, was a 'labouring man'.[18] Their rhetoric was often brutal.

The 'No Rent' manifesto scandalized many in Ireland, including the Church. McCabe, Archbishop of Dublin, claimed that 'Parnell's whole course of action was calculated to create a spirit of discontent, and that the latent Fenianism of the country had been called into life by his action'. The Archbishop of Tuam, McEvilly, spoke of 'keeping "godless nobodies" in their proper place', and Moran of Ossory 'characterised the ringleaders as atheists, communists, socialists, Fenians and... "a clerk from Dublin" who was unheard of "till the present agitation"'.[19] Davitt himself admitted that the appeal of the Land League to the Irish peasant mind was that of self-interest and not of self-sacrifice. But the League had the support of thousands of ordinary Irish men and women and could not be ignored. The 'No Rent' manifesto appeal could thus be credibly endorsed by Parnell as a kind of safety valve for the more extreme elements of the movement, in the expectation that nothing substantive would come of it.

Parnell was thus relieved to be temporarily away from the cut and thrust of the tactical manoeuvrings of the League and nationalist parliamentarians. 'I am very comfortable here', he wrote to Katie the day following his arrest, 'and have a beautiful room facing the sun – the best in the prison.' He was accompanied by men he liked – 'three or four of the best of the men in adjoining rooms' – with whom he could 'associate all day long, so that time does not hang too heavy nor do I feel lonely'. 'My only fear is about my darling Queenie', he continued. He had been 'racked with torture all to-day, last night, and yesterday, lest the shock may have hurt you or our child'. He urged her to write 'as soon as you get this that you are well and will try not to be unhappy until you see your husband again'. He told Katie that she could wire him at

Kilmainham, and that he had her 'beautiful face with me here' and he kissed it 'every morning'.[20]

Katie, on the other hand, did not benefit from supportive company. She had to pretend that all was well, especially to her children, her aunt and her husband. There is little record of any contact with her own family and it is likely that she was much on her own. She was desperate for news of her lover. He had arranged for a visitor to take his letters to her out of the jail; the gentleman then readdressed them to a 'Mrs Carpenter' at an address in London, where Katie collected them. Sometimes, she explained, Parnell sent a formal letter to Eltham, 'enclosing one addressed to some political or other personage'. If her spouse were at Eltham, she wrote, she would 'show him this note asking me to post enclosure on a certain date'.[21] This pretence would lend credibility to the possibility that Willie was still wary and not a *mari complaisant* at this point in time. Communication between Katie and her lover was therefore complicated.

Formal letters could be sent out of Kilmainham, but only after being approved by the prison governor. Anything political or anything secret – personal letters to Katie, for example – had to be smuggled out of the prison. Then Katie, pregnant and unwell, had to make her way to London to the secret address to collect her messages. The method was uncertain and risky. Indeed, shortly thereafter, the prison governor became suspicious of Parnell's helpful visitor, and forbade interviews without the close proximity of two warders. At this, the leader 'refused to see him at all under these restrictions'.[22] Thus there must have been days when she travelled to London to find nothing there for her at all. On 17 October Parnell wrote to Katie that he had received her two letters, which reached him 'safely after having been duly perused by the Governor'. Her last letter – directed to Morrison's Hotel – had also reached him. 'If you have not done so already', he continued, 'please inquire in London about the messages you were expecting, and about any others that may arrive in future, and let me know in your next whether you have received them.'[23] This 'official' letter, addressed to 'My Dear Mrs. O'Shea', was clearly intended to reassure her, but at the same time could be seen by others, including the prison governor. To further allay any suspicions, political or private, Parnell noted in his message that he had also written to Captain O'Shea in Paris.

Two days later, the leader wrote a private letter, to 'My Own Darling Queenie', in which he told her that he had received her 'charming little letter of last Tuesday', which he had been 'anxiously expecting for the last week'. He was obviously extremely worried about her. Receiving her news had 'taken an enormous load' off his mind. He expressed hopes of seeing her at Kilmainham, although this seems to have been in response to her own desire to travel to Ireland to visit him. He told her that 'for the present you had better not come over'. In fact the idea was preposterous, but he let her down gently, explaining that there were 'five or six other men in rooms adjacent to mine who find out about everybody who visits me'. 'Besides,' he added, 'you would not be permitted to see me except in presence of two warders, and it might only make you more unhappy.'[24]

That she was deeply unhappy there can be no doubt. Parnell's letters to her from prison are full of encouragement and solicitude. He urged 'Dearest little Queenie'[25] to keep up her spirits. A few days later, on 21 October, the leader wrote to 'My Own Darling Wife', reassuring her that he slept 'exceedingly well'. He was allowed 'to read the newspapers in bed in the morning, and breakfast there also, if I wish'. His main anxiety was for her. She must not mind his being in the infirmary – 'I am only there because it is more comfortable than being in a cell, and you have longer hours of association.' The infirmary was actually a 'collection of rooms', he explained, and each man had a room to himself. He was much better there, he told her, and had to think of 'little maladies... to give Dr. Kenny an excuse for keeping me in the infirmary'.[26] Dr Joseph Kenny was a well-respected medical practitioner who had studied at the Catholic University Medical School and at the College of Physicians and Surgeons in Edinburgh. He was Medical Officer to the North Dublin Union and a member of the executive of the Land League. Kenny became a good friend of Parnell's and treated a number of Land Leaguers in different prisons, before his own imprisonment.[27] Parnell was therefore under sympathetic medical supervision, however limited, and he was perhaps being perfectly honest when he told Katie that, far from being ill, he had 'never felt better in my life'.

The difficulty was communication. 'A very strict watch is kept', he wrote, 'and I have been obliged to exert my ingenuity to get letters out to you and to get yours in return.' The political prisoners were in trouble because of the 'No Rent' manifesto and stricter watch was being kept – fresh warders had been brought in. There was no question of a visit, as 'for five days more I am not to be allowed to see any visitor'. He was at his most reassuring, and told her that he would write to her again about a visit. He also claimed that the prison was not secure, and that he could 'get out whenever I like, but it is probably the best policy to wait to be released'. And he once again expressed his deep concern for his 'own dear little Wifie', asking her to 'sleep well and look as beautiful when we meet again as the last time I pressed your sweet lips'.[28]

The next few letters were formal ones, addressed to Mrs O'Shea. He was 'anxiously waiting', Parnell wrote on 26 October, to hear that she had 'quite recovered from the indisposition you speak of'.[29] Two days later, he sent another 'official' letter. Not having heard from her that week, he wrote to express his hope that she was better, 'and that the absence of a letter from you is not to be attributed to any increase in the indisposition of which you spoke in your last'.[30] This of course was a useful way to let her know that he had not received any incoming mail from her. But on 1 November, Parnell wrote that he had received her letters and telegram. He wished to reassure her that he had been 'rather indisposed' but was much better. He desired to let her know this 'lest you and other friends should be troubled by exaggerated reports in the newspapers'. There were to be no visits, he explained, although 'things may be relaxed again after a time'.[31]

Eventually, they resorted to the use of invisible ink, which, Katie recorded, 'saved an infinity of trouble and anxiety, as we could now write between the lines of an ordinary or typewritten letter without detection'.[32] The Governor once again became suspicious, however, and the friendly warder who posted Parnell's letters was dismissed. He was able, though, to reorganize his communications, and on 2 November Parnell informed her that he had succeeded in so doing, and requested that she 'always acknowledge receipt of my letters by their date'.[33]

Meanwhile, the Land League was in disarray, and a skeleton network operated underground. The activists were desperate for direction, and hoping to receive word from the prisoners in the jail. The American economist Henry George had arrived in November as correspondent of the New York paper, *Irish World*. In his private letters to his editor, Patrick Ford, George said that 'the men in Kilmainham' were 'managing to keep in touch with people outside but communication was becoming "increasingly difficult"'.[34]

The winter of 1881–2 became one of the most violent in living memory. To a great extent the crimes appeared to be committed by members of secret societies and groups. When the Land League discipline broke down – with its executive imprisoned and largely out of touch – agrarian anarchy reigned. The loss of the leader was badly felt. The newspaper *United Ireland* published a view of the imprisonment of 'our chief, our guide' in tones of high drama. 'Let them wring their hearts;' the paper mourned on 15 October, 'let them manacle the body of our beloved chief. His spirit is abroad in a million Irish hearts. His work is done; his lesson taught. It has sunk into our souls.'[35] Yet there was some uncertainty felt by members of the Land League executive and others about Parnell's true feelings about encouraging the Irish farmers to refuse to pay rent. After all, he was himself a landlord. William O'Brien later told the story of how Parnell, when asked about the response of his own tenants in Wicklow, would 'humorously' reply, 'they are standing by the "No Rent" manifesto splendidly'.[36]

Despite the overall congeniality of his companions, Parnell in fact had little in common with them. The Ladies' Land League furnished the men's rooms with curtains, furniture and books. Parnell liked to read, preferring the newspapers, but he chafed at his confinement because of the separation from the woman he loved. As one of his biographers, F. S. L. Lyons, has pointed out, the leader was 'living simultaneously at two levels of existence'. 'On the surface, he was the adored chief of a small circle of intimates... privately, in that strange correspondence with Katharine, with all its cloak-and-dagger paraphernalia of invisible ink and misleading cover letters, he was manifestly turning away from a movement which had served its purpose.'[37]

Parnell's letters reflected his anxiety about Katie. 'My own little Wifie', he penned, 'I so wish I could be with you to comfort and take care of you, but will you not try to care for yourself, my darling, for my sake?'[38] The next again pleaded with 'My Dearest Queenie' to 'take care of yourself and your King's child'.[39] On 21 November, Parnell wrote that he was 'relieved to know that my darling is a little less miserable', yet he was 'still very much troubled and anxious' about her.[40] 'Has *he* left yet', enquired Parnell, adding that it was 'frightful' that she 'should be exposed to such daily torture'.[41]

Meanwhile, O'Shea had in the previous June (at the time of the threatened duel) written to Gladstone with a proposal on the amendment of the Land Bill to compensate landlords who reached agreements with tenants. If such agreement were reached, O'Shea claimed, then the Parnellites would let the Bill through. The Prime Minister's reply had not been particularly encouraging:

We feel indebted to you for the earnest and just desire you feel to promote a prompt settlement of the Land question in Ireland, and for the zeal with which you have undertaken a difficult operation, in that view. But we do not see our way to any form of action on the basis you propose without raising difficulties, which might prove to be greater than any of those we have at present to encounter.[42]

O'Shea was determined to act as an important agent in the political process around the Irish land agitation and tried to parley his developing relationship with Parnell into an increasingly prominent position for his own newfound career. He was also still travelling to Spain, and Parnell promised Katie that he would try to arrange a visit to Kilmainham for her while her husband was away. He was concerned about her low spirits and tried to explain that communication was difficult. His messenger was looking 'very frightened', he explained on 29 November, so 'perhaps it will be safest for Wifie not to write again for a few days, until I see further, or until I can manage another address'. He could manage, he wrote, 'to write my Queenie two or three times a week'.[43]

Parnell constantly reassured her about his health, insisting that the exercise and congenial company were in fact doing him good. The Land League had been paying for improved food to be provided to them at a cost that had been estimated at £400 a week (and possibly more).[44] The normal prison diet was quite repulsive, but the main reason for making the fuss was to provoke the government to action, and to relieve the League of this considerable expense. As an immediate response, Anna Parnell launched a special sustenation fund, which by Christmas had reached the sum of £9,000. This was enough, they calculated, to provide every suspect held in custody in all the prisons with one good meal per day for a period of seventeen weeks.[45] 'You must not be frightened', wrote Parnell to reassure Katie, 'if you see we have all gone on P.F. [Prison fare].' She need not worry, as it would 'not be so far as we are concerned here, and will only be for a week as regards the others, but Wifie must not tell anybody that I have not done so, as it would create discontent amongst the others'.[46] Although he was no doubt seeking to allay her anxiety – and in the absence of her letters it is nevertheless obvious that she made no secret of her fears and worries in her correspondence with him – he also frequently told her that he believed that he had in fact gained weight.[47] On 3 December the leader wrote to Katie that he was 'exceedingly well', and was not 'really on prison fare, as we can get anything we want here'.[48]

Communication between the two continued to present difficulties. 'You ought to have had a note by the 1st explaining about P. fare, and suggesting caution until another means of communication can be found,' Parnell wrote on 3 December.[49] And a few days later, on 6 December, he assured her that her 'dear letter of the 1st' had reached him 'quite safely', but it would be a 'risk for her to write again to the same place'. In any event, he added, he would send her in his next communication 'a prescription which will enable you to write ordinary letters with something added'.[50] The following day he wrote that he would send the 'secret ink of which the prescription of on the other side'. There is a real sense that the leader rather enjoyed all this scientific experimentation and intrigue. 'No. 1 is for writing,' he went on, 'No. 2 for bringing it out.' The instructions continued regarding how to address the envelope, and Parnell added that the 'secret handwriting should be with a clean quill pen, and should be written lightly'.[51]

Katie was not so entertained by all this. On 14 December, Parnell wrote that he had been able to read her second letter 'perfectly' but added 'you frighten me dreadfully when you tell me that I am "surely killing" you and our child'. He was so distressed at Katie's letters and situation that he added this most extraordinary paragraph: 'Rather than that my beautiful Wifie should run any risk I will resign my seat, leave politics, and go away somewhere with my own Queenie, as soon as she wishes; will she come? Let me know, darling, in your next about this, whether it is safe for you that I should be kept here any longer.'[52] The next day, he wrote: 'Nothing in the world' was 'worth the risk of any harm or injury' to 'His Own Darling Queenie'. He was desperate with worry. 'How could I ever live without my own Katie?' he exclaimed, 'and if you are in danger, my darling, I will go to you at once.' Parnell told her that her letter had frightened him 'more than I can tell you' and urged her to tell him that she was better. He had received no news from her for 'several days'.[53] By the next day, he had received encouraging word, and wrote that her letter had 'relieved me very much'. He once again urged her to take care of herself, adding that they had 'both to live for each other for many happy years together'.[54] And on 21 December Parnell was 'very well and delighted to hear that Queenie is safe'.[55]

It is difficult to ascertain the whereabouts of Willie O'Shea at this time. On 22 December, Parnell wrote to Katie that he was happy that she had been 'relieved from some of the intolerable annoyance for a time'.[56] This could have been a reference to Willie's living arrangements. If so, the remark indicates that Willie was still staying at Eltham periodically. Clearly, Katie chose to emphasize how disagreeable she found these visits. She also obviously required more reassurance from her lover, which he duly provided. 'My darling', he penned, 'you are and always will be everything to me, and every day you become more and more, if possible, more than everything to me.' He did not receive, he promised her – possibly in response to a jealous query – 'any letters from any ladies I know, except for one from Mrs. S., shortly after I came here'. And he was 'glad to say that none of my "young women" have written'. The following comment gives a good indication that Willie O'Shea was indeed present with his family at times, and also that the two of them took pains to continue the deception of her spouse. 'Let me know as soon as he goes', Parnell wrote to Katie on Christmas Eve, 'and I will write you home.'[57] The deception possibly extended to the timing of her pregnancy. Parnell wrote to her on 30 December, 'My Own Queenie', telling her that he was 'very nervous about the doctors', stressing that she 'should at all events tell one of them the right time, so that he may be on hand, otherwise you may not have one at all'. It is a distinct possibility that, in an attempt to deceive Willie, Katie should have misinformed him about the dates of her confinement, and therefore would also have lied to her doctors despite the possibility of serious repercussions. As her lover pointed out, 'It will never do to run this risk.'[58]

Indeed, Parnell wrote again on 3 January 1882, insisting that 'Queenie' must 'be sure to have at least one doctor in February'. It is important to note, however, that as an inveterate hypochondriac, he might simply have been expressing his concerns for her health. As he pointed out, 'It will never do to let it trust to chance.'[59] He did feel 'very anxious' about her, he wrote on 7 January. 'You must tell the doctor, and never mind about ——,' he added. He also wondered whether she might be able to leave for London or Brighton at the beginning of February. 'London would be best', he proposed, 'if you could get him away on any pretext; but if you could not, Brighton would leave you most free from him.' Parnell was obviously unhappy that O'Shea was still around. 'It is perfectly dreadful that Wifie should be so worried at night,' he exclaimed. 'I had hoped that the doctor's orders would have prevented that.'[60]

Evidence that Willie O'Shea was a deceived spouse during this period has been found in Parnell's letters expressing disgust at his colleague's presence at Eltham. 'I do trust you have been now relieved for a time by his departure', the leader wrote to Katie on 11 January, 'and that you are getting a little sleep.' It is possible, of course, that Katie complained of her husband's attentions in order to placate her lover. It is clear from the correspondence that Parnell considered himself to be her husband, and Willie the interloper. It is very difficult to know where Katie stood on this. Aside from her assertions, there is no evidence that Katie and Willie were estranged at this time. It was an awkward situation. Katie might well have wished to play it safe by not alienating her husband, in case her lover remained for an indefinite period in jail. She had no way of guessing the outcome at this time. Parnell's health was fragile, and he was committed to a risky political process, where he might be arrested and re-arrested at any moment. What is certain is that the leader was convinced that Katie shared his horror at Willie's presence, which, Parnell claimed, was 'enough to have killed you several times over, my own Queenie'.[61]

Katie's 'continued loneliness and weariness' made him very unhappy, Parnell wrote on 17 January.[62] A few days later, on 21 January, he told her that he thought it would be 'much too risky' for her to go to Brighton, as it would be too far from the doctor. He reassured her that he would 'find means to see my Wifie wherever she is'. He also thought he and his colleagues would be released 'shortly'.[63] It is obvious that Katie continued to complain and worry about him, as his next letter of 23 January spoke of how her letter had made him 'very nervous about my own love again'. He feared 'poor Queenie has had a dreadful time of it, and our poor little child also'.[64] In the absence of Katie's letters, it is difficult to know exactly what was going on between them, but one thing is clear: that Katie leaned on and relied upon her lover to raise her spirits and give her comfort. There is little sign of a 'stiff upper lip' on her part and it does appear that Parnell spent much of his time worrying about her and striving to reassure her. It is also clear, however, that he just found the whole situation a lot less difficult than she did. His letters, although comforting and kind, are also full of remarks that indicate a cheerful disposition and outlook. On the whole, he seemed to be suffering a lot less than his 'wifie'.

On 28 January, Parnell confided that he did 'not know what to say' about Katie going to Brighton, but that she would 'decide best for herself'. He hoped that she would not worry about not seeing him as soon as she had hoped. He was well, he reassured her, and 'in the best of spirits'.[65] Meanwhile, caution remained important. The leader suggested a few days later, on 31 January, that Katie be very careful about writing for a few days.[66] The invisible ink seemed, however, to be working well. Parnell wrote to Katharine on 2 February that the 'writing between the lines comes out perfectly, and you need at no time write more heavily'.[67] The next day he once again reassured her that his health was fine. 'You really must try and sleep properly at night', he admonished, 'and stop worrying yourself about me. I can assure my darling there is nothing to feel unhappy about so far as my health goes.'

Indeed, a common theme to emerge from the leader's letters to Katharine was how well he felt physically at Kilmainham. He took plenty of vigorous exercise and rest. 'I really cannot remember when I have ever felt so well in my life,' he told Katie.[68] He made frequent and specific reference to ball-playing in the courtyard, pointing out that 'strong exercise always agreed with me'.[69] So although it was 'very very hard not to be able to see each other', his main concern, as he expressed on 3 February, was for her, 'that my poor Wifie should not have her husband with her now'.[70] But Katie continued to suffer. On 14 February her 'Own Loving Husband' wrote to her 'very much troubled' about her having become 'so thin'.[71] He often reproached himself 'for having been so cruel to my own love in staying so long away from her'. He had not believed that the movement would last, he claimed, but 'this wretched Government' had by their ineptitude kept things going. Next month, he believed, 'when seeding time comes, will probably see the end of all things and our speedy release'.[72]

As Katie's due date approached, the difficulties in communication must have been increasingly hard to bear. 'I had written my Queenie a nice long letter which she should have liked very much,' Parnell penned on 17 February, 'but an alarm came before my messenger arrived that we were all going to be searched, and I was obliged to burn it.' And the problem was in both directions. 'Queenie had best not write me direct at any time,' he warned. But he was waiting 'very anxiously' to get word that she was well, and beseeched her to take care of herself, and 'not run any risk by remaining at E [Eltham]'.[73] When Katie finally managed to get word through to her lover, his relief was intense. 'Oh, my Wifie', he wrote on 17 February, 'when I had your two short messages of the 14th your poor husband burst into tears and could not hold his head or think of anything until my darling's note arrived that everything was right.'[74]

Katie's baby, a daughter, was born on 15 February 1882. For some time after the birth there was no communication between Katie and Parnell. He wrote an 'official' letter to her on 5 March. It had been so long since he had heard from her, he lamented, that he sometimes wondered whether she had 'quite forgotten' him. Written in a kind of code, the letter went on to say that he had been 'prevented from receiving or sending letters for a week'.[75] But his main concern was to see Katie and their daughter. 'I shall love her very much better than if it had been a son,' he wrote on 16 March. After asking what Katharine intended to call the baby, he asked her to give 'papa's best love and innumerable kisses'. He had been 'training up' the chairman of the Prisons Board, he told her, to allow him to see his sisters in private. He had that day been able to see his sister Emily, 'for the first time', and he had done so 'with the intention of passing Queenie off as another married sister after a time'. A visit would reassure her, he declared, as to how 'happy and comfortable' he was.

His constant preoccupation was to allay her anxieties. He did not know whether he would be moved or not, but wherever he went he would be 'probably very well off'. Parnell also told her that he would send her his weight the next day with a certificate from the chief warder 'so that you may believe it'. He was confident that once the tenant situation had settled, the imprisoned Land Leaguers would be set free. And he was expecting her to look after herself for his sake. 'I want Queenie when I see her to be an even younger little Wifie than when I gave her that last kiss.' The idea of nursing the child herself was, he said, 'too preposterous'. He urged her to think of herself and to take 'great, great care of your husband's own little Wifie'.[76]

Meanwhile, reports of the unrest throughout Ireland reached him. The number of agrarian outrages continued to rise. Gladstone's government was aware of the failure of the suspension of habeas corpus. The British administration had, however, reached an impasse with Parnell. It suited neither side to have him imprisoned. Crime rates in Ireland had risen after his arrest and continued to be a huge problem. But it was difficult to find a way forward. The Irish leader remained quite comfortably in Kilmainham, reading *The Times, Engineer, Engineering, Pall Mall Gazette* and *Universe,*[77] while ministers tried to find a means to break the deadlock.

Parnell was also increasingly eager for the situation to evolve. His time of incarceration had provided him with opportunity for quiet reflection and he claimed to Katie that he was unhappy about the course the Land League had followed. By 14 February 1882 when he was, arguably, becoming increasingly anxious to see Katie, he wrote of how he reproached himself at having caused such a long separation. Although this is the sort of thing one would expect him to say in the circumstances, what followed caused an uproar when Katie published his letter in 1914. 'At least, I am very glad that the days of platform speeches have gone by and are not likely to return,' he wrote. 'I cannot describe to you the disgust I always felt with those meetings, knowing as I did how hollow and wanting in solidity everything connected with the movement was.'[78]

Katie in a sketch by
her mother, Lady Wood.

Rivenhall, Essex. Katie's childhood home.

Avondale, County Wicklow, Ireland. The family home of Charles Stewart Parnell.

rs Anna Maria Wood,
tie's 'Aunt Ben'.

tie's mother, the novelist
d artist Lady Wood.

Captain William Henry O'Shea, a Cornet in the 18th Hussars, before his marriage to Katie.

CHAPTER TEN

Lies and Subterfuge

*P*ARNELL'S EAGERNESS TO BE released was heightened by reports that Katie was unwell after the birth of her daughter. She had indeed been 'very ill', she later recalled.[1] Parnell learned of her illness when Katie's sister Anna wrote to him, saying that she had seen Katie recently. At Anna's report that her sister had not yet left her room, the leader was uncertain how to respond to Katie's sibling. 'What am I to say to her?' he wrote to Katie on 23 March 1882.[2] It is entirely unclear just how much Katie confided in Anna. There was certainly some ambiguity in the relationship between the sisters. Katie later claimed to Harrison that Anna had been aware of her situation as early as July 1881. She apparently told him that her sister had even been involved in settling an arrangement between all the parties at the time of the proposed duel (July 1881).[3] This seems most unlikely, as the correspondence between Parnell and Katie whilst he was in jail indicates quite clearly that O'Shea was still being deceived by the pair and no arrangement had been made.

Parnell's comment would seemingly denote that he did not know how much Anna knew – which reinforces the idea that Anna was not an intermediary the previous July, and certainly was not in his confidence. Katie herself was obviously not prepared to clarify the situation. Parnell's letter of 29 March to her said that he agreed to follow Katie's subsequent suggestion of how to handle Anna. He would write back to her, to say how sorry he had been to hear that Katie had not yet left her room. He would claim to have 'seen the event in the *Times*', and would express his hope that Katie 'would soon be quite well again.'[4]

Parnell wrote in the same letter that he hoped Katie could make an arrangement for 'him' (i.e. Willie) to 'keep away'. 'It will be too intolerable', he continued, 'having him about always.' The leader evidently wished to regularize their illicit relationship in some way. When he saw her again, or was released, he could 'consider the situation', but until then she had 'best make some arrangement'.[5] He was absolutely without doubt in his own mind that he was her husband and she his wife in all but name. On 5 November 1881, shortly after his arrest, Parnell had requested that Katie put her 'proper initials upon the inner envelope of her next letter, thus K.P.'.[6] But although he maintained this stance with Katie, he knew that things needed to be sorted out with Willie. 'I wrote yesterday to say that I think you had best make some arrangement about him pending my release,' he reminded Katie on 30 March, 'and when that takes place we can consider further.'[7]

In the meantime the relationship had still to be kept secret. Parnell wrote on 30 March, asking Katie for a lock of 'our daughter's hair'. Katie had decided upon Claude as a name and Parnell asked whether Sophie might make a 'nice second name'. It was the name of one of his sisters – whom he was said to be 'most like of the family', but, he worried, it might 'make suspicions'.[8] A week later Parnell asked Katie to give his 'best love and ever so many kisses to our little daughter'. He was, however, 'troubled about her health, and hope it will not make her permanently delicate'.[9]

This was the first warning about the baby's well-being. Two days later, on 7 April, Parnell wrote, saying, 'part of what you say about our daughter makes me very anxious indeed'. He hoped 'the poor little thing' would 'soon get over it'. He did not seem overly worried, though, and thanked Katie for the hair, which was 'absolutely lovely'. Parnell was 'so glad it is more like Queenie's than mine'. Although 'less beautiful than Wifie's', there was, he declared, a 'golden tint in it which is quite exceptional'. As ever, the leader's main concern was for Katie. He hoped his 'precious one' was 'getting strong again' and would have 'some good news to tell me of our little daughter when she writes next'.[10]

Claude did not thrive, however, and Katie wrote of how she 'faded from me'. The doctors were called in, as the baby's health worsened. Willie had 'no suspicion' of the child's paternity, she wrote, and only stipulated that the infant be baptized. Further evidence of Parnell and Katie's determination to preserve their secret was provided by Katie's declaration that she and her lover 'had long before agreed that it would be safer to have the child christened as a Catholic'.[11] Thus Claude Sophie (sometimes referred to as Sophie Claude), the offspring of two Protestant parents – if indeed she was Parnell's child – was baptized by a local Catholic priest, Father Hart. This seems to have caused Parnell no discomfort at all, but it is unlikely that Katie, the daughter of a clergyman, was entirely at ease with the charade. 'I made an altar of flowers in my drawing-room', she wrote.[12] Willie seemingly believed that Claude Sophie was his daughter and to refuse the baptism would have been impossible. Certainly, for O'Shea to have been so convinced of paternity means that he and Katie had been having sexual relations. Thus, all Katie's decisions had to be based on her deception.

In Ireland, Parnell hoped that the impasse between him and the British government was reaching an end. He wrote to Katie that 'D' [John Dillon] was going to go abroad,[13] and that he was trying to get O. K [O'Kelly] out of prison. O'Kelly was sick and, after securing his release, the leader hoped that he might be allowed to visit his mother, whose health was faltering.[14] It is interesting to note that however desperate Parnell may have been to see Katie, he made no great play of stating his desire to get his colleague and friend O'Kelly 'out first'.[15]

Releasing any of the prisoners posed a dilemma for Gladstone. Many members of the government and the Houses of Parliament believed that firm measures were required to deal with the Irish prisoners. Queen Victoria was particularly in favour of repressive action.[16] Since 1868, when the worst of the Fenian threats had subsided,[17] the monarch had deepened her dislike and distrust of the Irish. Although the Fenian campaigns in Canada, Ireland and England from 1865 to 1868 appear in retrospect to have been badly organized, this is not how they were perceived at the time. After Davitt's arrest in February 1881, Victoria was so preoccupied with Ireland that special arrangements were made to provide her with all Fenian material passing through the Foreign and Home Offices. On 1 March 1882 a shot was fired at her when she left Windsor railway station and, although the Prime Minister wrote to her of his shock, she did not believe that Gladstone was sufficiently firm. Reports of disturbances during the Land War had angered her, and she was furious at efforts made by the Irish MPs to block the Coercion Bill in Parliament. In an exchange with Lord Hartington (then Secretary of State for India), she wrote that she trusted 'that means will be found to prevent these dreadful Irish people from succeeding in their attempts to delay the passing of the important Measures of Coercion'.[18]

The Queen's relations with Gladstone were problematic and those with Parnell non-existent.[19] But the Irish leader had claimed while on a speaking tour in America in 1880 that the British sovereign had contributed 'nothing' to the famine relief efforts in the 1840s,[20] and, as 'Uncrowned King' of Ireland, he was increasingly viewed there as an alternative to an uncaring Victoria, thus widening the gulf between the monarch and her Irish subjects. The Queen was especially disenchanted after the assassination of Tsar Alexander II in March 1881, when American

Fenians had responded by making threats against the Prince and Princess of Wales. Unsurprisingly, the monarch refused a request by Lord Cowper to arrange a visit to Ireland by the Duke and Duchess of Connaught during a lull in agrarian upheaval in spring 1881.[21]

It was therefore difficult to argue for leniency and constructive debate. A convenient opportunity occurred, however, when Parnell's nephew – son of his sister Delia – died suddenly in Paris. Henry Thomson, aged twenty, had lived alone, spending his time composing music. His death had come unexpectedly after a high fever. Delia was devastated, and her brother applied to Forster for permission to attend the funeral in France. The decision to allow him parole indicated the government's willingness to break the deadlock. It was not a straightforward process. The Queen, for example, was among those who, despite her well-known firm family feeling, strongly objected to the decision to allow Parnell temporary freedom.[22]

For the Irish leader it was an opportunity to see Katie, and he left Kilmainham at 6 a.m. on 10 April, arriving that afternoon at Willesden Junction in London. There he was met, as arranged, by his colleagues Justin McCarthy (Deputy Leader of the Party), and Frank Hugh O'Donnell.[23] O'Donnell was an arrogant and clever Home Rule MP and journalist (known as 'Crank' Hugh by many of his colleagues), who had never supported Parnell's leadership. He once famously referred to Parnell as 'my wayward errant boy'.[24] O'Donnell was, however, a very important figure at this time in the Party. Also present for this meeting were P. J. Quinn (former Acting Secretary of the Land League in Ireland and already released from Kilmainham) and Frank Byrne (Secretary of the Land League in Britain).[25] The terms of Parnell's parole precluded him from engaging in open political activity. A meeting with these men was clearly in breach of that order. Parnell retired to McCarthy's house in Jermyn Street to discuss the failure of the 'No Rent' manifesto. When the leader was later asked whether he had spent the night in London, he replied in the affirmative. When questioned as to where, he had been evasive, saying that he had been with friends. When specifically asked whether it had been at the home of Justin McCarthy, Parnell said, 'No, it was not.'[26]

He was not at that time pressed to say where, nor did he volunteer the information. He had almost certainly gone straight to Eltham. 'I put his dying child into his arms,' wrote Katie.[27] The following day he had to travel, as was expected, to Paris. Before leaving the country, Parnell met with O'Shea. Years later, Parnell explained at a Special Commission that he had visited the Captain at his London flat. O'Shea was, he later explained, ill with an attack of gout, and had been unable to meet the Irish leader at Eltham.

Willie O'Shea now took it upon himself to act as intermediary between Parnell and the British government. He wrote to Gladstone on 8 April, to remind him of the proposal he had sent him the previous summer. This proposal had concerned the scheme whereby landlords might be compensated by the Exchequer in return for reducing their rents. In return for acceptance of this proposition, Parnell was prepared, the letter had stated, to cease opposition to the Land Bill then before the House. O'Shea was attempting in this next approach to revive terms of similar cooperation. His letter began by reminding Gladstone that the previous year 'all that was needed could have been done on a mere matter of detail. To save the situation now, great audacity would be required, but great audacity has often proved to be great statesmanship.'[28]

O'Shea and Parnell met one another on the evening of 11 April 1882. The Irish leader had spent the previous night with Katie at Eltham, and probably most of the following day. Biographers have made much of the pathos of Parnell and Katie spending this time together with the dying Claude. Katie herself said very little about it, but her book nevertheless conveys the impression that she was living in an isolated universe during this time. What must be remembered is that her other children were no doubt present, as were the household servants. Perhaps arrangements had been made to take the children away, but it is difficult to imagine where. Katie does not seem at this time to have been close to the rest of her family and Willie did not have them at his flat in Albert Mansions in London. It is most unlikely that Aunt Ben, who did not warm particularly to children, would have welcomed them to her home.

So, far from being alone to nurse and mourn the baby, Katie and her lover were probably in the midst of a busy household where life went on despite the baby's illness. That such illnesses were hardly uncommon needs also to be taken into account.[29] Although the event was no doubt tragic for the Irish leader, who believed that Claude was his only child (if the tale about Lizzie the barmaid were indeed untrue, that is), it was unlikely to have brought ordinary life at Wonersh Lodge to a standstill. Parnell could not, in any event, linger. His parole leave had been granted for the specific purpose of seeing his sister in Paris. And his mind was definitely on political matters. He met with Willie to discuss progress. Although O'Shea's letter to the Prime Minister had been written without the Irish leader's knowledge, Willie had opened a dialogue that Parnell was happy to develop. On 11 April, the Prime Minister wrote back to O'Shea. 'I do not see any mode of proceeding upon the lines which you have drawn', he replied, 'but the finance of the Irish Land Act must be dealt with during the present year and I hope that the plan will be such as to suit itself to whatever may be the scale of any possible operation.'[30] O'Shea refused to be discouraged. The important thing, he believed, was not the financial detail, but the principle of trading off some concession on the government's part in exchange for a commitment from Parnell to refuse to encourage violent acts in Ireland.

In this, the Captain was – possibly for the first time in his political career – on to something important. Both parties needed a way out. The British administration was deeply concerned at the escalation of agrarian violence in Ireland and the policy of coercion was not helping. Parnell wanted to be out of prison. The conditions at Kilmainham were not ones of extreme hardship, but neither were they overly pleasant. He and his colleagues were often ill. O'Shea could assure the Prime Minister, he wrote on 13 April, that he was in Parnell's confidence. 'The person to whom Mr Parnell addresses himself in many cases (much as I differ from him in serious matters of politics and policy)', the Captain wrote, 'is myself.' Willie was keen to position himself as an important mediator. He wrote that the Irish leader 'considers, I believe, that I am not without insight into Irish affairs, necessities and possibilities and he knows that no member of Parliament has nearly so much influence with the clergy of the country which that member represents, as I have attained.' He proposed that there was a possibility of some sort of cooperation. He then went on to make the extraordinary assertion that the leader had some eighteen months ago 'used every effort to induce me to take over the leadership of the party'. This was, however, only known to a very few individuals besides themselves.[31]

The reasons behind this assertion are unclear. Certainly, O'Shea wished to portray that he was an important person, and also that he had a special relationship with Parnell. The leader was spending time at Eltham. He travelled there on 10 April and again after his return from Paris on 21 April. In fact, O'Shea wrote to Gladstone that the Irish leader had spent the previous Tuesday 'partly at my house in Eltham and partly here'.[32] The fact that O'Shea knew and apparently encouraged these visits could indicate that he had come to accept the relationship between the leader and Katie. It is difficult to understand, however, why the couple had to take such pains to keep the affair a secret if this was the case. The Kilmainham correspondence convincingly shows that O'Shea himself was regularly present at Eltham. He either did not know what was going on, or he was completely aware, and his complicity extended to having Claude baptized in his own faith and making the birth announcement in *The Times*.

There was of course the spectre of Aunt Ben's goodwill. It has been estimated that at this time Willie O'Shea was personally receiving an income of £600 per annum from his wife's relative. There were in addition extra payments, by Katie's favour.[33] And underpinning the whole unsavoury edifice was the prospect of a large inheritance. Aunt Ben was at this time eighty-nine years old and there was presumably not long to wait.

Meanwhile, there was also political (and presumably personal) advantage to be gained. Parnell was now corresponding with both O'Sheas. He wrote to Katie on 13 April 1882 from the Grand Hotel in Paris. This was a 'private' letter, addressed to 'My Own Queenie'. There was a fever in Paris, he told her, which the doctor claimed was not infectious. He was 'obliged to go to the house, which has been well disinfected, to see my sister, who is very much cut up'. Parnell reassured Katie that the risk to him was minimal, as he had already had this fever 'very badly' when he was young, 'and they say people very rarely have it a second time, and then only slightly'. It was, he said, 'the ordinary typhoid, which doctors say is not catching'. He made no mention or enquiry about baby Claude, and merely told her that he would take a Turkish bath every day 'and adopt other precautions'.[34]

There was then an 'official' letter sent to her on 15 April, which informed Katie that Parnell did not plan on travelling for a couple of days, because he had caught a 'slight cold'. He was 'very glad' to have made the trip, as his sister was 'in a very low state', and his coming over had 'picked her up very much'. Once again there was no mention of the baby.[35] The following day, on 16 April, the leader wrote to tell her that due to the doctor's insistence, he would not travel as planned on the Monday but rather on Tuesday. He had dined with his sister, who was 'much better'. His own cold was, he reported, 'quite gone' and he believed that he had caught it 'from leaving off a flannel jacket which I used to wear when asleep in prison'. He had averted a 'bad chest cold', however, by taking two Turkish baths 'immediately I felt it coming on'. There was no reference to Claude in this letter, although he did tell Katie that he was staying in Paris under the name of Stewart and had 'not been found out yet'.[36] It is possible that Parnell was trying to make his way back to England without the knowledge of his colleagues or Willie O'Shea. In the two of his 'official' letters to Katie from Paris, he made vague references to travelling for a few days 'in the south or elsewhere' or commencing a journey 'to the country'.[37] This could have been coded reference to an attempt to see her secretly.

O'Shea had been busy in Parnell's absence. Gladstone had responded on 15 April to his letter of two days earlier. It was typical of the Prime Minister's magisterial way with words. He was positive, without communicating very much or committing to anything:

Dear Sir,

I have received your letter of the 13th, and I will communicate with Mr. Forster on the important and varied matter which it contains… I am very sensible of the spirit in which you write; but I think you assume the existence of a spirit on my part with which you can sympathise. Whether there be any agreement as to the means, the end in view is of vast moment, and assuredly no resentment, personal prejudice, or false shame, or other impediment extraneous to the matter itself, will prevent the Government from treading in that path which may most safely lead to the pacification of Ireland.[38]

O'Shea was actually encouraged by this missive, and he was determined to gain credibility through his allegedly close relationship with Parnell. He decided to cultivate the President of the Board of Trade, Joseph Chamberlain. O'Shea wrote to Chamberlain on 15 April, explaining that he did so 'as you appear to be a minister without political pedantry'. He enclosed a copy of the letter of 13 April that he had sent to the Prime Minister, and indicated to Chamberlain that an attempt made by the Liberal leaders 'might be met by the most influential Irishman of the day in a candid and moderate spirit'.[39]

By now, O'Shea had already developed a reputation as a somewhat *louche* and rather untrustworthy politician. His friends included other MPs who cared less for sound politics and more for manoeuvring. There were always a few men for whom Ireland represented ways to goad the government, or to gain some kind of tactical political advantage. The Tory MP Lord Randolph Churchill,[40] for example, was friendly with O'Shea at this time and exemplified the kind of 'light-hearted approach to political consistency' that O'Shea found sympathetic.[41]

However, Chamberlain was receptive to O'Shea's advances. He replied warmly, although sounding a note of caution. He agreed that the government had a responsibility to consult representative Irish opinion, but pointed out that 'the leaders of the Irish party must pay some attention to public opinion in England and Scotland'. It was as important to educate the public as to try to move the statesmen. Hitherto, Irish members had acted 'as if their object were to disgust, embitter and prejudice all English opinion'. 'The result', he added, 'is that nothing would be easier than to get up in every large town an anti-Irish agitation almost as formidable as the anti-Jewish agitation in Russia.' This could help no one, he wrote, and he should 'rejoice whenever the time comes that a more conciliatory spirit is manifested on both sides'.[42] The President of the Board of Trade had never been an enthusiastic supporter of coercion without reform of unjust laws.[43]

O'Shea was quick to respond to Chamberlain's encouraging reply. On 18 April he replied to the minister, telling him that he was in 'complete accord' with Chamberlain 'as to the duties of Irish representatives and the misfortune of the courses adopted by some of them'. Although he understood the 'reticences', O'Shea believed that 'what the French call the psychological moment ought not to be lost'. He had heard from Mr Parnell that morning. 'He says in confidence', O'Shea continued, 'that he hopes "something may come out of the correspondence and certainly the prospect looks favourable".' Evidently there was genuinely contact between Parnell and O'Shea. It is difficult to know just how much faith the Irish leader was putting into these negotiations, but he seemed amenable enough. After requesting permission to show Chamberlain's letter to his colleague, O'Shea wrote that Parnell 'will be with me at the end of the week'.[44]

Katie confirmed in her account that Parnell had indeed telegraphed Willie to let him know when he was returning to England. Her comment was that the leader 'wished to conciliate Willie as much as possible, and believed that his politics might now prove useful'. The conciliation must have been effective, as on the evening of 21 April the three of them gathered at Eltham. The two men were in deep discussion of how to break the deadlock between the Land League and the British government. Willie wanted her to join them, penned Katie, as if this were not an extraordinary scenario. She, however, 'would not leave my baby' so her husband and her lover worked out the terms of what would eventually become 'The Kilmainham Treaty'.[45]

In fact, Parnell had returned to Eltham a few days before Willie came down from London to join him. This means that either O'Shea did not know where the leader was, or he did know, and was not worried. In this case, his lack of anxiety would stem from either a total lack of suspicion, or complete connivance. Certainly, the Irish leader was always in the habit of keeping those around him in the dark about his movements. 'Mr Parnell is lost!' wrote the daughter of Chief Secretary Forster[46] on 13 April in Dublin. 'Not only was he too late for his nephew's funeral, but he has never arrived in Paris at all.' Florence Forster continued in her diary:

All his most faithful friends are waiting for him in vain. It is even said that in Paris nothing was known about the nephew's death and funeral, and that Mr Parnell's sister is at Nice, not Paris. Father suggests that he may have gone to her there – or it is possible that he may be all this time in seclusion in London, as he was once before when he was supposed to be in Paris. Anyhow, the papers are in a considerable flutter, and Mr Parnell's friends a good deal perplexed by this disappearance of their hero.

By the end of the day, however, Florence had noted, 'Mr Parnell has arrived in Paris and is staying with his sister.'[47] On 21 April, Florence, now in London, asked her father 'if anything was known of Mr Parnell'. Forster told her that it was secret, but Parnell was at that time in London, staying with Captain O'Shea, 'who communicated the fact to Mr Chamberlain'. When she asked whether Parnell had broken his word, the Chief Secretary explained, 'Well, not exactly.' Florence wrote:

What he is doing is not according to the arrangement he made with the Chief Secretary, which allowed a week or such time longer as might be necessary for him to attend his nephew's funeral. But it appears that Captain Barlow [at Kilmainham Gaol], rather overstepping his powers, asked him when he was leaving Kilmainham, 'how long do you want, a week or ten days or a fortnight?' to which Mr Parnell replied, ten days. He seems, however, to think that the offer of a fortnight having been made him, he is at liberty to take it if he wishes to do, provided he does not break the other conditions of his parole – not to take part in political matters.[48]

The Chief Secretary evidently believed that O'Shea was the key link to the Irish leader. He told his daughter that O'Shea had 'said something about Mr Parnell not being well' and that as a result he had intimated that should Parnell ask for a further leave of absence, he would grant it on health grounds. Parnell had declined, Florence reported, 'saying that if he stayed away longer he would lose his influence in Ireland, in which Father thinks he is right'. 'Meanwhile', she added, 'his "indisposition" does not seem to be anything serious.'[49] Forster had considerable pressures on him at this time. There were many in the House of Commons – and indeed the Cabinet – who felt that the Coercion policy in Ireland was a failure. Increasingly, there were those who directly blamed the Chief Secretary for this. The *Pall Mall Gazette* conducted an increasingly vituperative campaign against the Chief Secretary and in early April 1882 began to clamour for his resignation. And in Ireland, where newspapers each day carried stories of atrocities committed by all sides, 'Buckshot' Forster was reviled.[50]

The Prime Minister's lack of a completely dismissive response to O'Shea's overtures signified an opportunity to resolve the impasse. Parnell then chose to involve his second-in-command, Justin McCarthy, in the process. He wrote to him from Eltham on 22 April. In reproducing this letter, Katie did not remark on the fact that the leader wrote it after baby Claude had just died that night. Instead, she suggested that Parnell had left her just after the baby's death, and before departing had stolen in 'to kiss us both and say good-bye'.[51] In fact, the leader remained at Eltham for a few more days and did not return to Kilmainham until the evening of 24 April. There is no means of knowing the effect of the baby's death on Parnell, although from his letters it is clear that he believed that he was the father. He could not, of course, tell anyone. In his letter of 22 April, he simply asked McCarthy if he could meet him in London the following day and trusted that his colleague would 'have some news of result of Cabinet today'.[52]

Parnell wrote again to McCarthy after returning to prison. On 25 April, he sent him the draft treaty, which he proposed should be shown to Chamberlain. What is interesting about this communication is that O'Shea seems to have been completely circumvented in the negotiating process. Parnell wrote to Katie, also on 25 April, enclosing a letter he had received from the Captain. 'What', he asked her, 'do you think I had best say to it?'[53] He had told 'his friend' (meaning McCarthy) of the steps to take, so the process could, in Parnell's view, go on without O'Shea's participation.

And, indeed, O'Shea was not the only candidate for go-between during this delicate political process. There was plenty of opportunity for advancement in seeking to negotiate a settlement. Parnell and the Kilmainham prisoners had become national heroes. Gifts had continuously arrived for the leader whilst he was incarcerated. He received food, flowers and poetry as well as a music box that played 'The Wearing of the Green' and other rebel songs. Ballads were written and these were sung on street corners. One of the finest of the genre was 'The Blackbird of Avondale or the Arrest of Parnell':

The fowler way-laid him in hopes to ensnare him.
While I here in sorrow his absence bewail,
It grieves me to hear that the walls of Kilmainham
Surround the dear Blackbird of sweet Avondale.[54]

Frank Hugh O'Donnell also attempted to break the deadlock. O'Donnell was always quick to disparage the rank-and-file Irish Party members and he believed that he deserved to play a more important role in the party. He made contact with the Prime Minister's son, Herbert Gladstone (they did not in fact meet until 12 April), who noted the position presented to him by the Irishman:

The sum of what he said was this: The Land Act was succeeding. If amended in the way of arrears of rent it would prove a signal success. Crime was shocking to Parnell.

The Land League wished to withdraw the No Rent Manifesto. It was feared that unless the natural leaders of the people were released the whole country would get out of hand. Parnell and his colleagues were no longer irreconcilable. They would be content with a fair grant of Home Rule. If released, Parnell's influence would be a moderating one. The inference was that the League would fall in with the Land Act and come to terms with the Government.[55]

O'Donnell's motivations may have been self-serving, but the message he communicated to Herbert Gladstone did indeed broadly reflect Parnell's strategy. The leader wanted the Irish Parliamentary Party to be recognized as the elected representatives they undoubtedly were, and 'removed from a language of English political excoriation that tarred them all as murderous ruffians'.[56] This demand was not unacceptable to the Prime Minister, who realized that the coercion measures were failing, and preferred to have Parnell working against agitation and extremism. The difficulty now was reconciling the views of conservatives who shared Forster's more coercive outlook.

Forster's daughter recorded the Chief Secretary's increasing frustration with the softening of the hard line against the Irish prisoners. He was also dissatisfied with Cowper as Lord-Lieutenant, and had been hoping for a new appointment of someone more capable of sharing the burden. It was not only the Tories who disagreed with many of Gladstone's policies for Ireland. Within the Liberal Party itself there was a basic unwillingness to credit the Parnellites with any political *gravitas*. And of course the Land League rhetoric (and its concomitant encouragement to violence in many instances) did not help the Irish parliamentarian cause. It was in any event extremely difficult for many British politicians to accept that Parnellism was becoming a representative and therefore a perhaps legitimate (democratic) channel for Irish nationalist aspirations.

Gladstone wished, nonetheless, to generally reconsider the Liberal position vis-à-vis the Parnellites. One reason for this was because the Catholic Church hierarchy in Ireland had become less opposed to Parnell's politics and leadership. By the spring of 1882, it was becoming accepted that Parnell genuinely represented the views and aspirations of the majority of Catholics in Ireland. However, it is important to note that even though the Irish leader claimed to have a wider mandate for all of Ireland, Gladstone never accepted that Parnell represented either Ulster or southern Protestants.[57]

Katie professed to be pleased at this new direction in Anglo-Irish affairs. There was a benefit to her husband Willie, who could carve out an important role in the political developments. There was also a real opportunity for her lover to leave prison. 'I had never before ventured to influence Parnell in any way politically', she wrote, 'but now I greatly dreaded for him this latter policy of the extremists and the perpetual strain of watchfulness and control it engendered.'[58] She was determined to encourage him to find a way to leave jail. Aside from her own strong desire to have him near her, she was also worried about his health.

Parnell's sister Emily, although notoriously unreliable in other elements of her published recollections,[59] was convincingly adamant that her brother was suffering physically while incarcerated. She had been relieved to find that Parnell was 'in the best room which the prison afforded'. He had an armchair, 'by a bright, glowing fire'. On her first visit to Kilmainham, she had found Parnell sitting in the chair by the fire, absorbed in a book. But, despite the comforts, she noted that he looked 'paler and thinner'. Emily was happy to learn that like the other 'Suspects', her brother was eating and drinking what he liked – as long as it was paid for. She was also pleased to know that he and his companions played football and were able to 'indulge in any other recreation they preferred, and as much as they chose, in an enormous, well-ventilated hall, which had a balcony all round, and resembled an opera-house, minus the seats'. But in spite of these amenities, Emily noted that over the course of her brother's incarceration – during which she visited him regularly – his health deteriorated. 'I could not fail to perceive', she wrote, 'the change for the worse in his appearance, which each time was more and more apparent.'[60] Despite the freedom to congregate enjoyed by Charles and his colleagues, and the decent food, she believed that the six months her brother spent in jail was 'the most trying time he had passed'. Emily was entirely convinced that those months had shaken his constitution and undermined his health to such an extent that Charles Parnell 'never recovered the injurious effects of his imprisonment, but was ever after extremely delicate and subject to divers ailments and illnesses'.[61] This viewpoint coincided with that expressed later by Katie and was observed by many of Parnell's colleagues as well.

It was therefore very much in Parnell's best interest to be released, and, increasingly, that of the British government as well. The strategy of imprisoning the parliamentarians was not working and it was becoming clear that the Irish parliamentarians were seeking to control the violence, not encourage it. Naturally, it was politically undesirable to have the Irish Party members free to align with violent agitators, but the random violence – murders, maiming and killing of animals and the wanton destruction of property – was unacceptable. The rule of law in Ireland was being undermined and attempts at discipline were too often poorly implemented in a high-handed manner.

The Chief Secretary was unwilling to change the tactics unless the MPs concerned provided guarantees of future good behaviour before being released. This they were, unsurprisingly, not willing to do. The deadlock was broken, however, by the intervention of other parties who were less entrenched in their positions. Chamberlain had responded to O'Shea's approach by writing to the Prime Minister to share his view that 'an opportunity had occurred for a conciliatory policy'.[62] John Redmond had introduced a bill designed to extend the benefits of the 1881 Land Act to tenants whose rent was in arrears, as well as to those tenants whose leases dated from before 1870.[63] It was hoped that this movement from the Irish side might lead to further negotiations. Chamberlain and others believed that the proposal was a potentially positive sign of an Irish willingness to resolve the crisis. Gladstone replied on 19 April that he would forward Chamberlain's letter to Forster. Chamberlain subsequently met with the Chief Secretary, who authorized him to tell O'Shea that Parnell's leave might be extended.

O'Shea replied to this offer in a letter from Eltham written on 21 April. He explained that the Irish leader could not ask for an extension of his parole. The following day Chamberlain recorded that the Cabinet discussed the letters and the Irish proposals for the amendment of the Land Act. He offered once more to act on his 'own responsibility' with O'Shea and other Irish members 'to ascertain their views but distinctly without authority to negotiate or to do more than receive any information they might tender'.[64] This was the next step in what became the 'Kilmainham Treaty' brokered by Chamberlain with O'Shea and other parties. O'Shea clearly wished to make maximum use of this opportunity of first-hand negotiations with a member of the government. It is considered by many historians that it was particularly unfortunate that such a delicate task was entrusted to Captain O'Shea.

The complexity of the negotiation was obvious. On the one hand Chief Secretary Forster, while not entirely opposed to the idea of release, was becoming increasingly removed from the new direction embarked on by Gladstone and the rest of the Cabinet. His concern became focused on obtaining a requirement from Parnell for commitments and guarantees that his colleagues were reluctant to impose. The distance between their positions would soon lead to Forster's resignation. On Parnell's side there was also reason for hesitation and careful deliberation. Although he was undeniably anxious to rejoin Katie, he was too canny a politician to take reckless action. He knew that he needed to avoid a capitulation that would serve only to alienate his own nationalist support. There was also a real risk of leaving his followers and colleagues feeling betrayed if he seemed to negotiate his own release from prison.

These considerations required deft handling. That Willie O'Shea was quite unsuited for such manoeuvring can be observed from the later repercussions of his side of the negotiations. He sent Chamberlain a letter on 24 April in which he included a phrase that subsequently caused huge problems for the Irish leader:

'Mr Parnell is prepared in case of such an arrangement of the question of arrears to use his best exertions to stop outrages, the circulation or support of no-rent manifestoes, and intimidation generally.'[65] This was bad enough, but O'Shea also included a second letter in which he expounded further: 'If the country should not settle down as clearly and quickly as Mr Parnell is confident would be the case, I have reason to believe that he would *ipso facto* be brought to see the necessity of not offering an embittered opposition to the passage of temporary provisions aimed at individuals and localities tainted with crime.'[66]

O'Shea was obviously not in a position to make this claim. Although he had played a useful role in breaking the deadlock, Parnell was not relying on him to pursue developments. The leader had already met with his deputy, Justin McCarthy, before returning to jail. On 25 April, he sent his second-in-command a 'letter embodying our conversation' which he wished him to show, if 'desirable', to Chamberlain.[67] The enclosure, Katie recorded, was 'identical with the draft treaty – apart from a few verbal alterations'.[68] Parnell had determined to bypass Katie's husband. On 25 April – the same day as O'Shea was in communication with Chamberlain – he wrote to Katie enclosing a letter from Willie to him. He had already taken steps with McCarthy, he explained, 'so that the matter referred to in enclosed will probably go on all right without, or with, the further participation of the writer'.

It seems Parnell was intent on avoiding O'Shea altogether. 'I thought of writing him that I had received his note too late to reply for Wednesday', he continued, 'but that in any case my letter from Paris ought to be sufficient indication of confidence.'[69] In a letter pre-dated to 28 April he confirmed to O'Shea his decision to use McCarthy in the negotiations. He carefully phrased his position:

The accomplishment of the programme I have sketched would, in my judgement, be regarded by the country as a practical settlement of the land question, and would, I feel sure, enable us to co-operate cordially for the future with the Liberal Party in forwarding Liberal principles; so that the Government, at the end of the session, would, from the state of the country, feel themselves thoroughly justified in dispensing with further coercive measures.[70]

Nevertheless, Parnell was trying to give O'Shea the appearance of working with him. The Captain had travelled to Kilmainham on 29 April to see Parnell. The Irish leader explained to Katie that he had thought it best to give Willie this letter, 'as he would have been dreadfully mortified if he had had nothing to show'. Everything was going well, he reassured her, and he had received 'two letters from my own lovie yesterday'.[71]

That Parnell was so concerned at keeping O'Shea pacified would strongly indicate that the Captain had the upper hand in some way. He was either a victim of deception, or was exacting a heavy price for his cooperation. In any event, Katie was now desperate to get her lover back. She 'threw the whole strength' of her influence upon Parnell, 'and urged upon him the greater good for Ireland likely to accrue in the making by him of immediate peace'. Her 'great fear for him won his decision for peace', she recalled, 'and he wrote and signed the "letter" that Willie wanted to take to the Government.'[72]

CHAPTER ELEVEN

Two Husbands

HE TRICKY PROBLEM OF disguising Claude Sophie's paternity disappeared when the infant died. On 25 April 1882 Parnell wrote of his regret that he could not be with 'my Queenie' on the day the baby was buried. He had been thinking 'all day' of how 'desolate and lonely' Katie must have been. He wished that he might have been able to stay and comfort her, but hoped that their separation was soon coming to an end. Indeed, it was 'too terrible to think that on this the saddest day of all others – and, let us hope, the saddest that we *both* shall ever see again – my Wifie should have nobody with her'.[1]

And yet Katie was not alone, as Willie was present at the funeral and indeed wrote to Chamberlain: 'My child is to be buried at Chiselhurst this afternoon. Afterwards I shall return to Eltham and I do not intend to come to town unless you want me.'[2] Claude Sophie was buried in a Catholic cemetery.[3] Katharine wrote that the grave was headed by a granite cross and wreathed with clematis and white roses. She did not record who had attended the funeral, but it is obvious from O'Shea's letter to Chamberlain that he must have been present.[4]

The O'Shea family were naturally grieved by the loss. Willie's mother and sister Mary had been unaware of anything untoward in Claude's paternity. Mary wrote to her sister-in-law from Paris on 21 May, a warm, affectionate letter in which she expressed her sorrow at the loss of the baby. It is quite clear from her letter too that Katie was not alone at Eltham: she made reference to Aunt Ben, and to her kindness to Katie's children – the old lady had been 'so sweet a friend and so charming in all her ways towards you dear children, "the butterflies", most attractive description'. There had also been a visit to Katie's family from Lady Mary O'Donnell, who with her husband George was a great friend of the O'Sheas.[5] The O'Donnells were from County Mayo, and Mary later became godmother to another of Katie's daughters.[6] Lady O'Donnell had written to Mary about the visit, including a 'rapturous description of the little creatures'. She loved 'your dear little Claude, and shared your grief at losing her'.[7]

Mary's letter mentioned that 'William' (meaning Willie) would have told her of 'mamma's long and trying illness'. Mary could 'scarcely leave her for an instant'. The Bishop of Killaloe had called and enquired 'most kindly' for Katie; he had written, she said, to William 'offering his tribute of sympathy' on the death of 'your dear baby'. Mamma hoped that the children were well. 'Is dear little Carmen strong?' Mary enquired, 'And her amiable and devoted sister – how is she?' She and her mother hoped that 'their brother is in perfect health, no memory even of delicacy still'. Mary sent Katie 'mamma's love and kindest wishes for your health and comfort'.[8]

Katie wrote that she reproduced this letter to prove, 'I think very conclusively, that my little one's paternity was utterly unsuspected by the O'Sheas'.[9] And indeed, the letter, with its loving concern and devout prayers, does make the point that her in-laws were entirely unaware of the affair with Parnell. There has been suspicion that Gerard insisted on its inclusion as a means of proving his assertion that his father and family were duped by Katie and the Irish leader. What the communication does most forcibly, however, is draw attention to the high emotional costs of Katie's extramarital affair. Her in-laws prayed: 'all blessings may be granted to you and to those you love'.[10] Reading this cannot have been comfortable.

And the fact remains that Parnell could have chosen to be freed. He could at the very least have taken up Forster's offer of an extended parole leave. It would have been difficult to attend Claude's funeral, but not entirely impossible. At this time, he was working with Willie on the Kilmainham Treaty. Even if attending the funeral proved too awkward, the leader could have remained at Eltham, hammering out details of the negotiation. Members of the government would not have known the true reason for his remaining in England. It was Parnell himself who did not wish to cede political advantage, and thus returned to Kilmainham. This decision was later viewed by many of his supporters as evidence of the leader's commitment to the cause of Irish nationalism.

Parnell was conscious of the benefits that incarceration continued to bring him politically. Many of the extremists, and in particular the Irish-Americans, had been alienated by his initial support for the Land Act. Nationalists such as Patrick Ford and Patrick Egan had been pressing for a general strike against rents, and the leader's eventual support for the scheme had reassured them. This was critical to ensure an uninterrupted flow of funds from the United States. Signing the 'No Rent' Manifesto after being arrested had also helped Parnell send a placatory signal to the more extreme wings of the nationalist movement. So despite his many protestations to the woman he loved – his letters to Katie were tender and solicitous – he was clearly determined to reap the benefits of a jail sentence.

But Parnell became increasingly determined to end the stalemate with the government. The longer he and his colleagues stayed in prison, the more difficult it would be for both sides to resume a constitutional path. It is not clear how informed Parnell kept his colleagues of the negotiations. Davitt later claimed that all of them

– with the possible exception of O'Kelly – were kept in the dark.[11] But O'Shea informed the Prime Minister that the Irish leader '*had* communicated with his fellow prisoners before writing to O'Shea'.[12] O'Shea changed his story several times,[13] but whatever the truth of the matter Gladstone was certainly appreciative of the result. He wrote to Forster on 30 April about his impression of Parnell's letter, which had been communicated to them through O'Shea:

With great sagacity, Parnell goes on to state his other aims under the amendment of the Land Act. But he carefully abstains from importing any of them as conditions of the former remarkable statement. He then proceeds to throw in his indication or promise of future co-operation with the Liberal Party. This is a *hors d'oeuvre* which we had no right to expect, and, I think, at present no right to accept... On the whole, Parnell's letter is, I think, the most extraordinary I have ever read. I cannot help feeling indebted to O'Shea.[14]

The Chief Secretary did not agree with the Prime Minister's assessment. In fact, he was absolutely horrified at the direction in which the government was moving. On that same day, Forster had a conversation with the Liberal MP George Joachim Goschen (who later was increasingly at odds with his party and became a supporter of the Union and a Liberal Unionist) about the Irish situation. He expressed his surprise and dismay when Goschen told him that in the House there was 'surrender in the air'. A release of the prisoners – now referred to as 'political suspects' – would be a grave mistake. Forster's daughter Florence recorded her father's outrage:

One thing to be considered... is that such a course would be a tremendous step towards Home Rule. It would be equivalent to admitting that these men are what they claim to be – but are not – the leaders and representatives of the Irish people, and that the Govt releases them in order to effect what it cannot accomplish itself – the pacification of

Ireland and the maintenance of law and order. It will be open to Mr Parnell to represent the transaction in this light before the Irish people: 'I got you the Land Act – the Govt shut me up for what I had done – but now finding that they cannot quiet Ireland without my influence they have had to let me out, to help to amend the Land Act and pacify the country.'[15]

It was apparent to his colleagues that Forster would soon resign. The proposed release of the prisoners had gained the support of the Cabinet, despite the Chief Secretary's rigid opposition. There was increasing speculation of who might be Forster's successor. Many believed that Chamberlain would be appointed to the position. His interest in Ireland was well known, as was his opposition to Forster's unsuccessful policies. The Chief Secretary himself believed that Chamberlain would probably succeed him. Florence Arnold-Forster recorded on 3 May that this was the 'general impression'.[16] Willie O'Shea, on hearing that Chamberlain was hesitating over the possibility, made a point of writing to him that if he accepted it would be a 'point of honour with Mr Parnell to work as if for himself to ensure the success of your administration'.[17]

Then, on 2 May 1882, Parnell, O'Kelly and Dillon were released from Kilmainham. Gladstone had read a memorandum to his Cabinet, upon which they agreed:

The cabinet are of opinion that the time has now arrived when with a view to the interests of law and order in Ireland, the three members of parliament who have been imprisoned on suspicion since last October, should be immediately released; and that the list of suspects should be examined with a view to the release of all persons not believed to be associated with crimes.[18]

Forster dissented from this, naturally, and resigned his office, as expected. Lord Spencer was appointed as the new Viceroy to succeed Cowper, and Lord Frederick Cavendish, not Joseph Chamberlain, became the new Chief Secretary. The choice of Cavendish came as a surprise. He was the husband of a niece of Mrs Gladstone's and both the Prime Minister and his wife held him in great affection. Chamberlain recorded that he had been relieved not to have been asked. This is somewhat doubtful, as there was every indication that he was very keen. The overall reaction to Cavendish's appointment was not positive. The appointment was unexpected and did not provide Cavendish with a seat in Cabinet. This was because the Lord-Lieutenant (Viceroy), Spencer, already had a seat in Cabinet and it was firm tradition that only one of the two Irish ministers would be a member. So the Chief Secretary position – at this critical moment – was offered without a seat in Cabinet to a likeable and inexperienced former Secretary to the Treasury. In his favour, Cavendish was hardworking and very well connected (he was Lord Hartington's younger brother).[19]

But Chamberlain was taken aback, as was his great friend and political ally Sir Charles Dilke. Dilke recorded:

On May 3rd, Chamberlain, who had decided to take the Irish Secretaryship if offered to him, was astonished at having received no offer. At 11-30 p.m. on the same day, the 3rd, I found that the appointment had been offered to and declined by Hartington; but the offer to, and acceptance by, his brother, Lord Frederick Cavendish, came as a complete surprise both to me and to Chamberlain.[20]

It is difficult to know what the Prime Minister intended by this appointment. Certainly the signs pointed to a strengthening of the Whig influence in Cabinet – to the detriment of the Radicals. Although the Chief Secretaryship did not carry the usual weight of a Cabinet seat, Cavendish was a known favourite of the Prime Minister.

Parnell went immediately to Avondale on his release on 2 May. He was accompanied by O'Kelly, whose recollection of their arrival was published by Parnell's first biographer, Barry O'Brien. The household servants had all rushed out, crying with joy, to meet the newly released pair. O'Kelly was 'horribly affected' at the welcome, but was shocked by Parnell's cool indifference. 'I thought he was the most callous fellow I had ever met.' O'Kelly was even more taken aback by the reaction of the leader's sister, Emily Dickinson. 'I hung back', he recalled, 'as I did not like to be present at the meeting between brother and sister, but Parnell said: "Come along". Mrs. Dickinson was as icy as himself. She got up calmly as he entered, and said quite casually: "Ah, Charley, is that you? I thought they would never let you back again".' Parnell had then replied: 'Well, what did you think they would do to me?' O'Kelly was stunned by Emily's response: 'I thought they would hang you.' Parnell merely smiled and said, 'Well it may come to that yet.' O'Kelly recalled: 'That was the whole greeting. They then talked about family affairs.'[21]

In 1882, Parnell, like many Wicklow landowners, was suffering financially from the land agitation. Clearly, as head of the Land League, he could hardly exercise a harsh policy towards his tenants. Sufficient political capital was already being made by his opponents with regard to the inconsistencies of his politics and landowner status. In 1879, Parnell claimed that his tenants were 'paying him badly'.[22] The rents were reduced by 20 per cent the following year and Parnell issued a circular around this time, which stated: 'In order to obviate any error on the part of anyone representing him, henceforth until the Irish Land Question is settled on the basis of the Land League principles, no farm tenant shall be asked to pay higher rent than the poor-law or Griffith's valuation.'[23] The Avondale estate was mortgaged, and Parnell's political expenses were increasing. He was spending less and less time in Ireland and, although his land was not especially poorly managed, Avondale was not prospering in his absence.[24]

Katie made no mention of this visit to Avondale. On the contrary, in her account, she wrote that on his 'release from Kilmainham', the leader 'returned to me at Eltham'.[25] We now have the evidence that it was his decision not to remain with her for Claude's funeral, and furthermore that he did not rush to her side upon his release from jail. It must also be noted that Parnell could have avoided arrest altogether. He could have fled to England (as did two other Irish MPs, Arthur O'Connor and Biggar), where warrants for their arrest under the Protection of Persons and Property Act could not be served. He explained to Katie while in jail that although he could have avoided arrest by leaving Ireland, it 'would have been very difficult for me to have kept out of the country', and that 'on the whole I hope it will turn out all for the best'.[26]

The leader's actions spoke for themselves. His priority was to further the cause of Irish nationalist aspirations. It was to this end that he directed his efforts and arranged his life. That he also organized an alternative existence cannot disguise the fact that Parnell was ferociously ambitious and committed to political success. The risks that he took in pursuing an affair with the wife of a colleague should not be viewed as evidence that he was prepared to throw away his political position. Katie provided him with a secret life of cosy comfort and tranquillity. She looked after him, making sure that he had hot meals and dry clothes. For a lonely man who had been sent away from home at the age of seven, the joy of being looked after in such a way must have been tremendously gratifying. That Charles Parnell found Katie sexually alluring as well made her appeal all the more compelling. It seems unlikely, however, that he would have welcomed an atmosphere of morbid fuss over the baby's death. He had a horror of death and funerals. Instead, Parnell's correspondence to Katie after Claude's birth has, one of her biographers has astutely observed, 'a rather selfish preoccupation with the restoration of Katharine's sexual attractiveness to him'.[27]

Katie excelled in the art of taking care of the people in her life. Her devotion to her aunt had earned her a comfortable income not just for her family but for her husband's political career as well. She had the skills to keep Willie settled and acquiescent with the Eltham solution to the family finances. There is every indication by the choices she made that she was devoted to her children. Her determination to provide a family home at Eltham showed an unwillingness to give up her domestic responsibilities. There is every reason to believe that the children lived there quite happily, for they remained loyal and attached to their mother, even throughout the troubles that lay ahead.

Once Parnell was released, he resumed his political activity. He left Avondale with O'Kelly that evening and returned to Dublin. They were joined there by Dillon and crossed by the night-mail in time to appear in Parliament. Florence Arnold-Forster was present and described the scene at Westminster:

Never have I seen the House so crowded in every part – literally from floor to ceiling – Members standing in double rows in the galleries on either side of the House, the Peers' gallery filled to overflowing – even the standing room there occupied; in a short time Lady Brand's Gallery was also filled,[28] amongst others present being Lady Spencer, Lady Harcourt, Lady Rosebery, the Duchess of Manchester, Mrs Gladstone etc. The Prince of Wales and the Crown Prince of Denmark were over the Clock.[29]

Shortly after 5 p.m., the ex-Chief Secretary made his resignation statement. Just after Forster had begun his speech, Parnell entered the House and 'made his way to his seat in full view of all beholders and amidst the cheers of his own followers'.[30] As one of the Irish leader's biographers commented, Parnell 'was not a man who chose dramatic moments for entering assemblies, but one who made drama by being present; he could not have chosen a more exciting moment than that for his return to the Commons'.[31] Apparently, the cheers of the Irish members drowned out part of Forster's speech, but his daughter recorded that he was applauded at the end of it nevertheless. Then the announcement of the Cavendish appointment was greeted in the House by jeers and laughter.

Parnell's own speech had been brief. He declared that a settlement of the arrears question 'would have an enormous effect in the restoration of law and order in Ireland'.[32] The leader was being deliberately cautious, as his undertaking with Gladstone had gone further than many of his colleagues would have liked. The substance of the agreement – one could not call it a treaty – was an implicit recognition of a desire to end the Land War and revolutionary agitation. The choice to pursue a constitutional struggle for Home Rule, however, reflected generally the views of the majority of the Irish Party at this point. Once a good Land Act was secured, the need for agrarian violence would be removed. Parnell's Kilmainham agreement was a sensible recognition of this. The violence in Ireland was leading nowhere. In its place, a well-led constitutional movement, relying on astute parliamentary action – but with a barely repressed threat of agrarian and political revolution behind it – had a better chance of success.

The signs were positive. Chamberlain, for example, recalled that he 'believed in the sincerity of Mr Parnell'. He hoped that with the Irish leader's assistance the reforms required would be implemented. An Arrears Bill would be introduced.[33] This bill would provide funds to tenants with their rents in arrears, so that they too could benefit from the 'fair rent' as promised by the Land Act of 1881.[34] Although the Tories were far more doubtful about the direction the Prime Minister was taking, the overall momentum in the House was in favour of resolution and constructive engagement. In order to pursue this new departure, however, Parnell had to quell the more extreme elements of the nationalist movement. Katie had been exerting pressure on him for conciliation, and this is no doubt the course he favoured in any event.

There were, though, still those who disagreed with Parnell's strategy. Although the parliamentarians such as Tim Healy, Sexton and some others could be counted on to avoid inciting violence, there were still secret societies whose members felt no such constraints. To add to the difficulty was the fact that in America – the source of most of the Party's funds – there was more support for the left wing of the movement. Henry George, still writing for the *Irish World*, was dubious over the Kilmainham agreement. Within weeks he wrote: 'Parnell seems to me to have thrown away the greatest opportunity any Irishman ever had. It is the birthright for a mess of potage.'[35] George and his boss, Patrick Ford, were much opposed to the moderate direction Parnell espoused and they were not alone in this.

A secret Irish society known as the 'Invincibles' had for some time targeted Forster for a political assassination. Each time the attempt to murder him had been foiled by accidental circumstance. The last opportunity had been on Forster's departure from Ireland on 19 April. The Invincibles were waiting for him at Westland Row station, where he was to have taken the 6.45 boat train for Kingstown. Forster was completely unaware of the plot, but inadvertently saved his own life by agreeing to the suggestion of his Private Secretary, Henry Jephson, that they should travel to Kingstown together by an earlier train and have dinner there before taking the mail boat.

The new plan was to murder the Under-Secretary, Thomas Henry Burke.[36] The Invincibles intended to do so during a torchlight procession made on the evening of 5 May to celebrate Parnell and the release of Davitt from prison the previous day. Once again, they were unsuccessful and another attempt was planned. On the evening of 5 May, Lord Frederick Cavendish, the new Chief Secretary, travelled to Ireland to take up his new post. On the following day, the new Viceroy, Lord Spencer, made a state entry into Dublin accompanied by Cavendish. After the state procession, the gang set out once more to find Burke, their intended victim. The men divided into two groups and drove out to Phoenix Park. One group was in a cab and the other in a jaunting-car.[37] At the park, they divided further into more groups, one of which was composed of two men, James Carey[38] and a man called Smith. He knew Burke by sight and was to signal when the Under-Secretary appeared.

Meanwhile, the Viceroy rode off with his small mounted escort to the Viceregal Lodge in Phoenix Park. Cavendish was to join him there for supper, and decided to walk. He knew and liked Dublin, having spent time there ten years previously when his brother, Lord Hartington, had been Viceroy. Inside the park he was joined by Burke, who left his jaunting-car to accompany him on foot. It was about seven o'clock in the evening and there were many people in the park. There was a polo match, which Spencer had observed some time before. So too did Carey, as he was waiting for Burke to appear. Then, Smith and Carey, having recognized the Under-Secretary, drove on to the place where seven gang members lay in wait. First Smith and then Carey were ordered to leave. The seven men pounced on Burke and Cavendish as they walked past and butchered them with 12-inch surgical knives. The knives had been smuggled into the country sewn into the skirts of Frank Byrne's pregnant wife.[39]

The murders caused tremendous outrage in England and in Ireland. The assassins had not even known who Cavendish was. The randomness and frenzied nature of the attack left people stunned. The news was broken to the Prime Minister, who had been dining at the Austrian Embassy in London. He and his wife were horrified. Aside from the personal dismay felt by many, the political ramifications were obvious. As the journalist and Liberal politician John Morley recorded,[40] the immediate result of 'this blind and hideous crime was at once to arrest the spirit and the policy of conciliation'.[41] Morley, who as editor of *The Fortnightly Review* had considerable influence, was a supporter of Parnell. This was a terrible setback. All the hard-won progress made towards resolving the Irish situation was put into jeopardy. Lurid details of the attack emerged, which shocked the public further.

A Lieutenant of the Royal Dragoons was in the park at the time, exercising his dogs just a few hundred yards away from the scene of the attack. He told reporters that his thought had been that the group of men had been 'larking about'.[42] When the men left, he wondered why two of them did not get up. They were both dead. Burke had suffered two deep wounds to his neck. Several other cuts were made across his chest and shoulder blade. One of these was the fatal wound, which had pierced his right lung. Cavendish had received a cut across his arm of such brutality that it had fractured the bone. Other bones were penetrated in a series of deep wounds to his neck, shoulders, chest and back. He had clearly attempted to defend himself, and suffered a deep wound to the armpit when he apparently raised his arm to ward off the blows.[43]

Florence Arnold-Forster wrote:

Nothing can describe, no future historian can exaggerate, the all-penetrating thrill of horror and dismay and excitement felt in every corner of England this morning[44] [...] All the accounts from Dublin and indeed from every part of Ireland describe the attitude of the people as being one of genuine distress and consternation at the crime which has disgraced their country – the first political assassination in our country since the Murder of the Duke of Buckingham [in 1682].[45]

It was particularly the murder of Cavendish that caused consternation. Barry O'Brien wrote of how an old Fenian – 'a hater of the Land League and all its works' – had told him of an encounter in New York:

I went into a shop… a few days after the murder to buy something. I said casually to the man behind the counter: 'This is bad work.' He agreed, and denounced the crime in strong language. Here, at all events, thought I, is a man who has escaped the influence of the Land League. I turned to leave, and as I got to the door he added: 'What harm if it was only Burke? But to kill the strange gentleman who did nothing to us!' That was what he thought about it, and no doubt that was what a great many other Irish people thought about it too.[46]

The pride in Irish hospitality was badly dented. The Irish poet Katharine Tynan wrote of the despair shared by so many in Ireland: 'I remember mooning about the hedgerows feeling the very sunlight sick. All the innocent delights of the fields had blood upon them... One element in the feeling of that day was that the Irish sense of hospitality was outraged by the death of Lord Frederick Cavendish.'[47]

Parnell was appalled. He had left his colleagues the previous day and travelled to Eltham, where he had spent the night. Katharine recalled that she had accompanied him to Blackheath Station that Sunday morning, where he was planning to rejoin his colleagues in London. Katie wrote of Parnell's horror when he saw the news in the *Sunday Observer*, which he had just purchased at the station to read the coverage of Davitt's release from prison. Her immediate thoughts were 'for the awful significance of the horrible thing to my lover, just released from Kilmainham on the Treaty...' Parnell was in shock, but she encouraged him to continue his journey to London to convene with his colleagues. 'He turned heavily away', she continued, 'saying, "I shall resign," and I answered as I ran beside him to the platform, "No, you are not a coward".'[48] Once again, Katie's recollections demonstrate not merely the inaccuracy of her memory of events, but her tendency to assign herself a starring role in them. Parnell did not take advice from her. If he had, he would not have ended up in Kilmainham, or continued a risky career in politics. So we do not know what Katie's response to the crisis really was. There can be little doubt that Parnell wished to be with his colleagues. It is interesting to note that after just one night with Katie – after their lengthy and traumatic separation – he had planned to make his way back to London to do his work.

All accounts given by his contemporaries agree that the Irish leader was profoundly affected by the murders. As Morley wrote, 'No worse blow could have been struck at Mr. Parnell's policy.'[49] He needed to see his fellow party members and take stock of the new situation. Interestingly, he went straight to O'Shea's apartment in Albert Mansions. There he wrote a message to the Prime Minister in which he offered to resign. O'Shea delivered the message himself. Gladstone wrote back immediately to O'Shea, saying, 'My duty does not permit me for a moment to entertain Mr. Parnell's proposal, just conveyed to me by you, that he should if I think it needful resign his seat.' The Prime Minister was, however, 'deeply sensible of the honourable motives by which it has been prompted'.[50]

The Irish leader then went on to the Westminster Palace Hotel, where he met up with Davitt, Dillon and McCarthy. They began work on a manifesto to the Irish people, denouncing the murders in the strongest possible terms. Parnell was still considering resignation, but continued nevertheless to think ahead with his colleagues about next steps for the party. The expectation was that either Dilke or Chamberlain would be asked to replace Cavendish. Parnell set off with McCarthy to call on them. They went first to Dilke,[51] who recalled that he had found the Irish leader 'white and apparently terror-stricken'.[52] Davitt also recalled that the leader had been 'wild'.[53] Parnell's brother John corroborated these contemporaneous observations, stating that the 'blow was a terrible one for Charley. He was completely unnerved.'[54] Dilke told the pair that should he be offered the post of Chief Secretary, the events of the previous day would not make him refuse it. His preference was, however, for Chamberlain to take up the position. He wrote to his friend the following day, confirming this:

Still I would act or serve under you and if it were thought I could be of any use I would join you in Dublin on the day the House was up, and spend the whole autumn and winter with you as your chief private secretary. I could always have the work of my London post sent over in boxes.[55]

Parnell and McCarthy then went to see the other likely candidate for the Irish post – Joseph Chamberlain. Before they left, Dilke took McCarthy to one side and warned him that he did not think it safe for the Irish leader to walk about the streets. He might be recognized and held responsible for the murders.[56] Parnell was undeterred and the two made their way to see Chamberlain. He also told them that he was prepared to take up the position if offered to him. Chamberlain's account of the visit was written many years later, in 1891, and was possibly influenced by recollections made by O'Shea and published in *The Times* in August 1888.[57] He claimed that when Parnell came to see him the leader had been 'white as a sheet, agitated and altogether demoralized'.[58]

The recollections are important because it was at this moment, O'Shea later claimed, that he had asked for police protection for the Irish leader. Parnell was, according to O'Shea's later testimony, terrified at the course of events and fearful for his own life. O'Shea said that on that day he had called on the Home Secretary, Sir William Harcourt, to ask for protection at Parnell's explicit request. An extract from the diary of Lewis Harcourt (Sir William's son) records on 9 May 1882: 'Parnell has applied for police protection.'[59] When questioned about this at a later date, however, Parnell emphatically denied ever doing anything of the sort. He flatly denied any belief that his own life was in danger: 'Such a thing never entered into my mind for a single moment.'[60] It was some six years later that both he and O'Shea (now far more hostile to his leader) gave this contradictory evidence. Justin McCarthy's recollection of Parnell's demeanour and state of mind on that day would seem to confirm that the leader was not unduly flustered or frightened:

Captain O'Shea came in while we were talking. When we were leaving, Chamberlain gave us much the same kind of caution that Dilke had given. I suggested to Parnell that we should take a hansom, and I hinted the reason to him. He replied rather sharply that he would do nothing of the kind. He said he had done no wrong to anyone, and that he intended to walk in the streets like anyone else.[61]

On balance, it is McCarthy's account and the leader's own testimony that seem most convincing. Parnell was a cool and collected individual who kept his feelings under rigid control. He was certainly very alarmed by the turn of events. But so too were his colleagues, including the more radical ones. Davitt was appalled when he heard the news, calling it 'horrible', 'a calamity', 'a catastrophe' and a 'thunderbolt upon our cause'.[62] It is difficult to believe that such a private man as Parnell, who had particular cause to preserve his privacy, would deliberately seek out police protection because of the crime.

It is quite clear that O'Shea was determined to continue working alongside the Irish leader. It was possibly the only career path left to him. Since June 1881 he had been working to position himself as the conduit to Parnell.[63] However, many within the British political establishment were altogether unconvinced of O'Shea's credibility and character. The senior civil servant Edward Walter Hamilton (Gladstone's principal Private Secretary) recorded that O'Shea had offered once again to negotiate with the government during Parnell's parole in April 1882. 'He makes himself out to be Parnell's special confidant,' commented Hamilton. The problem, as Hamilton saw it, was that it was 'impossible' to have 'any direct dealings' with the Irish Party – they were 'probably not the least to be trusted'. Neither, in his opinion, was the Captain. Although O'Shea was a 'gentleman by birth and a brother-in-law of Sir E. Wood [Katie's brother]', he was not, in Hamilton's opinion, 'of the "straightest"'.[64]

Chamberlain later played down his relationship with O'Shea, but at this time – and throughout the 1880s – they met and corresponded regularly. O'Shea certainly felt that in Chamberlain he had a political ally. He hoped therefore that the Chief Secretaryship would be offered to him. On 8 May, however, the position was offered to Dilke. He refused to accept it, as the offer came without a seat in the Cabinet. Although Chamberlain, who was of course already in the Cabinet as President of the Board of Trade, urged his friend to take the job regardless, Dilke was adamant. The appointment was ultimately accepted by George Otto Trevelyan, previously Financial Secretary to the Admiralty and also a Radical, who took the post without the Cabinet seat.

Willie O'Shea was now even more determined to use his relationship with Parnell to glean some personal advantage. He requested police protection for himself as well as for the leader – both at his London residence at Albert Mansions and at Eltham. Although one biographer has argued that this would indicate that O'Shea knew and accepted that Parnell was Katie's lover, this assumption does not necessarily follow. In fact, the reverse is probably true. It is most unlikely that O'Shea would wish to advertise his wife's infidelity to Harcourt, the police and the British government. On the contrary, the evidence strongly suggests that at this point in time all three parties were keen to maintain appearances. In O'Shea's case, it is entirely possible that this was not a deceit. He may have been unaware of the resumption of sexual relations between his wife and the Irish leader after the fracas of the previous summer and the threat of a duel. There is of course the possibility that O'Shea – in the hopes of political and personal gain through his association with the Irish leader – simply turned a blind eye to what was going on. But if this were the case, his demand for police protection – with the surveillance that inevitably entailed – seems odd.

Parnell and his colleagues fully expected the British government to respond to the crisis with further coercive measures in Ireland.

Parnell was very keen to distance himself from the assassins and he denounced the murders in the House on 8 May 1882. The occasion was a sombre one and all the parliamentary members wore black. Florence Arnold-Forster was again present, although the House and its galleries were so crowded that she had to stand at the back of the Ladies' Gallery: 'When Mr Gladstone rose and began to speak in low broken tones, it was in a silence so profound that I, standing far back where I could not catch a glimpse of the speaker, could yet hear plainly every word he said; there were sobs from amongst the ladies round me.'[65]

For two years, from the summer of 1880, the problems of Ireland had held a foremost position in the politics of Westminster. With the Kilmainham agreement, many politicians had dared to hope that a breakthrough might occur. The Liberal government, which had planned to drop coercion, now introduced a Crimes Bill, which had the effect of reintroducing it. In addition to discouraging the government from withdrawing coercive measures against Ireland, the vicious and secret nature of the assassinations caused Parnell much alarm. Although the reports that he was personally afraid for his own safety may have been fabricated by his enemies, there is no doubt that the attacks caused him much consternation.

It was hugely important for Parnell to be in control of the independence movement, and to be seen to be in control of it. His stay in Kilmainham had enhanced his stature at home. It had also consolidated his position as a statesman who could negotiate with the British at the highest levels. He was appalled at the damage the murders had done. Katie immediately understood the problem, and wrote of how she had urged her husband to bring the leader down to Eltham. The two of them arrived, she recalled, 'both very gloomy and depressed'. In addition to that strain, there was the subterfuge to be maintained. Katie wrote that she and Parnell had greeted one another 'as though this were our first meeting since he came out of prison'.[66]

Katie had a good understanding of the dilemma her lover now faced. After pressing Parnell hard to conciliate – so that he could regain his liberty and some personal safety – she now found that the Irish leader was in a worse situation than before. She wrote that she had 'spent one of the most terrible days of my life considering the effect this awful crime would probably have upon my lover's career'.[67]

One effect was the speedy introduction of new coercive legislative measures to address the Irish situation. The new Crimes Bill proposed that trial by jury be replaced in certain cases by trial by three judges and the Lord-Lieutenant given authority to forbid public meetings and to suppress newspapers. In addition, increased powers were to be conferred on magistrates and incitement to crime was to be summarily punished if deemed necessary. One of the most offensive of the proposed clauses of this bill was that giving the police extensive search powers. Home Secretary Harcourt introduced the measures on 1 May in a speech that left no one in any doubt of the government's intentions to impose order in Ireland. But many of these decisions had been made before the murders – as had, indeed, the decision to release Parnell and the others. The change was in how contact was structured between the two sides.

Opportunities for Parnell – as a 'gentleman' – to exercise the reassuring impression he gave some British politicians were inevitably reduced. This undoubtedly increased his discomfort with the unpredictability of the extremist elements of the nationalist movement. It was contradictory to be considered a statesman of *gravitas* and influence in his dealings with the British establishment while being connected to gangs of marauding murderers. There was certainly speculation at the time (and later) that Parnell had clandestine links with some extremist groups, notably the Irish Republican Brotherhood (IRB).[68] It is a distinct possibility that Parnell chose to take the IRB oath shortly after leaving Kilmainham prison. It has been suggested that this event took place on 2 or 3 of May in the library of Trinity College, Dublin.[69] (Parnell's swearing of the oath would explain his panicked reaction to the murders and his immediate offer to resign from politics.)

Moreover Parnell's personal life was becoming more public. Dilke recorded in his diary that the Home Secretary, Lord Harcourt, had spoken of Katie's affair with Parnell at a Cabinet meeting of 17 May.[70] According to Dilke's recollections, the Home Secretary 'told the Cabinet that the Kilmainham Treaty would not be popular when the public discovered that it had been negotiated by Captain O'Shea, "the husband of Parnell's mistress." He informed the Cabinet that... after this it would hardly "do for the public for us to use O'Shea as a negotiator".'[71] Dilke was not present at this meeting; the information came to him, supposedly, from Chamberlain. The second-hand nature of the intelligence, together with the lapse in time before the publication of the diary, means that Dilke's assertion must be treated with scepticism. What is clear, however, is that rumours of the affair were becoming known in high political circles. Just a month later, Edward Hamilton (Gladstone's personal Private Secretary) lamented that 'Mrs O'Shea' seemed to be 'on very intimate terms with Parnell; some say his mistress'.[72]

CHAPTER TWELVE

Emissary to the Prime Minister

𝒦ATIE RECORDED THAT she had dinner with her husband and her lover after the pair returned – together – to Eltham from London on 7 May. The immediate retreat to Eltham of both O'Shea and Parnell seems strange. The timing is also rather odd. Katie wrote that the dinner took place 'that evening' (after she and Parnell had learned of the murders on the morning of 7 May). With all that we know from contemporaneous accounts, however, it seems unlikely that either O'Shea or Parnell left London to retreat to Eltham in the midst of all the political and personal reactions to the murders. It was a time for members of the Irish Party to reflect, to clarify their positions, and for individuals to adopt appropriate public and private responses to the tragedy. As we have seen, there was a huge amount of political discussion and manoeuvring taking place in the aftermath of the crisis.

Of course, it may be that after the trauma of the day the two men felt the need to remove themselves from the scene. Another possibility is that Katie was mistaken in her account, and that the dinner occurred some days later. In any case, Parnell, she wrote, 'sat gazing stonily before him'. Her husband was 'really sorry' for the leader. During the meal he told her of what had transpired during the day, 'and of Parnell's continuous threat... of retiring from public life altogether'. O'Shea appealed to her for help, she declared. 'I wish you would urge Parnell not to talk so, Dick;' he said, 'he can't resign his seat now, the thing's impossible; he must show that it simply does not touch him politically in any way.'[1] It should be noted that for Willie to call his wife by his pet name for her (and her reference to it in this account) would indicate that their mutual relations were warm and friendly. The play-acting taking place between the three thus continued, and Katie recalled her response: 'I turned to Parnell and said: "I do absolutely agree with Willie about it, Mr. Parnell. It would be throwing the whole country over and a reflection upon all who joined in that Treaty".'[2]

Katie's account continued with this story. As the maid left the dining room after serving the trio their coffee, a large picture fell to the floor. It was an engraving of the House of Commons in 1880, with its members, including Parnell and O'Shea. It hung immediately behind where the leader was seated, and hit the ground with such a crash that 'in the state of nervous tension' they were all in, the three leapt to their feet. 'Willie's chair was overturned', Katie wrote, 'as he jumped up; but Parnell's was steady, held in a grip that showed his knuckles white as he held it slightly raised off the floor, while he stood, half turned, staring at the picture as it lay among the splintered glass.' Although Willie laughed about it, Parnell was deeply unnerved. When she later asked him why, the leader replied, 'It was an omen, I think, darling, but for whom? Willie or me?'[3]

Of course the whole story, with its undertones of superstition and melodrama, may have been fabricated. What is interesting about it is the light the vignette sheds on the workings at Eltham that evening. The situation was remarkable: either the O'Sheas and Charles Parnell were complicit in a highly unorthodox arrangement, or Willie was wilfully blind, or Katie and Parnell were deceitful to a very high degree.

There was further evidence that Parnell was prepared to work closely with his rival, however unpalatable he may have found this. The two had cooperated in a strategy that seemed to have backfired after the murders. The situation for the Irish Party now looked dire. *The Times* remarked straight away: 'Not more than four days have elapsed since the policy of conciliation was thus set in motion and already we have its hollowness exposed by the tragedy in the Phoenix Park.'[4] It did not help that the assassins could not be traced. The Kilmainham agreement, with which O'Shea was so closely identified, came under attack. Gladstone was criticized and the government was forced to defend its actions. Lady Ely, Lady of the Bedchamber to Queen Victoria, told Florence Arnold-Forster that Her Majesty 'was terribly distressed by the news of Saturday, and very unhappy about Ireland – "you know, my dear, she has no confidence in Mr Gladstone"'.[5]

Accordingly, the Prime Minister announced that changes had to be made to the Irish policy after what had happened. The Crime Bill introduced by Harcourt was to take precedence over arrears legislation. The Parnellites determined to fight the coercive measures of the bill and the Irish leader denounced it on 11 May, 'speaking apparently in a white heat of passion'.[6] But the momentum had moved away from conciliation. There was now considerable approval in the House (and in Cabinet) for Forster's position and respect for his resignation. Two days were set aside in the House of Commons – 15 and 16 May – to discuss what was being miscalled the 'Kilmainham Treaty'. There was suspicion that between the comings and goings, and correspondence between the negotiators and the government, a deal had been done. The Tories – opposed to Gladstone's policies in Ireland and of course the government's Opposition party – were determined to cause maximum discredit to the Prime Minister and Liberals.

Gladstone was in an awkward position. His Cabinet was a coalition and he personally bridged the gap between confirmed Whigs such as Hartington and Radicals such as Chamberlain. The coalition was vulnerable and such weakness provided political opportunity to the Tories. The Prime Minister needed the cooperation and support of the Irish members, but the Irish Party were incensed by the draconian measures proposed by the bill. Chamberlain wrote that as 'the shock of the murders lessened their opposition became more bitter and obstructive'.[7]

The promise of the Arrears Bill – on which Parnell was so keen and had staked his reputation within his own party – was in danger of being lost sight of altogether. On 13 May Gladstone wrote to Chamberlain, expressing his belief that the Irish leader had an obligation to support the government in their difficulties and to refrain from obstructive measures over the bill. Parnell responded by asking for amendments – which, Chamberlain noted, did not seem 'unreasonable' to him or to the Prime Minister, but Harcourt was adamant.[8] The Home Secretary was supported in his intransigent position by the majority of the Cabinet – especially by senior members such as the Liberal Lords Spencer, Selborne (who later broke with Gladstone and became a Liberal Unionist) and Hartington. Gladstone was extremely disappointed, as was Chamberlain. By refusing to allow the Irish MPs any input into the strongest coercion bill ever introduced, it could only, in their opinion, foster ill will and delay much needed progress.

As Chamberlain lamented, 'with a feeling almost of despair':

we are to stick to our Bill in every point of the slightest importance, and not make any concession to that Irish opinion which we professed to be ready to consult. Parnell and his friends behaved very well over the second reading, in reliance on our statements that their amendments will be fairly considered in Committee. If this means that they are all to be rejected, the Irishmen will have good reason to think themselves ill-used. They will have nothing to lose by obstruction – having gained nothing by more moderate courses – and they will obstruct accordingly.[9]

Parnell and O'Shea, as co-negotiators of the agreement now under attack, were obliged to face the antagonism together. This collaboration came at a cost. On 15 May, the Arrears Bill was brought forward by the Prime Minister. There then followed an ugly scene in the House of Commons concerning the Kilmainham agreement. The Prime Minister was asked to produce the letters that were used as the basis for releasing the prisoners. Gladstone replied that certain letters had passed between members of the House, but was disinclined to produce them. When pressed, Parnell agreed to read out his letter to Willie O'Shea from Kilmainham. It was in this document, dated 28 April, that the leader had articulated the need for the arrears question to be addressed and for leaseholders to be admitted to the Land Act as a means of ensuring that efforts to quell the agitation would have effect.

This was not enough for Forster. Tim Healy recorded: 'Near by sat Forster, the dismissed Chief Secretary, his furrowed brow and gleaming eyes portending trouble. As Parnell ended Forster, towering to his feet, shrieked, "That's not the letter!"... The House of Commons has known many dramatic moments, but in my thirty-eight years there I never felt such emotion as that interruption. Parnell paled.'[10]

The Irish leader replied that he had not kept a copy of it himself, but that the member for Clare (O'Shea) had given him a copy. It was possible, he said, that one paragraph might be missing. When O'Shea said that he did not have the original document with him, the ex-Chief Secretary triumphantly produced it. There were demands for O'Shea to read out the document in full. This, after some hesitation, he did. The missing words included the allusion to cooperating in future with the Liberal Party. It was not technically a 'deal' as such, but it was sufficiently suggestive of one to give the Conservatives a means to make as much capital from Gladstone's embarrassment as possible. The Tories made great play from what was an inept handling of the whole business.

Florence Arnold-Forster was indignant at the position in which the whole debacle had placed her father:

But the worst was not over with the reading of the letter; later on in the evening the affair came up again, and this time – by way of showing plainly what there was in the Gladstone-Parnell understanding which had driven him to resign rather than be responsible for its consequences, Father felt bound to read to the House the Memorandum of his conversation with Mr O'Shea on that memorable Sunday morning. The effect of this incident was to renew tenfold all the disagreeables connected with the production of the letter; the true nature of the Government's new allies, and the unsatisfactory cause of their promised influence in stopping outrage were made known to the House and to the country, but it was at the cost of much pain and annoyance to Father, owing to the manner in which he himself had been made the instrument of disclosing the truth, of embarrassing his late colleagues, and affording unbounded delight to the Opposition.[11]

There were other casualties. Chamberlain's reputation, never all that secure, suffered.[12] The following day, on 16 May, the government was heckled once again on the subject of the agreement. There was particular concern over whether Davitt had been released as a condition of Parnell's implied support to the Liberals. Next to Parnell he was one of the best known of the Irish agitators and his Fenian past had not been forgotten. The Queen had protested in particular against Davitt's release.[13] 'Is it *possible*', she wrote furiously on 4 May to Gladstone, 'that Michael Davitt known as one of the worst of the treasonable agitators is also to be released? I cannot believe it!'[14]

By all accounts, 16 May was a dreadful day in the House. Arthur Balfour, the Conservative member for Hertford and a rising star in the party, was the nephew and Private Secretary of Lord Salisbury, leader of the Conservative Party (and future Prime Minister).[15] He famously attacked the Prime Minister, declaring that the treaty 'stood alone in its infamy', and that the government 'had negotiated in secret with treason'.[16] Florence Arnold-Forster noted that Balfour had been 'violent', Gladstone 'excited almost to passion', and that 'Mr O'Shea' had been 'personally insulting to Father'. Everyone had agreed, she recorded, 'that the afternoon had been supremely unpleasant and unprofitable'.[17] Katie wrote that the Prime Minister 'declined to express any opinion on Mr. Forster's conduct in bringing before the House a private communication received by him as a Cabinet Minister after he had left the Cabinet'. The premier had continued, she said, by saying he was 'in no better position to pass judgement upon such conduct than was any other member of the House – a comment that was received with loud cheers'. Forster had then 'hastily explained that he would not have done so had it not been for the statement of Captain O'Shea'.[18]

Chamberlain tried to smooth matters, but the debate was ill-tempered. Further discussions over the next days concerning this bill and the Arrears Bill were difficult. There were some serious rifts. Within the Cabinet itself, Gladstone and Chamberlain were pitted against Harcourt who favoured the harsh coercion policy, supported by Spencer. The other deep problem was that of trust. No one could deny the existence of Irish secret societies. Although Parnell was anxious to limit the impact of coercion, he was not unaware of the dangers these extremists presented. The leader's desire for cooperation with the Liberal government was not welcomed by all of the Irish nationalists, least of all Dillon and Davitt. Thus many government ministers distrusted any cooperation with the Irish members. The Cabinet was not in a position to rely on Parnell to deliver on his promises, however nebulous. The Irish leader needed to establish a relationship of trust with Gladstone, but to communicate with him openly was impossible.

Meanwhile, whatever was known or suspected by her husband, Katie's love for Parnell had deepened and that month she had just become pregnant with his child. As well as providing love and emotional support to the Irish leader, Katie presented other advantages. She was of course married to a Member of Parliament, and also connected to the political world through her brother Evelyn, whose military record by 1882 was very impressive. In addition to his numerous promotions, he had been awarded the Grand Cross of the Most Distinguished Order of St Michael and St George.[19] In November 1882, Evelyn Wood dined in Downing Street with none other than the Prime Minister. 'Mr. Gladstone followed me', he recalled, 'apparently intending to sit next to me; but a Naval officer slipped in between us, to our host's evident annoyance.' His host had later engaged him in conversation, however, and Wood wrote: 'I have never had a more interesting table companion than Mr. Gladstone.'[20]

Katie was clearly more than a match for her husband, whom she managed tactfully, and for the difficult Aunt Ben, whom she also managed rather well. Her seemingly boundless optimism was combined with a strong sense of self-regard. It is therefore entirely unsurprising that the ambitious Parnell would turn to his valuable asset: a well-connected, bright woman absolutely devoted to his interests. He had already tried to approach the government indirectly. On 22 May Parnell had spent an hour with Henry Labouchere,[21] a Radical who was trying to help form a partnership of sorts with the Irish nationalists. The leader told Labouchere that he really was 'most anxious to get on with the Government if possible'.[22] Labouchere wrote to his fellow Radical, Chamberlain, explaining that Parnell 'says that he is most anxious for a *modus vivendi*, and believes that if the present opportunity for establishing one be let pass, it is not likely to recur. He and his friends are incurring the serious risk of assassination in their efforts to bring it about.'[23]

But, despite Parnell's evident desire to seek such a compromise, there was further obstruction from the Irish members in Parliament when Harcourt refused to make concessions on the coercion measures. Labouchere told Chamberlain that the Irish leader was 'most anxious that Gladstone should not think that obstruction arises from any ill-feeling towards him'.[24] Parnell wanted the Prime Minister to know and understand the reality of the Irish Party's situation. There was much disagreement. In Paris, Egan was furious at the idea that the League was being watered down. Extremists in the party asserted that a policy of conciliation was getting them nowhere.

Parnell therefore decided to explore another approach to the government. Within days of the heated Kilmainham discussions in Parliament, Katie wrote to the Prime Minister. On 23 May she asked him to meet with the Irish leader. 'I am very anxious', she queried, 'to ask if you will permit Mr Parnell to have a few minutes *private* conversation with you.' She also asked Gladstone to meet with her personally: 'I believe if you would kindly manage to see me for a few minutes after the morning sitting today, you would forgive my troubling you.' That Parnell was masterminding the communication was made clear by Katie's insistence that the communication was a secret one – 'I am writing in perfect confidence', she continued, 'that you will not mention the subject of this letter to *anyone* – I have not, and shall not even to Captain O'Shea.'[25]

The weight given to Katie's intervention can be evaluated by the Prime Minister's courteous response. He did not question by what right she should be making queries on such sensitive affairs of state. There can be little doubt that his knowledge of her excellent family connections calibrated his reply. His answer was an assessment of the advisability of such a meeting, and his decision not to agree to her request.[26] Katie (undoubtedly guided by Parnell) returned to the attack. She was 'inexpressibly sorry' that the Prime Minister was 'unable to accede to my wish'. She ventured to suggest, however, that perhaps he would see *her*. In a letter of 26 May, Katie wrote 'to beg you will allow me to see you for a few minutes as soon as you conveniently can'.[27]

The Irish leader needed a breakthrough with the government. Arnold-Forster recorded on 18 May that the police believed that the Phoenix Park assassinations had been planned by Mr Egan from Paris. One reason for this theory was that the O'Donovan Rossa gang – suspected of the crime – were known to be very poor, and Egan had complete control of the American Land League money. These funds, as we know, were previously sent to Paris to avoid confiscation. Arnold-Forster wrote that Egan 'is said to have entirely broken with Mr Parnell, whose policy he would have no objection to defeat'.[28]

Katie's persistence resulted in a private meeting with Gladstone at Thomas's Hotel on 1 June.[29] He arrived 'punctually' at three o'clock, she recalled. They had 'a long talk about Parnell and about politics – chiefly, of course, as referring to Ireland'. Katie noted that the Prime Minister was 'extremely agreeable and courteous, and I remember very well the great charm of manner he possessed'. She thought that he was a 'very great old man… as his wonderful eagle's eyes showed just sufficient admiration in them to savour of homage without offence'. Katie wrote that she had made her position very plain: 'And I may say here that, with all the perfect courtesy of which, when he chose, he was past master, he knew before the conclusion of our interview, and allowed me to know that he knew, what I desired that he should know – that my personal interest in Parnell was my only interest in Irish politics.'[30]

Edward Hamilton was appalled that Gladstone had been 'inveigled' into meeting with Katie. It would, in his opinion, had been 'far better for Mr. G. to decline point blank to see her or communicate with her; but he does not take the view of the "man of the world" in these matters'.[31] It is not clear whether the Prime Minister knew that Katie was Parnell's mistress, although rumours were circulating. In addition to Harcourt's comment, the Foreign Secretary, Earl Granville, remarked to Gladstone that Mrs O'Shea was said to be Parnell's mistress.[32] But when Granville's nephew,

George Leveson Gower, referred to this, the Prime Minister was resistant to the notion. Leveson Gower had discussed the matter with Hamilton, who said he could not see his way to approaching the Prime Minister on such a subject. He had no objection, however, to Leveson Gower doing so. He later told of how he 'opened the matter with what delicacy he could, mentioning Parnell's connection with the lady; but the old man fired up at once, and made him an oration'. Leveson Gower repeated Gladstone's unequivocal response:

You do not mean, he said, to ask me to believe that it is possible a man should be so lost to all sense of what is due to his public position, at a moment like the present, in the very crisis of his country's fortunes, as to indulge in an illicit connection with the wife of one of his very own political supporters, and to make use of that connection in the way you suggest.[33]

We have no means of confirming what the Prime Minister knew, or chose to ignore about the relationship. What we do know is that now Parnell had both of the O'Sheas working on his behalf. Willie was still in frequent communication with Chamberlain. It is unlikely that Parnell expected much to come of this, but O'Shea was a useful conduit, who had a good working relationship with a member of Cabinet. And there is every likelihood, of course, that Parnell wished to keep O'Shea busy. As the Crimes Bill was acrimoniously discussed and debated, information thus passed from Parnell and the O'Sheas to Labouchere, Chamberlain, Gladstone and others. In return, the Irish leader was anxious to retrieve as much information as he could about Harcourt's position and the government's flexibility on amendments to the bill. Communication was difficult and complicated because of the enormous difficulty of a fundamental lack of trust.

This lack of trust extended also to the Irish Party itself. First, there were Members of Parliament, and indeed of the Cabinet, who did not believe that any member of the Irish Party could be trusted. There were others – such as Harcourt – who had no sympathy for the position of moderates such as Parnell. On 8 June the Home Secretary reported: 'Parnell is evidently disposed to be as moderate and conciliatory as he dares – the recalcitrants are Healy, Dillon and O'Donnell, but as yet P. seems to hold his own.'[34] As biographer Lyons dryly pointed out, 'that "P" should be given some assistance in holding his own appears never to have entered Harcourt's head'.[35]

The Irish leader was indeed struggling. He had told Labouchere (who passed it on to Chamberlain) that he was 'in a very difficult position between the Government and the secret societies'. These societies, he explained, were 'more numerous than are supposed'.[36] He also had cause to fear his colleagues. Davitt continued to argue forcefully for comprehensive land reform (something the landowner Parnell had never convincingly pushed for). In Paris, Egan – in situ with the funds – made the case for continued opposition to the government. If the government would not make concessions to the bill, Parnell's situation within the Irish nationalist movement would be at risk. Labouchere explained the leader's predicament to Chamberlain, writing on 3 June:

Egan, he [Parnell] says, wants to carry on the agitation from Paris, in which case it will be illegal; he wants to carry it on in Dublin, in which case it will be legal. If concessions are made he will have his way; if not, Egan will remain the master in Paris. Grosvenor[37] quite admits that it is most desirable to aid Parnell to remain leader.[38]

Katie claimed that she 'frequently' met with the Prime Minister during this time, 'taking him drafts, clauses and various proposed amendments (of Bills affecting Ireland) that Parnell proposed, altered, and suggested privately to Gladstone before putting them before the House'.[39] But her claim was hotly disputed by Gladstone's son, Herbert. In his account, *After Thirty Years*, he went to painstaking lengths to 'prove' that there were only three meetings between his father and Katharine O'Shea. These took place, he wrote, on 1 June, 29 August and 14 September 1882. The second and third interviews were held at 10 Downing Street. Others besides Herbert Gladstone have also observed that much of Katie O'Shea's recollection of her relationship with the Prime Minister is unreliable and in many instances exaggerated. However, the meetings – at this highly critical time – were undoubtedly important. There was no private contact whatsoever between the Irish leader and Gladstone. The first personal contact was not made until 26 February 1886.

In the spring of 1882, Parnell was trying desperately to create some form of alliance with the Liberals and Katie's role as go-between was obviously useful. The leader was doing his utmost to try to persuade the government to modify the proposed Coercion Bill. Katie obligingly ferried messages to and fro, and corresponded with both Gladstone and the Chief Whip, Lord Grosvenor. But the Prime Minister was not willing to accede to her frequent requests for meetings. Katie admitted as much, stating that this was because having a verbal account of Parnell's views put before him 'did not suit Gladstone', who 'had no intention of giving away his hand in regard to the Crimes Bill'.[40] Katie wrote to the Prime Minister on 22 June, requesting such a meeting. 'I have a letter I want to show you,' she declared, 'and there are a few things I should like to tell you as I think it better that you should know them.'[41]

Meanwhile, Willie O'Shea was also busily at work. His conduit was the Chamberlain/Dilke axis. O'Shea had formed a working friendship with Chamberlain which he now attempted to develop into a political partnership. The President of the Board of Trade was a canny politician, and his correspondence with the Captain reveals little commitment on his part. But he was sufficiently encouraging of O'Shea's efforts to act as a mediator between Parnell and the government to give the Captain grounds to push for more. O'Shea had also gained confidence after the relative success of the Kilmainham agreement. He seems to have completely ignored his responsibility for bungling the matter of Parnell's letter. This was typical of O'Shea. He had a remarkable ability to overlook his incompetence, and to move past each crisis to look optimistically to the future. Now he threw himself into the role of political mediator with enthusiasm.

Parnell, like Chamberlain, obviously did just enough to encourage him. On 25 May (the day before Katie made her approach to Gladstone), O'Shea confided to Chamberlain that 'Parnell has just spoken to me and given me the heads of his speech. If he keeps to them, all will be right.'[42] Both O'Sheas were now well in harness. On 16 June, Katie wrote to the Prime Minister that she was 'authorised to submit (privately) a written proposal for your kind consideration'. She continued to press for a meeting, asking whether she could hope to see him 'at Thomas' Hotel for a few minutes tomorrow?'[43] The next day she wrote again, clearly under the Irish leader's instructions, telling the Prime Minister she hoped 'that if you are unable to accede to the proposal in its entirety that you will not discard it altogether until I have had the pleasure of seeing you again'. If he was unable to see her on Monday, then she asked that he return the paper. She hoped that her 'anxious wish to save a useless waste of time in another quarter may plead for my having ventured to trespass personally on your time which I know to be of such inexpressible value to the nation'.[44]

The Irish leader played his cards close to the chest. It is likely that Katie was his sole confidante. Willie O'Shea wrote to Chamberlain on 23 June of his disappointment in Parnell, claiming that he was 'frequently in a "moony", drifting state of mind, nowadays, with which it is difficult to keep one's temper'. Frustratingly, the Captain found that the leader's 'amendments on the paper are inconsistent with views which he has expressed to me'.[45] He wrote to 'My dear Parnell', voicing his concern: 'A very considerable period of debate has now elapsed since at your request I informed the Prime Minister that there would be no obstruction to the Prevention of Crime Bill. I have therefore a special right to beg of you to carry out your engagement in its spirit as well as its letter.'[46] O'Shea seemed to sense that the power was slipping in another direction. He and Parnell were still in contact, however. O'Shea wrote to Chamberlain a few days later that he had spoken 'in the very strongest terms' to the Irish leader on 28 June. He confessed he could not 'understand him'.[47]

Katie continued her correspondence with Gladstone, who might have been somewhat perplexed at the two-fronted assault on the Irish question led by the O'Sheas. The odd situation once again begs the question of how much was known by the British political establishment at this point in time about the relations between Parnell and Katie O'Shea. T. P. O'Connor claimed that he was convinced that until the divorce case, Gladstone 'had no idea of the real state of things', adding that the Prime Minister was 'not the type of man to look for or to suspect illicit sexual relations'.[48] The Prime Minister's Junior Secretary, George Leveson Gower, later told Gladstone's son Henry that his father 'chose to disbelieve – or at any rate to disregard' the rumours.[49] The most likely interpretation is that the Prime Minister did not actually know of the extent of the affair in 1882. It was accepted that men had a private life, and indiscretions were permissible, if kept entirely secret. It was, however, a question of degree and discretion. Had Gladstone known that Katie and Parnell were possibly cohabiting, and that she was expecting the leader's child, he would certainly not have met her privately.

The Irish leader also opened up another line of communication with the government. He and Healy had a number of meetings with Labouchere. Through Labouchere and Chamberlain, Parnell sought to obtain concessions and amendments to the proposed legislation. Labouchere opined that the leader 'still is most anxious for the arrangement of some kind, which will enable him to throw in his lot with the Liberals, but he begs that the great difficulties of his position may be fairly weighed'.[50] There were many in the Irish Party (and in Ireland) who continued to voice considerable objection to any signs of overt cooperation with the British government. Parnell played his hand with great discretion and secretiveness.

Katie had moved into a new phase of her life, meanwhile. For more than five years she had lived a peaceful existence in the pleasant suburb of Eltham, looking after her children and Aunt Ben. Contact with Willie had, by her account, slowly diminished, although their relations were amicable. She occasionally went up to London to host dinner parties to help her husband's parliamentary career. In 1882, her eldest child, Gerard, was twelve, and had been sent to school at Blackheath some four years previously. The two younger girls, Norah, aged nine, and Carmen, aged eight, were educated at home by a German governess. Willie had rooms at Albert Mansions in London and visited Eltham at weekends. On Sundays he took the three children to Mass. Katie was a woman of energy and determination. There is every probability that she now found her settled life a little dull. Meeting the charismatic and handsome Charles Parnell had shaken her life immeasurably, and now she found herself swept up into the world of political intrigue.

She had been, by her own account, a political novice. In a remarkably short time, thanks to her relationship with Parnell, she was involved with politics at the highest level. The two spent hours going over his political positions, which she then conveyed to the Prime Minister. Although the political communications were Parnell's, it was Katie who tried to convince Gladstone to pay heed. She was 'grateful' for his letter, she wrote to the Prime Minister on 26 June, and 'deeply' regretted he 'should have come to any conclusion which will deprive me of the pleasure of meeting you'. She was still hopeful of another encounter: 'greatly as I have appreciated the happiness of seeing you, it is not from selfishness alone that I beg you will not "boycott" me altogether'.[51] On 5 July Katie was once again Parnell's voice. She 'would not venture to trouble you again so soon', she penned to Gladstone, 'but Mr P is anxious that I should let you know that centres of disturbance are being rapidly created throughout Ireland owing to loss by tenants of legal interest in their holdings through sale or expiring of period of redemption'. The leader also wished her to tell him 'that he will place new clauses on the notice papers for the Arrears Bill which will go far to meet these difficulties and he will do all he can to facilitate supply and the passage of the bill and also to prevent obstruction to other government business'.[52]

Willie continued to operate in parallel. On 28 June, he drew attention in a letter to the Irish leader to his frustration in the lack of discernible progress. 'My dear Parnell', he wrote:

With reference to the observation which you made to me yesterday afternoon, to the effect that the Prevention of Crime Bill is very complex and that the government have made no important concessions, I must point out that the Bill was quite as complex & the govt quite as uncompromising at the time when, at your request, I informed Mr Gladstone & Mr Chamberlain that it wd not be obstructed & when, later on, I mentioned to Sir W. Harcourt yr desire not to come into serious collision with the Govt. I again most earnestly beg of you to act fairly to myself, and in consonance with the promises of wh I have been on your behalf the bearer. Exasperation is growing very fast and it is clear that the Govt must shortly organise all-night sittings. The consequences may be deplorable. But this is altogether outside the graver question as between you and myself – the honourable fulfilments by you, at any risk, of an important pledge.[53]

The Captain's explicit reference to 'honourable fulfilments' by Parnell to him of an 'important pledge' is most significant. This is the first written indication of an agreement between the two men. It is difficult to know whether this agreement was political or personal – or both. But it is clear that Willie O'Shea believed that he and the Irish leader had a deal. He immediately reported to Chamberlain, telling him:

Parnell has just told me he hopes that I acknowledge he has done something to meet my views in insisting on his friends allowing the Clause to pass this evening, and it is only fair to him to let you know that he has told Hely [*sic*] he would walk out if that member forced a division on a previous amendment. Parnell complains that no concessions are made, and that Sir William Harcourt is *intransigeant* [*sic*].[54]

The Irish leader did just enough to provide the Captain with the impression that he was being cooperative. The real negotiations were taking place, however, with Katie as envoy. She recorded that Parnell would draft a memorandum, which she would then transmit to the Prime Minister. Although she was not therefore the author of these political messages, there is no doubt that Katie, an intelligent and capable individual, developed an expertise on the Irish political questions of the day. This, and her high self-confidence, enabled her to approach Gladstone and Lord Grosvenor with assurance. During the progress of another Crimes Bill in the spring of 1882, a series of letters were exchanged as heated debates continued. There were numerous sittings in the House devoted to discussion of the bill. Many of these sessions were acrimonious. Members of the Irish Party were very unhappy about the bill and fought bitterly to oppose many of its clauses.

Katie provided Parnell's explanation for some of the objections in a letter to Gladstone on 10 July. She wrote that some of the members had opposed an amendment to the bill – twenty-four had voted against it, while four others, she wrote, were in London but were not present in the House at the time of the vote. And of the rest of the party, 'fifteen had left to return home to business which had been neglected for the last two months'. Two others had been 'permanently absent for some time'. Mr Parnell believed, however, that he could 'keep as many men for the remaining stages of the Arrears Bill as for the Coercion Bill and he has sent telegrams to the absent ones urging them to return'.[55] The following day Katie wrote again, stating another change proposed by Parnell in the wording of the Arrears Bill. The leader considered his proposed change 'absolutely necessary to prevent many landlords defeating the bill and so foiling its compulsory character – if no other of his amendments are accepted, he is very anxious that this one should be'.[56]

Katie's memoir included many of the notes she had made during her discussions with Parnell. They are very detailed, and evidently make clear her understanding of the intricate negotiations. As a further development to his strategy of achieving results through political mediation, Parnell decided to turn away from some of the Land League's previous activity. He had already taken certain steps to do so. On leaving Kilmainham, he had been annoyed to find that the Ladies' Land League had spent heavily on providing funds for evicted tenants instead of reserving the money (mostly raised in America) for his parliamentary activities.

The Ladies' Land League had been formed at the urging of Michael Davitt early in 1881 and had as its effective head Anna Parnell, Charles's sister. Anna was a dedicated nationalist, and had been working hard for a Famine Relief Fund while staying with her mother in New York. Through 1880 she continued to fight for independence when she returned to Ireland in the late summer of that year. Davitt had worked with Anna Parnell in America and he proposed to the Land League executive that she should head up a Ladies' Land League. He was vehemently opposed in this by Charles Parnell, John Dillon and Thomas Brennan.[57] Davitt was, however, deeply concerned that the land agitation movement needed considerable reinforcement.

Charles had reluctantly agreed to the formation of the organization rather than see the results from land agitation dissipate. The Ladies' Land league (LLL) was formed and quickly comprised a group of talented, mainly middle-class women. They were well organized and straight away formed an executive council of thirteen.[58] The Treasurer was Kate Moloney, wife of the active Land Leaguer William Moloney (who was later imprisoned for his League activities). Hannah, Nannie and Virginia Lynch were also active LLL members. They came of a middle-class – but impecunious – family of Fenian sympathizers and all served the League in varying capacities. The sisters had turned to one of the few employment opportunities available to them and become governesses, although Hannah later became a successful novelist, literary critic and translator, also serving as the Treasurer of a Ladies' Land League set up in London.[59] Another member, the eighteen-year-old Jennie O'Toole, set off on 'missions' outside Dublin, along with Tessa Cantwell (stepsister to the dynamic Lynchs), who was herself only fifteen. O'Toole – as Jennie Wyse-Power – went on to lead a distinguished career in Irish politics.[60]

Anna Parnell had chaired the first LLL meeting in Dublin on 3 January 1881 and on 4 February the *Nation* published a letter signed by four members of the executive council. The letter declared that the law was soon to be suspended and that the leaders of the Land League would probably be arrested. There would be no one to help and protect evicted tenants. 'Therefore, the women of Ireland must step in to assist the evicted.' In order to do this, the ladies 'must form themselves in to branches and be ready (1) to give information on evictions in their district, (2) give advice and encouragement to unhappy victims, (3) collect funds and (4) disburse funds entrusted to them'.[61] The LLL was applauded as a ladylike charitable organization – dedicated to the 'alleviation of distress and suffering'.[62]

But Anna Parnell – like the clever and committed women who worked with her – had political goals. Like her brother, she did not espouse violence, but she did believe in fighting for justice. She began touring the country, addressing public meetings. Although

Anna Parnell was a shy woman who did not relish public speaking, she was strong-minded and opinionated, determined to do her duty. In her speeches, which were often attended by thousands of women as well as men, she urged the people of Ireland to be self-reliant and to stand up for their right to demand changes in land tenure. She spoke particularly to women, encouraging them to make a difference and to refuse to be intimidated or frightened, arguing that women could take responsibility for political change, and hoped that 'perhaps... when we are dead and gone and another generation grown up... they will point to us as having set a noble example to all the women of Ireland'.[63]

Charles Parnell was not a supporter of his sister's campaigning or of the LLL itself. John Dillon and Thomas Brennan (who was in charge of finances after Egan had left for Paris) were, along with Charles, increasingly hostile to the LLL as it became more independent of them. The purpose of collected monies was a critical issue. It was important to Parnell and his colleagues that money raised for the Land League be at least in part directed to political activities. But the fund-raising – especially as espoused by the LLL – focused on the plight of starving tenants and not on paying politicians to enact change. This was also the case with many of the funds originating from America. Many people who donated money to help those who were suffering in Ireland did not support radical land reform and would not have given money for such purposes.

Parnell understood this very well. On his arrival in New York on 2 January 1880 he had made a speech to open his fund-raising tour. 'We propose', he declared, 'then, to form two funds – one for the relief of distress, and the other for the purely political purposes of forwarding our organisation.' He acknowledged the difficulties this might present, and continued:

It has been suggested by a very influential paper in this city that we ought to devote our attention only to the relief of distress, and that we should only join the committee which has been proposed by the New York *Herald* for the relief of distressed Irish landlords and the British Government in general. But if we accepted this very good advice... I am afraid we should incur the imputation of putting the cart before the horse.[64]

Parnell and other Land Leaguers were determined to divert resources to political ends. During the tour, in March, Parnell had Healy draft a letter to Egan (Treasurer of the Land League) confirming this intention. He wrote:

I feel confident that, in addition to a very large amount for the charitable objects of my visit, such a sum will be entrusted to me for the purposes of our political organisation as will, if suitably invested, secure for the Land League a permanent income upon the capital, and thus enable it constantly and energetically to direct attention to the evils of the present land system until its destruction becomes inevitable.[65]

Fund-raising tours in the United States had become an important part of the nationalist struggle. The onset of the Great Famine had increased the flood of Irish immigrants into America – at a rate of about 100,000 in the 1860s[66] – and the Irish population had concentrated in the great urban centres of Pennsylvania, New York, New Jersey and New England. Much of the rhetoric associated with the influx was one of nostalgia and Anglophobia. The mass emigrations of the famine years were explained in terms of English oppression. The Irish-American press became very powerful and Irish-Americans came to dominate the Democratic Party. This large and growing expatriate community was characterized by its continuing preoccupation with politics 'back home' and by its ardent support for a wide-ranging variety of organizations that supported the struggle for Irish independence. These varied considerably in tone and in their espousal or rejection of extremism.[67]

It was thus of great importance for Irish nationalists to cultivate this Irish-American community, who were such a critical source of funds. In his quest for financial support there Charles Parnell was aided by his American parentage. His mother Delia had settled with daughters Fanny and Theodosia, after 1874, in the prosperous and attractive town of Bordentown, near Trenton, New Jersey. The town was on the banks of the Delaware River, and the three women lived comfortably at 'Ironsides', the home Delia's father had purchased in 1816. The house and its farm were on an estate located high above the river, about a mile and a half from the town. Ironsides was an attractive building, which has been called a 'rustic version of the grander neoclassical Avondale'.[68] The house had a large sitting room, a library and a dining room, all of which were furnished with Delia's many pictures, sofas and other furniture. The rooms boasted the original fine wood panelling and marble fireplaces.[69]

The New York that Charles visited in 1880 was a bustling metropolis of over 700,000 inhabitants.[70] Post Civil-War reconstruction, rapid industrialization and financial speculation had transformed it into an enormously wealthy city. The economic depression which had begun in 1873 was over.[71] Leading businessmen such as August Belmont, Jay Gould, William Vanderbilt, J. P. Morgan and the Rockefellers dominated. Ostentatious consumption and flaunting of wealth had become the norm: mansions were built along Fifth Avenue, and hostesses outdid one another with parties on an unprecedented scale. The season just after the war was marked by 600 balls – and for these an estimated $7 million was spent on clothes and jewellery.[72] The wealthy elite mingled at the theatre: stalls at Wallack's, the nation's leading playhouse, were in great demand. In the Union Square Rialto the gilded elite enjoyed opera performances at the Academy of Music, which hosted the American premières of *Aida* (1873), *Lohengrin* (1874), *Die Walküre* (1877) and *Carmen* (1878).[73] Fancy dinners at restaurants such as Delmonico's took place, at which generous hosts such as the speculator Leonard Jerome (who made and lost several Wall Street fortunes) presented the lady guests with expensive gold and platinum bracelets as party favours. Social climbing was rife, as new money struggled with the social arbiters of the wealthy old guard. The era of the 'dollar princesses' entered full swing. Daughters of wealthy Americans looked – along with their socially ambitious parents – to the Old World to secure their social position by marrying a titled man. In one of the first of such transatlantic alliances, Leonard's daughter Jennie married the son of Lord Marlborough, Randolph Churchill, in 1874 (and later became the mother of Britain's most famous statesman, Winston Churchill). Further exchanges of 'cash for titles' followed, with heiresses such as May Goelet, Consuelo Vanderbilt and the Yznaga sisters all casting their matrimonial nets overseas.[74]

Lavish personal consumption on horses, houses, boats and extravagant entertainments was accompanied by visible philanthropic activity. In 1880, the year of Parnell's fund-raising visit, the magnificent Metropolitan Museum of Art opened its doors. Across Central Park a group of prominent men, including Theodore Roosevelt, Sr (a leading glass importer and amateur naturalist), banker J. P. Morgan and corporate attorney Joseph Choate, set out to build an American Museum of Natural History.[75] Yet underpinning this opulent display of magnificence and wealth lay the underclass, most of whom lived in appalling conditions in the city's verminous slums. Many of these workers were Irish immigrants. The 'notorious cellars of Boston', and the 'wooden tenements (called "barracks") run up for the Irish immigrants in New York'[76] had reinforced from the 1840s an immigrant culture that retained a strong ethnic identification. And although the Irish immigrant population had, from about 1879, become more literate and modernized, they remained to a large degree excluded from the upper-middle and upper classes. Nevertheless, many Irish immigrants had climbed up the socio-economic ladder – moving on from the factory and mining jobs to become police officers, nurses or members of the civil service.[77] Irish immigrants and their descendants purchased property and invested heavily in the Catholic Church. There were also some Irish-American millionaires. But the 'subculture' mentality remained in force for the most part, and this group was thus a reliable source of funds for the Irish nationalist cause.

Fanny Parnell became increasingly involved in raising funds and awareness of Irish nationalist aspirations in the United States. As her daughter became more active in her nationalist activity, Delia joined in. Not known to be especially political – she was by most accounts a spoiled and self-centred woman – Delia Parnell was nevertheless used by some Irish-American groups to raise funds and bolster Irish nationalist aspirations. This development was not overtly encouraged by her son Charles, although Delia appeared with him on platforms during a tour he made in America in 1880. Her political involvement continued in October of that year with the foundation of the Ladies' Land League by Fanny in the United States. Delia was titular president of the new organization, although she was not involved in the management or policymaking of the institution. Ellen Ford, a committed nationalist – and sister of Patrick Ford – together with Fanny Parnell ran the organization. But, according to T. P. O'Connor, Delia Parnell's attendance at the Irish-American meetings in 1881 was extremely dedicated and she often spoke 'for an hour or more, patiently and indefatigably'.[78] Delia also travelled with Ellen Ford on tours for the Ladies' Land league and, throughout 1880 and 1881, became something of a minor celebrity in Irish nationalist circles.

Many branches of the LLL in Ireland and in America were named after her, but from late 1882 her public appearances became rare, and her discourse, never entirely coherent, even more erratic. There had always been a strong tendency to self-aggrandizement and eccentricity, and there was every possibility that Delia was enjoying the attention that her famous offspring generated. Her political beliefs were vague in the extreme, and her lifestyle was summed up by one biographer as 'rackety'.[79] The written accounts of her odd sayings and speeches, along with a seemingly complete inability to deal with her finances, lead to the impression that she was more of an embarrassment than an asset to the Irish cause. Delia had her supporters, nevertheless, eager to make use of the famed Parnell connection. T. P. O'Connor wrote that 'her speeches, without any disrespect, appeared to be somewhat rigmarole… but the immense respect felt for her personally, and for her son, always secured her an attentive, though puzzled, audience'.[80] On her way to Ireland in 1881, for example, Delia Parnell declared at a meeting in Liverpool that 'Ireland was the keystone of the universe and on it depended the future of the world'.[81] Although Delia (no doubt mercifully, for her children at least) faded from the political stage after 1882, accounts of her financial and personal woes appeared from time to time in the press. She relied increasingly on her daughter Fanny, who organized the house and farm at Bordentown, and in fact had sporadic contact with her famous son.

Charles Parnell issued a direct order to the LLL that spring to reduce expenditure on relief, legal aid and the construction of huts for evicted tenants in County Limerick. Anna Parnell simply ignored her brother's demand, and had the huts built anyway.[82] It was a trying time for the siblings. In July 1882, shortly after Charles had been released from jail, their much beloved sister Fanny died suddenly in Bordentown. Both Anna and Charles were devastated. Fanny was an acknowledged beauty and a talented nationalist poet. She had been working ardently to raise awareness and funds for the Irish cause in America. She wrote hundreds of letters, as well as composing verse, and campaigned tirelessly. Her politics were probably more radical than those of her brother, but she was attacked for her moderate position by hard-line nationalists.

The American Fenian William Carroll had written in disgust to Devoy in 1879:

It will be news to all Fenians that I ever met to learn that they would be satisfied with a Home Rule government and a British Queen. However, it is not Irish to contradict a lady, and so we leave Miss Parnell to see what she will see of Fenians' love for British Queens before she adds another twenty-two years to her present record of summers.[83]

It is difficult to ascertain the extremity of her political views. Radical Fenians in America did not like her brand of nationalism (many of them were critical of the entire family, including Charles). The Parnells were seen by some nationalists as pro-British and insufficiently radical. Despite this, Fanny had certainly become a political celebrity. Lockets with her portrait were sold in Ireland for a shilling each, and her poems graced every nationalist journal.[84]

Theodosia had left her mother and sister in the spring of 1880 to return with her brother Charles to England. She was to be married that summer, in Paris, to the English naval officer Claude Paget. Fanny and her mother had stayed on in Bordentown, busy with the Land League and travelling to address political meetings. As Fanny's health deteriorated, however, she found that these forays – which she much enjoyed – had to be curtailed. In April 1882, she had hoped to travel with Delia to Washington, as one of the official Ladies' Land League delegates to the second annual convention of the Irish Land League of America. But she was suffering from a recurring fever and had to cancel her trip. In June, however, she was sufficiently recovered to receive Davitt and the nationalist Home Rule MP William ('Willie') Redmond as her guests at Bordentown. She drove the carriage to the railway station herself on 11 July, and that evening brought them to admire the now abandoned estate of Joseph Bonaparte, who had previously settled there. This was where her grandmother, Delia II, had 'once suffered "all the ennui of paying court" without the charm of being at court'.[85] The two men left the next morning, accompanied by Delia, to travel to New York. Davitt was to be given a large public reception at the Harmony Hall.

Some days later, Fanny was back to her usual pleasant routine. On the evening of 18 July, she took her habitual walk with her two dogs, a brown setter and a black-and-white St Bernard. The next morning, she drove into the town to collect her mail, returned to the house and at noon sat down to lunch with her mother. She then fed her dogs and went to her room to rest. Later, her mother was unable to rouse her, and the doctor who was sent for pronounced Fanny dead. His diagnosis was that she had died of 'paralysis of the heart'.[86] She was thirty-two years old.

Katie read of Fanny's death in the morning papers and woke Charles Parnell to give him the news. He had been staying at Eltham and was sleeping after a late night in the House of Commons. Their routine, as she described it, was for the leader to sleep until four in the afternoon, after which he would join her for breakfast and 'chat' until it was time to return to Parliament. It is interesting to note that if Parnell was not to be 'roused' before four in the afternoon, the servants (and children) must perforce have known the leader was there. Katie knew that her lover would be very upset at the news. He had told her that Fanny was 'the cleverest and most beautiful woman in his family'. This Katie had taken as 'high praise', especially, she wrote, as Willie had met another of Parnell's sisters, Delia Thomson, and had told Katie that she was 'the most strikingly beautiful woman he had ever met'.[87]

Katie described how Charles Parnell was distraught at the news. He was 'terribly shocked' and 'utterly broke down'. She was unable to leave him and stayed with him all day.[88] Nevertheless he responded forcefully to the news that his sister's body was to be embalmed and then brought back to Ireland. He had Katie write a cable on his behalf forbidding the plan, and insisting that Fanny be buried in America, where she had died. Despite the pleas of thirty-five branches of the Land League in America, 'to grant the request of the Irish people of the United States... to bear her honoured remains to her motherland',[89] Parnell refused absolutely. He hated death, all talk of it, and funerals. He was horrified at the idea of embalming and these plans were abandoned. Fanny was buried in the underground vault of her mother's relatives, the Tudors of Boston, in Cambridge, Massachusetts.[90]

Anna Parnell was traumatized by the news. She and Fanny had been very close, the best of friends, and had worked together to promote the cause of Irish nationalism. Fanny's death occurred just as Anna was suffering the criticism of the Ladies' Land League by her brother and other members of the male executive of the Land League. She was disillusioned by this, and also by the attempts made by many dishonest tenants trying to extract money from the League. But the main problem was her brother Charles, who was relentless. He decided to cut off completely the Ladies' funds. In July, Anna learned that the money they were paying out for Land League purposes was not being covered by the funds held by Egan in Paris. The bank continued to honour their cheques, but the account was becoming very overdrawn. They soon had a negative balance of £5,000. Katie explained that Parnell had for some time been wary of the Ladies' League. He had written to his sister 'again and again' from prison, 'pointing out the crass folly for the criminality for which the Ladies' League, now, existed'.[91]

Katie wrote that the 'fanatic spirit of these ladies was extreme' and that in Anna it was 'abnormal'. Charles saw no way to save his sister, or the country, she claimed, 'but by fulfilling his threat of vetoing the payment of another penny to the Ladies' Land League'.[92] He believed, furthermore, that Anna and her Ladies' Land League were being used by his rivals, notably Dillon and Davitt.[93] Parnell wrote to Katie on 20 August 1882 from Dublin that the 'two D*s' had 'quarrelled with me because I won't allow any further expenditure by the ladies and because I have made arrangements to make the payments myself for the future'.[94] Anna was livid over her brother's summary decision to cut them off. She disbanded the Ladies' League, and refused to speak to Charles ever again. Katie recalled that Charles Parnell had 'much family affection' and had 'many times made overtures of peace to his sister, of whom he was really fond', but to no avail. The rift was absolute. On two occasions when they met accidentally, Anna resolutely turned away from her brother, and she steadfastly refused to reply to any of his letters.[95]

Charles Parnell knew exactly what he was doing. Closing down the Ladies' Land League was a calculated political move. He needed to distance himself from the extremists and the Ladies' Land League was too radical – and it had served its purpose. Despite Anna's obvious sincerity and devotion to the cause, as well as the dedication and hours of hard work volunteered by the members of the Ladies' Land League, they were expendable. Moreover, Parnell made certain to capitalize politically from his decision and briefed Katie to inform the Prime Minister during one of their meetings of the 'enormous sum these Lady Leaguers had expended'. She had then told Gladstone of 'the great difficulty Parnell had had in suppressing them'.[96]

The demise of the Ladies' Land League showed Charles Parnell to be a ruthless operator who sacrificed his relationship with his sister for his political ambitions. By so doing, he was able to successfully demonstrate his autocratic, aloof leadership style to the Irish Party, and to the Prime Minister. His political star was in the ascendant as he looked ahead to fighting for Irish nationalist aspirations.

CHAPTER THIRTEEN

The Go-between

K ATIE MET AGAIN WITH the Prime Minister at the end of the summer, on 29 August 1882. The meeting took place at his office at 10 Downing Street. 'Gladstone would not sit still when he talked to me', she wrote, 'but liked to pace up and down the long room with me.' On her entry, the premier would 'rise from his desk to greet me and, solemnly handing me a chair, would walk down the room to the door at the end'. This door, she remarked, 'was always open when I entered', but the Prime Minister would then 'close it firmly and, pacing back to the door of my entry, push it'. After this, she recalled, they 'paced up and down' while she 'voiced Parnell's instructions and listened to the G.O.M.'s[1] views, intentions, and tentative suggestions, always on my part keeping to "It is considered that, etc.," in giving Parnell's point, and always receiving "Your friend should, etc," or "I am prepared to concede to your friend, etc., in return".'[2]

He was extremely cautious, Katie observed, and when she asked him who was 'shut up in that room', Gladstone replied: 'Persons, or a person, you do not come to see, Mrs. O'Shea. Only a secretary or so, and occasionally, in these times of foolish panic, detectives.' And they could certainly not overhear any of the conversation, he told her, 'in answer to my look of inquiry'.[3] Herbert Gladstone, as we have seen, claimed that Katie wildly exaggerated these meetings and repudiated the idea that any pacing could have taken place at his father's office, demonstrating that the 'long room' was only 28'3" × 19'3" and, further: 'The idea of his walking up and down a room arm in arm with a lady while discussing politics, to anyone who knew Mr. Gladstone is ridiculous. Moreover the position of the furniture made it impossible.'[4] He asserted that phrases from Katie's account,[5] such as 'I had frequently to see him at Downing Street', his 'preparations always made me smile', and 'he always showed the marvellous charm of manner' were contrived attempts to make the relationship seem more than it was. He supposed that 'Mrs. O'Shea had an obvious purpose' and had 'wished to magnify the part she played and to create the impression that she had free access to Downing Street and possessed the close and unreserved confidence of Mr. Gladstone'.[6]

Hamilton noted that the interview of 29 August had been granted to 'Mrs. O'Shea' at 'her earnest solicitation'. It appeared, he wrote, that 'what she wanted most to press on the Prime Minister was the considerations of her husband's claims to be appointed Under-Secretary for Ireland'. His assessment was that 'This or some other place is very likely what has been at the bottom of O'Shea's overtures and negotiations and friendly professions all along.' He did not personally believe that Willie O'Shea was a suitable candidate, writing that although the Prime Minister 'thinks the Government is under *some* obligation to O'Shea', he could not 'admit this at all'. Indeed, Hamilton believed there 'never befell a greater misfortune than to have to take heed of that man's information'.[7]

'That man', however, was convinced that he deserved recognition and was not lacking in self-belief. O'Shea had written to Chamberlain some days previously, on 10 August, about helping to organize Irish support for a proposed piece of legislation.[8] He claimed to have 'arranged the matter of the tactics to be employed to get as strong an Irish vote as possible... with Parnell last night'. He added that it 'seems unnecessary' to have the Irish leader 'write a letter on the subject, my "full powers" having stood the test of events'.[9] Katharine continued her efforts to help him, writing to Gladstone on 15 September and enclosing a letter and a telegram from 'my husband' which she asked the Prime Minister to 'kindly read, and destroy, at your leisure'.[10] Willie's letter was addressed to his 'dearest wife'. In it he wrote of how it was still difficult for him to write due to a broken arm from which he was recovering. 'Yes', he said – and one must wonder whether it was in reply to a question put to him – 'I should like to be under-secretary very much and I think I might make a useful one.'[11] It is of course entirely possible that the letter was set up deliberately, to serve the dual purpose of convincing Gladstone that the O'Shea marriage was intact, and also to find a position for O'Shea.

At the time the suggestion was not completely unrealistic. Willie O'Shea had made a name for himself in the Kilmainham negotiations and not everyone in political circles considered his role to have been nefarious. The Prime Minister felt that the government owed him something. Both Joseph Chamberlain and Dilke were subsequently in frequent communication with the Captain, as was Labouchere. Parnell continued to treat him with courtesy. As an Irish MP, O'Shea naturally took a keen interest in Irish politics at Westminster. He argued against coercion in Ireland, and more than once travelled there to attempt to secure the release of some suspects.[12]

O'Shea's communications to Katie in the spring of 1882 were warm and affectionate. He addressed her by his unusual pet name for her (Dick), and signed himself 'Boysie', or even 'Your Boysie'. He told her about his activities, political and professional. He confided details about his doings and also his worries about financial difficulties. On 31 March he wrote that he had received her telegram, and would 'do nothing till I hear again about the shares'.[13] By 1 May, he was 'getting quite hopeless'; the 'dates of payments are staring me in the face'.[14] On 29 September he reported that he had '£100 coming due on October 17th, £300 on November 13th, and £300 on December 3rd at the National Bank'.[15] He still had an interest in the bank in Madrid, where things were not going well.

Willie was forthcoming in his correspondence with his wife, and shared his opinions and plans. He gave details of his discussions with Chamberlain about the Irish question, and about his own hopes for a position in Ireland. There is no doubt that he considered Katie his confidante. The information he provided to her in his letters about his dealings with Chamberlain, for example, tallies with that in his own letters of that time to Chamberlain. He was keen to spend time with his girls, whom he called 'the Chicks'. On 1 May he wrote to Katie that he was in negotiations with Chamberlain. He would try to 'run down to Eltham if possible' the following afternoon, 'unless I hear you are taking the Chicks anywhere'.[16] Katie was independent at Eltham, free to make her own plans with her children without consulting her husband. He clearly made a point of letting her know when he would be turning up.

Eltham was still his marital home and Willie was obviously fond of his children. While away in Ireland that summer, he sent 'Great love to chicks' on 26 August, 'Dearest love to chicks' on 31 August.[17] Later, after he had badly injured his arm, he told Katharine that he 'must write to chicks, and it is still laborious'.[18] During his stay in Dublin, he was keen to meet with political figures. He reported to Katie that he had spent 'a long time' with the Chief Secretary, Trevelyan. 'It was funny', he told her, 'to see his three boys playing cricket in the grounds of his lodge with constabulary sentinels at each corner.' The lodges, he observed, were 'charming places', but he had not been in the Under-Secretary's'. He had tried 'to get a photograph of it', but 'failed'.[19] The position of Under-Secretary was of great appeal to a man such as O'Shea.

At the head of this hierarchical micro-society was the Viceroy. He represented the monarch, and was always a high-ranking aristocrat.[20] The Viceroy worked and entertained in splendour at Dublin Castle in the capital. 'The splendour of the Castle Seasons', recollected society hostess Daisy Fingall, 'was greatly increased by the fact that the Lord Lieutenants brought over their own pictures, much of their own furniture, and their own plate.' This was, she wrote, 'often very magnificent'. In fact, the only times she had eaten off gold plate were at Buckingham Palace and at the Viceregal Lodge in Dublin.[21] The edifice supporting the Viceroy's stature was elaborate. There was a continual 'courtly ceremonial of state entries, audiences, investitures, levees, parades and entertainments'.[22] In addition to the 'courtly retinue of chamberlains, comptrollers, heralds and poursuivants'[23] there was an entire infrastructure of administrators to run Ireland. Willie was determined to gain the reward of a plum posting in Dublin for his work on attempting to help resolve the Irish problem. That such a position would include prestigious perks and advantages would be particularly welcome. His desire to see the lodge would most likely imply that he was planning to bring his family with him.

Parnell was also in Ireland at this time, but he avoided the Captain. O'Shea commented to his wife that although the leader was staying near by, he did not receive him or seek him out. The following letter sent by O'Shea to Katie on 31 August portrayed his trust in her and indicated his belief that she was in total sympathy with him:

My Dick,

I am longing to get home. No one knows I am writing, so say nothing in your letter about it to my people. Great number of inquiries, but Mr. Parnell, although in next street, never sent. P for pig! Gout come in old place, not bad. Dearest love to chicks. Great many telegrams.

Your Boysie

Am all right, but very helpless for present.[24]

His comment about Parnell implies that he expected his wife to agree with him. It certainly does not read as a letter to a woman expecting Parnell's child. O'Shea then wrote some days later that he had heard that 'Mr. Parnell' had gone to England. 'I merely say', the Captain commented, 'he never took the trouble to send a message or write a line.' Willie had seen Katie's letter to Aunt Mary, he continued, and one from their son Gerard. In a glimpse of domestic detail, he told his wife he was 'quite satisfied with fish, especially as I don't want the gout to go to my arm'.[25]

Meanwhile Katie continued to be in regular contact with her lover. Parnell wrote to 'My Own Queenie' from Morrison's Hotel in Dublin on 20 August 1882. He used Morrison's Hotel as his Dublin base, while Willie O'Shea preferred the more classic Shelbourne Hotel on St Stephen's Green in the city centre.[26] Parnell – who signed himself 'Your Own Husband' – explained that he had 'quarrelled' with Dillon and Davitt over his refusal to 'allow any further expenditure by the ladies'. The leader declared that the two had been 'in hopes of creating a party against me in the country by distributing the funds amongst their own creatures and are proportionately disappointed'.[27]

The 'Chief' had a reputation for being an enigmatic leader. He trusted very few people and he did not confide much in his colleagues. As his brother John pointed out: 'Charles kept his own counsel even as a boy. As a man this trait developed to such an extent that it was only on very rare occasions that one caught a glimpse of the real man beneath the courteous but frigid exterior... But it must be remembered that then, as ever, he was always a questioner rather than an informant. He wanted to get every scrap of information and every shade of opinion on any subject in which he took a real interest, but at the same time he did not like disclosing his own views.'[28]

Parnell's colleague T. P. O'Connor noticed this as well. 'Parnell was one of those magnetic personalities', he recalled, 'at once so taciturn, so inscrutable, and at the same time so hypnotic, that everything about him, even the most trifling, took your attention, and perhaps set you guessing.'[29] In order to pursue his political ambitions, he needed to spend time in Ireland and he was in Dublin that August, and either remained there or returned in October. He also travelled to his beloved family home at Avondale. And with the rare exception of 1883, Parnell never missed the opening of the grouse season in Ireland. Like his father before him, he hunted with friends every August at the family shooting-box in Aughavannah at the foot of the Wicklow mountains. Charles Parnell was a gracious host, whose simplicity was appreciated by those he favoured with his hospitality. Justin McCarthy recollected a visit to Avondale, where Parnell had prepared their picnic with no ceremony or fuss. 'With his own hand', he marvelled, 'Parnell took a loaf of brown bread, cut it into slices, buttered them, and then wrapped them in a paper parcel: this was to be our lunch.'[30]

Throughout September and October 1882 Charles Parnell was hard at work preparing the establishment of a new organization to replace the outlawed Land League. It was a battle for power that he was determined to win and he delayed making a decision. At a meeting at Avondale in September, Parnell finally agreed – after much urging by both Davitt and Dillon – to establish a new national organization. Davitt wanted land nationalization to be a key element of the new league's constitution. Parnell refused to accept this radical agenda. He imposed strict conditions on his agreement to call for a convention to set up a new organization. Davitt later recalled: 'Before Mr. Parnell consented to call such a convention he insisted that he should draft the programme or constitution in order that it should be more strictly constitutional than the Land League and that he should have the task of defining what the policy of the new organisation would be upon the land question.'[31]

Tim Healy wrote to his brother on 5 October that there was 'little less than a split between Davitt and Parnell'. Davitt had prepared a constitution of his own, Healy wrote, 'and Parnell remarked yesterday that he had one ready himself, and would not have Davitt's. If the Conference passes off safely it will be a relief.'[32] Healy drafted the constitution while Parnell lay sick in his hotel bedroom. The leader's intention was to distance himself from the extremists and to persist in trying to work with the Liberals, and he continued to use Katie as a conduit to Gladstone. According to Hamilton's diary, Katie informed the Prime Minister at their second meeting, on 29 August, that Davitt and Dillon 'were both "in great dudgeon" with Parnell by reason of his restricted action on land and national questions'. Hamilton also recorded: 'She regards Davitt as the incarnation of vanity and Dillon as a *tête montée*.[33] She of course reflects Parnell's views.'[34]

Parnell had been quite ill during his stay in Ireland. On 10 October he reassured Katie that the doctor had seen him, and told him that he had suffered an 'attack of dysentarial diarrhoea, but not of a severe character, and very little fever'. In any event, it was 'now quite over'. But this was not the first time he had suffered from intestinal illness. During his stay at Kilmainham he had also had much stomach trouble. At this latest recurrence, the doctor informed him that his 'stomach must have been getting out of order for some time'.[35] However, just a few days later, Parnell wrote that he had left his room for the first time and 'caught a slight cold, which threw me back somewhat'. Katharine had evidently complained of both her concern for him and her unhappiness. The leader confided that the 'dreary hours' of separation from her had been made worse 'by the knowledge that Wifie has been unhappy and anxious all the time'.[36]

Katie was in fact reliving the horrible circumstances of her previous pregnancy. It is not clear who fathered the child she was carrying, but it is certain that Parnell believed it was his. There is no indication, however, in Willie's correspondence with his wife – with all its hopeful speculation of Under-Secretary lodges in Ireland – that he knew she was pregnant by another man. At the age of thirty-seven and having lost a child some months previously, she was likely to be suffering a difficult pregnancy. She was also corresponding with both Parnell and her husband, each of whom demanded her full attention. And of course there was always the imperative need to tend to Aunt Ben, and to her children. Unsurprisingly, Katie wrote that '1882–83' had been 'a very anxious time for me'. Indeed, the 'nervous tension caused by the violence in the political world and the continual threatenings of violence, intrigue, and political force, made privately to Parnell, against him and others, was so great that, by the end of '83, if I had not had my lover's health to care for I should myself have broken down altogether'.[37]

Yet Katie continued to play an active role in Parnell's political strategy. The Prime Minister took note of what she told him. After their meeting on 29 August, Gladstone wrote to Spencer straight away, informing him of Parnell's falling-out with Dillon and Davitt, and of Katie's portrayal of the leader 'as thoroughly bent on legality'.[38] She wrote again to Gladstone on 22 September, confiding that Mr Parnell was expecting a large sum of money from America – £16,000 – which 'he was anxious to hand over to Mr Egan's successor who in the event of Mr Egan's resignation will be Mr P's own nominee'.[39] Obtaining control of the finances of the new organization was a critical achievement for Parnell and was secured by Egan's resignation as Treasurer that October. He further consolidated his leadership position at a conference held to establish the new national organization. This conference took place in Dublin on 17 October. The constitution, drafted by Healy under Parnell's instruction, and by the Nationalist politician and land agitator Timothy Harrington,[40] was presented to the conference, listing five major objectives: to pursue national self-government, to achieve land law reform, to establish local self-government, to extend the parliamentary franchises, and to develop and encourage the labour and industrial interests of Ireland.[41]

Parnell was elected chairman of the National League. Biggar was one of the Treasurers and Tim Healy the Secretary. In his speech, Parnell put Home Rule at the forefront of the league's objectives:

I wish to affirm the opinion which I have expressed ever since I first stood upon an Irish platform, that until we obtain for the majority of the people of this country the right of making their own laws we shall never be able and we never can hope to see the laws of Ireland in accordance with the wishes of the people of Ireland, or calculated, as they should, to bring about the permanent prosperity of our country. And I would always desire to impress upon my fellow countrymen that their first duty and their first object is to obtain for our country the right of making her own laws upon Irish soil.[42]

This strong stance was nevertheless a move away from a proto-revolutionary movement to one that was dominated by parliamentarians and committed to constitutional reform. It did not suit all members, and most of all alienated those on the left of the party who favoured substantive and radical change. Dillon left for the United States, not to return for three years. So too did Brennan, and Egan after he had handed over the Paris funds. Davitt was dismayed at what he saw as Parnell's effectual hijacking and subsequent stranglehold over the new movement. 'It was', he later wrote, 'in a sense, the overthrow of a movement and the enthronement of a man; the replacing of nationalism by Parnellism; the investing of the fortunes and guidance of the agitation, both for national self-government and land reform, in a leader's nominal dictatorship.'[43]

Katie's role as a go-between was particularly important at this juncture. Parnell wanted to ensure Gladstone was apprised of the developments. So keen was the leader to gain the Prime Minister's confidence that he had Katie send a copy of the proposed constitution to him before the conference met. 'I am requested by

Mr Parnell to give you the enclosed', she wrote on 6 October, 'in the hope that you will give it your consideration and kindly let me know if it, or any part of it, would be likely to meet your views – it is a summary of what in his opinion would settle the land question in Ireland.'[44]

Although Gladstone assured her in his reply of 10 October that he would 'make known the purport of your communication and its enclosure to one or two of my colleagues', he could make no promises or take any action. He was, as ever, cautious and courteous. In sending her this 'limited reply', he allowed himself 'the satisfaction of acknowledging the spirit and intent of the memorandum which, in the exercise of his right as a Member of Parliament, Mr. Parnell has framed and transmitted'.[45] Katie persisted. She wrote again to the Prime Minister on 20 October. She hoped that he would 'exonerate me from having troubled you unnecessarily in forwarding the communications I have sent you from time to time and I tell you that it has taken me two years to penetrate through the habitual reserve and suspicion of the Saxon of the author'. This she had done 'sufficiently to induce him to make his views known at all and thus shake himself free of the set by which he was surrounded'.[46]

Parnell, with Katie's help, sought to establish his position as a credible alternative to the violent extremists of Ireland. He sought reform through legislative change and wished to portray himself as a man with whom the British government could negotiate. The situation in Ireland had calmed down considerably. Under Spencer, the Liberals continued coercion, but it was coercion of a different nature and degree. The Crime Prevention Bill of 1882 (which was to last three years) 'provided for a special tribunal to try cases that were bound to be dismissed by juries, for the extension of summary jurisdiction and the treatment of incitement to intimidation as intimidation'.[47] Further judicial changes included the centralization of the magistracy and the reorganization of the special branch of Dublin Castle. Thus, under Spencer, Ireland was governed according to Liberal principles – habeas corpus no longer suspended, for example. And the newly founded National League was allowed to continue openly as a legal political party. Although the Nationalist MPs continued to denigrate British rule in Ireland, at the same time they sought and received recognition and legitimacy in the House of Commons. Despite this progress, it remained unthinkable for the Prime Minister to have direct contact with Parnell, who continued to associate with Irish nationalists who espoused views far more extreme than his own.

Katie's willingness to present herself as the face of acceptable Irish aspirations was thus of critical importance to the Irish leader at a time when he was pursuing two tactical paths. On the one hand, Parnell sought to harness the drive and furious ambitions unleashed by land agitation and fuelled by colleagues such as Davitt and O'Brien. On the other, he wished to portray himself, aided by Katie, as a politically heavyweight gentleman whose word could be relied upon, and who could realistically aspire to one day achieve independence through Home Rule for Ireland, with himself as leader. Katie's social connections, along with her conventional outlook – she was no revolutionary – combined to make her the perfect vehicle for this strand of Parnell's communications strategy. Her symbolic importance was particularly significant. Her involvement, as a middle-aged middle-class woman, in the movement for Irish independence provided a clear contrast to that of the murderers in Phoenix Park. Her unconventional lifestyle was not widely known, of course.

In addition to her work for Ireland's independence, Katie was also busy trying to help Willie get a job. Once more she asked the Prime Minister for his help. On 30 October 1882, Katie was 'constrained' to write again, she owned, by her husband's 'great anxiety to know if there is any hope for him respecting the appointment I mentioned to you some time ago of his being very anxious to fill'.[48] O'Shea was struggling to stay at the forefront of Irish affairs. He was in Ireland throughout that autumn and on 29

September he wrote to Katie from Newport House in Mayo of his frustration. 'I wrote to Mr. P. about his conference', he confided, 'but he has of course not answered my letter.' He was also worried about his business affairs, adding that he was 'sorry we cannot manage the bank any longer… I don't see any way out of it at all, and believe the end is at hand.' This letter was signed: 'Your Boysie'.[49]

'Boysie' continued to confide in his wife. On 17 October, he told 'Dick' that he had seen Trevelyan at Dublin Castle. 'He of course admitted me at once and was very civil,' Willie reported. He had then seen the Assistant Inspector General of Constabulary, who gave him the opinion of the heads of department on the newly appointed head of Special Branch, E. G. Jenkinson, who had previously been in the Indian Service. 'They call him "His Majesty the Lion of Pride",' O'Shea claimed. He added that Jenkinson knew 'nothing whatever of the country and assumes the command of everything, meddling and muddling all, but is an immense favourite with Lord Spencer'. O'Shea's pettishness in reporting this to Katie might be explained by the fact that Willie had been 'kept waiting an hour' by the new chief.[50] The perceived insult, and the fact that the Convention for the Irish National League was taking place that very day without him, gives us a realistic picture of the Captain's position.

Lack of money was always a preoccupation for him. He asked Katie if she could get her nephew, Matthew Wood, to rent him the flat at 1 Albert Mansions 'very cheap'.[51] There was little prospect of an immediate improvement of his situation, however. On 1 November, the Prime Minister wrote to Katie an entirely non-committal letter regarding her request for a position for her husband. He declined to add anything to his previous letter, which had promised nothing. 'In regard to the particular office', Gladstone informed her, 'I can add nothing to that former letter, for the Viceroy is, & I am not, primarily responsible for the appointment.'[52] In fact there was no chance whatsoever of Willie getting this position. On 3 November, Gladstone circulated a memo to his Cabinet colleagues:

I wish to represent to those of my Colleagues, who have any considerable amount of civil patronage at their disposal, that Mr O'Shea has rendered spontaneously considerable service to the Government, and to the country, by finding a way out of the very embarrassing predicament in which we found ourselves past spring through the imprisonment (necessary as it had been) of three members of Parliament. His desire is or has been to succeed Mr Hamilton in Ireland as Under Secretary. This appears to be out of the question. But the debt is real; and so is the desire to have it acknowledged. WEG Nov.3.82.[53]

That the Prime Minister's support for O'Shea was not shared by all was evidenced by the response of Gladstone's Private Secretary. He commented: 'Mr G. will not get much sympathy on this account from his colleagues.'[54] Spencer was unequivocal in his dismissal of the notion. 'I cannot for a moment conceive it possible', he stated in a letter to the premier, 'to entertain the idea of O'Shea being fitted to succeed Hamilton.' He did not mince his words, explaining: 'The Post is one which requires that highest administrative qualities of an experienced Official, and if I were to judge of Captain O'Shea from the volumes of letters which he pours in to the Chief Secretary and to myself on every conceivable subject, I can hardly think of a man more unfitted for the Place.'[55] Willie O'Shea was not offered the post.

Gladstone did not commit himself to Katie's attempts to form an unofficial nexus either. There is considerable uncertainty as to the Prime Minister's genuine response to the Katharine O'Shea/Parnell overtures. He later claimed, when asked by Barry O'Brien, that he had written 'no letters of importance' to Mrs O'Shea. 'I wrote letters acknowledging hers', he said, but stated all 'my communications with her were oral, and all my communications with Parnell were oral. I only received one letter from him.'[56] His Private Secretary Hamilton's contemporaneous notes would support this interpretation. He recorded on 23 September 1882, 'Mrs O'Shea will continue to volunteer writing under the inspiration of Parnell. It is a great piece of impertinence; and yet difficult for Mr. G. to forbid it.'[57]

Spencer was very unhappy about the correspondence. He wrote to the Prime Minister on 18 September that he was 'unpleasantly struck by Mrs. O'Shea's letter', adding that 'interesting as it is to get at the opinions of a man like Parnell on these subjects I feel it is playing with edged tools, and entering into indirect communication with one who indirectly by his own confession has influence with the worst men in the Kingdom, those who can stop or commit atrocious murders'.[58] The Prime Minister reassured him the next day, pointing out that 'Mrs. O'Shea's communications are wholly uninvited'. He felt, however, that the Irish leader had since his liberation determined not to encourage crimes 'and has endeavoured to influence his friends in the same sense'.[59] Spencer was still unhappy, and protested again the following week. Gladstone sent all of Katharine O'Shea's letters on to Spencer and, on 25 September, the Viceroy returned them, stating, 'I wish she would not write to you. I quite dread the fact of her communication leaking out. I say this knowing she writes without your invitation.'[60]

On 8 October, the Liberal leader, Lord Granville, protested as well. 'My dear Gladstone', he wrote, 'I fancied you had already put an end to the correspondence with Mrs. O'Shea. I quite agree that Dick Grosvenor would be the right channel.'[61] Lord Hartington wrote that he would go even further than Granville, in objecting to any private communications with the Irish leader. He stated emphatically on 14 October that he deprecated 'any such communications even through Trevelyan or R. Grosvenor... I venture to think that there exists now no sufficient reason for any communication with Parnell, other than across the floor of the House.'[62]

There is little doubt that Gladstone was not of this opinion. In his reply to Hartington, he pointed out that his 'recollection about the Cabinet is that there was informal conversation about it, but not any decision of any kind; much less that no communication should at any time be held with Parnell except across the table'.[63] He was not responding to Katharine O'Shea's overtures merely out of courtesy. Agrarian crime in Ireland had dropped dramatically after the Kilmainham releases, and fell continuously through to the end of 1882.[64] The Prime Minister believed that Parnell was a force for moderation in Ireland. The representation of the Irish leader's views, through the reliable conduit of Katharine O'Shea, was not unwelcome. It seems to have been the Prime Minister's policy, however, to deny any 'official' interaction with members of the Irish side of the negotiations. The senior Liberal politician, Lord Derby, had remarked of his surprise at the premier's secrecy on this matter.[65] He recorded in his diary entry of 2 May 1882:

I note it as odd that Gladstone should have denied officially that any negociation had taken place with Parnell: when to me he said distinctly that a Mr O'Shea had acted as the go-between, & had had interviews with Parnell in Kilmainham. It is possible that O'Shea volunteered his services, & so was not in the strict sense of the word employed: but surely that is rather a fine distinction? The very time of his going over was named: he crossed on Friday night, was at the gaol on Saturday, & returned Saturday night.[66]

And the Prime Minister knew that his interaction with Katharine could be misinterpreted. On 26 September he wrote to Spencer telling him, 'Some time ago I signified to Mrs. O'Shea that we had better not meet again. Her letters I cannot control but do not encourage.' He was at pains to point out, nonetheless, that he thought 'she has been of some use in keeping Parnell on the lines of moderation: and I imagine he prefers the wife to the husband as an organ'.[67] Katie continued to press upon the Prime Minister this commitment by Parnell to move away from violence. She enclosed three telegrams sent to her by the Irish leader for Gladstone to peruse. In the first, Parnell declared: 'You may reply that your wishes and advice will be strictly complied with and that I will not permit myself to be drawn or pushed beyond the limit of prudence and legality.'[68]

The situation in Ireland had calmed sufficiently by the end of the year to reassure Gladstone and his government. The Prime Minister confided to Edward Henry Stanley, the 15th Earl of Derby, in October that he 'believed the Irish people as a body to be loyal'.[69] Derby, a senior politician (and elder son of the Lord Derby who was thrice Prime Minister), had only recently changed his political allegiance in favour of the Liberals. He was by no means as sanguine as the Prime Minister on the benefits of the Land Acts (and, indeed, later became a Liberal Unionist). He recorded that Gladstone did foresee trouble for the future – 'there would be great noise & talk in parliament, & but little done'.[70] Although the problems of Ireland had dominated parliamentary time, the attention demanded was at times out of proportion to its importance. This of course was the objective of Parnell's political tactics – to place Ireland at the top of the government's agenda, and in this he and his party had been very successful. The Prime Minister was also anxious about other foreign affairs, and confided to Derby:

He thought the war of revenge between France and Prussia must come: he would not be comforted when I observed that the same threats had been used after Waterloo. He was deeply disappointed as to Italy, which he had expected to be the most conservative power in Europe, owing to the boundaries of Italy being for the most part fixed by nature: but, to the contrary, they were a disturbing element, anxious for military glory, & for the possession of territories beyond sea, which could be of no use to them. He talked of the treaty with France now pending, but in a tone of greater indifference than he showed on any other subject – observing that he had great doubts as to the policy of commercial treaties, but if we failed to make one with France the political effect would be bad – it might make a coolness between them. He confirmed something that I said as to the unceasing exertions of Bismarck in various ways to make mischief between England & France – saying that he (B.) had caused it to be signified to him (Gladstone) while in opposition, at the time of the Constantinople Conference, that he ought to press for the seizure of Egypt. At the same time Bismarck was telling the French that we meant to seize the country, & stirring them up to resist the attempt.[71]

In January 1883, however, Irish affairs once more claimed attention. The Dublin police made their first arrests for the Phoenix Park murders, and it soon became clear that they had correctly apprehended some of the culprits. James Carey, Joe Brady and Daniel Curley were among those arrested. These developments revived the coverage of the attacks in England, and the press and Conservative Opposition took advantage of the news to provoke a sensation of outrage against Irish nationalism. Parnell was savagely attacked by Forster in Parliament on 22 February. In a passionate speech, he claimed that the Irish leader bore some responsibility for what had happened. 'Do not let the hon. Member suppose that I charge him with having planned any murder, or with complicity with murder,' he argued. Forster then delivered the summary of his accusation:

But I wish there to be no mistake that this I do charge the hon. Member and his Friends with. He and they allowed themselves to continue the leaders – he the avowed Chief – of an organization which not merely ostensibly advised and urged the ruin of those who opposed them, and avowed that doctrine of 'Boycotting,' which was to make life almost more miserable than death, but which set on foot an agitation, which organized or promoted outrage and incited to murder, of which the natural result and outcome was murder, and the hon. Member ought to have known this to be the natural outcome.[72]

Forster's argument was that Parnell had chosen to associate with extremists, and had reaped benefit from their violence, without taking responsibility for it. He claimed that the honourable member for Cork

was content that the League should be thus organized, and that his power should be thus increased. This is the charge I make upon him – that he was reckless of the conduct of his colleagues, and was content to derive advantages from their violence, instead of doing what I should have thought any man of his education and position would have done – that is, that he would have declared, 'This is a wicked and dangerous matter, and I will disavow all connection with it'.[73]

Katie wrote that her lover showed her, on his return 'home', a 'fierce joy in the false move of his enemies and the scorn and contempt of the lack of control which could lead a politician of Forster's experience into such a *faux pas* as this personal attack on him'. When she asked him how he would respond, Parnell replied, 'I shall not answer. I shall let him hang himself with his own rope.'[74]

Parnell's only response to all of Forster's lengthy accusations that day had been confined to one interruption when he said: 'It is a lie.'[75] It was O'Kelly who reacted most. Four times he insisted: 'It is a lie,' despite the Speaker's call to order.[76] The Speaker therefore named Mr O'Kelly to the House as disregarding the authority of the Chair.[77] O'Kelly was asked to leave after 305 members voted for the motion to suspend him (with only twenty against).[78] The Irish leader, however, remained silent for most of the debate, 'trying', according to the journalist and political diarist Henry Lucy, 'not altogether successfully, to seem at ease with a sickly smile on his face'.[79]

Parnell was at his most aloof when he addressed the House the following day.

I have been accustomed, during my political life, to rely upon the public opinion of those whom I have desired to help, and with whose aid I have worked for the cause of prosperity and freedom in Ireland; and the utmost that I desire to do, in the very few words which I shall address to this House, is to make my position clear, to the Irish people at home and abroad, from the unjust aspersions which have been cast upon me by a man who ought to be ashamed to have devoted – ('Oh, oh!') [interruptions] – who ought to be ashamed, I say, to have devoted his high ability to the task of traducing me. I do not intend to reply to the questions of the right hon. Gentleman.[80]

He continued by dismissing Forster and his accusations, and in his address he made plain to the House that he felt he had nothing to answer for. Nothing he could say would matter to the House; therefore, as Henry Lucy recorded, Parnell 'spoke only for Ireland'.[81] In a stirring conclusion, he claimed that he was

confident as to the future of Ireland. Although her horizon may appear at this moment cloudy, I believe that our people will survive the present oppression, as they have survived many and worse ones. And although our progress may be slow, it will be sure; and the time will come when this House and the people of this country will admit once again that they have been mistaken – that they have been deceived by those who ought to be ashamed of deceiving them – that they have been led astray as to the right method of governing a noble, a generous, a brave, and impulsive people; and that they will reject their present Leaders, who are conducting them into the terrible course which, I am sorry to say, the Government appears to be determined to enter.[82]

This sharp reminder of his politics and loyalties served to reinforce the leader's status in Ireland. His disdain for the House of

Commons specifically, and for the British government generally, was applauded. In America, Parnell's position as a fighter was admired, even though there was little to show for it. This speech served as a warning to the government, and it served to enhance the leader's reputation among his supporters.

Willie O'Shea then added fuel to the fire by his intervention in which he pointed out an error made by the ex-Chief Secretary in his speech. 'Mark the contradiction,' he said, before querying why Forster had not kept 'a note of the whole conversation', and wondering whether this was because he wished 'to hoodwink his Colleagues?'[83] O'Shea's participation in this debate, and his clear public support of the Irish leader, are evidence of his continued commitment at this time to the Irish question. The Captain still hoped to capitalize on the success – as he saw it[84] – of his role in negotiating the Kilmainham agreement. The Irish question was of importance, especially because it occupied a great deal of parliamentary time. After lengthy discussions and addresses over the course of several days, on 26 February Lord Hartington appealed to the members 'to endeavour to restrict the remainder of this debate within reasonable limits'. He remarked that the House had 'now been discussing Irish subjects discursively for four nights', and pointed out 'that on account of the extremely short period that will elapse before Easter, and the amount of work there is to do', he urged the 'hon. Members to condense their observations, so as to bring the debate on the Address to a close during the early part of next week'.[85]

The Irish cause was receiving sufficient parliamentary (and Cabinet) attention to represent potential opportunity for political advancement. O'Shea certainly intended to make a name for himself. He continued pursuing the government on Irish questions during parliamentary sessions. On 26 February he asked the Chief Secretary if 'he had received any information respecting the alleged posting at the Ballydehob Post Office of a letter containing dynamite, and addressed to the Lord Lieutenant', to which

Trevelyan replied: 'I have not, Sir.'[86] O'Shea also kept on pressing for advancement through other means. On 4 March, Chamberlain replied to O'Shea, telling him that he had written to Lord Granville and would let the Captain know the result 'as soon as possible'. He wished 'the matter was entirely in my hands'.[87] Some ten days later, Katie wrote to the Prime Minister, enclosing 'part of a letter received from my husband today'. A telegram followed later the same day, in which she asked Gladstone not to trouble himself with the letter, explaining: 'He has just sent splendid report – regret having troubled you.'[88] The exact meaning of either of these communications is unclear; what is obvious is that the Captain continued to use his political friends and his wife to help his career behind the scenes.

We can guess that Willie aimed high, however. Katie wrote again to the Prime Minister on 15 June 1883. 'I have so long abstained from troubling you', she began, 'that I venture to hope I may be rewarded, and that you will kindly grant my request, and let me know if you can spare a few minutes to see me tomorrow either at Downing St or Thomas' Hotel at any time least inconvenient to yourself – in any case I hope you will not refer me to anyone else. I can assure you I do not desire to ask for the Viceroyalty!'[89] Another letter written to Gladstone on the same day was on a different subject entirely. In this, Katie referred to a conversation she had had with Parnell about 'useful measures for Ireland' that the government might consider.[90]

It is also of interest to note that, quite apart from the fact that Katie was writing to the Prime Minister on both her husband's and her lover's behalf, on 4 March 1883 she had given birth to another girl. The arrival of Clare Gabrielle Antoinette Marcia Esperance O'Shea was announced in *The Times* on 9 March: 'On the 4th inst, at Eltham, the wife of William Henry O'Shea, Esq., M.P., of a daughter.'[91] Katie did not mention this in her memoir, and the letters from Willie at this time do not appear in her chronicle. The sequence of his correspondence to her jumps from

e Irish Nationalist leader, Charles Stewart Parnell, in 1881.

JOSEPH G. BIGGAR.

ISAAC BUTT.

JAMES O'KELLY.

T. M. HEALY.

CHARLES STEWART PARNELL.

JUSTIN McCARTHY.

THOMAS SEXTON.

MICHAEL DAVITT.

T. P. O'CONNOR.

E. D. GRAY.

WILLIAM O'BRIEN.

TIMOTHY D. SULLIVAN.

TIMOTHY HARRINGTON.

JOHN DILLON.

Leading members of the Irish Home Rule Party in 1887.

...nell and Irish Land League leaders in Kilmainham Gaol, Dublin *c*.1881.

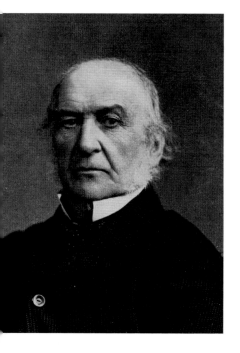

...Liberal leader and British Prime
...ister, William Ewart Gladstone.

The British statesman, Joseph Chamberlain,
a leading Radical Liberal.

THE RIVALS.   THE IRISH "VAMPIRE."

THE IRISH HORSE AND HIS MASTER (?)

Mr. Punch. "LEAVE HIM ALONE, JOHN; HE'S SAFE TO COME A CROPPER!"

Political cartoons from *Punch* depicting views on Irish Nationalism during the 1880s.

17 October 1882 to 20 October 1884, two years later. The letters then continue through to 1889.

What is even more extraordinary is the fact that not only does she omit to mention that she gave birth to Clare in March 1883, but also the birth of another daughter, Frances Katie Flavia Guadalupe, on 27 November 1884. Again, this birth was announced in the traditional way, in *The Times*, on 4 December 1884: 'On the 27th Nov., at Eltham, the wife of W.H. O'Shea, M.P., of a daughter.'[92] Willie himself seemed unperturbed by the arrival of Clare. In a letter to *The Times* on 8 March, just days after the baby's birth, he defended Charles Parnell from Forster's accusations. He wrote that whatever differences he and Parnell might have had 'on matters of politics and policy, he is my friend and I hope you will allow me to defend him'.[93]

O'Shea's ease of manner can be interpreted in only one of two ways. Either he was not aware of the possibility that Clare was not his own, or he was entirely complicit in his wife's adulterous relationship. One thing is clear. Both O'Shea and Parnell were in considerable financial difficulty. The Captain had already complained of a lack of funds. He and Katie were entirely reliant on Aunt Ben to provide for the family, as Katie could not rely on her husband for income. Equally, she could not turn to her lover for help. The previous November, Charles Parnell had filed a petition in the Landed Estates Court for the sale of his Wicklow property. In February 1883, just before Clare's birth, an order of sale was made, when charges on his property had reached £18,000 in mortgages, as well as the annuity of £100 per annum payable to Parnell's sister, Emily Dickinson.[94] The Irish leader was about to lose his home. His financial position was dire, and his economic prospects as a politician poor. He was therefore in no position to provide for Katie and the children.[95] However humiliating this proud man may have found the situation, he had no alternative but to comply with Katie's strategy of concealment.

O'Shea and Parnell continued to work together on Irish politics. The leader had declared his intention to lie low for a time; 'I see nothing for it', he told his colleagues, 'except to "duck" for these three years, and then – ah – resume.'[96] In fact, Parnell's strategy in Ireland was to build the party machine. The decisions taken at the October Conference in 1882 led to a new 'New Departure', and for the following several years he was engaged in helping to recruit members for the Irish Party. He was preparing for the developments in British politics that would bring about legislation to transform the electoral body. The Franchises and Redistribution Acts of 1884–5 were to add over half a million voters to the register in Ireland.[97] The Chief and his senior colleagues accordingly spent the years from 1882 to the general election of 1885 recruiting new men to join the party. These Parnellite MPs became part of an increasingly well-honed party machine. The men came from divergent backgrounds, such as farming, journalism, the law and the retail trade. They took a pledge to vote along party lines before standing for election and many of them were paid from party funds.[98] The candidates, after being approved by the national organization, were then sent out to stand for seats in various constituencies.

The Irish leader made a decision to take a dominant role in this political development, and as a consequence had to spend a lot of time in Ireland. During visits back to England he saw Katie. He had to be cautious, however. Despite Katie's later protestations to Harrison that her husband had known all about the affair after 1881, the correspondence reprinted in her book tells the opposite story. On 4 July 1883, Parnell wrote formally to 'Mrs O'Shea' from Avondale. 'I seize a vacant moment to write you a few words', he cautiously began, 'as it does not look as if Irish affairs would permit me to see you for some time longer.' He went on to ask her to forward an enclosure to Captain O'Shea, and ended by telling her that he intended 'to make it my first business to look up West Clare, and trust that Captain O'Shea may be able to meet me there'.[99]

In December that year, Katie rented a furnished house in Brighton for three months for herself and the children, and also selected a house for herself and Parnell. She recorded, however, that her husband had come down and insisted on her taking a house facing the sea in Medina Terrace. So, 'with difficulty' she got out of her previous arrangement, 'and certainly the house Willie chose was very much pleasanter, owing to its close proximity to the sea'.[100]

CHAPTER FOURTEEN

A Secret Life

HE O'SHEAS AND THE Irish leader continued to associate on various levels throughout 1883 and 1884. The births of the two girls – later accepted by O'Shea and others as Parnell's children – did not seem to cause any perturbations. Indeed, the Captain invited Parnell to stay with him in Brighton, where he had undertaken to stay with the children in December 1883, while Katie travelled back and forth to tend to her aunt. She makes no mention of it whatsoever, but one does wonder whether baby Clare was included in the Brighton ménage supervised by Willie O'Shea. The baby had been baptized in the Catholic faith at St Mary Magdalen Church in Brighton on 2 May 1883. Lady Mary O'Donnell – the same family friend who had sympathized over the death of Claude Sophie – stood, as we have seen, as godmother.[1] The pretence was thus being maintained. What Willie knew is impossible to ascertain. During this period, though, he and Parnell spent time together discussing a possible Local Government Bill. O'Shea wrote to Chamberlain on 8 December from Medina Terrace in Brighton, informing him that 'Parnell attached the greatest importance to my holding my tongue at present'. The leader foresaw 'scores of difficulties in the immediate future'.[2]

Parnell had managed to save himself from financial ruin. His predicament had become public knowledge in Ireland. The Avoca branch of the Irish National League resolved: 'in order to manifest our undying admiration of Mr Parnell, we propose to open a subscription list for the purpose of clearing off the inherited mortgage on his estate'.[3] With the enthusiastic support of William O'Brien, *United Ireland* launched a testimonial to raise funds for the leader. The nationalist Archbishop of Cashel, Dr Croke, gave it his approval,[4] and the fund garnered further support when the Vatican (the Pope disapproved of the involvement of the Church in the nationalist movement) condemned it.[5] By the end of 1883, £37,000 had been collected. This 'tribute' was presented to Parnell in Dublin on 11 December. An oft-repeated story tells of his ungraciousness in accepting the money. During a small ceremony with twenty other MPs at Morrison's Hotel, the Lord Mayor made a little speech before presenting the cheque. He was twice interrupted by Parnell, who asked whether the cheque was made out 'to order' and crossed, and he never finished his speech. Later that evening, at the ceremonial banquet, Parnell's remarks were confined to the political situation only. The only comment that he made consisted of two sentences that were hardly fulsome: 'I don't know how adequately to express my feelings with regard not only to your lordship's address, not only to the address to the Parnell National Tribute, but also with regard to the magnificent demonstration. I prefer to leave to the historian the description of tonight and the expression of opinion as regards the result which tonight must produce.'[6]

Much has been made of this apparent lack of gratitude by Parnell's biographers, especially after Healy's memoirs corroborating the event were published in 1929. It must be noted, however, that Healy had by this time turned against his political mentor. The more plausible explanation for the leader's ungracious conduct is that he was deeply embarrassed by the whole episode. His pride was undoubtedly wounded, but the need for the money took precedence. His ambiguity about accepting the gift was evidenced, however, by O'Shea's report to Chamberlain on 8 December. He reported that the government's policy, as exercised by Dublin Castle, was increasing Parnell's popularity, and, further, that 'the announcement which he is about to make, that he will hand over his "Tribute" (with the exception of the small amount taken from it to pay the mortgage on Avondale) to trustees for public purposes, will convert many waverers to his side'.[7]

Parnell's lack of funds – and there is evidence that he did spend his own money for political purposes – would explain why this proud and somewhat arrogant man accepted the subterfuge demanded by Katie. Losing the income stream as provided by Aunt Ben was simply not an option for the O'Sheas, nor, as we have seen, for Parnell. And Katie did spend money. Throughout her narrative, there is never any mention of scrimping or saving. She refers to renting houses, taking carriages and employing servants, with equanimity. Money seemed to flow freely in her household, and is never mentioned as an everyday constraint. In June 1885, for example, Katie paid for an advertisement in *The Times*, offering a sizeable £5 (about £350 in today's money) reward for the return of a fox terrier dog, 'Joe', who had 'probably followed a carriage or cart on the London road'.[8] Living in such close proximity to a wealthy relative – who did not stint on providing for every comfort – seems to have created for Katie a comfortable and secure cocoon. At the same time, her involvement in her lover's life provided an outlet for her considerable energy.

There were notable challenges for her to face, nevertheless. During the years 1882 to 1885, Parnell was frequently away. In 1883, he visited Ireland in June and July, and was there for much of December. In 1884 he travelled to Ireland in February, April, May, August and September. The following year, he was there for most of January, and 'almost continuously' from August to November 1885.[9] He needed to be in Ireland to campaign for Parnellite candidates. In July 1883, he was there to support Tim

Healy's campaign at Monaghan – an Ulster stronghold. Katie complained sufficiently strenuously to Parnell that he nearly abandoned the campaign to return to her. In the end, he was persuaded to stay and wrote to pacify her from Morrison's Hotel in Dublin. She claimed that he penned the following 'to allay the fears I had expressed in regard to certain political actions', but in fact the letter does not substantiate this – rather, it seemed designed to reassure a jealous lover. It also vividly demonstrates the difficulties Parnell faced in keeping Katie happy in their unorthodox arrangement:

When I received your note I at once determined to go over to you to-morrow morning and to give up my engagement to speak at the Cork banquet to-morrow night, as I knew my own was very much troubled about something, and felt sure that I could comfort and reassure her. I have since been besieged the whole evening by entreaties and threats not to throw over Cork, and it has been represented to me, and with truth, that half the result of the Monaghan victory will be lost if I leave Cork to the Whigs and my enemies. I have been very much perplexed and dragged in different ways, but have at this hour (2a.m.) made up my mind to ask my own Wifie to suspend her judgement for another twenty-four hours about whatever is tormenting her, to place some little confidence in her husband's honour and fidelity for that short time... I feel that I can ask this of my own Wifie, and that she will not withdraw her confidence and love from her own husband until he can return and defend himself.[10]

Such a letter reflects the ambiguities and cross-currents of the leader's life. At the same time that he was deepening his commitment to Katie, he sought to build bridges with the Catholic Church in Ireland. He spoke against the annual vote of supply for the 'godless' Queen's Colleges, 'non denominational institutions which had been a bugbear of the Catholic hierarchy for almost forty years'.[11]

The Irish university question had been troublesome for years.[12] The problem had been debated since the establishment of the Queen's Colleges in 1845. The degree-granting Queen's University was then incorporated in 1850. The militant Catholic bishops and clergy were from the outset firmly opposed to the colleges. That year, Rome forbade the Catholic clergy to hold office in the colleges. The Vatican also required the bishops to discourage Catholics from attending the colleges. The challenge thenceforth lay in devising a university system that would be acceptable both to the representatives of the Irish Churches, and to the British government. The Catholic hierarchy took a strong interest in the process, and held very definite ideas about the type of education to be provided to the growing number of middle-class Catholics. There was also a clear concern to achieve equality with their Protestant counterparts. After considerable disagreement and debate, the University Education (Ireland) Act was passed through Parliament in 1879. This provided for the replacement of the Queen's University by the Royal University as the degree-granting body – as part of a response to meeting Catholic demands for university education. The state-funded fellowships were from that point divided between the Queen's Colleges, the de facto denominational Magee College, Londonderry and the Catholic University (later reconstituted as University College, Dublin). The continued state funding of the Protestant Queen's Colleges – through the annual vote of supply – remained a source of frustration for certain members of the Catholic hierarchy in Ireland.

In July 1884, Parnell tried to intervene in a dispute over some property between the Vatican and the secular authorities of the Italian state.[13] In October 1884, this strategy bore fruit, when the Catholic bishops agreed to accept Parnell's Irish Party as their sole parliamentary representation on the educational issue. Their endorsement served to further consolidate Parnell's position as head of the National League. As one historian has noted, Charles

Parnell by 1884 'found himself master both of a regimented
parliamentary body and a national party machine'.[14]

Yet at this critical time in the consolidation of his political
ambitions, the 'Chief' was leading an increasingly complex double
life. T. P. O'Connor recounted how one evening Parnell and
O'Shea had arrived together at the London offices of the *Freeman's
Journal.* The journalist J. M. Touhy was then in charge of the
paper and told O'Connor an 'extraordinary story'. When the
leader and O'Shea had finished giving him the statement on the
political situation they had prepared, Parnell 'took a piece of
paper out of his pocket and, showing it to O'Shea, asked him
whether he should also supply this information to the *Freeman's
Journal.* O'Shea nodded an assent, and Parnell handed the
document to Mr. Touhy.' This document was 'an announcement
in due and also rather curt form of the birth of a daughter to
Mrs. O'Shea, the wife of Captain O'Shea, late of the 10th
Hussars'.[15] What must have seemed strange was that it was
Parnell who gave the editor the announcement, after receiving
O'Shea's approval to do so.

Katie meanwhile continued her correspondence with Gladstone.
On 19 July 1883, she sent the Prime Minister 'Heads of a bill,
which Mr Parnell has drawn up, and about which he is very
anxious'.[16] On 24 July, Katie begged that he would 'not take the
Irish estimates on Thursday'. She reasoned that if he did so, 'it
will bring all the Irish Party (who will shortly be scattered over
the country) back and it will cause a waste of very valuable time'.
Later, she suggested, the estimates 'might pass without a protest'.[17]
Katie's correspondence with the Prime Minister was more
intermittent during 1884, although she did continue to send
Gladstone papers forwarded by Parnell.[18] Katie also attended
parliamentary sessions as often as she could. As regards their
relationship, she and Parnell continued to exercise discretion.
Although Katie glossed over the details of their relations during
this period, she included telegrams from her lover sent in 1884

that indicate that the pair were careful to avoid Willie's suspicions. On 29 February, Parnell cabled to Katie that he was happy to accept her dinner invitation for that evening.[19]

Willie O'Shea accompanied Parnell to Avondale in May that year, thus establishing conclusively that at the time they were getting on well. On 30 May, Parnell telegraphed to Katie: 'Captain and I arrived safely.'[20] On 10 September, Parnell reported from Dublin that 'Willie is looking very well indeed, in fact much better than I have ever seen him before.'[21] A few weeks later, he sent her an "official" communication, which indicates that appearances were being maintained. This was not necessarily for the Captain's benefit, however. As the leader of the Irish Nationalist Party, Parnell was constantly aware that his mail could be intercepted. He wrote to the Quaker Nationalist MP Alfred Webb on 26 February 1883, stating that should he have anything 'particularly private' to communicate to him, Webb could address his letter 'with perfect safety' to Parnell's secretary, Henry Campbell, 'under cover' to John Dorrian. 'Any letter sent in this way', he ended, 'will reach me safely.'[22] Webb was an early member of the Home Rule League and an important figure in the struggle for independence. He and Parnell needed secure lines of communication.

Other communications which might be opened were treated cautiously, for professional and personal reasons. Parnell wrote to Katie on 28 October, addressing his letter to 'Mrs O'Shea'. In it, he informed her that he was staying at Dover for a few more days, and was then planning to travel on to the Netherlands, returning through Paris. 'If I thought that Captain O'Shea would be in England', he wrote, 'I should wait for him, but if not should take my chance of meeting him in Paris on my return.'[23]

At this time, throughout 1884, O'Shea and Parnell were continuing to meet regularly to discuss a number of Irish projects. O'Shea was in regular contact with Chamberlain, and led him to believe that he was very much in the Irish leader's confidence. In addition to his dealings with Parnell, Willie was also spending more time at the family home. Katie wrote that she was 'ill' (her euphemism for pregnancy) at this time, and that her husband 'was coming to Eltham a good deal'.[24] She and her lover had to be careful. In one communication, Parnell wrote that if 'he' – meaning O'Shea – went early, he could 'return perhaps early enough to see you this evening for a few minutes'.[25] In another, he told her that there 'ought to be no difficulty in my seeing you to-morrow, and I will manage it'.[26]

The lovers escaped when they could. Katie wrote of a visit to Hastings for a few days, when a friend of her aunt had come to stay, thus giving her 'freedom'.[27] Hastings was a charming town, with lovely Georgian terraces and a lively centre with many shops. Of course the main attraction was the sea, and the resort featured a pier as well as a promenade. 'We stayed at the Queen's Hotel', Katie recalled, 'and Parnell revelled in the sudden freedom from politics – casting all thought and care from him as we walked by the sea and gave ourselves up to the enjoyment of the fresh salt air.'[28] The elegant Queen's Hotel had been built in 1862, and stood on the seafront. Katie wrote that during their short visits to the seaside, she and her lover 'looked about for a house that Parnell could buy later on', but that 'as he always kept a regretful eye upon Brighton, where it was inexpedient that we should be seen much together, we never really settled on one for purchase'.[29] It is difficult to imagine where Parnell would have found the means to purchase a house in Brighton, although it is perfectly possible that the couple shared the pleasures of dreaming of a better future. There is, it must be said, something quite surreal about the Irish leader and Katie 'hunting round Sussex in the neighbourhood of Brighton… hoping to find a suitable country house'. Even the discovery, after Parnell had rented a house in Eastbourne, that 'a brother of his was living there'[30] does not seem to have deterred them. On their visit to Hastings, Katie described how her lover had bought her notepaper embossed with the monogram 'K.P.' in blue and gold.

Parnell 'declared it was a good omen, and bought me more boxes of it than I could use for many years'.[31]

While they enjoyed these snatched moments, Willie was preoccupied with carving out an important role for himself within the British government with some responsibility for Irish affairs. He pinned his hopes on his relationship with Chamberlain, with whom he planned to broker a deal with Parnell. The President of the Board of Trade was not averse to finding a solution to the vexing problem of reforming local government in Ireland, which had been promised as far back as 1881 in the Queen's Speech.[32] This was an opportunity that O'Shea lost no time in developing. His unofficial intervention – which was becoming something of an O'Shea specialty – was welcomed by Chamberlain because at the time the backdrop to Anglo-Irish relations was again unpropitious. Despite the 'New Departure' – when Irish parliamentarians were loosely allied with the Fenians in their common ambition for land reform and national independence – the American Clan na Gael had not abandoned its armed struggle. In Ireland, therefore, the ballot box coexisted with civil disobedience and agrarian crime (although the number of crimes decreased after the enactment of the Crimes legislation).

The Clan funded arms smuggling into Ireland, and between 1881 and 1883 its Revolutionary Directory put in place plans for a major dynamiting[33] campaign in England. Shortly after Forster's 1883 attack on the Irish leader, London experienced the onslaught of the Dynamitards. This was not the first time that England had experienced bombing activity. In 1881 a Skirmishing campaign, led by the revolutionary Jeremiah O'Donovan Rossa, had been launched. Rossa, a grocer from Skibbereen, County Cork, had founded the Phoenix Society, a literary and political group, in 1856. The Society was subsequently absorbed into the Fenian movement and Rossa was imprisoned from 1865 to 1871. He was released on condition of exile and went to America, where he edited the *United Irishman.* He organized his own Skirmishing Fund there.

Rossa directed the first nationalist bombing campaign in mainland Britain, which took place during 1881–5. Through a network of auxiliary organizations, such as the Emerald Club, he sent teams to England to light fires and place explosives. Not all Fenians agreed with this terrorist policy, and many denounced Rossa. Fenian ideology was predicated 'round the view of England as a satanic power on earth, a mystic commitment to Ireland, and a belief that an independent Irish republic, "virtually" established in the hearts of men, possessed a superior moral authority'.[34] This view was supported by the Irish-American immigrant groups, and underpinned by the revolutionary movements of post-1848 Paris. Adhering to this view of Irish nationalism made it difficult for many Fenians to condone violence. The greatest strength of Fenianism lay in its ability to remain on the moral high ground. An important part of the culture surrounding Fenianism reinforced its politics through a lively culture of ideological mythology.

Nationalist poetry, songs and memoirs drove the movement on a strong emotional rhetoric. The Fenians had a great talent for publicity and public occasion. The attempts of the English government to maintain control through coercion served to fuel the flames of patriotic fervour. Failed insurrections and risings did so as well. Demanding amnesty for political prisoners and launching daring rescue campaigns formed an important part of the revolutionary struggle. Violence that harmed civilians did not sit easily with the Fenian mentality. Rossa continued regardless. In January 1881, there was an explosives attack on Salford barracks in which four civilians were injured, including a boy of seven who died two days later. Another Rossa team next attempted to blow up the City of London's Mansion House on 16 March. The plot was foiled when a constable on duty discovered the bomb with its fuse still burning and put it out. On 16 May, a bomb was planted at the Liverpool Police Headquarters, but little damage was caused. And, on 10 June, the same team placed a large and heavy bomb against the door of Liverpool Town Hall, where once again a constable managed to foil the plan. The bomb was pulled away from the door and exploded in the street.

Rossa's campaign was largely ineffectual. It continued through 1882, however, when an unsuccessful attempt was made on Mansion House on 12 May. On 17 June a large cache of IRB arms was discovered at Clerkenwell. This discovery along with the persistent bombing campaign had by now succeeded in creating a climate of fear. It was exacerbated by the assassination of Tsar Alexander II in March 1881, and extra precautions had been taken to protect the Queen, on whom an assassination attempt was made in March 1882. The Phoenix Park murders had of course added to the atmosphere of brutality. By May 1883 the Irish-American journal *An Gaodhal* reported, 'England is now in a panic and every European monarch feels like a hunted stag'.[35] The bombings perpetrated by Rossa's men continued. In January 1883 there were simultaneous explosions in Glasgow, where a large gas storage tank was ruptured at the gasworks, causing injuries and extensive damage. Just two months later, in March, an attack was made on government buildings in London. Damage was done to the Home Office, Colonial Office, India Office and the Local Government Board (which received the most damage). There was further destruction of nearby buildings caused by flying debris. Parnell wrote laconically to Katie that there had been an explosion of a bomb at the Home Office 'just before I left; it blew down a large piece of the front wall and did a great deal of damage, they say'.[36]

The Clan – affiliated to the IRB from 1877 – was also making serious plans for a terror campaign, led by the Clan na Gael revolutionary, William Mackay Lomasney. On 30 October 1883, simultaneous bombs exploded in London: one on the Metropolitan Line of the Underground near Paddington Station and the other between Charing Cross and Westminster Underground stations.

There were extensive injuries caused to the passengers, who were cut and bruised by flying glass and woodwork. Carriages were wrecked. On 26 February the following year a bomb exploded at London's Victoria Station, causing great damage. When other left luggage offices were immediately searched, unexploded bombs were discovered at Charing Cross, Paddington and Ludgate Stations. It did not end there. Further attacks were made on London targets, including the office of the Irish Special Branch at Scotland Yard. And on 13 December, during the evening rush hour, an attempt was made to blow up London Bridge. In the New Year, a bomb was set off on 2 January outside Gower Street Underground station. On 24 January, there were attacks on the Tower of London and the Palace of Westminster.

By later in the year, many of the perpetrators had been arrested.[37] It was fortunate that most of the bombs had not achieved their aims because they were faulty. But the campaign did succeed in blackening the cause of Irish aspirations. The Clan's revolutionary activities were not representative of all Fenians. Many Irish nationalists in Ireland and in England were horrified by these attacks. In America, there was considerable dismay at the use to which funds had been put.[38] The violence did nothing to serve the cause of romantic nationalism, but Parnell was conspicuously silent. On 2 March, O'Shea wrote to Chamberlain that 'P. "regrets" your allusion to him re Dynamite… He believed the Dynamiters to be a small and insignificant gang, unable to do any real mischief except to the unfortunate passers by, and he considers it a fatal error to advertise the miscreants.'[39] The leader was deliberate in his refusal to condemn the attacks outright. He maintained his usual links with party supporters. On 3 March 1884, *The Times* reported that Parnell had 'consented to preside at the St. Patrick's Day dinner of the Irish societies of London'.[40]

This deterioration in Anglo-Irish relations, and the ensuing lack of English public support for Irish nationalism, was further intensified by the publicity engendered by the Maamtrasna murder case. In August 1882, a small farmer, along with his wife and three of his children, had been brutally killed in their cabin in a rural area of County Mayo. The massacre was either the result of a vendetta, or could have been the responsibility of a secret society. Either way, the crime horrified people in Ireland and in England, especially as it took place so soon after the Phoenix Park murders. The men held to be responsible were arrested and tried – three were hanged and five were given life sentences. One of the men hanged, Miles Joyce, had died protesting his innocence. It later transpired that the two other men who were hanged had confessed before their execution that Miles Joyce was not guilty. There was a public outcry, and Lord Spencer was prevailed upon to set up an inquiry. It was not considered sufficiently searching by the Irish public, and the Maamtrasna case was used by Parnell and his colleagues, notably Harrington, to attack the government.

Four days of parliamentary time, at the end of October 1884, were devoted to the case, much to the fury of the government. It was believed that Parnell was behaving as an irresponsible political opportunist and the situation was made worse when the Fourth Party somewhat cynically decided to support the Irish MPs. The Fourth Party was a group of four radical Tory backbencher activists: Lord Randolph Churchill, John Gorst, Sir Henry Drummond Wolff and Arthur Balfour. They campaigned for reform within the Conservative Party ('Tory democracy') and greater opposition to Gladstone's second Liberal administration. Public response in England was unsympathetic. The image of Ireland as a hotbed of seething, violent nationalism was reinforced. Added to this was the perception that the Irish leader was seeking to gain from the situation by putting pressure on the government and diverting attention from more pressing matters. *The Times* reported that Parnell

reiterated, in his cold and measured style, the charges and the demands which had been urged on Friday by Mr. Healy and his temporary allies of the Fourth Party. The facts, or allegations, which have already been discussed at length were again brought forward in a confused mass, with the object, or, at any rate, with the effect, of obscuring the real issue before the House. To that issue the attention of the House was recalled in a powerful speech by the Home Secretary... At the request of Lord Spencer, the Home Secretary assured the House, he had himself carefully considered the demand for an inquiry which had been pressed by the Irish Irreconcilables in the first instance upon the Lord Lieutenant and now upon Parliament. His decision was arrived at – and his statement is surely one which cannot be doubted – under the deepest sense of responsibility, and he had come unhesitatingly to the conclusion that there was no justification whatever for interfering with the administration of the law in the Maamtransa case.[41]

Parnell knew that he could afford to provoke the British administration. The forthcoming general election would introduce significant changes to the political landscape and balance of power at Westminster. Ireland had not been affected by the Reform Act of 1867, but the Irish leader expected that the outcome of the newly enacted franchise legislation – the Franchise Act of 1884 – would be that Ireland's newly enfranchised poor tenant farmers would send at least eighty Nationalist MPs to the House of Commons. He anticipated that all the stringent selection and promotion of loyal Nationalist candidates undergone since 1882 would result in bringing a political body to Westminster over which he would have iron control. He was therefore careful not to commit to any English politician or party before the election. He did, however, encourage O'Shea to explore possibilities for cooperation with Chamberlain on a scheme for local government in Ireland. He also communicated some of his thinking on Irish government through Katie, who continued to send letters to Gladstone.

Willie O'Shea meanwhile set out, in a letter to Grosvenor in October 1884:

1 That no member of Parliament has made greater efforts or sacrifices in support of the government than I have, for the last three years.

2 That I have saved the Government from innumerable inconveniences and obstruction.

3 That important government measures have been materially assisted, on one or two occasions perhaps actually saved, by my influence.

4 That some of the successes attained by the Government in important divisions have been considerably affected, and more than once swelled into triumphs by my recruiting powers.

5 That when I was absent after Easter, the government nearly came to grief.

6 That Mr Davitt thought it worth his while to go on a crusade through West Clare against a supporter of the Government so dangerous to politicians of his opinions as myself.

7 That I am detested by several of my countrymen in the House of Commons as the 'restraining influence', and because they have a shrewd suspicion that they have often voted for the government because of my management.

8 That I have not attended a meeting of Irish members of any political organization in London since the week before the 2nd reading of the Irish Land Act, and that I never receive intimations of such meetings or whips.[42]

O'Shea's main bargaining asset, however, was not any of the above, but rather his relationship with Parnell. It is unclear how aware this proud man was of that fact, but this is certainly how others viewed his importance. Chamberlain wrote: 'Mr. O'Shea declared himself to be the spokesman of Mr Parnell', as an explanation of his negotiations held with the Captain during 1884–5.[43] Chamberlain, whose interest in possible local government reform in Ireland dated back to 1879,[44] continued to pursue possibilities for change. O'Shea's offer to negotiate a deal with Parnell represented an opportunity to further the cause for reform with the expiration in 1885 of the much disputed

Prevention of Crime Act. Arrangements to prevent its renewal were to be welcomed. In September 1884 Chamberlain wrote to Dilke: 'we shall have an awful business over the renewal of the crimes act. I wish Spencer could see his way to let it drop but I imagine there is no hope of this.'[45] Chamberlain was keen in this connection to promote his blueprint for an Administrative Central Board for Ireland. O'Shea spoke to both Chamberlain and Parnell, and committed his version of their ideas to paper in a draft form on 27 November 1884.[46] O'Shea then sent the highly secret document to Chamberlain, who was appalled that the Captain had put in writing a discussion they had had on the subject – in 'an envelope which arrives open on both sides, whether by accident or design I know not'.[47]

Chamberlain was extremely cautious about the discussions. He knew that he was not representing the official government view in this matter. In the same letter, he clarified his position:

One thing, however, I must make clear: the time has not arrived for any negotiation or agreement. I am very glad to know Mr Parnell's views on local government which in principle seem to be the same as my own. If this turns out to be the case I shall be glad to find that we are working on the same lines. As to any support he may be able to give English Radicals in matters in which they are interested I will neither ask nor receive a pledge. Experience alone can show if there is any possibility of co-operation between the Irish Party and the English democracy.[48]

But O'Shea was unrelenting in his determination to achieve an agreement. He held discussions with Parnell, which he then summarized into memos that he pressed forward in his function as intermediary. He purported to represent Parnell's position accurately to Chamberlain, who was duly encouraged by the leader's readiness to negotiate. But Parnell was as cautious as Chamberlain. He also had other irons in the fire. In the lead-up to the election, throughout 1884, he toured Ireland to support

Nationalist candidates, in between visits to Eltham and to the seaside with Katie. He gave just enough encouragement to Willie for him to keep working for the scheme. Yet although Willie O'Shea went back and forth between Chamberlain, Dilke, and Parnell, ferrying proposals he had drafted, it was becoming increasingly clear by the end of 1884 that the negotiations were not going well.

Parnell took a big step back, and made his own position quite clear to the Captain. On 5 January 1885, before he left for a speaking tour to Ireland, he wrote: 'In talking to our friend [Chamberlain] you must give him clearly to understand that we do *not* propose this local self government plank as a substitute for the restitution of our Irish parliament... The claim for restitution... would still remain.'[49] This was a huge impediment to the process, for Chamberlain insisted that the central board would have some legislative powers. On this basis, the Irish leader later repudiated any agreement whatsoever to the scheme, claiming, 'Our view in 1882, and from which we never departed, was that the functions of the proposed council, should be purely administrative, and that it should not be accepted... as a substitute for a Parliament.'[50]

O'Shea was predictably unhappy at this clarification. He could see his chances of glory slipping away. In addition, he had got short shrift from another of his requests to Grosvenor,[51] and was fuming. 'I have been not only an out and out supporter of the Government', he wrote on 3 January, 'but its out and outset supporter, and it may be that the Government never had greater need of me than at the present time.'[52] Nevertheless, he persevered. There is no indication of how much he told Parnell in 1885 of Chamberlain's insistence on the legislative nature of the proposed board, a concept that the leader rejected in a further letter to O'Shea on 13 January 1885.[53] Certainly, Chamberlain later claimed that he knew nothing of these letters. In any event, the unofficial talks went on. On 28 April, the Captain recorded:

Chamberlain asked me to his room in House tonight. Explained situation. Spencer asks for renewal of Crimes Act for 3 yrs and offers an ineffective Local Govt Bill for Ireland. Chamberlain ready to agree to oppose this policy, and to make it on his own behalf and that of Dilke a question of their resignation (which wd no doubt influence Shaw Lefevre and Trevelyan to the same course) on condition of my obtaining Parnell's full support of the Irish Local Govt Scheme proposed by myself to Chamberlain in January last, and P's engagement to prevent obstruction to renewal of Crimes Act for 1 yr.[54]

The following day, O'Shea recorded that he had seen Parnell and 'made him above offer'. The leader had, however, told him he required 'time for consideration'.[55] It would not be long before the scheme was abandoned altogether.

O'Shea kept Katie informed of his progress. He shared his annoyance over what he saw as Parnell's intransigence over independence for Ireland. 'On Thursday I have the appointment with Chamberlain,' he wrote to 'My Dick' on 9 January. 'But you see that Parnell is inveighing against the Land Courts and promising the dupes "Liberty" in the immediate future, so he appears to have altogether shifted from common-sense again,' he lamented. There is no evidence of any estrangement at this point between him and his wife. 'Tell Norah', he added, 'I shall come down early to-morrow to spend her birthday with you all.'[56] It is difficult to know whether the fact that they corresponded was due to their living arrangement, or because she was, to his knowledge, cohabiting with Parnell.

Willie sent a telegraph to Katie on 2 March 1885, asking her to cable him how she was. Like her husband, she suffered from poor health. In her book, Katie frequently described problems she had with headaches and insomnia, as well as heart trouble. It is important to note that illness played an important part in all three lives: Parnell's poor health was notorious, but what is less remarked on is how frequently Willie and Katie also complained of being unwell. Gout plagued the Captain – he had a chronic painful condition that frequently caused him to be laid up, sometimes for weeks at a time. He never, however, entirely lost his energy and devoted himself with terrier-like obsession to the project at hand. 'If you see Gladstone to-day', he told his wife on 2 March 1885, 'tell him how Grosvenor annoyed me about post offices.'[57] In addition to portraying his discontent over the Chief Whip's lack of positive response, this comment indicated that the Captain was aware of his wife's contact with government channels, and indeed the Prime Minister. It also demonstrates that Katharine was in her husband's confidence, and that he fully expected her to be sympathetic. This communication has been interpreted by some biographers as evidence that O'Shea knew about such contact from its inception, which is not necessarily the case.

Katie was fully engrossed in Parnell's deliberations throughout 1885. She recorded that at this time the Liberal government 'was in a bad way', having 'narrowly escaped defeat on the vote of censure for its failure to relieve Gordon at Khartoum'.[58] The fall of General Gordon in Egypt had produced a public outcry against Gladstone and his Liberal government. After the difficulties in South Africa,[59] the dramatic defeat at Khartoum landed another blow to Gladstone's administration. Although the government had been elected on a largely anti-imperialist position, Egypt was important to Britain for strategic and economic reasons. By 1880 Britain took 80 per cent of Egypt's exports and supplied 44 per cent of its imports – and a third of that nation's total debt was in the hands of British bondholders.[60] The 'Dual Control' exercised by France and Britain, which gave nominal power to local rulers, the Khedives, was breaking down, as Mohammed Ahmed (the 'Mahdi') and his followers mounted a rebellion. By the end of 1883, most of the Sudan was in their hands and, in January 1884, the British government decided to evacuate and appointed Major-General Charles Gordon to put this in place. These orders lacked clarity and Gordon was often out of touch with the Cabinet, communicating his independent views directly to newspapers, where the public lapped up his defiance and his refusal to give in to the rebel forces. He was assassinated while besieged at Khartoum, on 26 January 1885. News of his death, of which first telegraphic rumours reached Britain on 5 February, caused an immediate sensation. Derby recorded the following day: 'The papers are of course full of Khartoum… Great exaggeration prevails, one article saying that no such calamity has occurred since the Indian Mutiny, another referring as a precedent to the destruction of the army in Afghanistan, 40 years ago.'[61] The Queen was livid, and sent a telegram *en clair* rebuking Granville, Hartington and Gladstone for Gordon's death.[62] Derby commented that this rebuke gave a 'strong hint as to H.M.'s feelings, which indeed we knew pretty well before'.[63] Victoria had written: 'These news from Khartoum are frightful and to think that all this might have been prevented and many precious lives saved by earlier action is too fearful.'[64] The Prime Minister's reply was magisterial in its icy politeness and ironic dignity: 'Mr Gladstone does not presume to estimate the means of judgement possessed by Your Majesty, but so far as his information and recollection at the moment go, he is not altogether able to follow the conclusion which Your Majesty has been pleased thus to announce.'[65]

There was no denying, however, that the fall of Khartoum was a military setback. It delivered a blow to Britain's imperial prestige and Gordon's death was used to criticize Gladstone and the Liberal Party. 'England stands before the world dripping with blood and daubed with dishonour,' the writer Robert Louis Stevenson wrote on 2 March 1885 to J. A. Symonds.[66] There was huge public outcry amid grief and rage. Gladstone's nickname, the G[rand] O[ld] M[an], became inverted to M[urderer] O[f] G[ordon].

To add to the Prime Minister's woes, Irish nationalists sought to make political capital of Britain's misfortunes despite the fact that Gladstone had made clear his intention to improve the political situation with Ireland, for which he was increasingly criticized.

Just days after the announcement of Gordon's death, William O'Brien addressed a National League meeting in Cork. Resolutions were adopted along the expected lines in favour of national independence and the abolishment of landlordism. O'Brien went on to declare, however, that there 'was not a capital in Europe in which the news of the fall of Khartoum was not received with joy and excitation (cheers), and with a secret wish and prayer of "More power to the Mahdi and his men"'. *The Times* reporter present recorded that this announcement was greeted with 'loud and prolonged cheers'.[67]

Parnell understood that this was a political opportunity. Katie wrote that the Cabinet at this moment was further divided over Ireland. She made no mention of the fact that her brother Evelyn was in Egypt during the crisis, first in the post of Sirdar of the Egyptian Army, and then as Chief of Staff to Lord Wolseley, who was sent out to relieve Gordon, arriving days too late. There is no mention in her account of any qualms she might have had in staking her reputation and good name with those of Irish Nationalists, many of whom reviled Britain and all things British. There is no mention of any fears she might have held on behalf of her brother, who faced considerable dangers in Egypt. Katie's account of what is as much her lover's life as her own describes a personal situation that by 1885 was one of apparent isolation from her brother, and possibly from other members of her family. And, indeed, it is difficult to imagine how she could have lived a 'normal' existence, with ordinary relationships. She was hiding not just her clandestine liaison with Parnell, but also her association with a politician directly or indirectly linked to known revolutionaries. This was in contrast to her husband Willie, who always maintained a slightly cynical detachment from the cause of Irish nationalism. (This was in fact to cause him considerable problems in the not too distant future.) He referred to his fellow Irish MPs as 'The Boys' and was inclined to be disrespectful of them.

Katie, on the other hand, threw herself wholeheartedly into the cause and made it her business to negotiate on Parnell's behalf. This was not as straightforward an enterprise in the mid-1880s as her subsequent account would imply. Images of Ireland and especially of nationalist Ireland were frequently negative in the British press during this period. The satirist magazine *Punch* had long been notorious in publishing caricatures of Irish peasants as simian beasts (although paradoxically these images were interspersed with those of an idealized, classical Hibernia). Even when printing cartoons of the aristocratic Parnell, the magazine at times represented him in 'traditional Paddy attire of billycock hat, breeches and pistol'.[68] The representation of Ireland in the British press was, as we have seen, quite complex. On the one hand, pictures dating back to the famines had flooded the press and influenced public perceptions of that island and its inhabitants. Political caricaturists in both *Punch* and *Vanity Fair* had then used the material provided by the growing numbers of Irish MPs to portray a stereotypical image of the Irish 'race'.

The presence in London during the 1880s of talented Irish writers and journalists, such as T. P. O'Connor,[69] Barry O'Brien and Justin McCarthy (who in addition to being a successful popular historian and novelist was editor of the *Morning Star* and leader-writer for the *Daily News*, as well as a Nationalist MP for the years 1879–1900), did, however, gradually change the more negative perceptions. The impact on the British understanding and appreciation of the richness of the literary and artistic merits of the Irish came somewhat later. In the 1890s the influence of authors such as George Bernard Shaw, Oscar Wilde and William Butler Yeats went some way to transforming older prejudices against the Irish.[70] But this was yet to come. In 1884–5, Katie's enthusiastic espousal of Irish nationalist politics would have been most unusual and very daring. She was clearly fully *au courant* of every development and nuance in the leader's thinking. She described Chamberlain's scheme for limited local government and pointed out that it had been 'ascertained indirectly that Parnell would accept this scheme, and would not oppose a moderate Coercion Act'. And indeed, she recalled, the Prime Minister was prepared to go yet further 'and give the National Council control over the police'.[71]

According to her account, the Cabinet voted against the proposals in May 1885, and this was 'the rock upon which the Government was to come to a wreck'.[72] Actually, the threat of Cabinet resignations had been hanging over Gladstone's coalition since mid-May. The government was defeated unexpectedly on 9 June over the beer-duty issue, by 264 votes to 252. It was the first result of an uneasy alliance between Parnell and the Conservatives. Thirty-nine members of the Irish Party voted against the government, as did six Liberal MPs. Another seventy of the Liberals (mostly Radicals) abstained, and thus some hours later the Cabinet resigned. The leader of the Conservatives, Lord Salisbury, formed a minority government pending a general election, and took office on 24 June.

Parnell had already made contact with members of the Tory Party. Although still conveying vague proposals to Chamberlain through the offices of O'Shea, at the same time he was developing a working relationship with the Conservatives. He met several times with Lord Randolph Churchill, who had adopted a radical position on the Irish question within the Tory Party. Churchill's aims have been likened to those of Chamberlain, another radical who sought to achieve political success on Irish issues. Churchill considered himself an Irish expert, having lived there when his father, the Duke of Marlborough, was Viceroy during 1876–1880.[73] The shifting balances of Salisbury's minority government, combined with Churchill's appetite for intrigue, presented a new opportunity for Parnell to manipulate British politics.

There is evidence that Parnell was playing both sides. He was in the advantageous position of holding out the promise of cooperation to either political party. Both the Liberals and the Conservatives had come to the view that the resolution of the long-standing Irish problem was critical to political success. Although the leader met with Churchill on several occasions, he also encouraged Chamberlain, who, now out of office, felt free to pursue bold plans for Ireland. Chamberlain continued to rely on Willie O'Shea to act as go-between. The Captain had been disappointed when the scheme for local government had foundered. He had hoped for the position of Chief Secretary, and blamed Parnell, writing to Katie on 17 March 1885 that he had just seen the leader, who appeared 'to funk making a treaty'. It was 'too bad', he lamented, 'as it is a great chance, especially as it would probably allow of my being Chief Secretary in the next Parliament'. 'P' had said he would think it over, Willie added, 'but he is unable, or unwilling, to face difficulties'.[74]

It was clear that Parnell was not alone in playing both sides. Katie was obviously still in her husband's confidence. In addition to his complaints about his health, and pathetic requests for her attention – 'Come if you can'[75] – Willie continued to share with her his optimism about the future. He wrote excitedly that Chamberlain had promised him the Chief Secretaryship on the formation of a new government after the general election. 'This is an enormous thing,' O'Shea exalted, 'giving you and the Chicks a very great position.'[76] Their contact was undoubtedly close at this point. 'I am very sorry to hear that your chest is still troubling you', sympathized Willie on 2 April, writing from Madrid, 'and I am afraid that as long as you have to cross the park in bad weather you cannot be safe.' However, his letter continued with an acknowledgement of their financial situation. 'Anything is better than making yourself ill,' he advised. 'Aunt is certainly very unreasonable.' Yet Aunt's demands had to be respected, as O'Shea's conclusion demonstrated: 'If Aunt accuses me of extravagance', he ended, 'you can truthfully tell her that my sister's illness was an immense expense to me. This hotel is simply ruinous, and I never have anything but 1s. 6.d wine. I must have a sitting-room to transact business.'[77]

Although O'Shea wrote confidently to his wife that 'Gladstone is very strongly in favour of our solution,'[78] she in fact was working with Parnell to broker a similar treaty with the Prime Minister. It is quite clear that Willie did not suspect this. On 4 May, he had confided that the reason he was 'anxious' about the local government scheme was because Chamberlain, if he had power, would offer him the position of Chief Secretary he so coveted. This, or an 'equivalent position if the name is abolished', was O'Shea's ambition, although he acknowledged that the 'boys' would have to agree to it. He then warned Katie: 'Gladstone ought not to know this.' He not only trusted her, but continued friendly domestic relations. Willie ended his letter by asking his spouse to let him know 'whether I am to take tickets for the conjurer [*sic*] for Wednesday'.[79]

In reality, no prospect of political advancement remained for the Captain. Although his patron, Chamberlain, along with Dilke, continued to promote the plan for a central government scheme for Ireland, the Conservatives were now in power and gaining momentum.[80] The new Viceroy, Henry Howard Molyneux Herbert, 4th Earl of Carnarvon, met with the Archbishop of Westminster, Cardinal Manning, on 24 June and was assured the Irish bishops 'all agree in favour of the Union with England'.[81] The Viceroy departed for Dublin on 29 June, confident that he had the Catholic Church's support. Carnarvon had held the office of Under-Secretary for the Colonies throughout 1858–9, and had been Colonial Secretary during 1866–8. He supported a limited measure of self-government for Ireland (but not Home Rule). Manning went further in backing the Conservative administration by refusing to provide Dilke with a requested letter of introduction to the Irish bishops. Dilke and Chamberlain had planned a trip to Ireland, an idea approved by the *Freeman's Journal*, which welcomed the Radical initiative in its columns on 23 June.[82]

Cardinal Manning's uncooperative stance was echoed by the pronounced hostility of William O'Brien's *United Ireland*. On 27 June, the editorial campaign against Dilke and Chamberlain began. A series of highly antagonistic attacks were published against the pair. Chamberlain was shocked and very angry. He and others understood that *United Ireland* was a 'Parnell' paper. He sent O'Shea a clipping of the offensive article, which stated, 'We plainly tell Messrs. Chamberlain and Dilke that if they are wise they will keep out of Ireland altogether. We do not want them here. Let them stop at home and look after their own affairs.'[83] Chamberlain simply footed the excerpt addressed to 'My dear O'Shea' with a series of exclamation marks. The Captain was horrified at this turn of events. He immediately replied to his friend:

My dear Chamberlain,

I have seen Mr Parnell. He told me he attributed the Article in United Ireland to his not having seen Mr W O'Brien before the latter's departure for the Continent – that the article was disapproved of by Messrs Sexton, T P O'Connor and O'Kelly – that there was internal evidence to show that it was not written by Mr Healy. But he went on to explain that he would do nothing to 'break up' his Party on the eve of a general election, and the only hope he would hold out was that he would 'do his best', and if he saw O'Brien, who would probably return soon, he would 'talk the matter over' with him & that it might yet be put right. At the same time he acknowledged the difficulty caused by United Ireland's having already taken up its own position.

Although I urged that for more than three years you had worked loyally, always doing, or doing your best for, everything I asked you on his behalf; and although I laid particular stress on the many assurances of (in my opinion) a most binding nature which I had taken you from him regarding the present business, he did not appear to be disposed to go any farther. I cannot, however, doubt that on reflection he will see the necessity of altering a position of political and personal *cruelty* to you and myself. Under the circumstances I did not see any advantage in alluding to the hostile spirit of his observations to a third person. It would be fatuous to believe that the Parnellites do not see through the insincerity of Ld R. Churchill or that they overlook every declaration of his except those made for the purpose of duping them. I am sure his tactics do not deceive Parnell, but O'Brien is his most dangerous rival, and the *democracy* in question loves a Lord.[84]

   This was a far cry from the collegiate days of 1883, when in the matter of a Bankruptcy Bill in Parliament, Chamberlain had been 'glad to recognise Parnell's perfect loyalty in this matter. It is only what I expected.'[85] O'Shea realized that political advancement was now unlikely. He was livid with Parnell, and wrote furiously to 'My Dick' that the leader was not to be trusted, and that Parnell had 'recently said that he is under no obligation or promise to me!!!!!' He explained that the marks were of 'admiration, not of surprise', as 'the man who, after promising to assist in every way Mr. Chamberlain's journey to Ireland, can let his paper the same week abuse him like a pickpocket, is not to be respected by Mr. C., and I have already told the *scoundrel* what I think of him'. O'Shea was angry at having looked 'such a fool'. He told his wife that he was 'worried, if not out of my wits, out of my hair'.[86] The following day he confided once more to his wife, that he had seen 'a great number of M.P.s of various parties' and 'One and all spoke in astonishment and disgust of Parnell's conduct towards me.' Willie also added the very pointed remark: 'None of them, of course, knew the absolute baseness of it.'[87]

   Katie, not surprisingly, made no reference to her response to Willie's outburst in her book. She can have been in no doubt as to his feelings. In addition to his letters to her, O'Shea told Chamberlain of his interview with the Irish leader on 27 June:

My dear Chamberlain,
   I need scarcely tell you that although my temper is that, not of an

angel, but of an archangel, I made believe to lose it yesterday afternoon. Mr Parnell sat under a tree for an hour and a half, reflecting on all my observations, and although he would not confess anything, I cannot help thinking he must take steps to prevent United Ireland (with which he professes to have no contact except through O'Brien) continuing the course commenced in the last number. My advice is do nothing, say nothing, until my return from Madrid on Tuesday week.[88]

O'Shea did not extend his anger with Parnell towards his wife, which indicates that either he was still oblivious of her relations with the leader, or he was wary of antagonizing her for fear of losing his income. But from this point forward, the Captain was increasingly suspicious of Parnell, and more hostile. The delicate balance that had been achieved since 1882 was profoundly damaged by O'Shea's perceived humiliation at the hands of Parnell. Their uneasy friendship was never to recover.

CHAPTER FIFTEEN

Desperate Measures

HE SUMMER OF 1885 was one of great activity and tensions
for the O'Sheas. Willie O'Shea frantically tried to preserve
his collaboration with Chamberlain, while Katie remained in
contact with Grosvenor. He had responded the previous year,
in May 1884, with a 'non-committal acknowledgement' of the
receipt of the memorandum for 'A Proposed Constitution for
Ireland', 'drawn up by Parnell' that she had sent to him at the
leader's instruction.[1] This document had many points in common
with that drawn up by the Captain. Throughout 1884 and in early
1885 both Willie and Katie were working on the same lines,
through different channels. There is every indication that the
Captain believed that his wife shared his aims and goals for his
own personal political objectives, which of course were closely
tied up with Chamberlain's proposed resolution of the Irish
question.

By the summer of 1885 it was becoming apparent to Willie that
his plan was not succeeding. On 11 July Chamberlain wrote to
O'Shea, stating that he thought 'that Mr Parnell is bound as a
gentleman & a man of honour to take steps to correct'[2] the negative
impression he had given towards Chamberlain's proposed visit to

Ireland, and indeed the proposed local government scheme. On 13 July the Captain replied that he had seen Parnell, and had a conversation with him about the 'whole subject'. The leader had assured him, he explained, that he very rarely interfered with *United Ireland*. 'It is but right to mention that throughout the conversation he expressed very kind personal feelings, and he concluded by observing that it must not be considered unreasonable, under the altered complexion of the situation, that he should take a few days for further reflection before giving a definite and definitive reply to the categorical questions in your letter.'[3]

But Parnell had other ideas. Unbeknownst to O'Shea, Parnell and Katie continued to correspond with Grosvenor after the collapse of Gladstone's administration on 9 June 1885. The Liberals hoped to be back in power shortly, and Gladstone was considering doing battle. The Irish question was an important part of either party's programme. Parnell was fully aware of this. At this point, the Irish Party was by no means exclusively wedded to the Liberals, and he did just enough to keep informal negotiations going with all sides, while secretly exploring the possibility of working with the Conservatives. He arranged to meet the new Viceroy, Carnarvon, at the end of July. Katie was fully in his confidence, and when Grosvenor wrote to her on 14 July, asking whether Parnell's proposed constitution would 'still hold good', she gave him Parnell's inconclusive reply. Grosvenor wrote again, 'asking for a plain answer'. This was at the moment 'impossible to give', she recalled, 'for the attitude the Tories would take up with regard to Home Rule was not yet certain'.[4]

Hamilton was suspicious of the Irish leader.[5] He recorded on 20 July that he had spoken to Gladstone, and wrote:

Parnell has thrown over the Central Board scheme, and declines to accept such a scheme as even a partial solution of the Local Government question. This complicates the situation as it makes a programme which might commend itself to Mr. G more and more problematical, and without a programme Mr. G will not commit himself to fighting again.[6]

The following day Hamilton had further conversation with Gladstone. The talk about Ireland was not encouraging. 'Parnell's change of front', Hamilton observed, 'will I hope open the eyes of Mr. G and Chamberlain to the absolute untrustworthiness of the man. He is slippery as an eel and cunning as a serpent. Mr. G has always pinned his faith too much to Parnell.'[7]

Chamberlain came to this conclusion by the end of July. He abandoned his proposed visit to Ireland, and instructed O'Shea to inform Parnell that as far as he was concerned, 'the matter was at an end'.[8] Although Chamberlain did not entirely abandon his proposals for Ireland, he made a speech on 8 September which referred to the lack of support for his scheme. 'The opportunity has passed away', he declared, adding, 'Mr Parnell, encouraged by the tory surrender, has raised his terms, and the national leaders have abandoned, at all events for the time, all care for local government.'[9]

Willie's prospects looked increasingly poor, while Katie worked with Parnell to secure maximum political advantage for him and the Nationalists. She recorded that after Parnell met the Lord-Lieutenant, he believed that the Tories 'were prepared to support a measure of local government for Ireland'. The question, she noted, was how far the Liberals would go to match the Conservative offer. On 4 August Gladstone himself wrote to Katie, asking whether the proposed constitution still represented Parnell's views. 'He was', she noted, 'urgent in asking for an answer.'[10] Hamilton was unhappy that the former Prime Minister had communicated directly with 'the lady' – 'a dangerous proceeding and one to which attach very strong objections'.[11]

The result was the confirmation that at this stage the Irish leader wanted nothing less than some sort of local legislature for Ireland. Gladstone replied to Katie on 8 August and made clear his unwillingness to strike a bargain with the Irish leader – and that 'into any counter-bidding of any sort against Lord R Churchill I for one cannot enter'. However, he was interested to know the views of the Nationalist Party, and was therefore looking forward to receiving from her a paper describing those views. The instructions on privacy would, he added, be observed by him.[12] The channel with Gladstone was thus open, and Katie continued to act as the go-between.

The formal adoption of a Home Rule policy – while not new – represented a radical political cleaving between Willie O'Shea and his wife. The Captain saw his future within the Liberal camp, and espoused moderate proposals for an increase in devolved responsibility within Ireland for Irish affairs. He did not, however, support a break from Britain. Katie, on the hand, was clearly prepared to follow Parnell's push for Irish legislative independence. In the course of 1885, Katie had a new room built on to her house at Eltham, which adjoined her sitting room and led into the greenhouse and garden. The room was to be Parnell's study, and he 'superintended every detail, saw that the cement was laid to the proper depth under the flooring and sent to Avondale for sufficient sweet-chestnut wood to have the room panelled half-way up and to make beautiful, heavy double-doors, window settings and the mantelpiece and fittings'.[13]

In her memoir, Katie skirted round the tricky subject of how she managed to accommodate this domestic felicity within her marriage and family. There is a large gap in the correspondence with her husband at this time. Testimony later provided in court by her servants, however, has provided additional detail on Katie's living arrangements.[14] During 1884 and 1885 she was attempting to live a clandestine domestic existence with Parnell. Willie was frequently abroad, in Spain or in Portugal. He also spent time in Ireland. Even when in England, O'Shea spent most of this time in London, at his flat in Albert Mansions, maintaining regular visits to his family at the weekends. Katharine's parlourmaid, Jane

Chapman, claimed under oath that while she was in employment at Eltham in July and August 1885, Mr Parnell was frequently staying at the house. She also stated that Captain O'Shea was not living there at the time.

Chapman answered the questions put to her. She confirmed that there was indeed a room in the house set aside for Mr Parnell's use. He used it 'constantly', and the door was locked when he and Mrs O'Shea were together in the room. She also claimed that Mrs O'Shea and Mr Parnell were often out together, 'sometimes as late as between 12 and 1 o'clock'.[15] Further confirmation of these arrangements came from the coachman, Richard Wise, who had been in Mrs O'Shea's employ from the spring of 1885 to the latter part of 1888. Wise stated that in addition to the horses belonging to Katie's children, there were horses named Dictator, President and Home Rule.[16] These were Parnell's horses.

What is striking about these accounts is the combination of Katie's overt and covert behaviour. She wrote that when Parnell sent over his horses, he also sent her a letter, addressed to 'Mrs O'Shea', asking if she would 'allow them to stand in your stables *for a few days*, until I can make other arrangements'.[17] The letters were written, Katie explained, 'in case the horses should be noticed arriving in Eltham and the fact reported to Captain O'Shea'.[18] But of course the arrival of horses would be noticed and Katie, an intelligent woman, would have been aware of that fact. She was probably not worried about the servants. The testimony makes very clear that she was their employer, not Captain O'Shea, or Mrs Wood. Servants were expected to gossip, perhaps, but certainly not to question their employer's behaviour. Katie O'Shea was providing her household staff with a living, and indeed they would require a reference from her in order to gain any future employment.

The danger was her husband. There had apparently been a fracas the previous summer, in 1884. Katie made no mention of this in her memoir, but O'Shea later claimed during their divorce case, in November 1890, that he had heard 'rumours' at that time, and had confronted his wife about her relations with Parnell. His recollection was that she had firmly denied them. He wrote nevertheless to the Irish leader on 4 August from the House of Commons Library:

You have behaved very badly to me. While I often told you that you were welcome to stay at Eltham whenever I was there, I begged of you not to do so during my absence, since it would be sure at the least sooner or later to cause scandal. I am making arrangements to taking my family abroad for a long time, and I hope they will be sufficiently advanced to allow of my asking for the Chiltern Hundreds[19] before the end of the Session.[20]

On 7 August Parnell had sent a cold riposte:

Dear Sir,

In reply to your letter, I do not know of any scandal, or any ground for one, and can only suppose that you have misunderstood the drift of some statements that may have been made to you. If you finally decide upon vacating your seat before the autumn Session, it would, I think, be most suitable if you could do so a few days before this present Session closes, so as to enable the writ to be moved and the election held during the recess. But if you do not intend to go abroad permanently before the termination of the autumn Session, there need be no hurry about creating the vacancy. If you should have any communication to make to me on this point please address me at Avondale, where I shall be after the 9th for the shooting.[21]

On the same day, O'Shea received a letter from Katie. Her communication, unlike that of Parnell, was heated:

I am very sorry that you should have waited in on my account, but after our conversation on Tuesday I could not imagine that you would expect me – in any case, I was feeling scarcely strong enough to travel again in the heat yesterday, and for the children's sake I should not like to die yet, as they would lose all chance of aunt's money, and, however good your appointment, they will scarcely have too much, I imagine, and certainly we have a better right to all she has to leave than anyone else.[22]

This was a salutary reminder, as no doubt it was meant to be. The Captain had grown increasingly reliant on regular cash injections channelled through his wife from Aunt Ben. He had also been waiting a long time for his children to inherit Aunt Ben's fortune. What caused Willie to react so precipitately at this time? He later vaguely claimed that 'rumours' had come to his attention, and certainly any whiff of a scandal always drew an immediate reaction from him.

It is important to note that in August 1884 Katharine was five months' pregnant. It was further stated in court – during the divorce case five years later – that O'Shea had left for Spain and Portugal in March and had extended his stay abroad due to illness. During this absence, he claimed, Parnell had gone to live at Eltham. In fact, parliamentary records show that O'Shea was in England throughout March. He intervened in parliamentary sessions on 6, 14, 17 and 25 March. He was also present in the House on 3 April.[23] After that date, however, the Captain made no intervention until 30 June, some three months later. He had told Chamberlain on 16 April that he was leaving for Madrid the following day.[24] O'Shea was probably away from mid-April until the end of June. He was an assiduous MP and regularly attended Sessions, so his absence was no doubt due to his travels. It is impossible to determine what exactly made him write to Parnell at the beginning of August.

O'Shea had already returned to England some time previously, so he had not just found out about his wife's living arrangements. It is entirely possible, however, that as Katharine's pregnancy became obvious, he may have confronted her and learned (or suspected) the truth. T. P. O'Connor recalled that Labouchere, with whom O'Shea was friendly, had repeated a story to him, as told by the Captain. This was to the effect that while O'Shea was living at Albert Mansions, and his wife at Eltham, she 'used to pay him [Willie] occasional visits… and – I need not be more precise, but suggest the humiliating and shameful compromises which married women who have a lover sometimes have to submit to'.[25] Labouchere was a known gossip, and not a reliable witness, as O'Connor himself admits. Still, it remains difficult to determine what exactly went on. Neither Katie nor her husband was reliable in their recollection of dates. She claimed that he had left in February 1884 to go to Lisbon, and implied that this was for an extended stay.[26] The parliamentary records show that in fact the Captain was in the House on 7, 19, 21, 25 and 29 February.[27] He could of course have travelled abroad for a short stay, or several visits of limited duration, but this is a quite different interpretation of what her memoir suggests.

O'Shea was in England at the time of the last child's conception. It is therefore possible that O'Shea might have believed that the baby was his. He may just as plausibly have thought that the two girls, Claude Sophie and then Clare, could have been his, but the third was not. It is also possible that his overriding concern was for discretion, and that another pregnancy, while his wife was spending so much time with the Irish leader, was carrying things too far in the public domain. His letter clearly refers to his anger over a 'scandal'. This last explanation is the most likely. Katie and her lover were settling down to a domestic arrangement that would have precluded any acceptance on Parnell's part of the kind of 'shameful compromises' to which O'Connor alluded. Once Parnell and Katie were living as man and wife, it would have been entirely out of character for the leader to knowingly condone such practices.

Of course, Katie may have continued a sexual relationship with her spouse without Parnell's knowledge. It is impossible to know her true feelings for O'Shea at this time. But the pattern that does emerge from the evidence is that Katie was drifting away from her husband and towards a new, permanent life with her lover. Parnell gave up his rooms in London and moved into Wonersh Lodge. He brought over his dogs from Avondale. Katie described a tranquil and pleasant life at Eltham. She grew white roses in pots in the greenhouse, 'in order to provide my exigeant lover with buttonholes'.[28] The pair took long drives in the countryside, where she tried to teach him the names of wildflowers, although she recalled fondly that 'he did not shine in any branch of botany'.[29] On rainy days, or if the leader felt unwell, he indulged his love of shooting. Katie recollected that he liked to 'amuse himself at home in my sitting-room with an air-gun', and that sometimes 'he would go to the farther end of my aunt's park, where there was a pond basin, dried up long before, and many happy hours were spent there, shooting in turn, with his revolvers'.[30]

'I had a private pitch laid out for him in a two-acre field', she wrote, so that he could indulge his love of cricket.[31] And indeed Parnell seemed happiest out of doors. Colleagues remembered that he seemed at his most at ease at his simple shooting-lodge or at Avondale. He was passionate about his hobbies – assaying metals and astronomy, and enjoyed the simple comforts of home. He 'was not in the least a well-read man', Katie recalled, and he 'took no interest in literature as such, but for works on subjects interesting to him – mining, mechanics, or engineering and (later) astronomy'.[32] This intensity and limited focus was noticed by others. 'He had an essentially strong but not a broad or comprehensive mind,' Davitt wrote. This mind was 'slow in grasping all the bearings of a problem, or in seizing upon the chances or dangers of a situation, but once it caught hold its power of concentrated application to the task before it made him a match for greater intellects within the sphere in which the issue was to be decided'.[33]

William O'Brien also commented on the leader's 'simplicity' and 'delicate reserve'.[34] As the Irish Party assumed greater political significance in 1885, the leader at the same time was tightening his firm hold on the Nationalists. Katie was able to provide him with the simple and quiet private life he needed. His health was always precarious, and he suffered badly from nervous strain. Katie wrote of how she had to calm him during the night:

When the attacks came on I went into his room, and held him until he became fully conscious, for I feared he would hurt himself. They were followed by a profuse perspiration and deep sleep of several hours. He was terribly worried about these nightmares, but I assured him that it was only indigestion in a peculiar form. 'You *really* think so?' he would reply, and when I told him that they would pass off with careful dieting he was reassured, and he followed my directions so implicitly as to diet that he soon proved me right.[35]

Katie was adept in providing the calm atmosphere and careful cosseting he needed. She was after all well skilled in this art. They remained much at home; naturally, Katie could not participate with her lover in any kind of a social life. Furthermore, she stated that Parnell's 'dislike of social life was so great that he would never accept an invitation that could be in any way avoided'.[36] McCarthy observed that his colleague

went very little into the social life of London, partly because he had a strong impression that English people in general disliked him, and that even where his host and hostess were thoroughly friendly, some of their guests might be reluctant to meet him. 'The truth is,' he said to me more than once, 'I am nervous about being disliked; I hate to be hated.'[37]

O'Shea's outburst in August 1884 was thus an irritant to Katie's well-organized household. She made no mention of how she and her husband resolved their conflict, but Willie was soon back at work on the proposed constitution for Ireland, which he hoped would seal his success.[38] By November, he had drawn up his memo and was meeting with the Irish leader to discuss political matters. Their relations were sufficiently restored for Parnell to send the following letter to O'Shea on 24 December 1884. It was addressed not 'Dear Sir', but rather 'My dear O'Shea', and in this communication Parnell thanked him for what was clearly an invitation, explaining that 'it would have given me a great deal of pleasure had I known in time'. He went on to say that he would look for O'Shea 'to-morrow at Eltham, unless I hear that you are unable to leave town, in which case I will call at Albert-mansions'.[39] The inference was plain – that neither man was actually at Wonersh Lodge, and that Parnell would only go there if O'Shea was to do so as well.

Matters seemed settled, and it was in early 1885 that Katie and Parnell took the more overt steps of living together. None of this – the construction of a new room, the arrival of horses and dogs – seemed to attract any further suspicion from the Captain. He was engrossed in the dealings with Chamberlain, and it was only when the deal with Parnell fell through that the situation once more deteriorated. There was another problem looming. For some time, Willie O'Shea had been losing the confidence of his constituents in Clare. Although his record as an MP was not altogether bad, his efforts to ingratiate himself with the Liberals and his habitual condescension to his Irish colleagues had not gone unnoticed. As Katie pointed out, her husband was, with 'his own set, in and out of the House', a popular man. He was 'witty, and his wit was a little cruel; a raconteur, his stories lost nothing in the telling, and as a diner out he was much sought after'. But his 'set', she explained, 'did not include the then Irish Party'. And indeed, for the Captain, 'it would have been sacrilege to himself not to be at all times perfectly dressed, and to dine out of evening clothes as bewildering as to dine in them would have been to the majority of those on the Irish benches'.[40]

The Parnellite MPs were, it has been demonstrated, 'poorer and from a lower social stratum than were most other British

M.P.s'.[41] Willie would not have found them particularly congenial company. He was also becoming increasingly unpopular with his own constituency. In June 1884, a branch of the Irish National League in Clare passed a resolution of no confidence in him.[42] To compound the problem, by the autumn of 1885, as the general election loomed, O'Shea was estranged from the leader after the failure of Chamberlain's scheme. On 22 August the Captain had informed Chamberlain that his political relations with Parnell 'had been strained owing to his withdrawal from the Irish local govt. scheme'.[43] On 3 September, O'Shea wrote more on the subject to Chamberlain from Holyhead. 'As you know, my relations with Parnell are very strained,' he stated. The leader had invited him to shoot at Avondale, he continued, but he had thought it 'well to refuse'. He was aware of some possible trouble with his seat. O'Shea was unhappy that some of his friends had come from Clare to Dublin to meet him and advised him to tone down his proposed constituency speech, reporting that the 'people are "wild", and will not listen to moderate counsel for the moment'. It is a measure of the Captain's obstinacy that his reaction to this was as follows:

I must ask you to consider whether in one of your forthcoming speeches you could possibly manage to give me a lift... What I want somebody to inform my deluded countrymen is that although a reasonable man, I am intensely Irish in sentiment and political design; that although not inferior in ability to other Irish members, I have been content constantly to efface myself in debate in order otherwise to gain substantial advantages for the Irish people; and that my influence, apart from the Kilmainham treaty, was a *more potent factor throughout the Parliament than the speeches and antics of those who now take to themselves the credit of everything that has been attained.*[44]

This attitude was unlikely to endear him to the constituents of Clare, and indeed the Captain resigned his seat in November.

Katie was frantic with worry. O'Shea absolutely refused to take the Nationalist pledge, which meant that the Irish Party would certainly refuse to support him. Even Parnell, now riding the high tide of popular opinion in Ireland, could not get support for a man who would not take the pledge. He had by chance met O'Shea in October 1885 while travelling from London to Ireland:

When I arrived at Euston I found him [O'Shea] on the platform before me, also T.P. [O'Connor], and we all then went over together. I asked the latter about the former's chances, and he was positive he had none, pledge or not. O.K. [O'Kelly] on my arrival was of the same opinion, and advised me strongly to let him go North or else make some provision for him outside politics. He called to see me next morning and told me he considered his chances very bad, also that nothing would induce him to take pledge. I said very little, and while we were talking over the situation O'S. tapped at door. He said he would like to consult O'K., so invited him in. The latter strongly advised him not to stand, and while conversation was proceeding, he informed O'K,. he would not take pledge, when O'K. told him at once that it was not in the power of mortal man to get him in for any National constituency without it, and that even I could not do it. He then decided to give it up, and it was arranged he should stand for a constituency in the North which we do not intend to contest, and where he will have a chance.[45]

The overt explanation for his support for O'Shea was that the Captain had been promised a safe seat by Parnell in return for his support on a critical parliamentary vote.[46] The Captain claimed that Parnell had made a 'distinct bargain' with him 'the night of the close division about Egypt'. Parnell had told him: 'If you vote with us against the Government I promise you your re-election without trouble or expense.'[47] This was the 'official' explanation for Parnell's determination to find a place for O'Shea. At what was clearly Parnell's instruction, Katie wrote on 23 October 1885 to Grosvenor, and also to the Prime Minister, begging for help. She asked the Chief Whip to support her husband's bid to stand as a Liberal candidate. Katie told him that Mr Parnell had promised that if O'Shea were adopted as the Liberal candidate for mid-Armagh, he would ensure the delivery of the Nationalist vote there for him, and would throw in 'his' (i.e. Nationalist/Catholic) votes for East Down, North Antrim, North Armagh, and North Derry to the Liberal candidates. In other words, the horse trade that the leader suggested was that he would effectively guarantee three seats to the Liberals in exchange for their support of O'Shea.[48]

Parnell hoped to avoid having to deal with the Liberal administration directly, which is why using Katie as a conduit was so useful. He told her that O'Shea would try to get selected for a seat in the North. 'He then wants me to go see Lord R. [Richard Grosvenor]', he continued, 'but I would much prefer not doing so, as it would very probably come out.' If Gladstone agreed, he told her, the 'best plan will be for you to write and tell W. that it is all right, so as to get me out of seeing Lord R'.[49] But the plan for a mid-Armagh seat did not work. Faced with rejection from the Nationalists and then the Liberals, the Captain was furious. He was also unwell, suffering from an attack of gout, and confined to bed at the Shelbourne Hotel in Dublin. He wrote angrily to Chamberlain on 8 November. 'Parnell called on me yesterday afternoon', he explained, 'and began to mumble something about sorrow that I had not seen my way to contest mid-Armagh and hope that an English seat might yet be found for me.' O'Shea was having none of it, he claimed, and told the leader that he did not want 'any more beating about the bush, that no man had ever behaved more shamefully to another than he had behaved to me, and that I wished to hold no further communication with him. He enquired whether I wished him to leave and I replied, most certainly. He then crossed the room and held out his hand. I informed him that I would not touch it on any account.'[50]

What emerges from this letter, even allowing for O'Shea's sense of self-importance, is the real venom he was feeling towards Parnell. This was echoed in his correspondence with Katie, to whom he confided that at a lunch with friends he had learned there was 'much talk in Dublin about my affair. All agree Parnell's conduct is loathsome.' The following is one of the strongest indications we have of O'Shea's possible lack of knowledge at this point on the extent of his wife's involvement with the leader. 'He has run away to England,' continued the Captain, perhaps unaware that Katie must know this, if Parnell was with her. 'As I have reason to believe, he may deny his having promised me to secure my re-election "without trouble".'[51]

The situation was turning into a crisis. On 24 October, Gladstone had replied to Katie's request to help her husband with a bland assertion that he would forward her request to Grosvenor. Although he professed he would be 'very sorry if Captain O'Shea should fail to obtain a seat in the new parliament', the former Prime Minister was unwilling to do or say more. 'You will I am sure understand… that if I were to go beyond this it would lead to much inconvenience and confusion of duties,' he explained. And as to the paper (Parnell's 'Constitution') she proposed to send him, 'if it is intended for me I shall be happy to receive it'.[52] This of course was the problem for Katie. Her role as credible mediator was in danger of being jeopardized by her blatant attempts to seek favour and to 'place' her husband.

She seemed prepared to go to tremendous lengths to help her increasingly disgruntled spouse, but it is difficult to know how much this anxiety was from fear of what he might do, or whether she still cared about him and was unhappy at his situation. In any event, she continued to exert pressure on both her lover and her political contacts to make progress. On 30 October, Katharine wrote again to Gladstone, reiterating that she was 'very anxious that Lord Richard Grosvenor should find a seat for Captain O'Shea somewhere'.[53] She pressed Grosvenor until he came up with the possibility of a seat in Liverpool. This meant, however, imposing a candidate on the local constituency. And O'Shea did not make matters easier. He was not especially cooperative or even appreciative of Katie's frantic attempts to find him a safe seat. At first, he refused to even contemplate an English seat at all. And it would have been hard for her to forget his bitter words, written to her on 2 November from Dublin:

All I know is that I am not going to lie in ditch. I have been treated in blackguard fashion and I mean to hit back a stunner. I have everything ready; no drugs could make me sleep last night, and I packed my shell with dynamite. It cannot hurt my friend [Chamberlain], and it will send a blackguard's reputation with his deluded countrymen into smithereens.[54]

Katie recounted in her memoir her desperate actions to remedy the situation. She had pinned her hopes on the Liverpool seat. Grosvenor had wired her on 9 November to say that he would write to Liverpool, and on 13 December the Liverpool agent, Wylie, told her that he had informed their Liverpool correspondent and had wired O'Shea. But on the same day Willie telegraphed his wife from Chamberlain's, where he was staying, to say that another man had been chosen and that he was planning to return to London. At this, Katharine 'threw all caution to the winds so far as Lord Richard and Gladstone were concerned and sent a peremptory message to Wylie asking where the former was'.[55] He then replied to her the next day, saying that Grosvenor was expected that morning. The Chief Whip – on receiving yet another message from Katie – replied to her 'with really natural irritation'.[56] This is hardly surprising, as she had no authority to intervene in such a manner into Liberal parliamentary affairs. O'Shea, on the other hand, had blithely gone to London. When pressed, he told Katie that he was ill, and needed to see the banker Sir Samuel Montagu about some business affairs.[57]

The Liverpool seat fell through, despite the support of Grosvenor and even, indirectly, that of Gladstone. Parnell was pressed to push for the Irish vote to get behind O'Shea, but the Captain was beaten by a few votes. Katie wrote of her 'bitter disappointment' at her husband's defeat, and was clearly suffering from nervous strain.[58]

It may have been after the stresses of the general election of 1885 that Parnell brought her an invalid couch (or he may have brought it during one of her pregnancies), returning 'home', Katie wrote, 'in broad daylight in a hansom-cab, triumphantly supporting one end of a large couch, the other end of which spread its upholstered length over the roof'. With the help of her maids, Parnell arranged the chair in Katie's sitting room, adjusted 'its complicated "rests" with earnest abstraction, after which he led the procession up to my room, and in spite of my amused protests carried me down and placed me on the couch amid cushions and shawls, and spent a happy evening in "watching me" as I lay comfortably on my new possession'.[59] Such domestic felicity, however, came at a cost.

Both the Conservatives and the Liberals had used the Irish question as an important part of their election campaigns. The Liberals had expected a large majority – and were disappointed by the result of the ballot box. The end result was that 335 Liberals, 249 Conservatives and 86 Home Rulers, or Nationalists, had gained seats. It was a blow for Gladstone, who had hoped for a strong majority. Instead, Parnell's Irish Party held the balance, if they voted with the Tories. This would require a tight party discipline, however, and that the Conservatives and Parnell cooperate – not a likely prospect. Many Tories were firmly against Home Rule. So, although the Irish leader was in a good bargaining position, he needed to capitalize on it in order to get the best deal possible from either side. To this end, he continued to negotiate behind the scenes with both parties.

The Liberals – and Hartington in particular – expected that with a large majority, the Irish would simply have to accept whatever was proposed. Given this, it would be acceptable to offer them quite a lot – short of Home Rule, however. For Gladstone, the election results presented an opportunity to reopen the whole Irish question. Derby recorded a conversation he had had with him in early October:

He said the plan of a central council put forward by Chamberlain would have been accepted by Parnell, who then thought he could do no better for the Irish cause: but R Churchill by seeking his alliance had induced him to raise his terms, and now he would be content with nothing short of a local parliament, having full powers of legislation.

The former Prime Minister was now entertaining new thoughts about the situation generally. Derby recalled:

He thought that question of Irish Union must be studied seriously. He had been reading old debates upon it, including Pitt's speech in proposing it to parliament, and he was not satisfied with the argument in its favour. He had come to the conclusion that the Union was a mistake, and that no adequate justification had been shown for taking away the national life of Ireland.[60]

Just a day or so before, Gladstone had received Parnell's proposed constitution for Ireland from Katie. He sent a discreetly guarded reply. But on 21 November, Parnell – in what some saw as an attempt to call Gladstone's bluff – instructed the Irish voters in England to support the Conservatives.[61]

Katie's intervention was again put to use. On 10 December 1885, she wrote to Gladstone. 'So much depends on your reply', she penned, 'that I hope you will pardon my writing you again on the subject of the scheme [Parnell's Constitution] I sent you sometime ago.' Her role was obviously subtle and quite critical. She could say what the leader – still ostensibly working with the Tories at this point – could not. It was of course a scheme, she explained, 'that Mr P could not bring forward himself and my object in writing is to ask if you can tell me in confidence if you consider a scheme based on the lines of the one I sent you a paper respecting, is at all possible'. Katie was also able to send a strong hint his way: 'I have private information that Mr P is to see Lord C[arnarvon] in a day or two.'[62]

The 'Grand Old Man' was a master of the game, and unimpressed by this veiled threat. Besides, he was hoping that Parnell might indeed do a deal with the Conservatives, who could perhaps be persuaded to take up Home Rule themselves. If Home Rule could be a non-party question, as he preferred, it would be more likely to succeed as a Tory measure, enacted with Liberal support. Gladstone sent a letter to Katie in which he told her that he was 'glad to hear that Mr Parnell is about to see Lord C. I have the strongest opinion that he ought if he can to arrange with the government for the plain reason that the Tories will fight hard against any plan proceeding from the Liberals.'[63] But the Conservative Prime Minister Salisbury was unequivocal. He told Churchill that Gladstone had sent to Balfour 'a marvellous letter saying he thinks "it will be a public calamity if this great subject should fall into the lines of party conflict" – & saying he desires the question should be settled by the present Government. His hypocrisy makes me sick.'[64]

While Katie corresponded at Parnell's behest with Gladstone, sending drafts and letters, she also continued her quest to sort out a position for her husband. She wrote to Grosvenor on 4 December, thanking him profusely for his help during the general election. This communication, written on her own account and no doubt at her own initiative (there is every chance that Parnell may not even have known about it), gives a hint of Katie's spirit and also her tenacity. 'I am really *grateful*', she wrote, 'for the trouble you have taken.' She hoped that there would be another opportunity for O'Shea. She pointed out that Mr Gladstone had told her in 1882 that he would remember O'Shea 'should a "suitable" vacancy become vacant. This is nearly 1886! Suitable is such an open question, isn't it?'[65]

Willie, meanwhile, was being left behind by events. On 17 December, Gladstone's son Herbert, who had much studied the Irish question, supplied information to the press to the effect that his father now supported Home Rule. This was known as the famous 'Hawarden Kite'. Herbert's motivation for doing this, on his own initiative, was presumably to force the pace of progress. The timing was seen by some as a cynical bid to get Irish support for Gladstone, but he remained calmly above the fray and avoided making any commitment to Home Rule. Instead, this master tactician chose to challenge the Conservatives on an unrelated issue, and defeated them in the House on 27 January 1886 by 329 votes to 250. This was all that was needed to bring down Salisbury's administration and, within forty-eight hours, Gladstone was requested by Queen Victoria to form a new government.

There was disappointment in store for Chamberlain (and, by extension, O'Shea). He had hoped for the Colonial Office. Instead, Gladstone gave him the minor appointment of the Local Government Board. To make matters worse, the post of Chief Secretary for Ireland was awarded to John Morley, a far more junior Radical. The Captain's dream of high position in Ireland was looking distinctly unlikely to be realized. Katie wrote that O'Shea turned to Parnell. She recalled:

And now came the demand we expected from Willie. He could not bear to be out of Parliament… and he went to Parnell in the House and insisted that his 'services in regard to the Kilmainham Treaty and also in acting between Chamberlain, Mr. Gladstone and himself' deserved the recognition of Parnell's support in again trying for an Irish seat.[66]

This is how Katie chose to explain her husband's justification for his demands.

The evidence suggests that by this stage Katie and Parnell's liaison was no longer entirely secret. In Liverpool, it was later alleged that a number of people heard Grosvenor reply to the question of why the Irish leader made an exception in supporting O'Shea. The Chief Whip had declared, 'Oh, he sleeps with O'Shea's wife.'[67] And there were further murmurings. In December, Parnell had been confronted by an angry crowd in Louth, furious that their local candidate, Philip Callan, had been defeated by a Parnellite candidate, Joseph Nolan. The leader had campaigned against him, and Callan had been incandescent. Raging at Parnell in front of the rowdy crowd, he shook his fist and launched into a bitter attack on him. The newspaper report was confused, but its key passage made oblique reference to Parnell's campaigning for O'Shea in Liverpool:

He [Callan] asked Mr Parnell, face to face, what was there in the character or private history – in the public character or private history – of Captain O'Shea, what was there superior in his political character or private history superior to that of Phil Callan and his wife that Mr Parnell should malign and traduce him (Mr Callan) and support with his best exertions Captain O'Shea (cheers).[68]

This was almost certainly a thinly disguised attack on the leader's relations with O'Shea's wife. There was no other apparent reason for Callan to introduce his own spouse into the discussion other than to make the inference about Katie. She recounted that Willie was angry that Parnell was not doing more during the general election to support his candidature and gave her version of events:

That Parnell had, and was pressing it so strongly as to jeopardise his own position he did not understand. His true reason for doing so – my desire – he did not know; nor did he know, what Parnell knew, that ugly rumour had already begun the campaign of brutality that, not daring to meet its foe in the open, wars with the dirty word, the filth flung at a woman's love and, with only the knowledge of its own motives and methods, the belief that where there is a wrong that wrong must surely be of the basest kind.[69]

Both she and Parnell understood what was needed: O'Shea had to get his seat, or he would turn nasty. The spectre of Aunt Ben's displeasure – and the ensuing loss of funds – was undoubtedly enough to keep the Captain quiet in public, but he would continue his vendetta against Parnell until he got satisfaction in the form of a public capitulation from the leader. It put Parnell in an utterly impossible position. O'Shea still refused to take the pledge, but a Nationalist seat was all the leader could get him. Parnell turned his sights to Galway, which was the only Irish seat available.[70] To intervene in this selection, however, was problematic. On 4 February 1886, *The Times* reported that the two candidates for the seat were Dr O'Connor (brother to Arthur O'Connor, MP) and Mr Doherty, an engineer from Dublin. Mr T. P. O'Connor, MP, was to arrive in Galway shortly, and a convention was to be held to choose between the two candidates, 'to whom it is believed that no opposition will be offered'.[71]

Willie still refused to take the pledge. He put pressure on Katie and threatened, she claimed, to travel to Ireland to be proposed in Galway by someone other than the leader. He was absolutely determined, Katie wrote, and indeed her account, while inaccurate in the details of how Willie leveraged his position, still conveyed some of the panic she felt at his behaviour:

In going over the problem with me, weighing up the pros and cons, Parnell said: 'I can force Willie upon Galway, but it will be such a shock to my own men that they'll not be the same again. Or I can leave it alone, and... and... will do almost as much mischief with him there. Queenie, you must see him again, and tell him I'll propose him if only he will consent to take the party pledge. Tel him I cannot insult the others by proposing him without this.' I did so, but it was no use. Willie was not well, and would not even discuss the matter, merely reiterating his intention to go to Galway the moment he could get his shoe on (he suffered much from gout), and his disgust at the ingratitude of 'the man he had let out of prison', to say nothing of Gladstone's, Grosvenor's and my own ingratitude. I went home, and on Parnell's return I told him of my failure.[72]

He reassured her that in the end it would not matter. He would force O'Shea on the Galway electorate. 'It will cost me the confidence of the party, but that much he shall have, and I shall be done with his talk of pledges.' He then told Katie that he had already planned earlier to propose O'Shea, and had informed O'Connor of his decision. 'You should have seen his face, my Queen', he said, 'he looked as if I had dropped him into an ice-pit.'[73]

CHAPTER SIXTEEN

The Turning Point

G ALWAY WAS A MEDIEVAL CITY on the west coast of Ireland. Bordered by the River Corrib, Galway had historically been a relatively prosperous place. Mercantile trading up to the seventeenth century had resulted in fortunes that had been converted into urban castles, rural tower houses and considerable land purchase. Galway citizens had, however, supported the Confederate side in 1642 and capitulated to Cromwellian forces in 1652 after a nine-month siege. The city remained Jacobite until 1691 when it surrendered without a siege. Galway lost a considerable amount of its wealth and prestige over the years that followed. Towards the end of the eighteenth century, though, the town had undergone rapid expansion. Victorian Galway was moderately prosperous, thanks in part to the great fishing tradition of the Claddagh, the seafaring suburb to the west of the town, and to a burgeoning population explosion in its surrounding areas. But the general trend was one of decline, and this was exacerbated by the famine years. The population dwindled, despite the town's success as a tourist centre as the gateway to Connemara, one of the loveliest regions of Ireland. This tourist trade was enhanced by the opening of the first railway connection to Galway in 1851.

The town also held one of the Queen's Colleges, which opened in 1849.

Katie made no mention of the huge problems caused by Parnell's decision to interfere in the Galway election. Although he was supremely confident he could tell the Galway constituency how to vote, he reckoned without the opposition of other senior party members. On 9 February, *The Times* reported that an 'unexpected and very serious rupture has occurred in the Home Rule ranks in reference to the Galway election'. It was 'more serious than the revolt of Mr Callan at Louth'. The *Freeman's Journal* had warmly endorsed Captain O'Shea, observing that 'in the present condition of Irish affairs no doubt the constituency and the public will attach full weight to the recommendation of Mr. Parnell, who has opportunities for judging the political situation not open to others'. *The Times* pointed out, however, that unlike the preferred candidate, O'Shea was 'an absolute stranger and suspected of being a Whig in the garb of a Nationalist'.[1] And, indeed, the local people had 'not yet recognized the special merits for which Mr. Parnell desires to have him elected'. Local feeling was running very high, the article continued, and the rupture had been 'rendered more marked and mysterious by the active intervention of Mr. Healy and Mr. Biggar, who arrived in Galway yesterday'.[2]

As soon as they had learned of Parnell's decision, Healy and Biggar had rushed to Galway to protest O'Shea's candidacy. Healy was in no mood to accept the leader's high-handed action. He had already gone behind Parnell's back to conduct a secret political intrigue with Labouchere the previous year. Healy had represented himself to Labouchere as the acting leader of the lieutenants of the Irish Party, who could negotiate without Parnell.[3] That this tentative collaboration had led to nought only contributed to Healy's bitterness. He and Biggar were, furthermore, convinced that the reason Parnell was beholden to O'Shea was because of his liaison with the Captain's wife. Biggar, in conversation with local nationalists in Galway, made reference to O'Shea as the husband of the leader's mistress, and Healy also made this reference to O'Shea's rival, local candidate Michael Lynch.[4] Although these disclosures were not made public, they were known and discussed at the time.

O'Connor recalled that Parnell had worked 'like a man possessed' to secure O'Shea's Liverpool seat. 'The great ambition of O'Shea,' he recollected, 'was to be returned to Parliament and above all to be returned as a Liberal. He had a constant and obstinate ambition far beyond his merits, intellectual or political.' The Captain had been encouraged by Chamberlain, O'Connor wrote, who was 'hostile to some of the actions of his own Government'. And it was also at this time that the leader 'began the use of O'Shea's wife as an intermediary between the Liberal Party and Parnell – interventions of which the colleagues of Parnell knew nothing'.[5] There were suspicions, O'Connor recalled, but 'No secret was better kept, and for so long, as the liaison of Parnell with Mrs. O'Shea… Whispers there were, but I can say with perfect accuracy that until the Galway election the story was not told.'[6]

At the Galway election, however, the story was told privately. Parnell chose to impose his personal authority, and most of the Irish Party followed his lead. William O'Brien put the situation clearly in a later letter to John Dillon, on 7 February:

Your feelings and ours about O'S. are, of course, the same – loathing. So is our feeling about the infamous way in which P. has put him forward and slighted the party. The question was, in the special circumstances of the moment, whether we should swallow O'Shea or utterly destroy our movement and party at its brightest moment for a personal reason which we could not even explain… We pressed Parnell by all possible means short of open revolt, but his answer was emphatic and he is plainly bound by some influence he cannot resist… It is a terrible pass but I think we cannot hesitate. Posterity would execrate us for wrecking this movement at such a moment for so miserable a cause.[7]

The betrayals were many. O'Shea was in essence blackmailing Parnell, who in turn used (or abused) his position to force the Irish Party to do his bidding. The leader even intimated that he would resign if O'Shea was not selected. This must prove that the Captain was aware of the adultery in 1885, although he later denied it. The Irish leader made a statement to the press after the divorce in November 1889 to that effect: 'Captain O'Shea was always aware that he [Parnell] was constantly there [at Mrs. O'Shea's house at Eltham] in his absence from 1880 to 1886 and since 1886 he has known that Mr Parnell resided there from 1880 to 1886.'[8] Still, at the time, the leader strove to maintain appearances by insisting that Chamberlain supported O'Shea, and that there were sound reasons for the Captain's election. O'Shea was duly returned on 10 February 1886. In the wake of this election was fury, bewilderment and much resentment in the Irish Party. As Thomas Croke, Archbishop of Cashel and himself a committed Nationalist, commented privately, the 'Galway affair was an ugly business', and 'provision should be made, somewhere, against escapades of this kind in future'.[9]

There was political capital to be made by anti-Nationalists. Unionist comments on the Galway election were scathing. A Catholic Unionist present during the debacle gave his view of events:

Parnell comes of the conquering race in Ireland and, he never forgets it, or lets his subordinates forget it. I was in Galway when he came over there to quell the revolt organised by Healy. The rebels were at white-heat before he came but he strode in among them like a huntsman among the hounds – marched Healy off into a little room, and brought him out again in ten minutes, cowed and submissive, but filled, as anybody could see, ever since, with a dull smouldering hate which will break out one of these days, if a good and safe opportunity offers.[10]

William O'Brien attempted to soothe Healy with an editorial in *United Ireland*:

Those who counted on defections from Mr. Parnell's side have been rudely undeceived. The shallow cockney journals who expected Mr. Healy to break into mutiny against the chief whom he had served from the first dawn of his power with the fidelity of a Crusader and the courage of a lion, have been taught how little they know of the depths of a nature whose ferocity is reserved for the enemies of Ireland, and whose key note is a tenderness of heart as fascinating as the fiery play of his intellect.[11]

But there was great residual bitterness. Labouchere summed it up for Herbert Gladstone:

Healy has been an ass in the O'Shea business. Harrington, O'Brien and O'Connor and the others were with him, but they knocked under to avoid a split. They now console themselves by saying that the Captain must have letters of Parnell about Mrs. O'Shea, and thus can make him do what he likes. I doubt this. When once Parnell gets an idea into his head, he sticks to it with the tenacity of a lunatic.[12]

At this time, Katie was preoccupied with Irish affairs at Westminster. She had continued to correspond with Gladstone on Parnell's behalf and on 23 January wrote that she was 'authorised by Mr P to tell you that he and the Irish members would be willing, since your speech on Thursday, to assist in ousting the govt if Mr P could have reasonable assurance that firstly you will be sent for by the Queen and secondly that you will form a Ministry'.[13] On 30 January, she informed Gladstone that Mr Parnell would, when the time came, 'be glad to learn from you through myself, or Lord Grosvenor the method you think best to adopt for the purpose of the full interchange of views you deem desirable and indispensable with regard to Irish autonomy'.[14]

Parnell and Katie were hoping to achieve a breakthrough with Gladstone. Most politicians and senior civil servants did not make efforts to really understand the Irish situation. Randolph Churchill had made much of his direct experience of Ireland, but he was unusual. The 'official mind' was disinclined to reward Irish violence and threats with land reform and independence. But Gladstone, especially during 1885–6, was determined to enact change. This change was not without its costs. The 'Irish Question' had, as we have seen, for years provided fodder for political intrigues and careerism. Now, Gladstone used his determination to achieve some form of Home Rule – including land reform – for Ireland as a means to force other politicians into compliance.[15]

From the moment of his third administration, Gladstone worked tirelessly on a definitive settlement for Ireland. The Government of Ireland Bill was introduced on 8 April, shortly before the Land Purchase Bill. Limited legislative independence for Ireland was proposed, although several important questions were left unresolved.[16] The roles of a Privy Council and the Viceroy were left undefined, as were many of the practical details of the executive. The major point of difference between Gladstone and Parnell was, however, that of finance. The Prime Minister wanted Ireland to bear one-thirteenth of imperial costs. This was eventually bargained down to one-fifteenth, although Parnell's demands to go down to one-twentieth were refused. But the overriding importance of the proposed bill was that it was actually being introduced at all. The historical significance of this should not be overlooked. Gladstone was the first British premier to recognize the legitimacy of the Irish right to self-determination. There was tremendous opposition. Churchill, once a supporter, now turned against Home Rule and vigorously campaigned against it. He supported the Unionists[17] and his now famous phrase, 'Ulster will fight; Ulster will be right,' was coined on 7 May in a public letter.[18]

And the opposition grew. Within the Liberal ranks, there was considerable dismay at the Prime Minister's initiative and, on 31 May, Chamberlain held a meeting with fifty MPs at which the Quaker Liberal MP (and former Cabinet member) John Bright[19] made a declaration against Home Rule, which was signed by forty-six of those present. Despite Gladstone's impassioned pleas on the bill's second reading on 8 June 1886, the measure was defeated by 341 to 311. It was found that ninety-four Liberals had voted against the government. The result was expected. Parnell had cagily hedged his bets by remaining in the background in the lead-up to the vote. His initial response to the measure had been reserved, and he – unsurprisingly – had points of disagreement. As it became apparent that the bill would not pass, there was little to be gained by fighting the detail.

Parnell kept a cool head throughout the deliberations. He showed throughout 1885 and 1886 that he was willing to deal with British politicians of all persuasions. He had demonstrated his fundamental political pragmatism by his willingness to work with both Liberals and Conservatives. The Irish leader had then gained Gladstone's confidence by convincing him of his essentially conservative direction. And, all along, Parnell had managed the tricky task of retaining the extreme elements of his party within the broad Nationalist alliance. For this he owed a great deal to Katie. Her correspondence with Gladstone and Grosvenor presented Parnell as a reasonable and trustworthy politician. The lines of communication were not obvious, as the Prime Minister could not be seen to meet with the head of the Irish Party. Using Katharine O'Shea as a credible and reliable conduit was a stroke of genius.

That the Prime Minister believed in the Irish leader's integrity at this point in time was certainly due in part to the relationship Katie helped to foster between the two men. On 25 March 1886, for example, at a critical time in the development of the Ireland Bill, Katharine wrote to Gladstone about a possible meeting between him and the Irish leader:

Mr Morley mentioned to Mr Parnell that he thought you might wish to see him. Mr Parnell acting on your letter to me, said he thought

Mr Morley could convey to you all that was necessary at present. But Mr Parnell wishes me to tell you that he will be happy to go to your room in the house or to see you in Mr Morley's room if you should care to see him at any time – perhaps Mr Morley's room would be best, as being less likely to be noticed, however, of course you will know best.[20]

At the time of such delicate negotiations, therefore, the appearance on 24 May of a small piece in the *Pall Mall Gazette* was particularly unwelcome. Entitled 'Mr. Parnell's Suburban Retreat', the article reported a collision that had taken place between Mr Parnell's carriage and a market gardener's cart. The incident had occurred while the leader was returning 'home' to Eltham. There was a direct assertion made. 'During the sitting of parliament the hon. member for Cork usually takes up his residence at Eltham, a suburban village in the south-east of London.'[21] This tittle-tattle had the potential to be enormously damaging. Just months previously, Dilke's career had been ruined when he was named as co-respondent in the Crawford divorce case, which was heard in February 1886.[22] The ensuing scandal precluded the offer of a post for Dilke in Gladstone's Cabinet.[23] The Prime Minister had written to his colleague on 2 February, expressing his 'profound regret that any circumstances of the moment should deprive me of the opportunity and the hope of enlisting on behalf of a new Government the great capacity which you have proved in a variety of spheres and forms for rendering good and great service to Crown and country'. It was fortunate for Dilke that the more sensational evidence – for example, Mrs Crawford's assertion that he had insisted on a threesome with her and his young maid – had not yet been made public. If so, it is unlikely that Gladstone would have gone on to state: 'You will well understand how absolutely recognition on my part of an external barrier is separate from any want of inward confidence, the last idea I should wish to convey.'[24]

O'Connor recalled how the journalist T. D. Stead became obsessed by sex scandals. 'He sought everywhere for the violator of the strict sexual code,' O'Connor wrote. 'It was he who drove Dilke first almost to madness and then to ruin,' he recollected. More worrying still, O'Connor remembered:

the almost sickening shudder which I felt one day I paid Stead a visit at the *Pall Mall Gazette*, of which he was then the editor, and he said to me broadly and in almost a casual way: 'The question I am now considering is whether I should ruin the Irish Party by exposing the *liaison* between Parnell and Mrs. O'Shea'. Speaking still in that same tone as of almost a commonplace occurrence, he told me that he had actually sent for Captain O'Shea and put the question to him whether it was true or not that his wife was the mistress of Parnell.[25]

This was just the sort of development to cause O'Shea acute embarrassment. The threat of a public scandal was damaging to his pride, but it was also a liability for Parnell and of course for Katie herself. It was at this time that her relationship with Willie deteriorated sharply. On 16 April 1886, she had written an extraordinary letter to the Prime Minister, begging him to help her find a position for her husband. O'Shea may have realized two months after his controversial election that he had been foisted on a constituency that did not want him. Furthermore, he faced a dilemma over the proposed Home Rule legislation. Once Chamberlain had set himself against it – leading to his inevitable resignation later – the Captain did not want to go on record to support it. On the other hand, he had been elected on a Nationalist ticket, making it highly inappropriate to vote against Home Rule.

Katie wrote to the Prime Minister on 16 April, stating that her husband's predicament was such that had he begged her 'to write and ask if you can and will give him the province of some colonial appointment, later on – the fact is that he is in very great pecuniary difficulties'. Katie's no doubt carefully considered phrasing was interesting: 'My Aunt, with whom I have been living for many years', she continued, had agreed to 'assist my husband out of his present difficulties, for my sake, if she can see any hope of his getting any lucrative occupation'. And she would never have troubled the Prime Minister about her husband, Katie added, if he had not 'kindly promised some years ago to remember him... hence his desire that I should write and beg you to give some hope of one kind. I fear that unless something can be done for him at once he will become so hopelessly embarrassed as to render it difficult to do anything later... I fear it will be difficult to get him any appointment if he is made a bankrupt, and I am afraid he will be, unless you can give me some hope for him.'[26]

It is impossible to know who was behind this request. Certainly it was a very odd letter. On 19 November of the previous year – a mere six months earlier – Gladstone had been prevailed upon to send a telegraph to Captain O'Shea publicly supporting his candidature in Liverpool.[27] Then O'Shea, after failing to get elected as a Liberal MP, had stood successfully for a Nationalist seat in Ireland. It may well have been Katie's plan to get her spouse a position that would take him away from London and away from her. He may have had other ideas. Just a fortnight after she had sent her letter to Gladstone, O'Shea wrote to Chamberlain that he could say anything he liked in Galway: 'I am the most popular MP that has represented the borough for a quarter of a century!'[28] Two weeks later he wrote to say that 'Mr Parnell asked Montago and Nolan on Friday to warn me that he believed I should be murdered if I voted against the bill. I saw him today but I declined to discuss political affairs.'[29]

The snippet in the *Pall Mall Gazette* about Parnell's living arrangements was an unwelcome attention, and O'Shea had immediately written to his wife, enclosing the offending paragraph. She sent an affectionate response, addressing her letter to 'My Boysie':

I received your letter and as I telegraphed I have not the slightest idea of what it means, unless indeed it is meant to get a rise out of you. I

saw the paper when I came home from Aunt's but I was so wet I thought
it best to change before I tellied [telegraphed] to you. I do not see that
it has anything to do with us, and I am inclined to agree with Charlie
whom I heard from this morning. He says in respect of Healy that 'it is
better to put up with a great deal of abuse rather than retaliate, for it is
ill fighting with a chimneysweep, for right or wrong you only get soiled.'
I should say the paragraph has been made up by Healy & Co to annoy
you but I don't see why it should do so. However it is not wonderful after
the notices I have received from some of the papers, from Romeike [Press
Agency] and I should advise you to hold on to your seat for I am (sure)
you will annoy the sweeps most by doing so. I was sure there would be
no end to their spite after your Galway success. We will call early
tomorrow and talk it over. Your K[30]

O'Shea recounted that, two days after this, his wife came into
London and handed him the following letter, stating that it was
from the Irish leader. It was marked 'private' and ostensibly written
from the Irish Parliamentary Offices in London:

May 26, 1886
 My dear Mrs O'Shea,
 Your telegram in reference to the paragraph duly reached me. I had
a couple of horses at a place in the neighbourhood of Bexley Heath but
as I am now unable to be much away from London, have turned them
out to grass for the summer. I am very sorry that you should have had
any annoyance about the matter and I hope to see you on Sunday. Kindly
return me enclosures when you have had time to read them.
 Yours very truly
 Chas. S. Parnell[31]

Later it was declared in court that Parnell and Katie had lied about
the leader's whereabouts, and that the above letter was a complete
fabrication, designed to mislead the Captain. It was further asserted
that Parnell and Katie had gone to the Wonersh Lodge stables and

removed his horses, harness and saddles to another stable 'lest Captain O'Shea should come down and find them there'.[32]

In fact Katie and her lover took further evasive action. In May 1886, Katie rented a house in Eastbourne, in St John's Road. The owner of the house, a builder, testified that a gentleman – whom he did not know – and a lady had come to view the house. The rental agreement for nineteen weeks was signed 'Katie O'Shea', and she paid the rent. While they were there, he recalled, he heard a rumour that the gentleman was Mr Parnell. 'There were two servants, two young ladies, and a young gentleman besides the gentleman and the lady.'[33] A cab driver confirmed that he remembered Mr Parnell living at No. 2 St John's Road. 'He often engaged my cab,' he claimed. 'I have driven him to the station, and on various occasions have driven him with Mrs. O'Shea, on one occasion to East Dene.'[34]

Katie wrote that she had taken the children to the seaside in May 1886, first at the Queen's Hotel, and then to the house in St John's Road. She made no secret of Parnell's presence. He enjoyed the bathing, she recollected, and was 'much distressed' that the 'weakness' of her heart prevented her from joining him. He was also disappointed that boating had the 'most disastrous effects' on her. 'He was boyishly determined that I should at any rate join him in some way in his sea "sports", and one May evening he insisted that if I went into the sea fully dressed it could not hurt me.' She was dubious, and held tightly to him as they waded out to sea. 'He held me tightly, laughing aloud as the ripple of waves and wind caught my hair and loosed it about my shoulders; and, as I grew cold and white, my wonderful lover carried me, with all the weight of my soaked clothing, back to the shore, kissing the wet hair that the wind twisted about his face and whispering the love that almost frightened me in its strength.'[35]

There was also a quiet and peaceful domesticity. Parnell's two horses were brought down from London. Katie does not give any reason other than the need for them, but their removal from her stables coincides with her husband's letter of remonstration. She and her lover were keeping out of Willie's way, and planning for a future together. 'We often drove out to Birling Gap', she wrote, 'a favourite haunt of ours – and there we selected a site for the ideal house of our dreams.' The couple were steering clear of O'Shea, but there is no evidence to suggest that they were exercising anything more than the usual discretion favoured by Parnell. There were the cab rides, the house rental, and Katie wrote of how they enjoyed conversations with the coastguardsman, 'who was always ready for a chat when we cared to hear his stories of the sea'.[36]

The couple were searching for a house, a seaside retreat, and they spent time touring the area. According to her account, they found a property, presumably during this visit. The house was built but not entirely finished, she recalled, on the cliffs towards Beachy Head. Parnell liked it so much that he took a three-year lease on it as soon as it was finished. He and Katie spent many happy hours, she remembered, going over the decoration and details of the house. Together they selected the Minton tiles for the hall, and the leader showed her how to lay the tiles one day. He did so with considerable energy and had finished the work by the time the workers returned. 'He then insisted upon my writing "Heatherbell Cottage" on a tile', she recalled, 'which he proceeded to inlay over the front door, earning the comment from the men working there that he seemed to know as much about the "job" as they did.'[37]

Parnell loved manual labour, and he loved the outdoors. Just as colleagues recalled his enjoyment of country pursuits, Katie wrote of how much this quiet man had enjoyed being out in the open, especially when the weather was wild. She recalled that he had a

great love of sea-storms, and when there was a gale blowing from the west, and rough weather assured, he loved to get me out to Birling Gap to listen to the roar of the sea and the screaming of the wind as it blew around us, nearly carrying us off our feet. He would tie his coat about me, and hold me firmly against the wind as it tore about us, and while we gazed out at the raging waves he would exclaim: 'Isn't it glorious, my Queen? Isn't it alive?'[38]

But Parnell was 'low and depressed all through the summer of this year', she wrote, and she became increasingly worried about him. She tried different diets 'without effect' and rented a house for him in London.[39] Later records tell a different story. From the summer of 1886, Katie and her lover lost their peaceful existence. Just when Parnell was enjoying the domesticity with Katie, this life came under attack from O'Shea.

The couple were trying to establish residences away from Eltham, presumably to escape Willie's attentions. Another seaside house was rented under the name of Parnell's secretary, Henry Campbell, at Eastbourne. The letter asking for the rental was, however, in Katie's handwriting. The owner of Moira House at Eastbourne testified that Mrs O'Shea and an unnamed gentleman had come to view the property. Mrs O'Shea had agreed to take the house for one year, and had chosen the wallpaper. She had also had trelliswork installed on top of the wall. The rent was paid for one year, by Mrs O'Shea. The couple also needed a London residence in which they could safely meet. To this end, some months later another house was rented in York Terrace, in Regents Park, in March 1887. It was let to Mrs O'Shea, and she paid the rent up to March 1889. Katie engaged a maidservant and a housekeeper to look after Parnell, and furnished the house with books and journals that would interest him.

Parnell rented another house in south-east London, in the suburb of Brockley, in January 1887, under the assumed name of Clement Preston. There was in fact some confusion over this rental. Parnell had originally told the agent that his name was Fox. He then said it was Preston. He refused to provide any references, but paid a deposit that was accepted. He took the tenancy of 112 Tresillion Road for one year, and a couple was hired to look after him at the house. Parnell interviewed the coachman himself and his wife, Susan Honey, was interviewed by Clement's 'sister', whom she later identified in court as Katie O'Shea.[40] It was clearly a fraught time for Katie and her lover. She gave no hint of these subterfuges in her book, but recalled that Parnell had never liked the house at Brockley. 'He wearily said he did not want to live in London unless I would live there too', she wrote, 'but, as I pointed out, that was impossible.'[41] 'I had had unpleasant letters from Willie', Katie later admitted, 'and the latter and I were not now on speaking terms.'[42]

The Captain was making life very unpleasant. He had already requested Katie not to have Parnell at Eltham. He penned on 26 April 1886:

With regard to Mr. Parnell, I believed your assurance, but I have scores of times pointed out to you, that however innocent in themselves, the frequent visits of a man to a woman, during the absence of her husband is an offence against the proprieties, and is sure sooner or later to be observed upon severely by society. I trust for Norah and Carmen's sake you have learnt the lesson.[43]

Matters worsened for the Captain. He continued through the spring of 1886 to oppose the Home Rule Bill. This caused huge upset for his Nationalist constituency and on 9 June 1886, just four months after his controversial election victory, O'Shea stood down, claiming that his objections to the bill had been 'too strong to allow him to support it', but that he believed 'that a measure will soon be carried which will satisfy the patriotic aspirations of Ireland and improve the material interests so gravely involved'. He was aware that his views were not shared by his constituents, and therefore 'honourable feelings suggest that he should resign his seat, which he accordingly does'.[44]

Relations between the Captain and his wife subsequently deteriorated. During the summer, O'Shea learned of further newspaper comment while he was away in Carlsbad, taking a cure for his gout. On 2 July he wrote to 'Dear Kate' to remonstrate that an American woman had read out an offending article (much to her embarrassment when she realized what the subject was), and that he had feigned to know nothing about it. 'I merely said that just as everybody of respectability avoided politics in America, so it must be when the worst features of American politics had been introduced into our country by filthy swine like Parnell and his crew.'[45] After his return to England, O'Shea wrote to Katie from Brighton on 20 August:

It will be advisable not to settle anything definite until my return. I hope to-day to conclude a provisional arrangement by which, should it be decided to carry into effect one of the proposals which you made the other day, I should be ready to take away the children on the 1st of October. Having most carefully weighed your second proposal, that we should live at Brighton or some place, and that you should go on frequent visits to Eltham [presumably to keep up a good relationship with Aunt Ben], I find the objections to it quite insuperable. One of them is that it would allow the scandal to continue unabated in another form.

He went on to suggest that Katie should seek some outside advice: 'I should think it will be necessary to seek the advice of a third person in the matter, so that nothing which can be suggested by unprejudiced prudence should be omitted in order to mitigate (if by any means possible) some of the effects of the deplorable situation on the future of the children.' The Captain asked her to make a list of her debts, so that he could assess their finances. He ended by stating that, although he hoped it was not necessary, 'I repeat that I forbid you to hold any communication, directly, or indirectly, with Mr. Parnell.'[46]

Katie's response was not printed in the newspapers, but a partial copy is in the archives of the National Library of Ireland. On 23 August, she sent 'Dear Willie' the following:

You have written me many mean and impertinent letters, but the last, which even you were ashamed to give me yourself, and obliged the children to convey to me, is one of the most mean and insolent you have ever written... You speak of provisional arrangements to commence from the 1st October, under which you will provide a home for myself and the children. I shall be obliged by your letting me know by return of post where the house is to be if away from Eltham my Aunt says she will not give one penny to me either for the support of myself or the children, or of course for yours either. She also says that she understood that she was asked to buy the lease and furniture, and pay for the rent of your rooms at Albert Mansions when you required them to live in. If you mean to take a house away from Eltham let me know & I must arrange with Anna [her sister] & Charlie [her brother] for one of them to come and live here. Of course in that case you will provide all monies for the children, and myself.[47]

This was indeed setting the matter straight for him. Katie knew, as did her husband, that he did not have the means to support his family. Further, Katie's withdrawal from Eltham would herald the arrival of one of her siblings, who would then be in closer proximity to Aunt Ben and her benevolence. If Willie insisted on antagonizing his wife, significant risks would be run. The children, aged sixteen down to the infants, were dependent on Katie's ability to provide for them. Her siblings were not well off, and neither was her lover. There is every indication that Katie was a practical woman. She understood her predicament, and her only hope was to persuade her husband that his best interest was in maintaining the status quo.

She and Parnell continued to dream of the day when they would be free. In the meantime, the situation was enormously stressful. They could no longer live together at Eltham. Parnell especially seems to have found the separation unendurable. Katie could not be everywhere, and she was much needed at Eltham. Katie was in anguish and described how, after seeing her lover in London, she would have to leave him behind. 'I went home haunted by his grave, considering eyes and his sad "You must not leave me here by myself; I don't want to be here without you!",' she remembered.[48] She would make 'flying visits to him, to sit with him while he ate his breakfast'.[49] His health declined, and Katie made changes to his diet. When these met with no success, she insisted that he consult a doctor. 'His nerves had completely broken down', she recorded, 'and I felt terribly worried about him.' She accompanied him, using his alias 'Mr Stewart', to see the famous surgeon, Sir Henry Thompson. Katie made no attempt beyond this to be discreet, and indeed took it upon herself to meet privately with this eminent doctor before allowing him to see 'my' patient, so that she could 'explain a little about Mr. Stewart's ill-health'.

Katie professed to be greatly comforted by the doctor's concern and advice:

Sir Henry Thompson warned me that it was most important for Mr. Parnell's health that his feet should be kept very warm, as his circulation was bad. When his feet became cold it upset his digestion, and this so disorganised his general health that he was then laid up for several days. I always insisted upon his frequently changing his shoes and socks when he was at home, and gave him a little black bag containing a change whenever he was sure to be away for a few hours, as I found that the trouble of the frequent changing was amply compensated for in warm feet and therefore better health.[50]

She was unable to abandon Parnell to the rented homes, and the life of subterfuge was causing them both considerable strain. Katie described long waits in train stations in order to snatch moments together. She even met him at the St Pancras Hotel. Again, there seems to have been no desire on her part to exercise discretion. She waited for the leader in his room, and 'made the waiter bring up a tray into the bedroom, with a cold bird, some tomatoes and materials for salad dressing, adding a bottle of still Moselle'. When

Parnell returned, she made him his supper, which they ate as a breakfast in the early dawn. Then Katie left to take the early train back to Eltham.[51]

Such a situation was unsustainable. She could not give up her lover, and Parnell was utterly devoted to her, as well as dependent. She wrote of how she frequently went to the House to take him to dinner in a restaurant, before driving him back. Katie would often 'promise to wait for him at some station, so that he could find me without observation. It would have been much more comfortable, of course, for me to have waited in a house or rooms somewhere, but people were so extraordinarily curious about Parnell that it would have been impossible so to get any peace unless we changed the address every week, and this would have been decidedly too expensive.'[52] The real reason, of course, was because of Willie. What Katie wanted was to re-establish her domestic tranquillity with Parnell, especially for the sake of his health and well-being. Because Aunt Ben was still alive, this had to be at Eltham.

But O'Shea was unrelenting. He wrote on 13 September 1886, telling his wife that she should see her solicitor, Mr Pym: 'Although I remember your telling me that Mr. Pym dislikes me, I do not consider that this would be any obstacle to his being professionally consulted.' This was, O'Shea later claimed, Katharine's response to his request that she consult someone reliable. She had suggested her brother Evelyn and Pym. The Captain went on to state that 'As, however, you say you are prepared to meet my views, I hope there need be no reference.' O'Shea made his position clear: 'All I want is that you should engage not to communicate, directly or indirectly, with Mr. Parnell, and that you should take Norah and Carmen to Eltham and prepare a room for me, so as to live in the house.'

This first condition had been suggested by Evelyn Wood, he continued, 'and the second affords the only chance of mitigating the effect of the scandal on the children'.[53] He was going to Paris and hoped that the arrangements would be made during his absence. 'I think it better and more quiet to write than to attempt the personal discussion which, of a matter of fact, is painful.'[54] The pair were almost certainly arguing bitterly. On 25 September, the Captain once again pressed his demand, in the 'interests of Gerard, Norah, and Carmen', that she should not communicate with Mr Parnell.[55] It is interesting that the two younger daughters, now aged three and a half and two, were not mentioned. That O'Shea let them go, by default, as it were, was later interpreted as proof that he knew they were Parnell's and not his children.

On 3 October, Katie sent an indignant reply:

Dear Willie,

I have been waiting for an answer from you, for, while I desired to meet your wishes as far as I can, I have not the slightest intention of allowing you to make the rest of my life utterly miserable by nagging at me from morning to night at Eltham. Of course you cannot, and do not, believe that I object to your living at Eltham because I wish to receive visitors there who you do not like, for you know as well as I do that I only desire to be left in peace with my children, and that peace I deserve and will have when at home.

She then issued a sharp reminder of where the money was coming from. 'If, however, you would prefer our living somewhere else say so, and we will try and do so, and run the risk of consequences as far as aunt is concerned.'[56] Willie was, in spite of this, determined to press his case. 'You say that you are anxious to meet my views', he wrote on 4 October, 'but you make no approach to them. The condition which is to me all important you refuse.'[57] Katie's reply was written in Eltham, according to O'Shea's lawyer, and it had no date. It read: 'I regard your last inquiry only as another method, under cover of an obscure newspaper paragraph, of renewing the demand which I have repeatedly and definitely refused to agree to.' On an even more ominous note, she added, 'I must ask you to immediately reply to my letters respecting

money matters, as I shall not get the money if you do not.'[58]
Another of Katie's letters, ostensibly written in early October,
was also produced. 'I was too tired and worried to write last night',
she argued, 'and I am beginning to feel the effects of the constant
wet feet, fog, and damp here. The things you mention seem so
petty after the real difficulty of existence, for they have no
existence, and I cannot understand how a busy man can give so
much time to them.'[59]

Katie's position had all along remained consistent. She avoided
an outright denial of adultery. Instead, she maintained that there
was no scandal – and indeed, if the two of them had, as she later
claimed, an arrangement, then there would be no scandal insofar
as Willie himself was concerned. If, however, there was public
knowledge of the affair, this might have been too much for O'Shea.
But some time in early October, she took a different line, and lied
to her husband. In an undated letter, written almost certainly on
9 October 1886, Katie replied to her husband's query – upon seeing
a paragraph in the *Sussex Daily News* stating that Mr Parnell had
been staying at Eastbourne with her – with an outright denial. 'I
know nothing about Mr. P's movements in reference to
Eastbourne', she asserted, 'and I do not see why I should be
expected to. I only know that his brother and family had a house
there before we left, and I imagine that the rumours (if any) have
originated from that.'

In addition to denying that they had been in Eastbourne
together, Katie wrote that she had seen in a newspaper that 'Mr.
P' had travelled to Ireland in the first week of August, and not
returned until his speech on the Queen's Speech in Parliament.
She knew he was in Ireland, as he had sent her some grouse.
Katharine then went on the attack: 'I am disgusted at your desire
and evident attempt to drag my name into a newspaper again when
it has not even been mentioned, and if my name is mentioned in
the newspapers again I shall take steps to prevent it in future,
whoever drags it in.' Once again she reminded him of their living

situation by ending, 'I am writing in haste as I have to go to my aunt about money matters.'[60]

The Captain replied on 10 October by telling his wife that he had made 'no attempt' to put her name in the newspapers. 'Indeed, one of the effects of its having been there has been to end my public life,' he claimed. He was also very sorry she had refused to consult her solicitor, he went on: 'I believe he would have advised you in the interest of your children to agree not to communicate with Mr. Parnell any more.' He regretted that she would not consent to his plan, but acknowledged that he had 'no means of enforcing it'. He did not think that it was to the advantage of the children for him to spend the winter at Albert Mansions in London, but he acceded to her proposal.[61] In fact, O'Shea recognized that he could not force Katie to have him live at Eltham. This, more than anything, is evidence that the couple were de facto separated at this point. And indeed their relations worsened as the year drew to a close. 'I am perfectly disgusted with your letter,' Katie wrote to her husband during this period. 'It is really too sickening, after all I have done. The only person who has ever tarnished your honour has been yourself.'[62] By December they were barely on speaking terms. Willie wrote on 12 December 1886, 'I shrink from the possible eventualities of discussion with you, especially as to-day before our daughters.'[63]

Now that their relations had broken down, O'Shea did not refrain from attacking Parnell. On 19 December he wrote to Stead at the *Pall Mall Gazette*:

It was stated in the *Pall Mall Gazette* yesterday that Mr. Parnell was staying on a visit with me. The fact is that I have had no communication whatsoever with Mr. Parnell since May. You have been deceived probably by some Parnellite, because there are dogs of his, I am told, who in return for the bones he throws them snap when they think it safe.[64]

On 20 December, the paper printed the following: 'Mr. O'Shea asks us to contradict the statement that Mr. Parnell is staying on a visit at his house.'[65] However, just two days later, the *Gazette* published this:

Mr. Parnell has been really ill. Of that we are credibly assured. Not, of course, that he was so ill as to know nothing about the Plan of Campaign... On the whole, notwithstanding the semi-official bulletin of the Press Association, he will do well to recover sufficiently to cross to Dublin before Christmas. What with Olympian religions at Hawarden and Eleuisan mysteries at Eltham, our composite party seems to be somewhat in a bad way.[66]

The paper was making sly reference to Gladstone's prolonged stay at Hawarden. He had retreated there on 22 September and had remained there ever since.[67] The dig at the 'Eleusian Mysteries' – ancient rites known for their highly secretive nature – at Eltham was unmistakable.

The *Gazette* referred to the Plan of Campaign, and suggested that the leader was fully aware of its nature. This Plan was a renewal of the land agitation. After the defeat of the Home Rule Bill, Gladstone had dissolved the Cabinet, and another general election was called. This time, the Liberal Unionists (who opposed Home Rule) joined with the Conservatives. The result was that the Conservatives won 316 seats, the Liberals 191, the Liberal Unionists 78, and the Nationalists 85. Salisbury formed a Conservative government and when Parnell proposed a Tenants' Relief Bill, in September 1886, it was thrown out. In response to the Conservative administration, some of his more militant lieutenants favoured a more aggressive strategy. T. C. Harrington, Dillon, O'Brien and others revived the proposal made earlier by Tim Healy. Basically, the Plan of Campaign called for tenants to unite in refusing to pay 'unfair' rents, and to instead pay the rent money into a central fund. This fund would then be used to finance the maintenance and legal costs of those tenants taken to court. It was a return to a more highly charged campaign on the Irish side, and the *Gazette* was referring to the fact that the leader had remained conspicuously silent on the matter. He expressed concern to O'Brien about the costs of the movement, and was also worried about the effect of agitation on British public opinion, and in fact the possible pernicious effect on the Nationalist-Liberal alliance.[68]

Indeed, Parnell was remarkably silent after the First Home Rule Bill failure in 1886. He made not a single public speech in Ireland until 1890. The leader's apparent withdrawal from the struggle was all the more astonishing because the situation was evolving quite dramatically. Arthur Balfour replaced the moderate Michael Hicks Beach as Chief Secretary in March 1887. Balfour was firmly committed to undoing the constitutional achievement of the Home Rule movement, namely its apparent move to respectability. To achieve this, he began by enacting coercion measures. On the day of his appointment, *The Times* had published the first of a series of articles accusing Parnell of being directly linked to crime in Ireland. Balfour immediately announced an inquiry into the series of allegations that followed, resulting in a Special Commission.

The Irish leader was at first determined to take no notice of the allegations. But a series of forged letters was published, linking Parnell to agrarian crimes, and he decided to take legal advice.[69] Katie wrote that she had strongly urged him to do so, and that he had been resistant. He was far more absorbed, she recalled, by his scientific experiments and using his 'wonderful little machine' to weigh 'infinitesimal specks of his morning's extraction of gold with the utmost accuracy'.[70] It is possible that O'Shea, who knew the journalist involved, was aware of the story as early as June, well before it went public. He was probably extremely concerned that Katie's association with Parnell, who he believed would be found guilty of criminality, would reach Aunt Ben's ears. This could explain his repeated insistence that she break off all contact.

Even though Parnell wanted to ignore the letters, the matter did not end there. In July 1888, one of his colleagues, O'Donnell, brought a libel case against *The Times*. The action failed, and had the added effect of bringing into the open new evidence against Parnell. The leader went on the offensive in the House, and the government responded on 17 July by announcing the launch of a Special Commission of investigation. Even more than Balfour previously, Salisbury showed a willingness to help the newspaper make their case. The Commission, with the backing of the Conservative government, and through the action of *The Times*, launched an extensive and unprecedented attack on the entire Irish Nationalist movement. The Commission was instituted not to establish the authenticity of the letters, but to test the claims made in them. It was thus a very significant political process by which the Tories hoped to destroy the Irish Party and tarnish the Liberals. As one historian has observed, the result was that the 'constitutional achievement of the parliamentary party between 1882 and 1886 was effectively negated'.[71]

Parnell was, however, triumphantly vindicated when it was proved sensationally on 22 February 1889 that a Richard Pigott had forged the letters.[72] Although fully exonerated, Parnell was too clever a political operator not to understand the real import of the investigation. The Irish independence movement had been put on trial, and discredited by the government. The link between the movement's aspirations and crime had been established, despite his own proven innocence. Much information on the Land War and the Land League had been exposed, especially on the role of the Fenians. The damage to the cause was done. The leader's quest for constitutional independence had been dealt a tremendous blow and he now virtually disappeared from the political scene.

CHAPTER SEVENTEEN

Legal Battles

*T*HE CASE DID NOT WORRY PARNELL MUCH', recorded Katie, 'except that it took up so much of our all too little leisure time, which was so precious to us.'[1] After the tumults of 1886, the two suffered when apart. From Avondale, on 30 August 1887, the leader wrote that he had been 'exceedingly anxious' about her. 'You seemed so very ill that it has been haunting me ever since that I ought to have stayed in London,' he continued. He was working on his new mine, he reported, but it would not be necessary for him to remain too long, 'so that whenever you are ready for me I can return'.[2] What is particularly interesting about this letter is that, first, he does not say that he wished he had remained at Eltham, but rather in London. And, second, that he was waiting for her to be ready for his return.

In June 1887, Katie had written to her son Gerard (now aged seventeen), giving an undertaking that she would meet his wishes with regard to Parnell. 'I agree', she wrote, 'that there shall be no further communication, direct or indirect.'[3] It was later stated in court that Katie's son had been shielding his mother, and had lied to his father about the leader's presence at Eltham in December 1886. Gerard had told the untruth, it was claimed, 'in the hope that no wrong was being committed and from a natural anxiety not to speak against his mother'.[4] He subsequently decided that his mother was not being fair to his father, and remonstrated with her, according to court reports. The situation was getting extremely complicated, as evidenced by Gerard's expression of his 'wishes' that his mother should cease communicating with Parnell.

In March 1887, Katie arranged an appointment for the solicitor Pym to see her aunt, who was planning to make a codicil to her will. Her intention was to leave everything to her niece. Maria Wood was now entirely dependent on her 'Swan', and Katie's brothers were getting suspicious. O'Shea later wrote of how they each had financial problems. In 1882, Evelyn Wood had asked his aunt for a loan of her silver plate (which she subsequently gave him). Charles had obtained a present of £2,000 'on the plea of poverty'.[5] Katie was concerned that they might try to intervene to get more of her aunt's fortune. She wrote to O'Shea in March that she agreed that Pym needed to see her aunt, but she was 'waiting to see if Charlie comes tomorrow or if anything happens in the way of their taking any further steps'. Katie also told her husband not to worry about another insinuation concerning Parnell's presence around Eltham, made on 26 February in the Tory weekly *St Stephen's Review*:

I should not be if I were you if you refer as I imagine to St Stephen's Review – no one thinks anything of St Stephens and that is so evidently the old rumour again that I think you will be very unwise if you take any notice of it. I do not understand what it means in the least but I am quite sure that if any one finds they have been able to take a rise out of you by it that they will go on for ever and with the family on the look out it is very important that it should be allowed to die its own death. I thought of writing to St Stephen's myself when I first saw it but I am sure it is not worth it and it is no doubt done to get a rise out of you...

In any case I should advise your waiting until the Codicil is done before you get into a correspondence with any of the Newspaper Scoundrels.[6]

On 7 April 1887 Maria Wood signed a new will, which was witnessed by her footman, Ezra Willsher, and her housemaid, Rosa Aldridge. This document read: 'I revoke my other will and codicils and I leave all my personal and real estate to my niece Katie O'Shea whom I appoint my executrix.'[7] The danger appeared to be over. But Willie must have sent his wife an unpleasant communication, for on 9 April she replied:

By the time I was able to leave Aunt it was too late to go up with any hope of finding you in and besides the bitter East wind had been almost too much for me – it has made all our colds worse. Norah has had a very bad cough. I hope to be in Town tomorrow but I will telegraph in the morning. I don't suppose our 'talk' about Gerardie will matter for a day or two, will it? As Gerardie says he told you that Grant is engaged until the end of this month and he is very anxious to go on with him until then and he is working very well. I did not consider that your last letter required an answer as it was one of the many gross insults you are fond of writing to me which would be better answered altogether, or not at all. Your assertion that I at any time 'concealed the fact of my being in the family way' is simply a foul lie – like many other things you have written to me.[8]

Relations between the two worsened. Although O'Shea was probably not expecting anything to come to him personally, no doubt he had hopes that his children would benefit from Aunt Ben's bequest. The new will circumvented that by leaving everything to Katie herself. O'Shea was certainly disappointed. He had good relations with his children, in particular with his son, Gerard, who now took action on his father's behalf. On 13 April he wrote to O'Shea from Eltham:

My dearest Father,

Although my news may not be pleasing to you, yet it must be told. On my return from London this evening I came in by the back way and as I came past the window of the new room that was built last year I heard the voice of that awful scoundrel Parnell talking to a dog. Grouse I suppose. So I asked my mother if it were, and she says that he has come to dine and will be gone presently. Perhaps I ought to have gone in and kicked him out, but I am anxious to avoid unpleasant scenes with my mother. And also I think it is better for you to know about it before giving him a thrashing as you of course, understand more about these things than I do. However, if you want me to kick him you only have to say so, and it shall be done at the first opportunity.[9]

O'Shea testified that he had called on his wife the very next day, 'and had a very painful interview with her'.[10] Katie wrote in response on 17 April that she expected him to 'clearly state what your definite wish is in reference to the subject of our conversation on Friday'. She added: 'At the same time I must tell you that if you put it in such an offensive manner as you did on Friday it will be impossible for me to accede to it both for my children's sake and my own, for you have no right to give such a reason for my not meeting any one.' The matter was complex, however. This was not just about the scandal. Katie then went on to point out that her aunt had made a new will, and enclosed a copy for Willie to peruse. She informed him that she planned to consult her solicitor in order to have 'his opinion as to whether it is sufficiently formal or whether it would be better to have a more formal one made by him carrying out her intention, in any case I believe it would be as well to have this one signed and witnessed by him'.[11]

O'Shea's immediate reply was to state that he had not known the contents of this or any other of Mrs Wood's wills. He hastened to make clear, however, the one thing on which he could credibly take a view. The effect of this will was, he claimed, 'that if she survives you the children will not have a penny of her money'. He advised that should this not be the intention, 'the new Will ought to state that in case you predecease her, she leaves her real and personal estate to your children'.[12] This would not benefit the

Captain directly or even indirectly, unless Katie died, but it was something, and in reply to Katie's request for his definite wish, the Captain recorded that he answered, 'Consult Pym.'[13] Katie sent him a cable the next day: 'Very well Charlie is coming see Aunt today cannot leave when he is here.'[14] Charlie's visit had to be managed, and Katie could not take the risk of leaving him alone with her aunt.

Meanwhile, Gerard was staying with his father in London. His absence was beginning to cause problems for Katie at Eltham. Her brother Charlie's visit was expected on 18 April. She could not come to London, she cabled her husband, 'as uncertain time Charlie will come and leave cannot go before he leaves'.[15] On 19 April Katie cabled her husband: 'Please send Gerard immediately unless he returns today Aunt declines to alter it [her will] he can go up again if you wish after all settled.'[16]

Gerard went to Eltham on 19 April, but then returned to his father in London. O'Shea was insistent that his wife should consult her solicitor. The absence of Gerard from Eltham was dangerous for Katie, whose position with her aunt could be seriously undermined if her behaviour was suspicious. Her brother's visits were thus most unwelcome. She went to consult Pym as Willie insisted. On 22 April, the solicitor sent the following to the Captain:

I have seen Mrs O'Shea and laid before her your wishes. She most indignantly and emphatically denies that you have or ever had the least ground for the very unworthy suspicions you have chosen to affix to her credit.

The particular friend you alluded to is and has been a rare visitor at her house and he only became a friend [in red: Parnell] of the family upon your introduction and by your wish. Were she now to forbid him the house it would involve her either in an admission that there had been some ground for your complaint or that she was behaving with a discourtesy which the past friendship and kind favors [sic] shewn to you by that friend do not deserve. She therefore, although anxious to do nothing to cause you annoyance, must decline to peremptorily close her doors on the few and far between visits this friend is ever likely to make. With regard to your eldest son, it seems highly desirable on every account that he should at once return home to continue his studies.[17]

Katie had clearly decided to brazen it out and stand up to her spouse, who was still primarily concerned with appearances. The Captain had written once more to Pym:

What I asked you to advise Mrs. O'Shea about was this and only this: That reports being wide and strong as to her relations with Mr. Parnell it would, for her children's sake, be expedient that she should declare her renunciation of communication with him. You have either given her this advice or you have not. However this may be, I understand that she refuses to recognise what I hold to be her duty to her children. Please return the correspondence which I sent you in confidence, and accept my apology for having sought to impose upon you a task which does not fall within the scope of professional duty.[18]

Pym returned the letters to the Captain, and wrote on 25 April that he would give advice to his client at his own discretion. He added: 'I trust by this time your eldest boy has returned home as otherwise I forsee [sic] his position with Mrs. Wood may be very seriously compromised.'[19]

O'Shea then wrote directly to Parnell on 29 April 1887:

It has come to my knowledge that in the face of the scandal which has been largely disseminated by your own associates, and which I have no reason to believe you have ever made any effort to curb, you continue to communicate with and to meet Mrs. O'Shea. I now personally call on you to discontinue all communication, direct or indirect.[20]

The Captain was by now seriously alarmed, as the situation seemed to be getting out of hand. On 27 April, Katie's brother Evelyn had written her a seemingly innocent letter. 'I have a suggestion about the Titled Deeds of some land which were mislaid to impart to you', he wrote, 'if it is convenient for you to come over – or shall I write it to your husband?'[21] This was certainly a threat. The brothers continued to apply pressure. Charlie paid another visit to his aunt in May. He recorded in his diary:

Then on to Eltham, Katie with aunt who was not well. I sent up to ask if she would like to see me, she sent to say she was not at all well but would like to see me. Katie looked black as thunder, evidently hated my coming. Aunt wished me to stay to luncheon and cheered up so much that she offered to drive me to the station altho' she had not left the house for 10 days. She took me to Blkheath and begged me to come again to see her.[22]

The danger was seemingly averted, for the time being. Willie, however, was not satisfied. Katie agreed to send letters to Gerard, reassuring him that she would meet his wishes about Parnell. These were sent in June. 'I am most anxious that everything should be made as pleasant as possible for you', she wrote, 'and that nobody should come here who is in any way obnoxious to you, and, therefore, I readily agree that there shall be no further communication, direct or indirect, with him.'[23] The following day, she also agreed, in reply to his request, to give up the lower stables. She hoped that this would satisfy him (and, more importantly, his father).

Pym wrote again to O'Shea on 25 August, stating that he trusted that Gerard had indeed returned home, 'as otherwise he foresaw his position with Mrs. Wood might be very seriously compromised'.[24] The Captain felt that the whole issue could be resolved if Katie simply agreed to give up her relationship with Parnell. He became obsessed by this. Katie at the same time was hugely frustrated. If Willie would not make such a fuss, there would be no difficulty. Both recognized, however, that an impasse had been reached. The result was that Parnell had to go away. It is little wonder that he was terribly ill at this time. Even the normally imperturbable McCarthy was taken aback at the leader's appearance in the House on 18 May 1887. He wrote: 'Only one impression was produced among all who saw him – the ghastly face, the wasted form, the glassy eyes gleaming…'[25]

Parnell's absence from daily living with Katie did not, however, have the result of increasing his political activities. Indeed, his colleagues complained of his infrequent appearances at this time. He was rarely in the House or at meetings with his colleagues. Even his beloved hunting trips were curtailed – this was because, Katie explained, he 'would never stay more than a few days, as he could not bear to be away from me longer. I used to wish it were possible for me to go to Ireland with him in order that he might enjoy his shooting to the full, but that was impossible.'[26] Somehow the two managed to snatch time together. Katie wrote that she would take her children down to Brighton 'for a few day's change' and that on these occasions her lover would stay at a place near Chain Pier. She recalled:

I remember one rough, stormy day when we had been much worried and were wondering whether the time of waiting we had imposed upon ourselves (that Ireland might not risk the leadership that seemed her only hope) till the way could be opened to our complete union before the world, was not to be too long for our endurance. It was a wild storm, and Parnell had to hold me as we slowly beat our way to the pier head… Then we stood looking at the great waves – so near, and shaking the whole pier-head in their surge. Parnell remarked that the whole place could not last long, and as I turned to get a fresh hold on him, for I could not stand against the wind, and the motion of the sea sickened me, the blazing fires in his eyes leapt to mine, and, crushing me roughly to himself, he picked me up and held me over the sea, saying, 'Oh my wife, my wife, I believe I'll jump in with you, and we shall be free forever.'

Katie responded by saying, 'As you will, my only love, but the children?'[27] And he had brought her back to safety. It is a strong indicator of how the stresses and strain of the subterfuge and O'Shea's attacks, as well as her brothers' intervention, were affecting Parnell. Gone was the cosy domesticity at Eltham, replaced by rented homes under assumed names, unfamiliar servants, and only snatched moments of Katie's time. Aunt Ben's astonishing longevity was, however, drawing to a close. This, despite Katie's claims in her book that her anxiety concerned the importance of the Irish leadership, was the real hold O'Shea had over her. She simply could not risk the scandal – which is no doubt why Willie kept referring to it in his correspondence.

But for Charles Parnell, Katie was his home. He spent little time in Ireland and had effectively abandoned Avondale. He travelled there in January 1888, and reported to Katie that his sister Emily was at Avondale on her own, and that his mother was expected that night. His sister was practically destitute, and separated from her alcoholic husband.[28] Emily had lived on and off at Avondale for years. By 1875, her husband's problems were such that the couple depended on her brother Charles for support. In 1884, soon after her husband's death, she had lived a peripatetic existence, and in 1886 had returned to live at Avondale. Debts accumulated by her husband had swallowed all of her money, and permanent residence at Avondale had become a necessity. She lived there with her daughter Delia until her brother's death. Although Charles was not especially close to any family members, he did not abandon them. When Emily's husband died in Belgium, Charles organized the removal of the body from Brussels, settled his affairs there and returned to Avondale to console his sister. After she took up residence at the family home, he spent time with her on his brief visits. They enjoyed long rides on horseback into the mountains.[29] But he clearly did not confide in Emily – and she spent much of her days alone at Avondale.

His mother Delia had fared little better in her own life. She had always found it difficult to manage her finances. Delia Parnell had inherited a good deal of property from her father and brother, but much of this had, apparently, been lost in the Black Friday stock market panic of 1873.[30] T. P. O'Connor, who was staying in New York that year, heard that Delia Parnell 'was an incessant gambler on the stock exchange'. He was also much taken aback by her changed appearance. She had gone from being 'very well-dressed' to wearing 'shabby clothes'. She claimed to have 'become almost a pauper'. Despite being awarded a pension in 1880 by the House of Representatives of $1,200 a year (later reduced to $600), Delia Parnell seemed incapable of resisting the lure of the stock market and was chronically unable to manage her money. On 5 March 1884 Charles had purchased the Bordentown estate from her for $20,000.[31] Despite this, there was major publicity when Delia Parnell then aired her financial embarrassments by asserting in July 1885 that Bordentown was to be put up for sale.[32] Ellen Ford was the prime instigator of a move to help her, when 'a number of New York ladies resolved to initiate a movement for a testimonial to Mrs Delia T. S. Parnell, in recognition of her services to the Irish cause and on account of her present financial embarrassments'.[33] There was further negative publicity when in February 1886 the *Washington Post* newspaper reported that the invalid Delia Parnell was living in penury in a tenement. The journalist claimed that Mrs Parnell had told him that she could no longer afford to live at Old Ironsides and that she had bequeathed it to her son Charles.[34] This was untrue, but reports of this made their way to Irish and English newspapers, no doubt creating intense embarrassment to the leader. Perhaps at his insistence, Delia Parnell travelled to Ireland the following September and remained at Avondale for over a year.[35]

But there was no one to meet her when she arrived at the family home. Although she had travelled through Dublin, where she had met the Lord Mayor and spoken to reporters, Delia drove off to

Avondale in a jaunting car accompanied only by Mr. P. O'Brien, MP. A witness of her arrival in Wicklow recalled: 'After the long journey there was no-one to meet her at the station, not even the "Uncrowned King", and as the car left the precincts of the railway, not a solitary cheer was raised. The bystanders, some dozen in number, seemed to gaze upon the lady as if she were a curiosity.'[36] Delia Parnell, with her rambling, erratic speeches, bizarre pronouncements and parlous finances, had indeed probably become something of an oddity. She must have returned to America after her stay at Avondale, as in November 1889 there were further statements in the New York *Herald* and *Standard*, reporting on Mrs Parnell's finances, health and the threatened loss of her home.[37] This news made its way across the Atlantic. Justin McCarthy wrote to his friend Mrs Campbell Praed:

Some of the tory Unionists took up the report and wrote as if Parnell, wallowing in wealth, had deliberately consigned his aged parent to starvation. The *St. James Gazette* was particularly brutal about 'son Charles'... Luckily, Parnell reads hardly any newspapers and so will not see most of the attacks against him and his family.[38]

Charles Parnell did, however, respond to this publicity about his mother. He gave an interview in which he stated he had been 'very much surprised' to learn of his mother's problems, 'and had at once cabled to his agents in New York to supply Mrs Parnell with funds'. The report continued:

He had had no reason to suppose that his mother was pressed for funds, as on previous occasions she had always applied to him and he had always promptly remitted the sum required. Since his last remittance, however, although she had frequently written him, the letters did not complain of any want of funds, or contain any application for money, but, on the contrary, indicated that she was in good spirits and spoke of her intention to realise the crops of the Bordentown estate, which had been stored during the last three or four years for a rise in prices, and which she anticipated would realise six or seven hundred pounds. Mr Parnell thinks that his mother's income and crops may have been attached to await the issue of some legal proceedings, and that the present alleged pressure may have arisen from that circumstance. With regard to the threatened sale by foreclosure of her Bordentown estate, Mr. Parnell does not think there is any risk of such a contingency... He has always found it very difficult to obtain exact information as to the condition of his mother's affairs and health... Mrs Parnell has always declined to reside anywhere but in America, although her son has frequently tried to induce her to live at Avondale, where he would have more chance of taking care of her.[39]

That Delia Parnell needed close supervision was hard to deny. Charles Parnell wrote to Katie during his January 1888 visit to Avondale that his mother was in the clutches of a friend whom Emily described as 'the worst sponge that ever got hold of my mother'. Parnell reported that 'Miss B.B.... drank nothing but whiskey, and took it to bed with her'. The party were up until six in the morning, dancing and performing theatricals in the cattle shed that Parnell had had built at Avondale, modelled on his own plans. This was his mother's idea. Charles was not overly preoccupied by his mother's condition. He was, however, 'very anxious' about his 'own love and so glad to get telegram today'.[40]

Katie's siblings had not given up on the idea of taking action to secure their own inheritances from Maria Wood. Their elderly relative was now taking opium for her pain,[41] and was very forgetful. She relied more and more on her companion. On 7 March 1888, she made yet another will, leaving all of her 'real and personal estate' to her niece, Katharine O'Shea.[42] Evelyn and Charles Wood decided to bring a petition claiming that Aunt Ben had lost her reason.

Katie turned to Gladstone. While the Conservatives were in power, Parnell had been waiting to see what could be achieved once the Liberals returned, and his relations with Gladstone were good. The former Prime Minister considered that a successful negotiation with the Irish leader could form an important plank in his strategy for dealing with Ireland if he returned to power. On 8 March 1888 the two had met for an hour and half. They had discussed a five-point plan for the future governance of Ireland. The Liberal leader recorded that Parnell had 'looked not ill, but far from strong'.[43] The meeting went well. Gladstone recorded approvingly that 'as a whole', Parnell's 'tone was very conservative'.[44]

Certainly, Katie felt confident to approach the Liberal leader on a personal matter. On 13 April, she wrote asking him for his help. She had twice been to see Gladstone's personal physician, Sir Andrew Clarke. At the first appointment she had waited two hours before he sent to say that he could not see her. 'I went again on Friday the 6th April', she wrote, and he had promised to come down to see her aunt the following day. He had done so, and promised to send her a favourable report. Before Sir Andrew had left, Katie wrote, 'he told me "it was a cruel thing" for anyone to say my Aunt was insane he thought her a most charming cultivated woman'. Although the physician had managed to keep out of court all his life, he was prepared to testify, but he begged Katie to prevent his involvement in a court case if possible. She had told him that she 'hoped and believed that the petition in lunacy would be withdrawn when he gave his report'. Katie wrote to Gladstone once more, however, when she did not hear from Sir Andrew. 'I now write to beg you will kindly write or in some way urge Sir Andrew to give his report at once.' Although she deeply regretted troubling Gladstone 'again', she claimed that her 'poor Aunt' was 'suffering so cruelly from suspense that I fear she cannot live much longer if it's continued'.[45] There is no record of Gladstone's intervention in this matter, but by the following week Katie had her report.

Sir Andrew Clarke had made his visit to Eltham on 7 April. In his report, filed on 20 April, he wrote that he had visited Mrs Wood for an hour and a half and conversed with her 'continuously for over half an hour'. He concluded that Mrs Wood was 'attentive capable of apprehension and reflection ready to reply coherent and logical free from illusions delusions and hallucinations full of old stories able to quote largely from the French poets and sometimes seasoning her reminiscences with flashes of quaint humour'. The doctor stated that the 'only defects which I was able to discover in my interview with Mrs Wood were her very imperfect sight and occasional forgetfulness of something previously said but capable of being recalled and a slight tendency to repetition'.[46] Katie wanted to be absolutely certain of success. On 1 May, she wrote asking for Gladstone's further assistance before the hearing on 7 May. 'Sir Charles Russell has been briefed', she wrote, 'and I write to ask if you will kindly mention the matter to him, or if you would prefer it will you kindly give me a letter of introduction to Sir Charles Russell.' Both she and her aunt, she stressed, were 'very anxious to ensure his presence and attention to her case, and I am sure this will be secured if you will kindly interest yourself in her favour'.[47] In the event, the petition was dropped for the time being.

O'Shea had undoubtedly aggravated his relations with Katie by giving evidence over his dealings with the Kilmainham Agreement in the Parnell and *The Times* legal action. Although he did not actually accuse Parnell of being linked to crimes, he had identified the handwriting of one of the letters as probably being the leader's. His testimony had left feelings of rancour on both sides. Chamberlain wrote to the Captain that Morley had told him at Westminster 'that Parnell believed that you had been at the bottom of the letters – forged them I presume. I told him that I was certain you had neither done nor said anything at that time to help the "Times".'[48] If Parnell believed this, however, there is no doubt that he would have shared his suspicion with Katie. It would have made her even more exasperated with her by now estranged spouse.

Piccadilly Office 60. Haymarket S.W.   Vincent Brooks Day & Son Lith.

MRS. PARNELL.

A portrait of Katherine Parnell, from 1891, standing against
a sea wall with ships in the bay in the distance.

The certificate for Katie's second marriage, citing her age, incorrectly, as forty.

Parnell's funeral in October 1891.

Parnell and Katie's youngest daughter, Katie.

nell and Katie's daughter, Clare.

ell's only known grandchild,
's son Assheton Maunsell.

Katie photographed on the south coast of England
in May 1914, shortly before the publication
of her memoir of Charles Stewart Parnell.

The Captain wrote to Chamberlain on 1 November 1888 that he had gone into the witness box the day before 'under a very heavy load of anxiety owing to matters in themselves apart from Charges and Allegations'.[49] Two days later, he wrote once more, stating that as he was going away, he 'had better tell you that the anxiety I felt was occasioned by the fact that Mrs O'Shea is under a written engagement not to communicate directly or indirectly with Mr Parnell and the latter under a written order not to do so with Mrs O'Shea'. The petition filed by Katie's brothers had only just been withdrawn, so the Captain was careful. He continued:

I daresay a great many people have some notion of the state of affairs, but I am most anxious for my children's sake that nothing about it should be actually published because a very large fortune for them may depend upon its not coming into print. I believe Mrs Wood of Eltham is worth £200,000 or more all left to them, and Sir Evelyn Wood and the rest of Mrs O'Shea's relations would use any weapon to change her will. She is 98. Years ago I begged that affairs should be arranged that *in no case* could I myself inherit of this money. It is on this account that I can safely say to you that the anxiety was in no way personal.[50]

O'Shea was spending very little time with his family. He travelled frequently to Spain, returning to England only for short visits. On 27 November 1888, he wrote to Chamberlain that his sole reason for coming to London was to see his son during his examination for the army. He was planning to return to Madrid for Christmas.[51] The breakdown of his marriage was now in the open. On 5 December, Chamberlain wrote to sympathize with O'Shea regarding the 'domestic anxieties which must have added very much to the wear and tear of the last few months. I have felt that I could not say a word to you on the subject until you spoke to me, but I have appreciated the strain to which you have been subjected.'[52]

He was not the only one under strain. Katie described that she had spent time helping Parnell with his lawyers for the

Commission. She went in to see his Counsel, George Henry Lewis. Lewis was a very successful solicitor, senior partner in his firm, and a specialist in libel cases. Labouchere wrote about the case to Herbert Gladstone, stating that 'Parnell is so touchy on the subject that it is impossible to enter upon it with him. The wife seems to have separated from the husband.' He also claimed in this letter:

Parnell insists to Lewis that he never sees Mrs. O'Shea now. Neither Lewis, nor his secretary Campbell have any notion where he lives. I left him a few days ago at about 12 at night. He had on a filthy flannel shirt, a still more filthy white coat with the collar turned up, and a pot hat. In his hand, he carried a shiney [*sic*] leather bag. I could not help thinking as he vanished into space, that he ran the risk of being arrested as the Whitechapel murderer.[53]

Katie provided unintended corroboration of this description of the leader's unkempt appearance. She wrote that Mr Lewis had asked Parnell to call and that at the meeting had told him that both he and his fellow solicitor, Charles Russell, 'were rather worried about his (Parnell's) clothes, and would he very much mind having a new frock-coat from Poole's for the trial!'[54] Katie described her and Parnell's amusement, but the evidence suggests that, without her constant care, the leader was bereft and unable to look after himself.

The difficulties were attenuated the following year when, in March 1889, Pigott's evidence was proved to be false. The response of Parnell's supporters was rapturous. And, when he entered the House of Commons on 1 March, Parnell was greeted by a standing ovation that Hamilton described as 'unprecedented' and 'rather overstepping the bounds of decorum'.[55] The Irish leader had been transformed from villain to hero. Although later testimony he provided was damaging to the image of Irish nationalism, it was a personal vindication for the leader. Public interest in the proceedings of the Commission collapsed. The correspondent of the *Daily Telegraph* reported on 2 March 1889: 'With the exodus of Pigott and the complete exposure of the forgeries, the glory of the Commission has departed. There were places to spare all over the court yesterday, and no ladies, eager and excited, occupied the narrow seats between the jury-box and their lordships.'[56]

Parnell was welcomed with open arms into the heart of the Liberal establishment. Salisbury[57] and the Conservatives, as well as Chamberlain and the Liberal Unionists, seemed defeated. The Irish leader was elected a life member of the National Liberal Club. On 8 March he was received at the Eighty Club, and a few days later at a great meeting in St James's Hall. Katie wrote that at both of these 'the enthusiasm was so great that the whole body of people present rose en masse as he entered, cheering, waving handkerchiefs, and shouting his name for some time before they allowed him to sit down'.[58]

O'Shea was in Madrid at this time. He wrote to Chamberlain on 9 March that, after seeing the newspapers, he supposed it was 'all up for the Times' case'.[59] His friend replied on 14 March that his own opinion had always been that when the newspaper 'failed to prove the letters, the public would lose all interest in the other part of the case, and I believe that that is just the present situation'. Although the effect had been 'to render the Parnellites exultant', he believed 'they are a little premature... My own private opinion is that six months hence it will all be forgotten, and that no permanent impression will have been made either way.'[60] The Captain remained in Madrid throughout March and April.

On 19 May 1889, Aunt Ben finally breathed her last; she was ninety-eight years old. After her death, Katie was free to live with her lover. They had, for 'various reasons', she wrote, had 'to relinquish any idea of living in the little house we had finished, with so much pleasure, at Eastbourne'.[61] Katie then rented a house near Mottingham until she could let out her house at Eltham. But the new house was damp, and Katie wrote of how they 'longed for the sea'.[62] They had previously rented the end house at Walsingham Terrace (No. 10) in Brighton and removed their things there. With her husband keeping a close watch on her, and after her promise to her son, she had not been able to live there with Parnell. Now that she had inherited her aunt's fortune, however, she was free to do as she pleased.

She and the Irish leader moved to Brighton, where she also took the house alongside No. 10. Parnell used the dining room as his own sitting room, she recalled, 'where he kept the roll-top desk I had given him for all his papers and political work, while down in the basement there was a room in which he had a furnace fitted up, and where we used to burn crushed ore before assaying it'.[63] Katie remembered this as a happy time. She and her lover took long walks with the dogs, and drove across the Downs to climb the hills. 'As we walked along hand in hand,' she recalled, 'we were gay in the glorious spring of the year, feeling that while love walked so closely with us youth could not lag too far behind, and in the wide expanse of the South Downs, which appealed so much to both our natures, we forgot all care and trouble.'[64]

Yet trouble was not far away, in the form of her increasingly bitter husband. Mrs Wood had taken care to keep the money away from O'Shea. In August 1889, he was ensconced in the Pump House Hotel at Llandrindod Wells and from there he wrote to Chamberlain, telling him that he would probably be going abroad within the next fortnight.[65] He then informed his friend in October that Katie's family had decided to take legal action contesting her aunt's will. While O'Shea had previously seen his interests to coincide with those of his wife in this matter, he was now estranged from her. He could be tempted by the possibility of getting some of the money for himself.

O'Shea explained the situation to Chamberlain in a letter sent from London on 13 October:

Some months ago Mrs Wood of the Lodge, Eltham, died, aged 98, leaving all her estate, real and personal, to her niece, Mrs O'Shea. The former consists of land in Gloucestershire, the latter of £145,000 in Consols.

While naturally anxious for my children's advantage, I have always endeavoured to have as little as possible to do personally with Mrs Wood's affairs. But Messrs Freshfield & Williams found that under my marriage settlement, and as my children's guardian, I must intervene in the suit of O'Shea v. Wood & another, consequent on my brother-in-law, Mr Charles Page Wood and Sir Evelyn Wood's disputing the will on their own behalf and of their sisters Mrs Chambers, Lady Barrett-Lennard and Mrs Steele. For them the Attorney General and Sir Henry James have been retained, for Mrs O'Shea Sir Charles Russell & Mr Inderwick, and I have told Freshfield & Williams to retain Mr Finlay for me. So there is every element of a *cause celebre* and of very heavy costs.

But as it concerns my character and is a gratifying instance of the appreciation of my conduct, I am chiefly desirous that my friends should know that notwithstanding the antagonism of our interests in the lawsuit, I am not only on terms of intimacy with Mrs O'Shea's family but that I possess their affection, esteem and sympathy in a very marked degree. These feelings constantly find expression, and last week at Belhus park (Sir J B-Lennard's) where almost the whole of Mrs O'Shea's family were assembled, they were very clearly exhibited before many persons belonging to the County and other strangers.[66]

This unwelcome development probably took Katie by surprise. That her family and estranged husband should unite against her – with such a high-profile legal team – was a cause for concern. A scandalous and public separation from her husband could be enough to create sufficient doubt in her good character to allow a challenge to the will. It was in her best interest to keep Willie on her side. The difficulty in so doing was now twofold. First, the affair was becoming public knowledge. This meant that the Captain had already lost face and was no longer threatened by the humiliation of disclosure. The second problem was that if her inheritance was at risk, O'Shea could decide that his chances were better with her siblings. If they promised him a personal settlement – which in all likelihood they did – he would be available to the highest bidder.

Chamberlain responded to O'Shea's letter sympathetically. 'I am sincerely sorry that you should have had such just cause for anxiety and trouble,' he penned, adding:

I fear that these things can not be hushed up in the days of 'P.M. Gazette' & 'Stars' & I am not sure that the boldest course is not always the wisest. However I have no right to express an opinion & it would not be worth anything unless founded on more information than I possess. I am glad that you have the sympathy & support of members of your wife's family. In the event of any publicity that is a strong point in your favour.[67]

O'Shea wrote to Chamberlain on 30 November 1889 that he had filed a petition. The previous week he had gone to Brighton with his son Gerard, he explained. Gerard had called 'unexpectedly' at one of the houses his mother had there 'and found a lot of Mr Parnell's things, some of which he has chucked out of the window. There was a dreadful scene and on our return to London we went to the lawyers and settled that an action should be immediately instituted.' O'Shea added that he had consulted his bishop, Cardinal Manning, on the matter, 'in order to get a dispensation from my church to commence an action'. He was sorry to say, however, that his lawyers had advised him that the Cardinal 'was trying to gain time and screen Parnell'.[68]

Chamberlain replied on 10 January 1890. His letter made clear that O'Shea could really have followed no other course at this point:

You know I have never presumed to refer to your private affairs in regard to which every man must judge for himself, but now that you have taken the decisive step I may be allowed to say that it seems to me to have been forced upon you, & that any further hesitation would have given rise to an accusation of complacency under an injury which no honourable man can patiently endure.[69]

The timing was dreadful. Parnell's relationship with Gladstone had so improved that he was invited to Hawarden in August. The Hawarden estate in Flintshire, North Wales, was Gladstone's rural retreat and family estate. To be invited to stay there was a tremendous privilege, and a mark of Gladstone's confidence in the Irish leader. Hawarden became the Liberal leader's 'hinterland', a retreat that had remained his wife's primary home throughout his political career. For William Gladstone himself, the estate was by and large the main centre of his life after 1850.[70] He famously felled trees there; in the 1870s, Gladstone's biographer Roy Jenkins points out, it became 'an almost obsessive form of recreation'.[71]

Nevertheless, Parnell did not go to stay with the Gladstones that summer, although he was invited again in October. The Liberal leader wished to discuss changes in the Home Rule plan of 1886, the land question, and their respective positions under the Commission.[72] In fact, the Irish leader did not actually stay there until the night of 18 December 1889. He and Gladstone spoke over the two days, and the Liberal leader sent an account of the successful visit to his colleagues: 'After very long delay, of which I do not know the cause, Mr Parnell's promised visit came off last week. He appeared well and cheerful and proposed to accompany (without a gun) my younger sons who went out shooting. Nothing could be more satisfactory than his conversation; full as I thought of good sense from beginning to end.'[73]

Gladstone's comment in his diary was equally positive. They had had 'two hours of satisfactory conversation', he recorded on 18 December, 'but he put off the *gros* of it'. The following day he had spent two hours more with the Irish leader. 'He is certainly one of the very best people to deal with that I have ever known,' was Gladstone's verdict.[74] The visit had gone extremely well. Parnell and Gladstone had had a solid four hours of bilateral discussion. Equally important, no doubt, was the favourable social impression the Irishman had made. At this grand stately home – in the autumn of 1878 guests had included the Dukes of Bedford and Argyll, the Duchess of Westminster and the Marquisal Baths[75] – Parnell had lived among his hosts, taking meals with them, and had clearly shone. Gladstone wrote that his guest 'seems to notice and appreciate everything'.[76]

But although Parnell had made a good impression on the Liberal leader, his own party were somewhat less convinced of his powers. His famed elusiveness reached new heights in 1889, when he regularly disappeared. Edward Byrne, of the *Freeman's Journal*, was in London in November 1889 and unable to find either Parnell or his Secretary, Campbell. Campbell did not reply to any of his notes, and Byrne recalled, 'As for the Chief, so far as I can make out he holds communication with nobody. He won't see or write to anybody.'[77] There was continuing speculation about the leader's health. This Parnell sought to put at rest by delivering a set of vigorous speeches at Nottingham and Liverpool. The leader's absences were unpredictable, and his whereabouts usually unknown. Despite this, he was, behind the scenes, seeking to re-establish better control over the party members, whose absences from Westminster had become alarming. Dillon and O'Brien had the excuse of being in and out of prison, and others had to make a long journey from Ireland to attend parliamentary sessions. But Parnell stressed the importance of attendance. He summoned meetings of the party in June 1888 and in August 1888, to discuss the matter. He wrote at the beginning of each session of the importance of assuring a strong Irish presence in the House. On 30 January 1890, the leader wrote to the *Freeman's Journal*, stressing the need for Irish members to devote 'constant and unremitting attention to their parliamentary duties'.[78] The leader needed to deliver Irish votes *en bloc* if he wished to maintain his bargaining power. He was also maintaining a reserve regarding the Plan of Campaign, which frustrated O'Brien and Dillon. The party was in danger of splintering, especially as the leader had turned against Healy. Dillon and O'Brien decided to break bail[79] and leave for France on their way to America to raise funds to support distressed tenants.

Parnell was thus at a critical juncture in his strategic plan to achieve some form of Home Rule for Ireland. His elusiveness added to his political mystique, as he sought to exercise control over the Irish Party. The news that O'Shea had filed for divorce, naming Parnell as co-respondent, was first disclosed in the Tory paper, *Evening News and Post*, on 28 December 1889. One of the paper's journalists called on Captain O'Shea. He was, according to the report, shown up to O'Shea's rooms. 'Breakfast was on the table', read the article, 'and Captain O'Shea's son was present.' In view of the 'confidential nature' of the enquiry, the reporter had asked to see the Captain privately, but he had insisted that the conversation could take place in his son's presence. When the journalist protested, O'Shea acquiesced, and confirmed the veracity of their report of the petition for divorce. The Captain then answered that their story was correct, and confirmed that he did not seek damages. He added, 'I am much obliged to your editor for having the courtesy to ask me before publishing the fact.'[80]

Just days later, on 3 January 1890, *The Times* took up the story, writing that a news agency had stated that 'Mr. Parnell was yesterday afternoon served at Messrs. Lewis and Lewis's offices with the citation and petition in the action for divorce brought by Captain O'Shea against Mrs. O'Shea and Mr. Parnell as co-respondent.'[81] Parnell responded straight away and gave an interview to the *Freeman's Journal*. He stated that he had been threatened with such proceedings by O'Shea in the past. He also asserted that the Captain had always been aware of his constant presence at Eltham in O'Shea's absence from 1880 to 1886. Parnell claimed that, since 1886, O'Shea had known that he resided there constantly.[82] This was the only time that the leader referred so specifically to the accusations.

Katie did not record her response to the petition, but O'Shea wrote to Chamberlain on 19 March that she and Parnell were 'obstructing to the best of their artifices'. His wife had 'feigned illness for 10 days, so as to evade service of an amended citation'. Her 'answers', he grumbled, would 'not be filed till the end of the month'. He was told that 'Mr Parnell expects to be able to postpone the trial until after the long vacation, say December next'. There had been 'over 200 declarations' taken for him, wrote the Captain, 'and the case against Parnell is overwhelming, not only in itself but owing to the treachery of the circumstances'.[83] A month later, on 17 April, O'Shea wrote to his friend that his spouse had not yet filed her response to the petition, and Mr Parnell had filed a 'simple denial just before the Easter vacation'.[84] Finally, on 2 August, O'Shea wrote to say that 'Having exhausted all the forms of obstruction, Mrs O'Shea has at last filed the particulars of her defence, and countercharges.'[85] Katie had made the surprising decision to accuse her husband of adultery with unnamed parties who included, most shockingly, her sister Anna. This was a surprising development, and was probably evidence of how angry Katie was with her sister for taking action against her in the probate case. It was clear that her own sister was taking the Captain's side. Many years before, Anna had mediated between Katie and her husband. Now she seemed to be supporting him at the expense of her sister. But Katie's ill-considered accusation was miscalculated. It meant that the divorce proceedings would be contested, and evidence provided to be heard in court. Instead of a quiet, discreet process, the accusations would require a response. Witnesses would be interviewed, and their testimony pored over. The scandal would be all over the papers.

Katie would have known that her husband's accusations could be proved. The petition specifically stated that adultery had been committed from April 1886 to the present date at Eltham, 34 York Terrace, Regent's Park, at Brighton, and at Aldington, Sussex. The most plausible explanation for her decision was that she hoped to frighten O'Shea into abandoning his action. The Captain wrote indignantly to Chamberlain expressing his dismay at Katie's accusations:

The latter are absolutely unfounded, the principal accusation being that in 1881 I committed adultery with one of her sisters! During the intervening nine years she has never hinted such a suspicion either to myself or to any member of the family. You can imagine the indignation of her brothers and sisters. Low as she had sunk with him before, I confess I was astounded when I heard of the depths to which Parnell has now dragged her. I am being subjected to every kind of injury and persecution; slander, gross extortion, attempts to corrupt witnesses of mine, unremitting shadowings.

My solicitors withal, are constantly plied with suggestions of compromise, 'no difficulty as to terms'! Another solicitor, whose practice is one of the largest in London, told me on Friday that a friend of his in the profession said to him a few days ago that he would make every effort in this direction, 'so as to avert a national calamity'.[86]

Chamberlain agreed that there was more at stake than his friend's marital problems. He wrote to O'Shea on 5 August 1890 that he did 'not wonder at the efforts which are made to bring about a settlement when so many interests are at stake'. He believed, however, that when these efforts 'finally failed', the 'co-respondent will not defend the case'.[87] And, indeed, Parnell's first response was to attack. He deliberately sought to link O'Shea's petition to the unsuccessful attempt by *The Times* to incriminate him. The idea he sought to disseminate was that he was once again falsely accused (although of course there is a glaring contradiction between this assertion and his admission that O'Shea had known about Parnell's living arrangements). At this time, the leader was still venerated and admired in Ireland and in England. O'Connor recalled how Parnell had been received at the Eighty Club, where he had famously made his peace with Lord Spencer. 'It was the shaking of hands between two nations, the burying of the historic animosities of England, the last consecrating touch to those life-long efforts, sometimes only partial in their effect, but always sincere in their intention, by which Mr. Gladstone had sought to pacify Ireland and consolidate the Empire.' Everywhere Parnell went, he was greeted by rapturous applause and cheers. O'Connor wrote that 'public bodies tumbled over each other in the desire to do him honour'.[88]

So there was initial reluctance to publicly disparage the Irish hero. There were, of course, those in the know who were well aware of the liaison. Hamilton recalled that Gladstone was concerned about the problem in March 1890. 'Mr. G is afraid that, from his not having asserted himself much lately, Parnell feels that matters may go so disagreeably for him in the impending divorce case that he may have to withdraw from public life and he had better commence to prepare for this.'[89] Editors such as Stead were convinced that Parnell was guilty of adultery. Colleagues such as Healy had long suspected the truth, and his friend and confidant, Harold Frederic, claimed in the *New York Times* as early as October 1888 that O'Shea was 'the despicable creature for whom Mr. Parnell in his ruinous infatuation created that ruinous split in the Irish Party at Galway three years ago'.[90] The journalist Alfred Robbins recalled being asked 'whether Parnell would be politically ruined by a divorce, the then recent Dilke instance being given as a promising precedent'. He replied that he did not believe so. Furthermore, 'the scandal was not new. It had not merely been talked of in private but alluded to in print for at least seven years; had been on every political lip during the Galway election episode of the spring of 1886; had been clearly hinted at in *The Times* the following year; and had been revived by the appearance of O'Shea before the Special Commission as a witness, not only politically but personally hostile to Parnell.'[91]

The nuances and worldly sophistication of some of the British elite were not, however, replicated in Catholic Ireland. Healy recorded that, in Ireland, O'Shea's accusations were regarded 'as a fresh persecution by *The Times*. Anyone who turns to the *Freeman* of that period will find resolutions from hundreds of branches of the National League expressing scorn at, and disbelief in them.' But Healy claimed that when he had subsequently asked Edward Ennis, then a member of staff,[92] why the paper encouraged 'a campaign of incredulity when everyone knew of the scandal', he had 'gloomily' replied: '"Oh, we have to keep up the pretence".'[93] There were those, such as Healy and the staff of the *Freeman*, who needed to support the leader in order to avoid a split in the party. There were also many in Ireland who wanted to believe in the Chief. He did nothing to dissuade this. With his famed imperturbable disdain, the leader allowed certain of his lieutenants to believe that nothing was amiss.

Davitt later wrote of how Parnell's colleagues 'shrank from approaching' on the matter, and that this 'extraordinary temper reflected the prevalent state of feeling in the ranks of his chief followers'. This had, he recorded, been due to the leader's 'growing reserve and absence from the party in recent years, and by the unwisely excessive adulation of his personality, which held him up as a man of a superior mould to the men whom he led'.[94] But there was more to it than that. Davitt recalled that at the last interview they were ever to have, the leader had assured him 'there was no peril of any kind to him or to the movement in Captain O'Shea's "threatened proceedings". He bade me to say to friends who might be anxious on the matter that he would emerge from the whole trouble without a stain on his name or reputation.'[95] Although Davitt acknowledged that those words were later denied by the leader, he insisted that they were spoken to him. He concluded that the Chief expected that O'Shea would withdraw his suit.

O'Brien was also reassured by the leader. On 14 January 1890, Parnell sent him the following: 'If this case is ever fully gone into, *a matter which is exceedingly doubtful,* you may rest assured that it will be shown that the dishonour and discredit have not been upon my side.'[96] Katie made no mention of the months leading up to the divorce. She and her lover were almost certainly convinced that O'Shea would not go through with it. And even men such as Justin McCarthy – who was very worried about the upcoming case – began to wonder whether it might be resolved. Perhaps the leader was innocent, after all:

It is beginning to be believed I don't know how or why that he will be able to come out of the whole affair triumphantly. I hope so with all my heart and soul. I had not thought that could be so. But he is a strange man quite capable of imposing on himself a powerful restraining law and not allowing a temptation to draw him too far.[97]

Katie's only chance was to convince the Captain to withdraw his suit, or to agree to a quiet uncontested divorce at a later stage. Of critical importance to a positive outcome of either of these possibilities was Katie's inheritance. O'Shea realized, however, that the money would not be his and that his chances might be improved by joining the Wood family side in their legal battle. If Willie O'Shea wanted a divorce, he could get one. Now that their relationship had broken down, 'Boysie' would have no compunction in hurting his wife and her lover, a man he thoroughly detested.

CHAPTER EIGHTEEN

Scandal and Re-marriage

𝒯HE MAJORITY OF THE Irish Party and indeed most of Ireland – including the Catholic clergy – were prepared to take their cue from the leader and wait. This wait was not for the findings of the divorce court, but rather for the grant of Home Rule. Gladstone and the Liberals were expected to return to power at the next general election, and the legislation which was to grant some degree of constitutional freedom to Ireland was eagerly anticipated. After years of struggle, the Irish Party was prepared for some form of independent government in Ireland. Gladstone and his party were committed to the process. The man believed responsible for this success was Charles Parnell.

But there were changing undercurrents in the Irish Nationalist movement that were not immediately obvious to Parnell. In February 1890, he was re-elected as sessional Chairman of the Irish Party. Joseph Biggar moved the re-election, and made 'a very feeling and sympathetic speech'. A week later, however, Biggar died. Justin McCarthy recorded after the funeral in Clapham: 'The service was solemn, intensely gloomy and I sat through it with darkening mind.'[1] The death of this large, engaging figure – whom the *United Ireland* had called the father of the Irish Party – was distressing for Tim Healy, and for those other party members who looked on him as a mentor. Biggar's robust common sense and stabilizing influence would be sorely missed. There were also some underlying problems between various members of the Irish Party that became apparent through 1889 and 1890. The relations between Parnell and the ambitious Tim Healy, for example, became more strained in the late 1880s. Some of the Nationalist radicals also felt increasingly estranged from the leader's pro-Liberal accommodating stance. Parnell's unpredictable attendances at Westminster – and absence from Ireland – did not help. And a further development of nationalist movement was the establishment in May 1888 of the *Irish Catholic* newspaper. This was the first time that Catholic nationalism had its own voice, and the late 1880s was marked by the emergence of a distinctly Catholic form of Irish nationalism.[2] This would have important repercussions for the Protestant leader.

Throughout 1890, Charles Parnell lived with Katie in Brighton. He maintained a low-key presence at Westminster, and spent little time in Ireland. In July 1889, he had admitted at Edinburgh that he had not spoken in Ireland 'for years and years'.[3] He was absent for the debates in Parliament at the end of the 1890 session when the Irish estimates – or budget – were debated. Parnell's continuation of his remote political and personal stance showed that he clearly discounted any threat of a leadership challenge from Healy. He was also seemingly dismissive of the gathering strength of Catholic proprietorial nationalism. The leader was biding his time, waiting for the legislation of Home Rule and preparing to maintain supremacy in its aftermath. He did not support radical land reform, which explained his reserved stance towards the Plan of Campaign.

His habitual hauteur had always extended to his personal life. Just five days before the divorce trial was to begin, Parnell met with long-time supporter John Morley in a Brighton hotel. After considerable discussion, Morley ventured to enquire whether 'certain legal proceedings' might lead to his disappearance from the leadership. Parnell had replied, 'Oh no. No chance of it. Nothing in the least leading to disappearance... The other side don't know what a broken-kneed horse they are riding.'[4] The leader was convinced that O'Shea was operating with his political opponents, and that the threatened proceedings would never come off.

This confidence convinced those of his supporters who needed to believe in him. He may even have succeeded in convincing Katie that all would be well. Parnell might indeed have convinced himself that he had broken no moral code. But for anyone beside Parnell, this was adultery, pure and simple. His simplistic view may have precluded an understanding of the complexity of Katie's situation. There remain considerable doubts as to the exact nature of her relations with O'Shea, particularly before 1886, and 'Boysie' and 'Dick' were perhaps not as alienated as Parnell wanted to believe. It is also entirely possible that Katie was less than generous with the truth over her relationship with Willie. She admitted as much to Harrison, telling him that Parnell 'considered himself a husband, and was sternly jealous in asserting the rights of his position in such ambiguities as were apt to arise in the occasional presence of Captain O'Shea and the necessity for keeping up appearances before the world'.[5]

It was a worrying situation. Katie knew her husband well, and they were no longer on speaking terms. Her usual tactics of soothing him and bringing him round were no longer possible. Her family had joined forces to attack her through the courts. The inheritance was at risk. The assets were frozen and she therefore did not have the means to pay Willie off. And by all accounts, her lover was imperturbable and, it would seem, almost unwilling to stare reality in the face. He was, however, according to Katie, determined she should get a divorce once she had been publicly named. It was his wish that they be married, and therefore he was probably hoping that Willie could be induced to allow Katie to quietly divorce him. 'He hated all the concealments and pretence of concealments,' Katie later told Harrison, 'although he was very good about it for my sake because of the difficulties I was in. He was always unhappy about the irregularity of my position and most anxious, if it could not be made right at once, at least to protect me and to make things easy for me in every way.'[6]

Katie also told Harrison that there would have been no divorce case as such except that her aunt had died and left everything to her 'in such a way that it was beyond Captain O'Shea's reach – so that it would be outside the effect of my marriage settlement'.[7] She had hoped that she could manage her husband. 'I was sure that I should be able to deal with it,' she recalled. 'With all that money coming to me I was certain that, if I was willing to make sacrifices, I could arrange everything.'[8] But she had failed. For many months she had had discussions with O'Shea, with her sister Anna as the intermediary, 'and there were quarrels and breakings-off and resumptions. And, in the end – up to the very last moment – if I could have got £20,000 to give Captain O'Shea, his charges against me would have failed and my countercharges against him would have succeeded.'[9]

O'Shea's communications to Chamberlain throughout the year confirm the confused state of affairs. He wrote on 15 August 1890 that he could not understand why Katie's solicitors (Greenfields) had retired from the case.[10] On 7 September, he wrote that although it had been several weeks 'since Messrs Greenfield threw up her case, she has not yet notified the appointment of fresh solicitors'.[11] And indeed, confirming Katie's later confidences to Harrison, O'Shea claimed that attempts had been made to bribe him, although he said that the amount was much higher:

Nobody except myself knows what a fight it was, or the influences religious, social and pecuniary that were brought to bear in the hope of 'squaring' me. The last offer was made to me through my son the evening before the trial, and was equivalent to over £60,000. Everything was done, of course, in the most careful way and for my children's sake I am bound to be dumb until after the probate suit.[12]

It is quite apparent from the facts that Katie and her lover did not have a well-thought-out strategy for handling the divorce. The most feasible explanation for this is that Katharine believed that her husband would agree to a deal, and the divorce would take place in discreet circumstances. Nothing could be further from what actually transpired. The preparation for the trial seemed a shambles. Harrison recounted that Katie threw over her solicitor, Sir George Lewis. Lewis had just emerged triumphant, defending Parnell in *The Times* trial, so this seems a surprising decision. Harrison commented that he never learned the reason for the falling out. He did comment, however, that Katie was 'of the "masterful" type of charming lady whose relationships with their expert advisers of all sorts are so often marked by conflict rather than co-operation until sheer incompatibility sunders them'.[13] Lewis later had apparently commented to a colleague that Mrs O'Shea 'is a very charming lady but an impossible one!'[14] Reginald Brett wrote that on 23 January 1890 Stead had called and was 'very low – from an interview with George Lewis. Mrs. O'Shea *wishes* to be divorced and to marry Mr. Parnell. Mr. Parnell, whether he wishes it or not, agreed.'[15]

The writer and poet Wilfrid Scawen Blunt (who had been a supporter of Irish Nationalist aspirations) reinforced this view some years later. He recounted that he had seen the Irish Nationalist politician Thomas Patrick Gill, who had spent much time with Parnell during the period of the divorce. Blunt wrote that Gill had told him

that Parnell had a complete case in defence against O'Shea, O'Shea having connived throughout and profited in a money way… He showed his whole defence to Gill before the trial. But Mrs. O'Shea would not allow him to defend himself, as she wanted a divorce so as to marry him. She was a woman quite unworthy of him, who had had other affairs before that with Parnell, and who neither sympathized with his politics, nor at all appreciated the height of his position.[16]

Who wanted the divorce is not clear, but what is obvious is that the pair were poorly prepared to defend the action. Parnell simply denied the accusations. Katie sought to counter-attack. She submitted her own allegations against the Captain on 3 June and 25 July – which is when she added an almost certainly false assertion that her husband had committed adultery with her sister Anna[17] – and again on 4 November 1890. Such an accusation was shocking. It is possible that Katie made this accusation in anger at her sister's participation in the Wood family's action against her. The fact that she and Anna were on seemingly cordial terms after the divorce would indicate that the assertion was untrue. Harrison recorded that Katie had seemed uncomfortable when he asked her about it – 'the accusation itself had been a blunder', he commented, and the 'topic was unwelcome'. He concluded that 'a clash during the negotiations had generated an unwonted heat – an ill-judged step. Certain it is that Mrs. Steele herself, in the very scanty evidence which she gave in the divorce trial, attributed the charge against herself to a falling out over some difference about the Probate action over Mrs. Wood's will.'[18]

There were rumours abounding over the case. The Liberals were reassured by Morley's conviction that Parnell would emerge unscathed as leader. The Irish Nationalists were driven by their need to believe in Parnell and remained confident. As the trial drew near, there was a report that the leader consulted a well-known divorce barrister, Inderwick, to get his opinion on whether he and Katharine O'Shea could retain custody of the two younger children and reside in a European country.[19] The picture that emerges from all the accounts is one of confusion. It seems likely that Parnell was not a great help in managing the process. Katie took the lead in the negotiations, no doubt because she was the only suitable interface with Willie, however much their relations fluctuated. It would appear also that she took the lead because she had to.

Katie recounted that at the last moment Parnell had insisted that they not appear in court. When they realized that O'Shea was proceeding with the action, their options were limited. Katie insisted consistently that Parnell wanted to marry her. There is no evidence to contradict this. If, however, they defended themselves, it would be proof of her husband's knowledge of the affair, or connivance. By law, if connivance were ascertained, the divorce would not be granted.[20] So Katie and the leader were in a bind. For Parnell to defend his honour, he needed to establish that he had not betrayed a colleague. Should he do so, however, then he and Katie would never be able to marry. What he tried to do, therefore, was to cultivate an air of mystery over the whole process, presumably in the hope that this tried and true tactic would somehow create enough uncertainty to allow it to blow over. This would explain his cryptic reassurances to his colleagues and the Liberals.

But what he failed to take into account was the extent of O'Shea's vindictiveness, and the folly of Katie's action in making the counter-charges. On 15 November, the Solicitor-General, Sir Edward Clarke, acting for O'Shea, stated that because he had just learned that the defendants were not to appear in court, 'the case now stood practically as an undefended one'. He went on to argue that, in these circumstances, 'although he was bound to prove by evidence such a case as would be sufficient for his Lordship and the jury to found a judgement upon, yet it would no longer be necessary for him to make the comments and to enter into the same amount of details which would have been required had the case been seriously contested on the part of the respondent and the co-respondent'. However, he went on, unlike Mr Parnell, Mrs O'Shea

did not content herself with that simple denial, but had made counter charges against her husband of adultery with different persons, including Mrs Steele, her own sister, and of cruelty, and had also put a statement upon the record which, whilst almost confessing that she had been guilty of adultery, imputed to him, that he had for a series of years connived at that adultery. It was remarkable that these charges had been repeatedly made. On June 3 Mrs O'Shea had filed particulars, and had repeated them on July 25 and on November 4.[21]

In the particulars filed on 4 November, Clarke stated, Mrs O'Shea had claimed:

The petitioner constantly connived at and was accessory to the said alleged adultery from the autumn of 1880 to the spring of 1886, by inducing, directing, and requiring the respondent to form the acquaintance of the co-respondent and to see him alone in the interest and for the advantage of the petitioner, by directing the respondent to invite the co-respondent to her house in the absence of the petitioner in his interest and for his advantage, both before and after he had accused her of adultery with the co-respondent, by his knowledge that the co-respondent was constantly at the house of the respondent in the petitioner's absence, and by leaving the co-respondent alone at Wonersh-lodge with the respondent on most of those occasions when the petitioner left to go to London or elsewhere.[22]

The Solicitor-General went on to explain that this was a 'very grave and serious statement for a wife to make', and that the 'mere abandonment at the last moment of such charges could not be any satisfaction to the husband who, having been originally gravely injured, had been subsequently grossly insulted by such pleadings being put on the record'. Clarke stated that he, 'as counsel to the petitioner, was in a position to absolutely and completely destroy any possible suggestion of that kind'.[23] The decision taken by Parnell and Katie not to appear in court meant that O'Shea's lawyers had a free hand to produce their witnesses and evidence which would not be cross-examined. Katie declared in her very scanty account of the divorce action that she and her lover had argued over this. 'Parnell would not fight the case', she wrote, 'and I could not fight it without him.' She claimed that the last time she had seen their Counsel, the eminent Sir Frank Lockwood – the day before the case began – he had 'begged' her to get Parnell to let him fight.

She agreed to do so, but recorded that she was suffering terribly from neuralgic headache. There can be no doubt that she was severely overwrought. Katie wrote revealingly of their journey back to Brighton in the train. Although Parnell 'had the power of putting himself absolutely beyond and above self-consciousness', she was only too aware of the 'gleam of so many eyes' watching them. She felt they were 'like animals watching from their lair'.[24]

She took to her bed, she recalled, and Parnell had nursed her tenderly. She tried once more to persuade him to fight the case, but he refused, telling her that they wanted the divorce. Katie wrote that she had broken down, and cried, saying that it was for him and his work. The leader told her that his life's work was 'Ireland's always, but that his heart and soul were mine to keep for ever – since first he looked into my eyes that summer morning, ten years before'. He declared that he had 'given, and will give, Ireland what is in me to give. That I have vowed to her, but my private life shall never belong to any country, but to one woman.'[25] When Katie awoke the next morning, she found her lover sitting by her bedside 'superintending the arrangement of "letters, tea and toast"'. In reply to her 'anxious query as to the time', Parnell had laughed quietly and told her, 'I've done you this time, Queenie; I sent the telegram long ago, and they must be enjoying themselves in Court by now!'[26]

What was happening in court would lead to a disaster for the leader. Uncontradicted by any cross-examination, O'Shea's witnesses told the whole sorry tale. The Captain was portrayed as an unsuspecting husband badly deceived by his wife and his colleague.[27] Parnell was pictured as a lying schemer who resorted to disguises and false identities to conduct his illicit affair. Most damning of all was the testimony by the cook, Caroline Pethers. She claimed that on one occasion her mistress had been in a locked room with Mr Parnell when Captain O'Shea 'rang the front door bell'.[28] O'Shea had gone into the dining room, and then upstairs. Ten minutes later, Mr Parnell was at the door, asking to see Captain O'Shea. 'Could he have gone down by the stairs?' asked the Counsel, 'No,' was the reply. 'There was a balcony outside the drawing room. There were two rope fire-escapes from the window. This happened three or four times. On these occasions Mr Parnell was in the sitting room, and he did not come down the staircase.'[29]

These sordid and unbecoming revelations were widely reported and shocked Parnell's supporters. The leader had been regarded as an honourable man. Indeed, he and Katie, ironically, had spent years building that impression. Even British ministers regarded him as a man of his word. The lurid revelations, which were catastrophically left unchallenged, caused great consternation. The hero of public life was found to be a liar and portrayed in the divorce court as a cad. The image of the leader scrambling down a fire escape was made much of. Parnell was jeered and ridiculed in the press and by his enemies. The risks he had taken, risks taken by a man previously renowned for his cautious politics, were viewed as evidence of a foolhardy infatuation, for which Katharine O'Shea was responsible.

There had been some doubt expressed by the jury over the Captain's part in the matter. He was questioned about his relationship with Katie, and his presence at the family home. But the jury were unanimous in their verdict to the effect that the respondent had committed adultery with the co-respondent, 'and that the petitioner had not connived at the adultery'.[30] An opinion in *Truth* commented on 20 November that, although the jury had acquitted O'Shea of connivance, he could not be acquitted of 'folly'. The Captain, the article claimed:

was perpetually writing to his wife, protesting against her allowing Mr. Parnell to visit her, and telling her that scandal had so coupled her name with his that even visits ought to be eschewed… Surely a man of Captain O'Shea's knowledge of the world might have taken means to verify these rumours more closely than by (for he is no recluse) asking his wife if they were true, when they were brought to his notice, and complacently accepting her denial.[31]

But the overall impression was that the pair had sinned and been found out. The publicity ensuing from the trial was received by a public which was scandalized by Katie's behaviour. Stead's recent, well-publicized newspaper campaigns against child prostitution had fuelled public scorn and horror for prostitution specifically, and for deviant sexual behaviour generally. The sensationalized accounts of Jack the Ripper in 1888 also contributed to a climate of disapproval of female sexuality. Much of the newspaper coverage of the killings had 'blamed "women of evil life" for bringing the murders on themselves'.[32] The movements of the 1870s and latter part of the nineteenth century to address 'social purity' attacked the double standard that allowed men to exploit women. The Social Purity crusades from the 1880s onwards were, however, mostly aimed at saving youth from sexual corruption. The crusaders (who included all the Christian denominations) demanded that public figures and political leaders should set a good example. Whilst the Prince of Wales was held to be immune from attack, others, such as Dilke, were loudly castigated.

Although many campaigners were battling to help women, the movement was for the most part focused on getting *men* to control their urges and to stop abusing women, or using prostitutes. The image of women was therefore still simplistic. There were the fallen women who needed to be helped, respected and protected. On the opposite side of the spectrum was the angel in the house. Even those Victorian feminists who fought hard to change the marital laws governing women's rights and property were more focused on enabling women to extricate themselves from bad marriages and abusive husbands, while in their arguments for giving women more rights there was an undercurrent of victimization.[33] Indeed, most advocates of women's rights were in alignment with the movements for 'social purity'. They wanted women to be free to occupy more of the public sphere, to feel safe on the streets and to be protected from lewd and exploitative male behaviour.[34]

But women who transgressed the social code by being neither victim nor saint were viewed with great hostility.[35] Women's sexuality was barely presumed to exist.[36] In society's eyes, Katie had conducted an adulterous relationship within the marital home – a huge sexual and social transgression.

This transgression was enshrined in law. A woman who committed adultery had injured her husband and, furthermore, an adulterous woman was deemed unfit to raise her children. Under Common Law, any mother found guilty of adultery was denied custody and even access to her children. On 18 November 1890, Mr Justice Butt ordered that Captain O'Shea should have custody of the children aged under sixteen. Lockwood asked the judge 'to reserve the question of the custody of the younger children'. He wished to bring 'certain matters to the knowledge of your Lordship'. Justice Butt replied that 'unless there is some reason to the contrary the custody of the children is always given to the innocent party'. The Solicitor-General stated that he believed he was 'entitled on behalf of Captain O'Shea to make a claim for the usual order'.[37]

The likelihood of this ruling would explain why there was some evidence that Parnell had become agitated before the trial. There are contemporary accounts that suggest that the leader had a severe falling out with Katie's Counsel (he himself was unrepresented). She made no reference to this in her book. But Lockwood told his colleague Alfred Pearse[38] that he had been infuriated by Parnell's late decision not to give evidence. Lockwood said that 'they' had wanted him 'to cross-examine O'Shea', but that he had 'declined to go on a foraging exhibition and to throw dirt unless they would go into the box to prove an issue'.[39] Parnell's strategy of maintaining a disdainful distance from the proceedings, while attacking O'Shea through Lockwood, was thus summarily rejected. The now Liberal Unionist (and previously Liberal Attorney-General) Sir Henry James (later Lord) recorded a discussion with Lockwood on 19 November. He had, according to James, asked his advice some days before the trial, and was open about what had transpired during the trial.

Lockwood confided to James that, after the first day at court, Parnell had called on him. 'He was very wild', wrote James, 'and attacked Lockwood, reproaching him with not having made an agreement with the Solicitor-General as to the children, saying "You could have done so, but you betrayed us".' Lockwood recounted that he had jumped up and said that 'no one should speak so to him'. The leader had then replied that Lockwood was 'bigger and stronger' than him, and accused Lockwood of thinking of throwing him out the window. Lockwood answered that indeed he was, and Parnell 'quietened down'. James recorded that Lockwood regarded the Irish leader 'as so wild and peculiar in his manner as to show signs of madness'.[40] And indeed there was a frantic quality to the leader's actions at this time. Katie recalled that he had continued to seem oblivious to the unfolding scandal. She wrote that the arrival of the decree nisi was celebrated, and Parnell 'declared he would have the "decree" framed'.[41] One positive aspect of the conduct of the trial was that – all going well[42] – within six months Katie would have a decree absolute and be free to marry her lover.

The verdict was not received with such pleasure by Parnell's colleagues, many of whom were horrified. The first instinct was, nevertheless, to stand by the leader. On the day after the divorce was pronounced, the Dublin branch of the National League passed a resolution that upheld Parnell's leadership. Parnell himself had been confident that he could ride out the crisis. Labouchere recalled the leader's claim to him that his 'people never will believe all this'.[43] In this he was partially correct. There was widespread reluctance to condemn the leader, who had done so much to try to bring Home Rule to Ireland. The initial response was one of shock and an instinctive closing of ranks. The *Freeman's Journal* continued to support the leader. The two established papers that did eventually turn on Parnell and call for his resignation did not do so straight away.[44] Lieutenants such as Tim Healy (who was ill with typhoid) made huge efforts to demonstrate their support. In a dramatic speech made on 20 November, Healy declared that Parnell had led the transformation of the Nationalist cause, and asked, 'is it now in this moment within sight of the promised land that we are to be asked to throw our entire organisation back once more into the melting pot?' He added that their 'English friends' should remember 'that for Ireland and for Irishmen Mr. Parnell is less a man than an institution'.[45] This deliberate attempt to set loyal Irishmen against English interference was at first successful.

Some days later, on 25 November, Parnell asserted his right to remain party leader when he was re-elected Chairman at Westminster on the eve of the new parliamentary session. It looked as though the leader had managed to overcome the scandal. He alluded to the divorce when he assured his colleagues that 'in a short period of time, when I am free to do so, I will be able to put a complexion on this case very different to that which it now bears, and I will be able to hold my head as high, aye, and higher, than ever before, in the face of the world'. The leader denied that he had ever deceived O'Shea, and claimed that the Captain had never been his friend.[46]

The leadership crisis had been only temporarily averted, however. In Ireland the Catholic Church had yet to pronounce. Meanwhile, there was great agitation in England. The Irish leader had become a laughing stock. Newspapers – and especially *The Times*, still smarting from the Pigott defeat – condemned Parnell outright. Even the Liberal papers, such as *Pall Mall Gazette*, were doubtful of the possibility of continuing to negotiate with the disgraced leader. Mary Gladstone wrote on 17 November of 'Awful blows', of which the 'most overwhelming of all' was 'Parnell's guilt in the O'Shea case. He and she undefended, and he has lived this life of lies all these years. A heartbreaking revelation.'[47] On 22 November, she wrote of how they had all 'waited and watched for Parnell's retirement. Papa's 1st words "It'll ne'er dae [do]", and he wrote at once to Mr. Morley saying he expected P[arnell] wd. at once ask for the Chiltern Hundreds. All England waited in suspense for this...'[48]

Gladstone soon realized that his supporters – and particularly the Nonconformist vote – would not support an alliance with the Irish Party as long as Parnell remained leader.[49] The Nonconformist Reverend Hugh Price Hughes of the West London Methodist Mission provided an example of the invective produced in opposition to Parnell. On 20 November his vitriolic piece was published in the *Methodist Times*:

We do not hesitate to say that if the Irish race deliberately select as their recognized representative an adulterer of Mr Parnell's type they are as incapable of self-government as their bitterest enemies have asserted. So obscene a race in those circumstances they would prove themselves to be would obviously be unfit for anything except a military despotism.[50]

There has been considerable debate over whether Gladstone could have resisted these kinds of attacks. He was certainly advised by Harcourt and Morley to respond decisively. Gladstone contacted Parnell's second-in-command, Justin McCarthy, and gave him his view that while Parnell was leader the Liberals would lose the forthcoming general election. Home Rule would therefore be put off until a time when Gladstone would no longer be able to lead the process. In order to avoid any accusation of dictating policy to the Irish Party, he desired McCarthy to convey the message to

Parnell. This McCarthy was unable to do – or, if he did so, the message had little impact. The leader's absences made it particularly difficult for his followers to respond to this crisis.

On 24 November Gladstone, encouraged by Harcourt and Morley, went further. He signed a letter – drafted in the main by Morley – in which he wrote that 'the continuance I speak of [that is, Parnell at the head of the Irish Party]... would render my retention of the leadership of the Liberal party, based as it has been mainly upon the prosecution of the Irish cause, almost a nullity.'[51] This crucial letter, which essentially said that, if Parnell stayed, Gladstone (and hopes for Home Rule) would go, was given to Morley. The leader remained so deliberately elusive that Morley was able to read him the document only after the committee meeting in which the leader was re-elected. After the meeting, the leader's response to Morley was that the letter did not matter. He told Morley 'that he must look to the future... that if he gave up the leadership for a time, he could never return to it; that if he once let go, it was all over'.[52] But he had been re-elected under false pretences. The members had known nothing of the Gladstone letter, which would have changed everything. And there were many members who believed that, if re-elected, the leader would do the honourable thing and resign in any event.

So, when Gladstone's letter was published immediately thereafter, there was an outcry and a sense of betrayal. The Irish Party was spilt into those who continued to support Parnell, and those who wished to depose him. The leader anticipated a battle ahead. He returned to Katie, and told her, 'I think we shall have to fight, Queenie. Can you bear it? I'm afraid it is going to be tough work.'[53] She wrote that she had agreed with him. 'But I must confess', she added, 'that when I looked at the frail figure and white face that was so painfully delicate, whose only vitality seemed to lie in the deep, burning eyes, my heart misgave me, for I very much doubted if his health would stand any prolonged strain.'[54] She recalled that she had 'burst out passionately', wondering why the scandal mattered now, after all the years. When her lover replied that 'they were afraid of shocking Mr. Gladstone',[55] she protested, claiming that Gladstone had known of their relations.[56] Parnell replied, 'Just so, but we are public reprobates now, it just makes the difference.'[57]

This was not strictly the case. In fact, Gladstone had been very much hurt by Parnell's lack of honesty. Hamilton recorded on 25 November that the Liberal leader had taken the Parnell business

much to heart. He feels he has been betrayed by a man for whom he always had a liking and indeed too fond a regard, and whose political veracity he never had reason to question. For Parnell had through J. Morley assured Mr. G. that he would come out of the O'Shea trial triumphantly. In short, Parnell had lied to Mr. G.; and Mr. G. could never forget or forgive that.[58]

Parnell, although ill, prepared to save his political career. The ruthless methods he adopted to do so reveal his determination to remain in power. Having duped many of the party members, and benefited from their sentimental and loyal initial support for 'the Chief', he planned to retain that influence. First, he decided to turn on the hard-won Liberal-Nationalist alliance. Just months after his famously successful visit at Hawarden, the leader issued a manifesto to the Irish people in which he was highly critical of Gladstone and the Liberals. Instead of promoting the alliance, which was to lead so promisingly to Home Rule, he appealed directly to the Irish public over the heads of the Irish Party. Parnell claimed that 'the integrity and independence' of some of these members had been 'apparently sapped and destroyed by the wirepullers of the English Liberal Party'. He demanded that Gladstone, foremost of the 'English wolves howling for my destruction', should not be allowed to influence the choice of Irish leader.[59]

The leader's repudiation of the friendly, informal agreements made with Gladstone was a sensation. Parnell made deeply negative (and almost certainly untrue, or highly exaggerated) claims about the Liberal leader's intentions for Home Rule. Katie wrote that, as she watched him labour over the draft, she 'deliberated for hours as to whether I ought to let him go on'. She wondered whether she should urge him to come abroad with her – to 'some sunny land where we could forget the world and be forgotten'. Katie claimed that she knew that he would come if she said she 'could not bear the public fight'. But, she continued, 'I knew that he would not forget; that he would come at my bidding, but that his desertion of Ireland would lie at his heart; that if he was to be happy he must fight to the end.'[60]

Parnell watched her while he wrote what was later called 'the public suicide of a great public man'.[61] 'I am feeling very ill, Queenie', he told her, 'but I think I shall win through. I shall never give in unless you make me, and I want you to promise me that you will never make me less than the man you have known.'[62] Davitt wrote that the secret behind the leader's 'immense influence and popularity' was that he was 'above and before everything else, a splendid fighter'.[63] In this instance, with his back against the wall, his combative instincts took over. Before publishing his manifesto he showed it to McCarthy and at that time made one of his very rare references to the O'Shea case. He told him that when the final divorce decree had been made

he meant to make a statement which would put him straight except for the actual crime. He would show that for twenty-three years of married life, O'Shea had in numbers of days, spent one year with his wife; that he had carried on with fast women, and had ill-used her; that he (Parnell) had found her a miserable woman, and that O'Shea had been quite willing to sell her to keep his seat in Parliament. He said: 'If I had defended the case, I should have sacrificed the one person whose interest I am bound beyond everything in the world to protect'.[64]

The manifesto was published on 29 November. Response in England was predictably horrified. There was a growing sense that the Irish leader was unbalanced and irrational. If his actions were not irrational, they were, in others' opinions, vindictive. Gladstone was disconcerted by this betrayal of private conversations, never intended for publication, and almost certainly misrepresented. It convinced him further that Parnell was dishonest and untrustworthy. The Earl of Derby recalled talking over the matter with Gladstone in December 1890. The Liberal leader

began to speak of Parnell, saying with a kind of grim humour: 'A large chapter has been added to my experiences of human nature in the last few weeks.' And he went on to express his astonishment at the breach of confidence, saying that in all their previous communications Parnell had shown himself to be entirely and even scrupulously truthful (I remember the exact words used.) I asked if he had not heard a good deal of the O'Shea business before? He said yes, but only reports, and he made it a rule to attach no importance to these, as anybody might be accused.[65]

In Ireland, Parnell's manifesto brought about public condemnation from the Catholic Church. His campaign thus grew even more risky. He had decided to bypass not only his own party and the Liberals, but also the clergy. Gladstone later told Hamilton that he 'knew no words strong enough with which to characterize Parnell's blackguard behaviour'.[66] The leader's only hope lay in the Irish people. He determined to press his case as the sole leader of the Irish nation. First, he had to attend the famous meeting in Room 15 at Westminster. All accounts of the frenetic lobbying beforehand in the House – by both Liberals and Nationalists – and the tense atmosphere during the days of the meeting describe a growing tension within the Irish Party. By 1 December, it looked as though Parnell's fate was preordained. The day before, a manifesto signed by five of the six Irish MPs who were in America[67] asked the party to repudiate Parnell. The influential Irish Archbishops Croke and Walsh also appealed for a change in leadership.[68] A lengthy and argumentative debate followed. Tim Healy had turned against Parnell, and led the increasingly bitter attacks on the leader.

Healy attempted to dismantle the concept that Parnell was their best chance of achieving results. He also sought to discredit the value of the leader's contributions to the nationalist cause. 'I say to Mr. Parnell his power is gone,' he declared. 'He derived that power from the people. We are the representatives of the people.'[69] Healy concluded by calling on the leader to withdraw. Katie wrote of the 'miserable treachery of Parnell's followers',[70] but she mostly blamed Gladstone. Parnell, on the other hand, felt no such resentment, according to her account. It was 'these fools, who throw me over at his bidding' that made him 'a little sad'.[71] Katie remarked that the matter of how long the Irish Party had known of her relations with the leader 'need not be here discussed. Some years before certain members of the Party opened one of my letters to Parnell. I make no comment.'[72]

The ruthless struggle continued over several exhausting and ill-tempered days. On the seventh and last day, bitter discussions began at noon. Soon there were unpleasant scenes. Tim Healy leaned forward 'scornfully to enquire: "Who is to be the mistress of the party?"'[73] This 'terrible interjection' was greeted by shock.[74] O'Connor wrote that members thought Parnell would strike Healy, and that Sexton 'felt the gravity of the remark so much that he confessed he hoped that Parnell would do so'.[75] Arthur O'Connor appealed to his friend the Chairman. Parnell replied, 'Better appeal to your own friends, better appeal to that cowardly little scoundrel there, that in an assembly of Irishmen dares to insult a woman.'[76]

After further futile debate, the meeting ended when forty-five members abandoned their leader and walked out, leaving a minority of twenty-seven Parnellites behind. The split had begun. The Irish Party would, arguably, never fully recover. Neither would Katie's reputation.

She described the subsequent frenzied efforts made by her lover to campaign personally in Ireland. Parnell and his followers had decided to assert that *they* were the legitimate Irish Party, and moved their battle to Ireland. This tactic, although plausible, had the great drawback of requiring the leader's physical presence to campaign for Parnellite candidates in by-elections. The adoption of platform speaking was a salient feature of nineteenth-century politics and the power of oratory to move minds during this period cannot be underestimated.[77] The leader set out for Kilkenny on 9 December. He was given a rapturous reception in Dublin, a city that remained loyal to him till the end. The poet Katherine Tynan was a great admirer. She described how on the morning of 10 December the leader had quietly seized control of *United Ireland*, which had turned against him. There was no struggle. That night, Parnell addressed the adoring crowds. Tynan wrote of the momentous event:

It was nearly 8.30 when we heard the bands coming, then the windows were lit up by the lurid glare of thousands of torches in the street outside. There was a distant roaring like the sea. The great gathering within waited, silent with expectation. Then the cheering began, and we craned our necks and looked out eagerly, and there was the tall, slender, distinguished figure of the Irish leader, making its way across the platform. I don't think any words could do justice to his reception. The house rose at him; everywhere there was a sea of passionate faces, loving, admiring, almost worshipping that silent, pale man.[78]

The next day, the anti-Parnellites seized the *United Ireland* offices. Parnell, his loyal friend Dr Kenny and his followers stormed the offices. 'At the sight of their Chief the crowd went wild,' Katie wrote, 'cheers for Parnell and curses for his enemies filled the air.'[79] The leader was held back from leaping the railings, and then with his supporters attacked the front door with a crowbar. The ferocity of this and other struggles took their toll on his health. Katie wrote with despair of how her lover travelled back from Ireland every Saturday to be with her, returning the next day to resume battle.

On one occasion, someone in the crowd threw lime in Parnell's face, later insisting it had been flour. Katie was indignant and frantic with worry. By the time she had received his 'reassuring message' she was, she recalled, 'nearly out of my mind'.[80]

As Parnell continued to campaign in Ireland, the attacks began on Katie:

From one end of chivalrous Ireland to the other, urged on more especially by a certain emotional Irish member of Parliament – the name of 'Kitty' O'Shea was sung and screamed, wrapped about with all the filth that foul minds, vivid imaginations, and black hatred of the aloof, proud Chief could evolve, the Chief whom they could not hurt save through the woman he loved![81]

The 'emotional' Member was Tim Healy, and his string of invective directed at Katharine O'Shea was, quite simply, astonishing. His biographer, Frank Callanan, has convincingly explained how cleverly the lawyer made political capital of the leader's illicit relationship.[82] Healy's strategy – highly successful – was to reduce and limit the political discourse in Ireland to one thing, and one thing only, the disgrace of Parnell and the O'Shea divorce. One insult after another was hurled at Katie's name and reputation. In an unrelenting series of scabrous sexual allusions, Healy led the charge against Parnell and his mistress for months. The debate was exceedingly low in tone. At every opportunity, Healy sought to degrade and belittle the pair. He was not alone. Other parliamentary colleagues joined in, as did large numbers of parish priests and many Nationalists.

The nationalist press could barely contain their scorn. 'Kitty O'Shea' was denounced as a fallen woman, a faithless wife. The epithets used to describe her included 'degraded', 'disgraced', 'shameless' and 'wretched'.[83] The *Irish Catholic* referred to 'the guilty leers of Kitty'.[84] An anti-Parnellite newspaper claimed that she had 'darkened the brightest page of Irish history; she wrecked the career of the most successful of Irish leaders; and plunged a united country into dissension'.[85] Katie claimed that these attacks hurt Parnell 'a little, it is true, but not very greatly'. He told her, 'It would really have hurt, my Queen if those devils had got hold of your real name, *my* Queenie, or even the "Katie" or "Dick" that your relations and Willie called you.'[86] Katie wrote that it was a 'little thing to bear for the man who loved me as never woman has been loved before'.[87]

It was untrue that Parnell was not hurt by these taunts and insults, besmirching the woman he loved. He turned on his enemies with fury in his political orations, as he fought two more by-elections (like the first, both resulted in defeat for his candidate). He referred to his former colleagues as 'miserable gutter-sparrows who were once my comrades... The miserable scum... The cowardly crew seeking to grip me by the throat... Away with such filth, away with such patriots, down with them.'[88] The rift was absolute and caused a rupture that took years to repair.

Katie and Parnell faced other difficulties. He was practically bankrupt, and her inheritance was frozen in probate. O'Shea had been awarded costs and on 22 April 1891 the Irish leader was presented with the Judge's Order for costs in the divorce case. Katie did not record that the leader later tried to evade paying these on the basis that he did not reside in England. Katie made little mention of how they managed financially during this period. Parnell was frequently away in Ireland, trying to save his career. On 24 June 1891, however, he and Katie at last formalized their union. Katie wrote of the trouble they took to avoid the newspaper correspondents, 'who hung about our house at Brighton with an inconvenient pertinacity'.[89] She and Parnell had made elaborate arrangements to send the two servants – who would act as witnesses – in advance to the town of Steyning by train. The leader was eager to evade the reporters, and Katie wrote that as her devoted maid Phyllis was fastening a posy on her breast, 'Parnell gently but firmly took it from her and replaced it with white roses he had got for me the day before. Seeing her look of disappointment he said, "She must wear mine today, Phyllis, but she shall carry yours, and you shall keep them in remembrance; now you must go!"[90]

Parnell then fetched the phaeton and his horse, Dictator, and escorted Katie out of the house. She fondly recalled that although her lover as a rule never noticed what she wore, that morning he told her: 'Queenie, you look lovely in that lace stuff and the beautiful hat with the roses! I am so proud of you!'[91] The pair rushed the 9 miles to the register office, where the Superintendent Registrar, Mr Edward Cripps, was awaiting them. The two maids arrived and Katie wrote that 'the little ceremony that was to legalise our union of many years was quickly over'.[92] The pair were besieged by reporters on their return. They managed to push through the throng, Katie wrote, and ate a quiet little wedding breakfast. The leader would not 'allow' her to have a wedding cake, 'because he said he would not be able to bear seeing me eat *our* wedding cake without him, and, as I knew, the very sight of a rich cake made him ill'.[93]

The marriage was reported in the papers the next day.[94] *The Times* wrote that Mr Parnell had obtained a special licence, and gave details of the event. Their Brighton correspondent had learned that a written statement was handed by Mrs O'Shea the previous evening, in which she confirmed their union, and also stated that the 'marriage will be solemnized later on at a London church, there have been some delay and difficulty in obtaining a license [*sic*] for the purpose'.[95] Katie did not record that she and her new husband were striving for a church blessing. On 25 June, Parnell wrote to Cripps and told him that he would be willing to 'give any clergyman willing to perform the ceremony in the church a fee of Ten guineas'.[96] Two days later, he wrote asking to have the ceremony conducted at the Steyning church upon his return from Ireland, on 8 or 9 July.[97] But on 7 July, Katie herself wrote to the Registrar, saying that she hoped she might have heard from him about whether the Bishop 'would consent to allow the Vicar to marry Mr Parnell and myself in his Church'. She enclosed a letter from her solicitor, Mr Pym, on the matter. Katie hoped that Mr Parnell would be back within a day or two, after the Carlow election, 'when he will no doubt see you or write to you respecting the marriage'.[98]

There then followed a gap in the correspondence, and on 6 August Katharine wrote once again to Cripps. She thanked him for his letter, and asked whether he would kindly meet Mr Parnell in London. There were clearly difficulties to resolve. 'He would then be able to arrange with you so much better than by letter', she explained.[99] Katie persevered and, on 28 August, sent Cripps a letter, asking him to call the following day, when Mr Parnell would be home.[100] On 31 August, Katie wrote to the Registrar, telling him that they were 'much obliged' for his letter, 'and we shall be glad if you will kindly ask Sir Th Thayer as you suggest, and let us know the result as soon as you conveniently can. My husband was obliged to go to Ireland but he will return this week.'[101] There is no further available correspondence on the matter, but the fact is that this ceremony never took place, suggesting that the obstacles were not overcome.

Later information provided by the *Sussex Daily News* offers more detail on the attempts made to have a religious ceremony. The Vicar of Steyning refused the couple's request for the ceremony, 'giving as his reason the result of the proceedings of the Divorce court'. The Reverend Arthur Pridgeon had also communicated on the matter with the Bishop of Chichester, who absolutely forbade it. The Reverend told the couple that he was, however, 'willing to comply with the Act of Parliament respecting the lending of the church for such a marriage, on the understanding that Mr. and Mrs. Parnell found a clergyman'. Despite such difficulties, the report continued, 'Mr. and Mrs. Parnell, however, were not moved from their purpose'. Arrangements had apparently been made to have the ceremony conducted at St James's Church in Marylebone.

They were awaiting permission from the Bishop and his granting of a licence.[102] The ceremony never happened.

The response in England to the marriage was generally positive. It was felt that the union could lead to a new beginning on a political level. The *Globe* observed:

Mrs O'Shea was the cause of the collapse of an important political faction; and it is not out of the question that Mrs. Parnell may be the cause of its re-establishment. Much more impossible things than this have happened in Irish history, in which personal sentiment has from time immemorial been so potent a factor. When Mr. Parnell's conduct is impugned on the score of morality, his friends will always be able to avail themselves of the answer that at any rate he kept himself unperjured, and that he took the first opportunity he could make of repairing the wrong he had done, so far as such wrongs can ever be repaired. It was on the moral high ground that he was thrown over by both Irish and English separatists; and now that he has done all that it is possible for any human being to reinstate himself in their political favour.[103]

The *Manchester Examiner* declared, 'there is no longer a "Kitty O'Shea" for Secessionists… to sneer at and taunt'.[104] The *Echo* commented that 'Mr. Parnell has done the right thing. He has married Mrs. O'Shea, and thereby done very much to atone for regrettable offences against the marriage law… The opposition which, naturally enough, came from the Irish priesthood against Mr. Parnell will now be softened, preparatory to its partial, if not general, removal.'[105]

But the reaction in Ireland was very different. There was no softening whatever. Very much to the contrary, Parnell's marriage confirmed his status as unrepentant adulterer. The *National Press* affirmed that 'the Pagan ceremony which the fallen man has gone through only sinks him deeper in his disgrace'.[106] The *Weekly National Press* condemned 'the empty mockery of marriage by which Mr. Parnell legalized his relations with the wealthy though degraded partner of his guilty pleasures'.[107] The *Kilkenny Journal* pronounced that Parnell had 'damned himself beyond redemption'.[108] Archbishop Walsh described Parnell's new wife as 'his partner in guilt', and declared that the marriage was 'a public compact for the continuance of their shameful career'.[109] Far from reconciling his supporters, Parnell's marriage confirmed the fears of those who had refused to believe the rumours of the divorce court. One observer noted that the union had done the leader 'incalculable harm in the eyes of the good Catholics, who regard it not as an act of reparation but as public admission that the worst was true'.[110]

The civil wedding had also offended Catholic sensibilities. Bishop O'Donnell's words summed up the Irish response to the union, and reinforced the feeling that Katharine Parnell would never be welcome there. He declared that the marriage was the 'climax of brazen horrors'.[111]

CHAPTER NINETEEN

Mrs Parnell

ESPITE PARNELL AND KATIE'S dreams, a visit to Ireland
looked unpromising. It would be a long time before 'King'
and 'Queenie' could expect a positive reception in his homeland.
In an interview on 27 June, the leader had told a reporter that he
had hoped to bring his wife to Ireland with him shortly, but that
she was a 'bad sailor' and in addition 'was compelled to remain as
near to her lawyers as possible, because of the coming trial of the
will suit between her and her brothers with regard to the Eltham
property recently left to her by her late aunt'.[1] But Parnell also
declared in that interview that he and his wife were 'perfectly happy.
As for myself, I can truly say that I am now enjoying greater
happiness than I have ever experienced in the whole of my
previous life.'[2]

There were, however, financial worries. On 29 July, a hearing
was held at the London Court of Bankruptcy, where Parnell
attempted to have set aside an order to pay £778 to Captain
O'Shea. His representative argued that Parnell had not been
resident in the jurisdiction of the court during the greater part of
the previous six months, but was based at Avondale in Ireland. He
argued further that his client had a counter-claim against the

Captain for £3,600 'in respect of money advanced to and paid for
and on his account between September 1889, and November 1890'.
The Registrar determined, however, that Mr Parnell, 'by having
rooms reserved for him in a house at Brighton, acquired a residence
in England, which gave the Court jurisdiction in relation to his
affairs'. There was no attempt made to substantiate Parnell's
counter-claim, 'and the Registrar dismissed the application with
costs'.[3]

The matter of their finances was pressing. In Ireland, Parnell
sought to raise a further mortgage on Avondale. He wrote to Katie
on 15 August, telling her she might 'fix the end of the year as the
time you and I would guarantee the payment of the costs'.[4] On 1
September 1891, he informed her that he did not think he could
get the loan from the Hibernian Bank within the fortnight, but
would 'hasten matters as much as possible'.[5] On 7 September, he
wrote that he had told Kerr, his manager at Avondale, that he could
not have the first one thousand of the loan, 'so you may reckon on
that amount'. The bank was to have given him the first payment
on that day 'but a hitch occurred on Saturday which I removed to-
day, and the board will meet to-morrow and ratify the advance'.[6]
The 'hitch' was that the bank was looking for further guarantees
from Parnell, who now had a sizeable overdraft on the estate,
managed by Kerr. The following day, Parnell wrote to the
Managing Director of the Hibernian Bank, in which he undertook
'to guarantee repayment to the Hibernian Banking Company of
Mr William Kerr's overdraft upon their branch at Wicklow to the
extent of £6000'.[7]

O'Shea was also short of funds. He had bought the lease on a
property in Chichester Terrace in Brighton and set up house there
with Gerard and Carmen in January 1891. Norah had, to his
chagrin, chosen to live with her mother. On 12 February, the
Captain lamented to Chamberlain that the absence of his eldest
daughter was 'a constant trial'. He was, however, much cheered by
the 'care and affection lavished on myself and my children who

are with me, by the family of the lady who was my wife'.[8] He was in financial straits, though, and later that month asked his friend to lend him £800. His lawsuits, he explained, had cost him £5,300 and, although he had paid his way all along, he now found himself 'in a corner, and a nasty one' for the want of £800 – of which £400 was required urgently.[9] Although Chamberlain lent him £400, it was with obvious reluctance. He told O'Shea that he would find him 'the first £400 of which you speak though the matter is not entirely free from difficulty'.[10] Clearly, the Captain continued to suffer financially. It was not until a year later, in March 1892, that he asked Chamberlain to see him about the payment of the debt.[11]

Katie and her new husband had, just before their marriage, also had to face the legal action taken by Henry Campbell. Parnell's former secretary brought a libel action against the *Cork Daily Herald* for printing an article which claimed that Campbell had undertaken the 'degrading duty of hiring houses for the immoral purposes of his master'.[12] The libel action succeeded, and the evidence established that Katharine O'Shea had been the one to use Campbell's name in 1886 to write to an estate agent at Eastbourne – without his knowledge or permission. This created further embarrassment for the leader, and he attempted to take the blame, in order to shield Katie. Parnell wrote a public letter to Campbell in which he took full responsibility. He claimed that he had obtained permission from Campbell to use his name, and had told Katharine O'Shea that he had that permission. He wrote this explanatory letter, he said, to 'vindicate this lady from the most unjust accusations made against her at the recent trial'.[13]

The leader's attempt to protect his bride-to-be backfired badly, however, as he then made allusion to her role as go-between with Gladstone. This was the first public mention of such a previously highly secret contact. The Dublin Unionist newspaper, the *Daily Express*, commented wryly that Parnell had presented Mrs O'Shea as 'a great diplomatist who in some mysterious way played the part of a benefactor to Irish nationalism'.[14] Dillon, who was imprisoned in Galway Gaol, was appalled. He wrote to O'Brien:

To me it seems a most indecent document. It is hardly possible to believe that P. is sane on this subject to flourish this wretched woman in the face of the country for such is plainly the significance of the letter – that Mrs. O'Shea has been entrusted by him with important political business. It is revolting and indeed I must say the revelations at the Campbell trial were very disgusting.[15]

In the public eye, this compounded Katie's two serious crimes. Members of the Irish Party blamed her for Parnell's 'fall'. Tim Healy, for example, denigrated her, reciting: 'Eight hours of work, eight hours of play, eight hours in bed with Kitty O'Shea.'[16] Her second transgression had been against the cherished institution of the middle-class family, a critical structure within Victorian society, where the rituals involved in running the middle-class household served to maintain the fabric of social stratification. As one family historian has explained, 'It was to middle class women that the job of maintaining genteel domesticity and thus the social status of the family – measured in both class and moral terms – was entrusted.'[17] It was no wonder that Willie O'Shea protested so vehemently about the effect of 'the scandal' on his children. Middle-class ideologies of domesticity were maintained through the rituals of gentility that Katie had disregarded, and what had been private decisions were now publicly vilified.

The most immediate problem for Katie, however, was managing her husband's precarious health. He was suffering badly from rheumatism and his chronic heart trouble. The journeys to and from Ireland were causing him physical pain. In September, on his return from campaigning, Katharine recalled that she was 'thoroughly alarmed about his health'. The 'tired, grey shadows were growing deeper upon his beautiful face', she lamented. She wished him to consult Sir Henry Thompson, but he refused. He was not ill, he insisted, but only tired. Katie wrote that she had told him that she believed that his fatigue was too much. She advised him 'that nothing, not even Ireland, was worth it, and I besought him now at last to give it all up, and to hide away with me till a long rest, away from the turmoil and contention, had saved him from the tiredness that would, I feared, become real illness if he went on'.[18]

Yet again, Parnell made a decision to prioritize his ambitions. He told his wife that if he gave in now, he would be 'Less than your King'. He would 'rather die', he stated, 'than give in now – give in to the howling of the English mob. But if you say it I will do it.' Katie recorded that she had made the sacrifice of not asking him to give it all up – she accepted 'that in the martyrdom of our love was to be our reparation'.[19] Parnell set off again to Ireland, and sent her a telegram from there, in which he was 'cheerful, though he said he was not feeling very well'.[20] When the leader returned on 2 October, he seemed 'very weak'. Katie recollected that she had been 'rather worried' that he had chosen to take a Turkish bath in London. He told her that he had had to have his arm in a sling while he was away, and also that his bag, containing a change of dry clothes, had gone missing, and he had had to sit in his wet clothes 'for some hours'. She had been 'much vexed' on hearing this, Katie wrote, 'for I always made such a point of his not keeping on damp things, and provided against it so carefully when starting him off'.[21]

Despite Katie's best efforts to nurse him, her husband sank quickly. She was by the next day 'terribly worried' and made him promise that he would take her away for a 'real honeymoon in a country where the sun is strong enough to get the cold out of your bones'. To this he agreed, telling her, 'So we will, Wifie, directly I get that mortgage through.'[22]

And indeed the lack of money undoubtedly added to his worries. He told Katie that he wished to write to his brother-in-law, Mr MacDermott (who was his solicitor), asking him about the mortgage he was trying to raise on the estate, 'as he wished to have the matter completed quickly'.[23] Katie made him promise to see a doctor, but he refused to allow her to send for Thompson in London, saying, 'No, the fee would be enormous at this distance.'[24] After two consecutive nights without sleep, the leader was convinced he was going to die. Katie stayed with him night and day. He seemed to rally, and then became very feverish. The local doctor, Jowers, had been called in and visited regularly, but there was little anyone could do, as Thompson later assured Katie. The damage had been done. The strain, the travelling and the 'worn out constitution' had taken their toll.[25]

Parnell became increasingly weak and, within days, was unable to leave his bed. Katie remained at his side, stroking his hand, while he fought the pain and tried to doze. She talked to him of the 'sunny land' where they would go when he had recovered. 'We will be so happy, Queenie', he told her, 'there are so many things happier than politics.'[26] After another sleepless night, the doctor called and advised that improvement would not be apparent for a day or two. He promised to call the next morning. But, late that evening, Charles Parnell 'suddenly opened his eyes and said: "Kiss me, sweet Wifie, and I will try to sleep a little"'. She lay down beside him, 'and kissed the burning lips he pressed to mine for the last time'. As she slipped her hand from under his head, he lost consciousness. The doctor came at once, Katie wrote, 'but no remedies prevailed against this sudden failure of the heart's action, and my husband died without regaining consciousness, before his last kiss was cold on my lips'.[27]

It was 6 October, just four days after he had returned home. He was forty-five years old. Katie had been married for less than three months. She was now a divorcee and a widow. The *Daily Chronicle* had commented on her wedding that Mrs O'Shea was

alas! among those whose bridal wreath has been twined with reeds of strife. But however much she may have erred, even in the fatal mistake of her first marriage, it is only just to say that she has borne with heroic self-restraint the punishment of brutal obloquy and cruel abuse which the leaders of the new Irish party have for the last year heaped upon her. She has had the good taste to live in sad seclusion after compassing her social death.[28]

Now, instead of reaping the reward for all her sacrifices and humiliations, Katie found herself alone. Not for long, however. Within hours of the news, the Irish Party and press sensationalized and mourned their leader's death. It came as a tremendous shock. Although it had been observed that in his last months the leader had looked increasingly weary and indeed unkempt, his demise was entirely unexpected. The news reached Ireland on 7 October. It was reported on 8 October that a contingent made up of Parnell's sister Emily Dickinson, John Redmond, Mr and Mrs Pierce Mahoney and John O'Connor had arrived in Brighton and had proceeded to Walsingham Terrace. 'Mrs. Dickinson', the *Evening Telegraph* reported, 'intends to use her influence in support of the request of Messrs Mahoney and Redmond, on behalf of their colleagues, that Mr. Parnell should be allowed to have a public funeral.'[29] Mr J. O'Kelly and Mr Joseph Nolan were already in Brighton, having arrived the previous night. Later, the article continued, a consultation had been held at the leader's address, where Mrs Parnell's solicitor was present, along with Redmond, Mahoney, O'Connor, Nolan and Mrs Dickinson.

Katie had little say in the matter and was in any event prostrate with grief. 'It was Mrs. Parnell's wish that the remains should be interred at Brighton, but she at once deferred to the wish of Mr. Parnell's colleagues that the interment should take place in Ireland, and that they should be accorded a national funeral.'[30] It was reported that Mrs Pierce and Mrs Dickinson were staying at Walsingham Terrace, and the funeral arrangements were being made by Messrs Redmond and Mahoney. Emily Dickinson later wrote that a 'small band of his followers' had rapidly appeared, and 'had taken possession of his body'. These people, she pointed out, 'in course of time deserted Charles after his burial by joining those who hounded him to death'.[31]

The leader's body was of great political and symbolic significance and was thus claimed by Parnell's followers immediately after he died. It is small wonder that Katie was later so bitter towards the Irish Party. At the last fateful meeting in Ireland at Creggs, Parnell had found little support from his supposedly loyal colleagues. Sophie O'Brien, the wife of Parnell's estranged colleague William O'Brien, wrote of that last meeting. 'The inner history of the last meeting… was piteous. He could find no man of importance in his party to accompany him. Many gave different pretexts, others evaded replying.'[32] The great leader – rejected by so many in the last months of his life, excoriated by his countrymen and in particular the clergy – was now hailed as the 'Chief'.

Men of state belong not to their families, but to the nation after their death. Winston Churchill's daughter, Mary Soames, wrote movingly of how her father's corpse became the property of the nation after he died. 'From the moment his body left his home,' she recalled, 'he, and all of us, became integral parts of a great pageant of state… Ever since his death we, his family, had realized that he belonged as much to others as he belonged to us – perhaps more – and that we were only a small part of the laying-to-rest of Winston Churchill.'[33] Public funerals are indeed important pageants of remembrance and are a critical element in the creation of the national myth. The Parnellites drew back their leader after his tragic and unexpected death. But in this process of swift rehabilitation, there was no place for his disgraced, English widow.

Katie was excised from Parnell's legacy. The part she had played in the great man's life was an embarrassment. The *Daily News* asserted that if Mr Parnell 'had died two years ago he would have bequeathed to our modern political history the memory of a career almost unique in the perfection of its triumph… He was not, however, graced so far by fortune. He outlived his triumph, and we say with sincere regret he outlived his reputation.'[34] *The Times* declared that had Parnell's death 'occurred only 12 months earlier we should have had to add that it extinguished one of the most noteworthy forces in contemporary politics'.[35] Justin McCarthy said in an interview: 'Until the Divorce court proceedings, I was the close friend of Mr. Parnell, and I admired him intensely.'[36] It was not merely that Katie was a reminder of all that had gone wrong, but her presence created an impediment to moving forward on Home Rule.

The split in the Irish Party had caused terrible damage to the cause of Irish nationalism. McCarthy and others were anxious to put their differences behind them. The effect of Parnell's death, he said, 'must be to draw us together'.[37] In Ireland the various factions raged at one another, however, as the Parnellite loyalists angrily insisted that none of the leader's enemies should attend the funeral. Threats were made that anti-Parnellites would be physically attacked if they came to pay their respects. But many of Parnell's colleagues were outraged, arguing that the funeral was a national event and that all should be able to participate. Far from healing old wounds, the preparations for the ceremony caused further ugly rifts. The language was intemperate. The *United Ireland* dramatically headlined 'Done to Death', to which the *Freeman's Journal* responded that this was 'an appeal to the passions of desperate or ignorant men'.[38]

Throughout these angry displays, Katie remained in seclusion. She refused to see anyone and was nursed by her daughter Norah. Such was the secrecy and withdrawal that rumours began to abound. Perhaps the leader was still alive, or maybe he had committed suicide? To end these stories, Katie allowed a statement to be made by Dr Jowers, in which he confirmed the cause of death as 'rheumatic fever (five days), hyperpyrexia, and failure of heart's action'.[39] Although there has continued to be some speculation about the exact cause of death, especially as it appeared to be so sudden, the diagnosis seems very plausible. Parnell's father had died at the age of forty-eight, of what was probably myocardial infarction. His grandfather, William, had died at forty-four after catching a chill.[40]

Parnell's supporters were determined to capitalize on the public enthusiasm for their former leader. In Dublin, where loyalty to Parnell had remained solid throughout, the preparations reached fever pitch. Parnell's brother-in-law was shocked, however, at the choice of a Catholic cemetery as the final resting place. He 'protested strongly' and sent the following telegram to Katie: 'Charles's father is buried in the family vault at Mount Jerome, where Charles should be buried also. It is proposed to bury him in the Roman Catholic cemetery of Glasnevin. May I insist on Mount Jerome.' He received the following reply: 'Many thanks, arrangements all made. Parnell.' But MacDermott pressed, and sent a 'strong remonstrance' to Mahoney, who was at Brighton. It was understood, the report observed, that Mrs Parnell was 'prostrated with grief, and the only relation of Mr. Parnell who is with her is Mrs. Dickenson [*sic*], who, it is believed, has been persuaded to agree to the proposed arrangements. Mr. T. Harrington, on being remonstrated with, said that Mr. Parnell's remains belonged to the nation, and the funeral was a national event.'[41]

The MP and Parnell loyalist Henry Harrison had travelled to Brighton to see if he could be of help to the Parnell household.[42] He described the scene at Walsingham Terrace as tragic, although he did not see Mrs Parnell for some weeks. She had taken to her room, and messages were brought to and from her by Norah. Harrison remained in a hotel near Brighton, and spent most of his days at Walsingham Terrace, where he made himself useful helping Norah with the huge number of telegrams, mail and visits. It was at this time that he first learned – with delight – of the existence of the two 'charming' daughters, aged six and eight, who were 'generally recognised and accepted as' Parnell's children.[43] They were living in the house next to No. 10, where

Parnell had resided, in No. 9. What also struck the helpful MP was how alone the widow was. There was no one to protect her interests, he observed. Apart from her maid Phyllis, and daughter Norah, who was only nineteen, Katie had no one. The younger children were minded by their nurse.

The picture that emerges is one of a deeply grieving widow who was overtaken by events. 'It was the wish of Mrs. Parnell that Mr. Parnell should be buried quietly and privately at Brighton,' reported one newspaper, 'but it was earnestly represented to her that the people of Ireland were (to put it plainly) entitled to attend the funeral… Mrs. Parnell gave way under these arguments.'[44] Her husband's body was removed from Brighton on Saturday, 10 October. Before the casket was sealed, Katie placed 'certain objects which her love and the pious observances of her grief prescribed for her'. She gave Harrison 'the wreaths and particular flowers' that she 'wished to lie close, specially placed at the last, upon the surface of the coffin'.[45] And that was the last Katie saw of her husband. The *United Ireland* reported that the 'scene in the house while the coffin was being borne down was peculiarly painful, the grief of Mrs. Parnell being heartrending'.[46]

The coffin was drawn by an open-sided funeral carriage to the station, then put into a van and taken on to Willesden, where the public were allowed to walk through the compartment to pay their last respects. The train moved on again and arrived at Holyhead for the Irish boat. The leader's remains were wheeled to the lower deck. A space had been cordoned off in the smoking saloon. A black cloth was draped over the coffin and the twenty-eight wreaths that had accompanied it were placed in front. One of these bore the legend 'Died fighting for Ireland' and another 'In fond memory of one of Ireland's greatest chieftains, who was martyred in the struggle for her independence'.[47] Rehabilitation was well on its way. There was no place at all for an English Protestant widow.

And less still on arrival in Dublin, where a great crowd stood to receive the Chief. They wore black crepe armbands tied with green ribbon and waited silently. The coffin was transferred to the train and brought into Dublin's Westland Row station. The large wooden case in which the coffin had travelled was removed, and people on the platform broke it into small pieces, which were taken by members of the crowd as relics.[48] The hearse, piled high with wreaths, moved on, followed by carriages of mourners. Throughout the morning, the leader's remains lay in state at City Hall. Outside stood thousands of mourners. The events were described by J. L. Garvin:

When the coffin at last appeared above the balustrades in front of the portico the scene was a strange one, and never to be forgotten. Every head was at once bared, the eyes of strong men filled with tears, which they vainly bit their lips to restrain, and a shadow of pallor seemed to flit distinctly over the sea of upturned faces.[49]

The powerful pageant continued. The hearse was followed by Parnell's horse, 'Home Rule'. The horse bore the saddle and bridle, and, as per the custom, Parnell's riding boots were placed in the stirrups, reversed. The first carriage contained Henry Parnell, Emily Dickinson and her daughter, and Mrs. J. E. Kenny. In the second were Mr Alfred MacDermott and his son, along with the estate manager, Mr Kerr. The third carriage held the two reverends who were to read the burial service at the cemetery. In the fourth carriage were the prominent Fenians John O'Leary, James Stephens and P. N. Fitzgerald. This 'remarkable prominence'[50] of the Fenians reinforced a positioning of the dead leader as secular and separatist (anti-Union). The funeral and its posturing were to set the tone for much of the Parnellism to come. And it further cemented bitter divisions between Irish Nationalists.

Following in the procession were the many carriages containing Parnell's colleagues, and many dignitaries. At the graveside, it was left to Harrison to follow Katharine Parnell's wishes, 'which were very clearly detailed' to him by Norah. He 'carried them out to the letter', he wrote. 'At the last moment, after the last solemn words of the Burial Service,' he recollected, 'I descended into the grave and placed wreaths and flowers with their attached scripts of burning grief on the coffin's surface over the Chief's heart.'[51] Katie's wreath was composed of white flowers, and on a card were her words of farewell: 'To my love, my dear husband, my king'.[52]

There was little time to grieve. The probate suit had become vital. Parnell had died without re-making his will after the marriage, which rendered it invalid. Although the leader had left his estate to Katie and their children, this was not enforceable. Harrison had insisted on finding legal representation for Katie, and had introduced her to a solicitor, Mr Hawksley. Katie needed to fight for her survival. John Howard Parnell, by default, inherited his brother's estate at Avondale. He travelled to Brighton a few days after the funeral. Harrison recorded that he remembered 'hinting broadly' to John Parnell 'how generous and becoming an act for him it would be to waive his legal rights as heir-at-law, so as to give effect to his brother's manifest intention. I struck no spark into him.'[53] And, indeed, John Parnell asserted his rights to Avondale. In his account, he made no mention of the ambiguity of his position, and no mention at all of his brother's children. He wrote merely that he had gone to meet his brother's widow, for the first time, to discuss 'the arrangement of Charley's affairs'. Also at this meeting were Katie's brother-in-law, Hawksley, her solicitor, and Mr Campbell, who had accompanied John Parnell from Ireland.[54]

John Parnell wrote of jolly evenings spent amicably playing chess, and made no reference to how he expected his sister-in-law and nieces to manage without their inheritance. Perhaps he believed that Katie would prevail in the probate suit. What is clear is that the pair seemingly never met again. 'That was the only time that I saw Mrs. Parnell, and I have had no direct communication with her since,' he recalled.[55] John Howard Parnell was determined to take his brother's place at Avondale, and his plans excluded his brother's widow and their children. He returned to the landed estate and tried a number of schemes to make it profitable. He failed entirely and, as early as March 1893, Alfred MacDermott had filed a petition for the sale of Avondale and, after much wrangling on John's part, it was sold in 1900.[56]

There was no help available from the other members of the Parnell family. Delia Parnell continued to reside in America, and made visits to Ireland in 1891 and 1894. By March 1896 she had rented out Ironsides and was living at Trenton. Financial worries continued to plague her and her pronouncements were bizarre. In the summer of 1896, American papers carried an interview in which she declared that her son 'was either assassinated by English agents or is still alive'.[57] Delia Parnell travelled to Avondale for the last time in 1896. In March 1897 efforts were made by some nationalist groups to raise funds for her, as it was reported that 'Mrs Delia Stewart Parnell and some members of her family are in deep distress'.[58] Emily Dickinson was still struggling to make ends meet and living at Avondale in impoverished conditions. By 1904 Anna Parnell, living in lodgings in London, was reduced to pawning her clothes and few remaining possessions to pay for her board and lodging. She was discreetly helped by Kate Moloney, who explained Anna's situation to John Dillon. Although the Irish Party was not prepared to officially recognize any obligation to the Parnell family, he agreed that a destitute Anna Parnell would be a serious embarrassment, and made arrangements to come to her aid, without her knowledge.[59] The other Parnells continued to live their separate lives and there is no evidence of any contact made with their brother's widow.[60]

Katie was made to put effort into securing her future. Willie O'Shea was living in Brighton, and still had technical custody of the two younger girls. Harrison was convinced that he was prepared to use this as a means of blackmailing his former wife to agree to a favourable settlement for him personally in the probate suit. He recounted that the Captain had sent a letter, through the offices of Anna Steele, reassuring Katie that she would be allowed to keep the younger children with her. The fact that he had post-dated his letter was for Harrison a sign that he wanted his former wife to agree to a request of his in court the next day. This supposition was, he said, confirmed by Norah, who then told him her mother 'will agree to anything, submit to anything, rather than lose the children'.[61] It is impossible to know whether Harrison's suspicions were correct.

What we do know is that the probate suit was settled out of court on 25 March 1892. Katie on the one side and her two brothers on the other agreed to share the £140,000 estate, with one half to each party.[62] There had been a 're-settlement of Mrs. Parnell's property', the court recorded, 'effected after the proceedings in the divorce suit of "O'Shea v. O'Shea and Parnell"' and the life interest of Katie's share was thus to be 'equally divided between her and Captain O'Shea'.[63] She must have been quite desperate, as her finances had deteriorated badly. Deprived after her aunt's death in 1889 of the usual steady stream of income, Katie had borrowed money on the expectation of receiving at least a partial inheritance. Once that was depleted, she had nowhere to turn. The Parnells could not or would not help her. Her own family was fighting her in court, and her former husband was practically destitute. As Harrison pointed out, the

secluded life of years, the Divorce Court tales and the divorce itself, the Irish Nationalism of Parnell, the Irish Split, with its turbid flow of obscene abuse of 'Kitty O'Shea', and the pending fight in the probate action were causes which, operating either severally or in combination, deprived her of any hope of help from social friends, political associates, or relations either of her own or of Parnell.[64]

Before the trial was to start, Katie moved, with her daughters Norah O'Shea, Clare and Katie and a maid, to the Inns of Court Hotel in Holborn. Norah, unlike her brother Gerard and sister

Carmen, had remained on her mother's side and did not join in the legal battle. Katie's health had been poor, Harrison recalled, but she was the principal witness at the trial upon which so much depended. Just before the trial began, her own solicitor, Hawksley, urged her to take the offer of settlement, Harrison wrote. Katie's Counsel, Sir Charles Russell, was concerned that a jury 'might be carried by an outcry that the Mrs. O'Shea who had deceived her husband so long was certainly also deceiving her aunt for years – that such a woman would be quite capable of exercising undue influence, and that list of large and increasing payments by the aunt to the niece during the last ten years might be taken to prove how the niece manipulated the aunt'.[65]

Katie agreed to the settlement, but only months later she was back in court, this time in a bankruptcy action. It is salient to draw attention to how incredibly dominated her life had become by litigation, and how unusual this was at the time. This was not the only legal action in which she was involved. Parnell had been one of the signatories on the account in Paris holding the Irish Party funds. When Parnell died, McCarthy had been able to withdraw all the funds in the London account. He tried to do the same for the balance in the Paris account, and received two objections, one from Mrs Parnell, and the other from Messrs Harrington and Kenny (both Parnellites). Katie was claiming expenses that her husband had incurred, that should be reimbursed from the Fund, including his overdraft at the Hibernian Bank. She took advantage of the fact that the funds were in France, and thus subject to the 'Code Napoléon', under which the heirs of the deceased had very strong rights to his goods. They also had the obligation to honour any debts.

Hawksley justified his client's position by asserting that Mrs Parnell had joined the action in order to have her late husband's estate 'reimbursed and indemnified to the extent Mr Parnell in his lifetime advanced moneys for the purposes of his party or incurred liabilities… the overdraft at the Hibernian Bank, the guarantee given to Mr Dawson, once Lord Mayor of Dublin, and one or two other trifling matters'.[66] This we know is not strictly accurate, although it could be that the solicitor was telling what he knew from Katie. She on the other hand knew full well that Parnell had intended to use the overdraft money for personal purposes, and also to pay debts on the estate. Nevertheless, Hawksley insisted to Harrington that his client was only doing 'her simple duty in protecting his estate. It is much to be regretted that she should on this account have been subjected to gross personal abuse from persons who have not the excuse of ignorance.'[67]

Healy was infuriated by the blocking of the funds in Paris. Less than a month after the leader's death, he made his most vicious attack on Katharine Parnell. In a speech to his Longford constituents, he told them that 'no more shocking incident has been heard of than this alliance between so-called Irish patriots and a proved British prostitute. I mince no words in dealing with this matter.'[68] Two days later, Parnell's nephew, Tudor MacDermott (son of Sophia) called Healy out of the Law Library of the Four Courts in Dublin. He called on Healy to apologize and demanded an undertaking that he would never again mention Katharine Parnell 'or I would thrash him as long as I could'. Healy asserted that as Katharine Parnell had put herself in the public arena by blocking the funds, he would have no compunction in using her name. At this, the twenty-year-old MacDermott proceeded to hit at him with a riding whip, until he was forcibly removed from the premises. When Healy was asked whether he wished to press charges against his assailant, he replied that he would not, as his attacker appeared to be drunk.[69]

Healy obviously wished to downplay the embarrassing incident. He was a practising barrister and senior politician, and his language with regard to Parnell's widow was extraordinary. The following night, he once again referred to Katharine as 'a proved British prostitute'.[70] For many members of the party, this was going too far. Dillon, an anti-Parnellite, nevertheless believed that the reference cost them much support. Redmond, a Parnellite, was horrified. Labouchere, who was in Ireland, intervened upon his return to England, by asking Gladstone to act. Morley agreed and urged the Liberal leader to do so. He said of Healy, 'I confess that I have always regarded his ferocities of the last twelve months with utter aversion and – what is more to the point – with the conviction that such brutalities really served the turn of Parnell's faction.'[71]

Gladstone wrote a letter, addressed to Labouchere – designed to be read to Healy:

I understood much complaint is made of Mr. Healy's references to the unhappy woman who has been, I cannot help thinking, at the very root of *all* the mischief. It is difficult to rein in a gallant horse at the exact moment when his work is done, nor can I for one blame allusions made early in the day to denounce a particular mischief. But the Almighty has smitten the woman heavily. Nor will her social punishment be slight. In his present position nothing can react on her behalf, unless it be displeasure and resentment at anything thought to be like hitting her when she is down. I cannot help hoping Mr. Healy may now feel he has done enough in this matter.[72]

Healy desisted from the very overt attacks as of this moment. This was probably the least of Katie's problems, however. On 24 November, just some months after the settlement of the probate suit, a statement of her affairs was issued by the Official Receiver of the Brighton Bankruptcy District. This statement showed her to have gross liabilities estimated at nearly £7,500, with a deficiency of over £2,000. The list of Katie's assets included cash in the bank of £2,300; cash in hand of £400; furniture worth £300; dividends of £200; and £4,870 worth of life interests. From this, the report read, had to be deducted £45 for rent, taxes, wages, etc. 'Loss of income consequent on the death of Mrs. Wood is the cause to which Mrs. Parnell assigns her failure,' the statement declared.

The conclusion of the report provided a summary of Katie's situation after the probate suit:

In consequence of that action, with the exception of the interest under her marriage settlement, the debtor was without means after Mrs. Wood's death in May, 1889; and money was borrowed and charges given on income in order to carry on litigation. In the meantime Captain O'Shea commenced divorce proceedings against the debtor, and obtained a decree nisi in November, 1890. There was then an application to vary the settlements, and terms were eventually arranged by which the debtor's interest in Captain O'Shea's property was extinguished and the remainder was again divided – a life interest in one moiety to Captain O'Shea and a life interest in the other to the debtor and then to the children of the marriage. The net result of this is that the debtor has a life interest in a sum of about £25,000, at present invested at 2½ per cent. In addition to this the debtor has a life interest in the leasehold property Wonersh-lodge, at present producing £75 per annum, and also a life interest in a further sum of £1,051, producing about £100 per annum. The debtor married Mr. C. S. Parnell in June, 1891, but that gentleman died suddenly in the October following intestate, and, although the debtor has an interest in his estate, it is doubtful whether anything will accrue from that source.[73]

At this time, Katie was living in a house at Bletchingley, near Reigate in Surrey. This was a charming town of medieval origin, which featured a historic castle, as well as a wide market square. The surrounding countryside was idyllic, and the town contained many lovely old buildings. But the owner of Katie's house was demanding payment of the rent. Her financial situation continued to be precarious. Much of her income was tied up in trusts. On 20 May the following year, there was yet further legal action taken on her behalf. An application was made to the High Court of Justice to have income from her trust settlement paid to her. Katie's request to release income was supported by her former husband,

and one of the children. Two trustees of the settlement, nonetheless, stated that 'Mrs. Parnell had already been largely overpaid her share of income'. There were complicated manoeuvres required, but Mr Justice North decided that there must be an order for transfer of her Consols fund into court, and after Mrs Parnell had executed a 'certain deed of appointment', the trustees needed to pay to her 'one moiety of the dividend'.[74]

Under a year later, O'Shea was also faced with bankruptcy. In his case, the situation was even more dire. The accounts furnished to the Receiver showed liabilities of £12,610, with assets estimated by the debtor at just over £4,000. O'Shea claimed that his income 'from all sources for several years past up to 1882 inclusive, averaged about £3,000 per annum, and for the year 1893 it was about £700'. For more than four years past, the report went on, the debtor had been involved in 'constant litigation, and in connexion therewith he has incurred very heavy law costs and expenses'. His insolvency was due to this, 'to loss of income, to liabilities incurred on bills accepted by him for the accommodation of others, and to his inability to realize debts due to him'. In November 1892, the report continued, the debtor had tried to discharge his liabilities by applying to the Probate Division for permission to give up his life interest in a marriage settlement. Trustees had opposed this, however, and the order was not made until March 1893. The trustees had then started proceedings in the Chancery Division – and this had prevented the money being paid out of court. O'Shea 'has lodged a proposal for a scheme of arrangement, by which his estate will become vested in a trustee for administration and distribution as in bankruptcy'. This was accepted by the Senior Official Receiver.[75]

On 7 March, there was further consideration of the legal action brought to execute the trusts of the marriage settlements of William O'Shea and Katharine Parnell. What was remarkable about this litigation against the trustees is that Mr Ingle Joyce acted for Mrs Parnell and two of her daughters; Mr Vernon R.

Smith for the son (who had attained twenty-one) and Mr A. R. Kirby for another daughter.[76] There is no further detail on this. In 1894, the ages of the children were as follows: Gerard, twenty-four; Norah, twenty-one; Carmen, nineteen; Clare, eleven, and Katie, ten. It is possible that Norah, having attained her majority, was represented on her own, or that one of the younger girls was not represented. And Katie was still involved in incessant litigation.

The financial problems continued for everyone. At a public examination on 17 March 1894, O'Shea testified to having liabilities of over £17,000, with assets estimated at just over £4,000. The report stated that the debtor 'who appeared to be in a delicate state of health was allowed to be seated during his examination'. The Captain claimed that in addition to his expensive litigation, he had not received the costs awarded to him after the divorce case. 'He considered that he still had a claim for the balance against the co-respondent's estate', O'Shea had declared, 'but he could not say whether it was a valuable asset, as he had not been able to discover anything about the estate.'[77] On 26 May, it was resolved that the arrangement O'Shea had proposed would be postponed, as some creditors had objected. On 26 June, the scheme was rejected as a result of the creditors' objections, and bankruptcy proceedings supervened.[78]

Katie was no more fortunate. It later transpired that one of the trustees, who was also her solicitor, Arthur Stopford Francis, had taken some of the money from her fund, and made out large loans to himself. In yet another court case, Katie and Gerard took action. In the King's Bench Division, a report of the case was presented on 4 April 1901. This explained that, in 1898, Katharine Parnell and three of her children had applied to release funds from her trust. They transferred these funds to a new trust to pay income to her and the children for life. A settlement was executed on 26 January 1899, of which Katie and her son Gerard were trustees. This settlement had a very wide investment clause, which was subsequently abused by Francis. Astonishingly, it transpired that

Katie had objected to the proceedings being taken against the respondent, and that she and Mr O'Shea still had absolute confidence in him.[79] This was contradicted by Katie's account. She claimed in her book that she had become suspicious of the trustee, and had sent Gerard to ask George Lewis for his help.

'Apart from the very serious loss it entailed upon me,' she recollected, 'the downfall of my trustee, clever, good-looking and altogether charming, was a great blow to us all. He had been so much a friend, and I and my son and daughters had trusted him so completely.'[80] O'Connor wrote that 'Mrs. Parnell' was 'not a woman who could ever be trusted with the management of money'. He recounted that upon discovering, through George Lewis, the fraud, she had insisted on helping the trustee, and had actually put up a sum of £3,000 to help defend him. 'Her efforts were in vain', he wrote, '... and she never got either the money of which she had been robbed or any of the three thousand pounds she had contributed to her despoiler's defence.'[81]

O'Connor claimed that, after Parnell's death, Katharine's mind 'varied' but was 'never quite normal'. Her state became 'so acute', he recounted, that soon after her husband's death, she was confined to a nursing home for two years. There is no corroborating evidence of this. O'Connor also wrote that Katharine had a 'mania for taking new houses... She took up all kinds of leases of houses, and every change of abode involved the removal of her large household – her daughters, her horses, her dogs, and her furniture.' He claimed that among the places she took houses after her husband's death, towns on the south coast of England for the most part, were: Brighton, Pangbourne, Folkestone, Hastings, Hove, Bournemouth, Maidenhead, Tremanton Castle, Saltash, Sea View on the Isle of Wight, Teignmouth, Chichester, Burnham, Worthing, and Littlehampton, adding 'but even this long list is not complete'.[82]

There were bankruptcy proceedings against her, at least once, he declared, and her goods were put up for auction. He had heard differing accounts of her state of mind, he wrote. 'She had, in spite of all her troubles, a certain strength of will which carried her through her many misfortunes, and, above all, through the death of the man to whom she gave such concentrated devotion.' On the whole she was 'fairly normal, except for an interval when she became mentally unbalanced'.[83] The details of Katie's life after she lost her husband are very sketchy. There is, as we have seen, sufficient evidence to ascertain that she was not financially secure. An overall picture of a restless, rootless life does emerge. She wrote herself in 1914 of how 'the space and beauty' of her childhood home at Rivenhall had left her 'with a sad distaste for the little houses of many conveniences that it has been my lot to inhabit for the greater part of my life'.[84]

Norah O'Shea stayed loyal to her mother and lived with her until Katie died. The census records of 1901 show that Katie was living in south Dorset, with a full household. In addition to Norah (aged twenty-eight) were her two younger daughters, Clare and Katie, aged eighteen and sixteen. The household was still reasonably prosperous, one imagines, with a complement of four servants. These comprised a cook, a housemaid, a coachman and a young boy of thirteen. Gerard and Carmen continued to live with their father, it is believed. The Captain died of chronic interstitial nephritis, leading to cardiac failure, in Hove on 22 April 1905.[85] *The Times* wrote of his role as an intermediary between Mr Parnell and Mr Gladstone, Mr Chamberlain and Mr W. E. Forster. It was observed, however, that after resigning his Galway seat, O'Shea had 'disappeared almost as completely from political life as his name has disappeared for many years past from public knowledge'.[86] T. P. O'Connor commented in his newspaper column that 'whatever his faults, Captain O'Shea was always personally a very agreeable man. Indeed, in the centre of the cyclone which he caused, his own very interesting personality has too often been entirely ignored. As a matter of fact, he was a man of very considerable abilities'.[87]

In 1896, Gerard O'Shea married his first cousin, Cristobel Barrett-Lennard. One of Katie's early biographers, who had conversations with surviving family members, wrote that this marriage took place because Gerard had seduced Cristobel, and she became pregnant. His uncle, Sir Thomas, had insisted that Gerard marry his daughter. The union was not a happy one, and their child was severely disabled.[88] Carmen married Dr Arthur Buck. He practised in Hove, and was the physician who signed her father's death certificate. He divorced her in 1914, and she married Edward Lucas. This second marriage also failed. Carmen was living alone in a flat in Worthing, when she was discovered dead of chronic pleurisy and heart disease on 23 December 1921.[89] There is almost no information on how much contact either Gerard or Carmen had with their mother. It is clear that Gerard was in touch with her, though, as he helped her some years later with the publication of her book on Parnell, published in 1914.

On 25 July 1907 the youngest of Katharine's children, her daughter Katie, married Louis Moule, a Lieutenant in the East Lancashire Regiment.[90] They travelled out to West Africa, apparently, and she did not return to England until after her mother's death. Clare, raised in part by the devout Norah, became a firm Catholic. She did not, however, grow up in the faith, as she made her Holy Communion very late, at the age of twenty, in October 1903. She was very religious and began contributing articles to the *Catholic Fireside.* Clare also had short stories accepted for publication, and her first novel, *The Story of Audrey,* was serialized in the *Monthly Magazine of Fiction* in 1904. She published too in 1906 an edition of lectures on the Holy Eucharist given by Professor Charles Coupe – who had given her religious instruction.[91]

Clare met a young Irish surgeon, Bertram Maunsell, who practised at Kettering General Hospital in Northampton. They met on 29 October 1907 and were married just a few months later, on 8 February 1908, at the Servite Church.[92] This seems to have been the only successful marriage of all of Katie's children by O'Shea and Parnell. The happy union was, however, sadly cut short. Clare gave birth on 16 November 1909 to a son, Assheton (who would be Parnell's only grandchild), and tragically died next day of a haemorrhage in a nursing home in London. Maunsell remarried and had more children,[93] but he later wrote to Assheton that he had never recovered from Clare's death. Assheton 'was several times taken to see his grandmother, Mrs. Parnell', according to a family descendant, Father John Maunsell.[94] He also recalled 'the faithful Aunt Nora [*sic*] coming down to see Assheton'.[95] On a further tragic note, Assheton was to die prematurely and without known issue of enteric fever in 1934, while serving in the army in India.

But information beyond these sparse details is absent. Katie was not among the mourners at Clare's funeral, although Gerard and Norah were present. A further fraud took place with Katie's money in 1906. Once again, a trustee made off with her funds. The amount that was salvaged was invested in the Grand Railway of Canada, which ceased to pay dividends in 1913.[96] Katie was thus without any means of support. Coinciding with this trauma was the publication in September 1913 of the letter Parnell had written to O'Brien about the upcoming divorce. In an introduction to this previously unpublished correspondence, O'Brien wrote:

It is notorious that it was the painful character of the uncontradicted evidence in the O'Shea v. Parnell divorce suit that turned the public condemnation of the great Irishman's fault into bitter indignation and disgust. It is now certain that if Parnell had been allowed to go into the witness-box the public verdict upon the entire transaction would have been altogether revolutionized. The fault would have remained, but the Irish leader would have been shown to be rather the victim than the destroyer of a happy home, and the divorce would never have taken place.[97]

This was too much for Gerard O'Shea, who continued to show great touchiness where his father's name and reputation were concerned. He immediately sent a letter to *The Times* in which he protested 'against the scandalous insinuations' made by William O'Brien in the *Cork Free Press* and subsequently reproduced in *The Times*. He asserted that O'Brien's deduction was 'a slander' upon his late father and his mother, 'and absolutely without foundation'. Then, in what was the first intimation of anything of the kind, he reproduced a letter from his mother, in which she declared that she was, as a result of 'the unwarrantable interpretation Mr. O'Brien has put upon the letter of my husband's he has published', proposing – with Gerard's consent – to publish 'as soon as possible myself the letters of my late husband, which, as you know, I had left directions should be published after my death'.[98]

The outcome of this was the announcement of the forthcoming publication by Messrs Cassell of two volumes, 'entitled "Charles Stewart Parnell: His Love Story and Political Life", by Katharine O'Shea (Mrs. Charles Stewart Parnell)'.[99] That this was undoubtedly a money-making exercise is evidenced by the fact that Gerard was clearly not so touchy about the prominence of 'Parnell' in the title. It was on this basis, of course, that 'remarkable facts of a character not hitherto made public'[100] were to be revealed, that the book was marketed. The *Daily Sketch* serialized the book in a number of sensational articles. With enticing headings such as 'Captain O'Shea's Challenge to a Duel' (7 May), 'Mrs. O'Shea as Secret Messenger from Parnell to Gladstone' (8 May) and, most sensationally of all, 'When Parnell Offered to Resign and Give Up Politics for Mrs. O'Shea's Sake' (12 May), Katie was at last having her say.

CHAPTER TWENTY

Revelations: Cashing In

KATIE'S BOOK CAUSED HUGE consternation when it was published in May 1914. The description of her role as unofficial go-between was very embarrassing for the Liberals. The Conservative press made as much capital as they could over the scandalous revelations. There were many objections on the grounds of decency. The *Daily Express* pronounced that the account of Mrs Parnell's husband 'is a tragic, pitiful revelation, a dragging down of idols, the telling of a story that ought never to have been told'.[1] *The Times* review described the work at length, and concluded that there was

something like desecration in baring the secret of that strong heart. There are women whom nothing on earth could move to such an act. Mrs. Parnell has not only bared her husband's secret; she has set it out with scraps of poetry and all the arts of a clever writer. She speaks of the deep pain the disclosure has cost her. Did Mr. William O'Brien's statements of last September necessitate it? Do they justify it or excuse it? Opinions and feelings, we think, will differ. Men – and women – must judge for themselves.[2]

There was some favourable comment as well. In London, the *Spectator* asserted that 'Anything tending to show the inner working of the mind of this most remarkable man is interesting even at this date.'[3]

In the United States, there were mixed reviews. The New York *Nation* pronounced that 'Botanizing on a mother's grave is nothing to this'.[4] The *Bookman* pointed out that the 'frankness of the narrative is more obvious than its good taste'.[5] 'The story startles and compels attention,' wrote the *Saturday Review*, adding, 'What the world will think of the author's discretion or taste in printing some of the love letters is a very different matter.'[6] But *The New York Times* wrote that this was a 'work of unusual standing among those which profess to describe, the relations between man and woman'.[7]

The memoir was a huge commercial success. Within days of the first print run, it had sold out. On 22 May, the publishers announced that 'The Most Remarkable Book of the Year' was being reprinted.[8] The lurid advertising, the sensationalist serialization, complete with illustrations such as the famous rose Parnell had supposedly preserved, and then the scandalized reviews, all contributed to a great success in financial terms. The book ran to three printings and was much discussed.

Henry Harrison was appalled by the publication. There had been some talk, he later wrote, of his writing, with Katharine's help, a biography of Parnell, just after he died. He had assumed that the idea had been discarded, and was astonished at some of the claims made in Katie's book. He published his own book, years later, in 1931. In *Parnell Vindicated: The Lifting of the Veil*, Harrison protested passionately against the content of Katharine's story. This version of events flatly contradicted what he had been told, he claimed. In addition, there were inconsistencies which he proceeded to analyse in great detail. Harrison tried not to blame Katharine too directly. He alluded to a lack of mental stability and judgement on her part. 'The end of her seventh decade was drawing near,' he explained, 'the surer touch of self-confident maturity had suffered an inevitable declension.'[9]

Harrison was also convinced that Gerard O'Shea had played a leading role in the composition of the work. The book 'was avowedly prepared and published at the instance of Captain O'Shea's son, who "was jealous of his father's honour"... Her book thus avowedly owed its origin to an O'Shea prompting, and it has in it not a little incorporated or interpolated matters of a pronouncedly O'Shea complexion.'[10] There was significance, he asserted, to the fact that the author's name 'Katharine O'Shea' was set in much bolder type than the subtitled 'Mrs. Charles Stewart Parnell'.[11] But Harrison's claim that Katharine was not responsible for the work, due to a lack of mental acuity, was not borne out by the evidence of a press conference which was held for the publication of the memoir.

The *Daily Mail* reported that at this interview Mrs Parnell '(Katharine O'Shea)' had 'an air of distinction and an unmistakable charm of manner'. Her 'vivacious eyes have a wonderful depth and fire', the article continued, 'and the face, fresh and mobile, is crowned with snow-white hair'. Katie declared that Parnell was a perfect lover, 'always most gentle, tender, and considerate; but even here he was sternly compelling, fiercely jealous, uncompromising and passionate, brooking nothing that stood between us, giving all and exacting all. To a woman of my temperament he was the ideal lover. Until I met him I could not dream that such happiness could be in real life.'

'The book is in no sense an apology,' she staunchly declared. She claimed that Parnell would have approved of the work. 'I had no idea at all of publishing', she said 'until Mr. O'Brien put that letter from my husband in a certain Irish paper and added as comment his own unreasoning imaginations.'[12] And indeed Katie used her book to give her own verdict on Parnell's colleagues, and on O'Brien. 'But now, after all these years,' she wrote, 'one of Parnell's erstwhile followers has arisen to explain to another generation that Parnell was not really such a man as this, that he was one of Ireland's eternal failures.'[13] She and her husband had been united, she declared, in their condemnation of the hypocrisy of those who had abused them. She and he had felt for them 'a contempt unspeakable'.[14]

In Ireland, the publication of the book was greeted at first by silence. The timing was especially unfortunate. In 1893 Gladstone had made another attempt at passing a Home Rule Bill. Although it was passed in the Commons (with difficulty), the Lords took just four days to reject it. The Prime Minister made no further attempt to enact the legislation. The opportunity for Home Rule was, for the time being, lost. The Parnell split had opened up divisions within the Irish Party as well as within the Liberal Party. In Ireland, the Nationalist movement took on a new direction, one that explicitly linked a Gaelic revival with independence. This 'new' nationalism was manifested by the foundation of the Gaelic League (1893), the Irish Literary Theatre (1899), the Abbey Theatre (1904) and the radical group Sinn Féin in 1907.

Divisions remained between the Parnellites, led by Redmond, and their opponents, led by McCarthy, Dillon, Tim Healy and William O'Brien. Even within this latter group, there were factions and the warfare between Healy and Dillon had come to a head in 1895. The Nationalist movement had thus continued to be fragmented, although many initiatives were taken during the period up to 1916.[15] After much struggle and internecine fighting, the campaign for Home Rule in Ireland reached its zenith between 1912 and 1914 under the leadership of Redmond. The Liberal Prime Minister, Henry Herbert Asquith, was prepared to introduce the Third Home Rule Bill. The opposition this time was from a new source, the die-hard Ulster Unionists. They were opposed to any legislation that granted Ireland independence.

In January 1913 they took decisive action. The Ulster Unionist Council decided to raise their own army, the Ulster Volunteer Force (UVF). It was to be made up of 100,000 men. By June of that year, the UVF was recruiting above expectations. The Unionists were supported in their struggle to reject Home Rule by the British Conservatives. Redmond had at first rejected any separate plans for Ulster. His position was not very strong, however, and by March 1914 Asquith had persuaded him to (most reluctantly) accept that the government should at least be prepared to initiate proposals for Ulster. The Irish Nationalists were once again faced with the prospect of a split. There were those who would follow Redmond's moderate and cooperative stance, and those who refused categorically to contemplate any special treatment for Ulster.

So when Katie's book was published in the spring of 1914, it was most unwelcome. One side of the Irish Party was becoming more radicalized (Sinn Féin) just as Redmond was hoping to achieve a constitutional breakthrough. The last thing he needed was the publicity given to a book that opened some of the worst wounds suffered by the party. Many in Ireland agreed.

A successful boycott of Katie's book was organized by the Dublin Vigilance Committee, a Catholic pro-censorship pressure group, and a meeting was held by the group on 14 June. British newspapers carrying notices of the book were boycotted and Catholic booksellers were asked not to stock the offending work. Although some advertising continued to appear in certain Dublin papers, it was, according to historian Roy Foster, 'the most effective voluntary black-out of a scandal by the press until the Abdication crisis'.[16] Only the *Independent*[17] published a view of this 'work of shocking character... giving the revolting details of a disedifying liaison... with an audacity and effrontery that must be repulsive to every decent man and woman'.[18]

The Irish *Nation* also published a response. 'We think this book ought not to have been written,' the article began. 'It can serve no useful purpose... Parnell's love-letters have, it is stated, been published with reluctance. Be it so. We can only regret that the reluctance was overcome.'[19] Although the book was largely ignored, there were people who avidly read it. William Butler Yeats, his father and Lady Gregory all devoured the work. Yeats as a poet was particularly inspired by the memoir.[20]

Katie made money out of the publication, and seems to have been entirely at ease with her revenge. She lived for another seven years in obscurity. It was as if the book, with all its controversy, was her last say on the matter. After all the years of scandal and notoriety, Katie faded quietly out of existence. On 1 February 1921, Norah, who had come from London to nurse her ailing mother, wrote to Harrison. He had not been in touch with the family, he recalled, save that John Redmond had informed him that Parnell's daughters had, when grown up, made themselves known to him. They had avowed themselves proud to be Parnell's children, Redmond had told him.[21] Norah informed him that her mother was 'dying, slowly and painfully, of heart disease'. Her mother 'had the happy delusion', she continued, 'that Parnell comes to her at night, when things are worst, and draws her "out of the black waves"'.

Norah continued:

She has never stopped mourning Parnell and I, knowing the misery of her heart and soul, have spent my life in keeping her from the follies of so many human ways of 'forgetting for a little while' when I could: and when I couldn't in nursing her back to health and sanity. Her periods of delusion have always been Parnell, Parnell, Parnell. Of course my point of view of Parnell and hers, and no doubt yours, is by no means similar, but in bringing up his two girls, Clare and Katie, for my mother's sake I have come to view a great man with inimical toleration. Your little playmate Clare died when her boy was born ten years ago. She married happily, a doctor in —, an Irishman. He has married again. Clare's boy is doing well at school, a clever little chap. His head is just the shape of his grandfather's like Clare's.[22]

On 5 February 1921, Katharine Parnell drew her last breath at a small terraced house in Littlehampton. It was a far cry from the faded splendours of Rivenhall. And, after all those years of promises and dreams, she had never travelled to the land of her 'King'. Instead, during the years after her husband's death, Katie seems to have drifted incessantly in small seaside towns. The money problems that plagued her led to lesser and lesser accommodation. Some biographers have interpreted Norah's delicate remarks as suggestive of an alcohol problem. This is possible, and would explain the chronic problem of funds. There is, however, no evidence of this. It does seem likely that her nervous temperament led to mental instability. A former employee of the seaside Royal Court Hotel, where she had stayed some eighteen months before her death, claimed that she had been 'the most eccentric woman he had ever known'. He asserted that she 'would get up at two o'clock in the morning to go to the front'.[23]

Katie's funeral took place on 8 February in Littlehampton. There were only four family mourners. They were her son Gerard and his wife, her daughter Norah, and her son-in-law Bertram Maunsell. It was a quiet and sad end to her notorious life. There were articles in the newspapers, commenting on the death of the 'Woman Who Changed Irish History'.[24]

There is little known about her children. After her mother's death, O'Connor recalled that Norah, now forty-eight, was left 'practically penniless'. He received an appeal to help her, and he wrote that he had found her some 'temporary employment, and she went as nursery governess for a while to a French family'. She was determined to train as a professional nurse, and did so, adopting her mother's maiden name of Wood.[25] Norah contracted the very painful disease of lupus erythematosus and died of septic pneumonia in July 1923. Norah O'Shea was buried beside her mother in Littlehampton Cemetery.[26]

Of Gerard there was little trace save a re-surfacing in May 1936 to object to a play about Parnell. As ever, his foremost sensitivity was over his father's reputation. 'No one had the temerity', he wrote, 'to publish in my father's lifetime that he was a blackmailer.'[27]

An 'interesting development' was later reported, that Gerard O'Shea had 'gone to Hollywood as technical adviser for the film now being made, which is based on the play'.[28] After this presumably profitable resolution of his objections, Gerard disappeared from public view and no more is known of his life.

Clare was dead, Carmen died soon after her mother, and Norah died some two years after Katie. There was further tragedy when, as we have seen, Katie's grandson, Assheton, died in 1934. He was unmarried, and left no known children. There remained the younger Katie O'Shea. She reappeared in an extraordinary newspaper interview in November 1937. There was possibly some public interest in Parnell after the successful play. The headline read 'Boarding-House Keeper Says "I was Parnell's Favourite Daughter"'. In what was by now firm family tradition, it went on, 'And Now My Money Has Gone'. Mrs Katherine Moule, aged fifty-two, claimed to be Parnell's youngest child. She was living in 'a bleak bedroom at the top of the house'. She declared that her mother had left her £2,000,[29] with which she had purchased the house in Mornington Crescent in London. Now the money had run out. Mrs Moule asserted that when her mother had died, her silence was seen as 'callousness'. In fact, she had been 'numb with unhappiness. She was wonderful to her children. No one could have had a better mother.'[30] Given the circumstances, it was a somewhat sad but perhaps fitting epitaph to Katharine Parnell's astonishing life.

EPILOGUE

When You are Old and Grey

Ireland is a small nation whose size, poverty and long-time colonial status have made it easy to dismiss as unimportant. Irish nationalism resembles nothing so much as a response to that kind of dismissal.

> William Michael Murphy, *The Parnell Myth and Irish Politics 1891–1956*, p. 3.

Just how important was Katie and Parnell's affair in the overall context of Irish Nationalist aspirations? The scandal and its political consequences certainly accelerated the collapse of Irish hopes of Home Rule legislation in the late nineteenth century. These ambitions were then crushed more severely by Parnell's untimely death. Many believed on both sides of the Irish Sea that Ireland's best expectations for constitutional reform were lost at this moment. This is probably overstating the case. Parnell was not necessarily needed to achieve Home Rule when Gladstone would return to power. But the myth of Parnell suggested that he was. And, further, it is an all too common feature of Anglo-Irish politics to give a supposed pivotal event, such as Parnell's death, too much weight. Roy Foster has questioned the idea of a turning point throughout Anglo-Irish history, 'after which nothing would be quite the same again'. He singles out 1885–6 as one such occasion, for example, and another in 1914, when it became clear that Asquith's Liberal government would not impose Home Rule on Ulster by force.

Foster challenges the idea of a turning point, stating that it has been one of the 'specific preoccupations'[1] in understanding and indeed anticipating the direction of Anglo-Irish relations. Although the fall of Parnell, with the ensuing extinguishment of nationalist hopes for Home Rule in the early 1890s, could be considered such a turning point, it fits neatly into the concept of a continuum of never-ending negotiations, which almost achieve a desired result, only to fail at the last hurdle. But one can also see, as Foster argues, that there have been in any event many such turning points, and that their outcomes have been complex and varied. It is probably too simplistic to say that this was such a turning point, or that, if so, it was indeed responsible for the failure of Ireland to achieve independence at this time.

However, there is no question but that peaceful, constitutional reform became far more elusive. The biggest problem for the Irish Party after Parnell's death was leadership. No one figure emerged to control the party as he had. Although the party was disciplined and not ineffective in the years after the split, it continued to suffer from internal power struggles. Redmond was in many respects a good leader, who pursued a constitutional strategy and maintained links with the Liberals, but he lacked Parnell's control and charisma. And the divisiveness had left a legacy of great bitterness. Under Parnell, separatist behaviour had been ruthlessly stamped out, and the battle was directed at the English – although, it must be noted, Parnell's own behaviour during the split actually encouraged separatism. So, although the phase of high Parnellism had been very effective, there had been dissent – much of which was exposed and further exacerbated during the rift after the leader's death.

The advent of the First World War postponed Irish independence yet further. By the time proposed legislation was ready for enactment, the Ulster position had become so deeply entrenched that separation was almost inevitable. There is thus a good case to be made that the momentum garnered under Parnell's leadership was lost to the cause of Irish nationalism, and lost for ever. What is possibly more interesting to observe is how the myth of Parnell and his downfall has become intricately associated with this failure to achieve some form of independence for Ireland in the 1880s. It has been argued that for many Irish nationalists, it was a source of consolation to blame Parnell's downfall for setting back the cause of Home Rule, rather than British reluctance to grant it and to wield their ultimate superiority in the decision-making process.[2]

But it can be seen that at the time Katie was assigned much of the blame. Her greatest transgression was this foray into the public sphere. She possibly could have continued her unorthodox lifestyle indefinitely. One could argue that her husband would never have been tempted to take advantage of her vulnerable situation if Parnell had not been such a famous man. Yet this is at the very heart of Katie's dilemma. All of the most exciting things happened to her because of her lover's position. The interaction with Gladstone, the late nights drafting documents, the parliamentary sessions – all these were part and parcel of a well-known politician's existence. And there is little doubt that Katie loved the fact that her lover was famous. Her book makes that perfectly clear. She may have loved Parnell the man, but she also loved Parnell the political hero. The nicknames of 'King' and 'Queenie' are really very telling. It is difficult to imagine that Katie did not harbour – encouraged by her lover – dreams of a high position once Parnell was in power.[3] And Katie was able to cash in on that celebrity status when she needed to, in 1914.

Katie thus seems to have faced a problem with very modern resonance. She enjoyed the benefits and allure of public success – albeit on the tailcoat of her lover. What she suffered when it all went wrong was the downside of celebrity. Her name became a byword in notoriety. She was publicly mocked and pilloried. Healy completely dehumanized and humiliated her, his excuse being that it was her own fault for placing herself in the public domain. Arguably, Katie did not overtly seek a public role for herself. However, she did not hesitate to use her contacts with public figures when she wanted something. She appealed to Gladstone and Grosvenor on numerous occasions, not just for Parnell, but also for her husband's advancement, and then for her own benefit when she needed a well-known physician to examine her aunt. She used the medium of a widely publicized and sensationalized book to make money when funds ran out. That she so obviously and callously traded on her notoriety and Parnell's fame was one of the reasons his colleagues were so incensed (and hurt) by the publication.

The very public nature of the scandal was of course made possible by the newspapers. Ironically, it was precisely through the press that Parnell had achieved much of his success. The press in Ireland had played a critical role in bringing the land agitation message throughout the country. Just as the provincial press had developed in England, the Irish provincial press grew dramatically throughout the nineteenth century. Between 1880 and 1886 alone, the Irish nationalist press swelled by 25 per cent, from forty-one to fifty-five newspapers.[4] The *Nation* was intensely loyal to the 'Chief' and editor T. D. Sullivan even went so far as to claim that Ireland's 'King' was twentieth in lineal descent from King Edward I.[5] McCarthy asserted that for the 'impressionable younger generation educated in the national schools "the newspapers were their evangel, Mr Parnell their saviour, and his lieutenants their apostles"'.[6]

Parnell grasped early on that he could use the press to communicate with a large and varied audience. His mythic status was achieved through the combination of his personal charisma and aloofness, alongside this mass mobilization tool. Parnell's mystique was cultivated by the Irish nationalist press, and even the British media contributed to his elevation in the public mind by continually singling him out. The negative press the leader received in England was also effective in adding to the Parnell myth. Publicity became the leader's most potent weapon, especially as it was built on very little personal information. Rather, the leader's frequent disappearances and remote demeanour enabled the press to create a mythic figure.

The charismatic leader holds power when people believe in his extraordinary qualities, but his hold on this authority is tenuous, and it is forfeited when he fails, or falls from grace.[7] Parnell's greatest transgression was, in the words of one historian, 'in dashing the dream people had of him, the unfettered faith in which he had been venerated in Catholic Ireland'.[8] Parnell asserted with confidence that his authority came from the Irish people. What he could not fathom is why the people would care about his personal living arrangements. He believed that his public and private lives were entirely separate. This of course was not true. The overlap was conspicuous on a number of levels.

He worked at various times closely with Willie O'Shea. He and the Captain shared a political vision for a period, and had the same colleagues. Whatever O'Shea's private arrangements were regarding his relations with his spouse, the fact that the leader was working closely with his mistress's husband was bound to create discomfort for those same colleagues. The second area of significant overlap from private to public and vice versa was that of the leader's finances. It has been seen that the Irish MPs had to be paid out of a central fund. Often the money used for such purposes had been raised to help struggling tenants. The application of Party funds was, however, nebulous. There were arguments over how the cash was to be distributed and over who had access. These arguments were exacerbated after the leader's death, as we have seen.

McCarthy wrote of how careless Parnell was with money. The leader was accustomed to paying many of his expenses from Party funds. It is not very clear where the personal and the professional diverged in his mind, and this is most probably because for him (and other senior members of the Irish Party) the demarcation was not plain. In essence, they were always working. The lines between public and private were quite blurred.

Thus on these levels alone Parnell's life was lived in both the public and the private sphere. He may have refused to believe that the two overlapped significantly, but his denial was not enough for many of his supporters. For Gladstone and the Liberals, he became a liability when the negative publicity surrounding his private life jeopardized the political process and his political partners. The mockery engendered by the details of Parnell's affair provided fodder to his enemies. Lord Hartington – who was himself living in an adulterous arrangement with the Duchess of Manchester – told the Queen when the scandal broke, 'I never thought anything in politics could give me as much pleasure as this does.'[9]

He was not alone in enjoying the scandal. There was an avid market for such stories. T. P. O'Connor had launched his radical paper, the halfpenny evening *Star*, in January 1888. He put a gossip column, entitled 'Mainly About People', on the very front page. This was a shocking innovation, and many of his rivals criticized the move, but sales rocketed. One of the main reasons for its success was the way O'Connor developed some of the techniques of the 'New Journalism'. One of the features of this new style was the personal factor. It had originated from America, where since the 1840s the *New York Herald* had successfully pioneered a breezy gossip column that featured stories of the rich and fashionable.[10] Its reporters sought out the 'floating gossip, scandal and folly'[11] of society. Although the penny press had hitherto furnished plenty of dramatic stories of crime, sensational trials and political and sexual misdeeds, this was the first attempt to create a market avid to learn more about the doings of the fashionable and wealthy. It was the first foray into the creation of a market for celebrity.

In Britain there had been an initial reluctance to follow this path. Gossip had remained confined to a select number of mainly political journals. But when O'Connor launched his column, its instant success was imitated, and celebrity culture was introduced to British society. T. D. Stead famously followed suit in sensationalizing the British press. By the time Katie's affair was exposed in public, there was a ready market for the shocking details. It was the ruin of Parnell, and the loss of her reputation and place in society. By the time she wrote her book, there was even more appetite for intimate details of her affair. The serialization pandered to its audience by actively promoting the more sentimental and lurid titbits it could extract from the story. In a thoroughly modern twist, Katie's story was marketed to a readership eager to learn more about the juicy human elements of her tale. It comes as no surprise that the book ended with Parnell's death. No one wanted to read about her sad decline thereafter.

Dramatic love stories have changed the course of history. Katie and Parnell's story is one. Another is Henry VIII's determination to marry Anne Boleyn – and a passionate desire for a son – that led to the establishment of the Church of England. A more modern example would be that of King Edward VIII's abandonment of the throne to marry the American divorcée, Wallis Simpson. Tales of adultery – such as the stories of Lancelot and Guinevere, Tristan and Isolde or Madame Bovary – have always held particular fascination. There is a magnificence in the large gesture and the extravagance of all-encompassing emotions that inspires song, poetry, great literature and opera. One of the deepest criticisms of Katie's book, however, was of the pedestrian nature of Parnell's letters and the mawkish sentimentality and domesticity they evoked. It was as though the big hero had sinned further, by not living a larger-than-life love affair to justify the risks he had taken. That Katie and her lover were portrayed in her book as a middle-class bourgeois couple completely spoiled the dramatic effect and eroded possible sympathy. It was painful for Irish men and women to accept that their dreams of long-awaited independence had been sacrificed on the altar of such a mundane affair.

Perhaps Katie's greatest punishment for her transgression lies in her legacy. Her children's lives for the most part were unhappy, with little trace left of their existence. William O'Shea has practically disappeared from history. As one reviewer astutely commented in 1914, 'Captain O'Shea is the embarrassing phantom of the story.'[13] Parnell, on the other hand, has been accorded heroic status in Ireland. His statue stands proud at the top of Dublin's O'Connell Street. There is a Parnell Street, and a Parnell Square. The Kilmainham Gaol Museum holds a collection of 'relics' belonging to him. He is revered as a great figure in the struggle for Irish independence.

Katie's legacy, on the other hand, is an international chain of Irish pubs, called 'Kitty O'Shea's'. Her name is so very much no longer her own that the pub group and the hotel giant Hilton went to court in 2002 over who had the right to exploit it commercially. The headline ran: 'Kitty O'Shea takes on Hilton'.[14] The remaining traces of her legacy are the notoriety for which she became a household name. She has gone down in history as the woman who caused the downfall of Parnell, and changed the course of Irish history. What I suspect she would have enjoyed, though, is the recognition by the world of the importance of her love affair. Katie always thrived on being the centre of attention – which is probably why she was one of the first of the modern 'celebrities'. I think that, like many of our present-day celebrities, being remembered at all would please her enormously.

Notes

PROLOGUE: MISTRESS OF THE IRISH PARTY

1. *The People*, Sunday 30 August 1925.
2. Katharine O'Shea (Mrs Charles Parnell), *Charles Stewart Parnell: His Love Story and Political Life, Volume II*, p.164.

CHAPTER ONE: A VICAR'S DAUGHTER

1. This is somewhat ironic, however, as Queen Victoria notoriously did not care for children. She was much put out by childbirth, and deeply resented her pregnancies as a constraint on her romantic relationship with her beloved husband, Albert. See Christopher Hibbert, *Queen Victoria: A Personal History*.

2. There is a great deal of information on this and other details of family background in Minna Evangeline Bradhurst, *A Century of Letters 1820–1920: Letters from Literary Friends to Lady Wood and Mrs. A. C. Steele.*
3. O'Shea, *Parnell, Vol. I*, p.12. Note: although these volumes are Katie's memoirs of Parnell, they are also the reminiscences of her own life.
4. K. Theodore Hoppen, *The Mid-Victorian Generation 1840–1860*, p.34.
5. For a life of Queen Caroline, see Flora Fraser, *The Unruly Queen: The Life of Queen Caroline.*
6. James Beresford Atley, *The Lives of the Victorian Chancellors, Vol. II*, pp.334–5.
7. Bradhurst, *A Century of Letters*, p.8.

8. See Fraser, *The Unruly Queen*, p.458.

9. Bradhurst, *A Century of Letters*, p.17.

10 See Atlay, *The Victorian Chancellors, Vol. II*, p.338.

11. Bradhurst, *A Century of Letters*, p.12.

12. Ibid., p.17.

13. Ibid., p.11.

14. O'Shea, *Parnell, Vol. I*, p.6.

15. Bradhurst, *A Century of Letters*, p.13.

16. John Angell James, 1856; cited by Hoppen, *The Mid-Victorian Generation*, p.437.

17. Hoppen, *The Mid-Victorian Generation*, p.437.

18. These replaced the missionary vicars-general who had governed the Catholic Church in England and Wales since the sixteenth century.

19. In 1770 there were probably around 80,000 Catholics in England and Wales. This figure dramatically increased to about 750,000 by 1851. There were in 1851 about 30,000 Jews, which increased to about 60,000 by 1882. Hoppen, *The Mid-Victorian Generation*, p.439 and pp.442–3.

20. Hoppen, *The Mid-Victorian Generation*, p.466.

21. Ibid., p.468.

22. Ibid., p.466. See Hoppen's chapter 'Godly People', pp.427–7.1 in this book for a comprehensive survey of religious life in the period 1846–86.

23. Bradhurst, *A Century of Letters*, p.17.

24. Ibid., p.26.

25. Maria Wood to Mrs Pascoe, August 1833, cited by Bradhurst, *A Century of Letters*, pp.20–1.

26. Bradhurst, *A Century of Letters*, p.23.

27. O'Shea, *Parnell, Vol. I*, p.7.

28. Bradhurst, *A Century of Letters*, p.23.

29. Ibid., p.25.

30. Ibid., p.22.

31. O'Shea, *Parnell, Vol. I*, p.21.

32. Bradhurst, *A Century of Letters*, p.x.

33. Ibid., p.x.

34. For this and other childhood memories, see Mrs Bradhurst's collection of Lady Wood and Mrs Anna Steele's letters, privately published as *A Century of Letters*.

35. O'Shea, *Parnell, Vol. I*, pp.12–13.

36. Bradhurst, *A Century of Letters*, p.xi.

37. Ibid., p.xi.

38. O'Shea, *Parnell, Vol. I*, p.14.

39. Bradhurst, *A Century of Letters*, p.19.

40. Ibid.

41. O'Shea, *Parnell, Vol. I*, p.4.

42. Ibid., p.11.

43. Ibid., pp.9–10.

44. Ibid., p.11.

45. Ibid., p.14.

46. Ibid., p.15.

47. Emma Wood to Mr E. S. Dallas (who worked for *The Times*) *c.*1873, cited by Bradhurst, *A Century of Letters*, p.182.

48. O'Shea, *Parnell, Vol. I*, p.17.

49. Ibid., p.18.

50. Bradhurst, *A Century of Letters*, p.26.

51. O'Shea, *Parnell, Vol. I*, p.7.

52. Ibid., p.7.

53. Ibid., p.2.

54. Ibid., p.9.

55. Ibid., pp.20 and 21.

56. Jane Jordan, *Kitty O'Shea: An Irish Affair*, p.7.

57. O'Shea, *Parnell, Vol. I*, p.14.

58. Bradhurst, *A Century of Letters*, p.103.

59. M. Baker, *The Rise of the Victorian Actor*; G. Taylor, *Players and Performances in the Victorian Theatre*; M. R. Booth, *Theatre in the Victorian Age* (all cited by Hoppen, *The Mid-Victorian Generation*, pp.392–3).

60. O'Shea, *Parnell, Vol. I*, p.31.

61. Bradhurst, *A Century of Letters*, p.104.

62. O'Shea, *Parnell, Vol. I*, p.29.

63. Ibid., p.30.

64. Ibid., p.30.

65. Ibid., pp.46–7.

66. Ibid., p.32.

67. Ibid., p.9.

68. Ibid., p.33.

CHAPTER TWO: THE PARNELLS OF AVONDALE

1. John's great-grandfather, Thomas Parnell (1625–86), was the son of a mercer and mayor of Congleton in Cheshire, who came to Ireland around 1660.

The Restoration refers to the return to Charles II in 1660 of the thrones of England, Ireland and Scotland after a series of complex struggles following the deposition in 1659 of Oliver Cromwell's son Richard (who had succeeded his father as Lord Protector following the defeat of the Royalists in the English Civil Wars of 1642–6 and 1648). In seventeenth-century Ireland – as indeed in later centuries – the religious persuasion of the English Regent was of enormous importance. The Restoration provided those individual proprietors with a claim on the King's favour with a return of their properties in Ireland. For others the results were mixed. The ensuing Acts of Settlement and Explanation modified the previous Cromwellian land settlements and, overall, Catholics were left with just over 20 per cent of Irish land – compared with 59 per cent in 1641. The Protestant landed class took on a dominant position, with an effective monopoly of public office until the King's brother, James II, a converted Catholic, succeeded him to the throne in 1685. James II reversed many of the changes that had so helped the Protestants in Ireland, and supported the appointment of Catholics to lead the army, judiciary and civil administration. These advantages were imperilled by James's hasty flight from Ireland after his defeat by William III (the Protestant Prince of the Dutch Republic, who was declared joint Sovereign of England, Ireland and Scotland after the Glorious Revolution of 1688) in the Battle of the Boyne on 1 July 1690.

2. The definition of who made up the eighteenth-century 'Anglo-Irish' was complex. Membership pf this group, according to historian Roy Foster, 'revolved round *Anglicanism*: this defined a social elite, professional as well as landed, whose descent could be Norman, Old English, Cromwellian or even (in a very few cases) ancient Gaelic. Anglicanism conferred exclusivity, in Ireland as in contemporary England; and exclusivity defined the Ascendancy, not ethnic origin. They comprised an elite who monopolized law, politics and "society", and whose aspirations were focussed on the Irish House of Commons' (R. F. Foster, *Modern Ireland 1600–1972*, p.170).

3. Sir John's opposition to the Act of Union did not extend to supporting Catholic emancipation. For a review of the complexities of his career and political positions, see Paul Bew, *Charles Stewart Parnell*, pp.4–5, and, more extensively, R. F. Foster, *Charles Stewart Parnell: The Man and His Family*, pp. 3–13.

4. R. F. Foster's book, *Charles Stewart Parnell*, is invaluable for detailed and accurate information on Parnell's maternal and paternal roots. See in particular pages 54–72.

5. Cited by Robert Kee, *The Laurel and the Ivy: The Story of Charles Stewart Parnell and Irish Nationalism*, p.17.

6. John Howard Parnell, *Charles Stewart Parnell: A Memoir by His Brother*, p.178.

7. These statistics are from K. Theodore Hoppen, *Ireland since 1800: Conflict and Conformity*, p.36. See also W. E. Vaughan, *Landlords and Tenants in Mid-Victorian Ireland*.

8. O'Shea, *Parnell, Vol. II*, p.51.

9. The fungal disease *Phytophthora infestans* arrived first in Belgium in June 1845. Its transmission was rapid, and first signs of it appeared in Ireland by September of that year. The potato was the staple diet of one third of Ireland's population – a very high percentage. Relief measures were instituted swiftly by government and by private organizations such as the Society of Friends. The prevailing ideology of the British government for non-intervention in market forces (laissez-faire) precluded a number of other measures, however. It was believed that strong intervention would trigger bankruptcy of local landlords and result in a dislocation of trade. The collapse of the potato economy would lead, many believed, to a much-needed agricultural reorganization through the consolidation of smaller landholdings and a concomitant removal of surplus population. There was also a concern that local landlords should face their obligations and that local taxation should go towards meeting the demands of relief. There was a persistent belief in England that the crisis had been caused by mismanagement and greed. A severe economic recession in Britain in 1847 did not help matters. In the first year of the famine, 1845–6, Sir Robert Peel's Tory government bought Indian corn meal from America to sell in government depots managed by grand juries and the Board of Trade. Lord John Russell's Whig administration took office in June 1846 and further extended the public work schemes, but refused to intervene in the internal food market or the continuing export of Irish agricultural product. It was not until February 1847 that food kitchens were set up throughout Ireland to feed the starving, many of whom died from diseases such as typhus and relapsing fever. At its peak 3 million meals were being provided daily, but from September of that year the government wound up the scheme, and insisted that further relief should come from workhouses. The death toll was horrific and there was much bitterness even after conditions improved. It would be wrong, however, to assert that the Great Famine was a uniform Irish experience. Various parts of Ireland bore the conditions very differently, and many farmers actually prospered. It is clear that Ireland's economy did not grind to a halt during this period. The progress of new, agriculturally based industries such as brewing, distilling and flour milling, along with the improvements in transport, communications and banking, would have to lead to a more nuanced interpretation of the Great Famine years. It remains, however, a subject of considerable (and vigorous) economic, political and historical debate. See, among many others, Connelly, ed., *The Oxford Companion to Irish History*; Foster, *Modern Ireland*; Hoppen, *Ireland since 1880*; Alvin Jackson, *Home Rule: An Irish History 1800–2000*.

There are very useful and informative first-hand accounts of a landowning landlord at this time in David Thomson with Moyra McGusty, eds., *The Irish Journals of Elizabeth Smith 1840–1850*.

10. See Foster, *Parnell*, pp.xiii–xx.

11. From an estimated 8.175 million in 1841, Ireland's population had dropped to under 5.2 million by 1881. The largest fall was in the decade 1841–51, when the population plunged to 6.5 million – a decline of nearly 20 per cent. This decrease continued, albeit less sharply (although it was followed by a further drop of 11.5 per cent the following decade) and the population went down to 4.2 million in 1926, when the trend slowly began to reverse. See W. E. Vaughan and A. J. Fitzpatrick, eds., *Irish Historical Statistics: Population, 1821–1971*, p.3.

12. Scandinavian involvement with Ireland went on for 400 years. The first Viking raid occurred in 795, and regular raiding continued over the next twenty-five years. After the 830s, larger groups were transported by bigger vessels and commonly terrorized one area for months, before returning to Scandinavia for the winter. The first permanent settlements (*longphorts*) were established in 841 and during the course of the ninth century Dublin developed into an important slaving centre. Dublin rulers such as Olaf the White (d. 871) and Ivar the Boneless (d. 873) were active in Scotland and Northumbria, returning to Dublin with valuables and slaves for the market. The Viking/Norse principal impact on Dublin was not in its raids, however, but the establishment of the town as an important trading centre. By 1172 Hiberno-Norse Dublin was an affluent town of craftsmen with nine churches in the town and another nine immediately outside it. The successful Anglo-Norman invasion of 1170 ultimately put an end to this prosperous epoch and the town received its first Royal Charter shortly thereafter. Dublin subsequently became the capital of Norman Lordship. See Connelly, ed., *The Oxford Companion to Irish History*, pp.159–63, and pp.579–81.

For details of population studies, see W. E. Vaughan and A. J. Fitzpatrick, eds., *Irish Historical Statistics: Population, 1821–1971*, p.5.

13. This 'monumental' edifice, with its embodiment of 'Burlingtonian ideas of classical propriety', cost £95,000. Construction began in 1729, and the building was 'deliberately far grander' than the Parliament at Westminster and 'achieved European primacy among buildings of this kind' (Foster, *Modern Ireland*, p.188).

14. The Act of Union comprised two identical measures passed in

1800 by the Irish and British Parliaments. The Act, negotiated under the supervision of Prime Minister William Pitt, provided that Ireland should be represented in the House of Lords by four bishops and twenty-eight peers, and in the House of Commons by 100 MPs (after 1832, this increased to 105 MPs).

15. The Duke de Stacpoole, *Irish and Other Memories*, cited by Elizabeth Bowen, *The Shelbourne: A Centre in Dublin Life for More than a Century*, pp.83–4.

16. See Bowen, *The Shelbourne*, pp.94–5.

17. See novelist Bowen's evocative descriptions of nineteenth-century Dublin life in *The Shelbourne*.

18. Foster, *Charles Stewart Parnell*, p.64.

19. Cited by Robert Kee, *The Laurel and the Ivy*, p.19.

CHAPTER THREE: KATIE WOOD AND WILLIE O'SHEA

1. See Joyce Marlow, *The Uncrowned Queen of Ireland: The Life of Kitty O'Shea*, p.12. Marlow had access to early family photographs.

2. O'Shea, *Parnell, Vol. I*, p.16.

3. Ibid., p.16.

4. Ibid.

5. Ibid., p.23.

6. Ibid.

7. Ibid.

8. Ibid., p.32.

9. Ibid., p.23.

10. Ibid., pp.33–4.

11. Ibid., p.34.

12. Ibid., p.35.

13. Bradhurst, *A Century of Letters*, p.3.

14. Ibid., p.6.

15. Ibid.

16. Ibid., p.21.

17. Ibid., p.30.

18. Ibid., p.33.

19. Ibid., p.36.

20. Peel (1788–1850) was born in Lancashire and entered Parliament as a Tory in 1809. He was Home Secretary during 1822–7, and 1828–30, and founded the modern police force in addition to reforming the penal laws. He was Prime Minister 1834–5 and 1841–6, when his repeal of the Corn Laws forced him and his supporters to break from the party. After the passing of the Reform Bill of 1832 (which he had resisted) he had reformed the Tories as the Conservative Party. After failing to convince his party to support him in 1846, he and his remaining followers formed a third party, the Peelites. The majority of them, including Gladstone, subsequently rejoined the Liberals.

St Patrick's College at Maynooth in County Kildare had been established in 1795 with government help. This was provided in the hope that Irish Catholic priests would no longer be trained in continental Europe (now increasingly seen as too revolutionary). Peel's proposed bill suggested that the annual grant be made a permanent charge on the consolidated fund and also that an additional £30,000 should be provided for buildings. See Hoppen, *The Mid-Victorian Generation*, p.443, and J. Wolffe, *The Protestant Crusade in Great Britain 1829–1860*, in Hoppen, *The Mid-Victorian Generation*, pp.443–4.

21. Hoppen, *The Mid-Victorian Generation*, p.443.

22. Ibid., pp.444–5.

23. Cited in ibid., pp.445–6.

24. Emma Wood to Mr Dallas, in Bradhurst, *A Century of Letters*, p.83.

25. Bradhurst, *A Century of Letters*, p.83.

26. O'Shea, *Parnell, Vol. I*, p.36.

27. Bradhurst, *A Century of Letters*, p.88.

28. O'Shea, *Parnell, Vol. I*, p.37.

29. Ibid., p.38.

30. Bradhurst, *A Century of Letters*, p.88.

31. O'Shea, *Parnell, Vol. I*, p.43.

32. Ibid., p.44.

33. Ibid.

34. Ibid., p.49.

35. Ibid., p.50.

36. Ibid., p.51.

37. Ibid., p.50.

38. Ibid., p.51.

39. Ibid.

40. Ibid.

41. Bradhurst, *A Century of Letters*, p.91.

42. See Susie Steinbach, *Women in England 1760–1914: A Social History*, p.53.

43. Anna retained his surname, however, and seems to have made the decision to add an 'e'. She used the name 'Mrs Anna C. [for Caroline] Steele'.

44. Bradhurst, *A Century of Letters*, p.86. Whether or not this tale is true, it does show that the Wood family seemed to have accepted Anna's position. This may be because Steel ill-treated her, and they were in Anna's confidence. Whatever the truth, Anna was sheltered by her family, and lived with them after this episode, which was undoubtedly shocking at the time.

45. Maria Chambers (née Wood) to Emma Wood, 15 March 1873, in Bradhurst, *A Century of Letters*, p.87.

46. Bradhurst, *A Century of Letters*, p.109.

47. O'Shea, *Parnell, Vol. I*, p.52.

48. Ibid.

49. Sir Thomas Barrett-Lennard gave Evelyn the £5,000 as a loan. Evelyn Wood, *From Midshipman to Field Marshal*, p.228, and Bradhurst, *A Century of Letters*, pp.81–2.

50. O'Shea, *Parnell, Vol. I*, p.54.

51. Ibid., p.53.

CHAPTER FOUR:
MRS O'SHEA

1. The political dimension of the anti-Catholic legislation is critical. James II (1633–1701) converted to Catholicism in 1669 and succeeded his brother Charles to the throne of England, Ireland and Scotland in 1685. His Catholic sympathies were treated with suspicion in England and he was overthrown in the revolution of 1688. He was replaced by the Protestant William III (1650–1702), Prince of Orange and husband of James's Protestant daughter, Mary (1662–94). Although the revolution was relatively bloodless in England, it led in Ireland to the three-year Williamite War, 1689–91. James II had the support of the French, and Louis XIV sent about 6,000 troops to fight in Ireland. William had to respond decisively to protect British interests. After successful battles, he finally secured victory after secret peace negotiations throughout 1690 that ended in 1691 with the Treaty of Limerick (3 October 1691). This agreement in effect secured the continued dominance of the Protestants in Ireland.

2. Exempt from this law were those Catholics covered by the Treaty of Limerick. Jacobite soldiers were offered free passage to France (from where they could continue their battle as the Irish Brigade), in exchange for surrendering their last stronghold in Limerick. For those who chose to remain in Ireland, there was a guarantee to keep their estates and to continue to practise their professions. If gentlemen or nobles, they would be allowed to continue to carry arms. Included in the concessions – which William deemed a fair price for releasing him from the costs of action in Ireland, which diverted him from his main enemy, France – were guarantees of religious freedoms for Catholics as had been enjoyed under Charles II.

3. This was an attempt to make the penal law self-enforcing. The discoverer legislation was in fact often used by Catholics and Catholic sympathizers to protect their land interests from Protestants.

4. This legislation proposed to admit Catholics to positions from which they were still excluded, despite the Catholic Relief Acts of 1778, 1782 and 1793. These positions included the right to be a Judge, King's Counsel, Sheriff of County, or to hold senior government offices, to be a member of the Privy Council, or to sit in Parliament. In Westminster, large parliamentary majorities had voted down petitions to end these exclusions in 1805 and 1808. The campaign for reform continued, and Grattan's emancipation bill of 1819 narrowly failed by only two votes. In 1821 an emancipation bill introduced by William Conyingham Plunket was passed in the Commons. There was, however, unrelenting hostility to emancipation from both the House of Lords and King George IV, which delayed the legislation until 1829. By then, the Catholic Association movement (which was established in May 1824, suppressed in March 1825 and relaunched in July of that year) had garnered massive public support in Ireland. See Connolly, ed., *The Oxford Companion to Irish History*, p.75.

5. This was not uniformly the case, however. For a full discussion, see, among others, Foster, *Modern Ireland*, pp.203–11.

6. Hoppen, *Ireland since 1800*, p.39.

7. O'Shea, *Parnell, Vol. I*, p.24.

8. T. M. Healy, *Letters and Leaders of My Day, Vol. I*, p.154.

9. I am grateful to Professor Patrick O'Shea, St Mary's University, Minnesota, for his help with this family history and genealogy.

10. O'Shea, *Parnell, Vol. I*, p.24.

11. Ibid.

12. This papal authority was manifested by the declaration of papal infallibility, for example, in 1870.

13. See Angela Bourke, *The Burning of Bridget Cleary: A True Story*, for a fascinating and scrupulous account of this tragic event, and of the cultural traditions still practised in nineteenth-century Ireland.

14. Bourke, *The Burning of Bridget Cleary*, p.28.

15. Ibid., pp.28–9.

16. O'Shea, *Parnell, Vol. I*, p.27.

17. Ibid., pp.27–8.

18. Cited by Joyce Marlow, *The Uncrowned Queen of Ireland*, p.17.

19. O'Shea, *Parnell, Vol. I*, p.27.

20. See Marlow, *The Uncrowned Queen of Ireland*, p.17. Marlow's book was published in 1975 and she had access to family records and oral history that has not been seen since by other biographers, and whose whereabouts appear to be unknown (see Bibliography, p.552.)

21. O'Shea, *Parnell, Vol. I*, pp.25–6.

22. Although some of Ireland's Anglican elite continued to go abroad for higher education, these numbers were small. Catholics and dissenters, however, looked outside Ireland – Catholics to the Irish colleges of continental Europe, and Presbyterians to Scotland. In the later eighteenth century, further attempts were made to cater for higher education within Ireland. A number of academies for Presbyterians were set up in Ulster, including Queen's Colleges in Belfast in 1845. The Catholic

University was founded by the Irish bishops in 1854 with papal encouragement (in 1850 Rome forbade clergy to hold office within the Queen's Colleges, which had now opened at Cork and Galway as well as Belfast; bishops were required to discourage Catholics from attending these institutions). This comprehensive rejection by Catholics of the Queen's Colleges led to the establishment of the Royal University of Ireland in 1882. In 1883 the Royal University and the Catholic University came under Jesuit control as University College, Dublin. See S. J. Connolly, ed., *The Oxford Companion to Irish History*, pp.78, 265–6, 467–70, 551–2.

23. This political label was used as a term of abuse by those referring to Catholics who, by playing a role in Castle life, were betraying their people.

24. This rank was replaced in 1871 by Second Lieutenant (but still used in some cavalry regiments).

25. It was, to be absolutely correct, the 'British' army only after the Act of Union with Scotland in 1707. For a good overview of the history of the British army, see David Chandler, ed., *The Oxford History of the British Army*.

26. O'Shea, *Parnell, Vol. I*, p.25.

27. Ibid.

28. Cited by Bradhurst, *A Century of Letters*, p.77.

29. Emma Wood to Lord Hatherley, in Bradhurst, *A Century of Letters*, p.76.

30. See Bradhurst, *A Century of Letters*, pp.76–7.

31. Cited in ibid., p.78.

32. O'Shea, *Parnell, Vol. I*, pp.26–7.

33. For a comprehensive study of barrack life, see French, *Military Identities: The Regimental System, the British Army and the British People c.1870–1900*, pp.190–226.

34. Ibid., p.224.

35. Such was the concern over costs that a Royal Commission was set up in 1901 to inquire into aspects of the life of army officers. See pp.(1903), X, Cd. 1421, 'Report of the committee appointed by the Secretary of State for War to inquire into the nature of the expenses incurred by officers of the army and to suggest measures for bringing commissions within reach of men of moderate means' and pp.(1903) X, Cd. 983, 'Minutes of evidence of the Committee appointed to consider the education and training of officers of the education and training of regimental officers of the Army'. I am grateful to Professor David French for sharing his considerable expertise in this area with me.

36. According to Katie, in O'Shea, *Parnell, Vol. I*, p.54.

37. Healy, *Letters and Leaders*, p.154.

38. O'Shea, *Parnell, Vol. I*, pp.53–4.

39. Ibid., p.53.

40. See Kathryn Hughes, *The Short Life and Long Times of Mrs. Beeton* for a comprehensive study of the establishment of a new middle-class household in the Victorian period; in particular chapter 5, 'Crockery and Carpets', pp.130–53.

41. See Judith Flanders, *The Victorian House: Domestic Life from Childbirth to Deathbed*, p.xxxix.

42. Kathryn Hughes, *The Short Life and Long Times of Mrs. Beeton*, p.140.

43. Willie O'Shea wrote to Joseph Chamberlain that Katharine's 'sole fortune … when I married her, was £120 per annum settled on herself' (UBL, Joseph Chamberlain Papers, JC8/1/160, 12 February 1891; cited by Jordan, *Kitty O'Shea*, p.9). It is important to note that we have only Willie's word for this. It was possibly the income from Katie's marriage settlement of £5,000.

44. O'Shea, *Parnell, Vol. I*, p.54.

45. Ibid., pp.54–5.

46. Ibid., p.55.

47. Ibid.

48. Ibid., pp.55–6.

49. Ibid., pp.56–7.

50. Ibid., p.57.

51. Ibid., pp.58–9.

52. Ibid., p.59.

53. Ibid., p.60.

54. Ibid., pp.60–1.

55. Ibid., pp.63–4.

56. Ibid., p.67.

57. Ibid.

58. Edward Robert Bulwer-Lytton, 1st Earl of Lytton (1831–91), was an English diplomat and poet, who wrote under the pseudonym Owen Meredith. He was the son of the novelist Baron Bulwer-Lytton. The 1st Earl of Lytton was in the diplomatic service from 1850 to 1875, when Prime Minister Benjamin Disraeli appointed him Viceroy for India. He was created an earl in 1880 for his services in the Afghan wars and was Ambassador to France until his death. He and his father were good friends of Lady Emma Wood and Anna Steele, and some of their correspondence was preserved in Mrs Bradhurst's *Century of Letters*.

59. Robert Lytton to Anna Steele, 4 May 1868; cited by Bradhurst, *A Century of Letters*, pp.145–6.

60. O'Shea, *Parnell, Vol. I*, p.66.

61. Lytton to Steele, 4 May 1868; cited by Bradhurst, *A Century of Letters*, p.146.

62. José Alvarez Junco and Adrian Shubert, eds., *Spanish History since 1808*, p.4.

63. See Gabriel Tortella, *The Development of Modern Spain: An Economic History of the Nineteenth and Twentieth Centuries*, pp.163–5.

64. O'Shea, *Parnell, Vol. I*, p.70.

CHAPTER FIVE:
GOLDEN OPPORTUNITIES

1. Ibid., p.71.
2. Ibid.
3. Ibid., p.72.
4. Ibid., p.73.
5. See the chapter on 'The Railway Revolution: Racing 1840–70', in Wray Vamplew, *The Turf: A Social and Economic History of Horse Racing*, pp.29–38.
6. Hoppen, *The Mid-Victorian Generation*, p.360.
7. See A. N. Wilson, *The Victorians*, p.409.
8. Hoppen, *The Mid-Victorian Generation*, p.360.
9. Humanitarian Christian groups made efforts in the early nineteenth century to 'remodel' what they saw as unacceptable leisure pursuits. The foundation of the RSPCA (1824), the Temperance Movement (1829) and the Lord's Day Observance Society (1831) were all attempts to promote a more 'civilized' society and to encourage the working masses to become more receptive to religious instruction and values. See Vamplew, *The Turf*, p.23.
10. Harold Perkin, *The Origins of Modern English Society, 1780–1880*, p.277. See also Harold Perkin, *The Rise of Professional Society: England since 1880*.
11. Vamplew, *The Turf*, pp.205–9.

12. Lowe's system was based on the premise that every single mare could be traced back to one of fifty mares in the *Stud Books* of 1791–1814, and he ranked these fifty according to the number of winners they had produced. His theory was the higher the rank, the higher the possibility of that mare's family producing a winning racehorse. See Vamplew, *The Turf*, pp.186–7.
13. O'Shea, *Parnell, Vol. I*, p.80.
14. Ibid., p.81.
15. Ibid., p.75.
16. Ibid.
17. Ibid., p.81.
18. Ibid.
19. The Badminton Library of Sports and Pastimes was published between 1885 and 1920. The original series – essentially a chronicle of Victorian aristocratic sporting pursuits – comprised twenty-eight titles, covering different sporting pastimes, published throughout 1896. In 1902, the series took on a modern hue when a volume on 'Motors and Motor-Driving' was added.
20. Cited by Vamplew, *The Turf*, p.184.
21. O'Shea, *Parnell, Vol. I*, p.83.
22. Bradhurst, *A Century of Letters*, p.161.
23. O'Shea, *Parnell, Vol. I*, p.84.
24. Ibid., p.85.
25. Ibid.

26. The first Lord Chancellor was possibly Angmendus, as early as 605, and other incumbents include St Thomas à Becket, St Swithin, Queen Eleanor, Cardinal Wolsey and Sir Thomas More.

27. Documents to which the great seal is affixed include letters patent, writs and royal proclamations.

28. Atlay, *The Victorian Chancellors*, p.367.

29. O'Shea, *Parnell, Vol. I*, p.86.

30. Lady Emma Wood to E. S. Dallas, undated, in Bradhurst, *A Century of Letters*, p.160.

31. Louis Napoleon, known as Napoleon III, was the grandson of Josephine, Napoleon I's first wife, from her first marriage to the Vicomte de Beauharnais. Louis Napoleon's mother, Hortense, was married to Louis, Napoleon I's brother. There was considerable speculation, however, as to the paternity of Louis Napoleon – some have even suggested that Napoleon I himself was his father. See William E. Echard, ed., *Historical Dictionary of the French Empire 1852–1870*; D. G. Charlton, ed., *France: A Companion to French Studies*; Pierre Goubert, *The Course of French History*.

32. Mrs George Cornwallis-West, *The Reminiscences of Lady Randolph Churchill*, p.27.

33. O'Shea, *Parnell, Vol. I*, pp.87–8.

34. Ibid., p.88.

35. Ibid., p.94.

36. Ibid., p.96.

37. Ibid., p.98.

38. Ibid.

39. Ibid., p.88.

40. Ibid., p.103.

41. Ibid., p.104.

42. Ibid., p.108.

43. Ibid., p.110.

44. There is a very large body of work on the separate spheres of Victorian Britain. Some of the most helpful books for an overview are: Susan Kingsley Kent, *Gender and Power in Britain, 1640–1990*; June Purvis, *Women's History: Britain, 1850–1945: An Introduction*; Steinbach, *Women in England*.

45. For more details on middle-class employment opportunities and philanthropic activities available to middle-class women of the period, see Steinbach, *Women in England*, pp.50–82.

46. O'Shea, *Parnell, Vol. I*, p.111.

47. Ibid., p.112.

48. Ibid., p.114.

49. Ibid., p.120.

50. Ibid., p.118.

51. Perkin, *The Rise of Professional Society: England since 1880*, p.38.

52. See also Hoppen, *The Mid-Victorian Generation*, pp.9–30; David Cannadine, *The Decline and Fall of the British Aristocracy*, pp.88–139.

53. O'Shea, *Parnell, Vol. I*, p.120.

54. Ibid., pp.120–1.

55. Ibid., p.122.

56. Healy wrote that Katie 'was supposed to have been endowed by a banker named Christopher Weguelin, once M.P. for Youghal. When Sir Evelyn proposed the match to his subaltern, O'Shea at first pleaded that he was too poor to marry, but was assured that Miss Wood possessed £30,000. In the divorce case of 1890 "Christopher's" name appeared in a letter which Mrs. O'Shea wrote to her husband: "You did not object to Christopher", she remonstrated. O'Shea's reply was: "Christopher is dead, Parnell is not"' (Healy, *Letters and Leaders*, p.154).

57. O'Shea, *Parnell, Vol. I*, p.123.

CHAPTER SIX:
THE RISE OF CHARLES
STEWART PARNELL

1. Ibid., p.125.

2. Ibid., p.133.

3. She did not record whether she was successful in obtaining the money from Aunt Ben, but many of Katie's biographers have assumed that the expenses were paid by her wealthy relative. It is probable, as the O'Sheas had no other means of getting such a large sum, and Willie would have found great difficulty in continuing the pursuit of his new-found parliamentary career if unable to honour his debt.

4. Franchise legislation continued, and a Redistribution of Seats Act in 1885 resulted in raising the Irish electorate to 738,000. See Connolly, ed., *The Oxford Companion to Irish History*, pp.205–6.

5. Irish, along with Scottish Gaelic and Manx, constitutes the Gaelic branch of the Celtic languages. The use of native Irish had enormously declined by the nineteenth century, when the majority of the population was bilingual. The revival of the language became linked with nationalism, and Irish regained its status as an official language in 1922.

6. O'Connell engineered an expulsion of the Young Irelanders from the repeal movement after disagreements on policy, in 1846. The repeal movement sought the repeal of the Act of Union.

7. Connolly, ed., *The Oxford Companion to Irish History* (new edn), pp.284–5.

8. The 1798 insurrection included four major outbreaks: County Dublin, eastern Ulster, County Wexford and the Connacht Rising.

9. The Defenders were a secret Catholic society, and at their origin the opponents of the Peep of Day Boys in County Armagh. From 1790, the Defender movement spread throughout Ulster and parts of Leinster, including Dublin city. Defenders allied with United Irishmen participated in the insurrection of 1798. The Defenders continued as a movement through the nineteenth century, as the Ribbonmen.

The Whiteboys movement was active from 1761 to the 1780s. Its members, who wore white shirts over everyday clothing, protested against enclosure of common land, tithes (especially on potatoes) and later on rents and evictions as well. 'Whiteboy' continued through the nineteenth century to be used as a general term for agrarian protesters.

'Ribbonmen' was a new name for the United Irishmen, as of 1811. The Ribbonmen were a secret underground network, which was probably a direct descent in many cases from the Defender society. The Ribbonmen were Catholics, and committed to an independent Ireland, by means of armed insurrection.

10. M. J. Kelly, *The Fenian Ideal and Irish Nationalism, 1882–1916*, p.1.

11. Ibid.

12. This Irish-American secret society was founded on 20 June 1867. It adopted a democratic structure (unlike the IRB) and promoted secrecy. Clan-na-Gael had a restricted membership, hierarchy, centralization of its funds, along with other accoutrements such as passwords, secret signs and symbols. Much of this is known due to the infiltration of the society's leadership by the English spy Henry Le Caron (Thomas Billis Beach). He was a member from 1876 and betrayed many of its secrets. See Séan McConville, *Irish Political Prisoners 1848–1922: Theatres of War*, p.331 (and fn 12, which refers to Beach's *Twenty-Five Years in the Secret Service*, London, 1892).

13. Engels commented, 'The only thing the Fenians still lacked were martyrs. They have been provided with these' (cited by McConville, *Irish Political Prisoners*, pp.134–5).

14. Kelly, *The Fenian Ideal*, p.2.

15. William Ewart Gladstone (1809–98) was the son of a Liverpool merchant and educated at Eton and Oxford. He first entered Parliament as a Conservative MP for Oxford in 1832. He was Prime Minister from 1868 to 1874, and enacted the Land Act of 1870. He had become a Liberal in 1859 and was once again Prime Minister during 1880–5, and 1886, during which time he attempted to resolve the Ireland question; he tacitly and later more openly accepted Parnell as the Nationalist leader through whom this could possibly be achieved. Gladstone virtually ended the Land War with his Land Act of 1881, but his subsequent attempts to enact Home Rule for Ireland in 1886 and again in 1893 (he was PM again during 1892–4) ended in failure – and split the Liberal Party – and he resigned in 1894.

See Jenkins, *Gladstone*, pp.289–90, for an interesting account of this comment by Gladstone.

16. The privileged position of the Church of Ireland had long been a contentious issue for both Catholics and Presbyterians in Ireland. After the Fenian insurrection of 1867, Gladstone addressed the question. It was found, through census returns and a series of parliamentary inquiries, that the Church's wealth and prestige were out of scale with its minority position and indeed with some serious pastoral and administrative failings. There was great objection both from the Queen and the Conservatives – and from the Church itself – but Gladstone's Irish Church Act became law on 26 July 1869. Connolly, ed., *The Oxford Companion to Irish History*, p.149.

The Landlord and Tenant Act (Ireland) of 1870 addressed the issues of Tenant Right. It further provided for similar rights elsewhere in the country. The Act also provided for compensation for tenants evicted – unless for non-payment of rent – and made provision for compensation for improvements made by a departing tenant. Connolly, ed., *The Oxford Companion to Irish History*, p.295.

17. Kelly, *The Fenian Ideal*, p.2.

18. Hoppen, *Ireland since 1800*. Hoppen adds that 'as in the 1850s', many of these MPs 'turned out to be at best fair-weather friends', p.123.

19. Cited by Hoppen, *Ireland since 1800*, p.123.

20. The complex and nuanced relationship between the Home Rule movement and Fenianism is particularly well addressed in Kelly, *The Fenian Ideal, 1882–1916*.

21. Parnell was in sympathy with the claims of the 'Manchester Martyrs', and famously declared in Parliament on 30 June 1876: 'I do not believe, and never shall believe, that any murder was committed at Manchester'. Hansard 3rd series, Vol. CCXXX, 30 June 1876, col. 808.

22. Paul Bew, *Charles Stewart Parnell*, p.19.

23. Donal McCartney, 'Parnell, Davitt and the Land Question', in Carla King, ed., *Famine, Land and Culture in Ireland*, p.71.

24. See W. E. Vaughan, *Landlords and Tenants in Mid-Victorian Ireland*, for a full discussion of tenant conditions.

25. It should be noted that Clan na Gael recognized the Supreme Council of the Irish Republican Brotherhood as the legitimate 'government' of Ireland.

26. One of the reasons for which the Fenians were drawn to Parnell, in spite of his political and constitutional rather than revolutionary ambitions, was possibly due to his success as a fund-raiser. He had garnered some £72,000 in North America during his tour in early 1880. See Alvin Jackson, *Home Rule: An Irish History 1800–2000*, p.40.

27. Cited by Jackson, *Home Rule*, p.41.

28. Patrick Ford was born in Galway in 1837 and emigrated to Boston with his parents to escape the potato famine in 1845. He left school early because of his father's need of financial assistance. A self-made man, he moved to New York City in 1870 and set up the *Irish World*. As editor, until 1913, of the paper – whose weekly circulation often rose above 100,000 copies – Ford was an important and very influential voice in the Irish-American community. He was a firm advocate of the Irish Nationalist movement and worked closely with Davitt on land reform.

29. The 'Skirmishing Fund' was one such, set up by O'Donovan Rossa and Patrick Ford in order to pay agents to 'lay English cities in ashes'. See R. Barry O'Brien, *The Life of Charles Stewart Parnell*, p.192.

30. Cited by R. Barry O'Brien, *The Life of Charles Stewart Parnell*, pp.192–3.

31. McCartney, 'Parnell, Davitt and the Land Question', in King,

ed., *Famine, Land and Culture in Ireland*, p.76.

32. Foster, *Modern Ireland 1600–1972*, p.405.

33. The generic term of Nationalist Party (1882–1922) included the Irish Parliamentary Party and its successive constituency organizations. Begun first under Isaac Butt – the Protestant founder of the Home Rule movement – as a loose group in the 1870s, it grew into a tighter and more strictly controlled group under the authoritarian leadership of Parnell. See S. J. Connolly, ed., *The Oxford Companion to Irish History*, pp.381–2.

34. The Transvaal was the seat of the growing unease. One of three republics that bordered on the British Cape Colony on the African continent, it had been recognized in 1852 as an independent republic by Britain. The inhabitants, Boers of Dutch descent, increasingly sought independence, fighting the British successfully in a series of conflicts. They were famously victorious in the Battle of Majuba Hill in 1881, following which they proclaimed their self-government. The discovery of gold in this region, in 1886, however, prompted the influx of British 'outlanders'. They were not absorbed into the local Boer population, and grew to harbour a number of grievances, chief among these being refused the right to vote. The republic began re-arming heavily, particularly after the aborted Jameson Raid by the British in 1895. Many British back home clamoured for war and jingoistic imperialism dominated the popular mood. See Thomas Pakenham, *The Boer War*.

35. O'Shea, *Parnell, Vol. I*, p.134.

36. See in particular R. F. Foster, *Modern Ireland*, pp.373–428; Paul Bew, *Charles Stewart Parnell*, pp.30–41; S. J. Connolly, *The Oxford Companion to Irish History*, pp.300–1.

37. After the death of the chairman Isaac Butt in May 1879, Shaw had served in that capacity. See also O'Shea, *Parnell, Vol. I*, p.134.

38. Among the twenty-three supporters were the influential members who became the core of the party, including the lawyer Tim Healy, T. P. O'Connor, Justin McCarthy, John Barry, Thomas Sexton, T. D. Sullivan and Joseph Biggar. Many of these supporters were dedicated Nationalists, and prepared to follow a more aggressive campaign for independence.

39. It has been argued that Parnell further benefited from the Reform Act of 1884. Its accompanying Redistribution Act failed to accord the constituent nations equal treatment: Ireland's declining population meant that she was over-represented. During the Edwardian period, there was one MP for every 66,975 persons in England, one for every 63,805 in Scotland, one for every 57,301 in Wales and, in Ireland, one MP for every 44,147. See G. R. Searle, *A New England? Peace and War 1886–1918*, p.120.

40. Henry Harrison, *Parnell Vindicated: The Lifting of the Veil*, p.254.

41. O'Shea, *Parnell, Vol. I*, p.135.

42. Ibid.

43. Ibid., p.136.

44. Lyons, *Charles Stewart Parnell*, p.128.

45. Parnell to K. O'Shea, 17 July 1880, O'Shea, *Parnell, Vol. I*, p.136.

46. The journalist, novelist, historian and politician Justin McCarthy (1830–1912) was born in County Cork. He worked for the *Cork Examiner*, 1847, and the Liverpool-based *Northern Daily Times*, 1859. He then contributed to the *Westminster Review*, and edited the *Morning Star*, 1864–8. He was Home Rule MP for County Longford and Vice-Chairman of the Irish Parliamentary Party, 1879. Although he led the majority faction after the Parnell split, he remained friendly with Parnell.

47. Henceforth referred to, more simply, as the Irish Party.

48. O'Shea, *Parnell, Vol. I*, p.137.

49. Searle, *A New England?*, p.122.

50. The Labour Party, founded in 1900, set up in 1903 a central fund from which to make payments to MPs, who, until then, had to be sponsored by their trade unions.

51. T. P. O'Connor (1848–1929) left Ireland in 1870 to become a journalist in London. In 1880 he became MP for Galway, transferring to a Liverpool (Scotland) seat in 1885, which he retained for the rest of his life. He was a key fund-raiser for the Nationalist Party during tours in the USA, and led the United Irish League of Great Britain.

52. T. P. O'Connor, *Memoirs of an Old Parliamentarian*, Vol. II, pp.61–2.

53. O'Shea, *Parnell, Vol. I*, p.137.

54. Ibid., p.138.

55. Kee, *The Laurel and the Ivy*, p.241.

56. O'Shea, *Parnell, Vol. I*, pp.139–40.

57. Charles Stewart Parnell left very little personal correspondence, and most of what we have has been provided by Katharine's memoir. While recollections by Parnell's family and political colleagues have provided some additional information, those authors for the most part did not know Katharine, and have therefore been unable to add much to our knowledge of her relationship with the Irish leader.

58. R. F. Foster has made a particularly interesting and very useful study of the authenticity of Katharine's memoir. See 'Love, Politics and Textual Corruption: Mrs. O'Shea's *Parnell*, in *Paddy and Mr. Punch: Connections in Irish and English History*, pp.123–38.

59. O'Shea, *Parnell, Vol. I*, pp.140–1.

60. Ibid., p.141.

61. Parnell to K. O'Shea, 9 September 1880, ibid., p.142.

62. Cited by Kee, *The Laurel and the Ivy*, p.49.

63. W. S. Blunt recorded in his published diary a conversation over lunch with John Dillon (who had been one of Parnell's chief lieutenants) on 10 March 1912:'[He] gave me a full history of Parnell's connection with Mrs. O'Shea. Parnell, he said, as a young man, was no paragon of virtue, but his loves had not before been with married women, nor had they been serious' (W. S. Blunt, *My Diaries: Being a Personal Narrative of Events 1888–1914*, p.381).

64. For a full discussion, see Frank Callanan, *T. M. Healy*, pp.52–5 and 638–9.

65. Michael Davitt, *The Fall of Feudalism in Ireland*, p.652.

66. William O'Brien (1852–1928) and fellow agrarian militant John Dillon (1851–1927) became Parnell's leading lieutenants. They reluctantly, but significantly, joined the opposition to him in 1891.

67. William O'Brien, *Recollections*, p.239.

68. William O'Brien, *The Parnell of Real Life*, p.57.

69. Justin McCarthy to Mrs Campbell Praed, 16 November 1890, in Mrs Campbell Praed, *Our Book of Memories: Letters of Justin McCarthy to Mrs. Campbell Praed*, p.256.

70. See Jane McL. Coté, *Fanny and Anna Parnell: Ireland's Patriot Sisters*, for a biography of these two sisters.

71. Timothy Michael Healy (1855–1931) was a member of the 'Bantry Band' – a tight political clan that included Tim's brother Maurice Healy, T. D. Sullivan, Donal Sullivan and William Martin Murphy. This group was also known as the 'Bantry Gang', and they were the most fiercely independent of the Nationalist MPs. Healy was a leading barrister and KC, and he gained a reputation as an outspoken political maverick. Although he began as an ardent Parnell supporter, he later turned viciously on the leader. He became the first Governor-General of the Irish Free State, 1922–8.

Healy vehemently denied in his memoirs that he was ever in Parnell's employ. He did, nonetheless, act as his Secretary in 1880 in America, where he corresponded and gave interviews on Parnell's behalf. See Frank Callanan, *Healy*, pp.32–8.

72. Timothy Daniel Sullivan (1827–1914) was a Nationalist politician, journalist and poet. A member of the 'Bantry Gang', he famously wrote the Nationalist hymn 'God Save Ireland' in 1867. He was the brother of Alexander Martin Sullivan, also a journalist and politician. T. D. Sullivan was a Parnell supporter in the 1880 election and member of the Home Rule League. He was MP for Westmeath (1880–5) and for Dublin College Green, and then West Donegal. A member of the Irish Parliamentary Party since its inception in 1882, he became an anti-Parnellite when the party split in 1891. He owned and edited a number of publications (*The Nation, Dublin Weekly News* and *Young Ireland*).

73. Cited by Foster, *Parnell*, p.256.

74. This will be discussed further, in chapter 12. Fanny Parnell (1849–82) was a poet and the founder of the New York Ladies' Land League in 1880. Like her sister Anna and mother Delia, she spent much of her life in America. She died suddenly of causes unknown at the age of thirty-two. Family members suggested that rheumatic fever was the cause – others have proposed that she may have taken her own life. See Foster, *Parnell*, pp.241–59.

75. Anna (1852–1911) later became disillusioned with the League, and published *The Great Sham* in 1907; the book recounted her unhappiness at the empty promises made to small tenants about land redistribution. She left Ireland in great bitterness after the closure of the LLL in 1882 and eventually settled in Cornwall. There will be more on the Ladies' Land League and on Anna Parnell in chapter 12.

76. Charles Parnell was never a great supporter of the LLL – a fact which Anna deeply resented. In addition to her increasing ambivalence about the LLL, however, the shock of her sister Fanny's death in July 1882 sent her into a physical and mental decline just at the time when the organization came under attack. She was therefore unable to defend it and deeply resented her brother for his determination to force the LLL into closure (more in chapter 12). See Foster, *Charles Stewart Parnell*, pp.260–84.

77. John Howard Parnell, *Charles Stewart Parnell*, p.181.

78. Foster, *Parnell*, pp.215–16. John Howard 'alone combined some attributes of both groups', p.216.

79. Ibid., p.223.

80. Emily Dickinson wrote a rather unfortunate and highly inaccurate memoir of her famous brother – almost certainly as a means of generating much needed income after his death. See Bibliography, p.556.

81. Cited by Foster, *Parnell*, p.231.

82. See William O'Brien, *The Parnell of Real Life*, p.58.

CHAPTER SEVEN: IRISH POLITICS

1. Parnell to K. O'Shea, 22 September 1880, O'Shea, *Parnell, Vol. II*, p.144.

2. Ibid., p.144. The story seems a bit odd, not least because of confusion over the dates. Lucy Goldsmith had a stroke on 17 September, and died four days later, on 21 September. Katie's reply to Parnell's request of 22 September to see her, stating that she could not leave due to her nurse's illness, would have been written after the servant's death. This discrepancy is a good example of the difficulty in relying on Katie's memoir for accuracy in dates and sequence of events. We have little in the way of corroborative evidence for many of the stories she told in this book.

3. Parnell to K. O'Shea, 24 September 1880, O'Shea, *Parnell, Vol. I*, pp.144–5.

4. Parnell to K. O'Shea, 25 September 1880, ibid., p.145.

5. T. P. O'Connor, 1887; cited by Paul Bew, *Charles Stewart Parnell*, p.10.

6. Parnell to K. O'Shea, 29 September 1880, O'Shea, *Parnell, Vol. I*, p.146.

7. Ibid., pp.145–6.

8. Ibid., p.149.

9. John Howard Parnell, *Charles Stewart Parnell*, p.263.

10. Ibid., p.264.

11. Ibid., p.265.

12. Ibid., p.266.

13. Ibid.

14. Ibid.

15. O'Shea, *Parnell, Vol. I*, p.150.

16. Ibid.

17. The word originates from Captain Hugh Cunningham Boycott. He was an English-born former soldier who had been appointed agent for Lord Erne's County Mayo estates in 1873. He came into conflict with the Land League at Lough Mask in 1880. He became one of the first, and most famous, victims of Parnell's tactic of consigning those who broke the Land League's code into 'moral Coventry'. Although Boycott tried to overcome the boycott, by drafting in Ulstermen to do the farm work, it required 1,000 troops to protect them.

18. Parnell to K. O'Shea, 'Tuesday' [n.d.], O'Shea, *Parnell, Vol. I*, p.152.

19. Parnell to K. O'Shea, 2 October 1880, ibid., pp.152–3.

20. Parnell to K. O'Shea, 4 October 1880, ibid., p.153.

21. Parnell to K. O'Shea, 5 October 1880, ibid.

22. Parnell to K. O'Shea, 17 October 1880, ibid.

23. Cited by Kee, *The Laurel and the Ivy*, p.259.

24. Ibid., p.261.

25. John Dillon (1851–1927) was qualified in medicine, although he lived by private means. He was MP for Tipperary 1880–3 and for East Mayo 1885–1918. He served four prison terms and his anti-landlordism dominated his career. He was the most influential Nationalist politician between Parnell and de Valera and an extremely accomplished parliamentarian (See Dramatis Personae). Dillon became leader of the anti-Parnellite movement in 1896, making way for John Redmond in 1900, with whom he cooperated for some years without compromising his brand of radical liberalism.

26. Cited by Kee, *The Laurel and the Ivy*, p.264.

27. Lyons, *Parnell*, p.141.

28. Cited by Bew, *Parnell*, p.42. Bew records that this and the following 'eulogy' by Duignan was reported in *Nation* on 2 January 1886: 'Ireland may say to him as Hamlet said to Horatio: "Give me the man that is *not passion's slave*, and I will wear him in my heart's core – ay, in my heart of hearts – as I do thee."'

29. Hops were a crucial ingredient in the brewing process. Katie's grandfather had made his fortune in this industry.

30. O'Shea, *Parnell, Vol. I,* p.151.

31. Ibid., p.150.

32. Ibid., p.151.

33. This is the most common name for the Chief Governor of Ireland after the Restoration. In the eighteenth century, Lords-Lieutenant were English politicians but Irish peers also served as Lords-Lieutenant in the nineteenth century. After 1772, the Lords-Lieutenant were permanently resident in Ireland. With the Chief Secretary, they were responsible for parliamentary management and after 1782 were accountable to the Cabinet in London. The Act of Union significantly reduced their powers (the possible abolition of the post was debated in Parliament in 1823, 1830 and 1844). The office survived, in an increasingly ceremonial capacity, until 1922. By the latter part of the nineteenth century the office of Chief Secretary was far more important politically. By 1900, the Chief Secretary acted as the main exponent of government policy in the House of Commons and was responsible for twenty-nine government departments. The position was known to be an extremely stressful one, involving much travel as well as a heavy workload.

34. William Edward Forster (1818–86) was raised by Quaker parents. In 1842 he had set up a woollen manufacture in Bradford, which eventually moved to a village in Yorkshire and became steadily profitable. Although Forster was expelled from the Society of Friends after marrying outside the faith, there were no hard feelings, and he retained his devotion to Quakerism, although not espousing its pacifism. Forster entered politics as a Radical MP in 1861, and was called to office as Under-Secretary for the Colonies in 1865. By the time Gladstone was returned to power in 1880, Forster had seen through a number of successful reforms and had become a high-ranking and well-respected Liberal politician. He was hoping for an appointment to Colonial Secretary. Instead, the Prime Minister wished him to take on the most critical office of Chief Secretary to the Lord-Lieutenant of Ireland, with a seat in the Cabinet.

35. *Freeman's Journal,* 25 October 1880; cited by T. P. O'Connor, *The Parnell Movement,* p.391.

36. Cited by R. Barry O'Brien, *The Life of Charles Stewart Parnell,* p.194.

37. Ibid.

38. Ibid., pp.195–6.

39. 'Coercion is the broad term for a suspension or modification of

ordinary or common law rights.'
See Alan O'Day, 'The Irish
Problem', in T. R. Gourvish and
Alan O'Day, eds., *Later Victorian
Britain, 1867–1900*, p.241.

40. O'Connor is referring to
Gladstone's diplomatic coup in the
Balkans, achieved after he
persuaded the Turks to give up the
small port of Dulcigno to the
Montenegrins.

41. T. P. O'Connell, *The Parnell
Movement*, p.392.

42. Cited by Roy Jenkins,
Gladstone, p.435. See this work for
a full depiction of Gladstone's
difficult relationship with his
sovereign, as well as an account of
her problems in dealing with the
evolving relationship between the
Crown and its ministers.

43. See Jenkins, *Gladstone*,
pp.289–90, for an interesting
account of this comment by
Gladstone.

44. The modern Afghan state
emerged in the mid-eighteenth
century. It became an area of
contention where British imperial
interests came into conflict with
those of expansionist Russia
(years of skirmishing, espionage
and intrigue between the two
countries without open conflict
were known as 'The Great Game').
The British objective was to secure
a stable, pro-British state to act as
a buffer against any further
Russian expansion towards India.

To this end, British (and Indian)
troops were present in the region
from 1839, leaving in 1842 after
defeats; they returned in 1878, and
left after serious losses were
sustained in the battles of 1880.
The third Afghan War broke out
in 1919. See T. A. Heathcote, 'The
British Army in India', in David
Chandler, ed., *The Oxford History of
the British Army*, pp.374–7.

45. Although Gladstone protested
that Britain should remain aloof
from the administration of Egypt,
the financial links were
considerable. In 1880, Britain took
80 per cent of Egypt's exports and
provided 44 per cent of its
imports. Gladstone himself had
significant investments there. See
Roy Jenkins, *Gladstone*, pp.507–8.

46. Nineteenth-century leading
military men included these
Anglo-Irish officers: Garnett
Wolesey (Commander-in-Chief of
the British Army), Field Marshal
Lord Roberts (of Khandahar) and
Field Marshal Lord Kitchener (of
Khartoum).

47. Cited by R. Barry O'Brien, *The
Life of Charles Stewart Parnell*,
p.203.

48. John Dillon and William
O'Brien often clashed with Parnell
over their agrarianism but became
reluctant anti-Parnellites in 1890.
In 1896, Dillon led the main anti-
Parnellite movement. In 1900 he
gave way to John Redmond, to

facilitate the reunion of parliamentary nationalism.

49. Thomas Sexton was the son of a policeman. He was largely self-educated and began his working life as a railway clerk. After becoming an MP in 1880, and a loyal Parnellite, he moved rapidly into the front rank of the party in the House of Commons. An ardent Land League supporter, he was often the party spokesman at Westminster, especially on matters of finance.

50. When Parnell returned to Cork from his tour of America earlier that year, a group of Fenians had marked their disapproval of his parliamentary and Land League alliance by declaring that he would not have their support. Many Fenians were unconvinced by Parnell's legislative tactics, and in open argument with him and his supporters.

51. Cited by Lyons, *Parnell*, p.139.

52. Parnell to K. O'Shea, 6 November 1880, O'Shea, *Parnell, Vol. I*, p.157.

53. Parnell to K. O'Shea, 4 November 1880, ibid., p.156.

54. Cited by Lyons, *Parnell*, p.125.

55. Cited by Kee, *The Laurel and the Ivy*, p.281.

56. Among many others, see Hoppen, *The Mid-Victorian Generation*, p.561.

57. Cited by Kee, *The Laurel and the Ivy*, p.282.

58. Parnell to K. O'Shea, 11 November 1880, O'Shea, *Parnell, Vol I*, pp.157–8.

59. Parnell to K. O'Shea, 11 November 1880, ibid., p.158.

60. One of the great difficulties in using Katie's book as a reference is the fact that the correspondence reproduced was not always properly, or even correctly, dated. At times, the letters were obviously out of sequence, and probably edited by her or Gerard O'Shea. This letter was placed between one dated 6 November, and another dated 11 November. Although Katie seems to indicate by its placement that it was written between those dates, we have no way of knowing whether this was the case. What is perhaps most interesting is the fact that she chose to place it thus.

61. Parnell to K. O'Shea, 'Monday' [n.d.], O'Shea, *Parnell, Vol. I*, p.157.

62. Ibid., p.151.

63. Ibid., p.152.

64. Gladstone's Second Cabinet, formed April 1880, included Sir William Harcourt as Home Secretary, W. E. Forster as Chief Secretary for Ireland, Marquess of Hartington as Secretary for India. See Appendix: A List of Cabinets 1880-1890.

65. Gladstone had invited Chamberlain to join his second administration in the last week of April 1880. The junior member for

Birmingham was then forty-four years old, and twice married, now widowed. He was a leading member of the radical wing of the Liberal Party and a successful reforming mayor of Birmingham. Before he entered politics at the age of thirty-two, he had successfully worked in the family's screw-business and built up a small fortune. He sold his shares a few months after gaining his first seat and devoted himself fully to politics. Chamberlain was a more enthusiastic supporter of coercive legislation during the land agitation than was his Prime Minister.

66. See Foster, *Modern Ireland*, pp.400–28, and Hoppen, *The Mid-Victorian Generation*, pp.667–90.

67. O'Connor, *The Fall of Parnell*, p.395.

68. Hoppen, *The Mid-Victorian Generation*, p.668.

69. This was a temporary measure to help tenants of small farms who were unable (as opposed to unwilling) to pay their rents. The bill was not popular and was opposed by the Whigs and others in the Commons. The Lords rejected the measure in August 1880 by 282 votes to 51.

70. O'Shea, *Parnell, Vol. I*, p.161.

71. Ibid., pp.162–3.

72. Throughout the nineteenth century, administrative or legal issues presented by Ireland were referred to as the 'Irish problem'.

The 'Irish question' presented a constant problem for the British administration, but was dealt with periodically rather than systematically. See Margaret O'Callaghan, *British High Politics and Nationalist Ireland: Criminality, Land and the Law Under Forster and Balfour*; in particular, pp.11–30.

73. *The Times*, 5 January 1880.

74. Forbes, Castle Forbes, Aberdeenshire, to the Editor, *The Times*, 5 November 1880.

75. 'From late 1879, nearly every lead cartoon [in *Punch*] had an Irish reference.' Foster, 'Paddy and Mr. Punch', in *Paddy and Mr. Punch*, p.186. See pp.171–94 for a full discussion of this.

76. See John P. Harrington, ed., *The English Traveller in Ireland: Accounts of Ireland and the Irish through Five Centuries*.

77. Anon. (The Special Correspondent of *The Times*), 'Letters from Ireland, 1886', in John P. Harrington, ed., *The English Traveller in Ireland*, p.302. The letters were published in book form in London in 1887. During his travels through Ireland, the correspondent was struck by the effects of the land crisis and wrote extensively of the agitation and boycotting. The civil unrest was having a negative effect on the tourism industry, he observed, in between admiring praise of the beautiful countryside.

78. Lyons, *Parnell*, pp.139–40.

79. Parnell to K. O'Shea, 4 December 1880, O'Shea, *Parnell*, *Vol. I*, p.163.

80. Ibid., p.167.

81. Ibid., p.149.

82. Details of the O'Sheas' domestic arrangements were provided during the divorce case and reported fully in *The Times*. See 17 and 18 November 1890, in particular.

83. For an excellent depiction of running the kitchen in the Victorian middle-class home, see Judith Flanders, the chapter on 'The Kitchen', pp.63–92, in *The Victorian House*.

84. Cited by Foster, *Parnell*, p.151.

85. Ibid.

86. His primary interest with the estate was not in its farming, but its industrial potential. This does not mean that he neglected the agriculture, as he stayed in contact with his agent, William Kerr, throughout his life and managed the estate from a distance. Parnell was far more interested in the sawmills he paid to have installed, and in quarrying. He became increasingly obsessed with his stone-quarrying business he set up there, and was also constantly seeking rich mineral deposits at Avondale. See Foster, *Parnell*, pp.149–215.

87. Parnell to K. O'Shea, 27 December 1880, O'Shea, *Parnell*, *Vol. I*, p.169.

Parnell to K. O'Shea, 28 December 1880, ibid., p.169.

88. Parnell to K. O'Shea, 27 December 1880, ibid., p.169.

89. Parnell to K. O'Shea, 28 December 1880, ibid., p.170.

90. Parnell to K. O'Shea, 30 December 1880, ibid., p.170.

91. Parnell to K. O'Shea, 3 January 1881, ibid., pp.170–1.

92. Ibid., p.168.

93. Ibid., p.169.

94. Maria Wood to Lady Wood, 25 October 1879, in Bradhurst, *A Century of Letters*, p.45.

95. O'Shea, *Parnell*, *Vol. I*, pp.171–2.

96. A habeas corpus was a writ requiring the production in court of a detained person. An English Act of 1679 confirmed that this procedure could be used as a defence against imprisonment without trial. Its suspension was therefore seen as a repressive measure. The interpretation and application of this legal procedure was of such importance in the Irish situation that it is useful to provide the following full explanation of habeas corpus in this context. 'In response to the challenges of the Defender and United Irish movements, Young Ireland and the Fenians, the right of habeas corpus was suspended by act of parliament for most of the period 1796–1806, during 1848–9, and again in 1866–9. The

Protection of Life and Property Act or Westmeath Act (1871), permitting the detention without trial of suspected Ribbonmen [a strongly sectarian Catholic organization] in Westmeath and adjoining counties, was seen as a novel use of the power of suspension outside periods of political emergency ... The Protection of Persons and Property Act of March 1881 temporarily reintroduced detention without trial; but the necessity of maintaining those so detained in relatively comfortable conditions led government to rely thereafter on the summary jurisdiction of the 1887 Crimes Act.' Connolly, ed., *The Oxford Companion to Irish History*, p.233.

97. The escalation of violence was frightening. There were assassinations, animals were tortured and groups of marauding young men imposed a type of gang rule in certain areas. It was, however, the threat of violence that was most disruptive, along with the moral intimidation. The League was careful to use moderate language, but its associated slogans and speeches were 'indissolubly linked with more violent rhetoric aired in the local speeches ... and with the long tradition of agrarian crime'. Foster, *Modern Ireland*, p.406.

98. Cited by O'Callaghan, *British High Politics and a Nationalist Ireland*, p.71.

99. See chapter 5. It is interesting to note that Charles Parnell was never enthusiastic about the LLL, despite (or because of?) his sister Anna's founding role. He was not known to admire strong, independently minded women. His choice of partner in Katie – a conventional woman who was happy to play a supporting role – is significant, and could explain his rupture with Anna, who disagreed with him publicly about the powers of the LLL.

100. Parnell's Reply to the Queen's Speech, 7 January 1881. See Hansard, H.C. 3rd s., Vol. 257, pp.193–203.

101. Cited by Peter Beresford Ellis, *A History of the Irish Working Class*, p.155.

102. Cited in ibid.

103. See, for example, Hoppen, *The Mid-Victorian Generation*, chapter 5, pp.127–66.

104. International Working Men's Association: this was formed in London in September 1864 and Marx was a prominent and leading member. The International was subsequently established in other cities, including Dublin and Cork.

105. Cited by Ellis, *A History of the Irish Working Class*, p.146.

106. The Prevention of Crime Act permitted trial for certain offences by a panel of three judges. It also created a legal offence of intimidation. The Criminal Law and Procedure Act of 1887 defined intimidation and conspiracy, and gave resident magistrates special powers of investigation and summary jurisdiction in districts proclaimed as disturbed. This legislation also empowered the Lord-Lieutenant to suppress subversive organizations. See Connolly, ed., for Insurrection Act, and Coercion Acts, *The Oxford Companion to Irish History*, pp.101–2, 260.

107. O'Callaghan, *British High Politics and a Nationalist Ireland*, p.75.

108. See O'Callaghan, *British High Politics and a Nationalist Ireland*, p.76, and McCartney, 'Parnell, Davitt and the Land Question', in King, ed., *Famine, Land and Culture in Ireland*, pp.79–81.

109. Cited by Conor Cruise O'Brien, *Parnell and His Party 1880–90*, p.58.

110. Cited by R. Barry O'Brien, *The Life of Charles Stewart Parnell*, p.215.

111. 'On the following day the prime minister moved, "That if upon notice given a motion be made by a minister of the crown that the state of public business is urgent and if upon the call of the speaker 40 members shall support it by rising in their places, the speaker shall forthwith put the question, no debate, amendment or adjournment being allowed" Hansard, 258.103. This resolution, somewhat amended, formed the core of new rules framed by the speaker and presented to the House on 9 February (ibid., 435).' Conor Cruise O'Brien, *Parnell & His Party*, p.59.

112. Cited in ibid., p.61.

113. O'Shea, *Parnell, Vol. I*, p.174.

114. Healy's account is the only one that describes this week, and it has been shown to lack accuracy. Healy was not a member of the executive and did not therefore attend their meetings.

115. Callanan, *Healy*, p.48. For a full account of this episode, see pp.46–55.

116. Parnell to K. O'Shea, 23 February 1881, O'Shea, *Parnell, Vol. I*, p.178.

117. Parnell to K. O'Shea, 23 February 1881, ibid. This was not necessarily a secret visit – the letter was addressed formally to 'Mrs O'Shea' and could therefore presumably be read by someone other than Katharine.

118. Parnell to K. O'Shea, 27 February 1881, O'Shea, *Parnell, Vol. I*, p.179.

119. Parnell to K. O'Shea, 1 March 1881, ibid., pp.179–80.

120. Conor Cruise O'Brien, *Parnell & His Party*, p.61.

121. Cited by Callanan, *Healy*, p.48.

122. Cited in ibid., pp.49–50.

123. Cited in ibid., p.52.

124. Cited by Conor Cruise O'Brien, *Parnell & His Party*, p.64.

125. Cited by O'Callaghan, *British High Politics and a Nationalist Ireland*, pp.78–9.

126. O'Callaghan, *British High Politics and a Nationalist Ireland*, p.79.

127. The Land Acts were passed over a period of fifty years and transformed landholding in Ireland 'from a system of territorial landlordism to one of owner occupancy'. Connolly, ed., *The Oxford Companion to Irish History*, p.295.

128. Parnell to K. O'Shea, 19 April 1881, O'Shea, *Parnell, Vol. I*, p.180.

CHAPTER EIGHT: PARNELL'S ARREST

1. *Evening Standard*, 14 October 1881; cited by Callanan, *Healy*, p.59.

2. Cited by Foster, *Modern Ireland, 1600–1972*, p.411.

3. Hoppen, *The Mid-Victorian Generation*, pp.367–71.

4. These figures provided in Judith Flanders, *Consuming Passions: Leisure and Pleasure in Victorian Britain*, pp.229–30. See pp.229–51 for a fascinating study on the development of Victorian seaside resorts.

5. Popular with the textile workers of Lancashire and Yorkshire, and other working-class holiday-makers, Blackpool was the 'queen' of mass-market resorts. In 1884, some 40,000 excursionists came each day during the season (mid-July to early September, plus Whitsun), in addition to the 70,000 resident summer visitors. Hoppen, *The Mid-Victorian Generation*, p.367.

6. O'Shea, *Parnell, Vol. I*, p.181.

7. Ibid., p.182.

8. The only period for which Parnell was absent without explanation at that time was at the end of May. He may well have spent most of the week in Brighton. He was in the House of Commons on 30 May, voting – as did Willie O'Shea – against the government.

9. Foster has written of Parnell's stone-quarrying and mining interests – see Foster, *Parnell*, pp.155–65.

10. O'Shea, *Parnell, Vol. I*, pp.184–5.

11. Parnell to K. O'Shea, 3 January 1881, ibid., p.171.

12. Cited by Kee, *The Laurel and the Ivy*, pp.318–19.

13. Herbert Gladstone Diary, cited by Kee, *The Laurel and the Ivy*, p.320.

14. Also known as the 'Primary Valuation', the 'Griffith's Valuation' – named after its director, the engineer and public servant Richard Griffith – this had been carried out in Ireland, county by county, between 1848 and 1860. The valuations, originally intended for taxation purposes, 'were set out in printed volumes, showing the occupants of land and houses, the persons from whom these were leased, and their area and value'. There was dispute over these valuations. Some felt that they were too high, although the valuations were in fact based on the 'unusually low agrarian prices recorded during 1849–52'. Connolly, ed., *The Oxford Companion to Irish History*, p.461. In 1881 the Irish Parliamentary Party and the Land League demanded rents set in accordance with these dated valuations. Strenuous objections were made by the landlords and others, as these valuations placed the land at estimates of at least 20 per cent below market rates. See O'Callaghan, *British High Politics and a Nationalist Ireland*, p.102.

15. Cited by Kee, *The Laurel and the Ivy*, p.363.

16. Pigott – described by Egan as 'for many years past the *bête noire* of Irish politics' – sold three titles: the *Irishman*, the *Flag of Ireland* and the *Shamrock*. Callanan, *Healy*, p.61.

17. Cited by Callanan, *Healy*, p.62.

18. O'Shea, *Parnell, Vol. I*, p.189.

19. Ibid., p.188.

20. Ibid., pp.188–9.

21. Testimony from the O'Shea divorce case was recorded in *The Times*; these records have been invaluable in reconstructing events.

22. *The Times*, 17 November 1890.

23. *The Times*, 17 November 1890. This statement was later greeted in court by laughter. O'Shea's statement is a contradiction of Katie's previous assertion that her husband had found Parnell's portmanteau, and sent it on to London. There may, of course, have been more than one piece of luggage.

24. *The Times*, 17 November 1890.

25. *The Times*, 17 November 1890.

26. O'Shea, *Parnell, Vol. I*, p.190.

27. Ibid.

28. Parnell to K. O'Shea, 20 July 1881, ibid., p.190.

29. Parnell to K. O'Shea, 22 July 1881, ibid., p.191.

30. Ibid., p.198.

31. Ibid., p.190.

32. Parnell to K. O'Shea, 1 August 1881, ibid., p.199.

33. Parnell to K. O'Shea, 17 August 1881, ibid.

34. Parnell to K. O'Shea, 10 September 1881, ibid., p.200.

35. Ibid., p.188.

36. *The Times*, 18 November 1890.

37. Hoppen, *The Mid-Victorian Generation 1846–1886*, p.671.

38. Foster, *Modern Ireland*, p.388. See pp.386–90 for a detailed analysis.

39. Ibid., p.389.

40. Cited by Kee, *The Laurel and the Ivy*, p.374.

41. Ibid., p.375.

42. Ibid.

43. Ibid., p.377.

44. Parnell to K. O'Shea, 7 October 1881, O'Shea, *Parnell, Vol. I*, p.201.

45. Cited by Kee, *The Laurel and the Ivy*, p.378.

46. Ibid., p.379.

47. Lyons, *Parnell*, p.165.

48. As we have seen, the Irish Parliament of 1782–1800.

49. Cited by Lyons, *Parnell*, p.167.

50. Parnell to K. O'Shea, 10 September 1881, O'Shea, *Parnell, Vol. I*, p.200.

51. Parnell to K. O'Shea, 25 September 1881, ibid.

52. Parnell to K. O'Shea, 4 October 1881, ibid., p.201.

53. See Foster, *Parnell*, pp.159–65.

54. Ibid., p.160.

55. Ibid., p.161.

56. Parnell to K. O'Shea, 7 October 1881, O'Shea, *Parnell, Vol. I*, p.201.

57. Parnell to K. O'Shea, 7 October 1881, ibid.

58. Cited by Jenkins, *Gladstone*, p.478.

59. O'Shea, *Parnell, Vol. I*, pp.194–5.

60. Parnell to K. O'Shea, 8 October 1881, ibid., pp.201–2.

61. Ibid., p.188.

62. Ibid., p.189.

63. Kee, *The Laurel and the Ivy*, p.389.

64. Parnell to K. O'Shea, 11 October 1881, O'Shea, *Parnell, Vol. I*, p.202.

65. There is some speculation about the absence of Katharine's letters to Charles Parnell throughout the entire memoir. Although some believe that the letters were buried with him, or that he did not preserve them for safety's sake, this is in my view unlikely. It is more plausible that Katie and her son were keen to present a sanitized and carefully edited version of the affair. There was also a considerable financial motive and the publisher would have been keen to emphasize the romantic and sensational elements of the tale. I suspect that Katie's letters were not included because they did not provide the evidence to support her story, and may even at times have contradicted it.

66. O'Shea, *Parnell, Vol. I*, pp.203–4.

67. Ibid., p.204.

68. Ibid., p.203.

69. Ibid., p.204.

70. 'The words in brackets appeared in the manuscript draft, evidently in error, and were deleted in the printed warrant which was actually handed to Parnell.' Lyons, *Parnell*, p.169.

71. Cited by Lyons, *Parnell*, p.169.

72. Parnell to K. O'Shea, 13 October 1881, O'Shea, *Parnell, Vol. I*, p.207.

73. Ibid., p.204.

74. T. W. Moody and Richard Hawkins, with Margaret Moody, eds., *Florence Arnold-Forster's Irish Journal*, p.273 (fn 1).

CHAPTER NINE: KILMAINHAM: PARNELL'S INCARCERATION

1. St John Ervine, *Parnell*, pp.180–1.

2. Some 955 were held in detention for some part of the following seven-month period. Alan O'Day, *The English Face of Irish Nationalism: Parnellite Involvement in British Politics 1880–86*, p.57.

Although the prison conditions for the 'political' interns were not especially harsh, the pernicious effects of prison life should not be underestimated. Health problems of varying degrees of severity for many of the prisoners were a constant concern. Poor ventilation, cramped living space, unfamiliar food and company as well as emotional strain and hardship played their part in affecting the well-being of the incarcerated parliamentarians and Land Leaguers.

3. Pat Cooke, 'Kilmainham Gaol: Interpreting Irish nationalism and Republicanism', in *Open Museum Journal*, Vol. 2, August 2000, p.5.

4. O'Shea, *Parnell, Vol. I*, p.210.

5. Ibid., p.206.

6. Ibid., pp.206–7.

7. Ibid., p.210.

8. Harrison, *Parnell Vindicated*, pp.123–4. Katie apparently said this to the author in 1891. He then did not actually publish the story until 1931. See Bibliography, p.558.

9. Harrison, *Parnell Vindicated*, pp.125–7.

10. Thomas Sexton (1848–1932) later represented West Belfast (1886–92) and North Kerry (1892–6). When he joined the Irish Parliamentary Party he became their chief spokesman on finance. A brilliant public speaker, he became known as 'Silvertongue Sexton', after Gladstone commented during the debate on the Land Bill of 1881 that Sexton's speech 'was the finest he had heard in the House of Commons'. D. J. Hickey and J. E. Doherty, *A Dictionary of Irish History since 1800*, p.527.

11. Parnell to K. O'Shea, 13 October 1881, O'Shea, *Parnell, Vol. I*, p.207.

12. Cited by Kee, *The Green Flag*, p.375.

13. O'Shea, *Parnell, Vol. I*, p.209.

14. Patrick Ford was Editor of the extreme Nationalist New York *Irish World*, and Egan, an ex-Fenian, was Treasurer of the Land League.

15. As R. F. Foster pointed out, one of the overlooked

achievements of the Ladies' Land League was its provision of a 'political baptism for a generation of radical Irishwomen who spoke on platforms, organized tactics, were denounced by the clergy and got arrested. Many of them would later be involved in the suffragette movement and Sinn Féin.' *Modern Ireland*, p.412.

16. A. B. Cooke and J. R. Vincent, 'Select documents; XXVIII Herbert Gladstone, Forster and Ireland, 1881–2 (11)', *Irish Historical Studies*, xviii, 69, March 1972, p.75. Cited by O'Callaghan, *British High Politics and a Nationalist Ireland*, p.92.

17. Quoted by Katharine O'Shea, in *Parnell, Vol., I* p.208.

18. See McCartney, 'Parnell, Davitt and the Irish Land Question', in King, ed., *Famine, Land and Culture in Ireland*, p.77.

19. McCartney, 'Parnell, Davitt and the Irish Land Question', in King, ed., *Famine, Land and Culture in Ireland*, p.77.

20. Parnell to K. O'Shea, 14 October 1881, O'Shea, *Parnell, Vol. I*, pp.210–11.

21. Ibid., p.215.

22. Ibid., p.215.

23. Parnell to K. O'Shea, 17 October 1881, ibid., p.211.

24. Parnell to K. O'Shea, 21 October 1881, ibid., pp.211–12.

25. Parnell to K. O'Shea, 19 October 1881, ibid., p.212.

26. Parnell to K. O'Shea, 21 October 1881, ibid., pp.212–13.

27. See Pauric Travers, 'The Blackbird of Avondale: Parnell at Kilmainham', in Donal McCartney and Pauric Travers, *The Ivy Leaf: The Parnells Remembered*, p.32.

28. Parnell to K. O'Shea, 21 October 1881, O'Shea, *Parnell, Vol. I*, pp.212–13.

29. Parnell to K. O'Shea, 26 October 1881, ibid., p.214.

30. Parnell to K. O'Shea, 28 October 1881, ibid., p.214.

31. Parnell to K. O'Shea, 1 November 1881, ibid., p.214.

32. Ibid., p.215.

33. Parnell to K. O'Shea, 2 November 1881, ibid., p.216.

34. Kee, *The Laurel and the Ivy*, p.395.

35. *United Ireland*, 15 October 1881; cited by Callanan, *Healy*, p.63.

36. Lyons, *Parnell*, p.180.

37. Ibid., p.187.

38. Parnell to K. O'Shea, 'Saturday' [n.d.], O'Shea, *Parnell, Vol. I*, p.219.

39. Parnell to K. O'Shea, [n.d.], ibid., p.220.

40. Parnell to K. O'Shea, 21 November 1881, ibid.

41. Parnell to K. O'Shea, 21 November 1881, ibid.

42. H. C. G. Matthew, ed., *The Gladstone Diaries with Cabinet Minutes and Prime-Ministerial*

Correspondence, Vol X, January 1881–June 1883, p.82.

43. Parnell to K. O'Shea, 29 November 1881, O'Shea, *Parnell, Vol. I*, p.221.

44. *Freeman's Journal*, 21 November 1881; cited by Lyons, *Parnell*, p.186.

45. See Lyons, *Parnell*, p.186.

46. Parnell to K. O'Shea, 29 November 1881, O'Shea, *Parnell, Vol. I*, p.221.

47. See, for example, Parnell to K. O'Shea, 18 November 1881, O'Shea, *Parnell, Vol. I*, p.220.

48. Parnell to K. O'Shea, 3 December 1881, ibid., p.222.

49. Parnell to K. O'Shea, 3 December 1881, ibid.

50. Parnell to K. O'Shea, 6 December 1881, ibid., p.223.

51. Parnell to K. O'Shea, 7 December 1881, ibid., pp.223–4.

52. Parnell to K. O'Shea, 14 December 1881, ibid., p.225.

53. Parnell to K. O'Shea, 15 December 1881, ibid., pp.225–6.

54. Parnell to K. O'Shea, 16 December 1881, ibid., p.226.

55. Parnell to K. O'Shea, 21 December 1881, ibid.

56. Parnell to K. O'Shea, 22 December 1881, ibid., p.227.

57. Parnell to K. O'Shea, 24 December 1881, ibid.

58. Parnell to K. O'Shea, 30 December 1881, ibid., p.228.

59. Parnell to K. O'Shea, 3 January 1882, ibid., p.229.

60. Parnell to K. O'Shea, 7 January 1882, ibid., pp.229–30.

61. Parnell to K. O'Shea, 11 January 1882, ibid., p.231.

62. Parnell to K. O'Shea, 17 January 1882, ibid., p.232.

63. Parnell to K. O'Shea, 21 January 1882, ibid., p.232.

64. Parnell to K. O'Shea, 23 January 1882, ibid., pp.232–3.

65. Parnell to K. O'Shea, 28 January 1882, ibid., p.233.

66. Parnell to K. O'Shea, 31 January 1882, ibid., p.233.

67. Parnell to K. O'Shea, 2 February 1882, ibid., p.234.

68. Parnell to K. O'Shea, 3 February 1882, ibid., p.234.

69. Parnell to K. O'Shea, 6 December 1881, ibid., p.223.

70. Parnell to K. O'Shea, 3 February 1882, ibid., p.234.

71. Parnell to K. O'Shea, 14 February 1882, ibid., pp.235–6. This is an example of the difficulty of interpreting the correspondence in the absence of Katharine's letters to Parnell. One can gather that she frequently wrote him of her fears and anxious state of mind. She also must have told him of her poor health. We know from his replies to her that she complained of poor sleeping, for example. This letter from Parnell would indicate that she also complained of losing weight. It gives a good indication of why the leader went to so much trouble to establish reliable and secret communications with Katie, and also why he constantly exhorted her to take care of herself, for his sake. Some of her critics have pointed out that she was a distraction and liability to Parnell at this critical moment of Ireland's quest for land and reform and independent rule.

72. Parnell to K. O'Shea, 17 February 1882, O'Shea, *Parnell, Vol. I*, p.236.

73. Parnell to K. O'Shea, 17 February 1882, ibid.

74. Parnell to K. O'Shea, 17 February 1882, p.237.

75. Parnell to K. O'Shea, 5 March 1882, ibid., pp.237–8.

76. Parnell to K. O'Shea, 16 March 1882, ibid., pp.238–9.

77. See Ervine, *Parnell*, p.190.

78. Parnell to K. O'Shea, 14 February 1882, *Parnell, Vol. I*, pp.235–6.

CHAPTER TEN:
LIES AND SUBTERFUGE

1. O'Shea, *Parnell, Vol. I*, p.237.

2. Parnell to K. O'Shea, 23 March 1882, ibid., p.240.

3. Harrison, *Parnell Vindicated*, p.124.

4. Parnell to K. O'Shea, 29 March 1882, O'Shea, *Parnell, Vol. I*, p.241.

5. Parnell to K. O'Shea, 29 March 1882, ibid., p.241.

6. Parnell to K. O'Shea, 5 November 1881, ibid., p.218.

7. Parnell to K. O'Shea, 30 March 1882, ibid., p.241.

8. Parnell to K. O'Shea, 30 March 1882, ibid., p.242.

9. Parnell to K. O'Shea, 5 April 1882, ibid., p.243.

10. Parnell to K. O'Shea, 7 April 1882, ibid., pp.243–4.

11. Ibid., p.244.

12. Ibid., pp.244–5.

13. Dillon had also been ill. Chief Secretary Forster had told Dillon's brother, 'The doors of Kilmainham are open if he likes to go to the Continent, but he must not stop here'. However, Dillon had refused to accept any terms and had made sure his refusal to do so was published in the *Freeman's Journal*, back in January 1882. Parnell's reference to the possibility of Dillon going abroad in April is therefore quite significant. See Kee, *The Laurel and the Ivy*, p.418.

14. Parnell to K. O'Shea, 7 April 1882, O'Shea, *Parnell, Vol. I*, p.244.

15. Parnell to K. O'Shea, 7 April 1882, ibid., p.244.

16. See McConville, *Irish Political Prisoners*, pp.255–66, for a very useful and quite fascinating discussion of Queen Victoria's attitude towards Ireland and the Irish, as well as an analysis of the consequences of this for Anglo-Irish relations.

17. A Fenian attack had caused further tragedy in England. An ill-fated rescue attempt was made on 12 December 1867 to free two Fenians held at Clerkenwell. The massive explosion – with no warning or regard for innocent life – caused twelve deaths and 120 injuries – a national tragedy in a poor community. All this contributed to enormous anti-Fenian sentiment in England. See McConville, *Irish Political Prisoners*, pp.120–39.

18. McConville, *Irish Political Prisoners, 1848–1922*, p.314.

19. Queen Victoria and Gladstone did not enjoy a good rapport. This had not always been the case. While Prince Albert was alive, Gladstone had been a royal favourite. But the situation had deteriorated during Gladstone's first premiership, due in large part to Benjamin Disraeli's successful attempts to turn the Queen against him. By his second premiership, in 1880, the monarch was a firm and partisan Tory who disliked her leading Liberal minister. This made the challenges faced by the premier – who was already at a disadvantage trying to hold together a very wide coalition of conservatives and progressives – even more daunting. And the relationship was time-consuming. It has been estimated that during 1880–5, Gladstone sent over 1,000 letters to the Queen, many in response to her (mostly censorial) correspondence of over 200 letters and 170 telegrams to him. Jenkins, *Gladstone*, pp.469–70.

20. James Loughlin, 'Nationality and Loyalty: Parnellism, Monarchy and the Construction of Irish Identity, 1880–5', in D. George Boyce and Alan O'Day, eds., *Ireland in Transition, 1867–1921*, p.36. This was an unfair accusation. As Loughlin points out, the 'widespread Irish view' that the Queen gave only £5 was incorrect. She actually contributed £2,500 personally (see footnote (2), p.244). Victoria was, nonetheless, a somewhat reluctant contributor and asked her Private Secretary, Henry Ponsonby, whether the entire amount of a £500 donation he had persuaded her to make had to go entirely to Ireland, given that there was 'so much distress in England'.

21. Loughlin, 'Nationality and Loyalty', p.39.

22. Royal Archives D32/13a, 15, 15a and 16: 13–18 April 1882; cited by McConville, *Irish Political Prisoners*, p.315 (fn 155).

23. Frank Hugh O'Donnell (1848–1916) was a Nationalist politician and author. He was initiated into the IRB and had a brief association with that movement. He worked as a

journalist in London and was Home Rule MP for Galway, then Dungaran, County Waterford. A most distinguished speaker, O'Donnell became a noted obstructionist. He was defeated by Parnell for the leadership in May 1880. O'Donnell refused to support the Land League and broke with the Parnellite wing of the party in 1881. He resigned his seat in 1885 and resumed his career in journalism. Hickey and Doherty, *A Dictionary of Irish History since 1800*, p.428.

24. Hickey and Doherty, *A Dictionary of Irish History since 1800*, p.428.

25. Although the others did not know it, Byrne was also 'closely connected' with a new Irish secret society, soon to be known as the 'Invincibles' that had been formed with the objective of assassinating leading members of the government administration in Ireland. Kee, *The Laurel and the Ivy*, p.420, and Lyons, *Parnell*, p.189. It should be noted that many Fenians in Ireland disapproved of assassination, in the belief that it was at odds with their ideals. See, in particular Kelly, *The Fenian Ideal*, p.16, for a discussion on Fenian disapproval on principle of assassinations.

26. Lyons, *Parnell*, p.189.

27. O'Shea, *Parnell, Vol. I*, p.245.

28. W. O'Shea to Gladstone, 8 April 1882; cited by Kee, *The Laurel and the Ivy*, p.419.

29. Infant mortality remained high in England (and elsewhere) throughout the nineteenth century. The *Journal of Statistical Studies* published in 1866 provided the data of 170 deaths per 1,000 births in England for the period 1860–1. These figures did not improve significantly until much later in the century. See L. Emmett Holt, M.D., LL.D., Professor of Diseases of Children, Columbia University, New York, in 'Infant Mortality, Ancient and Modern: An Historical Sketch', *Presidential address* before the American Association for the Study and Prevention of Infant Mortality, at the Fourth Annual Meeting, held at Washington, DC, November 14–17, 1913. Published in Archives of Paediatrics, 30:885–915, 1913.

30. Gladstone to W. O'Shea, 11 April 1882; cited by Kee, *The Laurel and the Ivy*, p.421.

31. W. O'Shea to W. E. Gladstone, *Private*, 13 April 1882; Gladstone Papers BL Add. MS. 44269, ff. 18–25: letter also reprinted in Joseph Chamberlain, *A Political Memoir*, pp.30–4.

32. W. O'Shea to W. E. Gladstone, *Private*, 13 April 1882; BL Add. MS. 44269, ff. 18–25.

33. See Henry Harrison, *Parnell, Joseph Chamberlain and Mr. Garvin*, p.156. Although Harrison was admittedly biased towards Parnell and against Willie O'Shea, this assertion was not disputed by O'Shea or any of his (few) supporters.

34. Parnell to K. O'Shea, 13 April 1882, O'Shea, *Parnell, Vol. I*, pp.245–6.

35. Parnell to K. O'Shea, 15 April 1882, ibid., p.246.

36. Parnell to K. O'Shea, 16 April 1882, ibid., pp.246–7.

37. Parnell to K. O'Shea, 15 and 16 April 1882, ibid., p.246.

38. Gladstone to W. O'Shea, 15 April 1882, in R. Barry O'Brien, *The Life of Charles Stewart Parnell*, pp.259–60.

39. Cited by Lyons, *Parnell*, O'Shea to Joseph Chamberlain, 15 April 1882, p.191.

40. Although a well-known politician in his own right, he achieved far more fame as the father of the celebrated British Prime Minister Winston Churchill.

41. R. F. Foster, *Lord Randolph Churchill: A Political Life*, p.82.

42. Joseph Chamberlain, edited from the original manuscript by C. H. D. Howard, *A Political Memoir 1880–92*, pp.34–5.

43. His great friend and political ally, Sir Charles Dilke, recorded on 12 January 1881: 'Chamberlain's position at this moment was that he personally did not believe in coercion, but that the feeling in the country was such that any Government would be forced to propose it, and he was not sufficiently clear that it was certain to fail to be bound as an honest man to necessarily oppose it. Dilke's Diary, 12 January 1881, in J. L. Garvin, *The Life of Joseph Chamberlain, Volume One, 1836–1885*, p.333.

44. W. O'Shea to J. Chamberlain, 18 April 1882, in Chamberlain, *A Political Memoir*, pp.35–6.

45. O'Shea, *Parnell, Vol. I*, p.247.

46. Florence Arnold-Foster was the adoptive daughter of the Chief Secretary and his wife. Although clearly biased in his favour, and increasingly indignant at how the outrages in Ireland were blamed on his coercive policies, she was an astute and intelligent observer. Her diary for the two-year period, 1880–82, provides a valuable source of information, as she was extremely well connected. She met everybody who was anybody in both England and Ireland and was her father's confidante, often walking with him to the House of Commons or to Dublin Castle. As one commentator noted, 'what most clearly emerges from her diaries is the profound sense of Christian responsibility which weighed Forster down as he bore his dreaded burden: solving Ireland'. Margaret O'Callaghan,

British High Politics and a Nationalist Ireland, p.87.

47. Florence Arnold-Foster, *My Irish Journal, June 1880–August 1882*, 13 April 1882, pp.447–8. This journal was published with the later title of *Florence Arnold-Forster's Irish Journal*, edited by T. W. Moody and Richard Hawkins with Margaret Moody. When quoting from the diary, I will refer to it by its original title and author.

48. Arnold-Forster, *My Irish Journal*, 21 April 1882, p.455.

49. Ibid.

50. Forster earned this epithet – unfairly, as it happens – because it was during his period of office as Chief Secretary that an earlier administrative decision was implemented. This allowed for police officers, on certain occasions, to use buckshot rather than the more lethal ball cartridge. See *Irish Historical Studies*, Vol. xvi, no. 62 (September 1968), p.238; cited by Robert Kee, *The Green Flag: A History of Irish Nationalism*, p.382.

It has been said that Forster's appointment was to be 'a classic instance of the cruellest dilemma that can face a liberal in politics. He was a paragon of Victorian liberalism, a man of the highest moral courage and personal integrity, a humane and tender-hearted man, of marked simplicity of life ... He was a firm believer in individual and political liberty and in social and international cooperation ... Yet, in an endeavour to pacify a distracted country, he felt it necessary to act in an increasingly despotic way in defence, as he believed, of those very social and political values with which his coercive regime was incompatible.' T. W. Moody, *Florence Arnold-Foster's Irish Journal*, pp.xvi–xvii.

51. O'Shea, *Parnell, Vol. I*, p.247.

52. Parnell to J. McCarthy, 22 April 1882, O'Shea, *Parnell, Vol. I*, p.252.

53. Parnell to K. O'Shea, 25 April 1882, ibid., p.253.

54. Cited by Pauric Travers, '"The Blackbird of Avondale": Parnell at Kilmainham', in McCartney and Travers, *The Ivy Leaf*, p.24.

55. Herbert John Gladstone, *After Thirty Years*, p.274.

56. O'Callaghan, *British High Politics and a Nationalist Ireland*, p.93.

57. O'Day, *The English Face of Irish Nationalism*, p.61.

58. O'Shea, *Parnell Vol. I*, p.256.

59. See 'A Note on Sources' in Bibliography.

60. Emily Monroe Dickinson, *A Patriot's Mistake*, p.107.

61. Ibid., p.108.

62. Chamberlain, *A Political Memoir*, p.36.

63. Although Redmond introduced the bill in the private members' ballot, it had in fact been drafted by Maurice Healy. Tim Healy was one of its sponsors.

64. Chamberlain, *A Political Memoir*, p.38.

65. O'Shea to Chamberlain, 23 April 1882, in Chamberlain, *A Political Memoir*, p.39.

66. O'Shea to Chamberlain, 23 April 1882, in ibid., p.40.

67. Parnell to Justin McCarthy, 25 April 1882, in O'Shea, *Parnell, Vol. I*, p.252.

68. O'Shea, *Parnell, Vol. I*, pp.252–3.

69. Parnell to K. O'Shea, 25 April 1882, in ibid., p.253.

70. Parnell to W. O'Shea, 28 April 1882, in ibid., pp.254–5.

71. Parnell to K. O'Shea, 30 April 1882, in ibid., p.255.

72. Ibid., p.257.

CHAPTER ELEVEN: TWO HUSBANDS

1. Parnell to K. O'Shea, 25 April 1882, in O'Shea, *Parnell, Vol. I*, p.253.

2. W. H. O'Shea to J. Chamberlain, 25 April 1882, J. Chamberlain Papers, JC 8/8/1/1, in Lyons, *Parnell*, p.176.

3. Although she was christened Claude Sophie, Katie referred to the infant as 'Sophie' when describing her resting place (O'Shea, *Parnell, Vol. I*, p.247). The name Sophie was chosen, according to Katie, as she was one of Charles Parnell's favourite sisters. Claude was, less suspiciously, the name of Lord Truro, one of Katharine's old friends. It is possible that Katie intended to call her daughter by her second name, Sophie, for everyday usage.

4. It is possible, of course, that Willie O'Shea's letter was in itself part of the conspiracy to deceive. It seems, however, an unlikely and rather contrived prospect. The explanation to Chamberlain, whom he did not know well, was unnecessary in the first instance. It should also be observed as a more general point that O'Shea was temperamentally unsuited to this kind of charade, and full of his own importance. For him to have set out to deceive astute political colleagues as well as his own sister and mother so deliberately seems highly implausible (but not impossible).

5. 'In 1881 O'Shea petitioned Gladstone on behalf of his "friend and kinsman" [he was apparently a distant cousin], the Baronet Sir George O'Donnell (spelt variously as O'Donnell or O'Donell), to use his old family title of Tyrconell. (See BL, Gladstone Papers, Add. MS 44269, ff. 1–2, 5 April 1881; ff. 13–14, 5 Aug 1881).' Jordan, *Kitty O'Shea*, p.239, f. 8.

6. It is highly unlikely that Lady Mary O'Connell would have taken on this responsibility had she known that their godchild, Clare, was in fact Parnell's child.

7. Mary O'Shea to K. O'Shea, 21 May 1882, in O'Shea, *Parnell, Vol. I*, p.248.

8. Mary O'Shea to K. O'Shea, 21 May 1882, in ibid., pp.248–9.

9. Ibid., p.247.

10. Mary O'Shea to K. O'Shea, 21 May 1882, in ibid., p.249.

11. Davitt, *The Fall of Feudalism*, p.353.

12. BL Add. MS. Gladstone Papers 33766 f. 71. Memorandum dated 5 May 1882 of conversation with O'Shea, who also stated that Parnell was 'now in earnest about putting down lawlessness, as he feels himself in danger of being supplanted by more violent men'. Conor Cruise O'Brien, *Parnell and his Party 1880–90*, pp.76–7 (also see fn 1).

13. On 30 April O'Shea told Forster that Parnell had told him that he had spoken to Dillon 'and had brought him round to be in full agreement with himself upon the general questions'. On 5 May O'Shea told Gladstone that Parnell's colleagues were aware of the leader's plans. Later, when testifying before the Special Commission into Parnellism and Crime (1887–8), he claimed that these negotiations were *not* known to Parnell's colleagues. See Lyons, *Parnell*, p.199 (and fnn 102, 103 & 104).

14. W. E. Gladstone to Forster, 30 April 1882, *Secret*, BL Add. MS. 44160 f. 160, in H. C. G. Matthew, ed., *The Gladstone Diaries, Vol. X, January 1881–June 1883*, pp.246–7.

15. Arnold-Foster, *My Irish Journal, June 1880–August 1882*, 30 April 1882, pp.467–8.

16. Ibid., 3 May 1882, p.473.

17. Cited by Kee, *The Laurel and the Ivy*, p.436.

18. John Morley, *The Life of William Ewart Gladstone, Vol. III*, p.65.

19. Spencer Compton Cavendish, Marquess of Hartington (later Duke of Devonshire), was a well-known and formidable Whig politician. He was famously three times offered the premiership and three times turned it down. His offices included: Postmaster-General, Secretary of State for India, the War Office.

20. Dilke Papers, 43936, 97, cited by Roy Jenkins, *Dilke: A Victorian Tragedy*, p.152.

21. R. Barry O'Brien, *The Life of Charles Stewart Parnell*, pp.268–9.

22. Cited by Foster, *Parnell*, p.182.

23. Ibid., p.183.

24. See ibid., pp.185–96, for more detail and analysis of Avondale finances.

25. O'Shea, *Parnell, Vol. I*, p.262.

26. Parnell to K. O'Shea, 14 February 1882, in ibid., p.235.

27. Jordan, *Kitty O'Shea*, p.62.

28. Mrs Brand's gallery refers to the Ladies Gallery at the House of Commons. Mrs Brand (from August 1881 Lady Brand), as wife of the Speaker, Sir Henry Brand (who held this position during 1872–84), controlled access to this gallery.

29. Arnold-Forster, *My Irish Journal*, 4 May 1882, p.475.

30. Ibid., p.476.

31. Ervine, *Parnell*, p.195.

32. Cited by Lyons, *Parnell*, p.205.

33. Chamberlain, *A Political Memoir*, pp.61–2.

34. Gladstone introduced an Arrears Act on 15 May 1882. It provided £800,000 to tenants to pay off arrears, so that they could benefit from the 'fair rent' as promised by the Land Act 1881. See Hickey and Doherty, *A Dictionary of Irish History since 1800*, p.18.

35. Cited by Kee, *The Laurel and the Ivy*, p.433.

36. Burke was one of the few Irish Catholics to have made a successful career in Dublin Castle and had been Under-Secretary since 1869. He was therefore regarded by some extremists as a traitor or a 'Castle Rat' and a 'legitimate' target for assassination.

37. Horse-drawn open carriage/cart.

38. James Carey was a builder and the owner of slum tenement property. He had presented himself as a candidate the previous year for Dublin Town Council. He later informed on his accomplices.

39. Byrne, it is recalled, was the Secretary of the Land League of Britain, and was one of the men who had met Parnell in London on the first day of his parole from Kilmainham.

40. John Morley, 1st Viscount (1838–1923), was Chief Secretary February–July 1886; 1892–95; and Lord President of the Council 1910–14. He was closely involved with the Irish question and Home Rule throughout his career.

41. See John Morley, *The Life of William Ewart Gladstone, Vol. III*, p.67.

42. *The Times*, 9 May 1882, p.6; cited by Jordan, *Kitty O'Shea*, p.74.

43. *The Times*, 9 May 1882, p.8; cited by Jordan, *Kitty O'Shea*, pp.74–5.

44. Arnold-Forster, *My Irish Journal*, 8 May 1882, pp.486–7.

45. George Villiers, 1st Duke of Buckingham, was a great favourite of King James I and VI of England and Scotland and one of the most rewarded royal courtiers in all history. He was murdered by a disgruntled soldier on 23 August 1628. Arnold-Forster, *My Irish Journal*, 8 May 1882, p.487.

46. R. Barry O'Brien, *The Life of Charles Stewart Parnell*, pp.273–4.

47. Katharine Tynan, *Twenty-Five Years: Reminiscences*, p.92.

48. O'Shea, *Parnell, Vol. I*, p.263.

49. Morley, *The Life of William Ewart Gladstone, Vol. III*, p.68.

50. Gladstone papers, BL Add. MS. 44545 f. 132, in H. C. G. Matthew, ed., *The Gladstone Diaries, Vol. X*, 7 May 1882, p.255.

51. There are some inconsistencies in the reports of the sequence of visits made by the pair. Chamberlain wrote that Parnell and McCarthy had come first to him, and then Dilke. This is contradicted in both Dilke's and McCarthy's records.

52. Cited by Jenkins, *Dilke*, p.153.

53. Ervine, *Parnell*, p.202.

54. John Howard Parnell, *Charles Stewart Parnell*, p.202.

55. Dilke Papers 43885, 234; in Jenkins, *Dilke*, p.154.

56. Lyons, *Charles Stewart Parnell*, p.209.

57. At this time, O'Shea had become increasingly hostile to Parnell.

58. Joseph Chamberlain, *A Political Memoir*, p.62.

59. See Chamberlain, *A Political Memoir*, p.63.

60. Charles Stewart Parnell's response, under oath, to examination by Mr H. H. Asquith, during the Special Commission 1888. Evidence reprinted in Harrison, *Parnell Vindicated*, p.326.

61. These recollections were published a year before O'Shea testified to the Special Commission. Cited by Lyons, *Parnell*, p.210.

62. Davitt Papers (Trinity College Dublin) MS. 9537/53; in McConville, *Irish Political Prisoners*, p.323 (fn 180).

63. Gladstone's principal Private Secretary, Edward Walter Hamilton, recorded on 18 June 1881 that O'Shea had made an 'extraordinary proposal' the other day, offering to 'effect a compromise between the Government and the Parnellites'. O'Shea suggested a government-subsidized reduction in Irish rents in exchange for 'hearty support for the Government in and out of Parliament' from the Parnellites, who would also 'stay outrages'. It was, Hamilton added, 'needless to say that the Government will not "look at" such a proposal'. Hamilton's following comment provides a useful indication of the 'official mind' at the time. He asks: how could the government 'demean themselves to bargain with such a fellow as Parnell, were the terms even feasible and fair?' Dudley W. R. Bahlman, ed., *The Diary of Sir Edward Walter Hamilton 1880–1885, Vol. I*, 18 June 1881, p.147.

64. Bahlman, ed., *Hamilton, Vol. I*, 16 April 1882, p.253.

65. Arnold-Forster, *My Irish Journal*, 8 May 1882, p.488.

66. O'Shea, *Parnell, Vol. I*, p.263.

67. Ibid.

68. In 1878 Davitt and John Denvir tried to recruit Parnell into the IRB and were told that he was determined never to join a secret society.

69. P. Maume, 'Parnell and the IRB Oath', in *Irish Historical Studies*, xxix, 1994–5, pp.363–70. Maume's assessment – and that of most experts – is that the evidence is inconclusive, but nonetheless plausible.

70. This diary, it must be noted, was not written up until some years later, in 1890. This is not to suggest that Dilke did not keep the diary regularly, merely that he could have been influenced by subsequent events when later editing the work.

71. Stephen Gwynn and Gertrude Tuckwell, *The Life of Sir Charles Dilke, Vol. I*, p.445; cited by Harrison, *Parnell Vindicated*, p.279.

72. Bahlman, ed., *Hamilton, Vol. I*, 20 June 1882, p.290.

CHAPTER TWELVE: EMISSARY TO THE PRIME MINISTER

1. The O'Sheas called one another by the pet names of 'Dick' for Katie and 'Boysie' for Willie. It is always of interest to check which salutations were used throughout their years of correspondence. The use of affectionate nicknames in their letters to one another almost invariably meant that relations between them were good. When things were not, they addressed one another more formally.

2. O'Shea, *Parnell, Vol. I*, pp.263–4.

3. Ibid., pp.264–5.

4. *The Times*, 8 May 1882, in Lyons, *Parnell*, p.212.

5. Arnold-Forster, *My Irish Journal*, 11 May 1882, p.492.

6. Ibid., p.494.

7. Chamberlain, *A Political Memoir*, p.64.

8. Ibid.

9. Ibid., p.65.

10. Healy, *Letters and Leaders of my Day, Vol. I*, p.161.

11. Arnold-Forster, *My Irish Journal*, 15 May 1882, p.498.

12. He was regarded as an outsider by many at Westminster. Many MPs from more traditional backgrounds questioned whether such a strong-minded man of business really understood the 'gentlemanly' arts of politics. After Chamberlain's appointment to the Cabinet, he nominated two of his brothers to membership of the Reform Club, frequented by Liberal members of the two Houses of Parliament. These nominations were held for two years, and were then blackballed by more than sixty members of the Club – perhaps by friends of Forster. Granville and Hartington were dismayed at the direction to which this kind of behaviour could lead, and convened a meeting of the membership to do away with blackballing. The Chamberlain brothers could then gain entry to the Club by majority vote. This meeting took place, however, in the wake of the news of Chamberlain's role in negotiating the Kilmainham agreement. Feeling against the proposed change ran high, and one member stated: 'there was no right more sacred in the eyes of every true-born Englishman than the right to black-ball anyone he pleased at a club election'. The proposal was rejected. Peter T. Marsh, *Joseph Chamberlain: Entrepreneur in Politics*, p.142.

13. Victoria was especially incensed by Davitt, whom she regarded as a dangerous and disloyal criminal. In January 1882 she had taken the highly unusual (and improper) step of getting her Private Secretary to bypass the government channels and get her information on Davitt from Cross, the former Home Secretary. See McConville, *Irish Political Prisoners*, pp.315 and 324–5.

14. Victoria to Gladstone, 4 May 1882; Royal Archives D32/56, in McConville, *Irish Political Prisoners*, p.324 (fn 183).

15. When the Conservative government of 1879 was defeated, there was much discontent in the party and a perceived lack of strong leadership. Balfour and three other Tory backbenchers, Lord Randolph Churchill, John Gorst and Sir Henry Drummond, formed the 'Fourth Party'. This was short-lived and not taken very seriously.

16. Max Egremont, *Balfour: A Life of Arthur James Balfour*, p.61.

17. Arnold-Forster, *My Irish Journal*, 16 May 1882, p.499.

18. O'Shea, *Parnell, Vol. I*, pp.267–8.

19. Wood went out on the Egyptian Expedition of 1882 and commanded the 4th Brigade and 2nd Division. He was thanked by both Houses of Parliament, and received the Bronze Star, 2nd class, Medjidie. He went out on the Sudan Expedition 1884–5 as Major-General on Lines of Communication. He was awarded the Grand Cordon of the Medjidie, 1st class, in 1885 and Knight Grand Cross of the Most Honourable Order of Bath in 1901. He was appointed General, Commanding 2nd Army Corps (later Southern Command) from 1901 to 1904, and Field-Marshal on 8 April 1903.

20. Field-Marshal Sir (Henry) Evelyn Wood, *Winnowed Memories*, p.20.

21. Henry Du Pre Labouchere (1831–1912) was the nephew of the Whig politician Henry

Labouchere, 1st Baron Taunton. He became a minor diplomat and then a Liberal MP. During a twelve-year break in his parliamentary career, from 1868 he gained renown as a journalist and publisher, notably through his personal weekly journal, *Truth*. He was rebellious and outspoken. During the 1880s he became a firm and vocal Radical. Labouchere tried to create a governing coalition between the Radicals and the Irish Nationalists that would exclude or marginalize the Whigs (led by Lord Hartington).

22. Cited by Kee, *The Laurel and the Ivy*, p.449.

23. Ibid.

24. Ibid.

25. K. O'Shea to Gladstone, 23 May 1882, Gladstone Papers BL Add. MS. 44269 ff. 75–8.

26. Gladstone to K. O'Shea, 23 May 1882, Gladstone Papers BL Add. MS. 44269 ff. 79–8.

27. K. O'Shea to Gladstone, 26 (?) May 1882, Gladstone Papers BL Add. MS. 44269 ff. 81–2.

28. Arnold-Forster, *My Irish Journal*, 18 May 1882, p.501.

29. There are numerous factual inaccuracies in Katharine's account of her meetings with Gladstone. She wrote for example that this encounter took place on 2 June. O'Shea, *Parnell, Vol. I*, p.269.

30. O'Shea, *Parnell, Vol. I*, p.270.

31. Bahlman, ed., *Hamilton, Vol. I*, 20 June 1882, p.290.

32. Earl Granville to W. E. Gladstone, 24 May [1882]; BL Add. MS. 44,174, f. 127; in Lyons, *Charles Stewart Parnell*, p.218.

33. W. S. Blunt, *My Diaries, Vol. II*, 25 October 1909, pp.280–1. George Leveson Gower apparently related this story to Blunt during a shooting-party.

34. Sir W. Harcourt to Earl Spencer, 8 June 1882, in Lyons, *Parnell*, p.222.

35. Lyons, *Parnell*, p.222.

36. Labouchere to Joseph Chamberlain, 16 May 1882, in A. L. Thorold, *The Life of Sir Henry Labouchere*, p.161.

37. The Liberal Chief Whip, Lord Richard Grosvenor.

38. Labouchere to Joseph Chamberlain, 3 June 1882, in Thorold, *Labouchere*, p.164.

39. O'Shea, *Parnell, Vol. I*, p.270.

40. Ibid., p.273.

41. K. O'Shea to Gladstone, 22 June 1882, Gladstone Papers BL Add. MS. 44269 f.90–1.

42. W. O'Shea to J. Chamberlain, 25 May 1882, UBL J. Chamberlain Papers: JC8/8/1/6.

43. K. O'Shea to Gladstone, 16 June 1882, Gladstone Papers BL Add. MS. 44269 fol. 84–5.

44. K. O'Shea to Gladstone, 17 June 1882, Gladstone Papers BL Add MS. 44269 fol. 87.

45. W. O'Shea to J. Chamberlain, 23 June 1882, J. Chamberlain Papers UBL: JC8/8/1/7.

46. W. O'Shea to Parnell, 23 June 1882, J. Chamberlain Papers UBL: JC8/8/2G1.

47. W. O'Shea to J. Chamberlain, 28 June 1882, J. Chamberlain Papers UBL: JC8/8/1/8.

48. T. P. O'Connor, *Memoirs, Vol. I*, p.231.

49. FCRO, Glynne Gladstone MSS, GG2165, Sir George H. Murray to Henry Neville Gladstone, 27 August 1934; in Jordan, *Kitty O'Shea*, p.84. Jordan's analysis of what Gladstone knew of the affair in 1882 is admirably thorough. Gladstone's sons were infuriated by Leveson Gower's claim, which was published in 1934 in a study of the Queen's Private Secretaries, Paul Emden's *Behind the Throne*. Herbert Gladstone had sworn in a court of law his denial that rumours of the relationship existed in 1882 (*The Times*, 3 February 1927, p.5). Jordan points out that Leveson Gower's story has some 'weak' points of detail, but that on the whole his 'story does ring true'. Furthermore, 'to his credit, he held out, warning that if a statement were issued denying Gladstone's awareness of the strong rumours in circulation in 1882, "I should be compelled to contradict it".' See Jordan, *Kitty O'Shea*, p.234 (fn 10).

50. Labouchere to J. Chamberlain, n.d. marked 'Thursd.', Gladstone Papers BL Add. MS. 44125 f.150, in Callanan, *Healy*, p.76.

51. K. O'Shea to Gladstone, 'Private', 26 June 1882, Gladstone Papers BL Add. MS. 44269 fol. 93–6.

52. K. O'Shea to Gladstone, 5 July 1882, Gladstone Papers BL Add. MS. 44269 fol. 97–8.

53. W. O'Shea to Parnell, 28 June 1882, J. Chamberlain Papers UBL JC8/8/2G2.

54. W. O'Shea to J. Chamberlain, 28 June 1882, J. Chamberlain Papers UBL JC8/8/1/9.

55. K. O'Shea to Gladstone, 10 July 1882, Gladstone Papers BL Add. MS. 44269 f 99.

56. K. O'Shea to Gladstone, 11 July 1882, Gladstone Papers BL Add. MS. 44269 fols. 104–5.

57. See Jane McL. Coté, *Fanny and Anna Parnell*, for a full study of the establishment of the Ladies' Land League, in particular pp.148–68.

58. The organization, made up of young women, was headed by an honorary president, Mrs Anne Deane. She was a middle-aged widow – patriotic and a cousin of John Dillon. See Coté, *Fanny and Anna Parnell*, pp.158–9.

59. Coté, *Fanny and Anna Parnell*, p.159.

60. See ibid., pp.159–60. I am grateful to Coté's excellent research on the LLL and its members.

61. Ibid., p.160.

62. The *Nation*, 5 February 1881, cited by Coté, *Fanny and Anna Parnell*, p.161.

63. The *Nation*, 21 March 1881, cited by Coté, *Fanny and Anna Parnell*, p.168.

64. William O'Brien and Desmond Ryan, eds., *Devoy's Post Bag, Volume I: 1871–1928*, p.475.

65. Parnell to Patrick Egan, 1 March 1880, in Callanan, *Healy*, p.33.

66. It is very difficult to know the exact number of Irish emigrants to the USA. Overall, the number has been estimated at approximately 5.5 million since the American Revolution. Between the onset of the Great Famine and 1891 about 3 million Irish arrived in America.

67. See Connolly, ed., *The Oxford Companion to Irish History* (new edn), p.276, and Foster, *Modern Ireland*, pp.358–62.

68. Coté, *Fanny and Anna Parnell*, p.89.

69. I am grateful to Jane McL. Coté's detailed descriptions of the house, furnishings and estate, including its history. See Coté, *Fanny and Anna Parnell*, pp.88–90.

70. Edward Robb Ellis, *The Epic of New York City*, p.326.

71. The world economy slumped in the 1870s, and the US economy fell with it. The depression lasted from 1873 to 1879. It was a catastrophe. Bankruptcies rose from 5,100 in 1873 to 10,478 in 1878 and by 1876 half of America's railworks were in receivership. Within one year, there were an estimated 3 million people unemployed. Edwin G. Burrows and Mike Wallace, *Gotham: A History of New York City to 1898*, p.1022.

72. Burrows and Wallace, *Gotham*, p.960.

73. Burrows and Wallace, *Gotham*, p.961. I am grateful to the authors for their fascinating study of the history of New York City.

74. See Elisabeth Kehoe, *Fortune's Daughters: The Extravagant Lives of the Jerome Sisters: Jennie Churchill, Clara Frewen and Leonie Leslie*, for more on the Jerome and Churchill families. See also Gail MacColl and Carol McD. Wallace, To *Marry an English Lord: The Victorian and Edwardian Experience*; and Amanda MacKenzie Stuart, *Consuelo and Alva: Love and Power in the Gilded Age* (London: HarperCollins, 2005).

75. Burrows and Wallace, *Gotham*, p.964. The authors make the interesting point that these men, along with A. T. Stewart, James Brown and William Dodge, were prominent, but 'not quite on a par with Rhinelanders, Livingstones, or Stuyvesants. Creating a natural history museum would strengthen their social position while underscoring their commitment to newly prized scientific values', p.964.

76. Foster, *Modern Ireland*, p.358.

77. Ibid.

78. Cited by Foster, *Parnell*, p.253. I am very grateful to Foster for his highly detailed study of Delia Stewart Parnell's life. See pp.225–40.

79. Ibid., p.231.

80. Ibid., p.235.

81. Ibid., p.236.

82. Anna Parnell to Mrs Lennon, 16 February 1908. In the private collection of Mrs Mary Slevin, Kiltyclogher, in Coté, *Fanny and Anna Parnell*, p.216.

83. Cited by Foster, *Parnell*, pp.246–7. As he points out, Fanny Parnell was in fact thirty years old at this time.

84. Ibid., p.246. See pp.241–59 for a full portrait of Fanny Parnell's life.

85. Coté, *Fanny and Anna Parnell*, p.221.

86. Ibid.

87. O'Shea, *Parnell, Vol. II*, p.44.

88. Ibid.

89. Cited by Coté, *Fanny and Anna Parnell*, p.222.

90. As Coté explains, there were frequent attempts made after Charles Parnell's death to have Fanny's remains brought back to Ireland for re-burial. All Fanny's heirs had to agree to this, however, according to an injunction taken out by her mother's lawyer. Anna always refused, as she believed, like her brother, that people should be buried where they had died. See Coté, *Fanny and Anna Parnell*, pp.223–4.

91. O'Shea, *Parnell, Vol. I*, p.261.

92. Ibid.

93. In fact, Coté makes a convincing case for the argument that the male executive of the Land League was threatened by the independence of the Ladies' League. When their overdraft reached £5,000, the women were told to sign a document that effectively rendered them 'subservient clerical assistants'. See Coté, *Fanny and Anna Parnell*, pp.218–19.

94. Parnell to K. O'Shea, 20 August 1882, O'Shea, *Parnell, Vol. II*, p.51.

95. O'Shea, *Parnell, Vol. I*, p. 261.

96. Ibid., p.273.

CHAPTER THIRTEEN:
THE GO-BETWEEN

1. 'Grand Old Man'.

2. O'Shea, *Parnell, Vol. I*, p.274.

3. Ibid.

4. Herbert Gladstone, *After Thirty Years*, p.301.

5. O'Shea, *Parnell, Vol. I*, pp.270, 274 and 275.

6. H. Gladstone, *After Thirty Years,* p.302.

7. Bahlman, ed., *Hamilton, Vol. I,* 29 August 1882, pp.326–7.

8. O'Shea wrote to Chamberlain that he had asked Labouchere to let him know that he had put down a question to Chamberlain 'as to the continuance of the heading in the submarine excavation near Dover' and the steps that Chamberlain proposed 'to take in order to bring to justice the person or persons guilty of this infraction'. W. O'Shea to J. Chamberlain, 10 August 1882, J. Chamberlain Papers UBL JC8/8/1/13.

9. W. O'Shea to J. Chamberlain, 10 August 1882, J. Chamberlain Papers UBL JC8/8/1/13.

10. K. O'Shea to Gladstone, 15 September 1882, Gladstone Papers BL Add. MS. 44269 fols. 114–15.

11. W. O'Shea to K. O'Shea, 13 September 1882, Gladstone Papers BL Add. MS. 44269 fols. 116–17.

12. See Kee, *The Laurel and the Ivy,* pp.459–61, for more on O'Shea's political activities in 1882.

13. W. O'Shea to K. O'Shea, 31 March 1882, O'Shea, *Parnell, Vol. II,* p.194.

14. W. O'Shea to K. O'Shea, 1 May 1882, ibid., p.195.

15. W. O'Shea to K. O'Shea, 29 September 1882, ibid., p.198.

16. W. O'Shea to K. O'Shea, 1 May 1882, ibid., p.195.

17. W. O'Shea to K. O'Shea, 26 and 31 August 1882, ibid., p.197.

18. W. O'Shea to K. O'Shea, *Sunday* n.d., ibid., p.198.

19. W. O'Shea to K. O'Shea, 26 August 1882, ibid., pp.196–7.

20. Some of the earliest occupants of this exalted post were the Dukes of Richmond, Bedford and Northumberland, and the Marquess Wellesley. David Cannadine, *Ornamentalism: How the British Saw Their Empire,* p.15.

21. Elizabeth, Countess of Fingal, *Seventy Years Young: Memories of Elizabeth, Countess of Fingal as Told to Pamela Hinkson,* p.76. Lady Fingall was originally a Burke from Moycullen in County Galway. In 1883 she married the 11th Earl of Fingall. The Fingalls were members of the landed aristocracy, who chose to remain in Ireland after independence. Lady Fingall (known as Daisy) was a renowned society hostess in Ireland and in England, where she knew many influential figures of the day.

22. Cannadine, *Ornamentalism,* p.15.

23. Ibid.

24. W. O'Shea to K. O'Shea, 31 August 1882, O'Shea, *Parnell, Vol. II,* p.197.

25. W. O'Shea to K. O'Shea, *Sunday* n.d., ibid.

26. It is entirely in keeping with the nature of the two men that when in Dublin O'Shea chose to reside at the posh Shelbourne

Hotel, and Parnell at the more modest Morrison's establishment. See Elizabeth Bowen, *The Shelbourne,* for a history of this classic Dublin landmark.

27. Parnell to K. O'Shea, 20 August 1882, O'Shea, *Parnell, Vol. II,* p.51.

28. John Howard Parnell, *Charles Stewart Parnell,* pp.125–6.

29. T. P. O'Connor, *Memoirs, Vol. I,* p.235.

30. Ibid.

31. Special Commission Brief, Davitt Proof, p.79; in Callanan, *Healy,* p.77.

32. T. Healy to Maurice Healy, 5 October 1882, in Callanan, *Healy,* p.77.

33. The best translation for this is someone for whom success, or ideas, has gone to their head.

34. Bahlman, ed., *Hamilton, Vol. I,* 29 August 1882, p.328.

35. Parnell to K. O'Shea, 10 October 1882, O'Shea, *Parnell, Vol. II,* p.52.

36. Parnell to K. O'Shea, 14 October 1882, ibid.

37. O'Shea, ibid., p.54.

38. Gladstone to Spencer, 29 August 1882, in Lyons, *Parnell,* p.229.

39. K. O'Shea to Gladstone, 22 September 1882, Gladstone Papers BL Add. MS. 44269 fols. 121–2.

40. As Honorary Secretary to the Irish Parliamentary Party, he drafted the Plan of Campaign,

which he published in *United Ireland* in October 1886. Thereafter he played – with Dillon and William O'Brien – a leading role in the land agitation. Harrington was called to the bar in 1887. He acted as Counsel for Parnell during the sittings of the Commission on 'Parnellism and Crime' in 1888–9. Harrington remained a loyal Parnellite throughout and after the split.

41. Lyons, *Parnell,* pp.235–6.

42. Cited by Barry O'Brien, *Parnell,* pp.283–4.

43. Davitt, *The Fall of Feudalism,* pp.377–8.

44. K. O'Shea to Gladstone, 'Private', 6 October 1882, Gladstone Papers BL Add. MS. 44269 fols. 124–5.

45. Gladstone to K. O'Shea, 10 October 1882, 'Private', Gladstone Papers BL Add. MS. 44269 f. 134, in Matthew, ed., *The Gladstone Diaries, Vol X,* p.348.

46. K. O'Shea to Gladstone, 'Private', 20 October 1882, Gladstone Papers BL Add. MS. 44269 fols. 137–8.

47. O'Callaghan, *British High Politics and a Nationalist Ireland,* p.93.

48. K. O'Shea to Gladstone, 30 October 1882, Gladstone Papers BL Add. MS. 44269 fols. 143–4.

49. W. O'Shea to K. O'Shea, 29 September 1882, O'Shea, *Parnell, Vol. II,* p.198.

50. W. O'Shea to K. O'Shea, 17 October 1882, ibid., pp.198–9.

51. W. O'Shea to K. O'Shea, 17 October 1882, ibid., p.199.

52. Gladstone to K. O'Shea, 1 November 1882; Gladstone Papers Add. MS. 44546 f. 31, in Matthew, ed., *The Gladstone Diaries, Vol X*, p.360.

53. Holograph, initialled by Granville, Kimberley, Harcourt and Spencer. Gladstone Papers, BL Add. MS. 44766 f. 134, in Matthew, ed., *The Gladstone Diaries, Vol. X*, p.361.

54. Bahlman, ed., *Hamilton, Vol. I*, 5 November 1882, p.357.

55. Spencer to Gladstone, 31 August 1882, in J. L. Hammond, *Gladstone and the Irish Nation*, p.307.

56. Barry O'Brien, *Parnell*, p.559. The amount of contact – via meetings or correspondence – remains difficult to ascertain. After the O'Shea divorce case, Gladstone made a number of comments, subsequently published, which questioned the importance of Katharine O'Shea's role as intermediary between himself and Parnell. This has been used by some Parnell biographers to question Katie's account. For a view on this, see Jordan, *Kitty O'Shea*, pp.86–7.

57. Bahlman, ed., *Hamilton, Vol. I*, 23 September 1882, p.344.

58. Spencer to Gladstone, 18 September 1882, in Hammond, *Gladstone and the Irish Nation*, pp.307–8.

59. Gladstone to Spencer, 19 September 1882, in ibid., p.308.

60. Spencer to Gladstone, 25 September 1882, in ibid., p.308.

61. Granville to Gladstone, 8 October 1882, in ibid., p.309.

62. Hartington to Gladstone, 14 October 1882, in ibid., p.311.

63. Gladstone to Hartington, *c.*15 October 1882 (n.d.), in ibid., p.311.

64. There had been 462 agrarian outrages in April and by October this had dropped to 111 that month. In 1883 the monthly total stayed lower – never rising above 100. See Kee, *The Laurel and the Ivy*, p.456.

65. Edward Henry Stanley (1826–93) was the 15th Earl of Derby, and the elder son of the Lord Derby who served the nation three times as Prime Minister. He took up the post of Colonial Secretary in December 1882. The 15th Earl served under Prime Ministers Disraeli and Gladstone, and kept full Cabinet diaries for that period. See John Vincent, ed., *The Diaries of Edward Henry Stanley, 15th Earl of Derby (1826–93) Between 1878 and 1893: A Selection.*

66. Vincent, ed., *The Diaries of Edward Henry Stanley*, 2 May 1882, p.420.

67. Gladstone to Spencer, 26 September 1882, in Hammond,

Gladstone and the Irish Nation, p.308.

68. Parnell to K. O'Shea, 15 (?) October 1882, Gladstone Papers BL Add. MS 44269 fols. 139–40.

69. Vincent, ed., *The Diaries of Edward Henry Stanley*, 28 October 1881, p.367.

70. Vincent, ed., *The Diaries of Edward Henry Stanley*, 28 October 1881, p.367.

71. Ibid., 28 October 1881, pp.367–8.

72. Hansard, Parliamentary Debates, 3rd series, 276 House of Commons Debates, cols. 618–19; 22 February 1883.

73. 276 H.C. Deb. 3s., col. 622; 22 February 1883.

74. O'Shea, *Parnell, Vol. II*, pp.60–1.

75. H.C. Deb. 3s., col. 628; 22 February 1883.

76. 276 H.C. Deb. 3s., col. 628; 22 February 1883.

77. Once a member was 'named' by the Speaker, another member could move to have that member suspended. That move could then be put to a vote, and if the majority so voted, the member would be asked to leave the House.

78. 276 H.C. Deb. 3s., cols. 628–9; 22 February 1883.

79. Cited by Kee, *The Laurel and the Ivy*, p.458.

80. 276 H.C. Deb. 3s., cols. 716–17; 23 February 1883.

81. Cited by Kee, *The Laurel and the Ivy*, pp.458–9.

82. 276 H.C. Deb. 3s., cols. 724–5; 23 February 1883.

83. 276 H.C. Deb. 3s., col. 725; 23 February 1883.

84. There was considerable residual unease in the House over the conduct of the government during the Kilmainham negotiations. The Opposition continued to press, in February 1883, for an official inquiry.

85. 276 H.C. Deb. 3s., cols. 811–12; 23 February 1883.

86. 276 H.C. Deb 3s., col. 854; 26 February 1883.

87. J. Chamberlain to W. O'Shea, 4 March 1883, J. Chamberlain Papers UBL, JC8/8/1/15.

88. K. O'Shea to Gladstone, 13 March 1883, Gladstone Papers BL Add. MS. 44269 fols. 171 and 178.

89. K. O'Shea to Gladstone, 15 June 1883, Gladstone Papers BL Add. MS. 44269 fols. 179–80.

90. K. O'Shea to Gladstone, 15 June 1883, Gladstone Papers BL Add. MS. 44269 fols. 182–5.

91. *The Times*, 9 March 1883.

92. *The Times*, 4 December 1884.

93. *The Times*, 8 March 1883.

94. Lyons, *Parnell*, p.244.

95. See Foster, *Parnell*, for a detailed analysis of Parnell's chronic financial problems; in particular Part IV, Section 3, 'Avondale and Parnell's Lifestyle', pp.185–96.

96. Cited by Lyons, *Parnell*, p.235.

97. As Roy Foster explained, these Acts, along with the 1883 Corrupt Practices Act, which reorganized electoral practice, made a big impact on Irish representation. In addition to the large number of new voters – mostly small farmers and agricultural labourers – there was 'an absorption of most Irish boroughs into the new county constituencies. Both processes might almost have been designed to facilitate the modernization of Parnellite politics.' Foster, *Modern Ireland*, p.416.

98. The establishment of a central party fund to pay members was adopted by Parnell in March 1884. The policy was put into effect after the 1885 general election. See Callanan, *Healy*, p.99.

99. Parnell to K. O'Shea, 4 July 1883, O'Shea, *Parnell, Vol. II*, p.65.

100. Ibid., p.66.

CHAPTER FOURTEEN: A SECRET LIFE

1. Parnell Collection, Kilmainham Gaol, Box 1E15.

2. W. O'Shea to J. Chamberlain, 8 December 1883, 'Private', J. Chamberlain Papers UBL JC8/8/1/20.

3. The *Nation*, 3 March 1883; *United Ireland*, 10 March 1883, in Lyons, *Parnell*, p.245.

4. His intervention, Lyons explains, was motivated by his desire to 'score points' off his 'brother' of Dublin, Archbishop McCabe (Cardinal McCabe in March 1882). McCabe was determined to steer the Irish clergy away from such political involvement, a course 'warmly endorsed by Pope Leo XIII'. Thomas Croke, Archbishop of Cashel, was a supporter of the Land League. He ignored this diktat, and went on to give enthusiastic support to William O'Brien when he successfully contested a by-election seat at Mallow in 1883. This earned Croke a reprimand from the Pope – although the Archbishop apologized, he was undeterred and supported a Parnellite for the Tipperary seat vacated by John Dillon. Croke 'enthusiastically approved' the Parnell testimonial, writing to the press on St Patrick's Day (17 March) 1883, enclosing his donation of £50. See Lyons, *Parnell*, p.245.

5. This was partly under British government influence, and was a demonstration of the Vatican's disapproval of the Irish Church's involvement in politics. Kee, *The Laurel and the Ivy*, p.467.

6. *United Ireland*, 15 December 1883, in Lyons, *Parnell*, p.246.

7. W. O'Shea to J. Chamberlain, 8 December 1883, 'Private', J. Chamberlain Papers UBL JC/8/8/1/20.

8. *The Times*, 2 July 1885.

9. See Foster, *Parnell*, p.150, for a very helpful reconstruction of Parnell's movements from 1875 to 1891.

10. Parnell to K. O'Shea, *Tuesday night* [n.d., probably around 4 July 1883], O'Shea, *Parnell, Vol. II*, pp.64–5.

11. Jackson, *Home Rule*, p.47.

12. See Senia Pašeta, *Before the Revolution: Nationalism, Social Change and Ireland's Catholic Elite, 1879–1922*, for a comprehensive study of this question.

13. Cardinal Manning intervened and convinced Parnell to let the matter rest. Jackson, *Home Rule*, p.47.

14. Ibid., p.48.

15. O'Connor, *Memoirs, Vol. I*, p.228.

16. K. O'Shea to Gladstone, 19 July 1883, Gladstone Papers BL Add. MS. 44269, fol. 186.

17. K. O'Shea to Gladstone, 24 July 1883, Gladstone Papers BL Add. MS. 44269, fols. 213–14.

18. K. O'Shea to Gladstone, 5 March 1884 and 7 May 1884, Gladstone Papers BL Add. MS. 44269, fols. 219; 221–2.

19. Parnell to K. O'Shea, 29 February 1884, cable sent from the House of Commons to Eltham, O'Shea, *Parnell, Vol. II*, p.68.

20. Parnell to K. O'Shea, 30 May 1884, cable sent from Avondale to Eltham, O'Shea, *Parnell, Vol. II*, p.69.

21. Parnell to K. O'Shea, 10 September 1884 (?), cable sent from Dublin to non-specified location, ibid., p.69.

22. Parnell to Alfred Webb, 26 February 1883, Jacob Papers, NLI 33143.

23. Parnell to K. O'Shea, 28 October 1884, O'Shea, *Parnell, Vol. II*, p.69.

24. Ibid., p.70.

25. Parnell to K. O'Shea, n.d., included in 1884 sequence, ibid., p.70.

26. Parnell to K. O'Shea, n.d., included in 1884 sequence, ibid., p.71.

27. Ibid., p.71.

28. Ibid., p.72.

29. Ibid., pp.72–3.

30. Ibid., p.73.

31. Ibid., p.72.

32. The Queen's Speech, 6 January 1881. See Hansard H.C. 3rd s., Vol. 257, cols. 5–7.

33. The production of dynamite dated back to 1867 when Alfred Nobel managed to stabilize its volatile and very dangerous explosive, nitroglycerine, such that it could be exploited commercially. Its use was seized upon by terrorists whose aims were to inflict random and ruthless carnage on civilians, in order to create pressure on the government to reach accommodation with them. As one historian pointed out, dynamite 'could have been tailor-made for the terrorist' (McConville, *Irish Political Prisoners*, p.127). It was one hundred times more powerful than gunpowder, and strategically placed small quantities could achieve major destruction. See McConville, *Irish Political Prisoners*, pp.326–7.

34. Foster, *Modern Ireland*, p.391.

35. *An Gaodhal*, 2, 8 (May 1883), p.312, in McConville, *Irish Political Prisoners*, p.345.

36. Parnell to K. O'Shea, 1884 (this is an error: the date is vague, and the bombing he refers to in this letter took place in October 1883), O'Shea, *Parnell, Vol. II*, p.70.

37. By the spring of 1886 the campaign was nearly over. Three of the perpetrators had accidentally blown themselves up, and twenty-five had been sentenced to penal servitude. See McConville's admirable reconstruction of the Dynamitard's campaign, *Irish Political Prisoners*, pp.326–60.

38. Irish-American Nationalist support was deeply fragmented. During this violent campaign, Patrick Ford's *Irish World* excoriated Parnell for his moderation. Some, but not all, members of Clan na Gael, who had supported Parnell in the past, were not prepared to condemn the dynamite attacks. And the Irish-Americans were known for their personal feuding, especially between Devoy and 'The Triangle' – Alexander Sullivan and two of his Clan associates. The fragmented nature of Irish-American support made it near impossible for Parnell to build alliances with the various sections. See Lyons, *Parnell*, p.247.

39. W. O'Shea to J. Chamberlain, 2 March 1885, J. Chamberlain Papers UBL JC8/8/1/38.

40. *The Times*, 3 March 1884.

41. *The Times*, 28 October 1884.

42. W. O'Shea to Richard Grosvenor, 19 December 1884, NLI MS. 5752, O'Shea.

43. Chamberlain, *A Political Memoir*, p.136.

44. See C. D. H. Howard, 'Joseph Chamberlain, Parnell and the Irish "central board" scheme, 1884–5', in *Irish Historical Studies, Vol. VIII*, 1952–3, pp.324–61, for a detailed reconstruction of these events.

45. J. Chamberlain to Dilke, 12 September 1884, BM Add. MS. 43875, f. 153v, in Howard, 'Joseph Chamberlain, Parnell and the Irish "central board" scheme, 1884–5', p.327.

46. J. Chamberlain Papers UBL JC8/8/1/28. This a rough draft of a Memorandum proposing to link the reform of local government boards in Ireland to the partial renewal of the Crimes Bill. The document was endorsed in O'Shea's handwriting, to read 'Drawn in agreement with C.S. Parnell – 1 Albert Mansions', 27 November 1884.

47. J. Chamberlain to W. O'Shea, 21 January 1885, Private, J. Chamberlain Papers UBL. JC8/8/1/37.

48. J. Chamberlain to W. O'Shea, 21 January 1885, Private, J. Chamberlain Papers UBL JC8/8/1/37.

49. Parnell to W. O'Shea, 5 January 1885, in Howard, 'The Irish "central board" scheme', p.334.

50. Parnell to *The Times*, 6 August 1888.

51. Willie O'Shea regularly made requests of Grosvenor and Chamberlain to make appointments of people he favoured or wanted to place in certain jobs. These attempts at patronage were usually met by polite refusals.

52. W. O'Shea to Grosvenor, 3 January 1885, NLI MS. 5752. O'Shea.

53. Parnell to W. O'Shea, 13 January 1885, Howard, 'The Irish "central board" scheme', p.335.

54. O'Shea Note, 28 April 1885, J. Chamberlain Papers UBL JC8/8/1/40.

55. O'Shea Note, 29 April 1885, J. Chamberlain Papers UBL JC8/8/1/40.

56. W. O'Shea to K. O'Shea, 9 January 1885, O'Shea, *Parnell, Vol. II*, p.203.

57. W. O'Shea to K. O'Shea, 2 March 1885, telegram, ibid., p.205.

58. Ibid., p.21.

59. The problems were in the Transvaal, one of the three republics that bordered the British Cape Colony in South Africa. The republic was one of the most industrialized and wealthy on the African continent. It was recognized as an independent republic by Britain in 1852, and an attempt was made to annex it in 1877. The inhabitants, Boers of Dutch descent, sought independence. They fought the British in a series of conflicts – and they were famously victorious at Majuba Hill in 1881. The victors then proclaimed their self-government by the Convention of Pretoria that April. Gladstone managed to keep the government together after this defeat, despite Conservative attacks. In February 1884 the London Convention granted further concessions to the Transvaal. The Boers were, however, still much dissatisfied. They repeatedly ignored the agreed frontiers and continued their expansion into 'native' lands. There was also growing resentment of Britain, which was to explode further after the discovery of gold in the Transvaal in 1886. See Thomas Pakenham, *The Boer War*, and Hoppen, *The Mid-Victorian Generation*, pp.657–8.

60. Hoppen, *The Mid-Victorian Generation*, p.659. Gladstone was himself a bond holder, and had a substantial investment in Egypt. By modern standards there is no doubt whatever that the Prime Minister had a serious conflict of interest. Yet at the time, his biographers have pointed out, his position was never concealed and, furthermore, of the fourteen Cabinet members, Gladstone was (along with Harcourt and Bright) the most reluctant to intervene in Egypt. See Jenkins, *Gladstone*, pp.507–9.

61. Vincent, ed., *The Diaries of Edward Henry Stanley*, 6 February 1885, p.749.

62. The Queen's complaint should have been sent in cipher, but in this instance was deliberately sent in plain words – Derby supposed that this was 'with the idea that the newspapers would get hold of it'. Vincent, ed., *The Diaries of Edward Henry Stanley*, 7 February 1885, p.750.

63. Ibid.

64. Cited by Jenkins, *Gladstone*, p.513.

65. Ibid., p.514.

66. Cited by Richard Davenport Hines, in the *Oxford Dictionary of National Biography*, under the entry for Charles George Gordon (1833–85) in online catalogue, at www.oxforddnb.com.

67. *The Times*, 9 February 1885.

68. Foster, *Paddy and Mr Punch*, p.185. See his chapter 'Paddy and Mr Punch' for a detailed analysis of representations of Ireland and the Irish in *Punch* and other British publications in the nineteenth century. Foster, *Paddy and Mr Punch*, pp.171–94.

69. O'Connor contributed regularly to the *Pall Mall Gazette* and was the founder of the very successful *Star*. He combined these activities with a long career as a Parnellite MP.

70. See *Conquering England: Ireland in Victorian London*, by Fintan Cullen and R. F. Foster, for a most interesting study of 'An Irish Power in London'. Of particular interest in this instance is the discussion on pages 14–20.

71. O'Shea, *Parnell, Vol. II*, p.21.

72. Ibid.

73. Randolph Churchill shed some of his *enfant terrible* posturing and partially reintegrated into the fold of the Conservative Party in 1885. In June of that year, he became Secretary of State for India under Salisbury's ministry. He still remained a political maverick, however, and was prone to attacking the government. There were also increasing reports of illness and mental instability. See R. F. Foster, *Lord Randolph Churchill*.

74. W. O'Shea to K. O'Shea, 17 March 1885, O'Shea, *Parnell, Vol. II*, p.206.

75. W. O'Shea to K. O'Shea, *Monday night*, 1885 [n.d., probably January], ibid., p.205.

76. W. O'Shea to K. O'Shea, n.d. [no doubt sometime during the Salisbury ministry, i.e. between June 1885 and February 1886], ibid., p.206.

77. W. O'Shea to K. O'Shea, 2 April 1885, from Madrid, ibid., pp.206–7.

78. W. O'Shea to K. O'Shea, 1 May 1885, ibid., p.209.

79. W. O'Shea to K. O'Shea, 4 May 1885, ibid., pp.209–10.

80. For a detailed reconstruction of the 'First Home Rule Episode', from 1884 to 1887, see, among other historical analyses of the period, the particularly impressive work by Alan O'Day: *Parnell and the First Home Rule Episode 1884–87*.

81. Manning to Carnarvon, 19 June 1885, Carnavon Papers MS 60829, in O'Day, *Parnell and the First Home Rule Episode*, p.57.

82. O'Day, *Parnell and the First Home Rule Episode*, p.56.

83. O'Shea, *Parnell, Vol. II*, p.212.

84. W. O'Shea to J. Chamberlain, 28 June 1885, J. Chamberlain Papers UBL JC8/8/1/47.

85. J. Chamberlain to W. O'Shea, 2 August 1883, Private, J.

Chamberlain Papers UBL JC8/8/1/16.

86. W. O'Shea to K. O'Shea, *Tuesday*, n.d. [almost certainly 28 June 1885], O'Shea, *Parnell, Vol. II*, p.213.

87. W. O'Shea to K. O'Shea, *Wednesday*, n.d., O'Shea, *Parnell, Vol. II*, p.213.

88. W. O'Shea to J. Chamberlain 28 June 1885, J. Chamberlain Papers UBL JC8/8/1/48.

CHAPTER FIFTEEN: DESPERATE MEASURES

1. O'Shea, *Parnell, Vol. II*, pp.20 and 18.

2. J. Chamberlain to W. O'Shea, 11 July 1885, J. Chamberlain Papers UBL JC8/8/1/49.

3. W. O'Shea to J. Chamberlain, 13 July 1885, J. Chamberlain Papers UBL JC8/8/1/50.

4. O'Shea, *Parnell, Vol. II*, p.23.

5. Hamilton had been appointed by Lord Salisbury to be Principal Clerk of the Finance Division of the Treasury. He remained at the Treasury for the rest of his civil service career; promoted to Assistant Financial Secretary in 1892, he was appointed Financial Secretary of the Treasury in 1902.

6. Bahlman, ed., *Hamilton 1885–1906* (hereafter referred to as Vol. II), 20 July 1885, p.1.

7. Bahlman, ed., *Hamilton, Vol. II*, 21 July 1885, p.1.

8. J. Chamberlain, *A Political Memoir*, p.157.

9. Cited by Howard, 'The Irish "central board" scheme', p.358.

10. O'Shea, *Parnell, Vol. II*, pp.23–4. The letter from Gladstone to which she refers was not printed in her memoir.

11. Bahlman, ed., *Hamilton, Vol. II*, 7 August 1885, p.2.

12. Gladstone to K. O'Shea, 8 August 1885, Gladstone Papers BL Add. MS. 44269 fol. 225.

13. O'Shea, *Parnell, Vol. II*, p.74.

14. For reasons that will be addressed later, none of the witnesses was cross–examined. It should be noted, however, that they were testifying in a court of law, under oath.

15. *The Times*, 18 November 1890.

16. *The Times*, 18 November 1890.

17. Parnell to K. O'Shea, 3 February 1885, O'Shea, *Parnell, Vol. II*, p.75.

18. Ibid., p.75.

19. Members of Parliament cannot directly resign their seat. Death, disqualification, elevation to the peerage, dissolution or expulsion are the only causes by which a member's seat can be vacated and thus any member who wishes to resign must go through the process of applying for a paid office of the Crown, which automatically disqualifies the member. There are two offices to which a member can apply for this purpose: Crown Steward and Bailiff of the Chiltern Hundreds and the Manor of Northstead. See House of Commons Information Office: Factsheet P11 Procedure Series, November 2002.

20. *The Times*, 17 November 1890.

21. Ibid.

22. Ibid.

23. See Hansard Records for those dates in the 3rd series.

24. W. O'Shea to J. Chamberlain, 16 April 1884, J. Chamberlain Papers UBL JC8/8/1/24.

25. O'Connor, *Memoirs, Vol. I*, p.229.

26. O'Shea, *Parnell, Vol. II*, p.68.

27. See Hansard, 3rd series, for those dates.

28. O'Shea, *Parnell, Vol. II*, p.47.

29. Ibid.

30. Ibid., p.48.

31. Ibid., p.49.

32. Ibid., p.244.

33. Davitt, *The Fall of Feudalism*, p.653.

34. W. O'Brien, *The Parnell of Real Life*, pp.10–11.

35. O'Shea, *Parnell, Vol. II*, p.46.

36. Ibid., p.245,

37. Harrison, *Parnell Vindicated*, p.84.

38. Katharine also skirted over the incident in her book, making no mention of it. The episode came to light years later, when the interchange of letters was produced at the divorce trial in 1890.

39. *The Times*, 17 November 1890.

40. O'Shea, *Parnell, Vol. II*, p.83.

41. O'Day, *The English Face of Irish Nationalism*, p.31. See chapter 2, 'The Composition of the Party', for more information on this.

42. The *Nation*, 21 June 1884, in Lyons, *Parnell*, p.312.

43. W. O'Shea to J. Chamberlain, 22 August 1885, J. Chamberlain Papers UBL JC8/8/1/54.

44. W. O'Shea to J. Chamberlain, 3 September 1885, J. Chamberlain Papers UBL JC8/8/1/56.

45. Parnell to K. O'Shea, 23 October 1885, O'Shea, *Parnell, Vol. II*, pp.85–6.

46. O'Shea's vote was almost certainly obtained for the close division on Egypt on 15 March 1884. O'Connor recalled that the government was under huge pressure to win the vote. A special sitting was convened, and the battle went on 'for hours, amid an excitement that increased with every moment, and that finally began to reach something like the frenzy of hysteria ... It was at such a moment that one had an opportunity of seeing what a potent factor in the destinies of the British Empire the Irish Parliamentary Party had become.' The Irish Whip, Mr Shiel, at first could promise only fifteen votes. 'After a while', however, 'his heart was rejoiced by a message from Mr. Parnell that he had succeeded in getting a promise from a member whose vote was considered doubtful that he would go with his Party even though it involved going against the Government. This, Mr Shiel calculated, raised the Irish vote to sixteen – which was, I believe, the number of Irish votes ultimately cast against the Government.' O'Connor, *Memoirs, Vol. I*, pp.332–3.

47. W. O'Shea to K. O'Shea, 19 November 1885, O'Shea, *Parnell, Vol. II*, p.101.

48. K. O'Shea to R. Grosvenor, 23 October 1885, BL Add. MS. 44316 fols. 63–7.

49. Parnell to K. O'Shea, 23 October 1885, O'Shea, *Parnell, Vol. II*, p.85.

50. W. O'Shea to J. Chamberlain, 8 November 1885, J. Chamberlain Papers UBL JC8/8/1/64.

51. W. O'Shea to K. O'Shea, 8 November 1885, O'Shea, *Parnell, Vol. II*, p.92.

52. Gladstone to K. O'Shea, 24 October 1885, Gladstone Papers BL Add. MS. 44269 fols. 230–1.

53. K. O'Shea to Gladstone, 30 October 1885, Gladstone Papers BL Add. MS. 44269, fols. 232–3.

54. W. O'Shea to K. O'Shea, 2 November 1885, O'Shea, *Parnell, Vol. II*, p.90.

55. O'Shea, *Parnell, Vol. II*, pp.92–3.

56. Ibid., p.93.

57. Ibid.

58. Ibid., p.103.

59. Ibid., p.71.

60. Vincent, ed., *The Diaries of Edward Henry Stanley*, 1 October 1885, p.815.

61. It is difficult to assess the impact of this. The Catholic clergy gave electoral advice along the same lines. Some Liberals spoke of losing twenty seats, which is probably an exaggeration. See Hoppen, *The Mid-Victorian Generation*, p.679.

62. K. O'Shea to Gladstone, 10 December 1885, Gladstone Papers BL Add. MS. 44269 fols. 237–9.

63. Gladstone to K. O'Shea, 12 December 1885, Gladstone Papers BL Add. MS. 44269 fols. 241–2.

64. Salisbury to Churchill, 24 December 1885, Marsh, *Discipline of Popular Government*, p.85, cited by Hoppen, *The Mid-Victorian Generation*, p.680.

65. K. O'Shea to Grosvenor, 4 December 1885, Gladstone Papers BL Add. MS. 44316 fols. 128–35.

66. O'Shea, *Parnell, Vol. II*, p.104.

67. E. R. Russell to Gladstone, 22 November 1890, BM Add. MS. 56,466, in Lyons, *Parnell*, p.320.

68. *Irish Times*, 4 December 1885, Lyons, *Parnell*, p.307.

69. O'Shea, *Parnell, Vol. II*, p.87.

70. T. P. O'Connor had in fact been elected for both Galway and Liverpool. He chose to take the Liverpool seat, leaving the Galway seat open for selection.

71. *The Times*, 4 February 1886.

72. O'Shea, *Parnell, Vol. II*, pp.106–7.

73. Ibid., p.107.

CHAPTER SIXTEEN: THE TURNING POINT

1. *The Times*, 9 February 1886.

2. Ibid.

3. See Callanan, *Healy*, for a comprehensive overview and analysis of the Healy/Parnell relationship.

4. O'Connor later claimed that Biggar made public reference to the affair, but John Muldoon, a journalist who was present, claimed that this was the extent of the disclosures made at that time. (Muldoon, then a student, was reporting the election for the *Galway Vindicator*. He later became a barrister and well-respected member of the Irish Party.) For more on what was known and said publicly and privately at the time, see, among many accounts, Callanan, *Healy*, pp.155–61, and Lyons, *Parnell*, pp.312–40.

5. O'Connor, *Memoirs, Vol. II*, pp.10–11.

6. Ibid., p.12.

7. William O'Brien to John Dillon, 7 February 1886, in T. W. Moody, 'Parnell and the Galway Election of 1886', in *Irish Historical Studies*, Vol. IX, 1954–5, p.327. This letter was in the Dillon Papers.

8. *Freeman's Journal*, 30 December 1889, in Moody, 'Parnell and the Galway Election of 1886', fn 2, pp.320–1.

9. Archbishop Croke to E. D. Gray, 10 February 1886, in Moody, 'Parnell and the Galway Election of 1886', p.338.

10. Quoted in W. H. Hurlbert, *Ireland Under Coercion*, vol. I, p.32; cited by Callanan, *Healy*, p.161.

11. *United Ireland*, 13 February 1886; cited by Callanan, *Healy*, p.161.

12. Labouchere to Herbert Gladstone, 10 February (1886), Viscount Gladstone Papers, BM, Add. MS. 46016 f.4.; cited by Callanan, *Healy*, p.160.

13. K. O'Shea to Gladstone, 23 January 1886, Gladstone Papers BL Add. MS. 44269 fols. 280–3,

14. K. O'Shea to Gladstone, 30 January 1886, Gladstone Papers BL Add. MS. 44269 fols. 284–91.

15. As one historian has noted, the 'Home Rule' episode of 1885–6 in this context 'should be seen, above all, as the most successful party purge in modern British history, with Gladstone brilliantly inventing ceaseless ways of ditching Liberal rivals to both his right and his left in order to prevent them from breaking up the party over the question of property'. Hoppen, *The Mid-Victorian Generation*, p.678.

16. Ireland was to have a unicameral legislature (the word 'parliament' was avoided), consisting of two bodies. The first was to be made up of twenty-eight Irish representative peers and seventy-five others elected for a ten-year period, with candidates having to be men of some substance, possessing either £4,000 in capital or owning property bringing in £200 a year. The second body was to consist of the existing 103 Irish MPs in addition to another 101 elected on a similar basis. Gladstone had after much thought concluded that it would be better to exclude the Irish MPs from Westminster – this presented so many practical problems, however, that he was forced to change his mind later.

17. Many British and Irish Unionists felt that Gladstone had neglected Ulster. Some wanted a special status for Ulster. The North Down MP, Thomas Waring, stated on 8 April: 'Irish loyalists were now part of one of the greatest Empires of the world … and were utterly determined that they should not be changed into colonials.' Cited by Jackson, *Home Rule*, p.62.

18. Cited by Foster, *Lord Randolph Churchill*, p.258.

19. A leading Liberal politician and great reformist, Bright was President of the Board of Trade, and also Chancellor of the Duchy of Lancaster. He objected to the Liberal government's foreign policy and when the British fleet attacked Egypt in 1882, he resigned from the Cabinet. He remained MP for Birmingham until his death in 1889.

20. K. O'Shea to Gladstone, 25 March 1886, Gladstone Papers BL Add. unbound MS. 56446 fols. 92–4.

21. *Pall Mall Gazette*, 24 May 1886.

22. For a full account of Dilke's life, see Jenkins, *Dilke: A Victorian Tragedy.*

23. Dilke was not the first politician so disgraced. Lord Palmerston was Prime Minister and nearly seventy-nine years old when he was cited by a radical Irish journalist as having committed adultery with his wife, Mrs Kane. This was in 1863, and Kane went on to lose his case. There was, however, a great amount of public hilarity, especially given Palmerston's age. One of the more popular jokes was: 'She was Kane, but was he Able?' Michael Diamond, *Victorian Sensation or the Spectacular, the Shocking and the Scandalous in Nineteenth-Century Britain*, p.134.

24. Gladstone to Dilke, 2 February 1886, Jenkins, *Dilke*, pp.232–3.

25. O'Connor, *Memoirs, Vol. I*, p.304.

26. K. O'Shea to Gladstone, 16 April 1886. Gladstone Papers BL Add. unbound MS. 56446 fols. 98–102.

27. Telegram on behalf of W. E. Gladstone to W. O'Shea at the Adelphi Hotel, Liverpool, 19 November 1885. NLI MS. 5752.

28. W. O'Shea to J. Chamberlain, 4 May 1886, J. Chamberlain Papers UBL JC8/8/1/70.

29. W. O'Shea to J. Chamberlain, 16 May 1886, J. Chamberlain Papers UBL JC8/8/1/71.

30. W. O'Shea to J. Chamberlain, 13 October 1889, J. Chamberlain Papers UBL JC8/8/1/127. O'Shea sent this as an explanation for his divorce suit, and included enclosures such as this letter to back up his account. The letter was also produced in court, and printed in *The Times* on 17 November 1890.

31. W. O'Shea to J. Chamberlain, 13 October 1889, J. Chamberlain Papers UBL JC8/8/1/127. O'Shea included in his letter to Chamberlain a copy of this letter from Charles Parnell to Katie O'Shea, dated 26 May 1886. The letter was also produced in court, and printed in *The Times* on 17 November 1890.

32. *The Times*, 17 November 1890. It bears repeating that none of this testimony was subjected to cross-examination. What is in doubt, nevertheless, is not the veracity of the statements, but the extent of

Captain O'Shea's knowledge and connivance.

33. *The Times,* 18 November 1890.

34. Ibid.

35. O'Shea, *Parnell, Vol. II,* pp.108–9.

36. Ibid., p.109.

37. Ibid., p.112.

38. Ibid., p.110.

39. Ibid., p.115.

40. *The Times,* 18 November 1890.

41. O'Shea, *Parnell, Vol. II,* p.125.

42. Ibid., pp.124–5.

43. W. O'Shea to K. O'Shea, 23 April 1886, produced in court, and printed in *The Times,* 17 November 1890.

44. *The Times,* 9 June 1886.

45. W. O'Shea to K. O'Shea, 2 July 1886, produced in court, and printed in *The Times,* 17 November 1890.

46. W. O'Shea to K. O'Shea, 20 August 1886, produced in court, and printed in *The Times,* 17 November 1890.

47. K. O'Shea to W. O'Shea, 23 August 1886, partial draft, NLI Tuohy 3882–3.

48. O'Shea, *Parnell, Vol. II,* p.125.

49. Ibid., p.126.

50. Ibid., p.116.

51. Ibid., pp.121–2.

52. Ibid., p.123.

53. O'Shea always referred to the 'scandal' rather than make any direct allusion to infidelity. This was to prove enormously significant when he later denied connivance in his wife's adultery.

54. W. O'Shea to K. O'Shea, 13 September 1886, produced in court and printed in *The Times,* 17 November 1890.

55. W. O'Shea to K. O'Shea, 25 September 1886, produced in court and printed in *The Times,* 17 November 1890.

56. K. O'Shea to W. O'Shea, 3 October 1886, produced in court and printed in *The Times,* 17 November 1890.

57. W. O'Shea to K. O'Shea, 4 October 1886, produced in court and printed in *The Times,* 17 November 1890.

58. K. O'Shea to W. O'Shea, n.d., probably early October 1886, produced in court and printed in *The Times,* 17 November 1890.

59. K. O'Shea to W. O'Shea, n.d., probably early October 1886, produced in court and printed in *The Times,* 17 November 1890.

60. K. O'Shea to W. O'Shea, n.d., probably 9 October 1886, produced in court and printed in *The Times,* 17 November 1890.

61. W. O'Shea to K. O'Shea, 10 October 1886, produced in court and printed in *The Times,* 17 November 1890.

62. K. O'Shea to W. O'Shea, *Sunday, December* [in 1886 sequence], O'Shea, *Parnell, Vol. II,* p.218.

63. W. O'Shea to K. O'Shea, 12 December 1886, O'Shea, *Parnell, Vol. II,* p.218.

64. W. O'Shea to W. Stead, 19 December 1886, ibid., p.219.
65. *Pall Mall Gazette*, 20 December 1886.
66. Ibid., 22 December 1886.
67. Gladstone remained ensconced at his country residence for an astonishing 125 consecutive nights. According to his biographer, Roy Jenkins, the Prime Minister 'was not giving up, but he was husbanding his energies, which he recognized to be in decline'. Jenkins, *Gladstone*, p.562.
68. See Jackson, *Home Rule*, p.71.
69. These letters were the handiwork of Richard Pigott, from whom Parnell had purchased the *Irishman* and the *Flag of Ireland*. Pigott had fallen on hard times, and turned against the leader. In the autumn of 1885 he had issued a pamphlet entitled 'Parnellism Unmasked', which had to be withdrawn for libel. Pigott had come to the attention of a former *Times* journalist, Edward Caulfield Houston, who subsequently agreed to pay him for evidence of the link between Parnell and crime. In April 1886 he gave Houston copies of five incriminating letters allegedly written by the leader. Houston then agreed to pay Pigott to retrieve the originals. He provided the letters to the journalist in July. By the end of the year the letters were in the possession of the manager of *The Times*. See, among other accounts, Kee, *The Laurel and the Ivy*, pp.521–3.
70. O'Shea, *Parnell, Vol. II*, pp.130–1.
71. O'Callaghan, *British High Politics and a Nationalist Ireland*, p.112. See her excellent chapter on the Commission, pp.104–21.
72. Pigott made a full confession, in the presence of a witness, to Labouchere on the following day, 23 February. He asserted that he had made the forgeries using genuine letters of Parnell's from the sale of the newspapers. Although he was theoretically under police watch, he left London and escaped to Paris and then Madrid. He shot himself in Madrid at the Hotel des Ambassadeurs just a week after his court appearance. Coincidentally, O'Shea was also in Madrid on that day.

CHAPTER SEVENTEEN: LEGAL BATTLES

1. O'Shea, *Parnell, Vol. II*, p.132.
2. Parnell to K. O'Shea, 30 August 1887, O'Shea, *Parnell, Vol. II*, pp.132–3.
3. K. O'Shea to G. O'Shea, 17 June 1887, produced in court and printed in *The Times*, 17 November 1890.
4. *The Times*, 17 November 1890.
5. W. O'Shea to J. Chamberlain, 30 March 1892, J. Chamberlain Papers UBL JC8/8/1/166.

6. Copy Letters and Other Documentary Evidence in the Divorce Case of Captain William O'Shea and Katharine O'Shea 1890, NLI MS. 35,982 982. [Note: This collection of documents is to be found on the reverse of a handwritten book on the First World War by C. G. B. Buckton.] K. O'Shea to W. O'Shea, [n.d., probably March 1887, according to sequence].

7. Will of A. M. Wood, dated 7 April 1887, NLI MS. 35,982.

8. K. O'Shea to W. O'Shea, 9 April 1887, NLI MS. 35,982.

9. G. O'Shea to W. O'Shea, n.d., NLI MS. 35,290; also reproduced in court (with several small discrepancies) and printed in *The Times*, 17 November 1890, with date stated as 13 April 1887.

10. *The Times*, 17 November 1890.

11. K. O'Shea to W. O'Shea, 17 April 1887, produced in court and printed in *The Times*, 17 November 1890.

12. W O'Shea to K. O'Shea, 17 April 1887, NLI MS. 35,982.

13. Extract from W. O'Shea's Diary, 17 April 1887, NLI MS. 35,982.

14. Telegram K. O'Shea to W. O'Shea, 18 April 1887, NLI MS. 35,982.

15. Telegram K. O'Shea to W. O'Shea, 18 April 1887, NLI MS. 35,982.

16. Telegram K. O'Shea to W. O'Shea, 19 April 1887, NLI MS. 35.

17. Pym to W. O'Shea, 22 April 1887, NLI MS. 35,982.

18. W. O'Shea to H. Pym, Esq., 22 April 1887, O'Shea, *Parnell, Vol. II*, pp.219–20.

19. Pym to W. O'Shea, 25 April 1887, NLI MS. 35,982.

20. W. O'Shea to Parnell, 29 April 1887, produced in court and printed in *The Times*, 17 November 1890.

21. Wood to K. O'Shea, 27 April 1887, NLI MS. 35,982, E.

22. Extract from Charles Wood's Diary, May 1887, NLI MS. 35,982.

23. K. O'Shea to G. O'Shea, 27 June 1887, produced in court and printed in *The Times*, 17 November 1890.

24. O'Shea, *Parnell, Vol. II*, p 220.

25. Cited by Callanan, *Healy*, p.179.

26. O'Shea, *Parnell, Vol. II*, p.151.

27. Ibid., pp.152–3.

28. See her book, *A Patriot's Mistake* (by Emily Dickinson), for a full – albeit probably rather inaccurate – account of her marital difficulties.

29. See Dickinson, *A Patriot's Mistake*, and Foster, *Parnell*, pp.219–22.

30. J. H. Parnell, *Charles Stewart Parnell*, p.138.

31. *Book of Deeds* for 1884, Clerk's Office, Mount Holly, Burlington County, New Jersey. I am grateful to Coté for citing this very useful information. Coté, *Fanny and Anna Parnell*, p.230 (fn 13, p.306).

32. *Herald* (New York), 22 July 1885; *Weekly Freeman*, 8 August 1885; cited by Foster, *Parnell*, pp.226–7.

33. *Herald* (New York), 15 July 1885; *Nation*, 1 August 1885; cited by Foster, *Parnell*, p.226.

34. *Washington Post*, 20 February 1886. Quoted in *Wicklow Newsletter*, 20 March 1886; cited by Foster, *Parnell*, p.227.

35. Foster, *Parnell*, p.228.

36. *Weekly Freeman*, 2 October 1886; cited by Foster, *Parnell*, p.228.

37. *Wicklow Newsletter*, 23 November 1889; cited by Foster, *Parnell*, p.228.

38. J. McCarthy to Mrs Campbell Praed, November 1889, McCarthy and Praed, *Our Book of Memories*, p.209.

39. *Wicklow Newsletter*, 30 November 1889; cited by Foster, *Parnell*, pp.229–30.

40. Parnell to K. O'Shea, 4 January 1888, O'Shea, *Parnell, Vol. II*, p.134.

41. O'Shea, *Parnell, Vol. II*, p.144.

42. Principal Probate Registry of Her Majesty's High Court of Justice: the last Will and Testament of Anna Maria Wood, signed on 7 March 1888; probate granted on 17 August 1892.

43. Matthew, ed., *Gladstone Diaries, Vol. XII*, 8 March 1888, p.104.

44. Ibid., p.105.

45. K. O'Shea to Gladstone, 13 April 1888, Gladstone Papers BL Add. MS. 44503 fols. 159–63.

46. Document in J. Chamberlain Papers UBL JC8/8/1/161. The report was sworn at 16 Cavendish Square in the County of Middlesex on 17 April 1888. It was filed 'In Lunacy' on 20 April 1888.

47. K. O'Shea to Gladstone, 1 May 1888, Gladstone Papers BL Add. MS 44269, fols. 310–12.

48. J. Chamberlain to W. O'Shea, 31 December 1888, NLI 5752.

49. W. O'Shea to J. Chamberlain, 1 November 1888, J. Chamberlain Papers UBL JC8/8/1/114.

50. W. O'Shea to J. Chamberlain, 3 November 1888, J. Chamberlain Papers UBL JC8/8/1/115.

51. W. O'Shea to J. Chamberlain, 27 November 1888, J. Chamberlain Papers UBL JC8/8/1/116.

52. J. Chamberlain to W. O'Shea, 5 December 1888, J. Chamberlain Papers UBL JC8/8/1/116.

53. Labouchere to H. Gladstone, 3 November (1888), Viscount Gladstone Papers, BL Add. MS. 46016, f. 136, in Callanan, *Healy* p.202. The sensational 'Jack the Ripper' murders took place at this time.

54. O'Shea, *Parnell, Vol. II*, p.134.

55. Jenkins, *Gladstone*, p.568.

56. *Daily Telegraph*, 2 March 1889, cited by Callanan, *Healy*, p.205.

57. See Andrew Roberts, *Salisbury: Victorian Titan*, pp.452–8, for a discussion of Salisbury's actions over the Parnell Commission.

58. O'Shea, *Parnell, Vol. II*, p.140.

59. W. O'Shea to J. Chamberlain, 9 March 1889, J. Chamberlain Papers UBL JC8/8/1/121.

60. J. Chamberlain to W. O'Shea, 14 March 1889, J. Chamberlain Papers UBL JC8/8/1/123.

61. O'Shea, *Parnell, Vol. II*, p.146.

62. Ibid.

63. Ibid., p.147.

64. Ibid., pp.148–9.

65. W. O'Shea to J. Chamberlain, 24 August 1889, J. Chamberlain Papers UBL JC8/8/1/126.

66. W. O'Shea to J. Chamberlain, 13 October 1889, J. Chamberlain Papers UBL JC8/8/1/127.

67. J. Chamberlain to W. O'Shea, 14 October 1889, J. Chamberlain Papers UBL JC8/8/1/129.

68. W. O'Shea to J. Chamberlain, 30 December 1889, J. Chamberlain papers UBL JC8/8/1/130.

69. J. Chamberlain to W. O'Shea, 10 January 1890, J. Chamberlain Papers UBL JC8/8/1/131.

70. See Jenkins, *Gladstone*, p.265.

71. Jenkins, *Gladstone*, p.396.

72. Gladstone to Parnell, 4 October 1889, Hammond, *Gladstone and the Irish Nation*, p.603.

73. Gladstone to Spencer, Ripon, Harcourt, Granville, Herschell, Kimberley, John Morley, Rosebery, Stansfield, Mundella, Campbell-Bannerman and Arnold Morley, 23 December 1889, Hammond, *Gladstone and the Irish Nation*, p.603.

74. Gladstone Diary Entries, 18 and 19 December 1889, Hammond, *Gladstone and the Irish Nation*, p.605.

75. Jenkins, *Gladstone*, p.419.

76. Cited by Jenkins, *Gladstone*, p.569.

77. Edward Byrne to Theophilus McWeeney, 26 November 1889, McWeeney Papers, NLI NS 21936, in Callanan, *Healy*, p.235.

78. Ibid., p.237 (and fn 113, p.671).

79. This resulted in the two of them being incarcerated in Galway Gaol from February to July 1891.

80. *Evening News and Post* 28 December 1889.

81. *The Times* 3 Jan 1890.

82. Callanan, *Healy*, p.241.

83. W. O'Shea to J. Chamberlain, 19 March 1890, J. Chamberlain Papers UBL JC8/8/1/128.

84. W. O'Shea to J. Chamberlain, 17 April 1890, J. Chamberlain Papers UBL JC8/8/1/143.

85. W. O'Shea to J. Chamberlain, 2 August 1890, J. Chamberlain Papers UBL JC8/8/1/144.

86. W. O'Shea to J. Chamberlain, 2 August 1890, J. Chamberlain Papers UBL JC8/8/1/144.

87. J. Chamberlain to W. O'Shea 5 Aug 1890, J. Chamberlain Papers UBL JC8/8/1/145.

88. O'Connor, *Memoirs Vol. II*, pp.184–5.

89. Bahlman, ed., *Hamilton Vol. II*, 21 March 1890, p.112.

90. *New York Times* 26 October 1888, cited by Callanan, *Healy*, p.243.

91. Alfred Robbins, *Parnell: The Last Five Years*, pp.132–3.

92. Edward Ennis, who became Registrar to the Lord Chancellor and later Under-Secretary for Ireland. Healy, *Letters and Leaders Vol. I*, p.317.

93. Healy, *Letters and Leaders Vol. II*, p.317.

94. Davitt, *The Fall of Feudalism*, p.635.

95. Ibid., p.637.

96. Parnell to W. O'Brien, 14 January 1890, William O'Brien, *Evening Memories*, p.466.

97. J. McCarthy to Mrs Campbell Praed, Jan 1890, McCarthy and Praed, *Our Book of Memories*, p.214.

CHAPTER EIGHTEEN: SCANDAL AND RE-MARRIAGE

1. Cited by Callanan, *Healy*, p.229.

2. See Callanan, *Healy*, pp.227–9. I am grateful for Callanan's analysis of the growth of Catholic nationalism in Ireland during this period, and for his work on the relationship between Parnell and other members of his party just prior to the O'Shea divorce.

3. *Nation*, 27 July 1889, Edinburgh, 20 July; cited by Callanan, *Healy*, p.237.

4. Kee, *The Laurel and the Ivy*, p.544.

5. Harrison, *Parnell Vindicated*, p.141.

6. Ibid., p.126.

7. Ibid., p.128. The passage of the Married Woman's Property Act in 1882 had given a married woman the right to hold all the property belonging to her at the time of her marriage, as well as that accrued by her thereafter, as her own separate property. This went considerably further than the milder reform of the Married Woman's Property Act of 1870, and was a radical departure from previous legislation, which held that all married women could not own property. See Stephen Cretney, *Family Law in the Twentieth Century*, pp.90–102.

8. Harrison notes that the estate was worth more than £140,000 – some £10 million in today's terms. Harrison, *Parnell Vindicated*, p.150.

9. Ibid., pp.128–9.

10. W. O'Shea to J. Chamberlain, 15 August 1890, J. Chamberlain Papers UBL JC8/8/1/147.

11. W. O'Shea to J. Chamberlain, 7 September 1890, J. Chamberlain Papers UBL JC8/8/1/148.

12. W. O'Shea to J. Chamberlain, 15 December 1890, J. Chamberlain Papers UBL JC8/8/1/152.

13. Harrison, *Parnell Vindicated*, p.140.

14. Ibid., p.108.

15. M. V. Brett, ed., *Journals and Letters of Reginald Viscount Esher*, i., p.142; cited by Callanan, *Healy*, p.248.

16. Wilfrid Scawen Blunt, *The Land War in Ireland: Being a Personal Narrative of Events*, p.463.

17. As we have seen, O'Shea informed Chamberlain of these accusations on 2 August 1890 (JC8/8/1/144).

18. Harrison, *Parnell Vindicated*, p.141.

19. Sir Edward Clarke, *The Story of My Life*, pp.290–1.

20. The principle was that marriage was a legally binding contract in which the state had a 'vital interest, transcending and operating independently of the will of the parties'. The public interest was protected by the clauses of the Matrimonial Causes Act 1857. It was then established that the court was to discard a petition if the petitioner 'had been accessory to or had connived at (or had condoned) the respondent's adultery or if the petition had been presented in collusion with the respondent'. Cretney, *Family Law in the Twentieth Century*, pp.176–7.

21. *The Times*, 17 November 1890.

22. Ibid.

23. Ibid.

24. O'Shea, *Parnell, Vol. II*, p.158.

25. Ibid., pp.159–60.

26. Ibid., p.161.

27. Kee makes the very interesting observation that one consequence of the absence of a defence was that O'Shea's carefully prepared evidence (and one must assume that he was confident that his letters, diary entries and witnesses would back up his version of events) was not presented in its entirety. Kee speculates that O'Shea's diary entries might have revealed a closer relationship with his wife – at least until 1886 – than she was perhaps prepared to admit to her lover. See Kee, *The Laurel and the Ivy*, pp.549–50.

28. *The Times*, 17 November 1890. In the absence of cross-examination, of course, there was nothing made of the fact that the Captain had had to ring his own doorbell. This may well have been the custom, but it may also have indicated that by this time he was, as Katharine claimed, a guest at Wonersh Lodge.

29. *The Times*, 17 November 1890.

30. Ibid., 18 November 1890.

31. *Truth*, 20 November 1890.

32. Judith R. Walkowitz (foreword by Catherine R. Stimpson), *City of Dreadful Delight: Narratives of Sexual Danger in Late-Victorian London*, p.218, cited by Thomas Prasch, 'Dangerous Sexualities in Victorian England', in *Journal of Women's History*, Vol. 6, No. 1, Spring 1994, p.91.

33. Nineteenth-century Victorian feminists crusaded to change the laws governing marriage. Much of this legislation denied rights to married women over their children and their property. The campaigns for marriage law reform in the nineteenth century resulted in some major new legislation, including the Divorce Act of 1857, and the Married Woman's Property Acts of 1870 and 1882. For a detailed study, see Mary Lyndon Shanley, *Feminism, Marriage and the Law in Victorian England, 1880–1895.*

34. See G. R. Searle, *A New England? Peace and War 1886–1918*, pp.70–4.

35. 'In June 1889 a small audience attended, wonderingly, the first unbowdlerized performance of Ibsen's *A Doll's House*, a private production at the Novelty Theatre, but only a small minority of women wanted to throw their respectability into doubt by attacking the institution of marriage as such. Even within the privacy of a discussion circle such as the "Men and Women's Club", set up in 1885, "liberated" women had little to say about a woman's right to sexual self-expression.' Searle, *A New England?*, p.72.

36. See Sheila Jeffreys, 'Women and Sexuality', in June Purvis, *Women's History: Britain, 1850–1945*, pp.193–216, for an interesting discussion on this topic.

37. *The Times*, 18 November 1890.

38. A. E. Pearse (later Sir Alfred) was a Liberal, who sat with Frank Lockwood for York. He had a conversation with Lockwood shortly after the divorce case. I am grateful to Frank Callanan for including this hitherto neglected account in *Healy*, p.250.

39. Cited in Callanan, *Healy*, p.251.

40. Lord Asquith, *Lord James of Hereford*, p.220.

41. O'Shea, *Parnell, Vol. II*, p.161.

42. The presentation of evidence of connivance during the ensuing six months would result in the refusal of the decree absolute.

43. Cited by Bew, *Parnell*, p.111.

44. Davitt's *Labour World* was the exception in making a call for Parnell's retirement. See Callanan, *The Parnell Split*, p.10.

45. Cited by Callanan, *The Parnell Split*, p.11.

46. Ibid., p.14.

47. Mary Gladstone (Mrs Drew), edited by Lucy Masterman, *Diaries and Letters*, 17 November 1890, p.413.

48. Mary Gladstone (Mrs Drew), edited by Lucy Masterman, *Diaries and Letters*, 22 November 1890, p.413.

49. Gladstone was attempting to achieve the 'immensely difficult feat' of bringing the Nonconformist vote to support Home Rule legislation that would result in the handing over of

Ireland to a predominantly Catholic regime. See Jenkins, *Gladstone*, p.571.

50. *Methodist Times*, 20 November 1890, in Jenkins, *Gladstone*, p.572.

51. Cited by Jenkins, *Gladstone*, p.573.

52. Cited by Callanan, *The Parnell Split*, p.19.

53. O'Shea, *Parnell, Vol. II*, p.161.

54. Ibid., p.162.

55. Ibid.

56. As we have seen, this is debatable.

57. O'Shea, *Parnell, Vol. II*, p.162.

58. Bahlman, ed., *Hamilton, Vol. II*, 25 November 1890, p.130.

59. Cited by Callanan, *The Parnell Split*, p.23.

60. O'Shea, *Parnell, Vol. II*, p.162.

61. Harold Frederic cabled this to the *New York Times*; cited by Callanan, *The Parnell Split*, p.25.

62. O'Shea, *Parnell, Vol. II*, p.163.

63. Davitt, *The Fall of Feudalism in Ireland*, p.652.

64. Cited by Callanan, *The Parnell Split*, pp.24–5. This is from a note of a conversation between R. M. Praed and Justin McCarthy, 29 November 1890, from McCarthy and Praed, *Book of Memories*, draft. Callanan points out that Praed referred to this statement being made at the time of the decree nisi, but it was in fact clear from the context that it was the decree absolute to which she referred. See *The Parnell Split*, fn 68, p.34.

65. Vincent, ed., *The Diaries of Edward Henry Stanley*, 3 December 1890, p.843.

66. Bahlman, ed., *Hamilton, Vol. II*, 3 February 1891, p.138.

67. The signatories were: W. O'Brien, J. Dillon, T. P. O'Connor, T. P. Gill and T. D. Sullivan.

68. The Irish bishops had at first a muted response to the divorce. This is believed to be because they were hoping that the greater good of Home Rule legislation would ensue, despite the scandal. There is also speculation that the Catholic clergy were waiting to see what the English response would be. A general reluctance to condemn the successful leader was evident in the early days. This was to change dramatically.

69. Cited by Callanan, *The Parnell Split*, p.38.

70. O'Shea, *Parnell, Vol. II*, p.163.

71. Ibid., p.164.

72. Ibid., p.165.

73. Callanan, *The Parnell Split*, p.52.

74. O'Connor, *Memoirs, Vol. II*, p.233.

75. Much to his professed chagrin, O'Connor was not present at these meetings, as he was in America. He wrote that he and the four other MPs there were able to see the cables as they arrived. 'We were as well aware of what was taking place in Committee Room 15', he wrote, '… as though we were present.' He lamented that history might have been different if they had all been there. The influence of 'two such important men as Dillon and O'Brien' might have resulted in a compromise, he wrote. O'Connor, *Memoirs, Vol. II,* pp.189–90; see also p.233.

76. O'Connor, *Memoirs, Vol. II,* p.233.

77. See Joseph P. Meisel, *Public Speech and the Culture of Public Life in the Age of Gladstone,* for an excellent study of this.

78. Katherine Tynan (Mrs Hinkson), *Twenty-five Years: Reminiscences,* p.326..

79. O'Shea, *Parnell, Vol. II,* pp.179–80.

80. Ibid., p.182.

81. Ibid., p.183.

82. See Callanan, *Healy,* for a comprehensive review of Healy's politically calculated destruction of Parnell, the man and myth, through venomous attacks on the affair, and on Katharine personally.

83. Cited by Donal McCartney, 'At the Graveside: Commemorative Orations: Katharine Parnell', in McCartney and Travers, *The Ivy Leaf,* p.99.

84. Cited by Callanan, *Healy,* p.311.

85. *National Press,* 2 November 1891, cited by Callanan, *The Parnell Split,* p.187.

86. This reads suspiciously as though subsequently invented by Katie. Parnell loathed O'Shea at this point. O'Shea, *Parnell, Vol. II,* p.183.

87. Ibid., p.183.

88. *Kilkenny Speeches,* December 1890, in *The Parnell Handbook.*

89. O'Shea, *Parnell, Vol. II,* p.250.

90. Ibid., p.251.

91. Ibid., p.252.

92. Ibid., p.253.

93. Ibid., p.254.

94. A curious and, if deliberate, rather endearing feature on the marriage certificate was the recorded ages of the celebrants. Parnell's age was recorded, correctly, as forty-four, while Katharine's was recorded – incorrectly – as forty (she was actually forty-five).

95. *The Times,* 26 June 1891.

96. Parnell to E. Cripps, 25 June 1891, NLI MS 35,290.

97. Parnell to Cripps, 27 June 1891, NLI MS 35,290.

98. K. Parnell to Cripps, 7 July 1891, NLI MS 35,290.

99. K. Parnell to Cripps, 6 August 1891, NLI MS 35,290.

100. K. Parnell to Cripps, 28 August 1891, NLI MS 35,290.

101. K. Parnell to E. Cripps, 31 August 1891, NLI MS 35,290.

102. This article appeared in the *Sussex Daily News* on 8 October 1891.

103. The *Globe,* in *Sussex Daily News,* 27 June 1891.

104. *The Manchester Examiner,* in *Sussex Daily News,* 27 June 1891.

105. The *Echo*, in *Sussex Daily News*, 27 June 1891.
106. The *National Press*, cited by Callanan, *The Parnell Split*, pp.126–7.
107. The *Weekly National Press*, cited by Callanan, *The Parnell Split*, p.127.
108. The *Kilkenny Journal*, cited by Callanan, *The Parnell Split*, p.127.
109. Cited by Callanan, *The Parnell Split*, p.127.
110. *Manchester Guardian*, 2 July 1891, cited by Callanan, *The Parnell Split*, p.128.
111. Cited by Callanan, ibid., p.127.

CHAPTER NINETEEN: MRS PARNELL

1. *The Times*, 27 June 1891.
2. Ibid.
3. Ibid., 29 July 1891.
4. Parnell to K. Parnell, 15 August 1891, O'Shea, *Parnell, Vol. II*, p.261.
5. Parnell to K. Parnell, 1 September 1891, ibid., p.262.
6. Parnell to K. Parnell, 7 September 1891, ibid., pp.262–3.
7. Parnell to John Mulligan, Esq., 8 September 1891, NLI MS. 39,928.
8. W. O'Shea to J. Chamberlain, 12 February 1891, J. Chamberlain Papers UBL JC8/8/1/160.
9. W. O'Shea to J. Chamberlain, 23 February 1891, J. Chamberlain Papers UBL JC8/8/1/162.
10. J. Chamberlain to W. O'Shea, 25 February 1891, J. Chamberlain Papers UBL JC8/8/1/163.
11. W. O'Shea to J. Chamberlain, 27 March 1892, J. Chamberlain Papers UBL JC8/8/1/165.
12. Cited by Callanan, *The Parnell Split*, p.124.
13. *The Times*, 26 June 1891. The letter was printed in the *Freeman's Journal* on 25 June 1891 (the day of Parnell and Katharine's wedding).
14. *Daily Express*, 26 June 1891; cited by Callanan, *The Parnell Split*, p.125.
15. *Daily Express*, Dillon to O'Brien, 'Thursday' with postscript marked 'Friday' (on 26 June 1891), containing the above, O'Brien Papers, NLI MS. 8555/1, cited by Callanan, *The Parnell Split*, p.125 (see fn 61, p.137).
16. Lampoon recited to Lady Lavery; cited by Callanan, *Healy*, p.309.
17. Shani D'Cruze, 'Women and the Family', in June Purvis, ed., *Women's History: Britain, 1850–1945*, p.54. See this chapter for an excellent study of nineteenth-century ideologies and policies on women and the family, pp.51–83.
18. O'Shea, *Parnell, Vol. II*, pp.263–4.
19. Ibid., p.264.
20. Ibid., p.265.
21. Ibid., pp.265–6.
22. Ibid., p.267.

23. Ibid., p.269. Katharine noted that the mortgage was never completed.

24. Ibid., p.268.

25. Sir Henry Thompson to K. Parnell, 10 October 1891, O'Shea, *Parnell, Vol. II*, p.272.

26. O'Shea, *Parnell, Vol. II*, p.274.

27. Ibid., p.275.

28. The *Daily Chronicle*, in *Sussex Daily News*, 27 June 1891.

29. The *Evening Telegraph*, 8 October 1891.

30. The *Evening Telegraph*, 8 October 1891.

31. Dickinson, *A Patriot's Mistake*, p.187.

32. Sophie O'Brien, *Recollections*, p.198, cited by Callanan, *The Parnell Split*, pp.172–3.

33. Mary Soames, *Clementine Churchill*, pp.541 and 543.

34. The *Daily News*, in the *Evening Telegraph*, 8 October 1891.

35. *The Times*, 8 October 1891.

36. The *Sussex Daily News*, 8 October 1891.

37. Ibid.

38. Both reported in *The Times*, 10 October 1891.

39. The death certificate was signed by Jowers, Katharine Parnell, and the Registrar, W. H. Spearing. *The Times*, 10 October 1891.

40. John Benignus Lyons (born in Mayo in 1922) was a consultant physician and neurologist until retirement from Sir Patrick Dun's. Since 1975 he has been professor of the history of medicine in the RCSI. He made a study of the medical causes of Charles Parnell's death and concluded that the Jower diagnosis was likely to be correct. 'The diagnosis of pneumonia offered in the late F. S. L. Lyons' biography seems to me unlikely other than as a terminal complication. Lobar pneumonia has a characteristic clinical picture and was then a commonplace which would have been readily recognised by Dr Jowers... The evidence of Bright's disease referred to by Sir Alfred Robbins is almost equally unconvincing. Lung cancer with involvement of the brachial plexus or a prolapsed cervical intervertebral disc are conditions to be included in the differential diagnosis; neither would be expected to terminate in cardiac arrest so characteristic of myocardial infarction, which emerges as the probable diagnosis. [...] If my submission is correct and the left arm pain was evidence of "coronary insufficiency", insistence on rest, avoidance of the testing meeting at Creggs and a prolonged convalescence might have at least postponed the dire consequences that ensued.' J. B. Lyons, *What Did I Die Of?*, p.99.

41. *The Times*, 10 October 1891.

42. Harrison's account, although first-hand and thus of great interest, was written many years after the event. See Bibliography, p.553.

43. Harrison, *Parnell Vindicated*, pp.102 and 103.

44. The *Sussex Daily News*, 9 October 1891.

45. Harrison, *Parnell Vindicated*, pp.97–8.

46. The *United Ireland*, 17 October 1891.

47. Kee, *The Laurel and the Ivy*, p.4. He has provided a vivid account of Parnell's last journey and burial, see pp.3–12.

48. Kee, *The Laurel and the Ivy*, p.5.

49. Cited by Callanan, *The Parnell Split*, p.182.

50. Kelly, *The Fenian Ideal*, p.63. See 'Parnell and the Fenians', pp.41–70, for a full discussion of this.

51. Harrison, *Parnell Vindicated*, p.99.

52. The *United Ireland*, 17 October 1891.

53. Harrison, *Parnell Vindicated*, p.109.

54. John Howard Parnell, *Charles Stewart Parnell*, pp.234–5.

55. Ibid., p.235.

56. In 1899 a scheme was launched to 'save' Avondale for the nation. There was considerable dispute over this. The Parnell family wanted it to be purchased for the family, claiming that 'political debts' had caused the financial problems in the first place. The Irish Party wanted it for 'the nation'. A fund-raising tour in America was organized, which raised $50,000. John Parnell became involved in arguments with John Redmond, however, and instead sold the estate in 1900 to a Dublin businessman called Boylan, on condition that he could purchase it back after two years. For two years John Parnell launched scheme after scheme to raise the funds to buy it back, with no success. After Boylan's death in 1904, the Board of Agriculture purchased the estate to start a forestry school there. The estate eventually passed into the hands of the Irish Forestry Commission and, in addition to the offices and classrooms, there is now a small museum in the house commemorating Parnell's career. See Foster, *Parnell*, pp.295–300, and Coté, *Fanny and Anna Parnell*, p.235.

57. This was an interview in New York on 28 July 1896, which was printed in Kansas *Current Remark* and quoted in *Wicklow Newsletter*, 22 August 1896. I am grateful to Foster for citing this. Foster, *Parnell*, p.300.

58. *Irish Weekly Independent*, 13 March 1897; cited by Foster, *Parnell*, p.300.

59. Anna Parnell was bitter about Davitt's account of the role of the LLL in his book, *Fall of Feudalism*, published in 1904. Anna's own account, *The Tale of a Great Sham*, attempting to put the record straight, was not published in book form until 1986, many years after her death. Anna Parnell drowned in September 1911 while swimming off the Capstone Headland in North Devon. See Coté, *Fanny and Anna Parnell*, pp.237–49.

60. Delia Parnell died in a terrible accident at Avondale in March 1897. She was sitting by the fire, and either fell into it or her clothes caught fire. She was found in flames, and died the next day from her injuries. By 1923 the remaining Parnell siblings had all died. For more details on their lives, see Foster, *Parnell*, pp.300–3.

61. Harrison, *Parnell Vindicated*, p.111.

62. Charles Wood and Sir Evelyn Wood were joined by a group of interveners, including sisters, brothers-in-law, sisters-in-law and cousins. Captain O'Shea was joined by Gerard and Carmen as interveners as well.

63. *The Times*, 25 March 1892.

64. Harrison, *Parnell Vindicated*, p.195.

65. Ibid., p.203.

66. Hawksley to ?, 29 October 1892, Harrington Papers NLI 40,620.

67. Hawksley to Harrington, 5 November 1892, Harrington Papers, NLI 40,620.

68. Cited by Callanan, *The Parnell Split*, p.187.

69. *The Times*, 4 November 1891.

70. Cited by Callanan, *The Parnell Split*, p.188.

71. Ibid.

72. Gladstone to Labouchere, draft, 24 November 1891, 'secret', cited by Callanan, *The Parnell Split*, p.189.

73. *The Times*, 24 November 1892.

74. Ibid., 20 May 1893.

75. Ibid., 24 February 1894.

76. Ibid., 7 March 1894.

77. Ibid., 17 March 1894.

78. Ibid., 23 June 1894.

79. Ibid., 4 April 1901.

80. O'Shea, *Parnell, Vol. II*, p.135.

81. O'Connor, *Memoirs, Vol. II*, p.324. It is important to remember that he did not know Katharine, and did not give the source for this information. His account of her latter years makes perfectly clear his perception of her as rather foolish and incapable. O'Connor did, however, claim to have kept in sporadic contact with Norah, and helped her after Katie's death, so he could have learned some of this directly from her.

82. O'Connor, *Memoirs, Vol. II*, pp.324–6.

83. Ibid., p.326.

84. O'Shea, *Parnell, Vol. I*, p.7.

85. Marlow, *The Uncrowned Queen of Ireland*, p.301.

86. *The Times*, 24 April 1905.

87. 'M.A.P. (Mainly About People)', edited by T. P. O'Connor,

6 May 1905, from Essex Record Office, Barrett Lennard Papers T/B 224/1.

88. Marlow, *The Uncrowned Queen of Ireland*, p.301. Further information on C. Barrett-Leonard is in the Parnell Archive in Kilmainham Gaol (KMG). She and Gerard separated and Cristobel lived with her daughter in a house on the estate at Belhus. Her daughter died in 1952, and Cristobel in 1954. Family sources believe that Gerard died some years before, and may have been buried in Spain, where he had cousins. KMG 21 MS IE 13 17.

89. Jordan, *Kitty O'Shea*, p.207.

90. *The Times*, 30 July 1907.

91. This information is from the Parnell archive held at Kilmainham Gaol (KMG). See KMG 10 BK IE 14 01. See fn 93 below for further information on this important archive.

92. KMG 21 LR IE 13 15.

93. His son John Maunsell, Assheton's stepbrother, was a Catholic priest. He held in his safekeeping a small number of objects that had belonged to Katharine and Charles Parnell. He agreed to give them to Sir Shane Leslie, an Irish historian who was writing a book on Parnell, in exchange for a small money gift. These items, he said, had been treasured by Katharine until her death, and she had wished them to

be given to her and Parnell's grandson. After Assheton's death, the objects remained in the hands of his father Bertram Maunsell, who died in 1941, when they came into the possession of his son John. See John Maunsell to Sir Shane Leslie, 25 January 1956, KMG IE 13 09. Of further intrigue in this collection was a family tree in which John Maunsell had inscribed the posthumous birth of a son (either miscarried or stillborn) to Katharine Parnell (undated). There is no record of such a birth, nor of any other corroborating evidence for this. Katharine would have been forty-six at the time, so it was not impossible, though improbable. A second family tree provided by Maunsell included no indication of this purported birth. See KMG 09 MS IE 13 21 and KMG 09 MS IE 13 20.

94. Father John Maunsell to Sir Shane Leslie, 25 January 1956, KMG IE 13 09.

95. Father John Maunsell to Sir Shane Leslie, 13 December 1966, KMG 21 LR IE 14 16.

96. Norah O'Shea to Harrison, 1 February 1921, Harrison, *Parnell Vindicated*, p.216.

97. *The Times*, 8 September 1913.

98. Ibid., 10 September 1913.

99. Ibid., 23 April 1914.

100. Ibid., 23 April 1914.

CHAPTER TWENTY:
REVELATIONS:
CASHING IN

1. *Daily Express*, 14 May 1914.
2. *The Times*, 19 May 1914.
3. *Spectator* (London), 112:912, 953 My 30; Je 6, 1914, in *Book Review Digest*.
4. *Nation* (New York), 99:551 N5 194, in *Book Review Digest*.
5. *Bookman* (New York), 40:320 N 1914, in *Book Review Digest*.
6. *Saturday Review*, 23 May 1923.
7. *New York Times*, 19:468 O 25 1914, in *Book Review Digest*.
8. *The Times*, 22 May 1914 (advertisement).
9. Harrison, *Parnell Vindicated*, p.13.
10. Ibid., p.12.
11. Ibid.
12. *Daily Mail*, 18 May 1914.
13. O'Shea, *Parnell, Vol. I*, p.viii.
14. Ibid., p.ix.
15. See, among others, Foster's *Modern Ireland*, pp.431–60, and Jackson's *Home Rule*, pp.80–174.
16. Foster, 'Mrs. O'Shea's Parnell', in *Paddy and Mr. Punch*, p.127.
17. This paper was owned by Parnell's enemy of old, William Martin Murphy.
18. Cited by Foster, 'Mrs. O'Shea's Parnell', in *Paddy and Mr. Punch*, p.127.
19. *Nation*, 23 May 1914, in KMG Box 1E15.
20. It inspired images for his works in *The Trembling of the Veil* and *A Vision*. See Foster, *Paddy and Mr. Punch*, p.123.
21. Harrison, *Parnell Vindicated*, p.214.
22. Norah O'Shea to Harrison, 1 February 1921, Harrison, *Parnell Vindicated*, pp.215–16.
23. *Weekly Dispatch*, 6 February 1921.
24. *Daily Mail*, 7 February 1921.
25. O'Connor, *Memoirs, Vol. II*, p.327.
26. Gerard O'Shea to Bertram Maunsell, 20 July 1923, KMG 20 LR IE 14 09. Maunsell annotated this letter sent to him, telling him of Norah's death. His note read that though Gerard was left the money to bury his sister, it cost Maunsell '£90 to stop his bankruptcy to pay the bill'.
27. *The Times*, 13 May 1936.
28. *Daily Telegraph*, 16 October 1936, in KMG 1E 15.
29. At least one biographer has pointed out that this was unlikely, given that the loyal Norah was left destitute. It is possible, however, that the £2,000 was a remaining trust for Katie.
30. *Sunday Despatch*, 7 November 1937, in KMG 1E 16 30.

EPILOGUE:
WHEN YOU ARE
OLD AND GREY

1. Foster, 'Knowing Your Place', in *Paddy and Mr. Punch*, p.80.

2. I am very grateful to Matthew Kelly for his incisive and helpful comments on this. As he points out, in the long run it was continued opposition by the House of Lords – and Irish unionism – that delayed Home Rule legislation, rather than Parnell's fall from leadership. British support for Irish legislative aspirations was central to Home Rule prospects.

3. It has been argued that Parnell possibly expected to retire from politics after Home Rule was enacted. There is, however, little indication of this in Katie's book, and Parnell's own actions in fighting his opponents so vigorously after the divorce would seemingly imply that he intended to hold on to his political power.

4. James Loughlin, 'Constructing the Political Spectacle: Parnell, the Press and National Leadership, 1879–86', in D. George Boyce and Alan O'Day, eds., *Parnell in Perspective*, p.225.

5. *Nation*, 2 January 1886, cited by Loughlin, 'Constructing the Political Spectacle', p.230.

6. Cited by Loughlin, 'Constructing the Political Spectacle', p.225.

7. See S. N. Eisenstadt, ed., *Max Weber on Charisma and Institution Building: Selected Papers*; see also Alan O'Day, 'Max Weber and Leadership, Butt, Parnell and Dillon: Nationalism in transition', in D. George Boyce and Alan O'Day, eds., *Ireland in Transition 1867–1921*, pp.26–9, for an excellent analysis of Parnell's charismatic leadership.

8. Alan O'Day, 'Max Weber and Leadership, Butt, Parnell and Dillon', in *Ireland in Transition*, p.29.

9. Cited by Jenkins, *Gladstone*, p.563.

10. The editor was in fact a Scot, James Gordon Bennett. See Roger Wilkes, *Scandal: A Scurrilous History of Gossip*, pp.86–117, for a very good study of the 'New Journalism'.

11. Cited by Wilkes, *Scandal*, p.87.

12. According to biographers, Carmen had three children by her first husband, Arthur Herbert Buck. See F. S. L. Lyons, *Parnell*, p.633, and Joyce Marlow, *The Uncrowned Queen of Ireland*, p.302, among others. There is, however, no further record of them.

13. *Saturday Review*, 23 May 1914.

14. RTE Business, 31 May 2002.

Sources for family trees:
Parnell Archive at Kilmainham Gaol, KMH, 09 MS. IE 13 20 and 09 MS. IE 13 21; R. F. Foster, *Charles Stewart Parnell: The Man and his Family*, pp.34, 46, 56 and 65–105; Jane Jordan, *Kitty O'Shea: An Irish Affair*, pp.214–5; *Burke's Peerage and Baronetage*, 107th edition, online at www.thepeerage.com

The Wood Family Tree

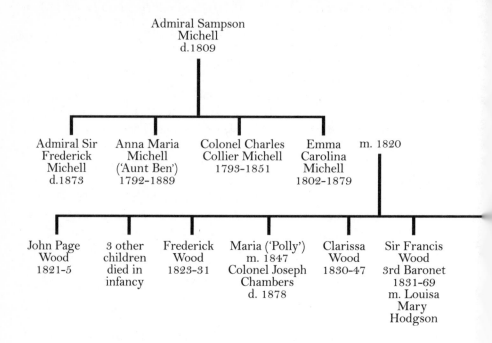

Admiral Sampson Michell
d.1809

Admiral Sir Frederick Michell d.1873 | Anna Maria Michell ('Aunt Ben') 1792-1889 | Colonel Charles Collier Michell 1793-1851 | Emma Carolina Michell 1802-1879 m. 1820

John Page Wood 1821-5 | 3 other children died in infancy | Frederick Wood 1823-31 | Maria ('Polly') m. 1847 Colonel Joseph Chambers d. 1878 | Clarissa Wood 1830-47 | Sir Francis Wood 3rd Baronet 1831-69 m. Louisa Mary Hodgson

The Parnell Family Tree

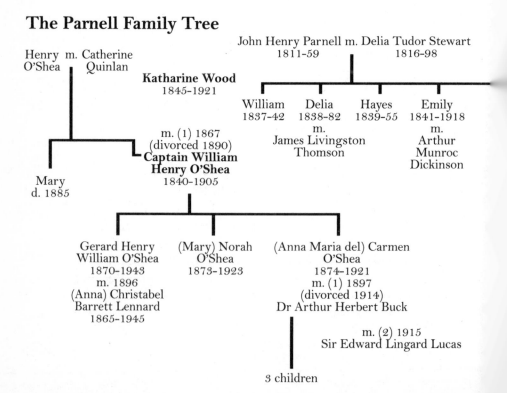

Henry O'Shea m. Catherine Quinlan

Katharine Wood 1845-1921

John Henry Parnell m. Delia Tudor Stewart
1811-59   1816-98

William 1837-42 | Delia 1838-82 m. James Livingston Thomson | Hayes 1839-55 | Emily 1841-1918 m. Arthur Munroc Dickinson

m. (1) 1867 (divorced 1890)
Captain William Henry O'Shea 1840-1905

Mary d. 1885

Gerard Henry William O'Shea 1870-1943 m. 1896 (Anna) Christabel Barrett Lennard 1865-1945 | (Mary) Norah O'Shea 1873-1923 | (Anna Maria del) Carmen O'Shea 1874-1921 m. (1) 1897 (divorced 1914) Dr Arthur Herbert Buck

m. (2) 1915
Sir Edward Lingard Lucas

3 children

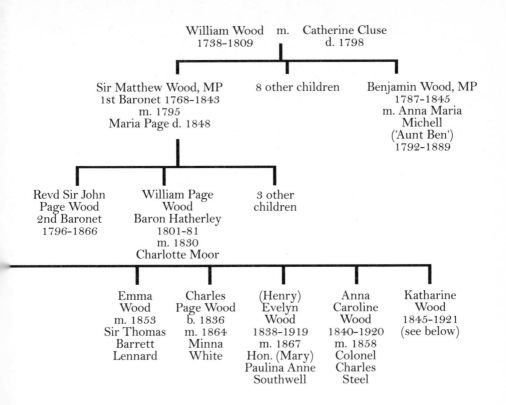

William Wood · m. · Catherine Cluse
1738-1809 · · d. 1798

Sir Matthew Wood, MP
1st Baronet 1768-1843
m. 1795
Maria Page d. 1848

8 other children

Benjamin Wood, MP
1787-1845
m. Anna Maria
Michell
('Aunt Ben')
1792-1889

Revd Sir John
Page Wood
2nd Baronet
1796-1866

William Page
Wood
Baron Hatherley
1801-81
m. 1830
Charlotte Moor

3 other
children

Emma
Wood
m. 1853
Sir Thomas
Barrett
Lennard

Charles
Page Wood
b. 1836
m. 1864
Minna
White

(Henry)
Evelyn
Wood
1838-1919
m. 1867
Hon. (Mary)
Paulina Anne
Southwell

Anna
Caroline
Wood
1840-1920
m. 1858
Colonel
Charles
Steel

Katharine
Wood
1845-1921
(see below)

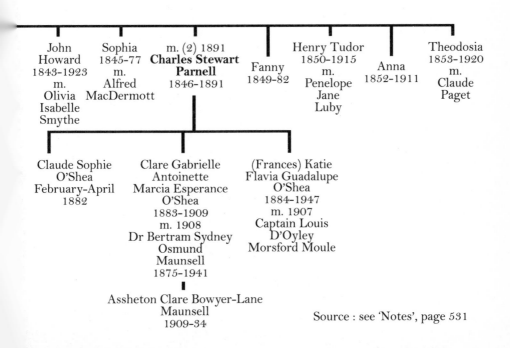

John
Howard
1843-1923
m.
Olivia
Isabelle
Smythe

Sophia
1845-77
m.
Alfred
MacDermott

m. (2) 1891
**Charles Stewart
Parnell**
1846-1891

Fanny
1849-82

Henry Tudor
1850-1915
m.
Penelope
Jane
Luby

Anna
1852-1911

Theodosia
1853-1920
m.
Claude
Paget

Claude Sophie
O'Shea
February-April
1882

Clare Gabrielle
Antoinette
Marcia Esperance
O'Shea
1883-1909
m. 1908
Dr Bertram Sydney
Osmund
Maunsell
1875-1941

(Frances) Katie
Flavia Guadalupe
O'Shea
1884-1947
m. 1907
Captain Louis
D'Oyley
Morsford Moule

Assheton Clare Bowyer-Lane
Maunsell
1909-34

Source : see 'Notes', page 531

Dramatis Personae

BRITAIN

BALFOUR, ARTHUR JAMES, 1ST EARL OF BALFOUR (1848–1930): Chief Secretary for Ireland 1887–91, and Conservative Prime Minister 1902–5, Balfour was elected as Conservative member for Hertford in 1874. From June 1885 to January 1886 he was President of the Local Government Board. In 1885 he moved to the new seat of Manchester East, which he held until 1906. His uncle, the Prime Minister Lord Salisbury, appointed him as Secretary of State for Scotland in August 1886 and he was Chief Secretary for Ireland in 1887. His Chief Secretaryship was to be very controversial. Balfour was deeply opposed to Home Rule, introducing and implementing energetic coercion and facing down Irish opposition in Westminster. He was particularly antagonistic to Parnellites, and had considerable success in breaking up the National League, although like Salisbury he was convinced of the need for palliative legislation and passed a number of Land Acts to improve the situation in Ireland. He became known as 'Bloody Balfour' by Irish Nationalists, however, after the 'Mitchelstown massacre' in 1887, when police fired on an angry crowd. In 1891 Balfour became First Lord of the Treasury and Leader of the House of Commons.

BANNERMAN, SIR HENRY CAMPBELL (1836–1908): Chief Secretary for Ireland 1884; Liberal Prime Minister. Campbell (who added Bannerman to his last name in 1871 to comply with a condition for inheriting his maternal uncle's estate) was elected Liberal MP for Stirling in 1868. From 1871 to 1874 and

1880 to 1882 he was Financial Secretary to the War Office. He was transferred to the Admiralty, where he worked during 1882–4 and was then appointed Chief Secretary for Ireland by Gladstone in 1884. He held this position for only seven months, until the fall of Gladstone's administration, but gained a strong reputation. Campbell-Bannerman hoped for compromise on the Irish question, but ultimately supported Gladstone. He held the Cabinet position of Secretary of State for War in 1886, and throughout 1892–5. He became Leader of the House of Commons in 1898, and Prime Minister 1905–8.

CARNARVON, HENRY HOWARD MOLYNEAUX HERBERT, 4TH EARL OF (1831–90): Conservative politician and landowner, and Colonial Secretary, during 1866–8 and 1874–8, Carnarvon supported the Disestablishment and the Land Acts of 1870 and 1881. He joined the Imperial Federal League in 1884 and was Lord-Lieutenant (Viceroy) of Ireland June 1885–February 1886. He was an advocate of a federal solution to Anglo-Irish relations, and promoted a policy of conciliation. His regime was a pacific one, and he met secretly with Parnell in August 1885 (Salisbury was aware of the meeting, but the Cabinet was not informed). Carnarvon's support for a limited form of self-government for Ireland was not shared by the Prime Minister or many of his colleagues, and he was not offered a post when a new government was formed in July 1886, bringing his political career to a close.

CAVENDISH, LORD FREDERICK CHARLES (1836–82): Cavendish was the second son of William Cavendish, 7th Duke of Devonshire, and brother of the Liberal politician Lord Hartington. Cavendish was Private Secretary to Lord Granville from 1859 to 1864; he entered Parliament as a Liberal for the northern division of the West Riding of Yorkshire in July 1865 and retained his seat until his death. He was Private Secretary to Gladstone – his wife's uncle by marriage – from July 1872 to August 1873, became a junior Lord of the Treasury, and was Financial Secretary to the Treasury from April 1880 to May 1882. He accepted the post of Chief Secretary to Ireland and took his oath at Dublin Castle on 6 May 1882. He and the Under-Secretary, Thomas Henry Burke, were murdered later that day in Phoenix Park, by a gang known as the 'Invincibles'.

CHAMBERLAIN, JOSEPH (1836–1914): Industrialist and politician, and a successful businessman and Mayor of Birmingham from 1873 to 1876, Chamberlain was elected Liberal MP for Birmingham in 1876. He soon made his mark in the House of Commons as a radical Liberal and Gladstone appointed him to the Cabinet, as President of the Board of Trade, in 1880.

Chamberlain had a strong interest in imperial issues; he was involved in some of the informal negotiations over the 'Irish question', acting, for example, as an intermediary over the Kilmainham Treaty, 1882. He was opposed to Home Rule as a breach of empire, but was a strong believer in the necessity of local government for Ireland. Chamberlain resigned from Gladstone's Cabinet over Home Rule in March 1886, and became leader of the Liberal Unionists, forming an alliance with the Conservatives against Home Rule.

CHURCHILL, LORD RANDOLPH HENRY SPENCER (1849–95): Conservative politician, and third son of the Duke of Marlborough, he was Acting Secretary for his father when the Duke was Lord-Lieutenant (Viceroy) of Ireland, 1877–80. Churchill retained a career-long interest in Ireland and Irish affairs. He was a strong supporter of the legislative union with Ireland. A well-known Tory radical – who briefly left the party to found, with three others, the 'Fourth Party' – Churchill was Secretary of State for India in 1885. He was later instrumental in the Tory-Home Rule accommodation, although he supported the Unionists after Gladstone announced his conversion to Home Rule, in February 1886. Churchill was Chancellor of the Exchequer and Leader of the House of Commons, June 1886, and promised an inquiry into Irish affairs. He resigned in December 1886.

COWPER, FRANCIS THOMAS DE GREY, 7TH EARL (1834–1905): Whig peer, politician and landowner, born into a family of great wealth, Cowper was Lord-Lieutenant (or Viceroy) of Ireland May 1880–May 1882. In December 1880 he prepared a memorandum for the Cabinet which urged the banning of the Land League, in addition to the suspension of habeas corpus and arms control. These coercive measures went beyond those recommended by Chief Secretary, W. E. Forster, and were not accepted. Cowper's appointment was not a very successful one. He was frequently at odds with Forster – who sought to have him removed from his position within a year after the appointment – and frustrated at the limitations of his position during a difficult period in Ireland. He initially resisted signing the papers releasing the Kilmainham prisoners in May 1882, and formally left office on 4 May 1882.

DILKE, SIR CHARLES WENTWORTH, 2ND BARONET (1843–1911): Writer and politician; before entering politics he made a world tour during 1866–7, and on his return he published *Greater Britain*, a record of his travels that brought him much attention – it ran to eight editions and its title became a catchphrase in imperialist debate. Dilke was elected to Parliament as a radical Liberal for Chelsea, a seat which he held throughout 1868–86. In 1869 he succeeded to the baronetcy and to proprietorship of the *Atheneum* and *Notes and Queries*. A close political ally of fellow radical Liberal Joseph Chamberlain, Dilke was Under-Secretary at the Foreign Office, 1880–82. Having refused the Chief Secretaryship to Ireland in April 1882, as it came without a seat in Cabinet, he entered the Cabinet as President of the Local Government Board in December of that year. Although many saw him as a future premier, his political career was cut short when he was cited as co-respondent in the scandalous divorce suit *Crawford vs Crawford and Dilke* in 1885–6.

FORSTER, WILLIAM EDWARD (1818–86): Elected Liberal MP for Bradford in 1861, Forster was Under-Secretary for the Colonies, November 1865–June 1866; he was Vice-President of the Council with responsibility for education in 1868, and was made a Privy Councillor. A leading front-bench radical in Opposition, Forster was then appointed Chief Secretary for Ireland in April 1880 – an immensely challenging time. He became distressed at being unable to help innocent victims of agrarian crime, and also with being associated with harsh coercive measures and legislation. Although he was fully supported by his Cabinet colleagues for the arrest of Parnell in October 1881, he was increasingly isolated in his obdurate refusal to compromise on key issues that would allow for the Irishman's release. He became the focus of bitter attacks in England as well as Ireland, and resigned over his disagreement with the negotiations between Parnell and the government in May 1882.

GLADSTONE, WILLIAM EWART (1809–98): A politician and statesman, he held the following offices: Colonial Secretary, 1845–6; Chancellor of the Exchequer, 1852–5, 1859–66, 1873–4 and 1880–2; Liberal Prime Minister, 1868–74, 1880–85, 1886, and 1892–4. Gladstone disestablished the Church of Ireland in 1869, passed two Irish Land Acts in 1870 and 1881, and passed Compensation, Arrears and Coercion Acts in 1880–2. He was committed to solving the 'Irish problem', and split his party over his conversion to Home Rule (losing the 1886 election). Despite his efforts, Gladstone was unsuccessful in passing Home Rule Bills in 1886 and 1893.

HARCOURT, SIR WILLIAM GEORGE GRANVILLE VENABLES VERNON (1827–1904): A politician and lawyer, he entered Parliament as a Liberal in 1868 and was appointed Home Secretary in 1880. In this capacity, Harcourt played a crucial role in moving forward the government bills for the maintenance of order in Ireland, especially after the Phoenix Park murders and subsequent 'outrages'. He was made Chancellor of the Exchequer briefly in 1886, a position he resumed in Gladstone's last administration, in 1892. He remained a senior figure highly influential in the government, and was one of the few opponents of Home Rule in the Cabinet to change his mind, deciding that compromise was preferable to coercion. In 1889 and 1890 he was deeply involved with Parnell. He was initially on his side and defended him against *The Times*. After the O'Shea divorce scandal, however, Harcourt was one of the Liberal leaders who advised Gladstone to sever links between Parnell and the Liberal Party.

LABOUCHERE, HENRY DU PRE (1831–1912): A minor diplomat during 1854–64, Labouchere was elected a Liberal MP for Windsor in 1865. Two years later he was returned for Middlesex, a seat he lost in 1868. He failed at Nottingham in 1874 and then had to wait until 1880 before entering Parliament again, representing Northampton (for the ensuing twenty-five years). In the meantime he gained renown as a first-class, witty journalist. His personal weekly journal *Truth*, started in 1876, gained a large audience and was famed for its inside information and exposés of the court and political establishment. After 1880 Labouchere became of the most powerful radicals in the Commons and worked with Joseph Chamberlain during 1880–85 to achieve an 'all-radical' government. He exploited his intimacy with the Irish Nationalists to campaign against moderate Liberals and was a determined supporter of Home Rule. When Chamberlain decided to vote against the first Home Rule Bill in 1886, it ruined Labouchere's attempts to bring Gladstone, Chamberlain and the Irish Nationalists into agreement.

MORLEY, JOHN, VISCOUNT MORLEY OF BLACKBURN (1838–1923): Morley had a successful career as a journalist, editor and writer – he was editor of a leading journal of opinion, the *Fortnightly Review*, 1867–82, edited the *Pall Mall Gazette* during 1880–83 and published a number of successful works. Morley took a close interest in politics and entered Parliament as a Liberal in 1883. By 1885 he was convinced that Home Rule was the only answer to the Irish question, and was one of the few prominent Liberals openly to support Gladstone's Irish policy. Gladstone appointed him Chief Secretary to Ireland in 1886, a position he resumed in the premier's third administration in 1892. The Parnell divorce had come as a disappointment, but Morley continued vigorously to support negotiations for Irish legislative independence.

SALISBURY, LORD (ROBERT ARTHUR TALBOT GASCOYNE CECIL) (1830–1903): Son of the 2nd Marquess of Salisbury, Robert Cecil was elected to represent Stamford as a Conservative in 1853 (he was granted the title Lord Cranborne on the death of his brother in 1865). Cranborne became Secretary of State for India in 1866, resigning the following year. In 1868 he succeeded his father as the 3rd Marquess of Salisbury and returned to government in 1874 as Secretary of State for India. In 1878 he became Foreign Secretary, and leader of the Conservative Party. At the general election of 1885 he became Prime Minister – replaced briefly by Gladstone in 1886 – but was then head of the governments throughout 1886–92, and 1895–1902. Salisbury's first, short ministry came in with the help of Parnellite votes, but he maintained his belief that self-government for Ireland was unacceptable. He was convinced that resolving the Irish question necessitated a firm hand and he reinvigorated coercion legislation with the appointment of his nephew Arthur Balfour as Chief Secretary in 1887.

SPENCER, JOHN POYNTZ, 5TH EARL (1835–1910): A close associate of Gladstone, Spencer was twice Lord-Lieutenant (Viceroy) of Ireland: from December 1868 to March 1874, and again from May 1882 to February 1886. During his first stint in Ireland, he was inexperienced but determined to achieve stability through land legislation. On leaving office he was encouraged by the seeming decline of Fenianism and agrarian crime. He was then Lord President of the Council with a seat in Cabinet from 1880 to early 1883, during which time he advised on Irish affairs. When he returned to the Viceroyalty in May 1882, Spencer oversaw a reorganization of the police forces and reform of the magistrate, and requested the appointment of an Under-Secretary for police and crime – by the end of 1882 the situation was relatively calm because of his actions. He changed his position and decided to support Home Rule after 1885, much to the astonishment (and considerable disapproval) of many of his colleagues and friends. Spencer was First Lord of the Admiralty, 1892–5.

TREVELYAN, SIR GEORGE OTTO, 2ND BARONET (1838–1928). A successful writer and historian, Trevelyan entered Parliament in 1865 as Liberal MP for Tynemouth and North Shields. He was returned at the 1868 election for Hawick, which he represented until 1886. He was appointed Chief Secretary for Ireland (without a Cabinet seat) after Cavendish's assassination in May 1882. Over the course of the two years spent at this stressful post – during which his hair turned white – Trevelyan answered over 2,000 parliamentary questions, many of them deeply hostile, on all aspects of Irish administration. He was moved to a less stressful position, as Secretary for Scotland, but resigned with Joseph Chamberlain over Home Rule in March 1886. Trevelyan was, however, uncomfortable in the Liberal Unionist camp, and to Chamberlain's dismay – and contempt – returned to the Gladstonian fold in 1887.

IRELAND

BIGGAR, JOSEPH GILLIS (1828–90): A Nationalist and politician, and a prosperous provision merchant from Belfast, Biggar was elected MP for Cavan in 1874. He joined the IRB in 1875, where he was a member of the Supreme Council until expelled in 1877 for refusing to quit Parliament. Known for pioneering 'obstruction' techniques in the House of Commons, he was also active in the Land League, where he was Treasurer from 1879. Biggar was a Presbyterian by upbringing but converted to Catholicism in 1877. He was an energetic performer in Parliament and very popular among the Irish members, who appreciated his honesty and good humour.

DAVITT, MICHAEL (1846–1906): A Nationalist and radical agrarian, Davitt was born in County Mayo. His family's eviction from their home in 1850 after falling into rent arrears led to their emigration to Lancashire. Davitt was brought up with an abiding hatred for landlordism. He began working at a mill at age nine, and lost his right arm in an industrial accident at the age of eleven. He subsequently returned to school and later became a book-keeper and typesetter. In 1865 he joined the IRB, and was involved in numerous Fenian activities, becoming the organizing Secretary and arms agent for the organization in England and Scotland. He was arrested in May 1870 and sentenced to fifteen years' penal servitude. Released in 1877, he renewed his connections with the IRB, travelling to the USA in 1878, where he met John Devoy. Davitt was instrumental in the development of the Land League and was a highly influential politician during 1879–82. After this time his impact declined, although Davitt's assessment of the land war as a straight fight between landlord and peasant – as expounded in his *The Fall of Feudalism* in Ireland (1904) – was very influential.

DEVOY, JOHN (1842–1928): A Nationalist and journalist, and a Dublin clerk, Devoy was imprisoned 1866–71 for his part in a Fenian conspiracy. After he was exiled in 1871, he became a highly efficient and determined organizer of

Irish-American support for Irish nationalism. Head of the revolutionary Clan na Gael in the United States, he founded the *Irish Nation* (1882) and the *Gaelic American* (1903) newspapers. Devoy also played an important role in the formation of the Land League. He and Michael Davitt launched the 'New Departure' in 1878/79. This was intended to link the IRB and Clan na Gael with the 'obstructionist' section of Home Rule MPs led by Parnell. Devoy and the Clan contributed substantially to the success of Parnell's US fund-raising. Devoy remained a key figure in the Clan and a supporter of separatist Irish nationalism, supporting the Friends of Irish Freedom – which raised large sums for the independence movement.

DILLON, JOHN (1851–1927): A Nationalist and politician, born in County Dublin to Catholic bourgeois parents, MP for Tipperary 1880–3 and for East Mayo 1885–1915, Dillon was a militant agrarian in the 1880s up to 1891. He was imprisoned six times and retained a career-long commitment to anti-landlordism. He was a member of the original committee when the Irish Land League was formed in October 1879, and in April 1880 joined the executive of the League. He was a close ally and friend of Michael Davitt. Dillon and William O'Brien frequently clashed with Parnell over their continued agrarianism, but were both reluctant anti-Parnellites in 1890. Dillon took an increasingly prominent role in the largest section of the divided Irish Nationalists and became the leader in 1896 upon the ageing Justin McCarthy's resignation. A passionate agrarian radical, he remained a fervent Home Ruler throughout his life. He resigned in 1899 to facilitate Party reunion, and supported John Redmond's election for the chairmanship in 1900.

EGAN, PATRICK (1841–1914): A Nationalist, prosperous Dublin baker and successful businessman, Egan was a committed Fenian, becoming involved with the IRB soon after its establishment. He was Treasurer of the IRB from 1873, although he and others resigned from that organization in August 1877. Egan, a close associate of Parnell, was one of the founders of the Irish Land League and at its foundation in 1879 was elected Treasurer. After the League was proscribed by the British government, he fled to Paris with their funds and remained there from February 1881 until the end of 1882. Learning that he was to be arrested, he fled to Holland and later the United States, where he continued to work for the Land League and to achieve Home Rule.

HEALY, TIMOTHY MICHAEL (1855–1931): A Nationalist and politician, born in County Cork and educated at the Christian Brothers School in Fermoy,

Tim Healy became a leading Dublin barrister and KC as well as an important and influential Nationalist MP – member (as was his brother Maurice) of the tight political clan known as the 'Bantry band'. He was in Parliament almost continuously between 1880 and 1918. Although initially a Parnell loyalist, he famously turned against the leader after the divorce trial in 1890–1, attacking him savagely and publicly. Known for his volatility and intense Catholicism, Healy subsequently found it difficult to work with other anti-Parnellite leaders. He was expelled from the National League in 1895. Healy played a major role in the reunification of the party in 1900, although his relations with the Chairman, John Redmond, were fraught. Healy later became the first Governor-General of the Irish Free State, 1922–8.

McCARTHY, JUSTIN (1830–1912): A Nationalist politician and writer, McCarthy was a successful journalist and editor, who also authored or co-authored more than fifty novels. He was born near Cork, and moved to Liverpool in 1853, then moved to London in 1860, where he was on the staff of the radical *Morning Star* until 1868. McCarthy took a close interest in Irish affairs, and entered Parliament in 1879 as a Home Ruler, becoming Vice-Chairman of the Irish Party in 1880 – a position which he held until December 1890. He was an original shareholder in *United Ireland*, and continued to write throughout his political career. He had both Liberal and Nationalist friends and, although he became a member of the Land League in 1881, he remained a political moderate. After the Parnell divorce, he led the withdrawal of the majority of Nationalist MPs, subsequently known as the anti-Parnellites, although he personally remained on good terms with the disgraced leader.

MURPHY, WILLIAM MARTIN (1844–1919): A businessman and politician, born in County Cork, Murphy made a large fortune from railway contracts and investments in Britain, South America and Ireland. He was Home Rule MP for the St Patrick's Division of Dublin, 1885–92, but Dublin stayed loyal to Parnell after the split, and Murphy, who opposed the fallen leader, lost his seat in 1892. An affluent, conservative Nationalist, he established the *Irish Catholic* and bought the *Irish Independent* in 1904. Murphy was founder of the Dublin Employers' Federation in 1912 and led the counter-attack against growing labour militancy – this culminated in the defeat of the unions in the famous Dublin lock-out of 1913.

O'BRIEN, RICHARD BARRY (1847–1918): A Nationalist, journalist and writer, born in County Clare, O'Brien went to London in 1869 to study for the bar.

Although called to the Irish bar in 1874 and the English bar in 1875, he concentrated primarily on his career as a journalist. O'Brien came to prominence with the publication in 1879 of *The Irish Land Question and English Public Opinion*, and he published a number of works on land legislation which contributed to the debate on this question. O'Brien supported Parnell in the split because he believed that he was the only leader of sufficient stature to run the party. He published his biography of Parnell in 1899 – this work was very valuable for its personal recollections and interviews, although it excluded any discussion of the subject's private life.

O'Brien, William (1852–1928): A Nationalist, journalist and politician, O'Brien was appointed by Parnell in 1881 as editor to the new weekly Land League newspaper, *United Ireland*. He wrote the famous 'No Rent' manifesto while imprisoned in Kilmainham Gaol with the other Nationalist leaders between October 1881 and April 1882. O'Brien was MP for Mallow in 1883–5, member for Tyrone South in 1886, for North East Cork in 1887–92, and for Cork City in 1892–5 and 1901–18. Although personally loyal to Parnell, he was unsuccessful in persuading him to resign from the leadership, and became, along with John Dillon, a reluctant leading anti-Parnellite.

O'Connell, Daniel (1775–1847): A Nationalist leader, known as 'The Liberator', born in County Kerry, O'Connell was from a Catholic landholding family. O'Connell was adopted by his uncle, the head of the O'Connell clan, who paid for him to attend the best Catholic colleges in Europe and made him his heir. O'Connell was set on a legal career, enrolling in London's Lincoln's Inn in 1794. He went to Dublin and entered the King's Inns in 1796, qualifying as a lawyer in 1798. He developed a reputation for radical political views, and was associated with the United Irishmen, although not a supporter of violent revolution. O'Connell became the most successful and famous barrister in Ireland and also campaigned extensively for Catholic emancipation. His adept use of popular mobilization to raise funds and structure countrywide agitation was very successful, and in 1829 Parliament passed the Roman Catholic Relief Act. This granted Catholic emancipation and O'Connell was elected to Parliament for County Kerry in 1830. He became a major figure in the House of Commons, and continued his extensive campaigning. Although he was later challenged by a new generation of Nationalists, and his campaign for repeal of the Act of Union did not succeed, O'Connell was revered by many throughout Europe as a champion of liberty.

O'CONNOR, THOMAS POWER (1848–1929): A Nationalist, journalist and politician (known as 'T. P.'), he became a Nationalist politician who combined his political career with that of a very successful London journalist, having left Ireland for London in 1870. His first book, a life of Benjamin Disraeli, appeared anonymously during 1876 – this vehement attack on the Prime Minister attracted considerable attention and, when it was published under O'Connor's name in 1879, its success provided him with an entrée into politics. He entered Parliament as a Home Rule candidate for Galway in 1880, transferring in 1885 to Liverpool (Scotland), a seat he retained until his death. O'Connor became a prominent parliamentary speaker and was from 1883 leader of the Nationalist Party in Great Britain. In 1888 O'Connor founded the *Star*, an evening journal noted for its radicalism. As well as founding a number of successful papers, he was the author of books such as *The Parnell Movement* (1886) and *Memoirs of an Old Parliamentarian* (1929). He was President of the Irish National League of Great Britain from 1883 to 1918.

O'GORMAN MAHON, THE (1800–91): A Nationalist politician, James Mahon adopted this title. Mahon was a Catholic gentleman from County Clare, who had been in O'Connell's campaign in 1828. He was MP for Ennis in 1847–52, and Home Rule MP for County Clare in 1879–85 and for Carlow in 1887–91.

POWER, JOHN O'CONNOR (1848–1919): A Nationalist and politician, he was a member of the IRB, and joined the Home Rule League in 1873 and encouraged other Fenians to give constitutionalism a chance. He was MP for Mayo in 1874 and a prominent obstructionist. He was expelled from the IRB in 1877 for refusing to leave the Home Rule Party. Power stood as a Liberal in the 1885 election – retiring from politics after he lost.

REDMOND, JOHN EDWARD (1856–1918): A Nationalist and politician, Redmond was Chairman of the Irish Parliamentary Party. Born in County Wexford to a family of the Catholic gentry (although his mother was of a Protestant family and had converted on marriage), Redmond was educated by the Jesuits. His father, William, was the MP for Wexford and John Redmond went to London to live with his father in 1876, becoming his clerk at Westminster. He entered Parliament in January 1881. He also qualified as a barrister and was called to the Irish bar in 1887 and was busy with agrarian cases. Redmond supported Parnell during the split, although as a conventional Catholic he was perhaps somewhat reluctant, and did not attend the fallen leader's last public meetings. Redmond became leader of the small Parnellite minority of MPs after the split and adopted a moderate political approach – dropping interest in radical agrarianism. He was elected Chairman of a unified party in 1900.

SULLIVAN, ALEXANDER MARTIN (1829–84): A Nationalist, lawyer and journalist, born at Bantry, County Cork, Sullivan went to Dublin in 1853 to pursue a career in journalism. He became assistant editor of the *Nation* newspaper in 1855, and by 1858 was its editor and sole proprietor. In addition to the *Nation*, Sullivan also published weeklies, such as the *Weekly News* and *The Emerald* and *Young Ireland*. These newspapers promoted a broadly based constitutional movement to win some form of Irish self-government, in which Sullivan hoped to play an important part. He was MP for Louth during 1874–80, and for Meath County during 1880–82. A. M. Sullivan was called to the Irish bar in 1876, although he chose to practise law in England. Two of his brothers, Timothy Daniel and Donal, were also involved in Nationalist politics and were – along with seven other MPs from their region – members of the politically ambitious 'Bantry Band'.

SOURCES

Joseph P. Finnan, *John Redmond and Irish Unity, 1912–1918*; R. F. Foster, *Modern Ireland*; S. J. Connelly, ed., *The Oxford Companion to Irish History*; F. S. L. Lyons, *Charles Stewart Parnell*; and Lawrence Goldman, Brian Harrison and Colin Matthew, eds., *The Oxford Dictionary of National Biography* (online version updated October 2007).

Appendix:
A List of Cabinets 1880–1890

GLADSTONE'S SECOND CABINET:
FORMED APRIL 1880

Prime Minister and First Lord of the Treasury: W. E. Gladstone
Chancellor of the Exchequer: W. E. Gladstone
Lord Chancellor: Lord Selborne (cr. Earl Selborne 1881)
Lord President: Earl Spencer
Lord Privy Seal: Duke of Argyll
Home Secretary: Sir W. V. Harcourt
Foreign Secretary: Earl Granville
Secretary for War: H. C. E. Childers
Colonial Secretary: Earl of Kimberley
First Lord of the Admiralty: Earl of Northbrook
President of the Board of Trade: Joseph Chamberlain
Secretary for India: Marquess of Hartington
Chief Secretary for Ireland: W. E. Forster
President of the Local Government Board: J. G. Dodson
Chancellor of the Duchy of Lancaster: John Bright

'Changes: *May 1881:* Lord Carlingford (Chichester Fortescue) succeeded
Argyll (resigned) as Lord Privy Seal. *May 1882:* Spencer, while retaining
his seat in the cabinet, became Viceroy of Ireland; Forster resigned as
Chief Secretary for Ireland (his successors were not in the cabinet). *July
1882:* Bright resigned as Chancellor of the Duchy of Lancaster and was

succeeded by Kimberley who combined the office with that of Colonial Secretary. *December 1882*: Gladstone resigned the Chancellorship of the Exchequer to Childers; Hartington succeeded Childers as Secretary for War; Kimberley succeeded Hartington as Secretary for India; Kimberley was succeeded as Colonial Secretary by Lord Derby and as Chancellor of the Duchy of Lancaster by J. G. Dodson; Dodson was succeeded as President of the Local Government Board by Sir Charles Dilke. *March 1883*: Carlingford succeeded Spencer as Lord President and combined that office with that of Lord Privy Seal. *October 1884*: G. O. Trevelyan succeeded Dodson (resigned) as Chancellor of the Duchy of Lancaster; *November 1884*: C. J. Shaw-Lefevre (Postmaster-General) was brought into the cabinet; *March 1885*: the Earl of Rosebery was brought into the cabinet, taking over from Carlingford as Lord Privy Seal.' (Hoppen, *The Mid-Victorian Generation*, pp.722–3)

Salisbury's First Cabinet: Formed June 1885

Prime Minister and Foreign Secretary: Marquess of Salisbury
First Lord of the Treasury: Earl of Iddesleigh (Sir Stafford Northcote)
Lord Chancellor: Lord Halsbury
Lord President: Viscount Cranbrook
Lord Privy Seal: Earl of Harrowby
Chancellor of the Exchequer: Sir Michael Hicks Beach
Home Secretary: Sir R. A. Cross
Secretary for War: W. H. Smith
Colonial Secretary: F. A. Stanley
First Lord of the Admiralty: Lord George Hamilton
President of the Board of Trade: Duke of Richmond
Secretary for India: Lord Randolph Churchill
Viceroy of Ireland: Earl of Carnavon
Postmaster-General: Lord John Manners
Vice-President (Education): E. Stanhope
Lord Chancellor of Ireland: Lord Ashbourne

'Changes: *August 1885*: Richmond was appointed to the new post of Secretary for Scotland; he was succeeded as President of the Board of Trade by Stanhope (whose successor as Vice-President (Education) was not in the cabinet). *January 1886*: Smith became Chief Secretary for Ireland while retaining his seat in the cabinet.' (Hoppen, *The Mid-Victorian Generation*, p.723)

GLADSTONE'S THIRD CABINET: FORMED FEBRUARY 1886

Prime Minister and First Lord of the Treasury: W. E. Gladstone
Lord Privy Seal: W. E. Gladstone
Lord Chancellor: Lord Herschell
Lord President: Earl Spencer
Chancellor of the Exchequer: Sir W. V. Harcourt
Home Secretary: H. C. E. Childers
Foreign Secretary: Earl of Rosebery
Secretary for War: H. Campbell-Bannerman
Colonial Secretary: Earl Granville
First Lord of the Admiralty: Marquess of Ripon
President of the Board of Trade: A. J. Mundella
Secretary for India: Earl of Kimberley
Secretary for Scotland: G. O. Trevelyan
Chief Secretary for Ireland: John Morley
President of the Local Government Board: Joseph Chamberlain

'Changes: *April 1886*: Chamberlain resigned and was succeeded by James Stansfield; Trevelyan resigned (his successor for Scotland was not in the cabinet).' (Hoppen, *The Mid-Victorian Generation*, pp.723–4)

SALISBURY'S SECOND CABINET: FORMED AUGUST 1886

Prime Minister and First Lord of the Treasury: Marquess of Salisbury
Lord Chancellor: Lord Halsbury
Lord Chancellor of Ireland: Lord Ashbourne
Lord President of the Council: Viscount Cranbrook
Chancellor of the Exchequer: Lord Randolph Churchill
Home Secretary: H. Matthews
Foreign Secretary: Earl of Iddesleigh
Secretary for War: W. H. Smith

Colonial Secretary: Hon. Edward Stanhope
First Lord of the Admiralty: Lord George Hamilton
President of the Board of Trade: Lord Stanley
Secretary for India: Viscount Cross
Chief Secretary for Ireland: Sir M. Hicks Beach
Chancellor of the Duchy of Lancaster: Lord John Manners

'Changes: *November 1886*: A. J. Balfour entered Cabinet as Secretary for Scotland. *January 1887*: Lord Randolph Churchill resigned as Chancellor of the Exchequer, to be replaced by G. J. Goschen. Lord Iddesleigh was dismissed as Foreign Secretary, being replaced by Salisbury, whose post as Lord President of the Council passed to W. H. Smith. The latter vacated his post as Secretary for War and was replaced by E. Stanhope, who in turn was succeeded as Colonial Secretary by Lord Knutsford. *March 1887*: A. J. Balfour was replaced as Secretary for Scotland by the Marquess of Lothian and became Chief Secretary for Ireland in place of Sir M. Hicks Beach (who nevertheless retained his place in the Cabinet). *May 1887*: Earl Cadogan entered the Cabinet as Lord Privy Seal and C. T. Ritchie as President of the Local Government Board. *February 1888*: Sir M. Hicks Beach was made President of the Board of Trade, replacing Lord Stanley. *October 1891*: W. H. Smith died, being succeeded as First Lord of the Treasury by A. J. Balfour, who was replaced as Chief Secretary for Ireland by W. L. Jackson.' (Searle, *A New England?*, pp.852–3)

Bibliography

A Note on Sources

By far the most important source of information on Katharine's life is her memoir of Charles Stewart Parnell. It is a curious work, apparently published in response to a letter that publicly criticized Willie O'Shea in 1913, effectively accusing him of connivance in his wife's adultery. Katie and Willie's only son Gerard took particular exception to this accusation and, it is believed, encouraged his mother to write and publish her memoir to refute it. Suggestions have been made by various parties that the memoirs were edited, even doctored or ghostwritten by him. It is very clear that the book was written to fulfil a purpose. What is less clear, however, is what exactly that purpose was, and how well the author (and/or her son) was able to adhere to it. The critical point, I believe, is that the two volumes provide wonderful insight into Katharine's early life. It is a powerful statement on Katie's part to dedicate the first 125 pages (thirteen chapters) to her own life, before even mentioning Parnell – bearing in mind that the book's title is *Charles Stewart Parnell: His Love Story and Political Life*. It is unlikely that Gerard would have had much to say or add to his mother's story of her early life. And there is a consistency to the author's voice, especially in the earlier memoir, that has been recognized by her biographers. It is probably a fair judgement to say that the earlier memoir can be trusted, in so far as allowance is made for Katie's agenda of justifying her later actions, and that the later memoir serves a useful purpose in adding to the Parnell story. Again, the problem of possible deliberate inaccuracies must be allowed for. A certain scrutiny must also be brought to bear on the authenticity and dating of the letters included in the book.

There are unfortunately few manuscript sources available, but those still intact are very helpful. Katharine's great-niece, Minna Evangeline Bradhurst, privately published a collection of family letters: *A Century of Letters 1820–1920: Letters from Literary Friends to Lady Wood and Mrs. A. C. Steele.* Many of these are to and from correspondents of Katie's mother, Emma Wood, and of Katie's sister Anna Steele. These letters, and the recollections in the work, are extremely useful in providing details of Katie's early life, and indeed of the lives and histories of Wood family members.

The British Library holds the archives of Katie's correspondence with Prime Minister Gladstone and a few other government correspondents. The National Archives of Ireland contain some interesting material on Katharine and Willie O'Shea, as well as on Charles Stewart Parnell. In particular, the archive at Kilmainham Gaol has a very useful collection of Parnell material and some artefacts passed down through his family. Correspondence between Willie O'Shea and Joseph Chamberlain is held at Birmingham University Library and yields interesting insight into O'Shea's motivation and behaviour.

Joyce Marlow published *The Uncrowned Queen of Ireland* over thirty-five years ago, in 1975. She made good use of manuscript and original material from a variety of sources. Her book benefited greatly from the help she received from family members, including Sir Richard Barrett Lennard, and particularly Christine FitzGerald, Katie's great-niece. The latter gave Marlow extensive access to family books, letters and photographs. Although some of these have ended up in the Essex Record Office (where they may be consulted) much seems to have disappeared from view. Marlow's biography is not a scholarly work and lacks footnotes for her many quotations, but it is well written with a clear aim for accuracy. It is thus of particular value for information on Katie's early life, which is otherwise poorly documented.

A recent biography by the literary specialist Jane Jordan provides much interesting detail on Katie's life. This work has been extensively researched and is useful for the wealth of information it provides on Willie O'Shea's motivations, and on Parnell's political world. This well-written book also provides a wealth of new detail on the later part of Katie's life after Parnell's death.

Other biographies of Katie include an earlier work by the novelist Mary Rose Callaghan. Biographies of Charles Stewart Parnell have also been of critical importance. Of the early works, that of R. Barry O'Brien, based on his personal acquaintance with the leader and on interviews with colleagues and contemporaries, has long been considered the best. Other contemporary works included those of Parnell's colleagues: Michael Davitt, John Devoy and St John Ervine. Later biographies include the impassioned work by Henry Harrison, who was eager to clear his leader's name. Seminal biographies by F. S. L. Lyons, Conor Cruise O'Brien and Roy Foster have contributed greatly to the knowledge of Parnell.

There is in addition an impressive amount of scholarly work on Irish history that has emerged in the past decade or so. Bodies of work that have been of particular interest and great benefit include those by Roy Foster, Alan O'Day,. Margaret O'Callaghan, Frank Callanan, Robert Kee, M. J. Kelly, Alvin Jackson, Theodore Hoppen, D. George Boyce and Carla King.

Primary Sources

British Library Additional Manuscripts (Add MS):
    Alverstone: 61737, 61738; Dilke: 43914, 43916; Gladstone: 44269, 44315,
    44316, 44503 and 56446; Harcourt: 21219; Hutton: 50086; Lytton
    (correspondence with Anna Steele): 59662; Morley: 48266, 48267;
    O'Shea Correspondence & Miscellany: 62114; Ramsay: 46450; Sir
    Evelyn Wood 61737, 61738
Essex Record Office: Barrett Lennard Papers: T/B 224/1/3
Kilmainham Gaol Archive: Parnell Collection: 09 MS IE, 10 MS IE, Box
    IE 15
Her Majesty's Court Service
Principal Registry of the Family Division:

Probate Department

The Wills and Grants for: The Right Honourable William Page Hatherley,
    The Reverend Sir John Page Wood, Sir Matthew Wood, and Anna Maria
    Wood

Decree Absolute Searches, Family Proceedings Department

Decree Absolute : Divorce of William Henry O'Shea and Katharine O'Shea
    (then Katharine Wood spinster); Co-respondent: Parnell
National Library of Ireland: Manuscript Collections: O'Shea, Parnell Papers
    and Miscellaneous Papers: MS 3882; 3883; 5752; 21679; 21936; 27666;
    31650; 33140; 33141; 33142; 33143; 33144; 33146; 33899; 35262; 35290;
    35982; 36681; 39928; 40014; 40620; 40624; 40618; 40651; 40653/3
University of Birmingham Library, Joseph Chamberlain Collection:
    JC/8/8/1/176; JC8/8/2G1-2

Articles, Pamphlets and Journals

The Accounting Historians Journal, 'The Financial Crises and the Publication
    of the Financial Statements of Banks in Spain, 1844–1868', by Mercedes
    Bernal Llorens, December 2004

Conquering England: Ireland in Victorian London, by Fintan Cullen and R. F. Foster (London: National Portrait Gallery, 2005)

Dublin Magazine, Vol. VI, No. 4, Oct.–Dec. 1931

Historical Research, Vol. 78, No. 201, Aug. 2005, 'Feminist and Anti-Feminist Encounters in Edwardian Britain', pp.377–99, by Lucy Delap

Irish Book Lover, Vol. V, November 1913, and June 1914; Vol. XIII, Oct, 1921

Irish Historical Studies, Vol. V, No. 19, March 1947

Irish Historical Studies, Vol. IX, 1954–5, pp.319–38, 'Parnell and the Galway Election of 1886', by Professor T. W. Moody

Irish Historical Studies, Vol. XXIX, 1994–5, pp.363–70, 'Parnell and the I. R. B. Oath', by Patrick Maume

Irish Historical Studies, Vol. XXXIII, 1998, pp.241–6, 'Letters of Mourning from Katherine [*sic*] O'Shea Parnell to Delia Tudor Stewart Parnell' (Select documents, 49), by John D. Fair

Irish Political Studies, 'Book Reviews', Vol. 21, No. 3, pp.384–6, 'Charles Stewart Parnell, F. S. L. Lyons', by Matthew Kelly

Journal of Women's History, 'Book Reviews', Vol. 6, No. 1, (Spring) 1994, 'Dangerous Sexualities in Victorian England', by Thomas Prasch, pp.87–97

Little Journeys, Vol. XVIII, No. 5, May 1906 (New York: Roycrofters, 1906)

Open Museum Journal, Vol. 2, August 2000

The Parnell Handbook: Containing Handy Notes and Useful Extracts from Speeches of Mr. C. S. Parnell, M. P., Before and After the Verdict in the Case of O'Shea v. O'Shea and Parnell (reprinted from 'The Irish Catholic'; Dublin: J. J. Lalor, 1891 (?))

Parnellism and Crime, Second and Revised Edition, Reprinted from *The Times* by George Edward Wright, London, 1887

Past and Present, May 1999, No. 163, pp.161–202, 'State, Civil Society and Separation in Victorian Marriage' by Olive Anderson.

Review of Reviews, London: The Review of Reviews 1890–1936, Vol. II: 1891, W. T. Stead, ed.

The Story of Room 15, by Donal Sullivan, MP; reprinted from the National Press Co., Dublin, 21 November to 5 December, 1891

MEMOIRS AND PUBLISHED LETTERS

Arnold-Foster, Florence, *My Irish Journal, June 1880–August 1882*, published as T. W. Moody and Richard Hawkins with Margaret Moody, eds., *Florence Arnold-Foster's Irish Journal* (Oxford: Clarendon Press, 1988)

Bahlman, Dudley W. R., (ed.), *The Diary of Sir Edward Walter Hamilton Volume I, 1880–1885; Volume II 1883–1885* (Oxford: Clarendon Press, 1972)

Ball, Stephen (ed.), *A Policeman's Ireland: Recollections of Samuel Waters, RIC* (Cork: Cork University Press, 1999)

Blunt, Wilfrid Scawen, *The Land War in Ireland: Being a Personal Narrative of Events* (London: Stephen Swift and Co., Ltd., 1912)

Blunt, Wilfrid Scawen, *My Diaries: Being a Personal Narrative of Events 1888–1914* (London: Martin Secker, 1933 (in one volume)/1919 (Vol. I), 1920 (Vol. II)

Bradhurst, Minna Evangeline, *A Century of Letters 1820–1920: Letters from Literary Friends to Lady Wood and Mrs. A. C. Steele* (London: R. E. Thomas and Newman, Ltd., printed for private circulation only, 1929)

Chamberlain, Joseph (edited from the original manuscript by C. H. D. Howard), *A Political Memoir 1880–92* (London: Batchwork, 1953)

Clarke, Sir Edward, *The Story of My Life* (London: John Murray, 1918)

Cornwallis-West, Mrs George, *The Reminiscences of Lady Randolph Churchill* (London: Edward Arnold, 1908)

Dickinson, Emily Monroe, *A Patriot's Mistake: Being Personal Recollections of the Parnell Family By a Daughter of the House* (Dublin: Hodges Figgis & Co., 1905)

Emden, Paul Herman, *Behind the Throne* (London: Hodder & Stoughton, 1934)

Fennell, Thomas, *The Royal Irish Constabulary: A History and Personal Memoir* (Dublin: University College Dublin Press, 2003)

Fingall, Elizabeth Countess of, *Seventy Years Young* (London: Lilliput, 1995/1937)

Gladstone, Mary (Mrs Drew), edited by Lucy Masterman, *Diaries and Letters* (London: Methuen & Co., Ltd., 1930)

Gladstone, Viscount, *After Thirty Years* (London: Macmillan, 1928)

Healy, T. M. (KC), *Letters and Leaders of My Day: Volumes I and II* (London: Thornton Butterworth, 1928)

Kelly, John (ed.), *The Collected Letters of W. B. Yeats, Volume One 1865–1895* (Oxford: Clarendon Press, 1986)

Matthew, H. C. G. (ed.), *The Gladstone Diaries: With Cabinet Minutes and Prime-Ministerial Correspondence, Volume X, January 1881–June 1883* (Oxford: Clarendon Press, 1990); *Volume XII, 1887–1891* (Oxford: Clarendon Press, 1994)

O'Brien, William, *Recollections* (London: Macmillan & Co., Ltd., 1905)

O'Brien, William, *Evening Memories* (Dublin and London: Methuen and Co., Ltd., 1920)

O'Brien, William and Ryan, Desmond (eds.), *Devoy's Post Bag 1871–1928* (Dublin: C. J. Fallon, Ltd., 1948)

O'Connor, T. P., *The Parnell Movement with a Sketch of Irish Parties from 1843* (London: Kegan Paul, Trench, & Co., 1886)

O'Connor, T. P., *Memoirs of an Old Parliamentarian*, in two volumes (London: Ernest Benn, 1929)

O'Shea, Katharine (Mrs Charles Stewart Parnell), *Charles Stewart Parnell: His Love Story and Political Life, Volumes I and II* (London: Cassell, 1914)

Parnell, John Howard, *Charles Stewart Parnell: A Memoir by His Brother* (London: Constable, 1916)

Porter, Mrs Adrian, *The Life and Letters of Sir John Henniker Heaton Bt by his Daughter Mrs Adrian Porter* (London: John Lane, 1916)

Praed, Mrs Campbell, *Our Book of Memories: Letters of Justin McCarthy to Mrs. Campbell Praed* (London: Chatto & Windus, 1912)

Sandford, Jeremy (ed.), *Mary Carbery's West Cork Journal 1898–1901, or 'From the Back of Beyond'* (Dublin: Lilliput, 1998)

Thomson, David with McGusty, Moyra (eds.), *The Irish Journals of Mrs. Elizabeth Smith 1840–1850* (Oxford: Clarendon Press, 1994)

Tynan, Katherine (Mrs H. A. Hinkson), *Twenty-five Years: Reminiscences* (London: Smith, Elder & Co., 1913)

Vincent, John (ed.), *The Diaries of Edward Henry Stanley, 15th Earl of Derby (1826–93) Between 1878 and 1893: A Selection* (Oxford: Leopard's Head Press, 2003)

Wood, Sir (Henry) Evelyn, *From Midshipman to Field Marshal, Vols I & II* (London: Methuen, 1906)

Wood, Sir (Henry) Evelyn, *Winnowed Memories* (London: Cassell, 1918)

BIOGRAPHIES

Abels, Jules, *The Parnell Tragedy* (London: Bodley Head, 1966)

Asquith, Lord, *Lord James of Hereford* (London: Ernest Benn, 1930)

Bew, Paul, *Charles Stewart Parnell* (Dublin: Gill & Macmillan, 1991/1980)

Brady, Margery, *The Love Story of Parnell & Katharine O'Shea* (Cork: Mercier, 1991)

Callaghan, Mary Rose, *'Kitty O'Shea': The Story of Katharine Parnell* (London: Pandora, 1994/1989)

Callanan, Frank, *T. M. Healy* (Cork: Cork University Press, 1996)

Coté, Jane McL., *Fanny and Anna Parnell: Ireland's Patriot Sisters* (Basingstoke and London: Macmillan, 1991)

Egremont, Max, *Balfour: A Life of Arthur James Balfour* (London: Phoenix, 1998/1980)

Ellman, Richard, *Oscar Wilde* (London: Penguin, 1988/1987)

Ervine, St John, *Parnell* (London: Ernest Benn, 1925)

Finnan, Joseph P., *John Redmond and Irish Unity, 1912–1918* (Syracuse: Syracuse University Press, 2004)

Foster, R. F., *Charles Stewart Parnell: The Man and his Family* (Sussex: Harvester, 1976)

Fraser, Flora, *The Unruly Queen: The Life of Queen Caroline* (London: John Murray, 2004/1996)

Gardiner, A. G., *A Life of Sir William Harcourt* (London: Constable & Co., Ltd., 1923)

Garvin, J. L., *The Life of Joseph Chamberlain* (London: Macmillan, 1932)

Gilmour, David, *Curzon* (London: Papermac, 1995/1994)

Harrison, Henry, *Parnell Vindicated: The Lifting of the Veil* (London: Constable, 1931)

Haslip, Joan, *Parnell* (London: R. Cobden-Sanderson, 1936)

Hibbert, Christopher, *Queen Victoria: A Personal History* (London: HarperCollins, 2001/2000)

Holroyd, Michael (ed.), *The Genius of Shaw: A Symposium Edited by Michael Holroyd* (New York: Holt, Rinehart and Winston, 1979)

Hughes, Kathryn, *The Short Life and Long Times of Mrs. Beeton* (London: Fourth Estate, 2005)

Jenkins, Roy, *Dilke: A Victorian Tragedy* (London: Papermac, 1996/1958)

Jenkins, Roy, *Gladstone* (London: Pan, 2002/1995)

Jordan, Jane, *Kitty O'Shea: An Irish Affair* (Gloucestershire: Sutton, 2005)

Judd, Denis, *Radical Joe: A Life of Joseph Chamberlain* (London: Hamish Hamilton, 1977)

Kee, Robert, *The Laurel and the Ivy: The Story of Charles Stewart Parnell and Irish Nationalism* (London: Penguin, 1994/1993)

Kehoe, Elisabeth, *Fortune's Daughters: The Extravagant Lives of the Jerome Sisters: Jennie Churchill, Clara Frewen and Leonie Leslie* (London: Atlantic, 2004)

Leonard, Hugh, *Parnell and the Englishwoman* (London: Penguin, 1991)

Lyons, F. S. L., *The Fall of Parnell 1890–91* (London: Routledge & Kegan Paul Ltd., 1962/1960)

Lyons, F. S. L., *Charles Stewart Parnell* (London: William Collins, 1977)

McCartney, Donal (ed.), *Parnell: The Politics of Power* (Dublin: Wolfhound, 1991)

McCoole, Sinead, *Hazel: A Life of Lady Lavery 1880–1935* (Dublin: Lilliput, 1996)

MacKenzie Stuart, Amanda, *Consuelo and Alva: Love and Power in the Gilded Age* (London: HarperCollins, 2005)

McKinstry, Leo, *Rosebery: Statesman in Turmoil* (London: John Murray, 2005)

Marlow, Joyce, *The Uncrowned Queen of Ireland: The Life of Kitty O'Shea* (London: Weidenfeld & Nicholson, 1975)

Marsh, Peter T., *Joseph Chamberlain: Entrepreneur in Politics* (New Haven and London: Yale University Press, 1994)

Morley, John, *The Life of William Ewart Gladstone: Vols I, II, & III* (London: Macmillan, 1903

O'Brien, Conor Cruise, *Parnell and His Party, 1880–90* (Oxford: Clarendon Press, 1957)

O'Brien, R. Barry, *The Life of Charles Stewart Parnell* (London: Thomas Nelson & Sons, 1911)

O'Brien, William, *The Parnell of Real Life* (London: T. Fisher Unwin, Ltd., 1925)

O'Connor, T. P., *The Parnell Movement with a Sketch of Irish Parties from 1843* (London: Kegan, Paul, Trench & Co., 1886)

Robbins, Alfred, *Parnell: The Last Five Years* (London: Thornton Butterworth, Ltd., 1926)

Roberts, Andrew, *Salisbury: Victorian Titan* (London: Weidenfeld & Nicolson, 1999)

Soames, Mary, *Clementine Churchill* (London: Doubleday, 2002/1979)

Strachey, Lytton, *Eminent Victorians*, edited by John Sutherland (Oxford: Oxford University Press, 2003)

Thorold, Algar Labouchere, *The Life of Henry Labouchere* (London: Constable & Co., Ltd., 1913)

Ziegler, Philip, *King Edward VIII: The Official Biography* (London: Collins, 1990)

SECONDARY SOURCES

Anglesey, The Marquess of, *A History of the British Cavalry 1816 to 1919, Volume II 1851 to 1871* (London: Leo Cooper, 1975)

Atlay, James Beresford, *The Victorian Chancellors, Vol II* (London: Smith, Elder & Co., 1908)

Berrisford Ellis, Peter, *A History of the Irish Working Class* (London and Sydney: Pluto, 1985/1972)

Bourke, Angela, *The Burning of Bridget Cleary: A True Story* (London: Pimlico, 2006/1999)

Bowen, Elizabeth, *The Shelbourne: A Centre in Dublin Life for More than a Century* (London: Vintage 2001/1951)

Boyce, D. George and O'Day, Alan (eds.), *Parnell in Perspective* (London and New York: Routledge, 1991)

Boyce, D. George and O'Day, Alan (eds.), *Modern Irish History: Revisionism and the Revisionist Controversy* (London and New York: Routledge, 1996)

Boyce, D. George and O'Day, Alan (eds.), *Ireland in Transition, 1867–1921* (London and New York: Routledge, 2004)

Brook, Stephen (ed.), *The Penguin Book of Infidelities* (London: Penguin, 1995/1994)

Bruce, Anthony, *The Purchase System in the British Army 1660–1871* (London: Royal Historical Society, 1980)

Buckland, Patrick (ed.), *Irish Unionisn 1885–1923* (Belfast: Her Majesty's Stationery Office, 1973)

Burrows, Edwin G. and Wallace, Mike, *Gotham: A History of New York City to 1898* (New York and Oxford: Oxford University Press, 1999)

Callanan, Frank, *The Parnell Split 1890–91* (Cork: Cork University Press, 1992)

Campbell, Christy, *Fenian Fire: The British Government Plot to Assassinate Queen Victoria* (London: HarperCollins, 2003/2002)

Cannadine, David, *The Decline and Fall of the British Aristocracy* (London: Papermac, 1992/1990)

Cannadine, David, *Ornamentalism: How the British Saw their Empire* (London: Allen Lane, 2001)

Chandler, David (ed.), *The Oxford History of the British Army* (Oxford: Oxford University Press, 1994)

Charlton, D. G. (ed.), *France: A Companion to French Studies*, 2nd edn (London and New York: Methuen & Co. Ltd., 1972)

Connelly, S. J. (ed.), *The Oxford Companion to Irish History* (Oxford: Oxford University Press, 1998) and Connolly, S. J. (ed.), *The Oxford Companion to Irish History* (new edition) (Oxford: Oxford University Press, 2004/2002)

Cretney, Stephen, *Family Law in the Twentieth Century: A History* (Oxford: Oxford University Press, 2005/2003)

Curtin, Nancy, *The United Irishmen: Popular Politics in Ulster and Dublin 1791–1978* (London: Clarendon Press, 1994)

Davitt, Michael, *The Fall of Feudalism in Ireland or The Story of the Land League Revolution* (London and New York: Harper & Brothers, 1904)

Diamond, Michael, *Victorian Sensation Or the Spectacular, the Shocking and the Scandalous in Nineteenth-Century Britain* (London: Anthem, 2003)

Easthope, Anthony, *Englishness and National Culture* (London: Routledge, 1999)

Echard, William E. (ed.), *Historical Dictionary of the French Second Empire 1852–1870* (London: Aldwych Press, 1985)

Eisenstadt, S. N. (ed.), *Max Weber on Charisma and Institution Building: Selected Papers* (Chicago and London: University of Chicago Press, 1968)

Elliot, Vivian (ed.), *Dear Mr Shaw: Selections from Bernard Shaw's Postbag* (London: Bloomsbury, 1987)

Ellis, Edward Robb, *The Epic of New York City* (New York: Coward-McCann, Inc., 1966)

Fanning, Clara Elizabeth (ed.), *Book Review Digest: Tenth Annual Cumulation: Book Reviews of 1914 in One Alphabet* (New York: H. W. Wilson, 1915)

Ferriter, Diarmaid, *The Transformation of Ireland 1900–2000* (London: Profile, 2004)

Fisher, Helen, *Anatomy of Love: A Natural History of Mating, Marriage, and Why We Stray* (New York: Random House, 1992)

Fisher, Trevor, *Prostitution and the Victorians* (London: Sutton, 1997)

Flanders, Judith, *The Victorian House: Domestic Life from Childbirth to Deathbed* (London: HarperCollins, 2003)

Flanders, Judith, *Consuming Passions: Leisure and Pleasure in Victorian Britain* (London: Harper Press, 2006)

Foster, R. F., *Modern Ireland 1600–1972* (London: Penguin, 1989/1988)

Foster, R. F., *Paddy and Mr. Punch: Connections in Irish and English History* (London: Allen Lane, The Penguin Press, 1993)

Foster, R. F., *The Irish Story: Telling Tales and Making it up in Ireland* (London: Allen Lane, 2001)

French, David, *Military Identities: The Regimental System, the British Army, and the British People* c. *1870–2000* (Oxford: Oxford University Press, 2005)

Gardiner, John, *The Victorians: An Age in Retrospect* (London and New York: Hambledon and London, 2002)

Githens-Mazer, Jonathan, *Myths and Memories of the Easter Rising: Cultural and Political Nationalism in Ireland* (Dublin and Portland, Or.: Irish Academic Press, 2006)

Goldman, Lawrence, Harrison, Brian and Matthew, Colin (eds.), *The Oxford Dictionary of National Biography* (Oxford: Oxford University Press, 2004); available online at www.oxfordnb.com

Goubert, Pierre, *The Course of French History* (London and New York: Routledge, 1991; first published 1984)

Gourvish, T. R. and O'Day, Alan (eds.), *Later Victorian Britain, 1867–1900* (London: Macmillan Education, 1988)

Greenwood, James, *The Wilds of London* (London: Chatto and Windus, 1874). This book was consulted on the following website: www.victorian london.org

Hammond, J. L., *Gladstone and the Irish Nation* (London: Longmans, Green & Co., 1938)

Harries-Jenkins, Gwyn, *The Army in Victorian Society* (London: Routledge and Kegan Paul, 1977)

Harrington, John P., *The English Traveller in Ireland: Accounts of Ireland and the Irish through Five Centuries* (Dublin: Wolfhound, 1991)

Harris, Michael and O'Malley, Tom, *Studies in Newspaper and Periodical History, 1995 Annual* (Westport, Connecticut: Greenwood Press, 1997)

Harrison, Henry, *Parnell, Joseph Chamberlain and Mr. Garvin* (London: Robert Hale Ltd., 1938)

Hickey, D. J. and Doherty, J. E., *A Dictionary of Irish History since 1800* (Dublin: Gill and Macmillan Ltd., 1980)

Hoppen, K. Theodore, *Ireland since 1800: Conflict and Conformity*, 2nd edn, (Essex: Longman, 1999/1989)

Hoppen, K. Theodore, *The Mid-Victorian Generation 1846–1886* (Oxford: Clarendon Press, 1998)

Jackson, Alvin, *Home Rule: An Irish History 1800–2000* (London: Weidenfeld & Nicolson, 2003)

Jeffrey, Keith, *The GPO and the Easter Rising* (Dublin and Portland, Or.: Irish Academic Press, 2006)

Jenkins, Roy, *The Chancellors* (London: Papermac, 1999/1998)

Junco, José Alvarez and Shubert, Adrian (eds.), *Spanish History since 1908* (London: Arnold, 2004/2000)

Kanner, Barbara Penny, *Women in Context: Two Hundred Years of British Women Autobiographers: A Reference Guide and Reader* (New York: G. K. Hall & Co., 1997)

Kee, Robert, *The Green Flag: A History of Irish Nationalism* (London: Penguin, 1972)

Kelly, M. J., *The Fenian Ideal and Irish Nationalism, 1882–1916* (Woodbridge, Suffolk: The Boydell Press, 2006)

Kent, Susan Kingsley, *Gender and Power in Britain, 1640–1990* (London and New York: Routledge, 1999)

Kiberd, Declan, *Inventing Ireland: The Literature of the Modern Nation* (London: Vintage, 1996/1995)

King, Carla (ed.), *Famine, Land and Culture in Ireland* (Dublin: University College Dublin Press, 2000)

Koven, Seth, *Slumming: Sexual and Social Politics in Victorian London* (Princeton and Oxford: Princeton University Press, 2004)

Larkin, Emmett, *The Roman Catholic Church in Ireland and the Fall of Parnell 1888–1891* (Chapel Hill: The University of North Carolina Press, 1979)

Lawson, Annette, *Adultery: an Analysis of Love and Betrayal* (Oxford: Oxford University Press, 1990/1988)

Legg, Marie-Louise, *Newspapers and Nationalism: The Irish Provincial Press 1850–1892* (Dublin: Four Courts Press, 1999)

Leslie, Shane, *The Irish Issue in its American Aspect: A Contribution to the Settlement of Anglo-American Relations During and After the Great War* (New York: Charles Scribner's Sons, 1917)

Lyons, F. S. L. and Hawkins, R. A. J. (eds.), *Ireland Under the Union: Varieties of Tension. Essays in Honour of T. W. Moody* (Oxford: Clarendon Press, 1980)

Lyons, J. B., *What Did I Die Of: The Deaths of Parnell, Wilde, Synge, and Other Literary Pathologies* (Dublin: Lilliput, 1991)

McCartney, Donal (ed.), *Parnell: The Politics of Power* (Dublin: Wolfhound, 1991)

McCartney, Donal and Travers, Pauric, *The Ivy Leaf: The Parnells Remembered: Commemorative Essays* (Dublin: University College Dublin Press, 2006)

MacColl, Gail and Wallace, Carol McD., *To Marry an English Lord: The Victorian and Edwardian Experience* (London: Sidgwick & Jackson, 1989)

McConville, Séan, *Irish Political Prisoners, 1848–1922: Theatres of War* (London and New York: Routledge, 2003)

MacDonagh, Oliver, Mandle, W. F. and Travers, Pauric, *Irish Culture and Nationalism, 1750–1950* (London: Macmillan, 1983)

Meisel, Joseph S., *Public Speech and the Culture of Public Life in the Age of Gladstone* (New York: Columbia University Press, 2001)

Moody, T. W. and Martin, F. X., *The Course of Irish History* (Cork: Mercier Press, 2001/1967)

Murphy, William Michael, *The Parnell Myth and Irish Politics 1891–1956* (New York: American University Studies, Peter Lang, 1986)

Norman, Edward, *A History of Modern Ireland* (London: Allen Lane, 1971)

O'Callaghan, Margaret, *British High Politics and a Nationalist Ireland: Criminality, Land and the Law under Forster and Balfour* (Cork: Cork University Press, 1994)

O'Day, Alan, *The English Face of Irish Nationalism: Parnellite Involvement in British Politics 1880–86* (Dublin: Gill and Macmillan, 1977)

O'Day, Alan, *Parnell and the First Home Rule Episode 1884–87* (Dublin: Gill and Macmillan, 1986)

Pakenham, Thomas, *The Boer War* (London: Abacus 2003/1979)

Pašeta, Senia, *Before the Revolution: Nationalism, Social Change and Ireland's Catholic Elite, 1879–1922* (Cork: Cork University Press, 1999)

Perkin, Harold, *The Origins of Modern English Society, 1780–1880* (London: Routledge, 1972)

Perkin, Harold, *The Rise of Professional Society: England since 1880* (London: Routledge, 1989/1990)

Purvis, June (ed.), *Women's History: Britain, 1850–1945: An Introduction* (London and New York: Routledge, 2004/1995)

Scott, Joan Wallach, *Gender and the Politics of History* (New York: Columbia Press, 1988)

Searle, G. R., The New Oxford History of England: *A New England? Peace and War 1886–1918* (Oxford: Oxford University Press, 2004)

Shanley, Mary Lyndon, *Feminism, Marriage, and the Law in Victorian England, 1850–1895* (London: I. B. Tauris, 1989)

Somerville-Large, Peter, *The Irish Country House: A Social History* (London: Sinclair-Stevenson, 1995)

Spiers, Edward, *The Army and Society 1815–1914* (London and New York: Longman, 1980)

Steinbach, Susie, *Women in England 1760–1914: A Social History* (London: Phoenix, 2005/2004)

Stewart, A. T. Q., *The Shape of Irish History* (Belfast: Blackstaff, 2001)

Stone, Lawrence, *Road to Divorce: England, 1530–1987* (Oxford and New York: Oxford University Press, 1995/1990)

von Stutterheim, Kurt, translated by W. H. Johnson, *The Press in England* (London: George Allen & Unwin, 1934)

Thomas, Donald, *The Victorian Underworld* (London: John Murray, 2003/1998)

Tortella, Gabriel, *The Development of Modern Spain: An Economic History of the Nineteenth and Twentieth Centuries* (Cambridge, Mass., and London: Harvard University Press, 2000)

Townshend, Charles, *Easter 1916: The Irish Rebellion* (London: Allen Lane, 2005)

Turner, E. S., *Unholy Pursuits: The Wayward Parsons of Grub Street* (Sussex: Book Guild, 1998)

Vamplew, Wray, *The Turf: A Social and Economic History of Horse Racing* (London: Allen Lane, 1976)

Vaughan, W. E., *Landlords and Tenants in Mid-Victorian Ireland* (Oxford: Clarendon Press, 1994)

Vaughan, W. E. and Fitzpatrick, A. J. (eds.), *Irish Historical Statistics: Population, 1821–1971* (Dublin: Royal Irish Academy, 1978)

Walkowitz, Judith, *Prostitution and Victorian Society: Women, Class and the State* (Cambridge: Cambridge University Press, 1980)

Warwick-Haller, Sally, *William O'Brien and the Irish Land War* (Co. Dublin: Irish Academic Press, 1990)

Weber, Max, *The Protestant Ethic and the 'Spirit' of Capitalism and Other Writings*, edited by Baehr, Peter and Wells, Gordon C. (London: Penguin, 2002)

Wilkes, Roger, *Scandal: A Scurrilous History of Gossip* (London: Atlantic, 2002)

Wilson, A. N., *The Victorians* (London: Hutchinson, 2002)

Yalom, Marilyn, *A History of the Wife* (London: Pandora, 2001)

Yeats, W. B., *New Poems: Manuscript Materials* edited by Mays, J. C. C. and Parrish, Stephen (Ithaca, NY, and London: Cornell University Press, 2000)

Index

Whig Party 3, 200, 219
Wilde, Oscar 294
Willsher, Ezra (footman of Aunt Ben) 353
Wise, Richard (coachman) 305
Wolff, Sir Henry Drummond 285
women
  domestic role 389–90, 410
  property 62, 389
  sexuality 389–90
Wonersh Lodge (Eltham) 425
  and Katie 72–3, 76, 91–3, 98, 115–16, 133–5, 202–3, 232
  O'Shea at 73, 76, 133–5, 145, 153–4, 166–8, 180, 184, 191, 195, 217–18, 232, 250, 280, 343–6
  and Parnell
    banned by O'Shea 135–7, 143, 339–42, 355–7
    and death of Claude 178–9, 186, 202
    and household servants 117, 137–8, 244, 304–5
    illness 98–100
    residence at 307–9, 311, 317, 328, 331, 335–6, 351, 354, 374
    rooms at 116, 304, 311
    visits to 100–1, 111, 116–17, 133–7, 143, 180, 184, 197, 208, 217–18, 356, 386
Wood, Anna see Steel, Anna
Wood, Benjamin 29–30
Wood, Charles (brother of Katie) 2, 5, 8, 14, 27
  finances 352, 355, 357, 362, 369, 445–6
Wood, Clarissa (sister of Katie) 2, 8
Wood, Emma see Barrett Lennard, Emma
Wood, Emma (mother of Katie)
  appearance 14–15

Wood, Emma (cont.)
  children 1–2, 8, 48
  and Evelyn 2, 10, 48–9
  family background 28
  financial situation 35
  as musician 10
  as novelist 10, 11, 14, 35–6, 73
  and O'Shea 33, 34–5, 67–9
  as painter 9, 14
  pets 37
  and Queen Caroline 4
Wood, Evelyn (brother of Katie)
  assault charge 36
  education 29
  finances 352, 362, 365, 369
  and Katie 2, 10, 48–9
    affair with Parnell 343–4, 356–7
  marriage 37–8
  military career 27, 47–9, 224, 293
  and O'Shea 32, 51, 69, 211
Wood family 1–16, 27–8
  amateur theatricals 13–14, 52
  financial situation 2–3, 6–7, 27, 29–30, 35, 51
Wood, Francis (Frank; brother of Katie) 2, 8, 25
Wood, Frederick (brother of Katie) 2, 8
Wood, Hon. Paulina (née Southwell) 37
Wood, Katherine see O'Shea, Katherine
Wood, Maria (née Michell; maternal aunt of Katie) 7–8, 10, 28–30, 48–9, 196, 255
  character 73–4, 92
  death 367, 368–9, 424–5
  financial aid to family 29–30, 35, 37, 52
  financial aid to Katie 30, 52, 62, 67, 70, 72, 78–9, 110, 143, 147, 181, 307

*Index compiled by Meg Davies
(Fellow of the Society of Indexers)*

TREATY AND HOW PARNELL WAS RELEAS...

S. O'SHEA'S STRUGGLE.

...and mentioning once more the reforms ...he insisted. The suggestion to settle the ...ifficulty by means of a loan over however ...rs repayment might be spread must be ...rejected.

...er he referred to in one to me written two ...others, but wifie must not tell anybody that I have not done so, as it would create discontent amongst the others. The man who has been taking care of me is going out to-morrow, and will be a loss to me. He has been very ill during the last week ...cated the night before last, so I sent O'Gorman Mahon to Forster about him, with the desired effect of getting his discharge. One of the others will supply his place to me, but not so well.

"Have not been weighed yet, but will to-morrow. I think wifie has my last weight. After eight at night I read books, newspapers, and write until about twelve or one, when I go to bed. I also think a good deal of my own darling during that time when everything is quiet, and wonder how soon I shall be with you again.

"The time is passing rather more slowly this month than the first, but still, it is not yet monotonous.

With me, of course, time passed far otherwise, and Parnell's anxiety on my behalf affected him more than his imprisonment.

"Though I am relieved to know that my darling is a little less miserable, yet I am still very much troubled and anxious about you. Has he (Captain O'Shea was staying at Eltham) left yet? It is frightful that you should be exposed to such daily torture. My own wifie must try and strengthen herself, and get some sleep for her husband's sake and for our child's sake, who must be suffering much also.

"I don't know who sent me the quilt; I am sending it

---

engendered—with the Coercion I... must, in the long run, inevitabl... indeed, England was prepared an unthinkable proposition.

So now I threw the whole s... fluence on the side of the treaty c... urged upon him the greater good to accrue in the making by h... peace. I was very anxious that h... by constitutional means, and h... establishing such amicable comm...

"Nothing in the world is... harm or injury to you. How... out my own Katie, and if yo... go to you at once." On th... ing day he urged: "I could... any arrangement or enter i... with Government unless I re... politics."

I was not to be perturbed... had been getting it from the Go... future they would be supplied f... do not receive any letters from except one from Mrs. S., shortly She wrote to sympathise, and ill. I replied after a time, were, but forgot to ask how sh... not written since. Am glad of my 'young women' have writ... write you home.

"Let me know as soon as h...

"Government are not likely to... but they will scarcely go out w... out first.

"I am very nervous about the should at all events tell one of time so that he may be on hand may not have one at all. It will this risk."

PARNELL:

THE LOVE S...
Written by his Widow, Katharine Parnell (Mrs. O'Shea).

"I WILL OFFER TO RESIGN," SAID PARNEL...

"IT IS AN OMEN!"

...rning point in Parnell's ...has come. Having im... ...l him in Kilmainham Gaol, ...Government have discovered ...cannot get on without him. ...ainham Treaty, drafted at ...hither Parnell had come on ...see his dying child, was ...sealed and delivered." The ...o "slow down" the agitation ...balanced by the promise

STUNNED WITH HORROR.

"The blood more stirs
To rouse a lion than to start a hare."
Shakespeare.

ON Parnell's release from Kilmainham he returned to me at Eltham, and on May 6 went to Weymouth to welcome Michael Davitt, who came out of Portland prison on that day. Parnell returned to Eltham that Saturday evening, and the next morning, Sunday, I drove with him to Blackheath Station, as he had to go to London to see ...tt and others. At the station I asked him to ...fore he left, and waited for

---

upon all who joined in... last roused himself and s... the G.O.M. and offer to... decision; the thing make... any good."

On the wall of the... hung a large engravin... All the members of the... picture, and among t... and Captain O'Shea. ...the room, after placin... side table, this pictu... behind Parnell, fell t... in the state of nerv... brought us to our ... overturned as he ju... steady, in a grip tha... held slightly raised ... half-turned, staring the splintered glass.

PARNEL...

Willie laughed, a... maid to pick up... goes Home Rule, ... a slight dash of th... developed in Par... smile turned to s... tense expression, ...tion of the fall:... the maid had sh... Parnell took the... hands and tried... said, "Mary (th... of the room, so... Parnell said ... other things. ...not really min... was only a r... was an omen... Willie or me... would not tal... believe in om... be "omens"... no more. S...

...UL KITTY O'SHEA.

...rriage I could see inside the station ...he half-turned and ...paper—the *Sunday* ...s before he brought ...rds that he wanted Michael Davitt. He ...he steps, and, as he ...t a curious rigidity ...olding the newspaper ...tely still that I was ...sickeningly afraid— ...eaning forward, called ...hen he came down the ...to the headline, said, ...rder of Lord Frederick

...g in, and tried to pull ...wful significance of the ...just released from Kil... ...ame home to me with a ...ss ashen, and he stared, ...crush-